CRITICAL SURVEY
OF
POETRY

CRITICAL SURVEY
OF
POETRY

English Language Series

REVISED EDITION
Sou-Win

7

Edited by
FRANK N. MAGILL

SALEM PRESS
Pasadena, California   Englewood Cliffs, New Jersey

Library of Congress Cataloging-in-Publication Data
Critical survey of poetry. English language series/edited
  by Frank N. Magill. — Rev. ed.
    p.   cm.
  Includes bibliographical references and index.
  1. English poetry—Dictionaries. 2. American
poetry—Dictionaries. 3. English poetry—
Bio-bibliography. 4. American poetry—Bio-
bibliography. 5. Poets, English—Biography—
Dictionaries. 6. Poets, American—Biography—
Dictionaries.
I. Magill, Frank Northen, 1907-
PR502.C85   1992   92-3727
821.009′03—dc20   CIP
ISBN 0-89356-834-1 (set)
ISBN 0-89356-841-4 (volume 7)

LIST OF AUTHORS IN VOLUME 7

CRITICAL SURVEY
OF
POETRY

ROBERT SOUTHWELL

Born: Norfolk(?), England; 1561
Died: London, England; February 21, 1595

Principal poetry

St. Peter's Complaint, with Other Poems, 1595; *Moeniae*, 1595; *The Complete Poems of Robert Southwell*, 1872 (Alexander B. Grosart, editor); *The Poems of Robert Southwell*, 1967 (James H. McDonald and Nancy Pollard Brown, editors).

Other literary forms

Besides writing poetry Robert Southwell wrote many religious tracts, including *Mary Magdalens Funerall Teares* (1591).

Achievements

Southwell's reputation as a poet in his own time is difficult to determine, since he was a priest in hiding and a martyr for his Roman Catholic faith. It is natural that the five manuscript compilations of his verses do not name the author, and that the two printed volumes, both published in the year of his execution, likewise do not name the author; one of them, however, gives his initials. The publishers may have thought that readers would associate the poems with Southwell, who was of much interest at the time, although the government tried to keep his trial secret. Early references to his verse, however, with a single exception, do not indicate knowledge of authorship. Southwell's name did not appear in an edition until 1620.

The musical quality of his verse is remarkable, considering that he almost forgot his native English during his long education abroad and had to relearn it when he returned to England as a priest in hiding. He has been described by Pierre Janelle as the "leading Catholic writer of the Elizabethan age," and one who might have developed into one of the greatest English writers if it were not for his death at thirty-four. His best-known poem is "The Burning Babe," and Ben Jonson is reputed to have said that if he had written that poem, he would have been content to destroy many of his.

Biography

Robert Southwell was born toward the end of 1561, according to evidence gathered from his admittance to the Society of Jesus and from his trial. His family was prosperous, and he spent his boyhood at Horsham St. Faith's, Norfolk.

In 1576, when he was about fifteen, he entered the English College of the Jesuit school at Douai; like many young Catholics of that period, he was sent to the Continent for his later education. He studied at the Jesuit College of

Clermont in Paris for a short time for his greater safety, returning to Douai in 1577, the year in which he applied to enter the Jesuit novitiate at Tournai. He was at first rejected, but was accepted into the novitiate in Rome in 1578, where he was a student at the Roman College and tutor and precept of studies at the English College. Forbidden to speak English, he spoke Latin and Italian, becoming very fluent in the latter and reading a great deal of Italian literature. He wrote Latin poetry, including religious epics, elegies, and epigrams.

His poetry in English was written during his English mission, from his return to England in July, 1586, to his arrest in June, 1592. He was stationed in London, working under a superior, Reverend Henry Garnet. Southwell occupied a house in London and provided lodgings for priests, meeting those coming into the country. He corresponded with the Reverend Claudius Aquaviva, General of the Society of Jesus, giving him reports of the persecution. He received much help from the Countess of Arundel, and his prose works were printed secretly. He met at intervals with his superior and other priests; one such meeting was raided, but they managed to escape.

He was betrayed by a fellow Jesuit who had been arrested after arriving in England and who described the appearance of Southwell, and by the sister of a Catholic friend with whom he was staying in Uxenden, north of London. This Anne Bellamy, of a loyal Catholic family, had been imprisoned and become pregnant while in prison, probably having been assaulted by the priest-hunter Topcliffe; she married Topcliffe's assistant and betrayed Southwell on the condition that her family would not be molested, a promise which was not kept. Southwell was arrested on June 25, 1592. Topcliffe wrote an exultant letter to the Queen about the importance of his prisoner and his intentions. Southwell was brought to Topcliffe's house and tortured many times. One of the tortures was being hung by the hands against a wall. He refused to identify himself or admit that he was a priest; in the absence of such identification, the family that had sheltered him could not be implicated. On Queen Elizabeth's instructions, he was moved to the Gatehouse Prison, where he was tortured and questioned by the Privy Council; but he always kept his silence. After he heard that there was other evidence against the Bellamys (they were imprisoned on Anne's evidence), he wrote to Sir Robert Cecil, a member of the Council, that he was a priest and a Jesuit. He did not want his silence to be misinterpreted as fear or shame of his profession. Imprisoned in the Tower of London, he was arraigned under the Act of 1585 for the treason of returning to England as an ordained Catholic priest and of administering sacraments. Weak as he was, he had to conduct his own defense, but he was constantly interrupted. He was convicted, dragged through the streets, and hanged, drawn, and quartered at Tyburn Tree on February 21, 1595, after praying for his Queen, his country, and himself. He was beatified by his Church in 1929 and canonized as a saint in 1970.

Analysis

Robert Southwell wrote his religious poetry with a didactic purpose. In the prose Preface to a manuscript, addressed to his cousin, he says that poets who write of the "follies and fayninges" of love have discredited poetry to the point that "a Poet, a Lover, and a Liar, are by many reckoned but three words of one signification." Poetry, however, was used for parts of Scripture, and may be used for hymns and spiritual sonnets. He has written his poetry to give others an example of subject matter, he says, and he hopes that other more skillful poets would follow his example. He flies from "prophane conceits and fayning fits" and applies verse to virtue, as David did. Perhaps his distaste for the stylized love poetry of his time explains the absence of sonnets in his writing. While Southwell's purpose in writing was didactic, he was often more emotional than purely intellectual. His poems are seldom tranquil. They tend to startle through his use of the unexpected, the fantastic, and the grotesque, and may thus be described as baroque. Southwell is also linked to the baroque movement in his use of Italian models and such themes as weeping, anticipating the seventeenth century Roman Catholic poet Richard Crashaw.

As might be expected, death is a recurring theme in his poetry, yet he makes the theme universal rather than personal, for his purpose was instructive and oral rather than merely self-expressive. In "Upon the Image of Death," for example, he speaks of what is apparently a *memento mori* kind of picture that he often looks at, but he still does not really believe that he must die; historical personages and people he has known have all died, and yet it is difficult to think that he will die. There are personal touches, such as references to his gown, his knife, and his chair, but all are reminders to him and to all of inevitable death, "And yet my life amend not I." The poem's simplicity and universality give it a proverbial quality.

His most inspired poems were about birth rather than death, the birth of the Christ-child. In Part VI of "The Sequence on the Virgin Mary and Christ," "The Nativitie of Christ," he uses the image of the bird that built the nest being hatched in it, and ends with the image of the Christ-child as hay, the food for the beasts that human beings have become through sin. His image of Christ is often that of a child, as in "A Child My Choice," where he stresses the superior subject he praises in the poem, compared with the foolish praise of what "fancie" loves. While he loves the Child, he lives in him, and cannot live wrongly. In the middle two stanzas of this four-stanza poem, he uses a great deal of alliteration, parallelism, and antithesis to convey the astonishing nature of this Child, who is young, yet wise; small, yet strong; and man, yet God. At the end of the poem, he sees Christ weeping, sighing, and panting while his angels sing. Out of his tears, sighs, and throbs buds a joyful spring. At the end of the poem, he prays that this Child will help him in correcting his faults and will direct his death. The prayer was of course meant to be didactic, but it assumes a very personal meaning because of Southwell's manner of death. The themes of the Nativity and of death are thus artistically linked.

As Vincent Barry Leitch has stated, the Incarnation serves as a paradigm of God's love for human beings and signifies God's sanctification of human life. There is thus a strong sense of the divine in human life in most of Southwell's poems, yet some of the poems are referred to as "desolation poems" because this sense of God in human life is absent. Sin is prevalent, and the sinner feels remorse. In "A vale of teares," for example, God seems to be absent, leaving people alone to work things out for themselves. The poem is heavily descriptive, describing a valley of the Alps and painting a picture of a dreary scene that is in keeping with a sense of loneliness and desolation. It is wild, mountainous, windy, and thunderous, and although the green of the pines and moss suggests hope, hope quails when one looks at the cliffs. The poem ends with an apostrophe to Deep Remorse to possess his breast, and bidding Delights adieu. The poem has been linked to the conventional love lyric in which the lover, in despair, isolates himself from the world, but it has also been linked to the Ignatian Exercises of the Jesuits.

Another poem on the theme of isolation and remorse is the long dramatic poem *St. Peter's Complaint*, comprising 132 stanzas of six lines each, based on an Italian work by Luigi Tansillo (1510-1568), *Le Lagrime di San Pietro* (The Tears of Saint Peter). Southwell wrote a translation of part of Tansillo's poem, entitling it, "Peeter Playnt," and two other poems, "S. Peters complaint," a poem of eleven stanzas, and "Saint Peters Complaynte," a poem of twelve stanzas. These three apparently represent stages in the composition of the long poem. In the translation, there is an objective rather than a first-person point of view, and Peter's denying Christ was an action in the immediate past in the courtyard, while reference is made to the suffering Peter will experience in the future. In each of the three original versions, Peter is the speaker and the time and place are indefinite. Much of the material in the "Saint Peters Complaynte" is incorporated in the long poem. The uneven quality of the long poem has caused Janelle to assign it to an early period of experimentation, but McDonald and Brown see it as an unpolished work left unfinished when Southwell was arrested.

In the long poem, St. Peter indulges in an extended nautical conceit, appropriate for this speaker, of sailing with torn sails, using sighs for wind, remorse as the pilot, torment as the haven, and shipwreck as the best reward. He hopes his complaints will be heard so that others will know that there is a more sorrowful one than they, and he lists all the unfortunate things he is, one to a line for a whole stanza, including "An excrement of earth. . . ." He says that others may fill volumes in praise of "your forged Goddesse," a reference to the literary fashion of praising some supposed love, who might not be real at all. St. Peter's griefs will be his text and his theme. Several times in his works, Southwell makes this distinction between the falseness of stylized love poetry and the reality of religious themes. St. Peter says that he must weep, and here Southwell employs hyperbole, for a sea will hardly rinse Peter's sin; he speaks of high tides, and says that all those who weep should give him their tears. The poem is heavily rhetorical, with many exclamations, parallelisms, repetitions, questions, and comparisons. St. Peter had not thought that he would ever deny Christ. In lines 673-677, Southwell characteristically begins a line with a word which had already appeared toward the end of the preceding line, thus patterning Peter's "circkling griefes." Peter compares himself to a leper with sores, and asks Christ's forgiveness. The taunts that Peter levels at the woman in the courtyard in the poem have been taken to suggest a parallel between her actions and those of Queen Elizabeth. Alice Mary Lubin, in a study of Southwell's religious complaint lyrics, says that this poem differs from the traditional complaint poem in that the complaining figure is separated from Christ rather than from a figure such as a lover, and that it differs from medieval religious complaint poems because it constitutes a statement of remorse rather than being simply a lament. A description of Peter's isolation occupies much of the poem. Lubin does not see the work as an ordered meditative poem; rather, it resembles an Italian "weeper" poem in subject, though not in treatment. She suggests analogues in *A Myrrour for Magistrates* (1559) and in the Old Testament Lamentations.

Southwell's most famous work, "The Burning Babe," combines several of his favorite themes, including the Nativity, isolation, guilt, and purification, into a vision poem that becomes a lament. He presents the material as a mystical vision. The occasion is presented dramatically, for it was a "hoary winter's night" and he was shivering in the snow when he felt the sudden heat that made him look up to see the fire. The dramatic contrasts continue, as he speaks of seeing a pretty baby; but it is in the air, not where a baby would be, and it is "burning bright," like a fire; the image is deliberately odd, ambiguous, and out of place. The next image, that the baby is "scorched" with great heat, turns the odd image into a horrible one, conveying the idea that the baby's body is no longer white but discolored from a fire that is not a mere metaphor. The fire is not from the air, but from inside the body, which means that there is no escape for the baby. The next image is ironic, for the baby cries copiously, as though the "floods" of tears could quench the flames, which they cannot do.

When the baby speaks, it is to lament that he fries in this heat although he is just born, and yet no one seeks to warm the heart at this fire, and no one but the baby feels this fire. Here the Christ-child is very much alone. It is not until the next line, however, that the baby is clearly identified as Christ, when he says that the furnace (the place where the fire is) is his breast, and the fuel is "wounding thorns." The ironic crown of thorns of the Crucifixion becomes fuel for the fire. His breast is kept burning because people wound him with thorns and hurt him through their mocking actions. The Crucifixion was a specific event, but the fire is a continuing torment, so the "wounding thorns" must be not only the crown of thorns but also the sins that people are continuing to commit.

Vision poems have often had a guide figure, someone who leads the viewer and explains the allegorical significance of the vision. Here the baby is both the vision and the guide, resulting in a kind of ironic horror. The image throughout this section of the poem is that of a furnace, a piece of technology used for creating and working things. The baby explains that the fire is love, a rather complicated idea, for it is the "wounding thorns" that keep the fire (the love) alive. Christ's love feeds on the wrongs of human beings. He loves human beings despite their sins, and indeed because of their sins. The smoke is sighs, His emotional dissatisfaction with what is happening, how people are acting. The ashes are the residue, the residual shame and scorn. The shame is Christ's embarrassment at being crucified and the equal embarrassment of the constant crucifixion He suffers because of continuing sin. The scorn is the rejection of His reality and the mission that He came into the world as a baby to accomplish, the taking of sins onto Himself. Thus the residue of the fire is the shame and scorn, not entirely consumed in the fire but left over and ever-present. Two personifications now enter the allegory. Justice puts the fuel on the fire, for it is not only that the sins and injustices of human beings be burnt, consumed, transformed in this way; but it is also Mercy that "blows the coals," that keeps the fire of love going strong by blowing air onto it. The imagery has changed from the "wounding thorns" causing the baby to be on fire, to the necessity and justice of burning up and burning away the wrongs of humans in the heat of God's love, which is kept going by His mercy.

The metals that are worked in this furnace are the souls of human beings, which have been defiled, but which are to be changed in the fire, thus representing another change in the imagery. Christ is now on fire to change them into something better, and He says that He will "melt into a bath to wash them in my blood." A bath is a cleansing, a purification, and after feeling the love of God, they will be purified by a cooling liquid, ironically not water, but Christ's blood, another touch of horror but also of love and glory. Saying that He would melt, a term meaning depart or disappear, but having special imagistic significance here because of the burning, the Christ-child vanishes. The reader is conscious that the baby will become the crucified Christ, and the poet realizes that it is Christmas. Southwell here makes the Christ-child the isolated one, most ironically, and develops the symbolism to make the reader feel remorse for his sins. The poem's startlingly grotesque subject clearly links it to the baroque movement.

Southwell's main themes were the opposing ones of the joyous Incarnation, with its joining of God and human beings; and the tragic desolation of feeling the alienation of self from God through sin. Striking images with strong emotion achieve a religious purpose of affecting the reader. In his short life,

Southwell wrote many fine poems in a language he had once forgotten. He referred very little in his poetry to the persecution that overshadowed his life, choosing to write instead of religious experiences that transcended time and place.

Rosemary Ascherl

Other major works

NONFICTION: *Epistle of Robert Southwell to His Father, Exhorting Him to the Perfect Forsaking of the World*, 1589; *Mary Magdalens Funerall Teares*, 1591; *His Letter to Sir Robert Cecil*, 1593; *A Humble Supplication to Her Majestie*, 1595 (written in 1591); *The Triumphs ouer Death*, 1596 (written in 1591); *A Short Rule of Good Life*, 1598; *An Epistle of Comfort*, 1605 (written in 1591); *A Hundred Meditations on the Love of God*, 1873 (written c. 1585; translation).

Bibliography

Janelle, Pierre. *Robert Southwell the Writer: A Study in Religious Inspiration.* 1935. Reprint. Mamaroneck, N.Y.: Paul J. Appel, 1971. Though a relatively "old" book, Janelle's biography—the first three chapters of the book—remains the standard account of the life of Southwell. The other chapters concerning Jesuit influence, Petrarchan origins, and Southwell's place among his contemporaries have stood the test of time. This scholarly volume contains an extensive bibliography, especially of primary sources.

Lewis, C. S. *English Literature in the Sixteenth Century, Excluding Drama.* Oxford: Clarendon Press, 1954. In a relatively brief overview of Southwell's poetic achievements, Lewis states that Southwell is of most historical interest as an early Metaphysical poet (his verse particularly resembles George Herbert's). Lewis also addresses the religious content of Southwell's poetry.

Martz, Louis L. *The Poetry of Meditation: A Study in English Religious Literature of the Seventeenth Century.* New Haven, Conn.: Yale University Press, 1954. 2d ed. New Haven, Conn. Yale University Press, 1962. Martz examines Southwell's meditative poetry which looks ahead to the religious poetry of the seventeenth century in its adapting "profane" poetic devices to religious poetry, its poetic meditations on the lives of Christ and Mary, and in its Ignatian self-analysis. He also demonstrates close ties between Southwell and George Herbert.

Moseley, D. H. *Blessed Robert Southwell.* New York: Sheed & Ward, 1957. A sympathetic biography drawn from late sixteenth century writings and records, which provides an understanding of the cultural, religious, and political climate in which Southwell lived and wrote. Supplemented by a chronological select bibliography of Southwell criticism.

Scallon, Joseph D. *The Poetry of Robert Southwell, S. J.* Salzburg, Austria: Institut für Englische Sprache und Literatur, 1975. Scallon's monograph provides chapters on Southwell's biography, his short poems (particularly those concerning Christ and the Virgin Mary), and the poems on repentance. *St. Peter's Complaint*, Southwell's best poem, receives extensive analysis. Contains a substantial bibliography.

STEPHEN SPENDER

Born: London, England; February 28, 1909

Principal poetry

Nine Experiments, by S. H. S.: Being Poems Written at the Age of Eighteen, 1928; *Twenty Poems,* 1930; *Poems,* 1933, 1934; *Vienna,* 1935; *The Still Centre,* 1939; *Selected Poems,* 1940; *Ruins and Visions,* 1942; *Spiritual Exercises (To Cecil Day Lewis),* 1943; *Poems of Dedication,* 1947; *Returning to Vienna 1947: Nine Sketches,* 1947; *The Edge of Being,* 1949; *Collected Poems, 1928-1953,* 1955; *Inscriptions,* 1958; *Selected Poems,* 1964; *The Generous Days,* 1971; *Recent Poems,* 1978; *Collected Poems, 1928-1985,* 1985.

Other literary forms

Although best known for his poetry, Stephen Spender has written a considerable body of drama, fiction, criticism, and journalism. The first of his six plays, *Trial of a Judge* (1938), was his contribution to the Group Theatre effort, in which his friend W. H. Auden was so heavily involved, and reflected the young Spender's socialist outlook. Most of the others—notably *Danton's Death* (1939), which he wrote with Goronwy Rees; *Mary Stuart* (1957), taken from the J. C. F. Schiller play; and *Rasputin's End* (1963), a libretto to music by Nicholas Nabokov—likewise dealt with broadly political situations and problems. Spender's published fiction consists of a collection of stories, *The Burning Cactus* (1936); a novel, *The Backward Son* (1940); and two novellas, *Engaged in Writing* and *The Fool and the Princess* (published together in 1958).

Spender's nonfiction prose comprises more than a dozen books, as well as hundreds of essays contributed to periodicals. The critical works have dealt mostly with the issues and problems of modern literature, beginning with essays written for *The Criterion* in the 1930's and *The Destructive Element: A Study of Modern Writers and Beliefs* (1935), and continuing through his study of T. S. Eliot (1975) and the selection of essays from various periods of Spender's career entitled *The Thirties and After* (1978). Especially notable among his other critical books are *The Struggle of the Modern* (1963), a study of modernism's complicated relationship to twentieth century literature in general, and *Love-Hate Relations: A Study of Anglo-American Sensibilities* (1974), which examines the connections between American and English literary sensibilities. Spender's journalistic writings include *Citizens in War and After* (1945) and *European Witness* (1946). He has also published an autobiography, *World Within World: The Autobiography of Spender* (1951).

Achievements

Several of Spender's poems stand among the most poignant of the twentieth

century. Those anthology pieces with which his name is most often associated—"Not Palaces, an Era's Crown," "Beethoven's Death Mask," "I think
continually of those who were truly great," "The Express," "The Landscape
near an Aerodome" and "Ultima Ratio Regum"—have helped achieve for
Spender greater recognition than for any of the other British poets who came
into prominence in the late 1920's and early 1930's, with the notable exception of W. H. Auden. Spender's stature rests also on his peculiar position
among poets writing through the Great Depression and after World War II.
More than the others, he emerged and has continued as an authentic voice
bridging the modernist and postwar periods. Even during the 1930's—when
Auden was the leader of the loose confederation of young writers to which
he and Spender belonged—it was Spender who in poem after poem voiced
most honestly and movingly the tensions informing the writing of poetry in
that troubled time. When Auden and Christopher Isherwood departed for
America in 1939, Spender remained as the foremost representative of the liberal values and lyric intensity which had marked the best poetry of the pre-
war years. More recently—especially with the death of the other figures making up the so-called Auden Group—Spender's verse, as well as his prose,
has taken on special interest, as a last link between contemporary British literature and an earlier period crucial to its development.

In many respects Spender's outlook and poetry have scarcely altered since
the 1930's. While many critics have regarded such want of development as
a mark of failure, in a sense it represents a strength. Presumably, Spender
has seen little reason to change his poetic method or to go beyond those
indisputably successful poems of his early adulthood because for him the
fundamental problems—poetic, political, and personal—have hardly changed
since that time. Interestingly, an audience has grown up that is scarcely aware
of Spender's poetic achievement and yet is very much fascinated by Spender
the essayist and lecturer. Because his most characteristic pronouncements to
this more recently acquired audience are closely related to the viewpoint
revealed in the early poems, they suggest the continuing value of those poems,
not merely as artifacts from an increasingly distant past but as permanent
sources of interest and pleasure.

Biography

Stephen Harold Spender was born in London on February 28, 1909. His
father was Harold Spender, a noted journalist and lecturer, and his mother
was Violet Hilda Schuster Spender, a painter and poet. The death of Spender's
mother when he was fifteen and of his father two years later, in 1926, brought
the four children, of whom he was the second-oldest, under the care of his
maternal grandmother, a pair of spinster great-aunts, and an uncle.

After attending University College School in London, Spender went to
University College, Oxford, in 1928, leaving in 1930 without a degree. Having

begun to write poetry in childhood and having determined to be a poet, he sought out the somewhat older W. H. Auden even before beginning at Oxford. Their friendship, marked by a mutual awareness of their differences in temperament and outlook, apparently developed rapidly; Spender himself published Auden's first book of poems in 1928 on the same handpress he used to bring out his own first book. He spent the summer vacation of 1929 in Germany, meeting many young Germans and observing social and political developments that would set the stage for the next decade.

The 1930's were a time of tremendous literary activity for the young Spender, periodically punctuated by travels throughout Europe. He achieved prominence as a leading member of the group of rising young writers clustered around Auden. Although Spender has claimed a singular position among the Auden group, during that time he behaved in a fashion broadly similar to that adopted by the others, briefly joining the Communist Party in 1936 and traveling to Spain in 1937 to observe the Civil War from the Republican side, and publishing poems and essays supporting a radical viewpoint and warning of the growing Nazi menace. By late 1939 he had joined Cyril Connolly as coeditor of *Horizon*, a post he held until 1941. The war years also saw Spender in the National Fire Service and later in the Foreign Service. In 1941, he married Natasha Litwin, his 1936 marriage to Agnes Marie Pearn having ended in divorce.

Since World War II, Spender has been occupied with numerous writing, editing, and translating projects, with extensive travel and university lecturing—particularly in the United States—and with his family life. From 1953 to 1966, he served as coeditor of *Encounter*, resigning when he learned of the Central Intelligence Agency's financing of that magazine. Spender's many public and literary honors include being named a Companion in the Order of the British Empire (C.B.E.) in 1962, receiving the Queen's Gold Medal for Poetry in 1971, and being given an Honorary Fellowship to University College, Oxford, in 1973. In 1970, he was appointed to the chair of English literature in University College, London.

Analysis

Stephen Spender seems always to have struck his readers as halting. Even in the relatively confident writing of his youth, he was the most likely of the Auden Group to avoid the extreme pronouncements to which his seemingly more self-assured contemporaries—especially Auden himself—were prone. Taken as a whole, his poetry appears to reflect a perpetual debate, an unresolved tension over what can be known, over what is worth knowing, and over how he ought to respond as a poet and as a citizen of a modern society. Taken separately, his poems—particularly the best and most representative ones—exhibit an attraction or a movement sometimes toward one side of an issue, and sometimes toward the other. Almost always, however, such commitment at least implies its opposite.

This tension itself may account for the continuing appeal of so many Spender lyrics, decades after they were written and after their historical context had passed. Obviously they conform to the demand for irony and ambiguity begun in the late 1920's by I. A. Richards and William Empson and prolonged until recently by their American counterparts, the New Critics. In this respect, if not in others, Spender established a link with the seventeenth century Metaphysical wits so admired by T. S. Eliot. The qualifying tendency of Spender's poetry connects him also with the postwar movement among a younger generation of British poets—notably Philip Larkin, Donald Davie, and Kingsley Amis—who have taken issue with Eliot's modernist ambitions and with Dylan Thomas' romantic gesturing.

The tentativeness of Spender's writing connects with so many diverse and often opposing tendencies in modern literature because it has its roots in the Romanticism underlying all modern literature. Like Romanticism, Spender's verse embraces a variety of conflicting impulses. Whether to write about private subjects or to take on more public concerns, and whether to adopt a personal or an impersonal stance toward the selected subjects, become central problems for Spender. He finds himself at some times, and in some poems, drawn to life's simple, civilian joys; at other times he is moved toward the grand actions of politics. Stylistically, he can be seen vacillating between directness and obliqueness, literalness and figurativeness, and realism and imagism. The conflicting pulls of pragmatism and idealism so evident throughout his career suggest a sympathy with virtually all strains of Western philosophy, especially since René Descartes. Underlying this inability, or unwillingness, to project a set posture is the drive toward inwardness seen in nineteenth century literature, a drive at once hastened and opposed by the great Romantics. The legacy of this drive and its attendant struggle constitute much of the drama played out in Spender's poems.

His writing in the 1930's suggests the same sort of shift evident in the other Auden poets and in many prose writers, such as George Orwell. It suggests, too, a process more of accretion than of drastic change, since the seeds of Spender's discontent with the posture of his earlier political poems lay in the poems themselves. Auden's poetry probably encouraged the young Spender to move from the unfocused idealism of his teens and to write more about the real world. Spender's poetry thus became noticeably contemporary in reference, with urban scenes and crowds, to the point that he could devote entire poems to a speedy train ("The Express") or an airship ("The Landscape near an Aerodrome").

Just as Auden found Spender too romantic, Spender found Auden too cool and detached from the often grim world which Auden had induced him to consider in his poems. Even at his most topical, even when most under Auden's influence, Spender refused to indulge in Audenesque wit or satiric bite. The characteristic feeling of the *Poems* of 1933 is one of commitment and seriousness. Where Auden might concentrate on the ridiculousness of society, Spender concentrates on society's victims and their suffering.

"Moving through the silent crowd" illustrates well the understated poignancy of which Spender was capable at this time in his career. Nearly empty of metaphor, it gains its effect through Spender's emphasis on emblematic detail and through the development of saddening irony. He frames the poem with his own vantage point, from which he observes the idle poor. The first stanza turns on his intimation of "falling light," which represents for him the composite disillusionment and wasted potential of the men silent in the road. In the second, he notices the cynicism implicit in such gestures as shrugging shoulders and emptying pockets. Such a scene leads him, in the final two stanzas, to develop the irony of the situation and to hint at a radical political stance. He notes how the unemployed resemble the wealthy in doing no work and sleeping late. Confessing jealousy of their leisure, he nevertheless feels "haunted" by the meaninglessness of their lives.

An equally strong element of social conscience colors many other Spender poems written before 1933. Generally they exhibit more eloquence and metaphorical sweep than the rather terse "Moving through the silent crowd." For example, in "Not palaces, an era's crown" he catalogs those purely intellectual or aesthetic considerations which he must dismiss in favor of social action. Such action he significantly compares to an energized battery and illustrates in a bold program of opposition to social and political tyranny. The short, forceful sentences of the poem's second section, where this program is described, contrast with the longer, more ornate syntax of the beginning. The hunger that Spender hopes to eradicate is of a more pressing order than that addressed by aesthetics or vague idealism, which he characterizes as sheer indolence. Only in the poem's final line, once his moral and political ambitions have been fully expressed, can he permit himself a Platonic image, as light is said to be brought to life.

Such insistence upon social reform, shading into radical political action, probably peaked in the period of 1935 to 1938, when *Vienna* and *Trial of a Judge* were appearing. Perhaps more notable than Spender's eventual repudiation of the unsuccessful *Vienna* is the fact that in so many of the shorter poems written during these years, especially those concerned with Spain, he turned increasingly from the public subjects, the outwardly directed statements, and the didactic organization marking the earlier poems. Where his critique of life in England might be construed as supportive of Communism, the picture he draws of Spain during the Civil War largely ignores the political dimension of the struggle and focuses instead on the suffering experienced by civilians in all regions and of all political persuasions. While a strain of political idealism continues, the enemy is no longer simply capitalism or even Adolf Hitler; rather, for Spender it has become war and those persons responsible for inflicting a state of war on the helpless and innocent.

One of his most effective poems from Spain, "Ultima Ratio Regum," exhibits a didactic form, even ending with a rhetorical question; but it carefully avoids condemnation or praise of either side. Read without consideration for Spender's original reasons for going to Spain, his angry and moving account of a young Spaniard's senseless death by machine-gun fire condemns the Republicans no less than the Insurgents and ultimately centers on the impersonality of modern war, which reduces to statistical insignificance a formerly alive and sensitive young man. Similarly, "Thoughts During an Air Raid" deals with Spender's own feelings while taking cover and with the temptation to regard oneself as somehow special and therefore immune from the fate threatening all other people in time of war. If Spender here argues for a more collective consciousness, it is but a vague and largely psychological brotherhood. As in "Ultima Ratio Regum," the viewpoint here is wholly civilian and pacifist. Even "Fall of a City," which clearly and sadly alludes to a Republican defeat, suggests more the spirit of freedom which Spender sees surviving the fall than any political particulars or doctrine attending that spirit. There Spender derives his residual hope not from a party or concerted action, but from the simple handing down of memories and values from an old man to a child. If anything, this poem reflects a distrust of large-scale political ideologies and action and of the dishonesty, impersonality, and brutality that they necessarily breed.

In his autobiography Spender writes of having been puzzled by civilian enthusiasm for both sides in the Spanish struggle. Like Orwell, he was also disturbed by Republican atrocities against civilians. Such disillusioning discoveries no doubt contributed to the reluctance with which he viewed England's struggle against the Nazis even after the war had begun. Conceding the need to counter the German threat, Spender in his war poems nevertheless stressed the pain, rather than the glory, of that necessity. Such was his perception of that pain that he found it necessary in "The War God" to ask and answer questions which, after Munich or the invasion of Poland, even the most war-wary Englishman probably would no longer have considered. One almost gets the impression that Spender is concerned with convincing, or reminding, himself more than anyone else of the reasons behind the war, so obvious is the logic of the poem. Even "Memento," his more effective response to the death camps, betrays the same lingering pacifism as its surreal images describe the victims' horror and helplessness.

Perhaps Spender's most remarkable—and his most reluctant—war poem is his response to the fall of France, "June 1940." Even as Britain is most threatened, he finds it necessary and appropriate to invoke the ghost of World War I to express his skepticism about the impending defense against Hitler. The first section of the poem combines a lyrical description of the delights of the English summer with suggestions of the war's distance from that pastoral scene. Spender has the "grey" survivors of the earlier war note the difference between the trench fighting of their youth and the newer, more mechanized European war of which they have heard only very little. He shows boys bicycling around village war memorials and the Channel "snipping" England from France. The scene and mood change drastically in the next section, with the slightly surreal account of the "caterpillar-wheeled blond" charging over birds' nests in France that very day, and with the lengthy series of voices arguing the need to counter the Nazi horde with armed resistance. Such arguments persuade the old soldiers, sitting in their deck chairs since the poem's beginning, that the struggle against Germany is just and that the alternative is an imprisoned England.

Even so, Spender characterizes the old veterans' response as "disillusioned" to prepare the reader for the poem's audacious ending. In six short lines he overturns the style, the premises, and the conclusion of the earlier dialogue. A dead soldier from the Great War suddenly testifies to the purgatory of guilt to which participation in that earlier struggle against Germany has doomed him, to imply that the arguments justifying the current war represent only a seductive parallel to earlier warmongering, and that even defeating Hitler will not wholly justify the impending struggle or absolve the English of war guilt. While the conclusion implied by the logic of the poem may not be that England ought to surrender, it certainly cuts very thin any moral advantage the English might claim in resisting. Again Spender ultimately focuses his attention on the burden—in this case a moral one—placed on the individual by collective action.

"June 1940" represents only the most blatant evidence of Spender's departure from the spirited socialism and anti-Nazism of his earlier poems. The general drift of his writing after 1934 had been clearly in that direction. His poems had dealt increasingly with personal problems and situations. In *Forward from Liberalism* (1937), he had articulated his dissatisfaction with the socialist creed, a dissatisfaction based principally upon what he saw as the necessary antipathy to the individual person which politics, and especially leftist politics, inevitably aroused. Before too long he was able, in *The Creative Element: A Study of Vision, Despair, and Orthodoxy Among Some Modern Writers* (1953), to attribute his earlier political orthodoxy to liberal guilt induced by the misery of the poor during the Great Depression.

The ease with which such renunciation and self-analysis seems to have come after the late 1930's suggests the limited nature of Spender's commitment to politics even when he seemed most political. The tension between individual and collective viewpoints which becomes central to the Spanish Civil War poems and to "June 1940" is at least implicit in most of his earlier writing, as well.

It is true that in his criticism Spender repeatedly questions the wisdom of the modernists' avoidance of politics, particularly by T. S. Eliot and William

Butler Yeats, whom he so admired as a young man. In this regard, "An Elementary School Classroom in a Slum" constitutes Spender's gloss on Yeats's "Among School Children," first in the type of school the younger poet chooses to visit, and second in his refusal to turn the visit into an occasion for personal theorizing, as Yeats did. Spender's allusion to "Sailing to Byzantium"—where he asserts that he will not transform the street beggars into "birds" on his "singing-tree"—attacks Yeats even more directly.

The grammar of this assertion, however—indeed, of many ostensibly political statements by the young Spender—guarantees, perhaps intentionally, some confusion of purpose and does so so often that it seems reflective of a confusion in Spender himself. "In railway halls, on pavement near the traffic" is the very poem in which he seems to mock Yeats for the Irishman's indifference to public affairs. The poem is governed by an "I" whose statement of poetic intent ultimately reflects more on himself than on the plight of the poor. Not only does the subject of the poem thus become poetry—something that Spender could deplore in Yeats—but also in a sense the poet becomes the hero. This is not to criticize Spender, but merely to point out, ironically, how much his focus approaches Yeats's after all. The first-person perspective of so many other early Spender poems ties the public to the private and prevents any purely political orientation from taking over.

"Moving through the silent crowd" illustrates even more strikingly this same tension. While the observed poor are rendered sympathetically, the reader can never forget the observer. The marked return, in the final stanza, to his viewpoint and his troubles—where three of four lines begin with "I'm," and where each of the parallel clauses develops the poet's dilemma—clearly raises a question as to the ultimate object of sympathy here. This does not mean that the poem reflects merely self-pity or that Spender might not want to get outside himself; however, the poem finally becomes an exposure not only of poverty, but also of the poet's inability to close the perceived gap between himself and the poor. He concludes with a sense of his distance from them; all he can do is sympathize and be "haunted" by them. Because he appears as helpless as they, though in a somewhat different sense, his helplessness becomes at least as important as theirs as the subject of the poem. Without the personal perspective, the poem seems to ask, Of what validity is political or social criticism? At the same time, the poem's fixation with the observer's perspective places in serious doubt the efficacy of whatever criticism he may construct.

Another dimension of Spender's uncertainty comes in his treatment of contemporary civilization, particularly in those celebrated early poems dealing with technology. Although Auden probably influenced Spender in this direction, Spender seems never to have been so comfortable as Auden with the up-to-date world, particularly as an element of his poetry. Such discomfort largely escaped his first readers, who found his apparent acceptance of material progress a welcome departure from old-fashioned nature poetry. A. Kingsley Weatherhead rightly suggests, in *Stephen Spender and the Thirties* (1975), that many writers of that decade wrote a covert kind of nature poetry even as they purported to repudiate the values of the Georgian poets. They did so, Weatherhead says, by taking a critical look at contemporary civilization and thereby implying retreat as the only viable alternative.

While this no doubt is true of Spender, his retreat often takes very subtle forms. Sometimes it resides largely in the terms with which he commends an aspect of twentieth century technology. "The Express," for example, appears to celebrate the beauty and speed of a fast-moving train and, thus, to confirm the benefits of modern applied science. An examination of the poem's progression, however, reveals considerable dissatisfaction with the external world for which the train has been manufactured. Perhaps the whole idea of a lyric poem's appropriating something so utilitarian as an express train might seem an implied criticism of utility; certainly Walt Whitman's "To a Locomotive in Winter" and Emily Dickinson's "I like to see it lap the miles" can be seen as backhanded compliments. Even so, Spender's train poem seems of a different order in that it places the train much more realistically—with references to stations, to gasworks, and to Edinburgh. A good deal of the poem's language is very literal. Even Spender's initial nonliteral description ascribes utility to the train's beginning: it is cast as a queen issuing a "plain manifesto" to her subjects.

The image of such public action yields to more private behavior in the poem's second sentence, where "she" is said to "sing" with increasing abandon as she gathers speed. In the third and final sentence, she sings enraptured, exceeding the bounds of nature by flying in her music. The shape of the poem is thus the progression of its metaphors. Because that progression is vertical— away from the earth, into a state of Platonic grace suggested by music, again reminiscent of Yeats—the poem becomes a celebration of imaginative and self-absorbed retreat from the mundane and empirical reality in which the express actually resides. Even as Spender praises the train, he gives equal praise to a place where the express could not possibly exist. The two objects of praise coexist, as do the two kinds of language by which they are represented. There is no evidence that the speaker of the poem—significantly *not* represented as "I"—does not believe he is praising the express on its own terms. On the other hand, the progression of the terms he uses, particularly the metaphors, suggests that he in fact admires principles quite antipathetic to those upon which the express runs, and that perhaps he can find the express tolerable only by transforming it into something it is not and cannot be.

Poems such as "The Express," "The Landscape near the Aerodrome," and "Pylons" suggest a flight from the material values upon which modern popular culture is founded. In this they can have even greater pertinence now than when they were written. An examination of other early poems suggests a wish, or at least a need, to escape the human element as well. For all of their apparent humanism, they propose a withdrawal from the very society that Spender would help redeem, and confirm the Marxist critique of Romanticism as an elevation of private concerns at the expense of the public good. They bring to mind, too, Hugh MacDiarmid's indictment of the Auden group's ultimate lack of political commitment.

Certainly, it seems no accident that Spender has written so much about Romanticism and especially about Percy Bysshe Shelley. His discussion of the modern poet's difficulties in reconciling the Romantic ideal of the individual imagination and sensibility with a public, collective age seems almost an abstract of poems such as "Without that one clear aim, the path of flight" or "From all these events, from the slum, from the war, from the boom." In the first of these, a sonnet, Spender complains of being choked and imprisoned by social reality, of needing desperately to escape on the "wings" of poetry. So politically suspect a motive for writing, which he reinforces by other Platonic images suggestive of Shelley, informs the second poem. There Spender expresses a faith, not in reformist action, but in the power of time to obliterate the memory not only of wrongdoing but also of those who would correct it. What might have horrified Thomas Hardy thus consoles Spender. In "Perhaps," he takes comfort in the more escapist position that troubling public events may be only fantasies. Even "I think continually of those who were truly great," so often cited as the epitome of 1930's selflessness, suggests that Spender's characteristic way of coping with social problems is to forget them: to ignore the present by dreaming of the "truly great."

Individual poems and the collective poetry of Spender rarely show him consistent in this regard. His struggle with the irreconcilables of individual and group, private and public, and realism and idealism have their stylistic level, as elegances of metaphor and syntax frequently accompany and undermine his call for action in the present. To an age grown increasingly aware of the limitations, if not the futility, of collective behavior and of the traps into which both leader and follower can fall, Spender poses the dilemma of the morally and socially sensitive individual. For this reason he commands a not inconsiderable place among the poets of this century.

Bruce K. Martin

Other major works

LONG FICTION: *The Backward Son*, 1940.

SHORT FICTION: *The Burning Cactus*, 1936; *Engaged in Writing* and *The Fool and the Princess*, 1958.

PLAYS: *Trial of a Judge*, 1938; *Danton's Death*, 1939 (with Goronwy Rees); *To the Island*, 1951; *Mary Stuart*, 1957; *Lulu*, 1958; *Rasputin's End*, 1963; *Oedipus Trilogy: A Play in Three Acts Based on the Oedipus Plays of Sophocles*, 1983.

NONFICTION: *The Destructive Element: A Study of Modern Writers and Beliefs*, 1935; *Forward from Liberalism*, 1937; *Citizens in War and After*, 1945; *European Witness*, 1946; *Poetry Since 1939*, 1946; *World Within World: The Autobiography of Spender*, 1951; *Shelley*, 1952; *The Creative Element: A Study of Vision, Despair, and Orthodoxy Among Some Modern Writers*, 1953; *The Making of a Poem*, 1955; *The Struggle of the Modern*, 1963; *Love-Hate Relations: A Study of Anglo-American Sensibilities*, 1974; *Eliot*, 1975; *The Thirties and After*, 1978; *Journals, 1939-1983*, 1985.

Bibliography

Blamires, Harry. *Twentieth Century English Literature*. Rev. ed. New York: Schocken Books, 1985. This standard account of the development of English literature devotes only four pages to Spender, but it represents the judgment of the last quarter of the century and places the poet well in his generation and cultural context. Includes an index, a useful list for further reading, and a chronology.

Connors, J. J. *Poets and Politics: A Study of the Careers of C. Day Lewis, Stephen Spender, and W. H. Auden in the 1930's*. New Haven, Conn.: Yale University Press, 1967. Connors concentrates on the political activities and influence of these three figures. Politics, however, directly affected their poetry, and Connors points this out accurately and in detail. Supplemented by a complete and easy-to-use index.

Hynes, Samuel. *The Auden Generation: Literature and Politics in the 1930's*. New York: Viking Press, 1976. Like J. J. Connors, Hynes examines the interphase between politics and literature, but he is more concerned with the literature. His broader scope covers the entire spectrum of literature and looks hard at its social functions during a period of intense propaganda. Includes an appendix and full notes.

Maxwell, D. E. S. *Poets of the Thirties*. London: Routledge & Kegan Paul, 1969. Maxwell's work is a classic on the period, re-creating the complex world of that time with clarity and insight. The book, a marvelous cornucopia of anecdotes, clearly underlines Spender's role. The index helps readers connect details.

Thurley, Geoffrey. "A Kind of Scapegoat: A Retrospect on Stephen Spender." In *The Ironic Harvest: English Poetry in the Twentieth Century*. London: Edward Arnold, 1974. Provides a good synthesis of the changing estimate of the enduring value of Spender's poetry. This account is even-handed and comprehensive and places Spender well in the context of the 1930's.

Weatherhead, A. Kingsley. *Stephen Spender and the Thirties*. Lewisburg, Pa.: Bucknell University Press, 1975. Covers most aspects of interest in Spender's work and life and is the most comprehensive single source. Weatherhead knows his subject well and develops it with sympathetic detail. His bibliography is still useful.

EDMUND SPENSER

Born: London, England; c. 1552
Died: London, England; January 13, 1599

Principal poetry

The Shepheardes Calender, 1579; *The Faerie Queene*, 1590, 1596; *Complaints*, 1591; *Daphnaïda*, 1591; *Colin Clouts Come Home Againe*, 1595; *Astrophel*, 1595; *Amoretti*, 1595; *Epithalamion*, 1595; *Fowre Hymnes*, 1596; *Prothalamion*, 1596; *The Poetical Works of Edmund Spenser*, 1912 (J. C. Smith and Ernest de Selincourt, editors).

Other literary forms

Like most Renaissance writers, Edmund Spenser usually prefaced his poems with dedicatory letters that complimented the recipients and also provided helpful interpretations for other readers. Further indications of Spenser's theories about "English versifying" appear in his correspondence with Gabriel Harvey: *Three Proper, and Wittie, Familiar Letters* (1580) and *Foure Letters and Certaine Sonnets* (1586). Although *A View of the Present State of Ireland* was written in 1596, it was not published until 1633, thirty-four years after the author's death. In this treatise, Spenser presented a clear picture of Elizabethan Ireland and its political, economic, and social evils. The serious tone of this work deepens the significance of the Irish allusions and imagery throughout Spenser's poetry.

Achievements

The inscription on Spenser's monument hails him as "the Prince of Poets in his time," but his reputation as "poet's poet" continued among his Romantic peers three centuries later. What was praised and imitated changed with time, but the changes themselves suggest the extent of Spenser's achievements. His popularity among his contemporaries was documented not only in commentaries written during his lifetime but also in William Camden's account of Spenser's funeral, during which mourning poets threw into his tomb their elegies and the pens with which they had written these tributes. Among his fellow Elizabethans, Spenser first gained renown as a love poet, a pastoral writer, and a restorer of the native language—all three of these roles already enacted in his early work, *The Shepheardes Calender*, in which he demonstrated the expansiveness of rural dialect and English unadulterated with continental vocabulary. Later, in a more courtly work, *The Faerie Queene*, Spenser still sought variety in language more through native archaisms than through foreign idiom. Despite its simplicity of diction, *The Shepheardes Calender* contained an elaborate academic apparatus that demanded recognition for its author as a serious poet. The fact that Spenser took his work seriously was also manifested in various levels of satire and in metrical experimentation which strengthened what Philip Sidney described as his "poetical sinews."

Seventeenth century imitators echoed Spenser's allegorical and pastoral elements, his sensuous description, and his archaic phrasing. These early Spenserians, however, did not fully comprehend their model. Their servile imitations of surface themes and complex metrical forms temporarily diminished Spenser's reputation and probably stimulated later eighteenth century parodies. The serious side of Spenser, however, gradually received more notice. In *Areopagitica* (1644), for example, John Milton extolled him as "a better teacher than Scotus or Aquinas," and when the neoclassicists praised him, it was primarily for allegorical didacticism. In the nineteenth century, admiration of Spenser's moral allegory yielded to delight in his metrical virtuosity and the beauties of his word-pictures. When such great Romantics as Sir Walter Scott, Lord Byron, and John Keats imitated the Spenserian or "Faerie Queene" stanza form, they demonstrated anew the strength and flexibility of Spenser's metrical inventiveness. Modern holistic criticism continues to find deeper levels of Spenserian inventiveness in structural intricacy, allegorical ingenuity, and both narrative and descriptive aptness.

Biography

If allusions in his own poetry can be read autobiographically, Edmund Spenser was born in London in 1552, apparently into a mercantile family of moderate income. In 1561, the Merchant Taylors' School opened with Richard Mulcaster as its first headmaster, and in that same year or shortly afterward Spenser was enrolled, probably as a scholarship student. From Mulcaster, Spenser learned traditional Latin and Greek, and also an awareness of the intricacies and beauties of the English language unusual among both schoolboys and schoolmasters of that time. Later, Spenser as "Colin Clout" paid tribute to Mulcaser as the "olde Shephearde" who had made him "by art more cunning" in the "song and musicks mirth" that fascinated him in his "looser yeares." Even before Spenser went to Cambridge, fourteen of his schoolboy verse translations had been incorporated into the English version of Jan van der Noot's *Theatre for Worldlings* (1569).

At Pembroke College, Cambridge, Spenser took his B.A. degree in 1573 and his M.A. in 1576; little else is known about his activities during that period except that he made several lifelong friends, among them Gabriel Harvey and Edward Kirke. Both Harvey and Kirke were later among Spenser's prepublication readers and critics, and Kirke today remains the most likely candidate for the role of "E. K.," the commentator whose glosses and arguments interpret enigmatic passages in *The Shepheardes Calender*. The Spenser-Harvey letters reveal young Spenser's theories on poetry and also his hopes for the patronage of Philip Sidney and Sidney's uncle, the Earl of Leicester, Queen Elizabeth's favored courtier. Harvey's greetings to a woman, whom he addresses as "Mistress Immerito" and "Lady Colin Clout," also suggest that Spenser was married about 1580; nothing more is known of the first wife, but there are records of a son and a daughter at the time of Spenser's second marriage to Elizabeth Boyle in 1594.

When Spenser found himself unable to gain an appointment as a Fellow at Cambridge, he accepted the post of secretary to John Young, Bishop of Rochester. In 1580, he went to Ireland as secretary for Arthur Lord Grey, the newly appointed Lord Governor. When Grey was recalled from Ireland two years later because his policies did not control the Irish rebellion as the English court desired, Spenser remained behind. For several years he moved into minor offices in different sections of the country; about 1589, he became "undertaker" of Kilcolman, an estate in Cork. As an "undertaker," Spenser received a grant of land previously confiscated from an Irish rebel, agreeing to see to the restoration of the estate and to establish tenant farmers on it. Love for Kilcolman is reflected in his poetry even though his days there were shadowed by litigation with an Irish neighbor who claimed the property and by a new outbreak of rebellion which eventually destroyed the estate and forced him to leave Ireland about a month before his death in 1599.

With the exception of *The Shepheardes Calender*, all of Spenser's major poetry was written in Ireland. The landscape and the people of his adopted country are reflected in imagery and allusions; political and economic conditions appear in various guises, perhaps nowhere so strongly and pervasively as in Book V of *The Faerie Queene*, the Book of Justice. Although Spenser lived most of his adult life far from the court of Elizabeth, he maintained constant contact with events and friends there. His strongest bid for court recognition came in *The Faerie Queene*, with its creation of Gloriana, the Fairyland reflection of the living Queen of Britain, who rewarded him for his portrait of her by granting him an annual pension. Two of Queen Elizabeth's favorites played major roles in Spenser's later years: Sir Walter Raleigh and Robert, Earl of Essex. Raleigh, who owned an estate neighboring Spenser's Kilcolman, frequently encouraged the poet's work in a general way and, if there is any validity in Spenser's famous prefatory letter, influenced specific changes in the structure of *The Faerie Queene*. Essex financed the poet's funeral and his burial in the Poet's Corner of Westminster Abbey in 1599.

Analysis

By an eclectic mingling of old traditions, Edmund Spenser created new poetry—new in verse forms, in language, and in genre. From the Middle Ages, Spenser had inherited complex allegorical traditions and a habit of interlacing narrative strands; these traditions were fused with classical myth and generic conventions, some of them transformed by continental imitators before they reached Spenser. This fusion of medievalism and classicism was in turn modified by currents of thought prevalent in Tudor England, especially by the intense nationalism that manifested itself in religion, language, politics, and international affairs.

To some extent, Spenser's poetic development evolved naturally from his deliberate selection of Vergil as his model. Like Vergil, he started his published career with pastoral eclogues; like him, too, he turned, in his last major work, from shepherds to great heroes. Before Spenser evoked classical muses in his epic, however, the tradition of Vergil had picked up romantic coloring and allegorical overtones from continental epics, especially Ludovico Ariosto's highly allegorized *Orlando furioso* (1532). Spenser himself announced the three-way pattern adopted for *The Faerie Queene*: "Fierce wars and faithful loves shall moralize my song." Long after Spenser's death his admirers continued to compare him with Vergil, often to Spenser's advantage. Vergil provided stimulus not only for the pastoral and epic genres in which Spenser wrote his two major works but also for the mythical allusions that permeate most of his work and for the serious use of poetry, especially in political and religious satire and in the reflection of nationalistic pride. Vergil's exaltation of Augustus and the Roman Empire accorded well with the nationalism of Elizabethan England, a nationalism poetically at its zenith in *The Faerie Queene.*

Vergil's sobriquet "Tityrus" became for Spenser a means of double praise when he hailed his fourteenth century predecessor Geoffrey Chaucer as an English Tityrus, the "God of shepheards." Rustic language, interlocked narratives, and experiments in vernacular quantitative verse forms in *The Shepheardes Calender* all reflect Chaucerian influence; in a less direct way, the vogue of courtly love in medieval and Renaissance literature was also channeled partly through Chaucer. During the two centuries between Chaucer and Spenser, love poetry became permeated with a blend of Petrarchan and Neoplatonic elements. Petrarchan lovers taught Spenser's shepherds to lament over their ladies' cruelty, to extol their beauty, and to describe their own pains, anxieties, and ecstasies with conventional images. The more sensuous aspects of love remained central to many of the *Amoretti* sonnets and to several set pieces in *The Faerie Queene*, such as Acrasia's Bower of Bliss and Busiranes' Mask of Cupid; but idealistic Neoplatonic concepts also emerged here. Such Neoplatonic concepts undergird the *Fowre Hymnes*. The first two hymns praise erotic human love and the inspirational force of feminine beauty; the other two deprecate these more earthly powers, elevating in their place the heavenly love and beauty of Christ, the source of all true human love and beauty.

In *The Faerie Queene*, too, idealistic Neoplatonic elements assume more pervasive significance than do Petrarchan motifs. The Platonic identification of the good and the beautiful, for example, is often manifest, especially in Gloriana, Una, and Belphoebe; and the true and false Florimels of Books III-V exemplify true and false beauty, the former inspiring virtuous love and marriage and the second inciting sensuous lust. Although Books III and IV are called the Books of Chastity and Friendship, their linked story dramatically demonstrates variant forms of love. The concept of love as either debilitating or inspiring reflects one of the mythical traditions transmitted from antiquity through the Middle Ages: the double significance of Venus as good and evil love. As the goddess of good, fruitful love, Venus herself frequents the Garden of Adonis, where nature is untouched by deceptive art, where spring and harvest meet, and where love flourishes joyfully. In her own temple, Venus listens to the sound of "lovers piteously complaining" rather than rejoicing.

Renaissance pageantry and Tudor emblem books contributed to the pictorial quality with which Spenser brought myths to life—classical tales, rustic folklore, and his own mythic creations. One of the most picturesque of Spenser's new myths describes the "spousals" of the Thames and Medway rivers, a ceremony attended by such "wat'ry gods" as Neptune and his son Albion; by other rivers, remote ones such as the Nile and the Ganges, Irish neighbors such as the Liffey and the Mulla, and streams that paid tribute to one of the betrothed rivers; and by Arion, accompanied by his dolphin and carrying the harp with which he provided wedding music. Scenes like these exemplify the artistry with which Spenser created new poetry out of old traditions.

Classic and contemporary models, rural and courtly milieu, universal and occasional topics—from such a mixture Spenser formed his first major work, the "little booke," which he dedicated to Sidney and which he signed "Immerito," the Unworthy One. *The Shepheardes Calender* went through five editions between 1579 and 1597, none of them bearing Spenser's name. Such anonymity fits common Renaissance practice, but it may also have had additional motivation from Spenser's awareness of sensitive topical allusions with too thin an allegorical veil. Contemporary praise of Spenser indicates that by 1586 the anonymity was technical rather than real. In his twelve eclogues, one for each month of the year, Spenser imitated conventions that Renaissance writers attributed to Vergil and to his Greek predecessors: debates between rustic speakers in a rural setting, varied by a singing match between shepherds, a lament for the death of a beloved companion, praise of the current sovereign, alternating exultation and despair over one's mistress, and veiled references to contemporary situations. A fifteenth century French work, translated as *The Kalender and compost of Shepherds*, probably suggested to Spenser not only his title but also the technique of emblematic illustration, the application of zodiacal signs to everyday life and to the seasons, and the arrangement of instructional commentary according to the months. Barbabe Googe's *The Zodiake of Life* (1565) strengthened the satirical and philosophical undertone of the calendar theme.

Despite the surface simplicity connoted by its nominal concern with shepherds, Spenser's book is a complex work. Not the least of its complexities are the paraphernalia added by "E. K.": the dedicatory epistle, the introductory arguments (for the whole book and for each eclogue), and the glosses. Although the initials themselves make Spenser's Cambridge friend Edward Kirke the most likely person to designate as the mysterious commentator, the Renaissance love for name-games does not exclude other possible solutions of the identity puzzle. Even Spenser himself has been suggested as a candidate for the enigmatic role. Many of E. K.'s annotations supply information essential to an understanding of the poet's cryptic allusions, to the identification of real-life counterparts for the characters, and occasionally to a modernization of archaic diction. Some annotations, however, are either accidentally erroneous or pedantically misleading: for example, several source references and the etymology for "aeglogues." E. K. derives the term "eclogues" from "Goteheardes tales" rather than from "conversations of shepherds," the more usual Renaissance understanding of the term; in actuality, "eclogues" are etymologically short selections which convention came to associate with pastoral settings.

The twelve separate selections could have produced a sense of fragmentation, but instead they create a highly unified whole. The most obvious unifying device is the calendar framework, which gives to the individual poem their titles and their moods. Another source of unity lies in the shepherd characters who appear repeatedly, especially Colin Clout, a character borrowed from the Tudor satirist John Skelton and used by Spenser as his own persona. Colin appears in four of the eclogues and is the topic of conversation in three others; his friendship for Hobbinol (identified by E. K. as Harvey), and his love for Rosalind (unidentified) provide a thread of plot throughout the twelve poems. Moreover, the figure of Colin represents the whole life of "everyman"—or at least every poet—as he passes from the role of "shepherd boy" in "January" to that of the mature "gentle shepherd" in "December."

In his general arugment, E. K. establishes three categories for the topics of the eclogues: plaintive, recreative, and moral. The four selections which E. K. classifies as plaintive are those in which Colin's is the main voice. "January" and "June" are laments about his futile love for Rosalind; "December," too, is a conventional love plaint, although it adds the dimension of Colin's approaching death. "November," one of the most highly structured eclogues, is a pastoral elegy for Dido, the daughter of one "greate shephearde" and the beloved of another "greate shepheard Lobbin." E. K. pleads ignorance of the identity of both shepherds, but most critics identify "Lobbin" as a typical anagram for Robin (Robert Dudley) plus Leicester, thus suggesting a covert allusion to a love interest of Elizabeth's favorite, the Earl of Leicester.

The first of the three recreative selections, "March," is a sprightly, occasionally bawdy, discussion of love by two shepherd boys. "April" starts out with a description of Colin's lovesickness but then moves on to an encomium on "fayre Elissa, Queene of shepheardes all," a transparent allusion to Queen Elizabeth. The singing contest in "August" gives Spenser an opportunity to exploit shifting moods and an intricate variety of metrical patterns.

It is sometimes difficult to interpret the satire in the eclogues which E. K. classes as "moral" because of the ambivalence of the dialogue structure itself and because of the uncertain implications of the fables included in four of the five moral selections. Besides, misperception on the part of the characters or the commentator can be part of the comedy. In "May," "July," and "September," different pairs of shepherds discuss religious "shepherds," making clear allusions to contemporary churchmen. In contrast to the sometimes vehement satire in these religious eclogues, the debate on youth and age in "February" has a light, bantering tone. As a statement of Spenser's views on poetry, "October" is perhaps the most significant "moral" eclogue. When the disillusioned young poet Cuddie complains that his oaten reeds are "rent and wore" without having brought him any reward, the idealistic Piers tries to convince him that glory is better than gain. He encourages Cuddie to leave rustic life, to lift himself "out of the lowly dust," but Cuddie complains that the great worthies that "matter made for Poets on to play" are long dead. The ambivalence of the pastoral debate is particularly evident here because the two voices apparently represent a conflict within Spenser himself. The inner Piers has an almost Platonic vision of poetry and sees potential inspiration in the active life of the court; but the inner Cuddie, fearing the frustrations of the poet's role, resigns himself to the less conspicuous, less stimulating rural life.

In a sequel to the eclogues, *Colin Clouts Come Home Againe*, Colin describes to his friends a trip to London, apparently a reflection of Spenser's trip to make arrangements for the publication of *The Faerie Queene*. The question-and-answer format allows Colin to touch on varied topics: the level of poetic artistry in London, conventional satire of life at court, topographical poetry about the "marriage" of two Irish rivers, and Platonic deification of love. Although this more mature Colin is less critical of court life than the earlier one had been, Ireland rather than England is still "home" to him.

Any study of *The Faerie Queene* must take into account the explanatory letter to Raleigh printed in all early editions under the heading: "A Letter of the Author's, Expounding his Whole Intention in the Course of this Work. . . ." The fact that the letter was printed at the end rather than the beginning of the first edition (Books I-III only) suggests that Spenser was writing with a retrospective glance at what was already in the printer's press, even though he was also looking toward the overall structure of what had not yet been assembled. Raleigh had apparently requested such an explanation, and Spenser here clarified elements which he considered essential to understanding his "continued Allegory of dark conceit." These elements can be summarized as purpose, genre, narrative structure, and allegorical significance.

In carrying out his purpose "to fashion a gentleman or noble person in vertuous and gentle discipline," Spenser imitated other Renaissance conduct books which set out to form representatives of different levels of polite society, such as those peopled by princes, schoolmasters, governors, and courtiers. By coloring his teaching with "historical fiction," Spenser obeyed Horace's precept to make poetry both useful and pleasing; he also followed the example of classic and Renaissance writers of epic by selecting for the center of that fiction a hero whose historicity was overlaid by legend: Arthur. Theoretically, an epic treats a major action of a single great man, while a romance recounts great deeds of many men. Kaleidoscopic visions of the deeds of many great knights and ladies within the separate books superimpose a coloring of romance, but the overall generic designation of *The Faerie Queene* as "epic" is possible because Arthur appears in the six books as a unifying hero. Through Arthur, the poet also paid tribute to his sovereign, whose family, according to the currently popular Tudor myth, claimed descent from Arthur's heirs.

Although the complexity of the poem stems partly from the blending of epic and romance traditions, Spenser's political concern added an even greater complication to his narrative structure. He wanted to create a major role by which he could pay tribute to a female sovereign in a genre that demanded a male hero. From this desire came two interlocked plot lines with Gloriana, the Faerie Queene, as the motivating force of both: the young Arthur "before he was king" was seeking as his bride the beautiful Queen of Fairyland whom he had seen in a vision; meanwhile, this same queen had sent out on quests twelve different knights, one for each book of the epic. At strategic points within these separate books Arthur would interrupt his quest to aid the currently central figure. Since Spenser completed only six of the proposed twelve books, the climactic wedding of Arthur and Gloriana never took place and the dramatic dispersion and reassembling of Gloriana's knights occurred only in the poet's explanation, not in his poem.

Patterns of allegory, like patterns of narrative, intertwine throughout the poem. By describing his allegory as "continued," Spenser did not imply that particular meanings were continuously retained but rather that central allegories recurred. In the letter to Raleigh, for example, Spenser explains that in his "general intention" Gloriana means glory, but in a more "particular" way she is "the glorious person" of Elizabeth. Spenser is not satisfied to "shadow" Elizabeth only as Gloriana. In the letter and in the introduction to Book III, he invites Elizabeth to see herself as both Gloriana and Belphoebe, "In th'one her rule, in th'other her rare chastity." Less pointedly, she is also "shadowed" in Una, the image of true religion (Book I); in Britomart, the beautiful Amazonian warrior (Books III-V); and in Mercilla, the just queen (Book V). The glories of Elizabeth thus appear as a pervasive aspect of the "continued allegory," even though they are represented by different characters. Allegorical continuity also comes from Spenser's plan to have his twelve knights as "patrons" of the "twelve private moral virtues" devised by Aristotle, with Arthur standing forth as the virtue of magnificence, "the perfection of all the rest." The titles of the six completed books indicate the central virtues of their heroes: holiness, temperance, chastity, friendship, justice, and courtesy.

Historical and topical allusions appear frequently. Only when such allusions link references to Arthur and Gloriana, however, do they form a continuous thread of allegory. In the Proem to Book II, "The Legend of Sir Guyon, or of Temperance," Spenser encourages Elizabeth to see her face in the "fair mirror" of Gloriana, her kingdom in the "land of faery," and her "great ancestry" in his poem. In Canto X he inserts a patch of "historical fiction" in which Arthur and Guyon examine the chronicles of Briton kings and elfin emperors, the first ending with the father of Arthur, Uther Pendagron, and the second with Tanaquil, called "Glorian . . . that glorious flower." Spenser prefaces his lengthy account of British history (stanzas 5-69) with a tribute to his own "sovereign queen" whose "realm and race" had been derived from Prince Arthur; he thus identifies the realm of the "renowned prince" of this story as the England of history. The second chronicle describes an idealized land where succession to the crown is peaceful, where the elfin inhabitants can trace their race back to Prometheus, creator of Elf (Adam) and Fay (Eve), and where Elizabeth-Gloriana can find her father and grandfather figured in Oberon and Elficleos. The "continued" historical allegory looks to the wedding of Arthur and Gloriana as blending real and ideal aspects within England itself.

Topical political allegory is most sustained in Book V, "The Legend of Artegall, or of Justice." In this book Elizabeth appears as Queen Mercilla and as Britomart; Mary Stuart as Duessa (sentenced by Mercilla) and as Radigund (defeated in battle by Britomart): Arthur Lord Grey as the titular hero, Artegall; the Earl of Leicester as Prince Arthur himself in one segment of the narrative. Several European rulers whom Elizabeth had either opposed or aided also appear in varied forms. Contemporary political problems are reflected in the story of Artegall's rescue of Irena (Ireland) from the giant Grantorto (literally translated as "Great Wrong"), usually allegorically identified as the Pope. Spenser's personal defense of Lord Grey shows through the naïve allegory of Canto XII, where Artegall, on the way back to Faery Court, is attacked by two hags, Envy and Detraction, and by the Blatant Beast (Calumny). Spenser thus suggests the cause of the misunderstandings that led to Elizabeth's recalling Grey from Ireland. Elizabeth's controversy with Mary Stuart, doubly reflected in Book V, also provides a significant level of meaning in Book I, "The Legende of the Knight of the Red Crosse, or of Holinesse."

A closer look at the tightly structured development of Book I shows more clearly Spenser's approach to heroic and allegorical poetry in the epic as a whole. On the literal level of romantic epic, Gloriana assigns to an untrained knight the quest he seeks: the rescue of the parents of a beautiful woman from a dreaded dragon. The plot traces the separation of Red Cross and Una, Red Cross's travels with the deceptive Duessa (duplicity), Una's search for Red Cross, the reunion of Una and her knight, the fulfillment of the quest, and the betrothal of hero and heroine. Vivid epic battles pit Red Cross against the serpentine Error and her swarming brood of lesser monsters, against a trio of evil brothers (Sansfoy, Sansjoy, and Sansloy), against the giant Orgoglio (from whose dungeon he must be rescued by Prince Arthur), and eventually against one of the fiercest, best-described dragons in literature. In Canto X, Red Cross learns his identity as St. George, changeling descendant of human Saxon kings rather than rustic elfin warrior. Red Cross's dragon-fight clearly reflects pictorial representations of St. George as dragon-slayer.

All three levels of allegory recognized by medieval exegetes are fully developed in Book I: typical, anagogical, and moral. Typically, Una is both the true Chruch of England, and Elizabeth is the protector of this Church; Duessa is the Church of Rome and Mary Stuart, its supporter. Red Cross is both abstract holiness defending truth and a figure of Christ himself. Arthur, too, is a figure of Christ or of grace in his rescue of Red Cross—here a kind of Everyman—from Orgoglio, the forces of Antichrist.

Anagogical or apocalyptic elements appear primarily in sections treating Duessa and the dragon and in Red Cross's vision of heaven. Duessa, at her first appearance, reflects the description of the scarlet woman in the Revelation of St. John, and the mount given her later by Orgoglio is modeled on the apocalyptic seven-headed Beast. The mouth of the great dragon of Canto XI belches forth flames like those often pictured erupting from the jaws of hell in medieval mystery plays. Red Cross is saved from the dragon by his contacts with the Well of Life and the Tree of Life, both borrowed from Revelation. Before Red Cross confronts the dragon, he has an apocalyptic vision of the New Jerusalem, a city rivaling in beauty even the capital of Fairyland, Cleopolis.

The moral level provides the most "continued" allegory in Book I. Red Cross-Everyman must develop within himself the virtue of holiness if he is eventually to conquer sin and attain the heavenly vision. When holiness is accompanied by truth, Error can be readily conquered. When holiness, however, is deceived by hypocrisy (Archimago), it is easily separated from truth and is further deceived by duplicity (Duessa) masquerading as fidelity (Fidessa). Tempted to spiritual sloth, Red Cross removes his armor of faith and falls to pride (Orgoglio). He must then be rescued from the chains of this sin by grace (Prince Arthur), must be rescued from Despair by truth, and must be spiritually strengthened in the House of Holiness, conducted by Dame Caelia (heaven) and her daughters Fidelia, Speranza, and Charissa (faith, hope, and charity). Only then can he repent of his own sins and become holy enough to conquer sin embodied in the dragon.

If Book I best exemplifies self-contained, carefully structured allegorical narrative, Books III and IV exemplify the interweaving common in medieval and early Renaissance narrative poetry. Characters pursue one another throughout the two books; several stories are not completed until Book V. In fact, Braggadochio, the cowardly braggart associated with false Florimell in this section, steals Guyon's horse in Book II and is judged for the crime in Book V. Belphoebe, too, introduced in a comic interlude with Bragga-dochio in Book II, becomes a central figure in the Book of Chastity. Belphoebe blends the beauty of Venus (Bel) with the chastity of Diana (Phoebe); her twin sister, Amoret, is a more earthly representation of Venus, destined to generate beauty and human love. Britomart, the nominal heroine of Book III, embodies the chastity of Belphoebe in her youth but the generative love of Amoret in maturity. Despite complex and not always consistent allegorical equations applicable to these central characters, Spenser moves them through their adventures with a delicate interlacing of narrative and allegorical threads typical of the romantic epic and its most entertaining level.

The sonnet sequence *Amoretti* ("little love poems") and the *Epithalamion* (songs "on the marriage bed") together provide a poetic account of courtship and marriage, an account which tradition links to actualities in Spenser's relationship with Elizabeth Boyle, whom he married in 1594. References to seasons suggest that the "plot" of the sonnet sequence extends from New Year's Day in one year (Sonnet 4) through a second New Year's Day (Sonnet 62) to the beginning of a third winter in the closing sonnet (Sonnet 89), a time frame of about two years. Several sonnets contain references which tempt readers to autobiographical interpretations. In Sonnet 60, "one year is spent" since the planet of "the winged god" began to move in the poet; even more significantly, the poet refers to the "sphere of Cupid" as containing the forty years "wasted" before this year. By simple arithmetical calculations, biographers of Spenser have deduced from his assumed age in 1593 his birth in 1552. Two sonnets refer directly to his work on *The Faerie Queene*: Sonnet 33 blames on his "troublous" love his inability to complete the "Queen of Faery" for his "sacred empress" and Sonnet 80 rejoices that having run through six books on Fairyland he can now write praises "low and mean,/ Fit for the handmaid of the Faery Queen."

Collectively and individually the *Amoretti* follow a popular Renaissance tradition established by Petrarch and imitated by numerous English sonne-teers. In metrical structure, Spenser's sonnets blended Italian and English forms. The five-rhyme restriction in the Italian octave-plus-sestet pattern (abbaabba cdecde) was adapted to fit the English pattern of three quatrains plus couplet; instead of the seven rhymes used in most English sonnets, the interlocked rhymes of the Spenserian quatrains created a more intricate, as well as more restricted, form (abab bcbc cdcd ee).

Although Spenser's metrical pattern was innovative, most of his conceits and images were conventional; for example, love is related to a judicial court (Sonnet 10) and to religious worship (Sonnets 22 and 68); the beloved is a cruel causer and observer of his pain (Sonnets 20, 31, 41, 42, and 54) and the Neoplatonic ideal of beauty (Sonnets 3, 9, 45, 61, 79, and 88); love is warfare (Sonnets 11, 12, 14, and 57), a storm (Sonnet 46), sickness (Sonnet 50), a sea journey (Sonnet 63). The poet at times promises the immortality of fame through his praise (Sonnets 27, 29, 69, 75, and 82); at other times he simply rejoices in the skill which enables him as poet to offer his gift of words (Sonnets 1 and 84). Even the kind of praise offered to his beloved is traditional. In Sonnet 40, "An hundred Graces" sit "on each eyelid" and the lover's "storm-beaten heart" is cheered "when cloudy looks are cleared." Elsewhere, eyes are weapons (Sonnets 7, 16, and 49) and a means of entanglement (Sonnet 37). The beloved is a "gentle deer" (Sonnet 67) and a "gentle bee" caught in a sweet prison woven by the spider-poet (Sonnet 71); but she is also a cruel panther (Sonnet 53) and a tiger (Sonnet 56). Physical beauties are compared to precious metals and gems (Sonnet 15), to sources of light (Sonnet 9), and to the sweet odors of flowers (Sonnet 64). Classical myths color several sonnets, identifying the beloved with Penelope, Pandora, Daphne, and the Golden Apples of Hercules (Sonnets 23, 24, 28, and 77) and the poet-lover with Narcissus, Arion, and Orpheus (Sonnets 35, 38, and 44).

In typical Petrarchan fashion, the lyrical moments in the *Amoretti* fluctuate between joy and pain, between exultation over love returned and anxiety over possible rejection. The sequence ends on a note of anxiety not in keeping with a set of poems conceived as a prelude for the glowing joy of the *Epithalamion*. Despite clear references to the 1592-1594 period of Spenser's life, it seems unlikely that all eighty-nine sonnets were written during this period or that all were originally intended for a sequence in praise of Elizabeth Boyle. The *Epithalamion*, however, is clearly Spenser's celebration of his own wedding at Kilcolman on St. Barnabas' Day (June 11), 1594.

In its basic form and development, this marriage song is as conventional as the sonnets with which it was first published; but it is also original and personal in its variations on tradition. Classical allusions, for example, are countered by the homely invocation to nymphs of the Irish river and lake near Spenser's home (lines 56-66), by the imprecation against the "unpleasant choir of frogs still croaking" in the same lake (line 349), and by some of the attendants: "merchants' daughters," "fresh boys," and childlike angels "peeping in" the face of the bride. Although allusions to classical gods and goddesses heighten the lyric mood, other elements retain a more personal touch.

Structurally, Spenser adapted the *canzone* form. As used by Dante and Petrarch, the *canzone* consisted of a series of long stanzas followed by a short stanza (a *tornata*) responding to the preceding stanzas. Within the stanzas one or more three-foot lines varied the basic five-foot line; the *tornata*, too, had one short line. A. Kent Hieatt has demonstrated in *Short Time's Endless Monument* (1960) the ingenuity with which Spenser varied the basic *canzone* structure to reflect units of time in general and to relate poetic divisions with night/day divisions on the longest day of the year in southern Ireland. Hieatt points out that variations in verse form correspond to days in the year (365 long lines), hours in the day (24 stanzas), spring and fall equinoxes (parallel diction, imagery, and thought in stanzas 1-12 and 13-24), degrees of the sun's daily movement (359 long lines before the *tornata*, corresponding to 359 degrees of the sun's movement as contrasted with 360 degrees of the stars' movement), and the division between waking and sleeping hours (indicated by a change in the refrain at the end of stanza 17). It is variations within stanza 17 that most personalize the time element to make the "bedding" of the bride occur at the point in the poem representing nightfall on the poet's wedding day, the day of the summer solstice in southern Ireland. At the end of the stanza, the refrain, which had for sixteen stanzas been describing the answering echo of the woods, changes to "The woods no more shall answer, nor your echo ring": all is quiet so that the poet-bridegroom can welcome night and the love of his bride.

The collection of moralizing, melancholy verse entitled *Complaints* reflects an as yet not fully developed artistry in the author. Although published in the aftermath of fame brought by *The Faerie Queene*, most of the nine poems were probably first drafted much earlier. The most significant poem in this volume was probably the satirical beast fable, "Prosopopoia: Or, Mother Hubberd's Tale." Following the tradition of Giovanni Boccaccio and Geoffrey Chaucer, the poet creates a framework of tale-tellers, one of whom is "a good old woman" named Mother Hubberd. In Mother Hubberd's story, a Fox and an Ape gain personal prosperity through the gullibility of farmers, the ignorance and worldliness of clergymen, and the licentiousness of courtiers. About two-thirds of the way through, the satire turns more specifically to the concern of England in 1579 with a possible marriage between the twenty-four-year-old Duc d'Alencon and Queen Elizabeth, then forty-six. The marriage was being engineered by Lord Burleigh (the Fox of the narrative) and by Jean de Simier, whom Elizabeth playfully called her "Ape." This poem, even more than *The Shepheardes Calender*, demonstrates Spenser's artistic simplicity and the Chaucer-like irony of his worldview. Burleigh's later hostility to Spenser gives evidence of the pointedness of the poet's satiric barbs. "Virgil's Gnat" also exemplifies a satiric beast fable, this time with Leicester's marriage as the target, hit so effectively that Spenser himself was wounded by Leicester's lessened patronage. In "Muiopotmos: Or, The Fate of the Butterfly," beast fable is elevated by philosophical overtones, epic machinery, and classical allusions. Some type of personal or political allegory obviously underlies the poem, but critical interpretations vary widely in attempting to identify the chief figures, the Spider and the Butterfly. Despite such uncertainty, however, one message is clear: life and beauty are mutable.

Mutability permeates *Complaints*; it is even more central to the posthumous fragment known as the "Mutabilitie Cantos." The publisher Matthew Lownes printed these two cantos as "The Legend of Constancy," a fragmentary Book VII of *The Faerie Queene*. Lownes's identification of these two cantos with the unfinished epic was apparently based on similar poetic form, an allusion to the poet's softening his stern style in singing of hills and woods "mongst warres and knights," and a reference to the records of Fairyland as registering mutability's genealogy. There are, however, no knights, human or elf, in these cantos. Instead, Jove and Nature represent allegorically the cosmic principle of Constancy, the permanence that underlies all change. Despite the philosophical victory of Nature, one of the most effective extended passages in the cantos represents change through a processional pageant of the seasons, the months, day and night, the hours, and life and death.

The principle of underlying permanence applies to Spenser's works as well as to the world of which he wrote. In his shepherds and shepherdesses, his knights and ladies, his own personae, and even in the animal figures of his fables, images of Everyman and Everywoman still live. Time has thickened some of the allegorical veils that conceal as well as reveal, language then new has become archaic, and poetic conventions have become freer since Spenser's poetry first charmed his contemporaries. Despite such changes, however, the evocative and creative power that made Spenser "the Prince of Poets in his time" remains constant.

Marie Michelle Walsh

Other major works

NONFICTION: *Three Proper, and Wittie, Familiar Letters*, 1580; *Foure Letters and Certaine Sonnets*, 1586; *A View of the Present State of Ireland*, 1633 (written in 1596).

MISCELLANEOUS: *The Works of Edmund Spenser: A Variorum Edition*, 1932-1949 (Edwin Greenlaw, *et al.*, editors).

Bibliography

Berry, Phillipa. *Of Chastity and Power: Elizabethan Literature and the Unmarried Queen*. London: Routledge & Kegan Paul, 1989. This example of feminist critical theory supplies a fascinating analysis of Elizabeth I and her relationship with the male writers who sought to make her fame immortal. Berry analyzes the works of Edmund Spenser in relation to those of John Lyly, Sir Walter Raleigh, George Chapman, and William Shakespeare.

Bieman, Elizabeth. *Plato Baptized: Towards the Interpretation of Spenser's Mimetic Fictions*. Toronto: University of Toronto Press, 1988. Offers a clear and insightful reading of Spenser in relation to the Christian and Platonic sources that inform his thought. Bieman offers subtle and rich readings of the *Fowre Hymnes* and the "Mutabilitie Cantos."

Hamilton, A. C., et al., eds. *The Spenser Encyclopedia.* Toronto: University of Toronto Press, 1990. This 858-page volume represents the cooperative efforts of Spenserian scholars to compile a series of articles on every aspect of Spenser's life and work. The superbly indexed volume also offers many useful articles on the history of England and on literary theory and practice.

Heale, Elizabeth. *The Faerie Queene: A Reader's Guide.* Cambridge, England: Cambridge University Press, 1987. Offers an up-to-date guide to Spenser's *The Faerie Queene*, the first great epic poem in English. Emphasizes the religious and political context for each episode. One chapter is devoted to each book of *The Faerie Queene*. An index is supplied for characters and episodes.

Heninger, S. K., Jr. *Sidney and Spenser: The Poet as Maker.* University Park: Pennsylvania State University Press, 1989. In this study of mimesis, or imitation, S. K. Heninger considers the transmutation of allegory to fiction. Examines the aesthetic elements in art, music, and literature, analyzes the forms of Spenser's major works and considers the relationship between form and content. This lengthy, 646-page study of Renaissance aesthetics offers an essential background for understanding Spenser's art.

Patterson, Annabel. *Pastoral and Ideology: Virgil to Valery.* Berkeley: University of California Press, 1987. Offers a learned and graceful introduction to the three great types of poems given authority in classical tradition: the pastoral, the georgic, and the epic. Patterson supplies a careful reading of Spenser's *The Shepheardes Calender* that illustrates its political commentary on the church and state.

Wells, Robin Headlam. *Spenser's "Faerie Queene" and the Cult of Elizabeth.* Totawa, N.J.: Barnes & Noble Books, 1983. This study of Spenser concentrates on the ways in which the moral and political allegory in the poem are parts of a continuous pattern of meaning. Wells contends that the idea of praise is fundamental to the poem and that for the first time it gives voice to the national myth.

WILLIAM STAFFORD

Born: Hutchinson, Kansas; January 17, 1914

Principal poetry

West of Your City, 1960; *Traveling Through the Dark*, 1962; *The Rescued Year*, 1966; *Eleven Untitled Poems*, 1968; *Weather: Poems*, 1969; Allegiances, 1970; *Temporary Facts*, 1970; *Poems for Tennessee*, 1971 (with Robert Bly and William Matthews); *Someday, Maybe*, 1973; *That Other Alone*, 1973; *In the Clock of Reason*, 1973; *Going Places: Poems*, 1974; *North by West*, 1975 (with John Haines); *Braided Apart*, 1976 (with Kim Robert Stafford); *Stories That Could Be True: New and Collected Poems*, 1977; *The Design in the Oriole*, 1977; *Two About Music*, 1978; *All About Light*, 1978; *Things That Happen Where There Aren't Any People*, 1980; *Sometimes Like a Legend*, 1981; *A Glass Face in the Rain: New Poems*, 1982; *Smoke's Way: Poems from Limited Editions, 1968-1981*, 1983; *Roving Across Fields: A Conversation and Uncollected Poems, 1942-1982*, 1983; *Segues: A Correspondence in Poetry*, 1983 (with Marvin Bell); *Stories and Storms and Strangers*, 1984; *Listening Deep*, 1984; *Wyoming*, 1985; *Brother Wind*, 1986; *An Oregon Message*, 1987; *Fin, Feather, Fur*, 1989; *A Scripture of Leaves*, 1989; *How to Hold Your Arms When It Rains: Poems*, 1990; *Passwords*, 1991.

Other literary forms

In addition to poetry, William Stafford has published an autobiographical account of his conscientious objector service during World War II, *Down in My Heart* (1947), and has edited poetry volumes and authored chapters in collections of critical analysis. Stafford's *Writing the Australian Crawl: Views on the Writer's Vocation* (1978) and *You Must Revise Your Life* (1986) contain essays on writing and the teaching of writing, as well as interviews with Stafford that were originally published in literary magazines.

Achievements

Stafford is considered one of the most prolific of contemporary American poets. Although he was forty-six years old when his first collection of poems was published in 1960, he more than made up for this late start in the next decade. Stafford's second volume, *Traveling Through the Dark*, won the National Book Award for Poetry in 1963. In 1970, Stafford was named consultant in poetry to the Library of Congress. Throughout his career, he has received numerous awards and honors, such as the Shelley Memorial Award, a Yaddo Foundation Fellowship, a National Endowment for the Arts grant, a Guggenheim Fellowship, a Danforth Foundation grant, the Melville Cane Award, and the American Academy and Institute of Arts Award in Literature.

Widely recognized as a spontaneous, ..atural poet, Stafford has greatly influenced the world of literature with his views on the teaching of writing. Equating the act of writing with coming to know the self, Stafford says that writing consists of finding the way as the process unfolds. He can indulge his impulses—knowing that they will bring recurrent patterns and meaning—because in back of his images is the coherence of the self. In his distinguished career as a professor, Stafford put such views into practice in his teaching and made them available to a wider audience through lectures, interviews, and his many published essays on the process of writing.

Biography

On January 17, 1914, William Edgar Stafford was born to Earl Ingersoll and Ruby Mayher Stafford in Hutchinson, Kansas. With his younger brother and sister, Stafford grew up in a series of small Kansas towns—Wichita, Liberal, Garden City, El Dorado—as his father moved the family from place to place in search of work. Earl and Ruby Stafford were nonconformists who held strong moral and spiritual beliefs. They instilled in their children a deep sense of individuality, justice, and tolerance. From long hours with his father in the Midwestern countryside, Stafford developed his love of nature. He credits his mother, and the gossipy stories she loved to tell, with helping him perceive the intricacies of language. Although certainly not scholars, both parents loved books, and the whole family raided the local library each week, vying for their favorites.

As an adolescent during the Depression, Stafford was already helping to support his family: raising vegetables, working as an electrician's helper, and delivering newspapers (at one time their only source of income). After high school, Stafford attended junior college and then enrolled in the University of Kansas, waiting on tables to pay his way. During his undergraduate years, Stafford began his habit of writing daily and began to translate his social and political beliefs into action. He participated in a demonstration against segregation in the university cafeteria and, when World War II broke out, registered as a conscientious objector.

Stafford spent the war incarcerated in conscientious objector camps in Arkansas, California, and Illinois, working on soil-conservation projects and fighting forest fires. These were formative years for him, a time of introspection, for Stafford was acutely aware of his unorthodox position against a generally popular war. He rigorously examined the tensions between the outer life of daily appearances and the inner life of conviction, developing a deep patience and an abiding sense of integrity. In order to write before the day's labor began, Stafford arose before dawn; this habit continued into later life. While at a camp in California, Stafford met, and soon married, Dorothy Frantz, a minister's daughter. When the war ended, the couple returned to the University of Kansas, and Stafford began work on his M.A. degree. He submitted an account of his conscientious objector experiences as his thesis project, which was subsequently published as his first book, *Down in My Heart.*

After graduation, Stafford taught high school briefly, worked in a church relief agency, and kept writing stories and poems. From 1948 to 1950, he was an instructor in English at Lewis and Clark College in Portland, Oregon. He then moved, with his wife and small children, to the University of Iowa, where he studied under Robert Penn Warren, Randall Jarrell, Reed Whittemore, Karl Shapiro, and others.

Stafford considered these years to be his reference point for how others lived the literary life. His own writing habits and perspective on the world of letters, however, had already been clearly established. When Stafford left Iowa in 1952, he took with him firmly held, idiosyncratic attitudes about writing and how it should be taught. In 1954, when he received his Ph.D. from Iowa, Stafford was already teaching English at Manchester College in Indiana. Next, he taught briefly at San Jose State College and then returned to Lewis and Clark College, beginning a teaching career there that lasted for almost twenty-five years.

Since Stafford's first book of poems, *West of Your City*, he has published many collections with his major publisher, Harper & Row; more than twenty-five other books or chapbooks of poetry with small presses; several collections of prose; short pieces of critical analysis; and interviews. He has traveled widely, lecturing and reading his work in the United States and abroad. During the Vietnam War, university students in America discovered Stafford's pacifist beliefs, and he was in great demand on college campuses. Precisely because of these beliefs, however, Stafford never became the antiwar poet that the students were seeking. In 1980, Stafford retired from teaching to become professor emeritus at Lewis and Clark College. Since then, in addition to giving numerous readings and lectures, he has continued to publish new collections of poems.

Analysis

William Stafford is a poet of the personal and the particular. With an optimistic outlook, he writes personally but not confessionally, and his particulars are sometimes regional but not provincial. Stafford writes most often in the first person, both singular and plural, and his poems are characteristically quite short. They investigate the processes of everyday life, looking through specific situations and happenings to uncover universal connections between humans and nature. Although Stafford celebrates nature in his work, this is not an end in itself; rather, it is a means to transcend surface manifestation and uncover the underlying unboundedness of life. In this sense, Stafford has been called a wisdom poet, one who uses nature in pursuit of a higher truth. His poems present situations, objects, and people that entice the reader to go beyond the towns and settlements of life—where what one knows can be readily seen—and search for what lies at their edges, in the wilderness, to listen to the silence one can come to understand, perhaps, as one's own self.

Although much of Stafford's work grows out of personal memories, a strictly biographical reading can be misleading. His work does not lend itself strictly to chronological investigation, either, for Stafford's key themes and metaphorical language in his first published collection are still characteristic of his later volumes. In addition, the order in which Stafford's poems have been published does not necessarily reflect the order in which they were written. He does not prepare his collections as thematic, structured volumes; rather, he views them as groupings of self-sufficient fragments. It is the incremental progression in individual works, not collections, that interests Stafford, and his focus is on the process of writing rather than on meaning or content. Though criticized for such an internal perspective, Stafford maintains a steadfast unwillingness to analyze his work intellectually. He believes that one should not defend or value what one has written but rather abandon it; others must decide about its significance.

Because Stafford's vision of life has remained essentially stable throughout his literary career, themes, images, and even words reoccur in his poems and take on specific significance, forming almost a shorthand language in themselves. Stafford's major theme is the spiritual search for the self, represented metaphorically as the search for "home." It is a quest for unity with the Absolute, which he associates with the adjectives "deep," "dark," and "silent." Subthemes are his focus on family and small-town living, much of which can be traced to his Kansas boyhood; the sacredness of nature and of wilderness, often in contrast to war, technology, and human alienation; and the exploration of truth as it unfolds through the common activities of daily life.

Stafford has been criticized for his overt simplicity and for his prose style. On the surface, many of his poems do seem to reflect an idyllic Midwest childhood, a longing for the uncomplicated (and perhaps a bit romanticized) past when people lived in greater harmony with nature. Stafford certainly does write in a conversational style. Yet it is this surface accessibility that invites the reader to enter the poems. Once the reader is in, Stafford hints at deeper levels of reality and may ask his readers to do or be or imagine seemingly impossible things. Many poems have a parablelike quality and present rather didactic messages, often in the last line. After the surface message is delivered, however, the silence resounds. Stafford is a poet who roams far into his own wilderness. He dreams, and he tests his dreams through the process of telling their stories. Because Stafford's clear vision is firmly rooted, he has the flexibility to follow where imagination and the sounds of language take him.

Published in 1947, Stafford's first book, *Down in My Heart*, is a spiritual autobiography of his four years in conscientious objector work camps during World War II. Within the context of narratives about firefighting, an altercation with a mob in a small town, and a pacifist wedding, he reveals the concerns of a man alienated from the majority of his countrymen by his social and political beliefs. This volume sows seeds that sprout as major themes in his later poetry. Stafford presents his metaphorical "home" as ultimately free from any particular location in his narrative about building yet another work camp. He also touches on other ideas that will unfold as significant poetic themes, such as the power of storytelling, the nature of the hero, sound and silence, and interactions between the individual and society.

Stafford's first volume of poetry, *West of Your City*, presents a poet of already mature voice, with a strong sense of his material. Running through these poems, arranged in three sections called "Midwest," "Farwest," and "Outside," is the theme of "home." For Stafford, "home" certainly means the security of the Kansas towns of his boyhood, and the persona of many poems in this collection and the poet himself are very similar. Stafford begins "One Home" with the line "Mine was a Midwest home—you keep your world" and moves through references to his personal history. His vision of home also extends, however, beyond the secure Kansas settlements into the adventure of wilderness at their edges. He concludes, "Kicking cottonwood leaves we ran toward storms./ Wherever we looked the land would hold us up." Running toward adventure, the speaker finds home wherever he looks. Venturing into the wilderness, into what is unknown, the individual has the chance to get a glimpse of what is closest to him, what he can ultimately know best because it is what he is—the self.

The well-known poem "Bi-focal" presents the sense of double vision that pervades virtually all Stafford's work as it unfolds his theme of underlying legends. The poem begins, "Sometimes up out of this land/ a legend begins to move." It locates "the surface, a map of roads/ leading wherever go miles" and "the legend under,/ fixed, inexorable,/ deep as the darkest mine." The poem concludes, "So, the world happens twice—/ Once what we see it as;/ second it legends itself/ deep, the way it is." This poem contrasts what is seen—what seems to be real on the surface of life—with the unseen, what is "deep." "Deep" is clearly defined as the way the world is. The speaker in the poem, like the poet, is able to see both levels, but it is the deeper way of seing that Stafford emphasizes in his work. He does so not by denigrating the surface details, but rather by penetrating them and revealing their more profound essence and the silence of legends at their source. The poems in *West of Your City*, written mostly in the first person, draw heavily from Stafford's memories. Yet the personal details expand to include his reader's life. Even the title of the volume demands the reader's attention: not west of "my" —the poet's—city, but west of the reader's.

Stafford's second collection, *Traveling Through the Dark*, established his reputation and won the National Book Award in 1963. Themes from the first collection reoccur, the subject matter is again straightforward, and the tone is gently conversational. Stafford's voice here is less tentative, more sure, but still it asks questions, encouraging the reader to travel past the everyday world of light into the dark wilderness where the real journey takes place. His image of darkness is firmly established here, and it is not a negative one. He associates darkness with depth, silence, and intuition, the edges toward which life always progresses, the edges beyond which greater understanding of the self may be found.

In this volume, Stafford transcends the boundaries of time and space, of past and future, and explores what he finds in the gaps. He moves beyond what he can see, to listen for what language has to tell him. The poem that gives the volume its title is one of Stafford's most famous works and has been frequently anthologized. It is characteristic of Stafford in that its form and narrative are simple, yet underneath lies more complexity. While driving a mountain road at night, the speaker in the poem comes upon a dead deer. He stops and gets out, confident that he should roll the animal over the edge of the cliff in order to clear the narrow road for cars that will follow his. As he comes closer and touches the deer, however, he finds that there is an unborn fawn waiting, still alive. The man begins to have doubts about what is right action. Should he do what might seem to be best on the surface—push the doe over the cliff and avoid further accidents on the road? Or is it possible to try to save the fawn? If so, would it be the right thing to do? Described with characteristic understatement, the moment of decision is swift: he decides to push her off.

"Traveling Through the Dark" has been read as a poem of conflict between nature and society, symbolized by the car. The speaker clearly sympathizes with the fawn, which "lay there waiting,/ alive, still, never to be born." Yet he accepts the forces of technology that caused the problem and realizes that the safety of the next passersby—in cars again—depends on his clearing the road. It has been noted that the personified car, which "aimed ahead its lowered parking lights" and under whose hood "purred the steady engine," is actually the most alive thing in this poem. This may be the ironic voice of a pragmatist who sees nature as something for human beings to use as they please. A more expanded reading, however, would bridge the Nature-society dichotomy somewhat by allowing nature to include the car and, by extension, society as well. From such a perspective, the car is both a symbol of death (a significant theme of subject-object unity in Stafford's poetry) and a symbol of life, a part of "our group" in the road. The poem uses the word "swerve" twice. Once the meaning is literal, the anticipated physical movement of further cars coming upon the carcass in the road. The second time, though, it is the speaker who swerves, and his swerving is internal. Having "thought hard for us all—my only swerving," he makes a decision. Yet what is he swerving toward, or away from?

It may appear that the speaker's dependence on progress is greater than his ability to control it. Even so, for the moment that he considers saving the fawn, he swerves away from society toward nature. Yet perhaps the swerve is in the opposite direction. Perhaps he is swerving from a more simplistic view of nature toward an understanding that encompasses the interests of society within its purview. From his upbringing and especially as a result of his years doing conscientious objector service during World War II, Stafford characteristically considers all sides of his questions. Perhaps the speaker in this poem comes to recognize his own part in the process of the narrative. Is he only the man who finds the dead deer, or does he also bear part of the responsibility for the killing? Underlying the obvious choice to be made— what to do with the deer—may be a suggestion that longing to return to the old ways and escape from society is not really much different from embracing progress without a firm connection with the simplicity and order of nature at its base. There is also the suggestion that Stafford himself may still be making his decisions. When asked about this poem, Stafford responded, "Choices are always Hobson's choices. All you have to do is get a little more alert to see that even your best moves are compromises—and complicated."

Still, the poem ends on an optimistic note. There is still time to prevent further disaster, the speaker decides, and he pushes the doe "over the edge into the river." It is interesting that the poem ends on the image of the river, which, in Stafford's linguistic shorthand, is consistently used as a metaphor for the changing nature of life.

Stafford's voice has been criticized as being simply his real-life "I" speaking normally but in a privileged position, and "Traveling Through the Dark" has been cited as a representative example of the poet firmly in control of all meaning. In refuting this attack, Dick Barnes agrees that Stafford does speak normally, but suggests that artists such as Stafford speak out of a solitude that others can barely imagine, "where the self is dead and the soul opens inward upon eternity. What makes [the artist's] act complete is that, speaking that way, he listens at the same time, and in listening joins any others who may be hearing in a kind of casual communion." Barnes uses "self" here in a relative sense: with death of the self, the individuality that keeps one localized to time and space is no longer restricting the soul.

Stafford, in his wilderness quest, may be in search of something even greater than mere removal of restriction. His death metaphor represents a creative force, a unity of subjectivity and objectivity. A reading of Stafford's work from the perspective of growth of consciousness might suggest that the death of the "self" is first found in the transcendental experience of unbounded awareness that is beyond the limitations of the relative states of consciousness—waking, dreaming, and sleeping. Repeated direct experience of this state of pure consciousness is the basis for the individual's growth toward higher states of consciousness. The "self" rises to the value of the "Self," providing the stable foundation for the eventual unity of subject and object that Stafford is seeking in his poetry.

The Rescued Year was Stafford's second collection with Harper & Row, which—over the years—became his major publisher. It shows a stability of vision, and Stafford has said that he considers this to be his most unified volume. Fourteen of the poems had already appeared in *West of Your City*, and some had been included in Stafford's Ph.D. dissertation, "Winterward." Others were written at the same time as poems in his earlier volumes. The poems reprinted from *West of Your City* reemphasize Stafford's major interests: home, the quest journey, sound and silence, duality of vision, memory and reality, the power of the story. One of these reprinted works, "Listening," defines the nature of the father image in Stafford's poems, which has been associated with the more intuitive, deep, unseen values of the wilderness. "My father could hear a little animal step,/ or a moth in the dark against the screen,/ and every far sound called the listening out/ into places where the rest of us had never been." Listening goes beyond seeing. The father understands more from what he hears in the darkness than the rest of the family could learn from what "came to our porch for us on the wind." The son could watch his father's face change when the understanding came, when "the walls of the world flared, widened." With even this secondary experience of silence, the son was changed. "My father heard so much that we still stand/ inviting the quiet by turning the face." From the father, the son learns to want to hear the sounds of the underlying processes of nature. The son learns patience. In "Listening," the speaker sees little, for little comes to him on the porch, within the familiar. Seeing his father listen, however, he and the other children are inspired to wait "for a time when something in the night/ will touch us too from that other place." They are waiting to be able to hear the silence themselves. This sequence of seeing, touching, listening is reminiscent of "Traveling Through the Dark," as the speaker first sees the doe, then touches her warm side, and then hears the wilderness listening. Learning from his father, as a representative of deeper levels of reality, is a theme in many of Stafford's poems.

Over a third of the poems in *The Rescued Year* deal with Stafford's boyhood and a Kansas setting. "Across Kansas" tells of traveling through the night as his family sleeps. Driving past the town where he was born, the speaker says, "I drove down an aisle of sound," locating his sense of memory and reality within the sense of hearing. Once he has this experience of sound, even what he sees has more meaning. The speaker "owns" his face more, and he sees his self in everything that the light struck. Again, as in many poems, the last line is telling. "My state still dark, my dream too long to tell." The traveling is through a darkness much deeper than the Kansas night.

Stafford's imagination creates the story of his reality in much of this volume. Yet the collection also focuses on more contemporary issues, as in the long poem "Following the Markings of Dag Hammerskjöld: A Gathering of Poems in the Spirit of His Life and Writings." Some critics have objected to this new subject matter. Considering the confusing time in which this collection was published, however, even Stafford's warnings in such poems as "At the Bomb Test Site" seem gentle.

With publication of *Allegiances*, critics and scholars started to ask for more discrimination, for Stafford to publish only his best work. Then as now, however, Stafford preferred to let the reader decide what was good. In this volume, his allegiances are generally to people, places, and objects from the rural plains. Stafford suggests that truth is inherent in the common things, if one goes deep enough. His real hero is the common man. In the poem that gives the volume its title, he says, "It is time for all the heroes to go home/ if they have any, time for all of us common ones/ to locate ourselves by the real things/ we live by." He describes the journey to taste "far streams" where one can touch gold and "come back, changed/ but safe, quiet, grateful." Some have criticized this volume for a sort of blurred perspective that reflects less connection between Stafford's inner and outer lives. Some poems in *Allegiances* do deal with the social and political climate at the time—the assassination of Martin Luther King, Jr., bombings, television news, and the like—but the volume is hardly overtly revolutionary. What it does seem to suggest is that, at a precarious time in the world, Stafford had come to expect moral guidance from himself and other serious writers.

The first poem in *Someday, Maybe*, "An Introduction to Some Poems," suggests that this volume will take a changed direction. It begins, "Look: no one ever promised for sure/ that we would sing. We have decided/ to moan." The speaker—clearly Stafford—expresses disillusionment. He is trying to turn his dreams into stories to give them strength. He suggests that the reader should do that too, "and hold them close at you, close at the/ edge we share, to be right." Many of the stories are based on Indian legends, or legends that Stafford fashions. These, perhaps, may offer some direction from a time when people were more in touch with nature than they were in the early 1970's. Though Stafford does not use poetry directly as a political vehicle, his concerns are underlying, and he searches into language for a way of dispelling his doubts about the world. In "After That Sound, After That Sight," the speaker says that "after that sound, we weren't people anymore," and "we are afraid to listen." This is not the optimistic Stafford one has come to expect. Yet poetry—language—is reliable. In "Report from a Far Place," Stafford says words are "snowshoes" with which he can still step across the world. They "creak, sag, bend, but/ hold," and "in war or city or camp/

they could save your life." He thus invites others to follow their tracks.

Stories That Could Be True: New and Collected Poems let critics and scholars see Stafford's work to that date as a whole. The new poems, such as "Song Now," tell the story of the speaker who returns from a far place, from both "Before" and "After," to find a home in the present, where "silence puts a paw/ wherever the music rests." The poem concludes, "Guitar string is:/ it can save this place." Despite growing disillusionment over the changes that are occurring in American society, Stafford continues to seek a reintegration in this volume. With a growing acceptance of death—a significant theme—comes an awareness of the primacy of the present and the desire to live it. The stories are put before the readers not so that they can come to know them in themselves, but so that they can, perhaps, come to know their own story better. The meaning of the story, for Stafford, is in its telling.

In *A Glass Face in the Rain: New Poems*, Stafford brings the process of storytelling, the process of writing, to the forefront. In his dedication poem, he says that the volume is intended for everyone, but especially for those on a "parallel way." These are the people readers do not see often, he says, or even think of often, "but it is precious to us that they are sharing/ the world." This volume was published after *Things That Happen Where There Aren't Any People*, a collection of more impersonal poems that focus on nature without human presence. Here, once again, however, Stafford's poems are grounded in the world of humanity. In "Glimpses," the speaker is definitely in the present and his presence there matters. "My debt to the world begins again," he says, "that I am part of this permanent dream." Stafford's part of the dream of life is to write poems. This collection continues to develop his acceptance of his own death, considering a future world that he will not be alive to see. Stafford has expanded his desire to be part of the process, and now he wants to communicate. In "Tuned In Late One Night," the speaker begins, "Listen—this is a faint station/ left alive in the vast universe./ I was left here to tell you a message." In "A Message from Space," he is trying to hear a message from the heavens, but when the message comes, it is surprising. "Everything counts," it says. "The message is the world."

In 1987, Stafford published a seventh volume with Harper & Row, *An Oregon Message.* Now the message has become explicit, and Stafford wants the reader on his side. He precedes the poems with a brief prose explanation of how he writes, "Some Notes on Writing;" it is the first time such a preface has been included in a volume of his poetry. In it, he says that "it is my habit to allow language its own freedom and confidence" even though such poems may bewilder readers who "try to control all emergent elements in discourse for the service of predetermined ends." He continues, "I must be willingly fallible in order to deserve a place in the realm where miracles happen." Stafford is, by extension, inviting the reader, too, to deserve a place in the miracle.

People and places from Stafford's past again figure prominently in this volume. He seems to be taking stock of them in a new way, though, seeking deeper integration than before. He blends the past, present, and future together, and a sense of playfulness emerges. In "Thinking About Being Called Simple by a Critic," Stafford alludes to William Carlos Williams' plum poem in his first line, "I wanted the plums, but I waited." While he waits, he hears the echo of a critic who said "how stupid I was." As Stafford probes the truth of these words, he starts to enjoy them and decides that the critic must be a friend: "Who but a friend/ could give so sternly what the sky/ feels for everyone but few learn to/ cherish?" Stafford feels rightly put in his place—and delights in it. He goes to the refrigerator, opens it, sees that "sure enough the light was on," and reaches in to get the plums.

Yet there is also a didactic tone in this volume. Stafford is ready to tell what he has been hearing in the silence all these years. In "Lie Detector," he says that the heart proclaims "the truth all the time, hidden but always/ there," because it is "acting the self, helplessly true." He concludes the poem in a celebration of the present: "At night, no one else near, you walk/ . . . your heart marching along/ with you, saying, 'Now,' saying, 'Yes,'/ saying, 'Here.'" The last poem in the collection, "Maybe Alone on My Bike," is representative of Stafford's blending of the serious and the playful. As he rides home ("maybe alone"), he says, "I listen," and reflects back at the distance he has traveled, thinking of the splendor and marvels of life as it reveals itself. He intones, "O citizens of our great amnesty:/ we might have died. We live," but then comes back to concrete narrative with his concluding line: "and I hear in the [bicycle] chain a chuckle I like to hear." Stafford is still listening, he is still finding meaning, and what was quiet bliss is now bubbling up to the surface as delight. Delight extends into Stafford's eighth collection with a major publisher, *Passwords*. These poems from the heart invite the reader to continue to make serendipitous discoveries through language, memory, and feeling.

Stafford has written in the same voice all of his life. Critics generally consider him to be a poet of place or a poet of myths. Yet he creates his own myths, and he is at home everywhere. He has said that the crucial parts of writing have to do with what is shared by human beings rather than their superficial differences. By exploring the great diversity the world has to offer, Stafford glimpses a unified vision of nature at its depths. Resting on an undercurrent of optimism, he unfolds this field of all possibilities, locating playfulness in the serious, imagination in the practical, profundity in the commonplace. In doing so, he takes the chance of being misunderstood, but that is part of the way he views the process of writing. Though he may seem to be giving messages to his readers, Stafford is simply inviting them to find their own way. He says that he prefers not to assert his poems, but to have them "climb toward the reader without my proclaiming anything." He hopes that "sometimes for every reader a poem would arrive: it would go out for him, and find his life."

Jean C. Fulton

Other major works

NONFICTION: *Down in My Heart,* 1947; *Friends to This Ground: A Statement for Readers, Teachers, and Writers of Literature,* 1967; *Leftovers, A Care Package: Two Lectures,* 1973; *Writing the Australian Crawl: Views on the Writer's Vocation,* 1978; *You Must Revise Your Life,* 1986; *Writing the World,* 1988.

EDITED TEXTS: *The Voices of Prose,* 1966 (with Frederick Caudelaria); *The Achievement of Brother Antonius: A Comprehensive Selection of His Poems with a Critical Introduction,* 1967; *Poems and Perspectives,* 1971 (with Robert H. Ross); *Modern Poetry of Western America,* 1975 (with Clinton F. Larson).

Bibliography

Holden, Jonathan. *The Mark to Turn.* Lawrence: University Press of Kansas, 1976. This volume, the first book-length study of Stafford's work, is a useful overview of his major themes and technique. Holden focuses his close readings on poems from Stafford's first published collection and the four collections with his major publisher that followed. The ninety-one-page study includes a biography.

Kitchen, Judith. *Understanding William Stafford.* Columbia: University of South Carolina, 1989. This comprehensive volume is accesible for the student as well as the good nonacademic reader. In addition to a short biography and overview of Stafford's work, it presents detailed analysis of seven of Stafford's major collections and also considers his chapbooks and distinguished small-press editions. This 175-page work concludes with a detailed bibliography of primary and secondary sources.

Lensing, George S., and Ronald Moran. "William Stafford." In *Four Poets and the Emotive Imagination: Robert Bly, James Wright, Louis Simpson, and William Stafford.* Baton Rouge: Louisiana State University Press, 1976. This scholarly volume defines a body of poetry termed "Emotive Imagination" and discusses its emergence within the tradition of American poetry. The chapter on Stafford considers his work from a mythic perspective, both as a reflection of Native American myths and as archetypal poetry that explores the traditional quest theme.

Nordstrom, Lars. "A William Stafford Bibliography." *Studia Neophilologica* 59 (1987): 59-63. Although it is difficult to assemble an exhaustive bibliography because Stafford publishes frequently with small presses, this relatively complete one includes both primary and secondary sources. In addition to prose and poetry collections, it lists critical studies, symposia, interviews, doctoral dissertations, film, and reference materials.

Pinsker, Sanford. "William Stafford: 'The Real Things We Live By.'" In *Three Pacific Northwest Poets.* Boston: Twayne, 1987. This chapter begins with a biographical sketch and then unfolds a book-by-book analysis of six of Stafford's collections, offering close readings of representative poems to support more general conclusions. It includes a selected bibliography.

Stitt, Peter. "William Stafford's Wilderness Quest." In *The World: Hieroglyphic Beauty: Five American Poets.* Athens: University of Georgia Press, 1985. This excellent chapter develops Stafford as a "wisdom poet" and explores his process-rather-than-substance view of writing. It includes an interview with Stafford originally conducted at his home in 1976 and updated in 1981 at the Bread Loaf Writers' Conference.

GERTRUDE STEIN

Born: Allegheny, Pennsylvania; February 3, 1874
Died: Paris, France; July 27, 1946

Principal poetry

Tender Buttons: Objects, Food, Rooms, 1914; *Geography and Plays*, 1922; *Before the Flowers of Friendship Faded Friendship Faded*, 1931; *Two (Hitherto Unpublished) Poems*, 1948; *Bee Time Vine and Other Pieces: 1913-1927*, 1953; *Stanzas in Meditation and Other Poems: 1929-1933*, 1956.

Other literary forms

Most of Gertrude Stein's work did not appear until much later than the date of their completion; the plays and theoretical writings in the following partial list bear the date of composition rather than of publication. *Q. E. D.* (1903); *Three Lives* (1905-1906); *The Making of Americans* (1906-1910); *Matisse, Picasso and Gertrude Stein, with Two Shorter Stories* (1911-1913); *Geography and Plays* (1908-1920); "Composition as Explanation" (1926); *Lucy Church Amiably* (1927); *How to Write* (1927-1931); *Operas and Plays* (1913-1931); *The Autobiography of Alice B. Toklas* (1932); *Lectures in America* (1934); *The Geographical History of America* (1935); *What Are Masterpieces* (1922-1936); *Everybody's Autobiography* (1936); *Picasso* (1938); *The World Is Round* (1938); *Paris France* (1939); *Ida, a Novel* (1940); *Wars I Have Seen* (1942-1944); *Brewsie and Willie* (1945). Much of her writing, including novelettes, shorter poems, plays, prayers, novels, and several portraits, appeared posthumously, as did the last two books of poetry noted above, in the Yale Edition of the Unpublished Writings of Gertrude Stein, in eight volumes edited by Carl Van Vechten. A few of her plays have been set to music, the operas have been performed, and the later children's books have been illustrated by various artists. There exists no recent complete bibliographical listing of her complete works, or of scholarly articles about her, except as appendices to major studies, notably by Richard Bridgman and Michael J. Hoffman.

Achievements

Stein's contribution to art, and specifically to writing, is as great as that of Ezra Pound or James Joyce. It is, however, diametrically opposed to that of these figures in style, content, and underlying philosophy of literature. She advanced mimetic representation to its ultimate, doing away progressively with memory, narration, plot, the strictures of formalized language, and the distinction among styles and genres. Her view of life was founded upon a sense of the living present that shunned all theorizing about meaning and purpose, making writing a supreme experience unto itself. For the first fifteen years of her artistic life, she worked at her craft with stubborn persistence while carrying on an active social life among the Parisian avant-garde. She became influential as a person of definite taste and idiosyncratic manners rather than as an artist in her own right. Her parlor became legend, and writers as diverse as Ernest Hemingway and Sherwood Anderson profited from her ideas. In the 1920's she was the matron of the American expatriates and her work, by then known to most writers, was either ferociously derided or enthusiastically applauded.

It was the poetry of *Tender Buttons* that first brought Gertrude Stein to the attention of the public, though after 1926, novels, critical essays, and prose portraits increasingly circulated. She secured a place in American letters with the publication of *The Autobiography of Alice B. Toklas* (1933), which was also a commercial success. She did not receive any official recognition during her lifetime, except as a curiosity in the world of letters.

Literary criticism has traditionally simply skirted the "problem" of Gertrude Stein, limiting itself to broad generalizations. There exists a group of Stein devotees responsible for preserving the texts, such as Robert Bartlett Haas, Carl Van Vechten, Donald Gallup, and Leon Katz. Stein's work has been illuminated by two indispensable scholar-critics, Richard Bridgman and Donald Sutherland; and there are useful interpretive suggestions in studies by Rosalind Miller, Allegra Stewart, Norman Weinstein, and Michael J. Hoffman. Stein's major impact has been upon writers of later generations, especially in the late 1950's, through the 1960's, and up to the present time; the poetry of Aram Saroyan, Robert Kelly, Clark Coolidge, Jerome Rothenberg, and Lewis Welch is especially indebted to Stein. New insights into this revolutionary writer in the wake of global revisions of the notion of writing and critical thinking have been offered in short pieces by S. C. Neuman, William H. Gass, and Neil Schmitz. Today, a place of eminence is accorded to Stein's fairy tales and children's stories, the theoretical writings, the major works *The Autobiography of Alice B. Toklas* and *The Making of Americans*, the shorter works *Three Lives* and *Ida, a Novel*, and finally *Tender Buttons*, considered by many to be a masterpiece of twentieth century literature.

Biography

Gertrude Stein was born in Allegheny, Pennsylvania, on February 3, 1874. Her grandfather, Michael Stein, came from Austria in 1841, married Hanna Seliger, and settled in Baltimore. One of his sons, Daniel, Gertrude's father, was in the wholesale wool and clothing industry. Daniel was mildly successful and very temperamental. He married Amelia Keyser in 1864, and had five children, Michael (born in 1865), Simon (1867), Bertha (1870), Leo (1872), and Gertrude (1874). In 1875, the family moved to Vienna, and three years later Daniel returned to America, leaving his family for a one-year stay in Paris. In 1879, the family moved back to the United States and spent a year in Baltimore with Amelia Keyser's family. In 1880, Daniel found work in California, and the family relocated again, in Oakland. Memories of these early moves would dot Gertrude's mature works. Leo and Gertrude found that they had much in common, took drawing and music lessons together, frequented the Oakland and San Francisco public libraries, and had time to devote to their intellectual and aesthetic interests. When in 1888 their mother died of cancer, Leo and Gertrude found themselves more and more detached from the rest of the family. In 1892, Daniel Stein died and the eldest son, Michael, took the family back to Baltimore; but the Steins began to scatter. In 1892 Leo entered Harvard, while Gertrude and Bertha stayed with their aunt, Fannie Bachrach. Michael, always patriarchal and the image of stability, married Sarah Samuels and later moved to Paris, where he became a respected member of the intellectual elite, maintaining a Saturday night open house at their apartment in rue Madame. Matisse's portrait of Michael is now in San Francisco.

Gertrude was a cuddled and protected child. At sixteen she weighed 135 pounds and later in college she hired a boy to box with her every day to help her reduce. Her niece, Gertrude Stein Raffel, recalls that her heaviness "was not unbecoming. She was round, roly-poly, and angelic looking." During her adolescent years she became very introspective and critical, and was often depressed and concerned with death. Already emotionally independent, owing to her mother's protracted invalidism and her father's neglect and false representation of authority, Gertrude saw in her brother Leo her only friend. Their bond would not be broken for another twenty years, and she would follow him everywhere, the two delving into matters of mutual interest.

In 1893, Gertrude Stein entered the Harvard Annex, renamed Radcliffe College the following year. She gravitated toward philosophy and psychology, and took courses with such luminaries as George Santayana, Josiah Royce, Herbert Palmer, and William James. In 1894 she worked in the Harvard Psychological Laboratory with Hugo Münsterberg. Her interest in psychology expanded and in 1896 she published, together with Leon Solomons, a paper on "Normal Motor Automatism" which appeared in the *Psychological Review*. A second article "Cultivated Motor Automatism," appeared two years later. In 1897, Gertrude followed her brother to The Johns Hopkins University and began the study of medicine. She specialized in brain research and was encouraged to continue, even though by 1901 her dedication had waned. She attempted four examinations, failed them, and withdrew without a degree.

In 1902 Gertrude traveled, first to Italy, then to London, where she met Bertrand Russell. She spent much time in the British Museum Library studying the Elizabethans, especially William Shakespeare. In the meantime, Leo also abandoned his studies, reverting to an earlier passion for history. A specialist in Renaissance costume, he was drawn to contemporary art, and when, in 1904, he and Gertrude saw a Paul Cézanne exhibit in Florence, they started buying paintings; Leo became a major collector of Henri Matisse. The two settled in the now-famous apartment at 27 rue de Fleurus, where

Gertrude Stein's literary career began, though her first sustained effort, *Q.E.D*, written in 1903, would remain unpublished until 1950. In 1905, while working on a translation of Gustave Flaubert's *Trois contes*, she wrote *Three Lives*. During that period she met Pablo Picasso, who would be very influential in her thinking about art, and with whom she would remain friends for decades. The following year he painted the famous portrait now at the Metropolitan Museum. These days of intense work and thinking saw Gertrude Stein fast at work on her first major long novel, *The Making of Americans*, which she completed in 1910.

Her trips abroad and throughout France from the home base in Paris became an essential part of her existence. In 1907 her brother Michael introduced Gertrude to Alice B. Toklas, who soon became her secretary, going to work on the proofs of *Three Lives*. Alice learned to use a typewriter and the following year, in Fiesole, Italy, she began to copy parts of the manuscript of *The Making of Americans*. Leo, intellectually independent, was moving toward his own aesthetic, though he was still busy promoting new American and French talents. As a painter Leo was not successful, and he came eventually to dislike all contemporary painters except the Cubists. In 1913 he moved from the rue de Fleurus apartment, and with him went all of the Renoirs and most of the Matisses and Cézannes, while Gertrude kept the Picassos. Leo's place had been taken by Alice, who stayed with Gertrude until her death in 1946.

The writer first began to be noticed as a result of Alfred Stieglitz's publication of her "portraits" of Matisse and Picasso in *Camera Work* in 1912. That year she spent the summer in Spain, capturing the sense of her idea of the relationship between object and space, with which she had been struggling. Here she began the prose poem *Tender Buttons*, which brought her to the attention of most of her contemporaries, eliciting varying reactions. She continued to write "portraits" while visiting Mabel Dodge in Florence, at the Villa Curonia. At the Armory Show in New York in 1913, Gertrude was responsible for the presentation of the Pablo Picasso exhibit. When the war broke out, she was in London, where she met the philosopher Alfred North Whitehead. She continued to work intensely, mostly on poetry and plays, and visited Barcelona and Palma de Majorca. In 1916 Gertrude and Alice returned to France and the next year did voluntary war relief work in the South. In 1922 she was awarded a "Medaille de la Reconnaissance Française."

With the appearance of her first collected volume, *Geography and Plays*, in 1922, her fame among the cognoscenti was assured, together with a lively controversy over her truly original style. She was invariably visited by the younger expatriate artists from America, and her parlor became a focal point for the exhange of ideas. Sherwood Anderson introduced her to Hemingway in 1922, and the younger writer learned much from her about the craft of writing. Hemingway was influential in securing publication of parts of *The*

Making of Americans in Ford Maddox Ford's magazine, *Transatlantic Review*. (The nine-hundred-page work was later abridged to half its size by her translator into French, and the shorter version was published in 1925 by Contact Editions, Paris.) Her relationship with Hemingway, however, because of conflicting temperaments, was short-lived; their friendship soon degenerated into bickering.

Gertrude Stein entered another phase of her life when she was asked to lecture in Oxford and Cambridge in 1926. The text of the conference, entitled "Composition as Explanation," constituted her first critical statement on the art of writing; she subsequently returned to a personal exposition of her ideas in *How to Write* (1931), breaking new ground at the stylistic level. This period of major intellectual and thematic upheaval witnessed several transformations in her art. She began to devote more time to the theater, and eventually tackled the difficult task of writing about ideas in the little known *Stanzas in Meditation and Other Poems* (written in 1932 but not published until 1956). In 1929 she left Paris and moved to Bilignin. Her *Lucy Church Amiably* (written in 1927) had not pleased her, but *Four Saints in Three Acts* (1934), with music by Virgil Thomson, was successfully produced in New York. After publication of the well-received *The Autobiography of Alice B. Toklas* (1933), she traveled to America for a lecture tour. Her *Lectures in America* (1935) dealt with her philosophy of composition.

Compelled to close her apartment at rue de Fleurus shortly after her return to France, Gertrude and Alice moved to rue Christine; with the onset of the war in 1939, however, they returned to Bilignin. During the war, the two women lived for a time in Culoz, where they first witnessed the German occupation and then the arrival of the Americans that would be experiences recounted in *Wars I Have Seen* (1945). In December, 1944, she returned to Paris, only to leave soon afterward to entertain American troops stationed in occupied Germany. Her views on the American soldier and the society that produced him changed considerably during these two years. In October, 1945, she traveled to Bruxelles to lecture. Weary and tired, she decided to visit her friend Bernard Fay in the country. Her trip was abruptly interrupted by her illness and she entered the American Hospital in Paris, where, after an unsuccessful cancer operation, she died on July 27, 1946.

Analysis

It is customary to refer to Gertrude Stein's poetry—and her work in general—with the qualifiers "abstract," "repetitive," and "nonsensical," terms which, in view of the predominance of multilayered levels of signification in twentieth century art, do little if any justice to a most remarkable literary achievement. The proper evaluation of Stein's work requires a willingness to rethink certain basic notions concerning art, discourse, and life, a task that is perhaps as difficult as the reading of Stein's voluminous production itself.

Her work, however, is really not excessively abstract, especially when one considers that her poetic rests upon the fundamental axiom of "immediate existing." Nothing could be more concrete than that. Whatever she may be describing, each unit is sure to be a complete, separate assertion, a reality immediately given—in the *present*, the only time there is.

Repetition is insistence: a rose is a rose is a rose is a rose: each time it is new, different, unique, because the experience of the word is unique each time it is uttered. Stylistically, this entails the predominance of parataxis and asyndeton, words being "so nextily" in their unfolding. Repetition of the *same* is often supplanted by repetition of the *different*, where the juxtaposition is in kind and quality. An example of the latter is the following passage from *A Long Gay Book* (1932):

> All the pudding has the same flow and the sauce is painful, the tunes are played, the crinkling paper is burning, the pot has cover and the standard is excellence.

Whether operating at the syntagmatic or at the paradigmatic level, as above, the repetition serves the purpose of emphasizing and isolating *a* thing, not simply *any*thing. The break with all previous associations forces one to consider *this* pudding and *this* sauce, allowing a concretization of the experience in *this* particular frame of the present. If the content appears to have no "logical" coherence, it is because it is not meant to, since the experience of the immediate does not warrant ratiocination or understanding of any sort. Art in Gertrude Stein is perception of the immediate, a capturing of the instantaneity of the word as event, sense, or object. The notion is clearly nonreferential in that art does not need a world to know that it exists. Although it occasionally refers to it, it does not *have* to—in fact, the less it does, the better. What is of paramount importance is that this self-contained entity comes alive in the continuous present of one's experience of it, and only then. The influence of Stein's painter friends was unequivocal. Not all discourse that links the work of art to history and other realms of life is, properly speaking, a preoccupation of the artist: it does not constitute an aesthetic experience, remaining just that—criticism, sociology, and philosophy. Meaning is something that comes after the experience, thanks to reflection, to the mediation of reason, and the standardization of logic and grammar; it is never given in the immediacy of the poetic expression. Gertrude Stein's writings attempt to produce the feeling of something happening or being lived—in short, to give things (objects, emotions, ideas, words) a *sense* that is new and unique and momentary, independent and defiant of what an afterthought may claim to be the "true" meaning or sense of an experience or artistic event. From this perspective, can it still be honestly said that Stein's work is "nonsense," with all the negative implications usually associated with the epithet?

Gertrude Stein had from very early in her career a keen sense of the distance that naturally exists between objects and feelings as perceived, and their transposition into conventional formalized speech. Her first novel, *Q.E.D.* (*Quod Erat Demonstrandum*), written in 1903 and known after 1950 as *Things as They Are*, while it dealt with the then taboo topic of lesbianism in a *ménage à trois* of three women, is already shorn of such typical narrative features as symbolism, character development, climax, and descriptions of setting, though it is cast in an intelligible variation of standard prose. At the limits of the Jamesian novel, what happens among the characters and the space of emotional relatedness is more important than the characters as characters. The focal point is the introspection of these human natures and all elaborations and complications of feelings remain internal, intimate, within the consciousness of the individual being described or, most often, within the dialectic of the relationship. Doing away with all contingent background material meant zooming in on the poetic process itself; but for all practical purposes the author is still struggling within the precincts of the most sophisticated naturalism: she is still representing, in the tradition of Henry James and Gustave Flaubert, two authors whom she admired greatly. The characters are at odds with the author: they are white American college women constantly preoccupied with the propriety of their very relationship and therefore demand of the author a polite, cultivated, and literary realization.

The problem of the language to employ in writing is dealt with in the next work, *Three Lives*, where the progressive abandonment of inherited expressive forms is much stronger and can be said to constitute a first milestone in Gertrude Stein's stylistic development, especially in "Melanchta," the last of the three stories.

Here Stein describes a love story set among lower-class blacks where she can explore the intensity of "uneducated" speech and where, as Donald Sutherland quite aptly points out, there exists "a direct relationship between feeling and word." Typical of her entire literary career, at the time of publication the printer inquired whether the author really knew English! In *Three Lives*, Stein was "groping for a continuous present and for using everything again and again." This continuous present is immediate and partakes of the human mind as it exists at any given moment when confronted with the object of writing. It is different from the prolonged present of duration, as in Henri Bergson, where aspects of human nature may enter. At the stylistic level, punctuation is rare and the present participle is employed as a substantive for its value in retaining the sense of process, of continuity in a present mode that knows no before and no after. This "subjective time" of writing is paralleled by similar developments in the visual and plastic arts, from which Stein drew copiously. Her admiration and appreciation of what Cézanne had done for painting was matched by the unrelenting support that she bestowed upon the upcoming younger generation of artists, such as Picasso, Matisse, Juan

Gris, and Francis Picabia. Cézanne had taught her that there are no less important areas on a canvas *vis à vis* the theme or figure that traditionally dominated representational painting, and he returned to "basics," such as color, tone, distribution, and the underlying abstractions, reaching out for those essentials in the welter of external detail in order to capture a sense without which there would be no painting. Picasso went even further, forsaking three-dimensional composition for the surface purity of plane geometry, ushering in Cubism. For Stein, perception takes place against the *tabula rasa* of immediate consciousness, and Cubism offered the flatness of an interior time which could be brought to absolute elementalism, simplicity, and finality.

Q.E.D. and *Three Lives*, for all their stylistic experimentation, are clearly works of prose. In *Tender Buttons*, however, Stein blurs the distinction between prose and poetry. She works with "meaningless" babble, puns, games, rhymes, and repetitions. Much as in Lewis Carroll and Tristam Tzara, the word itself is seen as magic. In a world of pure existence, dialogue disappears, replaced by word lists and one-word utterances. Interactions of characters are no longer tenable, and people give way to objects. The portrait is supplanted by the still life, and the technique of composition is reminiscent of Picasso's collages, *not* of automatic writing. The intention seems to be to give the work its autonomy independent of both writer and reader: one sees and reads what one sees and reads, the rest being reconstruction from memory or projections of the viewer's intellect. The effort is ambitious: to see language being born. Disparate critical ideas have been invoked to "interpret" *Tender Buttons*, and it is likely that Norman Weinstein (*Gertrude Stein and the Literature of Modern Consciousness*, 1970), comes closest when he summons the studies of Jean Piaget, the Sapir-Whorf language hypothesis, R. D. Laing, and the dimension of schizophrenia. On the opposite bank, Allegra Stewart (*Gertrude Stein and the Present*, 1967) reads the work as a Jungian mandala and relates the alchemical correspondences to all of the literary movements of the epoch, such as Dada, Futurism, and so on.

"A jack in kill her, a jack in, makes a meadowed king, makes a to let." The plastic use of language permits the bypassing of the rule where, for example, a substantive is the object of a preposition. The infinitive "to let" appears as the object of a verb and is modified by the indefinite article "a." If analysis emphasizes the dislocation, the derangement, of standard usage, suggesting that alternative modes of expression are possible and even revealing, no matter how unwieldly, it should also note the foregrounding of "events" in an atemporal framework, where even nouns are objects that do not need the passing of ages to be what they are. Sense, if not altogether certain meanings, can be obtained only in the suspended perception of the reading, especially aloud.

This effort to see and write in the "continuous present" requires, Stein said, a passionate identification with the thing to be described: a steady, trancelike concentration upon the object will first of all divest it of all its customary appellations and then permit the issuing forth of words and structures that alone can speak as *that* thing in front of the observer. In "Poetry and Grammar" (1935), Stein says: "Poetry is concerned with using with abusing, with losing with wanting, with denying with avoiding with adoring with replacing the noun. . . . Poetry is doing nothing but using losing refusing and pleasing and betraying and caressing nouns." In this spirit of reevaluation of the nature and process of naming things she will then go all out in making sure that the things she looks at will by themselves elicit the way they are to be called, never being for a moment worried that such a process may be at odds with the limited range of possibilities offered by conventional reality; she did not only want to rename things, but to "find out how to know that they were there by their names or by replacing their names." As Shakespeare had done in Arden, the goal was to create "a forest without mentioning the things that make a forest."

With this new discovery, for the ensuing twenty years she kept busy revisiting timeworn forms and models of poetic expression, charging them with fresh blood and impetus. The underlying magic would be constant: "looking at anything until something that was not the name of that thing but was in a way that actual thing would come to be written." This process was possible because Stein had arrived at a particular conception of the essence of language: it is not "imitation either of sounds or colors or emotions," but fundamentally an "intellectual recreation." The problem of mimesis and representation was forever behind her, and the idea of *play* became fundamental in her work.

The third stage of Stein's poetry came in the late 1920's and early 1930's, at a time when she was both very happy at receiving some recognition, and much depressed about some new problems of her craft. Of the three materials that she felt art had to deal with, sight, sound, and sense, corresponding to the spatial, the temporal, and the conceptual dimensions of the mind, she had up to then worked intensely on the first two, relegating the third to the background by ignoring it or by simply rejecting it as a response to conventional grammatical and logical sense. At times, she handled the problem of sense by mediating it through her theoretical writings, especially after 1925. With the ending of the "Roaring Twenties," however, much of the spatiality in literature also disappeared. Painting became intellectual, poets became religious or political, and the newer waves did not seem to hold much promise. Stein had also reached a conclusion concerning works of art: that there are no masterpieces containing ideas; in philosophy, there are no masterpieces. Ideas and philosophy require almost by definition a mediated, sequential array of items over time and in history, ideas being *about* something or other. For a poetic of the unique, concrete thing—again, against all claims that Stein's is a poetic of the abstract—the task of dealing with ideas, which are by nature abstract, posed no small problem. Still, owing also to her attention to religious thought and the artistic implications of meditation, communion, trance, and revelation, she felt the need to come to terms with this hitherto untrodden ground. Stein set about writing a poem of ideas without all of the historical and philosophical underpinnings and referents that accompany works such as Ezra Pound's *The Cantos* (1925-1972) and T. S. Eliot's *The Waste Land* (1922). True to the credo that art is immanent and immediate, she wrote *Stanzas in Meditation*, a long poem made up of five parts and running to 163 stanzas, some a line long, others extending over several pages.

Remarkably little has been written about this forgotten but truly major composition, for the difficulty once again is the unpreparedness of criticism to deal with another of Stein's innovations: instead of writing *about* ideas, she writes *the* ideas: thinking, in other words, does not occur in the mind *after* reading the words on the page, but the words themselves *are* the ideas, making ideas partake of the human mind instead of human nature. The old reliable technique of stopping the momentous thoughts on the page as consciousness becomes aware of them creates once again the typical situation with Stein's art: one experiences ideas as one reads; one cannot lean back and expect to put together a "coherent" whole. There are in fact no philosophical terms in the traditional sense and no organization as such. Norman Weinstein writes that "The poem is not *about* philosophy, but *is* philosophy set into motion by verbal action." The disembodied, fragmentary, and discontinuous vision of the Cubists is here interweaved with the process-philosophy of William James and Alfred North Whitehead. Stylistically, each line tends to be objective and stable and corresponds to what in prose is the sentence. As the lines build up into a stanza, they swell with tension, and, like the paragraph, constitute a specific unit of attention. The poem will occasionally evidence images and allow symbols, but these are accidental, perhaps because the idea itself can best or only be expressed in that particular fashion. According to Sutherland, the poem can be entered in a tradition that lists Plato, Pindar, the English Metaphysicals and Gerard Manley Hopkins. The poem can be read by simply beginning at random, which is perhaps the best way for the uninitiated to get a "sense" of it and familiarize themselves with the tone, lyricism, and surprisingly deceiving content. The technique of repetition is still present, revealing new contexts for given words, and Stein coins new expressions for ancient truisms. The text is a gold mine of brilliant aphorisms: "There is no hope or use in all," or "That which they like they knew."

From the time of the appearance of *The Autobiography of Alice B. Toklas* (1933) to the publication, shortly before her death, of *The Gertrude Stein First Reader and Three Plays* (1946), thirteen other books came out, among which were the highly successful and important *The Geographical History of America* (1936) and *Everybody's Autobiography* (1937). During these years Stein's major efforts were directed to the problem of self-presentation and the formal structure of autobiography. She put the writer on the same ground as the reader, ending the privileged position of both biographer and auto-biographer. She continued to elaborate the poetic of impersonal, timeless, and spaceless writing, assuring that experience, flow, and place remain within the confines of the continuous present of perception. Her poetry during this period was chiefly written for children, rhymed and chanted and playful, with no pretense at being anything more than a momentary flash in the con-tinuum of life, a diversion, a game. Many of these works were published either as limited editions or posthumously in the Yale Edition of her un-collected writings, where they can now be read in chronological sequence.

Peter Carravetta

Other major works

LONG FICTION: *Three Lives*, 1909; *The Making of Americans*, 1925; *Lucy Church Amiably*, 1930; *A Long Gay Book*, 1932; *Ida, a Novel*, 1941; *Brewsie and Willie*, 1946; *Blood on the Dining-Room Floor*, 1948; *Things as They Are*, 1950 (originally known as *Q.E.D.*); *Mrs. Reynolds and Five Earlier Nov-elettes, 1931-1942*, 1952; *As Fine as Melanctha*, 1954; *A Novel of Thank You*, 1958.

PLAYS: *Geography and Plays*, 1922; *Capital Capitals*, 1929, 1968 (published); *Operas and Plays*, 1932; *Four Saints in Three Acts*, 1934; *Lucretia Borgia*, 1939; *The Gertrude Stein First Reader and Three Plays*, 1946; *In Savoy: Or, Yes Is For a Very Young Man (A play of the Resistance in France)*, 1946; *The Mother of Us All*, 1947 (opera); *Last Operas and Plays*, 1949; *In a Garden: An Opera in One Act*, 1951; *Selected Operas and Plays*, 1970.

NONFICTION: "Composition as Explanation," 1926; *How to Write*, 1931; *The Autobiography of Alice B. Toklas*, 1933; *Matisse, Picasso, and Gertrude Stein, with Two Shorter Stories*, 1933; *Portraits and Prayers*, 1934; *Lectures in Amer-ica*, 1935; *Narration*, 1935; *The Geographical History of America*, 1936; *Ev-erybody's Autobiography*, 1937; *Picasso*, 1938; *Paris France*, 1940; *What Are Masterpieces*, 1940; *Wars I Have Seen*, 1945; *Four in America*, 1947; *Reflec-tions on the Atomic Bomb*, 1973; *How writing is Written*, 1974.

CHILDREN'S LITERATURE: *The World Is Round*, 1939.

Bibliography

Bloom, Harold, ed. *Modern Critical Views: Gertrude Stein*. New York: Chelsea House, 1986. Bloom's perceptive introduction to this collection of critical essays, as well as chapters from a number of full-length studies of Stein's work, describes her as the greatest master of dissociative rhetoric in mod-ern writing. The essays, written by leading Stein scholars, deal with bio-graphical as well as feminist intellectual and physical issues. Concludes with a useful chronology of Stein's life and work.

Bridgman, Richard. *Gertrude Stein in Pieces*. New York: Oxford University Press, 1970. This lengthy work is one of the most valuable assessments of Stein's achievement in modern times. Bridgman's study, essentially a biography, discusses each of Stein's works chronologically and analyzes them in the context of her personal life. Vastly informative, objective, and crucial to any preliminary reading. Includes a bibliography and appendices.

DeKoven, Marianne. *A Different Language: Gertrude Stein's Experimental Writing*. Madison: University of Wisconsin Press, 1983. In this relatively brief work, the author reads Stein's work chronologically through its major periods and devises "genres" such as "lively words," "voices and plays," "melody," and "landscape" to describe her experimental forms. Viewing the incoherence and unrestrictive play in the writing as essentially positive forces, DeKoven argues that Stein's writing successfully overcame conventional expectations of meaning and form. Contains notes and an index.

Dubnick, Randa. *The Structure of Obscurity: Gertrude Stein, Language, and Cubism*. Urbana: University of Illinois Press, 1984. Dubnick's interdisciplinary study deals not only with Gertrude Stein but also with cubism, structuralism, and semiotics. The author distinguishes between Stein's prose (genuine cubism), which exaggerates syntax and minimizes vocabulary, and poetry (synthetic cubism), which abbreviates syntax and extends vocabulary. Includes a bibliography.

Gass, William H. "Gertrude Stein: Her Escape from Protective Language." In *Fiction and the Figures of Life*. New York: Alfred A. Knopf, 1970. In a brilliant assessment of Stein's writing, in particular her use of language, Gass presents a rigorous defense of Stein's intellectual reach. Convincingly examines why she was first wrongly and uncritically admired, then censured by many without reason.

Kellner, Bruce. *A Gertrude Stein Companion: Content with Example*. Westport, Conn.: Greenwood Press, 1988. This lengthy and exhaustive study on Stein's life and work introduces the novice and the somewhat conversant reader to a variety of sources for approaching Stein's work. An insightful introduction entitled "How to Read Gertrude Stein," is followed by a series of critical essays on her writing, a bibliography of her published writing, biographical sketches of her most prominent friends and acquaintances, as well as her observations on a variety of subjects. Contains an annotated bibliography and numerous illustrations.

Neuman, Shirley, and Ira B. Nadel, eds. *Gertrude Stein and the Making of Literature*. New York: Macmillan, 1988. These essays by eleven Stein scholars provide new approaches and perspectives on the full range of her work. Includes modernist and postmodernist theory and practice, explications of little-read works, and assessments of the process of composition from notebook to manuscript to printed page. The wide variety in subject matter makes this a valuable addition to Stein's criticism.

GERALD STERN

Born: Pittsburgh, Pennsylvania; February 22, 1925

Principal poetry

The Pineys, 1969; *The Naming of Beasts and Other Poems*, 1973; *Rejoicings*, 1973; *Lucky Life*, 1977; *The Red Coal*, 1981; *Father Guzman*, 1982; *Paradise Poems*, 1984; *Lovesick: Poems*, 1987; *Learning Another Kingdom: Selected Poems*, 1990.

Other literary forms

While Gerald Stern is known almost exclusively for his poetry, he has also written a number of perceptive essays.

Achievements

Unlike the poems of many of his contemporaries, those of Stern explode upon the reader's attention with a high and impassioned rhetoric. The poems seem to tumble forward like trees in a flood, snaring, collecting, and finally sweeping subject matter one would have thought only peripherally connected to the main thrust. By using an engaging conversational tone, combined with the frequent use of repetition to sweep together myriad details, Stern's poems display a direct link to the poetics of Walt Whitman. Moreover, a psalmist's zest for parallelism and anaphora disclose a debt to biblical poetry and reinforce the pervasively spiritual, specifically Jewish, sensibility of Stern's work. His frequent use of surrealistic images, meanwhile, reveals a debt to twentieth century Spanish poets, and his love of humble specifics shows him to be a descendant of Ezra Pound and William Carlos Williams. The poems are, among other things, evidence of an immense curiosity about life set against the depersonalizing matrix of twentieth century history.

Eschewing the drift toward, on the one hand, hermeticism, and, on the other, the poetry of confession, Stern's poems, by capitalizing on many of the features of "open" poetry (in various of its historical incarnations), have shown a way for poetry to become equal to the task of transforming both memory and modern history into art. Although it is but one way, Stern's poetic is both stimulating and eminently suitable for representing and interpreting the variousness of American life in a way that encompasses both the tragic and the humorous into its fabric.

Biography

Born in 1925, Gerald Stern grew up in Pittsburgh. He attended the University of Pittsburgh and Columbia University and began his working career as an English teacher and a principal. After spending a number of years in Europe, mainly Paris and London, during the 1950's (though with a stint as an English teacher in Glasgow, Scotland), he returned to the United States and began teaching at Temple University in 1957. He also taught at the University of Pennsylvania, Indiana University of Pennsylvania, and Somerset County College in New Jersey. Stern would divide his time between his home in eastern Pennsylvania and the Writers' Workshop of the University of Iowa where he was a professor of English. Among his awards are a fellowship in creative writing from the National Endowment for the Arts (1976) and the Lamont Award (1977).

Analysis

Rejoicings announces most of the themes and much of the style of Gerald Stern's subsequent, better-known work. Already present are the tutelary spirits who people his later poems and the tension between his love of "high" culture as represented by various philosophers and poets, all heroes of the intellect and art, and his yearning for spontaneity and the "natural," represented by home-grown resources, as in "Immanuel Kant and the Hopi":

> I am going to write twenty poems about my ruined country,
>> Please forgive me, my old friends,
> I am walking in the direction of the Hopi!
> I am walking in the direction of Immanuel Kant!
> I am learning to save my thoughts—like
> one of the Dravidians—so that nothing will
> be lost, nothing I tramp upon, nothing I
> chew, nothing I remember.

While holding most of the Western intellectual tradition in high respect, Stern equally holds its neglect of emotion, intuition, and experience to be responsible for much of the misery to which human beings are taught to accommodate themselves. Thus, many of the poems in the collection have an aspect of unlearning about them, even as they continue to extol the finer mentors of Western tradition. Others look for a "third" way somehow to be negotiated between the mind/body dichotomy, as in "By Coming to New Jersey":

> By coming to New Jersey I have discovered the third world
> that hangs between Woodbridge Avenue and Victory Bridge.
> It is a temporary world,
> full of construction and water holes,
> full of barriers and isolated hydrants . . .

The "third world" of experience is one to which he will return again and again, finding it populated with all the things that are of little consequence to the heave of civilization: birds, flowers, weeds, bugs, and the like, as well as human detritus—the junkyards of America, superseded and yet everywhere visible as testimonials to other dimensions of life.

Although Stern had been publishing steadily for many years, the publication in 1977 of *Lucky Life* proved to be a watershed in his career. Expansive and ebullient, slyly melodramatic and hyperbolic (whether depicting the tragic, the nostalgic, or the mundane) but always wonderfully readable, the poems appeared during a period when the 1960's loose aesthetic had been exhausted, and the predictable return to formalism was just getting under way. The book seemed in some ways to partake of neither, though this is only a partial truth, for the poems are certainly more informed by the openness of the 1960's than by the subsequent swing the other way. By reaching back, through Whitman, to the psalmists, and imbuing the various techniques of poetic repetition with a dizzying parade of disjunctive images, emotional outbursts, jeremiads, and tender soliloquies, *Lucky Life* seemed to point the way to a new kind of democratic poetry, a kind of Whitman modernized and extended: "I am going to carry my bed into New York City tonight/ complete with dangling sheets and ripped blankets;/ I am going to push it across three dark highways/ or coast along under 600,000 faint stars."

Just as Whitman found American possibility teeming in New York, Stern, a century and a half later, locates it in the moral imperative to preserve its authentic and unrepeatable artifacts (as well as the national character that went into making them), as in "Straus Park":

> . . . if you yourself go crazy when you walk through the old shell
> on Stout's Valley Road,
> then you must know how I felt when I saw Stanley's Cafeteria
> boarded up and the sale sign out . . .

To this he opposes "California," that state of mind "with its big rotting sun": "—Don't go to California yet!/ Come with me to Stanley's and spend your life/ weeping in the small park on 106th Street." California is not a state of mind but a fact of life—to some, an ideal (to the poet, the wrong one). Still, it is possible to carry some of Stanley's memories even to California: "Take the iron fence with you/ when you go into the desert./ . . . Do not burn again for nothing./ Do not cry out again in clumsiness and shame."

The feeling for nostalgic way stations, for what, in a more somber locution, is sometimes called tradition, informs the poet's subject matter in a personal but dynamic way that is nevertheless always under threat by the rise of anonymity, conformity, and the pervasiveness of substitutes. These poems, then, are atavistic expressions of grief and longing for the return of the authentic: "What would you give for your dream/ to be as clear and simple as it was then/ in the dark afternoons, at the old scarred tables?" Characteristically, the poet often identifies this longing and grief with his Jewishness, as when he stops to examine a road kill in "Behaving Like a Jew": "—I am going to be unappeased at the opossum's death./ I am going to behave like a Jew/ and touch his face, and stare into his eyes,/ and pull him off the road." Led by a detour to a dilapidated coffeehouse called (the poem's title) "This Is It" ("the first condemned building in the United States"), the poet talks to its owner, a "coughing lady," and commiserates with her over the collapse of the neighborhood. He listens to the stories of her youth, about her dog "and its monotonous existence," and proclaims, "Everyone is into my myth! The whole countryside/ is studying weeds, collecting sadness, dreaming/ of odd connections. . . ."

Sometimes, Stern begins his nostalgia on an ironic note before devolving into seriousness, as in "If You Forget the Germans":

> If you forget the Germans climbing up and down the Acropolis,
> then I will forget the poet falling through his rotten floor in New Brunswick;
> and if you stop telling me about your civilization in 1400 B.C.,
> then I will stop telling you about mine in 1750 and 1820 and 1935 . . .

After a list of such playful give-and-take, the poet shifts key: "Here are the thoughts I have had;/ here are the people I have talked to and worn out;/ here are the stops in my throat." The real theme—the search for happiness amid the ubiquity of details and through the murderous lurch of time—is discovered in a journey into the poet's own typically broken past, narrated in a mock travelogue ("If you go by bus . . ."). Yet after a series of perplexing directions, he admonishes, "Do not bury yourself outright in the litter." Instead, he says, in an ending that finds echoes in Christian liturgy:

> Sing and cry and kiss in the ruined dining room
> in front of the mirror, in the plush car seat,
> a 1949 or '50, still clean and perfect
> under the black dust and the newspapers,
> as it was when we cruised back and forth all night looking for happiness;
> as it was when we lay down and loved in the old darkness.

Happiness is the subject of the title poem: "Lucky life isn't one long string of horrors/ and there are moments of peace, and pleasure, as I lie in between the blows." With age and the accretions of scars and memories, happiness becomes more problematical: "Each year I go down to the island I add/ one more year to the darkness;/ and though I sit up with my dear friends . . ./ after a while they all get lumped together." Announcing that "This year was a crisis," the poet lumbers through memories of past vacations, through dreams of getting lost on South Main Street in a town in New Jersey, of looking for a particular statue of Christopher Columbus, of sitting at a bar listening to World War II veterans, then dreams of himself sitting on a porch "with a whole new set of friends, mostly old and humorless." There follows a burst of apostrophes: "Dear Waves, what will you do for me this year?/ Will you drown out my scream?/ Will you let me rise through the fog?" The poem ends on a note of provisional affirmation:

> Lucky life is like this. Lucky there is an ocean to come to.
> Lucky you can judge yourself in this water.
> Lucky the waves are cold enough to wash out the meanness.
> Lucky you can be purified over and over again.

With the publication of *The Red Coal* in 1981, some critics believed that Stern had fallen into self-imitation and saw the poems as mannered in their style and sometimes bombastic in their treatment of subject matter. For example, the critic for *The New York Times Book Review* asserted, "In poem after poem he sets up for himself some temptation over which he wins a lyrical triumph. The invariability with which he clears those hurdles makes one suspect that the fences have been lowered." A dissenting view, however, would simply note that, in a poem, all triumphs are "lyrical," for in what sense could they be "actual"? Perhaps the insinuation of repetition is the more damaging. While it is true that Stern's poems offer little in the way of stylistic variation, their range is impressive.

Simply to list the place-names and people who gather to Stern's poems like flocking birds is to suggest the presence of a poet with wide cultural affinities and concerns. While all the figures and places could, with skepticism, be seen as a form of name-dropping, it is more likely that they play a totemic role, suggesting whole ranges of other experience anterior to the specific subject matter. Nicolaus Copernicus, Isaac Stern, Jascha Heifetz, Emma Goldman, Eugene V. Debs, Pablo Picasso, Vincent van Gogh, Casimir Pulaski, Galileo, Albert Einstein, Fyodor Dostoevski, Guillaume Apollinaire, Hart Crane, Ezra Pound, Thomas Jefferson, Gustave Flaubert, Wyndham Lewis, Maurice Ravel, Aleksandr Nikolayevich Scriabin, Antonio Vivaldi, Eugene O'Neill, Johann Wolfgang von Goethe—all these and many more haunt the poems like figures in a pantheon.

As for the kind of mind necessary for the poet's—and, by extrapolation, modern man's—survival, Stern compares a model of Galileo's to one of his own in a poem intriguingly titled "I Remember Galileo": "I remember Galileo describing the mind/ as a piece of paper blown around by the wind,/ and I loved the sight of it sticking to a tree/ or jumping into the back seat of a car." At first, he says he watched paper "for years," as if to test the adequacy of the metaphor, but "yesterday I saw the mind was a squirrel caught crossing/ Route 60 between the wheels of a giant truck." The squirrel escapes, but not before "his life [was] shortened by all that terror." The poet decides that "Paper will do in theory," but the alert, capable squirrel, "his whole soul quivering," finishes his mad scramble across the highway and escapes up his "green ungoverned hillside."

Such seizures and terror, often encountered in retrospect, are usually made over to the poet's advantage, as in "The Red Coal," the title poem, whose central image (most likely derived from the biblical story of the infant Moses, who chose Pharaoh's tray of burning embers over a tray of rubies) presides like a second sun over the poet's difficult but intellectually and spiritually formative years traveling with his friend, the poet Jack Gilbert:

> I didn't live in Paris for nothing and walk
> with Jack Gilbert down the wide sidewalks
> thinking of Hart Crane and Apollinaire
>
> and I didn't save the picture of the two of us
> moving through a crowd of stiff Frenchmen
> and put it beside the one of Pound and Williams
>
> unless I wanted to see what coals had done
> to their lives too . . .

The incandescent coal represents the yearning for knowledge, "as if knowledge is what we needed and now/ we have that knowledge." On the other hand, the coal almost certainly guarantees pain for those who would be its avatars: "The tears are . . . what, all along, the red coal had/ in store for us." Yet the tears are not the result of futility or disappointment; they are the liquid registers of experience as it imposes itself upon time, the baffling sea change of the body and mind that puts even the most familiar past at a strange remove: "Sometimes I sit in my blue chair trying to remember/ what it was like in the spring of 1950/ before the burning coal entered my life."

Many of the poems in *The Red Coal* cast a backward look over the poet's life, coming to terms with the effects of his commitment, "getting rid of baggage,/ finding a way to change, or sweeten, my clumsy life." That clumsiness, that self-estrangement, appropriately finds an equivalence, and hence an inward dialogue, with the lowly and dishonored things of the world, from weeds and animals (including insects and spiders) to Emma Goldman inveighing against the tyranny of property and the injustice toward winos whose lives the bright and aggressive world has cast aside. Such pity and commiseration are particularly strong in Stern and at times take on a marked spiritual coloring. In "The Poem of Liberation," the poet observes a large "vegetable garden planted in the rubble/ of a wrecked apartment house, as if to claim/ the spirit back before it could be buried/ in another investment of glass and cement." In "Dear Mole," the title animal is compared to John Ruskin, "always cramming and ramming, spluttering in disgust/ . . . always starting over,/ his head down, his poor soul warbling and wailing." A monkey appears in "For Night to Come":

> All morning we lie
> on our backs, holding hands, listening to birds,
> and making little ant hills in the sand.

> He shakes a little, maybe from the cold,
> maybe a little from memory,
> maybe from dread.

As the day passes, they "watch the stars together/ like the good souls we are,/ a hairy man and a beast/ hugging each other in the white grass."

Between the 1981 collection, *The Red Coal*, and the 1984 *Paradise Poems*, Stern published a book-length dramatic poem, *Father Guzman.* Cast in the form of a half-demented conversation between a savvy fifteen-year-old street urchin and a Maryknoll priest—both prisoners in a South American jail— the poem is an energetic, if at times prosy, political dialogue that touches on the likes of Christopher Columbus, Simón Bolívar, and Abraham Lincoln, and by way of Plato, Ovid, Campanella, Goethe and Dante. Father Guzman, whose head has just been cracked by rifle-butts of the National Guard, sits in his cell and confronts the taunts of the Boy, a native; from the initial exchange extends an impassioned conversation of forty pages. Foulmouthed and in-the-know, the Boy begins the poem by extolling his hero (Bolívar) and his affiliation (anarchist). Father Guzman replies that in the room where he was beaten were two American policemen carrying looseleaf notebooks. He compares them with flies and suggests that their incarceration is the result of the same oppression:

> You know the common fly
> has 33 million microorganisms
> flourishing in its gut and a half billion more
> swarming over its body and legs? You know
> that Bolivar left to his vice-presidents
> the tasks of pity?

Father Guzman concludes that Bolívar was "a Caesar" and "that the Mellons plan to betray the universe/ that Nelson Rockefeller was an ichneumon and/ David Rockefeller is a house fly." This makes the Boy sit up, and, weakly suggesting that his admiration of Bolívar results from the fact that both were orphans, changes the subject to "Venus, Bolívar's favorite goddess." Father Guzman understands how the mythology of heroes is such that even tyrants and demagogues can appeal to the masses through the lens of "love," a lens capable of distorting everyone equally:

> but I have seen enough
> of what you call love to last me a lifetime;
> and I have read de Rougement and Goethe,
> but I prefer to talk about this slum
> and the nature of oil capitalism . . .

The Boy, buoyed on the crest of his own postpuberty, continues unconcerned, by listing his "favorites": Plato, the Ovid of *Amores*, the author of the *Kama*

Sutra ("The section on plural intercourse/ really turns me on"), and other *maestros* of love. Father Guzman responds that he would like the Boy to experience the pornographic trenches of New York ("you would love New York City"). He admits that he, too, "wanted to burn [his] seed . . . to die!": "What Raleigh fought for, what the insane Spaniards/ dreamed of for a lifetime. I saw the/ issue of their violent quest." The Boy shifts again ("There is true love in the universe, you know that!/ Think of Dante! Think of the Duke of Windsor") but demurs and admits, "you I love more than my own flesh and blood."

In the second section, Father Guzman asks the Boy, "Why is life/ a joke to you?" The Boy replies that he would simply like to go for a swim and forget about history. Father Guzman interjects: "Listen to me! Without a dream you'd die!/ This slime of ours would fill/ the whole world!" The Boy says that his dream is to live "without misery and sickness and hunger." Father Guzman turns the talk to Utopias and Tommaso Campanella's *La cittá del sole* (1602; *The City of the Sun*, 1637), saying that he "worship[s] his spirit," but concedes that he does not like "the Caesar Complex . . ./ and all that control, in industry, education, and art,/ control of the mind, even of the heart." The Boy characteristically focuses on the control of the heart and exclaims, "I hate policemen! I can't stand them/ looking at you as if they knew/ what you already had in your pockets." Father Guzman wonders why, "in the whole history of the world/ there have never been two months of kindness?" and steers the talk to his admiration of Charles Fourier, "one of the true madmen of love/ and one of the great enemies of repression." The Boy asks Father Guzman what he believes in, and Guzman replies, "my heart is still old-fashioned and I want/ people to be happy in a world I recognize . . ./ . . . where souls can manage a little . . ./ without shaming themselves in front of the rats and weasels."

In section 3, the Boy puts on a dress and convincingly impersonates Father Guzman's former lover, who explains that she left him "when I saw your sadness and confusion." Dramatizing the ritual in painful detail, the Boy concludes, "There's nothing sadder than talking to the dress." They then act out an exchange between the American ambassador (Guzman) and the president (the Boy). The talk then turns to El Dorado. "Gomez" admits that there is no El Dorado but asserts that the dream is nevertheless a good one because it is idealistic, a kind of Grail. The "Ambassador" explains that in North America there is no such dream and consequently the jails are "like hotels": " . . . They sit there,/ all those priests and rabbis, weeping/ in the hallways, lecturing the police."

"Gomez" shows his machismo by describing tortures that he has invented and tries to justify the graft and nepotism he has installed in his country when the Boy breaks through: "I can't do it! I quit!" Guzman concurs, "I don't know how we started in the first place." Yet the pair play one more charade, with Father Guzman playing the part of Columbus: "I challenge anyone on horseback or foot/ to deny my rights to take this place by force." "Columbus" tells the Boy that he can bring him more than he has ever dreamed. The Boy claims not to understand the meaning of Columbus and wonders if in his cynicism he has been too hard on his country: "After all,/ we've changed, haven't we?" Exhausted by the heat of their encounter, the Boy begins to think of exile, and Father Guzman recommends New York: "Brooklyn's the place for you! I understand/ Flatbush is having a comeback. You could go/ either to Brooklyn College or N.Y.U." The poem ends with both prisoners looking at a star, and Father Guzman makes the comment, "Campanella is probably washing himself/ in the flames. Dante is probably/ explaining the sweetness to Virgil." The Boy replies, "It is a beautiful night. Life is still good./ And full of pleasure—and hope—"

Despite the unconvincing precocity of the Boy and Father Guzman's pervasive profanity, both in thought and in speech, the poem manages to dramatize most of Stern's previous themes: love of pleasure and exploration (as symbolized by poets and philosophers), the striving for justice, sympathy for the downtrodden, and hatred of exploitation and greed, especially that which is institutionalized by politics. It is a bold essay into history, poetry, and psychology, and though one can hear the poet's private voice coming through at times, it marks a welcome change from the Whitman-like first-person poems that so markedly characterize the earlier work.

In *Paradise Poems*, Stern works to bring his poems to a higher rhetorical pitch and, frequently, a longer format. A deeper, more elegiac strain runs through the poems, and the most notable poems are formal elegies for poets W. H. Auden ("In Memory of W. H. Auden") and Gil Orlovitz ("At Jane's"), the Yiddish actor Luther Adler ("Adler"), the photographer Alfred Stieglitz ("Kissing Stieglitz Goodbye"), and the poet's father ("The Expulsion"). In the elegy for Auden, the younger Stern plays Caliban to Auden's Prospero, as he waits outside for Auden's "carved face to let me in," hoping, like all young poets, to get the master's nod but realizing "that I would have to wait for ten more years/ or maybe twenty more years for the first riches/ to come my way, and knowing that the stick/ of that old Prospero would never rest/ on my poor head. . . . " Though Auden is "dear . . . with his robes/ and his books of magic," Stern understands that "I had to find my own way back, I had to/ free myself, I had to find my own pleasure/ in my own sweet cave, with my own sweet music."

By contrast, "At Jane's" sets the death of the impoverished and neglected poet Orlovitz against Stern's rising success. Orlovitz's death in a New York City street is portrayed as a stylish exit, adding a note of poignancy to his loss: "He fell in the street/ in front of a doorman; oh his death was superb,/ the doorman blew his whistle, Orlovitz climbed/ into a yellow cab, he'd never disappoint/ a doorman."

Stern, meanwhile, finds himself "brooding a little . . . / saying inside/ one of Orlovitz's poems/ going back again/ into the cave." Later, in a contrapuntal image of American-style safety and success, Stern finds himself among the tea-and-chatter of inconsequential, provincial literary life: "I wore my black suit for the reading, I roared/ and whispered through forty poems, I sat like a lamb/ in a mayor's living room, I sat like a dove/ eating cheese and smiling, talking and smiling . . . "

"The Expulsion" alludes to the expulsion from the Garden into history and memory. The paradise here is the "paradise of two," father and son. The expulsion also means coming to terms with the fact and significance of mortality. Stern's father has lived the exile of countless immigrants: memories of the old country, the myriad adjustments and new fittings needed for life in America, the striving for success, and then death—almost a cliché—in Florida. It is, in many ways, a typical life, yet it is horrifyingly disjunctive, with so many losses trailing after it, that death itself is somewhat anticlimactic: "He had/ fifty-eight suits, and a bronze coffin; he lay/ with his upper body showing, a foot of carpet." Yet this life partakes of a paradise that is only revealed with the father's passing: "My father/ and I are leaving Paradise, an angel/ is shouting, my hand is on my mouth." That paradise will now become a fixture of memory and art, a fertile and yet minatory place:

> Our lives are merging, our shoes
> are not that different. The angel is rushing by,
> her lips are curled, there is a coldness, even
> a madness to her, Adam and Eve are roaring,
> the whole thing takes a minute, a few seconds,
> and we are left on somebody's doorstep . . .

Already this paradise is becoming "the secret rooms, the long and brutal corridor/ down which we sometimes shuffle, and sometimes run."

The universality of exile is the theme of "The Same Moon Above Us," perhaps the most interesting poem in the collection. Here, the figure of Ovid, whose exile from Rome began a literary tradition that modern poets as different as Osip Mandelstam and Derek Walcott have found resonant with significance, is superimposed on the figure of a bum, "a man sleeping over the grilles" of New York. The point is to transform the exile into something triumphant, which these poets, to the greater glory of art, were able to do and which the bum, in his way, must also do: "The truth is he has become his own sad poem." When Stern writes "I think in his fifties he learned a new language/ to go with the freezing rain," one does not know whether this refers to the bum or to Ovid. Yet there is no confusion, for the harder one looks at the bum struggling among the garbage, the more Ovid comes into view, and vice versa. The poem is a haunting meditation on displacement and survival-by-transformation, no doubt the chief theme of this century's most valued poetry.

While Stern has never been bashful about either his ecstasies or his laments, the 1987 volume *Lovesick* explicitly sustains both categories, as the triple pun in the title suggests: that love brings to our attention the priority of life (that is, prior to all, including poetry); that the full acknowledgment of that life by means of our love of it can become a burden—although a blessed one; and that the poet is not afraid to reiterate the "luck" attendant on these seeming truisms. Stern's poems frequently hint that the difference between truisms and the truth is often a matter of perspective, with our century unfortunately specializing in conversions of the latter into the former. This attention to perspective further suggests the pervasive nostalgia for an Old World sensibility, through which the thought of his poems often loops on its way to the subject.

The volume, indeed, begins with a revisionist point of view toward a familiar subject, a dead dog ("The Dog"). The "speaker" is the dog—a persona unattempted by most contemporary poets, though Philip Levine and Thom Gunn come to mind—who moreover negotiates its soliloquy posthumously. Thus, Stern has set forth a potentially bathetic situation that he neatly escapes by turning the tables on the curiosity seeker, who is both the reader (and, by allusion, the speaker in "Behaving Like a Jew") by exposing anthropomorphism for what it is: an attempted escape from our obligation to love the world by coopting it in our own (linguistic) image. Thus, the dog is both knowing and superior, for it can rely on no such escape:

> I hope the dog's way
> doesn't overtake him, one quick push,
> barely that, and the mind freed, something else,
> some other thing, to take its place.

The dog's ploy is to ask for a mutual recognition: "great loving stranger, remember/ the death of dogs . . . give me your pity./ How could there be enough?" In doing so, it questions the sophisticated reader's learned disposition to exclude whole categories of emotion by grossly and obtusely dismissing them as "sentimental." This is not to say that Stern wishes to give sentimentality, as it were, a second chance. Rather, his poems serve as ironic reminders that the objects of rationality have taken more than their share of an intensity originally meant for emotion. This is the "pity" that we "naturally" assign to objects of rationality.

By "pity," with its moral overtones, the reader is also meant to understand *sympathy*—or, in Keatsian terms, "negative capability." As with Keats, Stern's sympathy extends to the nonhuman kingdoms of plant and animal. In fact, Stern may be said to start there, since it is all the more a matter of sympathy to transcend human limitations to celebrate the virtues of the truly "other." In "Bob Summers' Body," Stern conveys this same feeling toward another kind of otherness, as he watches the corpse of a friend being cremated:

> He turned over twice
> and seemed to hang with one hand to the railing
> as if he had to sit up once and scream
> before he reached the flames.

Seeing death in terms of life has the advantage of emboldening us so that thoughts of it do not "make cowards of us all," as Hamlet imagined. In Stern's revision, "there is such horror/ standing before Persephone with a suit on,/ the name of the manufacturer in the lining." Such horror has its humor, too, for humor often follows from a rearrangement of perspective. In the end, though, the death is a "plush darkness," not only naturalized but humanized as well—one might even argue, "accessorized," thanks to the cozy adjective "plush." A similar fellow-feeling arises in "This Was a Wonderful Night," where the poet appears to indulge in innocent, fanciful conversations and matter-of-fact pastimes, until it is clear that all the principal figures with whom the poet interacts are dead:

> This was a wonderful night. I heard the Brahms
> piano quintet, I read a poem by Schiller,
> I read a story, I listened to Gloomy Sunday.
> No one called me, I studied the birthday poem
> of Alvaros de Campos.

Nevertheless, the poet is happy to be "singing/ one or two songs . . . going east and west/ in the new country, my heart forever pounding." The motion of *Lovesick*, in spite of the trademark forays into the past and into the dimension of the other, is an ascending one, culminating in one of Stern's best poems, "Steps." In this poem, the poet remembers, and cites his body as testimony ("I gasp and pant as if I were pulling a mule"), the fact of steps (as well as actual steps) whose climbing took their toll ("The thing about climbing/ is how you give up") in order to return the fact of elevation:

> I gave up on twenty landings,
> I gave up in Paris once, it was impossible,
> you reach a certain point, it is precise,
> you can't go further; sometimes it's shameful, you're in
> the middle of a pair of stairs, you bow
> your head. . . .

Remembering steps in Pittsburgh, in Greece, West Virginia, and elsewhere, the poet knows that the climb, in spite of its real and allegorical exactions, is the only path to the empyreal:

Imagine Zeus
in West Virginia, imagine the temple to Hera
in Vandergrift, P. A. My heart is resting,
my back feels good, my breathing is easy. I think
of all my apartments, all that climbing; I reach
for a goldenrod, I reach for a poppy. . . .

The image of the poppy (which the poet chews in the poem's final line) confers a feeling of restfulness, and serves as a kind of general benediction for the lovesickness, for "the hands/ that held the books, and the face that froze, and the shoulders/ that fought the wind, and the mouth that struggled for air" ("All I Have Are the Tracks"). "Steps" serves as well as the final poem of *Leaving Another Kingdom: Selected Poems*, a volume that brings together substantial portions of each of his five books.

Stern's has been one of the more refreshing voices to emerge in American poetry since the 1960's, a voice neither too refined to proclaim its ecstasies nor too decorous to lament its sorrows. Sorrow and ecstasy are, after all, the two horizons of emotional exchange, but they are all too frequently bred or shouldered out of existence by the daily grind, and Stern, a historian of emotions, has clearly sought, throughout his career, to restore them. Because his poems are impatient with limitation, it is perhaps tempting to regard them as the enemies of restraint—restraint by which many believe the gears of civilized life are oiled. One must consider, however, that the battle between freedom and restraint is an ancient contest, and the struggle will doubtless persist as long as human beings exist. Stern's importance will not be decided on the basis of his beliefs but on the strength of his art. The son of Whitman, and yet his own man, Stern has produced an instrument capable of intimating, as perhaps no other contemporary American has, the sheer fullness of life in the twentieth century. That he has not substantially modulated this instrument may be a valid criticism. On the other hand, the persistence with which he repeats his enormous embrace of the world in poem after poem suggests a loyalty to his means that is equal to his loyalty to his vision.

David Rigsbee

Bibliography

Glaser, Elton, ed. "Gerald Stern Speaking." *Akros* 8-9 (1984): 5-30. This text consists of edited and arranged comments by Stern made in answer to questions about his work from students at Akron University. This is a good introduction to the eclectic side of Stern and provides, as well, insights into the sources of literary energy in his poetic practice.

Hillringhouse, Mark. "Gerald Stern: Ten Poems and an Interview." *The American Poetry Review* 13 (March/April, 1984): 19-30. This extensive interview, which took place in 1982, provides a good first-person summary of the career up to, and including, *Paradise Poems*. Stern speaks to specific thematic and compositional features of his poems and to his concerns with biography, the past, Jewish writing, and his relationship to other contemporary poets.

McCorkle, James. *Conversant Essays: Contemporary Poets on Poetry*. Detroit: Wayne State University Press, 1990. Larry Lewis discusses English poetry's preoccupation with the loss of Eden in his essay, "Eden and My Generation." Here Lewis lists Stern's *Lucky Life* as one of the works he says does *not* reflect a fall from Eden. Instead, he sees Stern's *Lucky Life* rooted in a sense of home and place.

Pinsker, Sanford. "The Poetry of Constant Renewal and Celebration: An Afternoon's Chat with Gerald Stern." *The Missouri Review* 5 (Winter, 1981/1982): 55-67. Reprinted in Pinsker, *Conversations with Contemporary American Writers*. Amsterdam: Costerus, 1985. In this short but valuable interview, which appeared after the publication of Stern's award-winning *Lucky Life*, the poet responds to questions about his relationship to Whitman, Romanticism, and what Pinsker calls "Jewish" Romanticism.

Somerville, Jane. *Making the Light Come: The Poetry of Gerald Stern*. Detroit: Wayne State University Press, 1990. This, the first full-length study of Stern's poetry, pays particular attention to the function of the "eccentric" speaker of the poems—the controlling principle in a "poetry of performance." While acknowledging the role of biography, artistic predecessors, and philosophical sources, Somerville focuses on the function of biblical materials as central to an understanding of Stern's work. The book follows a thematic organization, beginning with Stern's poetic modes, then turns to his treatment of "nostalgia" and, in successive chapters, three elemental roles enacted by the speaker: gardener, rabbi, and angel. The text is supplemented by a somewhat perfunctory (and incomplete) bibliography and an index.

Stern, Gerald. "What Is This Poet?" In *What Is a Poet?*, edited by Hank Lazer. Tuscaloosa: University of Alabama Press, 1987. This document, the product of a symposium on contemporary American poetry held at the University of Alabama in 1984, comes close to being a "testament" of the poet's beliefs and is therefore a valuable document toward any serious study of Stern's poetry. The poet addresses a wide spectrum of concerns but emphasizes his education as a poet, including his reading of the Romantics (Keats and Shelley) and their American counterparts (Emerson and especially Whitman), and the Modernists (Eliot, Crane, and Pound). This essay is especially recommended for those wishing to see the vitality of tradition in a frequently revolutionary poet.

Vinson, James, and D. L. Kirkpatrick, eds. *Contemporary Poets*. 3d ed. New York: St. Martin's Press, 1980. Part of the entry on Stern, by Gaynor F.

Bradish, is a statement by the poet in which he chooses "The One Thing in Life" (from *Lucky Life*) to express his artistic position. Bradish describes Stern's poetry as written in the confessional mode and "deeply felt." Notes Stern makes considerable use of repetition for rhetorical effect.

Wojahn, David. "The Red Coal." *Poetry East* 6 (Fall, 1981): 96-102. Describes these poems as investigating the meaning of memory, which is both their strength and their weakness. Notes that Stern's most successful poems are his long ones, which are all the more compelling because of the momentum gained along the way.

WALLACE STEVENS

Born: Reading, Pennsylvania; October 2, 1879
Died: Hartford, Connecticut; August 2, 1955

Principal poetry

Harmonium, 1923, 1931 (with fourteen additional poems); *Ideas of Order*, 1935; *Owl's Clover*, 1936; *The Man with the Blue Guitar and Other Poems*, 1937; *Parts of a World*, 1942; *Notes Toward a Supreme Fiction*, 1942; *Esthétique du Mal*, 1945; *Transport to Summer*, 1947; *The Auroras of Autumn*, 1950; *Selected Poems*, 1953; *The Collected Poems of Wallace Stevens*, 1954.

Other literary forms

Wallace Stevens' significant achievement is in his poetry, but he did write several experimental one-act verse plays, a number of essays on poetry, and numerous letters and journal notes which contain perceptive comments on his work. In 1916 he published in the magazine *Poetry* his first one-act verse play, *Three Travelers Watch a Sunrise*, for which he received a special prize from *Poetry*; in 1920 the play was performed at the Provincetown Playhouse in New York. A second verse play, *Carlos Among the Candles*, was staged in New York in 1917 and later published, again in *Poetry*. A third play, *Bowl, Cat, and Broomstick*, was produced at the Neighborhood Playhouse in New York in the same year but was never published during the poet's life. Between 1942 and 1951 he gave a series of lectures on poetry at Princeton and other universities, and these were collected in *The Necessary Angel: Essays on Reality and the Imagination* (1951). Later essays, as well as a number of uncollected poems and plays, appeared in *Opus Posthumous* (1957). The poet wrote excellent letters, and his daughter, Holly Stevens, collected and edited the best of them in *Letters of Wallace Stevens* (1966). In *Souvenirs and Prophecies: The Young Wallace Stevens* (1977) she presented important entries from the poet's journal (1898-1914). Focusing upon the relationship between the imagination and reality, Stevens' canon is highly unified; the prose and the plays help illuminate the difficult poetry.

Achievements

Although Stevens never has had as large an audience as that enjoyed by Robert Frost and did not receive substantial recognition until several years before his death, he is usually considered to be one of the best five or six twentieth century poets writing in English. *Harmonium* reveals a remarkable style—or, to be more precise, a number of remarkable styles. While critics praised, or more often condemned, the early poetry for its gaudiness, colorful imagery, flamboyant rhetoric, whimsicality, and odd points of view, one also finds in this volume spare Imagist poems as well as abstract philosophical poems which anticipate his later work. The purpose of his rhetorical virtuosity in *Harmonium* and in subsequent volumes was not merely to dazzle the reader but to convey the depth of emotion, the subtle complexity of thought, and the associative processes of the mind.

Strongly influenced by early nineteeth century English poets, Stevens became a modern Romantic who transformed and extended the English Romantic tradition as he accommodated it to the twentieth century world. *Harmonium* and subsequent volumes reveal his assimilation of the innovations of avant-garde painting, music, poetry, and philosophy. One finds in his canon, for example, intimations of Pablo Picasso, Henri Matisse, and Henri Bergson, and of cubism, Impressionism, Imagism, and Symbolism. Such influences were always subordinated to the poet's romantic sensibility, however, which struggled with the central Romantic problem—the need to overcome the gulf between the inner, human reality and outer, objective reality. A secular humanist who rejected traditional Christianity, arcane mysticism, and the pessimism of *The Waste Land* (1922) and the *Cantos* (beginning in 1925), he succeeded as a Romantic poet in the modern world. His contribution to poetry was recognized in 1950 with the award of the Bollingen Prize and in 1955 with the National Book Award and the Pulitzer Prize for *The Collected Poems of Wallace Stevens*. His reputation has continued to grow since his death in 1955.

Biography

On October 2, 1879, in Reading, Pennsylvania, Wallace Stevens was born to Garrett Barcalow Stevens and the former Margaretha Catherine Zeller. Wallace Stevens' father was a successful attorney who occasionally published poetry and prose in the local papers.

In 1897 Stevens was graduated from Reading Boys High School and enrolled at Harvard as a special student with the ambition to become a writer. He published stories and poetry in the *Harvard Advocate* and the *Harvard Monthly* and became acquainted with the poet and philosopher George Santayana, whose books provided support for his belief that in an agnostic age poetry must assume the role of traditional religion. After completing his special three-year course in English at Harvard, he joined the staff of the *New York Tribune*, but failed as a reporter.

In the fall of 1901 he entered the New York Law School and, after passing the bar three years later, began legal practice. He was not successful as a practicing attorney, however, and in 1908 he joined the New York office of the American Bonding Company. The next year he married Elsie Moll.

In 1916 Stevens joined the Hartford Accident and Indemnity Company and moved to Hartford, Connecticut, which was to be his permanent residence. He now led a double life. During the day he was a successful businessman, while at night and on weekends he was a poet. Few of his associates in the insurance world knew of his second career. Beginning in 1914 his work had begun to be published in *Poetry* and the other little magazines. At this time he became acquainted with an avant-garde group of writers and artists, including William Carlos Williams, Alfred Kreymborg, and Marcel Duchamp. His involvement in the business world, however, permitted only occasional participation in the activities of literary groups.

In 1923, at the age of forty-four, Stevens published his first volume of poetry. *Harmonium* was largely ignored by the critics, however, and he wrote only a few poems in the next five or six years. In 1924 his only child, Holly, was born, and subsequently he devoted his time to his family and to his business career. In 1931 Alfred A. Knopf reissued *Harmonium*, and in 1934 Stevens was promoted to vice-president of his insurance company. With his business career secure and with *Harmonium* receiving some recognition, he began to write and publish again. By the time *The Auroras of Autumn* appeared in 1950, his reputation had been firmly established. Even after the mandatory retirement age of seventy, he continued to work at his insurance company, and rejected an offer to be the Charles Eliot Norton lecturer at Harvard for the 1955-1956 academic year because he felt that if he accepted he might be forced to retire. He died in 1955, two months before his seventy-sixth birthday.

Analysis

Wallace Stevens frequently alludes to or quotes from the English Romantics in his letters and in his essays, and there is little doubt that this twentieth century poet is working within the Romantic tradition. The best evidence for the contention that he is a twentieth century Romantic, however, is his poetry. Repeatedly, one finds in his work the "reality-imagination complex," as he calls it. While one can see the central beliefs of William Wordsworth and John Keats in Stevens' poetry (celebration of nature, acceptance of mutability, rejection of supernatural realms, and belief in the brotherhood of man), the foundation of his Romanticism is his Wordsworthian imagination. The function of this imagination in Stevens' poetry is to make sordid reality, what Wordsworth calls "the dreary intercourse of daily life," palatable without resorting to mysticism. It is a difficult task; failure results in a profound alienation ("dejection" in the language of the Romantics).

Stevens does not merely repeat what Wordsworth and Keats have accomplished in their work but extends the Romantic tradition. He differs from his predecessors in his radical nontranscendentalism. In a May 30, 1910, letter to his wife he quotes from Keats's "Epistle to John Hamilton Reynolds": "It is a flaw/ In happiness, to see beyond our bourn,—/ It forces us in summer skies to mourn,/ It spoils the singing of the Nightingale." This idea is the premise of all Stevens' work. He takes the secular Romanticism of Wordsworth and Keats to its logical conclusion.

Stevens' poem "Of Modern Poetry" provides a good introduction to both his theory and his method. The modern poem whose origin goes back to the discursive odes of Wordsworth and Keats is "the poem of the mind in the act of finding/ What will suffice." This modern meditation shows the process of the mind confronting reality, searching for a secular solution to the individual person's feeling of meaninglessness. Before the Romantic period (1789-1832) this was not a major problem, and thus there was no need for this type of meditation. Or, as Stevens says: "It has not always had/ To find: the scene was set; it repeated what/ Was in the script." Now the poet ("the actor") is "a metaphysician in the dark," the man of vital imagination who seeks to redeem ugly reality and overcome his alienation by secular meditation. It is a meditation which will not descend to negation or ascend to supernaturalism ("below which it cannot descend,/ Beyond which it has no will to rise").

The meditation utilizes conversational speech, "the real language of men," as Wordsworth says in the Preface to the *Lyrical Ballads* (1800), or the "speech of the place," as Stevens states here, and seeks its affirmation in everyday reality. Yet this "poem of the act of the mind" may create heightened moments in everyday reality, "spots of time," as Wordsworth calls them in *The Prelude* (1850). It is these "spots of time" that often allow the imagination to redeem reality by ordering it, enchanting it, transforming it, or creating a feeling of stasis, of permanence beyond time. By these heightened moments and by the process of the meditation itself, the imagination strives to rectify the individual's sense of loss.

In short, Stevens expands the Wordsworthian-Keatsian discursive act of the mind in a radical fashion. In a number of his acts of the mind the only unifying element is the solitary mind searching for what will suffice to ease its alienation. In these acts of the mind the imagination can create moments of illumination which help regenerate the poet—and regeneration is the central goal of modern meditations, those "poems of our climate."

"Poems of Our Climate" reveals the function and limitation of a spot of time in a secular Romantic meditation. In the first six lines of the poem the mind seizes a specific, seemingly ordinary moment and freezes it into a timeless moment, reminiscent of the stasis in the beginning of "Ode on a Grecian Urn." Unlike Keats however, Stevens does not linger over this moment that the imagination has endowed with meaning. He does not wait until the fourth stanza to grow disenchanted but instinctively feels that this cannot be a permanent state—"one desires/ So much more than that." The evanescent and heightened quality of the frozen moment ("The light/ In the room more like a snowy air,/ Reflecting snow") immediately becomes the monotony of "Cold, a cold porcelain, low and round,/ With nothing more than the carnations there."

Stevens must reject this "cold pastoral" because one needs more than purity ("this complete simplicity"). One does not want to be stripped of all his "torments." The vital individual (the "vital I") is "evilly compounded"—an identity forged out of a world of pains and troubles, of good and evil experience.

The spot of time is a temporary relief from the banality or ugliness of reality, but it cannot be a permanent state. The "never-resting mind" always feels the compulsion to return to reality to remeditate and recompose it. "The imperfect is our paradise" might be Stevens' twentieth century reformulation of Keats's essential feeling in "Ode on Melancholy." Like Keats, he is ambivalent—both bitter and delighted over man's existence. Instinctively he desires to escape to an ideal state, but intellectually he realizes the impossibility of doing so. Man finds meaning only in human reality, which is by definition imperfect. Strip life of its torments and it becomes banality; conceal the dark side of existence or the "evil" aspects of one's nature and vitality is erased. Pure stasis untainted by life would be meaningless, and an art that mirrored this would be meaningless too. Stevens believes that art should express pain, struggle, and conflict, and thus he prefers the modern poets of "flawed words and stubborn sounds" to the "bawds of euphony." Stevens' poetry is a continual search; it is a continual oscillation between the depths of depression and heightened moments of affirmation. "[The mind] can never be satisfied, the mind, never" concludes Stevens in "The Well Dressed Man with a Beard."

Stevens sees external reality as the Other outside the self. "Large Red Man Reading" is a poem that reveals the crucial importance of the regenerative capacity of the imagination and the need to embrace the everyday world and reject the supernatural. As he seeks to reconcile himself to an earthly reality devoid of supernatural inclinations, Stevens contrasts the vital man of imagination (the large red man reading) with those who are "dead" to the imagination, "the ghosts." Ghosts as symbolic of those dead to the imaginative life occur elsewhere in his work. In "Disillusionment of Ten O'Clock," for example, Stevens complains that "the houses are haunted/ By white night-gowns" who do not "dream" (that is, imagine) of catching tigers "in red weather," as an old sailor does. In the ghostly realms of the modern world life is colorless—a dreary intercourse of daily life without imagination. In "Large Red Man Reading" the ghosts seem to recognize that a life without the imaginative interaction between the mind and reality is worthless. After leading a dull life on earth, they had hoped to find their paradise in heaven, but they have become dissatisfied with heaven ("the wilderness of stars") and returned to earth. They returned to hear the "large red man reading," for he is the vital individual of the imagination, a true giant in a paltry age. (Reading and study symbolize meditation, or the life of the imagination, in Stevens' poetry.)

In the course of the meditation it becomes clear why the ghosts have returned to earth. Heaven lacked the reality of earthly existence, its joys and its torments. The ghosts want to hear the large red man read from the "poem of life" in all its prosaic beauty and banality—"the pans above the stove, the pots on the table, the tulips among them." In contrast to the mythic abstraction of heaven, the ghosts would eagerly reach out for any sensory knowledge ("They were those that would have wept to step barefoot into reality"), even though this knowledge might mean pain ("run fingers over leaves/ And against the most coiled thorn") as well as pleasure. Stevens has mocked, with good-natured humor, the traditional belief that people desire to go to a paradisiacal heaven after dissatisfaction with the sinful, painful life on earth. The ghosts return to earth for the true paradise of an ever-changing sensuous reality ("being") heightened by the imagination ("reading").

The imagination's attempt to redeem reality is, however, not always completely successful—stalemate or even defeat are possibilities. Stevens is a darker poet than the critics have made him out to be—despite the fact that modern criticism has largely overcome the once popular cliché of the insouciant hedonist of impressionistic, pictorial poems. Often his poems of naturalistic celebration end on a tentative note of affirmation, for the ugly side of reality is an able match for the imagination; the mind can never completely transform reality into something purely positive. Furthermore, in a significant number of his acts of the mind, a sense of loss threatens to dominate. It is in these poems of "the whole of Harmonium," as he would have preferred to call his canon, that one finds a profound sense of loss ("the burden of the mystery," as both Wordsworth and Keats called it) as the very genesis of the work. In these works the imagination must grapple with "dejection," ascertain its causes or roots, and seek to resolve it as far as possible. These meditations of Stevens' are different from his others only in degree. Here, however, the imagination does not appear as potent as in his other acts, and spots of time do not seem to have the intensity, or the frequency, that one finds in his other meditations.

Stevens does not have only one attitude toward this sense of loss—and certainly not one type of "dejection" poem. His imagination takes a variety of forms and attitudes. It is probably a mistake to stress a chronological development in his attitude toward the burden of the mystery, although a case might be made for some lessening of humor and flamboyance and a gradual movement toward an autumnal tone during his career. Instead, one should stress the variety and complexity of his response. To show that his attitude toward the problem is much more complex than is usually thought, one must examine several of his poems, from his earliest to those written just before his death. Finally, it will also become clear that despite the sophistication of his responses to the problem, he was always a secular romantic who rejected the leap into transcendence and refused to submit to existential despair.

At the heart of "Sunday Morning" (1915) is a profound sense of loss, evoked by abandonment of traditional religious belief. Modern human beings can no longer justify suffering and death with Christian certitudes. This complicated meditative poem struggles with the problem at length, pondering questions that are central to Stevens' work. How does one dispel his anxiety when he realizes that all past mythologies are irrelevant? If there is no afterlife, how does one come to terms with death? Even as Keats did, Stevens overcomes his desire for the supernatural and puts his faith in humanist values.

"In the very Temple of Delight/ Veiled Melancholy has her sovran shrine," Keats had proclaimed in "Ode on Melancholy," and Stevens more vehemently reiterates this idea that life is process and there can be no separation of opposites, no separation of pleasure and pain. "Death is the mother of beauty," Stevens' speaker twice asserts in the course of the meditation. The very transiency of things makes them valuable; paradoxically, it is death that makes things beautiful. Stanza VI, reminiscent of Keats's "Ode on a Grecian Urn," shows that a heaven without mortality is a false paradise devoid of life. "Does ripe fruit never fall?" asks the frustrated speaker. The boughs will always hang heavy with fruit in "that perfect sky," and we can only "pick the strings of our insipid lutes" in this monotonous heaven, just as Keats's boughs will never shed their leaves and his bold lovers will always remain in the frustrating position of being poised over each other in the first stage of their lovemaking, a lovemaking of perpetual anticipation, not consummation.

Stevens believes that death is necessary for a true paradise because life can be enjoyed only when there are cycles of desire and fulfillment or disappointment. Death also has some positive value because it makes man aware of his common humanity, what Stevens significantly calls "heavenly fellowship." Wordsworth, in "Lines Composed a Few Miles Above Tintern Abbey" and "Ode: Intimations of Immortality from Recollections of Early Childhood," had expressed similar sentiments; but Stevens' attitude is more extreme. He supposes that the rejection of God results in a world that is intrinsically meaningless, whereupon one realizes that one must return to man as the only source of value.

"Sunday Morning" presents, in short, a radical humanism that Wordsworth and Keats had anticipated a century earlier. Instead of religion ("the thought of heaven") Stevens offers naturalistic reality, the "beauty of the earth." A person's emotional contact with nature is a substitute for rituals performed before an invisible deity. The only immortality that has any meaning for modern human beings, the poet argues, is the permanence of nature as felt in the seasonal cycle—nothing endures as "April's green endures." Depression and disillusionment are as natural as joy and hope, and memory of these opposite feelings helps form one's "soul" or identity. Echoing Keats, Stevens suggests that "all pleasures and all pains" are involved in one's responses to nature. In short, one's intense responses to external reality are "measures destined" for the "soul."

"A Postcard from the Volcano" (1936) is a meditation with a profound sense of loss at its foundation; about the precise nature of this loss, however, there is no critical agreement. The poem is as perplexing and intriguing as its bizarre title; to understand it, one must account for the sense of loss and explain the shift of tone at the end of the work.

"A Postcard from the Volcano" is divided into two parts by the ellipsis. The first part presents the problem: the poet feels dejected because he realizes that after his death the imaginative expression of his life in poetry will seem foreign to the new generation. The poet will have become an irrelevant ghost, such as Stevens has elsewhere mocked as the antithesis of the vital life of the imagination. The world of the past, especially that world interpreted by the poet's imagination, will become meaningless to the children of the present.

They will "pick up our bones" but will never be able to comprehend that these once had vitality and a keen sense of participation in the moment ("that these were once/ As quick as foxes on the hill"). They will not be able to perceive the impact of the past on the present, or realize how one can change his world through the manipulations of language. "We knew for long the mansion's look/ And what we said of it became/ A part of what it is."

Stevens pauses in his meditation. The pause seems to give birth to a new feeling—a change finally occurs when the mind swerves away from its dejection to a reconciling thought in the last two lines. Admittedly, the children ("still weaving budded aureoles") will have an innocent view of reality in which everything is viewed one-dimensionally. They will reiterate the poet's meditations and never comprehend his vision. They will say of his world that it seems "As if he that lived there left behind/ A spirit storming in blank walls,/ A dirty house in a gutted world"—they will see the poet as a mere ghost ranting without an audience. Yet Stevens' meditation shifts in the last two lines to a partial reconciliation. While the poet's vision will seem irrelevant and "run down" to the children, it will also be one with "A tatter of shadows peaked to white,/ Smeared with the gold of the opulent sun." That is, they will feel intuitively some of the vitality of the dead poet's vision. They will not intellectually understand the world of the past (it will be a "shadow" to them), but some of the remnants of the past will seem "smeared with the gold of the opulent sun" and consequently reveal the vitalistic imagination of the dead poet.

In "The Course of a Particular" (1951) Stevens presents a bleak winter landscape. The speaker in this matter-of-fact meditation does not appear to be much concerned with the "nothingness of winter." In fact, the speaker seems to be intellectually aware of the sense of loss but to remain emotionally tranquil, as if he had become accustomed to it. While the nothingness of the winter landscape becomes a "little less" because the poet can accept it more each day, he still feels he should try to humanize the sense of loss. He tries and then pauses. The attempt is half-hearted—"there is a resistance involved."

The humanizing metaphor of the crying leaves does not make the scene more human or more real to him. He tries to imagine harshness and the human responses to it, but the attempt does not work. Stevens discovers here that he cannot rewrite Percy Bysshe Shelley's "Ode to the West Wind" in the

1950's. All he feels is a dull monotonous winter scene; he cannot despair over a cold, inanimate universe. In "Sunday Morning" the separation of the self from nature was the cause for alienation, but now Stevens simply takes the separation for granted. He cannot pretend to be part of nature, even for a moment; if he says he is part of nature he immediately feels "resistance." He can no longer make the effort. Instead of attempting ennobling interchange of the imagination and reality, he concentrates on the particulars of reality before him. Winter is merely winter, wind-blown trees, snow, and ice.

In the final two stanzas the poet tries to transform the scene, but the cry of the leaves has no supernatural ("divine") significance, nor mythic ("puffed out heroes") significance, nor human significance. The "crying" leaves are simply leaves being blown by the wind; they do not transcend their phenomenological meaning. To imagine them crying is unsatisfactory. Finally, the poet asserts that the cry is simply the shrill winter wind and concerns no one at all. The poet has accepted the nothingness of modern life; the cry of the leaves does not symbolize a sense of loss but is simply another detail of reality.

The sense of loss in "Farewell Without a Guitar" (1954) is subdued. In lesser hands, this poem would have quickly degenerated into sentimental melancholy or nostalgia. Yet Stevens, with his few spare images, evokes a genuine feeling; like Hemingway, he expresses the most elemental emotions by cutting language to the bone. To do otherwise would be to luxuriate in an excess of emotion.

In "Farewell Without a Guitar," he suggests that things have come to their natural finale. While there is a sense of loss, there is also a sense of completion and fulfillment implicit in the meditation. The poem is so titled because Stevens' farewell is not accompanied by the music of lush poetry. Loss (and acceptance of it) is evoked without gaudy imaginative embellishment.

The paradise of spring yields to the autumnal terminal—youth to death, gaudy exuberance to spare imagism, celebration to farewell. Autumn is described as "The thousand leaved red," suggesting its beauty and naturalness, not the desolation of bare trees and cold, lifeless days. "Thunder of light" in the second stanza presages the storm of the third stanza and suggests that this storm is a virile one, one of power, not enervation. The oxymoronic metaphor might also suggest a heightened consciousness of reality, a consciousness that occurs when one comes to the end of life. The riderless horse is an apt image for the symbolic death of the man of imagination, the end of the poet's career. Stevens had previously symbolized the romantic poet, or the man of imagination, as "a youth, a lover with phosphorescent hair,/ Dressed poorly, arrogant of his streaming forces," who madly passes by on his horse the literal-minded Mrs. Alfred Uruguay ("Her no and no made yes impossible") on her slow donkey.

There will be no more imaginative excursions now. Only memories and past acts of the mind remain. Yet this activity of the mind and the memory of the past sensory contact with reality ("The blows and buffets of fresh senses/ Of the rider that was") now seem to form "a final construction"—a kind of spot of time that serves as the only immortality one can know. Sensuous reality in the present is heightened by this "construction"—a construction created out of the interchange of past sensuous reality ("male reality"), the imagination ("that other"), and the instinct for affirmation of the romantic poet ("her desire").

The autumnal sense of loss, rooted in Stevens' realization that he has come to the end of his career, is really transformed into an acceptance of loss, the celebration of his own farewell; it is reminiscent of Keats's "To Autumn." Reality is viewed in its most sensuous aspects, and affirmed. Reality had also been accepted in "The Course of a Particular," but it hardly appeared positive there. In contrast, in Stevens' final poems, mere existence ("mere being" or a life of process) is accepted and found affirmative.

Stevens differs from most twentieth century poets in his romantic faith in the power of the imagination to affirm mundane reality, or at least to make it palatable. He sees the imagination as the source of man's salvation in a godless world. Tough-minded and skeptical, he is not the kind of Romantic abhorred by T. E. Hulme, Ezra Pound, and the Imagists. He is not a visionary Romantic in pursuit of transcendent realms; he believes that the modern poet can reside only in the everyday world.

In his book of essays *The Necessary Angel* (1951), he states that the poet must avoid "the hieratic" and must "move in the direction of the credible." Without completely immersing himself in a sordid everyday world or escaping to an ideal world, the twentieth century romantic strives for the necessary balance between the imagination and reality. In his Preface to William Carlos Williams' *Collected Poems, 1921-1931*, reprinted in *Opus Posthumous* (1957), Stevens gives the best description of the "romantic poet nowadays": "he is the hermit who dwells alone with the sun and moon, but insists on taking a rotten newspaper."

Allan Chavkin

Other major works

PLAYS: *Three Travelers Watch a Sunrise*, 1916, 1920 (performed); *Carlos Among the Candles*, 1917; *Bowl, Cat, and Broomstick*, 1917.

NONFICTION: *The Necessary Angel: Essays on Reality and the Imagination*, 1951; *Letters of Wallace Stevens*, 1966; *Souvenirs and Prophecies: The Young Wallace Stevens*, 1977.

MISCELLANEOUS: *Opus Posthumous*, 1957 (Samuel French Morse, editor).

Bibliography

Bates, Milton J. *Wallace Stevens: A Mythology of Self.* Berkeley: University of California Press, 1985. A study of Stevens' life and works that attempts to show how he transformed his biography into a "fable of identity." Bates traces several "selves" found in the poems. This readable, biographical approach to studying the poems discusses the familial, philosophical, and aesthetic background of the poet. Family papers and letters are used extensively. The parallels between Stevens' life and poetry are excellent in the account of the poet's growth and development.

Bloom, Harold. *Wallace Stevens: The Poems of Our Climate.* Ithaca, N.Y.: Cornell University Press, 1977. This full commentary on almost all Stevens' poetry refers to his precursors such as William Wordsworth, Percy Bysshe Shelley, John Keats, Ralph Waldo Emerson, and especially Walt Whitman. A chapter on American poetics from Emerson to Stevens explores the prevalent themes of fate, freedom, and power. Includes an index of Stevens' work.

Kessler, Edward. *Images of Wallace Stevens.* New Brunswick, N.J.: Rutgers University Press, 1972. A study of the significant images in Stevens' poetry in which each chapter focuses on a particular image or group of images: "North and South," "Sun and Moon," "Music and the Sea," and so on. Good bibliographical references are included in the footnotes and a bibliography is included in notes following the text.

Morse, Samuel F. *Wallace Stevens: Poetry as Life.* New York: Pegasus, 1970. This study relates Stevens' life to his poetry and introduces his poetic ideas, theories, and methods. This is the authorized critical biography commissioned by Stevens' widow and daughter. Supplemented by a short select bibliography.

Rehder, Robert M. *The Poetry of Wallace Stevens.* Basingstoke: Macmillan, 1988. A fifty-page biographical introduction is followed by chapters on each of Stevens' major books. This volume is a good introductory study that gives a broad view of the poet's life. It includes extended readings of several of the major poems and comments on Stevens' style, but few references are made to other works on the poet. Much of the biographical material is taken from Peter Brazeaus' *Parts of a World* (1983) and Holly Bright Stevens' *Souvenirs and Prophecies* (1976).

Riddel, Joseph. *The Clairvoyant Eye: The Poetry and Poetics of Wallace Stevens.* Baton Rouge: Louisiana State University Press, 1965. This skillful reading of the major poems sees Stevens' view of a poem as an "act of Mind" and portrays the poet as being able to be looked at from several critical postures—particularly philosophical, historical, and structural. The study includes an account of his theory of imagination and how it relates to the changes and developments in his style. Each chapter begins with a commentary on the context of the particular phase under discussion and ends with a reading of one of the major poems.

Vendler, Helen. *On Extended Wings: Wallace Stevens's Longer Poems.* Cambridge, Mass.: Harvard University Press, 1969. Vendler's study concentrates on the problems defined by the poems themselves and not the social, biographical, or historical contexts. Analyzes the longer poems in chronological order and focuses on style, form, and internal evolution.

ROBERT LOUIS STEVENSON

Born: Edinburgh, Scotland; November 13, 1850
Died: Apia, Upolu, Samoa; December 3, 1894

Principal poetry
Moral Emblems, 1882; *A Child's Garden of Verses*, 1885; *Underwoods*, 1887; *Ballads*, 1890; *Songs of Travel and Other Verses*, 1896.

Other literary forms
Robert Louis Stevenson is primarily remembered for his prose fiction, although he was a notable essayist and enjoyed a small reputation as a poet. Stevenson also tried his hand at drama and collaborated with William Ernest Henley in the writing of four plays (*Deacon Brodie*, 1880; *Beau Austin*, 1884; *Admiral Guinea*, 1884; and *Macaire*, 1885), and with his wife, Fanny Van de Grift Osbourne Stevenson, on one (*The Hanging Judge*, 1914). His first published works were his early collections of essays, *An Inland Voyage* (1878), *Edinburgh: Picturesque Notes* (1879), *Travels with a Donkey in the Cévennes* (1879), *Virginibus Puerisque* (1881), *Familiar Studies of Men and Books* (1882), and *The Silverado Squatters, Sketches from a Californian Mountain* (1883). He published four more volumes of essays, *Memories and Portraits* (1887), *Across the Plains* (1892), *A Footnote to History* (1892), and *In the South Seas* (1896). His short stories are collected in *The New Arabian Nights* (1882), *More New Arabian Nights* (1885), *The Merry Men and Other Tales and Fables* (1887), and *Island Nights' Entertainments* (1893). Of his novels, the four romances of adventure, *Treasure Island* (1883), *Kidnapped* (1886), *The Black Arrow* (1888), and *Catriona* (1893; American title, *David Balfour*), along with his psychological work, *The Strange Case of Dr. Jekyll and Mr. Hyde* (1886), firmly established him as a master storyteller and assured him a place in popular culture for the several generations of readers (and viewers of film adaptations) whose imagination he captured. His lesser romances (*Prince Otto*, 1885, and especially those written in collaboration with his stepson, Lloyd Osbourne, *The Wrong Box*, 1889, *The Wrecker*, 1892, and *The Ebb-Tide*, 1894, as well as the uncompleted *St. Ives*, 1897) are of a much lower order than his major novels, *The Master of Ballantrae* (1888) and the unfinished *Weir of Hermiston* (1896).

Achievements
Stevenson's unquestionable literary achievements as a storyteller and as an accomplished essayist in an age of prolific essayists overshadow his prominence as a poet who excelled in occasional verse, who perfectly captured the impermanent and various moods of childhood, and who, in *Underwoods*, exerted a profound and lasting influence on Scots poetry of the twentieth

century. "Tusitala," "the teller of tales," as the Samoans called him, achieved a measure of fame as an essayist, sometimes as a controversialist, but was most at home writing the tales of adventure and romance upon which his reputation justly rests. His uncompleted masterpiece, *Weir of Hermiston*, and *The Master of Ballantrae* rank him as a serious novelist of the first order who dealt with the complexities of human personality in its own depths and as it is subject to both inexorable fate and the buffets of history. His extraordinarily penetrating study of the divided self, "the war in the members," has made his creations Dr. Jekyll and Mr. Hyde household words. His tales of adventure, especially *Treasure Island*, *Kidnapped*, and *Catriona*, have become classics not only for youth but also for those who would *recapture* their youth. Enjoyment, in a word, characterizes the purpose and effect of much of Stevenson's fiction; it is also the principal object of much of his poetry.

One does not read—certainly one does not reread—Stevenson's poetry for its examination of adult life's complexities or its wrestling with the ultimate questions which each generation must ask for itself. These concerns are certainly present in some of the poetry but do not dominate it. Rather, in the bulk of Stevenson's verse, one reads to find an emotion crystallized, an occasion noted, a fleeting mood artfully captured and rendered. One reads the poetry primarily to enjoy a highly realized sense of childhood, a freshness and naïveté that is usually full of wonder, sometimes on the verge of joyous laughter, and often tinged with an almost inexpressible sadness. Stevenson is unmistakably a minor poet who has something in common with William Ernest Henley and Rudyard Kipling, other minor poets of the age, as well as with the early William Butler Yeats. A. E. Housman's poetry owes a clear debt to Stevenson's.

Biography

Robert Louis Stevenson was born to Thomas and Margaret Isabella (Balfour) Stevenson in Edinburgh on November 13, 1850, the midpoint of the Victorian age. Thomas Stevenson, destined to be the last of a line of illustrious Scottish engineers, had hopes that his only child would take up that profession. His hopes proved to be unrealized when Stevenson switched from a sporadic study of engineering to a sporadic study of the law at Edinburgh University. Never a strong child, Stevenson spent much of his childhood and, indeed, much of his adulthood either undergoing or convalescing from long and serious bouts of illness, chiefly respiratory disorders. His early life and education were overshadowed by illness, confinement, and frequent changes of climate. His youthful wanderings after health and sun led to later trips to France, Switzerland, and America, and, finally, to the South Seas in 1888 where he ultimately built a house, "Vailima," in Samoa. There he remained until his death from a cerebral hemorrhage in 1894. His recent biographers make much of his turbulent adolescence and hint of his several early love affairs, especially the platonic affair with Fanny Sitwell whom he met in 1873 when she was newly separated from her husband. The more important woman in his life was the American, Fanny Van de Grift Osbourne, whom he met at Grez, France, in 1876, and married in California in 1880. From the time of his marriage (which drew him away from such friends as Charles Baxter, Sidney Colvin, and William Ernest Henley) until his death, Stevenson passed his time in constant writing, constant illness, and nearly constant travel. Periodically exiled from Scotland by its harsh climate and finally leaving it forever in 1888, Stevenson often returned there imaginatively to find sources for both his prose and his poetry. He was survived by his mother, his wife and her children, Lloyd Osbourne, and Isobel Osbourne Strong Field. The latter two wrote reminiscences of him.

Analysis

Robert Louis Stevenson himself, in a letter to his cousin R. A. M. Stevenson (September, 1868), wrote what is both a summary of his evaluation of Horace and Alexander Pope and a just index of his own intentions and later poetic achievement: "It is not so much the thing they say, as the way they say it. The dicta are often trivial and commonplace, or so undeniably true as to become part of orthodox boredom; but when you find an idea put in either of them, *it is put in its optimum form.*" Stevenson's poetry is often about the commonplace—childhood, partings, reunions, homesickness, felicitations, greetings, friendship, the open road, the sea—but it is a crafting of common experience into heightened language and optimum form. His verse usually achieves its effects by a rigid application of meter and fixed rhyme scheme, although on occasion he breaks into a Whitmanesque style with a force far exceeding that of his more conventional poetry. Even in conventional poetic forms, however, he generally succeeds in lifting ordinary sentiment to a higher plane by the very simplicity, directness, and clarity of his language. This is one aspect, for example, of *A Child's Garden of Verses*, accounting for its appeal to adults as well as to children.

Stevenson's is a poetry of sentiment. At times, the sentiment appears to be artificial posturing that ranges from melancholy to high spirited. He does not make intellectual demands of his readers, but he does ask them to listen carefully; indeed, listening to his poems read aloud is the way most people first come to him. He also asks his readers to participate in the moment as he captures it, if only for that moment's sake. The quality of that moment is often twofold; it has the permanence that poetry can give it, and it vanishes as it is apprehended by the reader.

One can find no better starting place for examining Stevenson's poetry than his envoy "To Any Reader" in *A Child's Garden of Verses*. Here, in eight rhymed couplets he encapsulates the sentiment of the volume. The reader is first carried back to childhood; Stevenson likens the reader's watchful care over the child in the verses to that which mothers exercise over their children as they play. Then, reminded of the commonplace event of a mother knocking at the window to get her child's attention, the reader is told that the child in the book will not respond in the familiar way. The child is there in the garden in one sense, but not there in another: "It is but a child of air." Stevenson suggests that, however much one might observe and watch over his child, he cannot successfully intervene in his child's life or break out of the historical confinement in which, as an adult, he finds himself. The moment one tries to do more than fix his attention upon the child, to have the child in the verses give ear to his concerns, warnings, admonitions, or summonses, the child vanishes; he becomes "grown up," and is "gone away."

The reader must proceed warily in *A Child's Garden of Verses* and not disturb the moments of the fifty-eight poems but, rather, enjoy them for what they are, privileged to observe and fleetingly share them before they dissolve, as they will when one tries to bring adult reflection to bear on them. Stevenson creates an ideal and somewhat idealized world of childhood—a special childhood, to be sure, but also a universal one. Although it is clear that the volume has for its background his own holiday visits to his maternal grandfather's house, Colinton Manse, near the Water of Leith, and is dedicated to Alison Cunningham ("Cummy"), his childhood nurse, to read the poems for the autobiography they contain would be to miss their point as poetry. Further, the child who narrates the poems is, above all, a persona created by a man in his thirties, a persona that is sometimes the object of gentle irony (in "Looking Forward" and "Foreign Children," for example) and often (although children actually do this) speaks with a wisdom beyond his years (in "The Gardener" and "System").

Each poem, in the words of "From a Railway Carriage," "is a glimpse and gone for ever!" In those glimpses Stevenson renders portraits that are quite new in children's literature. Neither out to produce a didactic primer nor to condescend to children, he does provide childlike insights while retaining for his narrator a sense of wonder about the world. Just as, literarily speaking, the child was the invention of nineteenth century literature, so this child is a new invention who speaks in a language which the adult has outgrown. Where Charles Baudelaire, for example, had written of the philosophy of children's toys in "Morale du joujou," Stevenson goes to the heart of the matter in such poems as "The Dumb Soldier," "The Land of Story Books," and "The Land of Counterpane."

Stevenson's *Underwoods*, best known for its Scottish dialect poems, also contains many occasional pieces in English that are of some interest, because in them is found a preeminent prose writer paying tribute, returning thanks, or commemorating a gift, a death, a visit, an illness. Much the same can be said of *Songs of Travel*. The Scots poems (Book II) are, by contrast, more interesting as poems in their own right. "A Lowden Sabbath Morn" and

"Embro Hie Kirk" are perfect in their resonances of Robert Burns's language, style ("the Burns stanza"), treatment of common religious themes, and, in the latter, religious controversy. Full of humor and hominess, like his earlier "pieces in Lallan" addressed to Charles Baxter, the poems in Scots lack an overall seriousness of purpose that might raise them from the status they achieve as minor poetry.

His *Ballads* amply illustrate that Stevenson's forte was prose. The South Seas ballads "The Song of Rahero" and "The Feast of Famine" are, in his words, "great yarns" that suffer primarily because, as he wrote, they are "the verses of a Prosater." "Heather Ale" is a curious retelling of a Pictish legend and "Christmas at Sea" is the story of a young man's first voyage in icy waters; it is not, except for the poignancy of the last two lines, remarkable. Stevenson is much more in his element in "Ticonderoga: A Legend of the West Highlands." Here his storytelling ability comes to the fore, as does his undoubted ability to catch the conversational tones of the Scots language. The ballad has all that one could wish for—a murder, a test of honor in the face of ghostly visitation, far-flung travel and military exploits, inevitable fate, and the eerie sense of supernatural forces at work. Yet, like the other ballads, "Ticonderoga" would be better suited to Stevenson's prose than to his mechanical verse.

Except for a very few poems (notably, "Requiem" and the poems in Scots), the master of prose succeeded best as a poet when he sought to recapture the evanescent moments of youth. Stevenson's poetry takes its place far below that of the greater Victorians. His poetry is not a reminder to man of his precarious place in the universe or of the tenuous grasp he has upon civilization. His poetry does, however, express the sheer delight, the cares, the rewards, and the experience itself of childhood. Like the child of *A Child's Garden of Verses* the reader looks to Stevenson the novelist and poet with a fondness for the magic of his "dear land of Story-books."

John J. Conlon

Other major works

LONG FICTION: *Treasure Island*, 1883; *Prince Otto*, 1885; *The Strange Case of Dr. Jekyll and Mr. Hyde*, 1886; *Kidnapped*, 1886; *The Black Arrow*, 1888; *The Master of Ballantrae*, 1888; *The Wrong Box*, 1889; *The Wrecker*, 1892 (with Lloyd Osbourne); *Catriona*, 1893; *The Ebb-Tide*, 1894 (with Lloyd Osbourne); *Weir of Hermiston*, 1896 (unfinished); *St. Ives*, 1897 (completed by Arthur Quiller-Couch).

SHORT FICTION: *The New Arabian Nights*, 1882; *More New Arabian Nights*, 1885; *The Merry Men and Other Tales and Fables*, 1887; *Island Nights' Entertainments*, 1893.

PLAYS: *Deacon Brodie*, 1880; *Admiral Guinea*, 1884; *Beau Austin*, 1884;

and *Macaire*, 1885 (with William Ernest Henley); *The Hanging Judge*, 1914 (with Fanny Van de Grift Stevenson).

NONFICTION: *An Inland Voyage*, 1878; *Edinburgh: Picturesque Notes*, 1879; *Travels with a Donkey in the Cévennes*, 1879; *Virginibus Puerisque*, 1881; *Familiar Studies of Men and Books*, 1882; *The Silverado Squatters, Sketches from a Californian Mountain*, 1883; *Memories and Portraits*, 1887; *Across the Plains*, 1892; *A Footnote to History*, 1892; *Vailima Letters*, 1895; *In the South Seas*, 1896; *The Letters of Robert Louis Stevenson to His Family and Friends*, 1899 (2 volumes), 1911 (4 volumes); *The Lantern-Bearers and Other Essays*, 1988.

Bibliography

Binding, Paul. *Robert Louis Stevenson*. London: Oxford University Press, 1974. A sensitive, well-written biography of the poet and author of *Treasure Island* and many favorite books and stories. Binding relates his strict religious upbringing in Scotland, his marriage to Fanny Van de Grift Osbourne, an American divorcée whom he met in Paris, and their travels in the Pacific from California to Australia. Ink drawings accompany each chapter.

Calder, Jenni. *Robert Louis Stevenson: A Life Study*. New York: Oxford University Press, 1980. A richly detailed, engaging biography of "Tusitala"— the teller of tales, as the Samoan natives called Stevenson. Calder concentrates on the personal history, leaving literary criticism to other writers. She sympathetically presents Fanny Van de Grift Osbourne, Stevenson's wife, who travelled on many journeys with her popular husband. Includes thirty-three photographs, notes, and an index.

Eigner, Edwin M. *Robert Louis Stevenson and the Romantic Tradition*. Princeton N.J.: Princeton University Press, 1966. Eigner shows the influence of the nineteenth century prose romance on Stevenson's work. The poet and novelist freely admitted his debt to other writers (William Hazlitt, Charles Lamb, William Wordsworth, Nathaniel Hawthorne, and Michel Eyquem de Montaigne) in the development of his famous style. In eight chapters, Eigner discusses "serious romance" as a teacher of moral values and a source of Stevenson's ideas on mysticism, realism, law, and nature. Contains an index.

Hennessy, James Pope. *Robert Louis Stevenson*. London: Jonathan Cape, 1974. Out of the more than twenty-five hundred letters (often long ones) that Stevenson wrote in his forty-four years, Hennessy has created a fascinating life portrait. Stevenson's struggles with illness, his love for friends and good conversation, his gallant Scottish mother, and his American wife— all are here in brilliant detail. Supplemented by a select bibliography and an index.

Kiely, Robert. *Robert Louis Stevenson and the Fiction of Adventure*. Cambridge, Mass.: Harvard University Press, 1964. Well known and loved as a poet and writer of adventure stories, Stevenson appears to modern critics surprising for his pessimism, his maturity of thought, and his polished style. He foreshadowed Joseph Conrad in many ways. In five chapters, Kiely discusses the aesthetic belief "art is rational," and the use of fantasy, comedy, and symbolism in Stevenson's work. Includes a select bibliography, notes, and an index.

Soposnik, Irving S. *Robert Louis Stevenson.* New York: Twayne, 1974. This useful book treats the forms in which the versatile Stevenson wrote. Following a chapter of biography, Soposnik reviews the essays, poems, stories (with a separate chapter on Dr. Jekyll and Mr. Hyde), and novels. The poems reveal a personality that wants to soar to the heights but is condemned to a lonely journey in life. The child's voice of *A Child's Garden of Verses* expresses feelings of wonder and longing. Contains notes, a bibliography, and an index.

JAMES STILL

Born: Double Creek, Alabama; July 16, 1906

Principal poetry
Hounds on the Mountain, 1937, 1939, 1968; *The Wolfpen Poems*, 1986.

Other literary forms
James Still's highly acclaimed novel *River of Earth* appeared in 1940. *Sporty Creek* (1977) continues the story of the family introduced in *River of Earth*. Still's short stories are collected in *On Troublesome Creek* (1941), *Pattern of a Man* (1976), and *The Run for the Elbertas* (1980). Like his novels, the short stories are admired for their deceptively simple narrative technique, skillful character delineation, and psychological insight. They have been compared to the stories of Anton Chekhov, Katherine Anne Porter, and Bernard Malamud. The exact, colorful language of Still's novels, short stories, and poems is often achieved through the artful use of folk speech, examples of which are found in two collections of Appalachian riddles and rusties (playful, formulaic uses of language): *Way Down Yonder on Troublesome Creek* (1974) and *The Wolfpen Rusties* (1975). *Jack and the Wonder Beans* (1977) is a delightful retelling of "Jack and the Beanstalk" in the local idiom. In *The Wolfpen Notebooks: A Record of Appalachian Life* (1991), Still draws from the notebooks which he has kept for more than fifty years, recording the distinctive expressions and customs of the Appalachian region.

Critical attention has been more often directed to Still's novels and short stories than to his poems. Still is rightly admired for his prose, however, because he is first of all a poet. After reading his novel *River of Earth* and the poems in *Hounds on the Mountain*, Katherine Anne Porter said in a letter that the two books should be read together. The novel was "an extension of the poems" while the poems were "further comment on the experience that made the novel." Still's poems, then, are doubly deserving of critical attention. Rewarding in themselves, they also belong to any assessment of his total achievement.

Achievement
Still's poems, short stories, and novels have consistently received high critical acclaim. *Hounds on the Mountain* was reviewed favorably in *Poetry*, *The Atlantic Monthly*, *The New York Times Book Review*, and other newspapers and journals, while *The Wolfpen Poems* was praised by James Dickey in the *Los Angeles Times Book Review*. Still has been the recipient of a number of awards, honors, and prizes. These include two Guggenheim Fellowships, the Southern Authors Award, and the Marjorie Peabody Waite Award of the Amer-

ican Academy and Institute of Arts and Letters for the "continuing achievement and integrity of his art." He has received a number of honorary doctorates. Scholarships and fellowships have been established in his name, including fellowships funded by the Andrew W. Mellon Foundation for Advanced Study in the Humanities and Social Science and in Appalachian Studies at the University of Kentucky. In 1981, Still received the Milner Award, given by the Kentucky Arts Council, in recognition of outstanding leadership in the arts. Still's poems are part of the continuing discovery, through literature, of America's native anthropology.

Biography

James Still was born in Double Creek, Alabama, in 1906. He attended Lincoln Memorial University and Vanderbilt University in Tennessee, and the University of Illinois, earning B.A. degrees in both arts and sciences, and the M.A. degree in English. Since the early 1930's he has lived in Knott County, Kentucky (except for time spent in travel and in military service in Africa and the Middle East in World War II). His home on Dead Mare Branch is a two-story log house built before 1840, given to him for life by a farmer and dulcimer maker named Jethro Amburgey. Still served as librarian for the Hindman Settlement School and has taught at Morehead State University and a number of other institutions.

Still has kept his private life and his life as a writer separate—in order to remain "intact." Those who know him as a teacher and writer know little about his day-to-day life among neighbors, for the most part farmers and coal miners, who know next to nothing about him as a writer. To them he is a farmer, a gardener, and the librarian at the Hindman Settlement School. Still's success in keeping separate his private life and his life as a writer has resulted in misunderstandings about both his life and his writing.

Because he has lived an apparently isolated life and made no effort to advertise himself or promote his writing, or even to accept awards and honors, and because he has published infrequently, Still has been perceived as a hermit-writer. This is a misperception. His failure to accept the award of the American Academy of Arts and Letters, and an invitation to be Phi Beta Kappa poet at Columbia University in the 1940's, contributed to his reputation as a recluse. According to Still, he declined in both instances because he lacked bus fare and suitable clothing for the occasions.

While he appeared to be living an isolated life at the Hindman Settlement School, Still was a constant reader of *The Nation, The New Republic*, and *The New York Times.* He was publishing in *The Atlantic Monthly, The Yale Review, Poetry*, and many other magazines and journals. At this time he numbered among his friends Marjorie Kinnan Rawlings, Katherine Anne Porter, Elizabeth Madox Roberts, and Robert Frost. Still considers himself fortunate to have lived in Knott County, Kentucky, lucky to have been assigned post office box 13 at Hindman. "Hindman was surely the only place you could cash a check at four a.m. and call for your mail at midnight. The cashier was an early riser, the postmaster an insomniac."

The notion that Still is a recluse in flight from modernity is mistaken. Cosmopolitan in his tastes and habits, he has read several hours a day for more than fifty years. His favorite writers are the Scandinavians and the Russians, especially Anton Chekhov, Nikolai Gogol, and Ivan Turgenev. He has traveled, spending ten winters in Mexico, Guatemala, Honduras, and El Salvador studying Mayan civilization. His advice to anyone wishing to write is to learn to type. When reminded that William Shakespeare did not type, his response was: "What might Shakespeare not have additionally accomplished with a Coronamatic 2000 with a pop-out ribbon!"

Because Appalachia has been the object of numerous sociological studies concerned with poverty and economic exploitation, there have been efforts to interpret Still's writing as sociological or political. Still resists these efforts, although he is not politically unaware. He helped distribute food and clothing to beleaguered strikers in Wilder, Tennessee, in 1930. He lived in east Kentucky during the time of the mine wars. He worked, as a temporary replacement, for the Emergency Relief Administration in the mid-1930's. "To live in that time and place . . . was to be politically aware," Still says. He cites the poems in *Hounds on the Mountain* as evidence of his awareness ". . . that at least in my area something was there that would not last much longer. . . . We were living in the nineteenth century, so to speak, and the twentieth would not long be denied."

Instead of a political consciousness, Still has brought the temperament, habits, and, to some extent, the methods of the scientist to bear on his writing. In his notebooks he has recorded every facet of the community in which he has lived. He considers himself "something of a botanist" and experiments with the development by natural selection of the wild strawberry and wild violet. The grounds around his house on Dead Mare Branch he describes as a "cross between a botanical garden and an experiment station." Where writing is concerned, however, he has no theories regarding artistic creation, recommends no methods or techniques. He cannot imagine having been influenced by other writers, and he is not interested in grooming a protégé. When his advice is solicited, he stresses preparation and familiarity with tools of the trade. "A writer gets ready to enter the profession, just as a truck driver learns to operate a truck. I'm fairly certain Chopin didn't compose his works on the piano with one finger, or even two. The preparation is the point." Still advises against looking too closely "into the springs of creativity." The creative process—if it is a process—remains a mystery to him, and he is content with that. When he talks about how he writes, however, his imagery suggests the scientific approach. The writing does not begin until he touches the "quick" of the material, as with a scalpel.

Analysis

"I have gone softly," James Still writes in *Hounds on the Mountain*. He compares himself to a child walking on "a ridge/ Of sleep . . . a slope hung on a night-jar's speech." He is a child "with hands like leaves" and eyes "like swifts that search the darkness in a perilous land" ("With Hands Like Leaves"). The similes define Still's unobtrusive approach to his material, his way of blending in, of becoming invisible as a speaker in the poems, insisting upon objectivity and exactness of detail. In "Eyes in the Grass" the eyes are those of a speaker unnoticed by either bird or insect. The speaker is "lost to any wandering view"; he is "hill uncharted"; his breathing is the wind; he is "horizon . . . earth's far end."

This approach to a people and a place, and Still's achievement as a poet, can be appreciated only in comparison with the way in which the southern Appalachian region of America has been typically depicted. The French critic Roland Barthes maintains (*Mythologies*, 1972) that there is an inherent difficulty in writing about mountains and mountain people, the result of a bourgeois Alpine myth which causes writers and readers to take leave of their senses "anytime the ground is uneven."

Whatever the cause or causes, southern Appalachia appears in American writing as a veritable funhouse of distorted and contradictory images which have since the mid-nineteenth century suited the needs, motives, and perspectives of abolitionists, social workers, Protestant missionaries, industrialists, and entrepreneurs. Southern Appalachia was known through an either/or literature, as either a place of problems, poverty, and peculiar people, or as a preserve of fundamentally American virtues and values, sterling Anglo-Saxon and Anglo-Celtic qualities. The region entered the popular American mind during the 1880's by way of local colorists (chief among them Mary N. Murfree, who wrote under the pseudonym "Charles Egbert Craddock"), who noted the quaint and sensational aspects of an old-fashioned way of life. By the 1920's a careful student of southern Appalachia remarked that more was known about the region that was not true than about any other part of the country.

At a time when it was fashionable, indeed almost obligatory, for poetry about southern Appalachia to be either a witless romanticizing of mountains and mountain people, or proletarian verse, Still walked softly. He presented no diagnosis of economic ills, preached no social gospel, offered no program. He declined to participate in the either/or literature, ambitious to do no more—and no less—than to show people in their place and tell how it was with these people at a particular time.

As a consequence, Still's poems discover neither merely a landscape of beauty and wild freedom nor only visual blight, exploitation, and hard, unrelenting conditions. All these things are caught in a vision that is both local and universal. Still's poems embody certain universal themes implicit in the experience of people in a particular place and time—the themes of endurance, perseverance, and self-preservation under harsh and perilous circumstances.

Details and images create an impression of a difficult life at subsistence level. In "Court Day," the hill folk rise and set out toward the county seat before dawn, when the day is still "dark as plowed earth." The road into town is a stony creek bed. The waters of Troublesome Creek are a "cold thin flowing." The fields of the county poor farm are "hungry" ("On Double Creek"). Descriptions of coal camps suggest unyielding, inhospitable conditions. Coal camp houses are "hung upon the hills" ("Mountain Coal Town"). Underground, the miners are "Breaking the hard, slow-yielding seams" of coal ("Earth-Bread"). Life is not only difficult and meagerly provided for; it is also somehow blighted. Chestnut trees are "cankered to the heart" ("On Red Bird Creek"). The ridges in "Journey Beyond the Hills" are "stricken and unforested." Early morning hours are "gaunt," the mist "leprous," the day "lean" ("The Hill-Born").

Danger and death are ever-present. Death sits "quiet upon a nest" in "Year of the Pigeons." The furrows of the county poor farm are "crooked as an adder's track" ("On Double Creek"). Stars in the night sky over a mountain coal camp are "cool as the copperhead's eyes." The underground shift of the miners is an "eight-hour death," a "daily burial" ("Earth-Bread"). The quarry in "Fox Hunt" is "gaunt and anxious," his life imperiled by the hounds. In the title poem the fox turns at the head of a cove to confront the hounds. The fox's blood laves "the violent shadows" of that place, and even the dry roots "questing beneath the earth."

Life under such conditions is characterized by stark contrasts—between the bitterness and sweetness of experience; between toughness and tenderness. Beauty and blight, untrammeled freedom and imprisonment coexist. The "starveling trees" in "The Hill-Born" bear sweet fruit. In "Horse Swapping on Troublesome Creek" the mare is spavined, while the foals have "untamed hearts" and "toss unbound heads/ With flash of hock and unsheared flowing manes." The stark contrasts of this life are implicit in the details of "Infare." The groom is "sunbronzed, resolute and free." His bride is "sweet apples from high green orchards." The old who have gathered for this wedding party have "ashy" faces and "rheumy" eyes. The wildness and freedom found in this place exist, paradoxically, in a setting that imprisons. Still refers to the "prisoned waters" of Troublesome Creek ("The Hill-Born") and to "men within their prisoning hills" ("Journey Beyond the Hills").

From birth to death the circumscribed life of man and beast is difficult, uncertain, constantly endangered. A foal is dropped "under the hard bead/ Of the crow's eyes" ("On Buckhorn Creek"). Life is vulnerable to powerful natural forces, as suggested by "Spring-tides surging to the naked root" (The Hill-Born"). The forces of nature continue to work on people, plants, and animals even after death. In "Rain on the Cumberlands" the speaker passes "broken horns within the nettled grass/ . . . hoofs relinquished on the breathing stones/ Eaten with rain-strokes." Rain sweeps down the nests of pigeons that have succumbed to the depredations of men and animals, until "not a slate-blue feather blows on any hill" ("Year of the Pigeons"). The dead are not spared the unrelenting harshness of conditions; they lie "under the hard eyes of hill and tree" ("Graveyard"). The dead are "quartered with the roots/ That split firm stone and suck the marrow out,/ And finger yellowing bones" ("Death on the Mountain").

The characteristic response to these adverse and unrelenting conditions is to endure, to carry on, as suggested by "Horseback in the Rain." The speaker is wet, hungry, lonely. His horse's hooves clatter on stone. Yet he has little choice but to "Halt not. Stay not./ Ride the storm with no ending/ On a road unarriving." The poem "Heritage" expresses a determination to stay on in the "prisoning hills" even though "they topple their barren heads to level earth/ And the forests slide uprooted out of the sky."

The response is not only to persevere, but also to preserve something of one's self and one's experiences. "Child in the Hills" emphasizes the perseverance of the child in a man who has "drifted into years of growth and strange enmeshment." The music of the "Mountain Dulcimer" preserves not only the sounds of mountain life—the ringing anvil, the creak of saddlebags and oxen yokes—but also the stillness, "Bitter as salt drenching the tongue of pain."

The characteristic qualities of his style blend with Still's ever-present themes in the representative "Spring on Troublesome Creek." The restraint and understatement of the opening line is gently insisted upon by repetition that suggests conversation, or a ballad: "Not all of us were warm, not all of us." Subsequent lines illustrate Still's simple diction and objective reporting of concrete details: "We are winter-lean, our faces are sharp with cold/ And there is a smell of woodsmoke in our clothes;/ Not all of us were warm, though we hugged the fire/ Through the long chilled nights." The poem concentrates Still's themes of endurance, perseverance, and self-preservation: "We have come out/ Into the sun again, we have untied our knot/ Of flesh." Here too is Still's tendency to see people and place as parts of one subtly interdependent whole. In this poem the condition of the people resembles that of the animals and plants that have also endured the winter. "We are no thinner than a hound or mare,/ Or an unleaved poplar. We have come through/ To grass, to the cows calving in the lot."

In a poem entitled "Anecdote of Men by the Thousand," Wallace Stevens writes: "There are men of a province/ who are that province." Still's poems suggest a similar identity between people and place. People are like the hills; their physical features, characteristics, and qualities mirror their environment. In the poem "On Troublesome Creek," men wait "as mountains long have waited." Hills are like the people. In "Court Day," the hills are so near they seem like people crowding close at the open courthouse window. The ridges in "Journey Beyond the Hills" are "heavy-hipped."

Like the dress of Stevens' woman of Lhassa, Still's poems are "an invisible element" of a place "made visible." Making himself almost invisible as a speaker in the poems, concentrating not on sensibility, or on social and economic views, Still allows an elusive element of a place and people to come into sharp focus. This elusive element, the theme of endurance, perseverance, and self-preservation implicit in the life he writes about, is rendered visible not only in the content of the poems but also through style and structure. The economy and concreteness of expression, the spareness of style, reflect not only the laconic quality of folk speech but also the conditions of the life from which the language comes. Structure and content, style and theme are blended in a genuine expression of a people and a place.

Fresh in his expression and point of view, Still has avoided the superficiality and sensationalism of local colorists and propagandists. Local colorists give the impression of having looked at mountain people and noted the quainter aspects of their traditional life. Reformers emphasize the deplorable circumstances resulting from the inadequacies of that traditional life, or from its destruction through the incursion of mercantile interests. Still gives the impression not merely of having looked at a place and a people but of having lived with them. While the local colorists and proponents of social and economic points of view say "they," Still says "we."

At its best, according to the novelist Wilma Dykeman, the literature of the Appalachian region is "as unique as churning butter, as universal as getting born." Such a combination of uniqueness and universality, found in the best literature of any time and place, is present in Still's poems. They are poems in which abstractions consist of what particulars ultimately mean. Like all genuine poems, they are, as William Carlos Williams puts it, "a vision of the facts."

Jim Wayne Miller

Other major works

LONG FICTION: *River of Earth*, 1940, 1968, 1978; *Sporty Creek*, 1977.

SHORT FICTION: *On Troublesome Creek*, 1941; *Pattern of a Man*, 1976; *The Run for the Elbertas*, 1980.

NONFICTION: *The Wolfpen Notebooks: A Record of Appalachian Life*, 1991.

CHILDREN'S LITERATURE: *Way Down Yonder on Troublesome Creek*, 1974; *The Wolfpen Rusties*, 1975; *Jack and the Wonder Beans*, 1977.

Bibliography
Cadle, Dean. "Pattern of a Writer: Attitudes of James Still." *Appalachian*

Journal 15 (Winter, 1988): 104-143. Cadle presents notes from conversations he had with Still between December, 1958, and December, 1959. Includes Still's views on writing; also has photographs of Still, his house, and neighbors and friends.

Dickey, James. Review of *The Wolfpen Poems*, by James Still. *Los Angeles Times Book Review*, December 7, 1986, 1, 19. Dickey states that this poem establishes Still as the "truest and most remarkable poet of mountain culture." Notes his sincerity and modesty and commends him for the feel of the country in his poems. Sees the strength of *The Wolfpen Poems* collection in that it underscores the necessity of Appalachian culture and its values.

Fletcher, James Gould. "Camera in a Furrow." *The New Republic* 91 (July 28, 1937): 343. When this review of *Hounds on the Mountain* was written, Still was a young poet, and Fletcher alludes to this in his critique. Comments on the monotony and lack of fire in the poems but acknowledges his attention to details and background knowledge of his subject.

Foxfire 22 (Fall, 1988). This special issue on Still concentrates on *The Wolfpen Notebooks*; it contains an interview and selections from the book (not yet published at the time of the issue).

Harriss, R. P. "Granite Appalachian Poetry." *New York Herald Tribune Books* (July 4, 1937): 5. Harris compares Still to Robert Frost and states that it is not easy to align Still with other living Southern poets. In reviewing *Hounds on the Mountain*, Harris says the poems "hark back to archaic mountain farms"; a notable exception is "Court Day," which is a contemporary look at mining towns. Praises Still for being articulate but not in a glib way.

The Iron Mountain Review 2 (Summer, 1984). This issue devoted to Still contains an interview with Still as well as essays on his poetry ("James Still's Poetry: 'The Journey of a Worldly Wonder,'" by Jeff Daniel Marion) and short fiction and a Still bibliography.

Marowski, Daniel G., and Roger Matuz, eds. *Contemporary Literary Criticism. Vol. 49.* Detroit: Gale Research, 1988. The entry on Still mentions that he is highly regarded for his prose and verse, which documents Appalachian life. Comments favorably on the "restrained and evocative qualities" of *The Wolfpen Poems.* Contains excerpts from reviews of his work spanning fifty years.

Miller, Jim Wayne. "Jim Dandy: James Still at Eighty." *Appalachian Heritage* 14 (Fall, 1986): 8-20. A profile of Still emphasizing his views of life and literature and his achievement as a writer; contains biographical information and frequent humorous interjections of local sayings and quotations.

MARK STRAND

Born: Summerside, Prince Edward Island, Canada; April 11, 1934

Principal poetry

Sleeping with One Eye Open, 1964; *Reasons for Moving*, 1968; *Darker*, 1970; *The Story of Our Lives*, 1973; *The Sargeantville Notebook*, 1973; *The Late Hour*, 1978; *Selected Poems*, 1980; *The Continuous Life*, 1990.

Other literary forms

Mr. and Mrs. Baby and Other Stories (1985) is a collection of short stories with a bent for fantasy; another work of fiction, *The Monument* (1978), is primarily prose but contains a few dozen poems integral to the discourse. Mark Strand has translated poetry into English, the most noteworthy volumes of which are *Eighteen Poems from the Quechua* (1971) and *The Owl's Insomnia: Poems by Rafael Alberti* (1973). He has edited or coedited anthologies of poetry, the most important of which is *The Contemporary American Poets: American Poetry Since 1940* (1969). His books on art include *William Bailey* (1987) and *Art of the Real: Nine American Figurative Painters*, (1983). His most successful book for children is *The Planet of Lost Things* (1982).

Achievements

From early in his career as a poet, Mark Strand has been received with respect by critics. His poetry, while grounded in a reality that borders on the surreal, manages to evoke sensations and sensitivity, flavored with a taste for the abstract and bizarre, which convey the haunting, factual nature of the human psyche. Although his poetry is clearly unusual in this ability, and while he has been given a series of awards and other recognitions, his work has not received the final honor—that is, his poems have not been commonly anthologized. Strand has been awarded two Fulbright fellowships (1960 and 1965), followed by grants from the Ingram-Merrill Foundation, the National Endowment for the Arts, and the Rockefeller Foundation in 1966, 1967, and 1968, respectively. In 1974 he was honored with a Guggenheim Fellowship and won the Edgar Allan Poe Award for *The Story of Our Lives* from the Academy of American Poets. The National Institute of Arts and Letters made another award in 1975, as did the Academy of American Poets in 1980. In 1987 Strand was awarded a MacArthur Fellowship. Continuing his duties in teaching the following decade, he was made poet laureate of the United States in 1990.

Biography

Although a Canadian by birth, Mark Strand moved to the United States in

1938, when he was four years old, and has remained there most of the time since then. He has consistently described his parents, Robert Joseph and Sonia Apter Strand, as "bookish," intellectual types who emphasized education and the humanities in his childhood. The youth at first fought his parents' influence in this regard and sought to become an athlete, although he was interested in art from an early age. He grew up in the country, spending much time without the companionship of other children. In 1954 he entered Antioch College in northern Ohio, where he immediately came under the influence of Nolan Miller, his freshman English teacher and a respected critic, editor, and writer. In his college years his attraction to and involvement with poetry became undeniable; he discovered that he liked reading it as well as writing it, and, whether consciously or unconsciously, set upon a career course that would eventually lead to the announcement that he had been appointed poet laureate of the United States by the Library of Congress.

The intervening years we characterized by a series of professional achievements not only in the classroom but also as a poet, translator, writer of fiction, editor, and art critic. Strand has been the recipient of numerous awards and fellowships, most of which were made by national committees or organizations.

Specifically, he earned a bachelor's degree in fine arts from Yale University in 1959, where he also received the Cook Prize and the Bergin Prize. Upon graduation, he was appointed a Fulbright Fellowship and spent a year at the University of Florence. In 1961 he was married to Antonia Ratensky, from whom he was divorced in 1973; the marriage saw the birth of one daughter, Jessica. While teaching as an instructor for three years at the University of Iowa, he earned his third degree, a master of arts, in 1962. He has taught at the University of Brazil, Mount Holyoke College, the University of Washington, Yale, Brooklyn College, Princeton University, Brandeis University, the University of Virginia, Wesleyan University, and Harvard University. Since 1981 he has taught at the University of Utah.

In the early 1960's Strand's first poems were accepted for publication by East Coast literary establishment magazines, particularly *The New Yorker*. He has consistently published poetry since then, with his works appearing in nearly a dozen volumes. In 1976 he was married to Julia Rumsey Garretson, and with her he had a son, Thomas Summerfield. Ostensibly, Strand's children's books were written in part for his own children, after the fashion of Charles Dickens.

Analysis

Mark Strand's poetry is entirely characteristic of the age in which he writes. Solipsism, alienation, and self-definition are the principal concerns. His work manifests a certain self-involvement that often goes over the line into narcissism. Many of his poems are an inner-self dialogue that reaches into the realm of clinical schizophrenia. He is unable to define himself, finally, except as a sensitive one searching for a definition. He does not sound a barbaric yawp over the rooftops of the world so much as he makes a distinguishable whimper from the closet of his bedroom. Overall, Strand's poetry fits quite clearly, quickly, and neatly into the packaged, near-formulaic modes of poetry manufactured in the second half of the twentieth century. Nevertheless, he has a voice, experience, and expression all quite his own, and certain identifiable attributes of his work do serve not only to separate it from the works of others but also to make it deserving of the attention it has received.

Strand's work depicts, to use his own word, the sourceless "darkness" that pervades human existence. In this depiction fear is present, to be sure, as are oversensitivity, bifurcation of identity in the voice of the poet(s), spiritual nakedness, a strange combination of fantasy and the almost-surreal, and an elusive peace that never exists in the conscious and remains undiscoverable in both the subconscious and the unconscious. Strand's poetry, then, is not distinctive so much in its subject matter or the ideas it expresses as in the techniques he employs: he thus has a far different domain from those of other poets writing in this subgenre of late modernism and postexistentialism.

Two poems from Strand's first published collection, *Sleeping with One Eye Open*, demonstrate most of these qualities. In "The Tunnel," the speaker of the poem is aware of a second self lurking, perpetually lurking, in the front yard of his house, itself a metaphor for his body. The primary persona of the poem experiences angst in both his ability and his inability to confront the other persona of his own self. He shines a flashlight at it, opens the door for a direct confrontation (which turns out to be more of a peek), makes obscene gestures at the other, leaves it suicide notes, tears up his (their) living-room furniture, and, finally, decides to dig a tunnel to escape to a neighbor's yard. The attempt fails; there can be no communication or contact with an other until he has first set his own house in order. The poet finishes digging the tunnel to find himself immobilized. He does not enter this escape route, although it is fully prepared; the poem ends with him aware that he is still being watched by the other self, now not in immediate physical visibility, and knowing that he will not leave the other after all. The self will remain fractured, and the fear will not go away. Escape is not possible, because it would be at least a partial enactment of suicide, which is unacceptable, accomplishing nothing.

In "Poem," the primary persona is again visited by the secondary self, who sneaks into his house (again a metaphor for the poet's body), climbs the stairs to the bedroom, where the poet is not sleeping but waiting, and announces that he is going to kill him. In this companion poem to "The Tunnel," the situation is reversed and enhanced. In the first poem the primary consciousness of the poet's existence tries only to escape the second consciousness and chooses not to do so. In "Poem," the second self succeeds in confronting the first one to announce not escape, but murder. Both halves meet with failure. The would-be murder of self is to be carried out by mutilation: the second self starts cutting away at the body, beginning with the toenails and proceeding upward, to stop only when "nothing is left of me," at least emotionally. The mutilating self stops when he reaches the neck; that is, he leaves the head to go on thinking, and he departs. Predictably, the poem ends just as the first one did. Both selves are left only to go on in a dual existence of irresolution and terror.

Strand revisits the same motifs and existence in many of the poems that were collected in *Reasons for Moving*. These are particularly evident in "The Man in the Mirror," a longer poem of thirty quatrains in which the poet reveals his innermost thoughts while routinely confronting himself in a mirror. The reflection first becomes an image, then an embodiment with a personality of its own, as the poet tries to define himself and find meaning in his life. The voyeuristic narcissism and the fact of the fractured self struggling for union and self-comprehension provide the framework, context, and message of the poem. The poet views himself in the mirror on his living-room wall, contemplating the meaning of what he sees—his other self. The emergence of identities is evident early in the poem: "I remember how we used to stand/ wishing the glass/ would dissolve between us." Yet this wistful attempt at merging the two parts is incomplete, therefore unsuccessful. "But that was another life./ One day you turned away/ and left me here/ to founder in the stillness of your wake." The body of the poem is then a matter of recording a list of ways in which he had tried to cope with this wake. He watches and studies the other self; he tries to forget him; he is driven to walking around the house, performing strange actions. The other continues to be present, but pointlessly so. Finally, as in the case of the two poems already discussed, the poet gives up; he knows that "it will always be this way./ I stand here scared/ that you will disappear, scared that you will stay."

Strand published "The Dirty Hand" in the same collection. This poem is, for both the poet and the reader, an experience in the self-involvement of narcissism and masturbation. The poet bemoans the fact that his hand is dirty and cannot be cleaned, ostensibly for the reason that he will simply get it dirty again: the stain of the flesh cannot be removed, because the flesh itself is dirt. He is aware of no guilt, only uncleanness. Repeatedly, he washes his hand (notice that the poet never refers to the hand in the plural; only one hand is problematic), scrubbing and polishing yet unable to remove the dirt from its nature. He tries to hide the hand from others, an endeavor that meets with little success, and he cannot hide the hand from himself either. The intensity of the problem increases, until finally he recognizes that he cannot live with it and proclaims that he will cut it off, chop it into pieces, and throw it into the ocean. This desire to rid himself of his nature, however, is not the main thrust of the poem, which ends with the wish for "another hand" to come to take its place, not at the end of his arm but by fastening itself to his arm. The poet wants someone else to assume the role of self-involvement, which leaves him unclean.

Darker, which was published in 1970, remains Strand's best collection of poetry. These poems focus on the fear and dread of the human conscious that occurs because of the immobility he had recognized and written of in earlier poems. Aware that it is not enough to maintain that individuals are trapped in fear, the poet turns to the "darker" realization that there is no change, no hope, and no progress. In his earlier poems he had recognized as much, but he now turns to dealing with the consequences of such a realization. Previously, he had expressed himself as entrapped; in *Darker*, the poems worry with the meaning of that permanent and irreversible entrapment.

The third poem in *Darker* is called "Giving Myself Up." In it the poet lists a series of some dozen items that he "gives up," parts of his body as well as his "smell" and his "clothes." The poet gives up every matter of importance to his self-involvement, even the "ghost" that lives in his clothes. The poem concludes, "And you will have none of it because already I am beginning/ again without anything." His surrender to fear, the hopelessness of isolation, and the immobility caused by having two identities accomplishes nothing. He has finished without anything and will start again without anything. He knows that he is hopelessly trapped in a cycle from which there is no escape—only a minimal comprehension of the process. Along with the other side of his schizophrenic self, he will begin again only to reach the same purposeless point later. Giving up to the other self will not let him out of his present state. Thus one answer is given to the problem of existing in permanent entrapment: self-abnegation will not work.

A second meaning of this fixated condition is similarly expressed in several other poems in *Darker*, particularly "Black Maps." Here, the poet maps out his existential life against a background of blackness. He begins the poem by recognizing that his birth (here called "arrival") is unacknowledged either by the "attendance of stones," an image representing the kinds of mental torture and persecution the poet later experiences, or an "applauding wind" thus he asserts that nature takes no joy from the appearance of the individual. "Nothing will tell you/ where you are" either at the time of birth or later in life. Individuals struggle and cope alone in a present that "is always dark." In this life all "maps are black," and life is a voyage only into the surrounding emptiness. By attempting to study these maps of the dark night of the soul, the poet learns only that "what you thought/ were concerns of yours/ do not exist." The cares and worries of this life are unimportant, because they have no physical or mental reality. In fact, the poet concludes, "Only you are there." Once again, the poet addresses his other self, the recognition of which entirely prevents him from any spiritual mobility. Only a dual loneliness pervades.

Also in *Darker* is a short poem that is in many ways Strand's bleakest expression of his condition. He writes "My Death" from the perspective of the other side of the grave. He asserts that sadness, confusion, and waste are commonplace, expected elements of the event, of which he is consciously aware. The poet seemingly enjoys the chaos he precipitates among his friends and relatives by telling them that he had tried to commit suicide several times. He shocks them into leaving: "Soon I was alone." The poet is now returned, by his own will and force and intention, to his original state: nothing is gained from death, not even momentary relief from the condition he has had in life.

In *The Story of Our Lives* Strand presents a new way of looking at his state. On the one hand he is given to the usual self-involvement; on the other there is a rather complete self-detachment. The title poem, the best in the collection, can be rightfully interpreted in a straightforward manner. The narrator of the poem is addressing someone, presumably a woman whom he loves and to whom he is probably married. He tells her that they have been reading "the story of our lives;" that is, the frame of this long poem is to explore the possibilities of what it would mean to be able to read their lives as though they were recorded in a book, here ostensibly a novel. They jointly read on, learning of themselves as their plots and plights unfold.

The poem, which is one of his better and more readable pieces, is written in seven stanzas of some twenty lines each. In the first one, Strand reports to readers (and undoubtedly to himself) that the *"we"* of the poem are trying to find meaning and direction in their "lives" by reading in a book where, at least, what happens is known. The *"we"* here garners two legitimate interpretations. First, it is clearly the poet himself and the lover whom he is addressing. At the same time, Strand has constructed the poem so as to legitimize it as another fractured-self conversation typical in his works. In either case, the personas of the poem are sitting together on a couch in their living room, knowing that "the book of our lives is empty"; the furniture is never changed; even the rugs become "darker" through the years as "our shadows pass over them." The second stanza opens with "We are reading the story of our lives/ as though we were in it/ as though we had written it." Life is just as vacuous in the novel as in their other, daily existence. The poet recognizes early that if such a book did exist, it would be unable to reveal meaning for him; that, perhaps, would be somebody else's life (or lives). In all stanzas except the first one, a few random passages from the imagined book are interwoven into the poet's own lines so as to make evident the futility of the endeavor. Because the book offers nothing new, the poet records that "it wants to divide us."

In the third and fourth stanzas, the other self becomes both bored and tired and falls asleep, as it is written in the book. The primary narrator-self reads on to see what will happen; of course he learns that the answer is, more or less, nothing. People fall asleep and people wake up—their lives remain empty whether they be well rested or not. By the fifth stanza, the poet has given up on finding something in the book that would foretell purpose in his (their) existence; he wishes only for a "perfect moment," one in which he could have momentary relief from the dark. Were there such a moment, so he ponders, he could then perpetually live and relive it by always starting at the beginning of the book and reading to that point. Such a moment is not to be found; it does not exist in their lives and cannot be found in a record of their lives. The concluding stanzas of the poem reinforce such a stance. The poet and his companion are left with loneliness and despair. They grow tired of reading the book, of studying the "tired phantoms" that occupy the "copy" as well as inhabit their own bodies. Thus they determine to accept this truth, realizing that "they are the book and they are/ nothing else."

Selected Poems is a collection that, as would be expected, contains his best poems, and the volume does serve well to represent Strand's life's work to 1980. Five new poems appeared in this publication, the most important of which is the unusual "Shooting Whales." The poet recalls an event from his childhood in which he, his father, and other family members get in a boat to watch fishermen who have gone out to shoot whales in St. Margaret's Bay. They are out all day, and as they are returning, after dark, their boat's engine dies. The speaker's father takes the oars and rows all the way home, speechlessly. That night the young speaker lies in bed envisioning the whales moving in the ocean beneath him: "they were luring me/ downward and downward/ into the murmurous/ water of sleep." His existence, then, is made akin to that of the whales; they are like singing mermaids who would lure him into the depths of his later darkness, self-involvement, and loneliness.

Strand did not publish another volume of poetry for ten years. *The Continuous Life* displays a variety in form and content. Many of the poems are ostensibly prose but qualify as poems, if at all, because each of their meanings is conveyed poetically, through a series of images. More noticeably, there is less focus on split personality and psychosis. Though the poet never gets out of himself to the extent that his subject matter is actually another person, he does focus on external people and conditions in some poems in this volume. A few of these poems are not even written in first person; some are recordings of conversations, almost in dramatic form; two or three of them are called "letters."

The majority of the thirty poems in *The Continuous Life* are composed in the same vein as those already discussed here, with little tampering with previous themes. In the poem "The Continous Life," Strand gives advice about what parents should tell their children. First, he instructs, "confess/ To your little ones the night is a long way off"—that is, tell them of death but explain that it is far in the distant future. His second advice is to inform them about how "mundane" life is, and he then offers a list of household chores and implements. Parents should also explain that life is a period "between two great darks," birth and death. In the meantime, individuals conduct a great "search" for "something . . . , a piece of the dark that might have been yours." Finally, the poet recognizes the existence and reality of "small tremors of love through your brief,/ Undeniable selves, into your days, and beyond." It is unusual for Strand to acknowledge the existence of love, or even of "small tremors of love," which here arguably counter the darkness upon which the bulk of his work focuses. The poet sees love, possibly, as an experience that can give partial and momentary relief in the present.

"The End," the short poem that concludes *The Continuous Life*, serves as a final comment about Strand's life, and therefore his poetry, "Not every man knows what he shall sing at the end," writes the poet in such a way as to suggest that he does. He then gives a short list of typical activities of life that come to an end when a man becomes eternally "motionless" and it is "clear that he'll never go back." The poem concludes, "Not every man knows what is waiting for him, or what he shall sing/ When the ship he is on slips into darkness, there at the end." The poet knows what awaits him at his end and what song he will then sing. Strand has explored his death sufficiently, he foresees, to know that he will comprehend and experience the darkness at that time just as he has lived his life. It will truly change nothing.

The poetry of Mark Strand is distinctive not so much in content as in approach. His contribution to twentieth century American poetry is the singularity in method and mode of expressing ideas common to other poets of his time. He stands apart from others, however, specifically through his estranged—though assuredly successful—mixture of the haunting darkness of reality with the fantastic and sexual, with self-alienation whose form is self-involvement, and with a recognition of the bifurcated personality, neither side of which can be subject functionally to the other. The mark of the superior quality of his works is that somehow he convinces the reader that life truly is this way and that the experiences he describes, however bizarre, are experiences that they share.

Carl Singleton

Other major works

LONG FICTION: *The Monument*, 1978.

SHORT FICTION: *Mr. and Mrs. Baby and Other Stories*, 1985.

NONFICTION: *Art of the Real: Nine American Figurative Painters*, 1983; *William Bailey*, 1987.

CHILDREN'S LITERATURE: *The Planet of Lost Things*, 1982; *The Night Book*, 1985; *Rembrandt Takes a Walk*, 1986.

TRANSLATIONS: *Eighteen Poems from the Quechua*, 1971; *The Owl's Insomnia: Poems by Rafael Alberti*, 1973; *Travelling in the Family: Poems by Carlos Drummond de Andrade*, 1986.

EDITED TEXTS: *The Contemporary American Poets: American Poets Since 1940*, 1969; *New Poetry of Mexico*, 1970; *Another Republic*, 1976 (with Charles Simic).

Bibliography

Bloom, Harold. "Dark and Radiant Peripheries: Mark Strand and A. R. Ammons." *Southern Review* 8 (Winter, 1972): 133-141. This article is formally divided into four main sections: the introduction and conclusion briefly compare the poetry of Strand and Ammons, while the second section is given to Strand and the third to Ammons. Critical commentary is provided for the title poems of Strand's first three volumes: *Sleeping with One Eye Open, Reasons for Moving*, and *Darker*. Bloom focuses upon the "dark" elements of Strand's work.

Cooper, Philip. "The Waiting Dark: Talking to Mark Strand." *The Hollins Critic* 22 (1984): 1-7. This article does not record line by line an interview with the poet; rather, Cooper makes use of an interview from which he quotes frequently and extensively in articulating his own understanding of Strand's poetry. Specifically, he finds it humorous, dreamlike, and haunting, while finding the central theme of Strand's work to be elusive.

French, Robert. "Eating Poetry: The Poetry of Mark Strand." *The Far Point* 5 (1970): 61-66. French interprets Strand's poetry in general in context of the opening poem in *Reasons for Moving*. "Eating Poetry" is seen not as a poem to be criticized singularly but as a springboard for understanding Strand's theory of poetry and poetic techniques. Several poems from *Reasons for Moving* and *Darker* are taken up. French also provides comments about the influence of Franz Kafka upon Strand.

Gregorson, Linda. "Negative Capability." *Parnassus: Poetry in Review* 9 (1981): 90-114. Gregorson discusses poems selected from Strand's *Selected Poems*. She focuses on the rhymes and meters of the poetry, as well as the imagery. Also included are some critical analyses of the poet's use of prosody. Her overall effort is to trace the developing forms and formats of the recognizably better poems.

Howard, Richard. "Mark Strand." In *Alone with America: Essays on the Art of Poetry in the United States Since 1950*. Enl. ed. New York: Atheneum, 1980. Howard writes critically of Strand's first two collections of poems, *Sleeping with One Eye Open* and *Reasons for Moving*. He sees the second volume as an outgrowth and continuation of the first one. Howard focuses on the duality of Strand's nature and his inability to reconcile the different aspects of his personality.

Olsen, Lance. "Entry to the Unaccounted For: Mark Strand's Fantastic Autism." In *The Poetic Fantastic: Studies in an Evolving Genre*, edited by Patrick D. Murphy and Vernon Hyles. New York: Greenwood Press, 1989. In this short article of some ten pages, Olsen interprets much of Strand's work in terms of fantasy. He deals specifically with poems taken from *Sleeping with One Eye Open* and *Reasons for Moving*. The critic sees many elements of science fiction in Strand's poems, as well as metafiction.

Strand, Mark. "The Education of a Poet." Interview by Nolan Miller. *The Antioch Review* 39 (1981): 106-118. Strand's freshman English teacher, Nolan Miller (a scholar and professor at Antioch College, where the poet earned his B.A.), interviews his former student. Early sections of the interview reveal the poet's attitudes toward reading, literature, and education. He also discusses the role and function of poetry.

SIR JOHN SUCKLING

Born: Whitton, Twickenham, England; February, 1609
Died: Paris, France; 1642

Principal poetry

Fragmenta Aurea, 1646; *The Last Remains of Sir John Suckling*, 1659.

Other literary forms

Between 1637 and 1641 Sir John Suckling completed three plays: *Aglaura* (1638), *The Goblins* (1638), and *Brennoralt* (1646). *The Sad One*, an unfinished fragment, was written sometime earlier. *Aglaura* was published in 1638 in folio format; none of the other plays was printed during the poet's lifetime. Most of Suckling's fifty-odd letters are personal in subject matter, but two of them—one to "A Gentleman in Norfolk" and one to Henry Jermyn—are essentially political tracts dealing with the Scottish Campaign of 1639 and the opening of the Long Parliament in 1640, respectively. Suckling was also the author of "An Account of Religion by Reason," a defense of Socinianism that attempts to reconcile biblical revelation with the mythologies of the ancients. Suckling's letters and "An Account of Religion by Reason" are collected by Thomas Clayton in *The Works of Sir John Suckling: The Non-Dramatic Works* (1971).

Achievements

During his lifetime, Suckling's reputation as courtier and rakehell overshadowed his literary endeavors. His attacks on the Neoplatonic amatory conventions of the 1630's led him into poetic skirmishes with Edmund Waller and a swarm of lesser poets; his much vaunted dislike of the aged and ailing Ben Jonson earned him the enmity of the Sons of Ben. In his satire "The Wits," Suckling took on the entire Caroline literary establishment, with a good word for no one but Lucius Cary, Viscount Falkland. Such combativeness, joined with the theatricality of his personal life, isolated Suckling from his fellow poets and his work elicited few of the usual encomia from contemporaries. The raciness and adolescent flippancy that are the hallmarks of his style, moreover, constitute a reaction against the prevailing Caroline tastes that was little appreciated in his own day.

Suckling's style, however, was precisely suited to the poets of the succeeding generation, and the Restoration wits found in him a model for their own aspirations. In John Dryden's *Of Dramatic Poesie: An Essay* (1668), Eugenius argues that the ancients "can produce nothing so courtly writ, or which expresses so much the conversation of a gentleman, as Sir John Suckling"; William Congreve and John Wilmot, Earl of Rochester, both praised his ease and naturalness. Restoration poets eagerly imitated "The Wits," using it as the pattern for their own literary squibs; they also appropriated the ballad stanza that Suckling introduced into formal poetry.

Although enthusiasm for Suckling waned during the eighteenth century, he continued to command a firm place in the poetic pantheon. Samuel Johnson praised him for not falling into the metaphysical excesses of poets such as Abraham Cowley. Since that time the critical estimation of Suckling has remained relatively constant: although a minor poet, he was a good one, and several of his lyrics are frequently anthologized.

John Dryden undoubtedly exaggerated Suckling's achievement, but his recognition of the part that Suckling played in transforming English poetic diction is valid. Suckling's ability to capture the rhythms of colloquial speech in rhymed verse represents a real innovation in seventeenth century poetry. Although his attitudes toward women and love are often cynical and occasionally grating, his earthy common sense usually comes across as a necessary antidote to the stylized Neoplatonism of so much amatory verse of the 1630's. In similar fashion, Suckling's embrace of native literary forms such as the ballad and the riddle serves as a corrective to the classicizing tendencies of Renaissance poetry. Suckling's oeuvre is small, but the role he played in English poetry was a pivotal one: his experiments in diction and essays in satire furthered the shift from a Renaissance to a Restoration aesthetic.

Biography

John Suckling was born in February, 1609, into a prominent gentry family. His father, also Sir John, was a longtime member of Parliament who held a number of minor positions at court; in 1622, he purchased the office of Comptroller of the King's Household, which he occupied until his death in 1627. The poet's mother, Martha, was the sister of Lionel Cranfield, later first Earl of Middlesex and, until his impeachment in 1624, Lord Treasurer of England. Although his mother died in 1613, Suckling maintained close ties with the Cranfield family; his uncle's disgrace, countenanced by the royal favorite the Duke of Buckingham, alienated Suckling from the inner circles of the court.

Suckling matriculated at Trinity College, Cambridge, between 1623 and 1628; he was admitted to Gray's Inn in 1627. He may have served in the English expedition against the French on the Ile de Ré in 1627 and definitely fought in Lord Wimbledon's regiment in the Dutch service in 1629-1630. In October, 1631, Suckling joined the embassy to Gustavus Adolphus led by Sir Henry Vane, who was negotiating with the Swedish monarch for the return of the Palatinate to Charles I's brother-in-law, the Elector Frederick. Vane sent Suckling to England in March, 1632, with dispatches for the King. His mission complete, Suckling remained in England and plunged into a course of gambling and womanizing that lasted for the rest of the decade. During this period, according to John Aubrey, Suckling invented the game of cribbage. In order to recoup the vast sums he lost at cards and bowling, Suckling entered into a prolonged courtship of the northern heiress Anne Willoughby. Although the King supported his suit, Suckling's prospective in-laws did not; after a series of challenges, threatened lawsuits, and pitched battles between the two families and their allies, Suckling ceased his attentions. Shortly after this abortive courtship, Suckling entered into a relationship with the woman he called "Aglaura," probably Mary Bulkeley of Beaumaris, Anglesey. Despite the intensity of feeling that Suckling expresses in his few surviving letters to Aglaura, the affair flickered out by 1639, when Mary married a local squire. During the remainder of his life Suckling's closest emotional ties were with his Cranfield relatives, his uncle and his cousin Martha, Lady Cary.

Suckling had begun writing poetry during adolescence, but the lyrics for which he is best known were composed during the mid-1630's. In 1637, he turned seriously to drama; his tragedy *Aglaura* was produced with great fanfare in February, 1638, by the King's Company at Blackfriars. Suckling provided *Aglaura* with a tragicomic ending for a performance before the King and Queen in April, 1638; the play was printed in a lavish folio edition later that year.

The outbreak of trouble in Scotland in 1639 put an end to Suckling's literary activities. Raising a troop of one hundred horsemen, whom he clad at his own expense in white doublets and scarlet breeches, Suckling joined King Charles in the north. Because of illness, perhaps dysentery, he saw little action and was later accused of cowardice in the campaign. With the Treaty of Berwick in June, 1639, Suckling returned to London and was elected to the Short Parliament as an MP for Bramber, Sussex, in a by-election. Suckling returned to the border country in August, 1640, for the Second Bishops' War. After the defeat of the King's forces at Newburn he participated in the general retreat, during which he reportedly lost his coach and a wardrobe worth £300 to the Scottish commander Leslie.

With the opening of the Long Parliament in November, 1640, Suckling began to assume a more active role in politics. He became involved in a conspiracy to stage a coup d'état which would have dissolved Parliament and returned effective political power to the king. The plans of the plotters were discovered; after a preliminary examination by the House of Commons, Suckling fled to France on May 5, 1641. A writ for his arrest was issued the same day. Suckling arrived in Paris on May 14, but nothing is known of his subsequent activities. Although the exact details of his death are unclear, the most plausible account is that he committed suicide by poison sometime in 1642.

Analysis

Sir John Suckling was a poet of reaction. Assuming the role of roaring boy at the Caroline court, he assaulted with an almost adolescent glee the conventions, literary and amatory, that prevailed during the 1630's. Suckling challenged the fashionable cult of Platonic Love with a pose of libertinism. He rejected the sophisticated Continental models employed by Ben Jonson and Thomas Carew in their lyrics, introducing in their stead native, "subliterary" forms such as the ballad and the riddle. Finally, Suckling rejected the title "poet," vaunting his amateur status in a pursuit that he implied had become increasingly dominated by ungentlemanly professionals. For the greater part of his short poetic career, Suckling was an iconoclast rather than an innovator, more certain of what he was attacking than what he proposed to offer in its place. In the final poems, however, he achieved a balance between the successive waves of idealism and cynicism that rocked his short life. This newfound confidence in his art manifests itself most clearly in the good humor and good sense of "A Ballad upon a Wedding."

Thomas Clayton divides Suckling's poetic career into four periods. The earliest poems, discovered by L. A. Beaurline in manuscript in the late 1950's, consist of a Christmas devotional sequence and two meditations upon faith and salvation written before or during 1626. These pieces are derivative and not of great literary value, but they do suggest the young Suckling's receptiveness to influences and stylistic options open to him. Two of the eleven poems are important inasmuch as they forecast the themes that will run through Suckling's best-known lyrics. In "Faith and Doubt," the speaker contemplates the Christian mysteries of the incarnation and redemption; suspended between a desire to believe and an inability to move beyond the rational, he prays for the experience vouchsafed the apostle Thomas—the confirmation of faith through the senses. The speaker's troubled doubt serves as a prologue to the pose of libertine skepticism that Suckling later adopted in his amatory verse. Even more central to Suckling's poetic vision, perhaps, is the exuberant description of rustic customs and superstitions in "Upon Christmas Eve." With a sensitivity reminiscent of Robert Herrick, Suckling testified to his rural upbringing and his obvious delight in country life. Beneath the elegant courtliness of later poems this theme will persist, eventually reemerging in "A Ballad upon a Wedding."

The poems that Clayton assigns to the years 1626 to 1632 are a mixed lot, suggesting that the young Suckling was still in search of a personal style. While a number of these pieces represent essays in popular, usually humorous, forms—the riddle, the character, the ballad—others are serious attempts at the type of lyric that flourished at court. A final group fuses the popular and courtly strains in parody or, more rarely, in a delicate mixture of humor and compliment. With only a few exceptions, the poems exhibit a preoccupation with love and sexuality.

The short riddle "A Candle" is essentially an adolescent joke that allows the poet to talk bawdy but evade the consequences. In a series of double entendres, Suckling describes the "thing" used by "the Maiden Female crew" in the night; to the discomfiture of the reader, the answer to the riddle proves to be "a candle." The poet is obviously intensely interested in sex, but apparently too unsure of his poetic powers to deal with it directly. The same type of double entendre informs "A Barley-break" and three characters— "A Barber," "A Pedler of Small-wares," and "A Soldier." In "A Soldier," the speaker offers his love to an audience of ladies, combining bluster with a winning naïveté. The assertion "I cannot speak, but I can doe," with its obvious pun on "doe," well describes Suckling's own position in the early 1630's—willing and eager to besiege the ladies, but unskilled in the language of amatory gallantry.

Suckling's attempts to write conventional love lyrics underscore the truth of the admission in "A Soldier." While technically correct, these pieces seem flat after the exuberance and leering smuttiness of the riddles and characters. "The Miracle," for example, is an uninspired rehash of the Petrarchan fire and ice paradox. "Upon the first sight of my Lady Seimor," an exercise in Caroline Neoplatonism, is a stillborn blazon. In *"Non est mortale quod opto: Upon Mrs. A. L.,"* Suckling tackles the same theme that Carew treats so successfully in "A Divine Mistress," that of the woman who is so perfect that the poet can find no way to approach her. Whereas Carew wittily solves the dilemma by praying to the gods to grant his lady "some more humanitie," Suckling blunders badly with his closing couplet, "I love thee well, yet wish some bad in thee,/ For sure I am thou art too good for me." The acquisition of "some bad," unlike "humanitie," can only mar the lady's perfection. Carew effects an accommodation between poetic convention and amatory pragmatism without compromising either; Suckling, facing the same dilemma, is forced to choose between them.

What is interesting about these poems written in an unblinking platonic vein is that they are contemporaneous with the characters and ballads. The disjunction between love and sexuality, moreover, assumes a literary form inasmuch as Suckling reserves his bawdiness for the "subliterary" genres. In Suckling's mature style, the gap is bridged: courtly verse forms are employed to set off the very grossness of the "country matters" they discuss. In "The deformed Mistress," Suckling weds the high-flown diction and exotic imagery of the serious blazon to the most unattractive physical blemishes with striking effect:

> Her Nose I'de have a foot long, not above,
> With pimples embroder'd, for those I love;
> And at the end a comely Pearl of Snot,
> Considering whether it should fall or not.

"Upon T. C. having the P." reemploys the fire and water conceit of "The Miracle" in unexpected fashion: the subject of the poem is Carew's difficulties in urinating when he has the pox. The best of these pieces is "Upon my Lady

Carliles walking in Hampton-Court garden," a dialogue between T. C., presumably Tom Carew, and J. S., Suckling himself. While T. C. deifies the countess and falls into raptures over her beauty, J. S. mentally strips her until she is as naked as Eve in her first state. The degradation of Lady Carlisle from goddess to mortal woman to whore becomes complete when J. S. suggests in the final lines that countless fools have enjoyed the favors of this leading court beauty; if he and T. C. are men, they will do likewise rather than contenting themselves with merely praising her charms. The humor of the poem should not distract the reader from the serious problem it raises. J. S., claiming that he is not "born to the Bay," disavows the title of poet; instead, he assumes the role of the plain-dealer who refuses to acquiesce in the fictions purveyed by Caroline lyricists. The dialogue dramatizes the opposition between "speaking" and "doing" that first appears in "A Soldier"; it also represents the externalization of an internal conflict inasmuch as Suckling, with little success, had for several years been penning the same platonic sentiments that he here fobs off on T. C. The attack on poetic conventions seems as much designed to conceal Suckling's inability to conform to the prevailing mode as to herald a new epoch in English lyric.

Between 1632 and 1637, Suckling composed the lyrics for which he is best remembered. Although most of these poems trade upon the blunt, skeptical attitude toward love that he affects in "Upon my Lady Carliles walking in Hampton-Court garden," others deal with love seriously, often in terms of the amatory Platonism that he had seemingly rejected. In the mid-1630's, Suckling was still searching for a congenial lyric stance, one that would allow him to reconcile love and sexuality, innocence and experience. Both Platonism and libertinism prove in the end to be inadequate solutions to the problem, since Suckling is uneasy with the one and much too strident in the other.

In the song "Honest Lover whosoever," the speaker gently prescribes the proper platonic behavior for the youth who aspires to amatory correctness. The effect is one of humorous indulgence; Suckling treats the absurdities of young love with the same bemused tolerance that Geoffrey Chaucer displays in Book I of *Troilus and Criseyde* (1382). The two poems "To his Rival" display the same comic delicacy, but it is a delicacy that begins to cloy. In "Why so pale and wan, fond Lover?," however, Suckling finds a formula that combines sympathy and humor in a winning way. After counseling a pining young lover in the arts of seduction, the long-suffering speaker finally loses patience: in the last line he dismisses the unyielding woman with the exclamation, "The Devill take her." The use of comic reversal for purposes of closure becomes a standard element in Suckling's lyrics; the formula provides the perfect means for the poet to indulge his platonic sentiments while protesting his superiority to them with a wink or a leer.

Darker in tone are the libertine lyrics, those which insist that love is a mere physical act without moral or spiritual implications. Suckling employs an argumentative style that superficially recalls the elegies, songs, and sonnets of John Donne, but the argument is less metaphorical and logically innovative than that of the elder poet. The tendency of these poems is to reduce love to mere appetite. In "Sonnet II," love is described as a good meal. In "Womans Constancy" lovemaking is compared to bees extracting pollen from a flower: "One lights, one tastes, gets in, gets out." Suckling reaches his nadir in "Loves Offence," in which he arrives at the conclusion that "love is the fart/ of every heart." The two "Against Fruition" poems present Suckling at his most cynical. In "Against Fruition I," the speaker argues against sexual consummation, not because of any moral or philosophical scruples, but because fruition compares unfavorably with the more exquisite delights of sexual anticipation. The speaker argues that "Women enjoy'd (what s'ere before th'ave been)/ Are like Romances read, or sights once seen." This mistress, reified rather than deified, reappears throughout Suckling's lyrics of the mid-1630's. "Against Fruition II," an address to a mistress, is disturbing in its violence. One wonders how the lady should deal with the paradox, "Shee's but an honest whore that yeelds, although/ She be as cold as ice, as pure as snow." Suckling provides no answer to the dilemma. The subversion of the platonic arguments to a libertine end renders the "Against Fruition" poems a fascinating intellectual exercise, but they prove to be a poetic dead end.

In the final years of his life, Suckling at last found a framework within which he could reconcile his own hateful contraries. In the prose "Letter to a Friend" and "An Answer," both undoubtedly written by Suckling, "Jack" attempts to dissuade his friend "Tom" from marriage with the usual libertine arguments. Tom, however, has the last word: turning the libertine commonplaces upside down, he argues that the "ravishing *Realities*" of marriage far surpass the "pleasing *Dreames*" of the sort that Suckling champions in "Against Fruition I." The reconciliation of idealism and skepticism is here suggested rather than achieved; yet, the recognition that love and sexuality are not necessarily incompatible prefigures the high-spirited synthesis of "A Ballad upon a Wedding."

In both style and substance, "A Ballad upon a Wedding" returns to the poems of the late 1620's. Suckling revitalizes the tired tradition of the epithalamium by describing an aristocratic wedding through the eyes of a yokel. The poem, written in an eight-eight-six ballad stanza, is remarkable for its exquisite imagery; in employing the homely details of rural life—mice, Katherine pears, a young colt—to blazon the bride's beauty, Suckling rediscovers the themes and techniques of his early Christmas poems. Coupled with the freshness of the imagery is a relaxed, accepting attitude toward the problem of love and sexuality that had bedeviled Suckling throughout his career. The poem closes with a comic reversal: the naïve speaker demonstrates that he is not so naïve after all when he speculates on what takes place in the nuptial chamber once the ceremony is over:

> At length the candles out, and now
> All that they had not done, they do:
> What that is, who can tell?
> But I beleeve it was no more
> Than thou and I have done before
> With *Bridget*, and with *Nell*.

The speaker's sexual awareness does not vitiate his fundamental innocence, nor does the bride's sexuality vitiate the romantic idealism that she inspires in the early parts of the poem. The real and the ideal are integrated into a comprehensive vision of love.

Aside from "A Ballad upon a Wedding" and one other epithalamium, Suckling's final poems deal primarily with literary affairs. As with love, Suckling achieves a balanced, mature outlook toward his position as a poet only with a struggle. "The Wits," probably composed during the summer of 1637, describes the scramble for the laureateship touched off by the death of Jonson in August of that year. Employing the same ballad form he had used in "A Ballad upon a Wedding," Suckling lampoons all the chief Caroline pretenders to wit. Jonson and Carew come in for some especially hard knocks; only Lucius Cary, Viscount Falkland, escapes the general opprobrium, perhaps because by this time he had given over poetry for philosophy. Suckling alone is absent from the convocation: a bystander tells Apollo,

> He loved not the muses so well as his sport;
> And
> Prized black eyes, or a lucky hit
> At bowls, above all the Trophies of wit.

Angered at this information, the deity promptly declares Suckling an outlaw in poetry. No role, perhaps, suited Suckling better. Falling back on the role of plain-dealer he had perfected in his lyrics, Suckling rejects the poetic establishment but at the same time betrays his anxiety that he does not quite measure up to its standards. In the last poems, however, Suckling demonstrates a growing willingness to accept his vocation. In "An Answer to some Verses made in his praise," he sheds his customary *sprezzatura* and, with convincing modesty, accepts the tribute of another poet. Suckling at long last takes his place among the wits he had feigned to scorn less than two years earlier.

The outbreak of civil war cut short Suckling's career. Before his death in 1642, however, he had achieved a poetic and personal maturity: his last poems, which suggest a new accommodation of the conflicting motives so evident in the earlier works, are also his best. Suckling's small oeuvre of some eighty poems is erratic in quality. Those pieces that argue doctrinaire positions on love and life tend to be his worst: the poems taking the stock platonic line are insipid, the libertine exercises too often grating. Yet, Suckling displays throughout his work a sure sense for the comic and a sensitivity to rural life matched in this period only by Herrick. Suckling's poems record his progress, sometimes halting but always fascinating, toward a sure sense of himself and his art.

Michael P. Parker

Other major works

PLAYS: *Aglaura*, 1638; *The Goblins*, 1638; *Brennoralt*, 1646; *The Works of Sir John Suckling: The Plays*, 1971 (L. A. Beaurline, editor).

MISCELLANEOUS: *The Works of Sir John Suckling: The Non-Dramatic Works*, 1971 (Thomas Clayton, editor).

Bibliography

Beaurline, L. A. " 'Why so Pale and Wan': An Essay in Critical Method." In *Seventeenth-Century English Poetry: Modern Essays in Criticism*, edited by William R. Keast. Rev. ed. London: Oxford University Press, 1971. Beaurline sees the poem as a dramatic lyric with a "facetious" (in the sixteenth century sense) narrator whose wit reflects unity in situation, character, argument, and language. Beaurline also discusses the poem as a response to the more complex Metaphysical poetry.

Clayton, Thomas. " 'At Bottom a Criticism of Life': Suckling and the Poetry of Low Seriousness." In *Classic and Cavalier: Essays on Jonson and the Sons of Ben*, edited by Claude J. Summers and Ted-Larry Pebworth. Pittsburgh, Pa: University of Pittsburgh Press, 1982. Clayton's essay provides an overview of Suckling criticism and proceeds to analyze four poems: the early "Upon St. Thomas's Unbelief," "An Answer to Some Verses Made in His Praise," "Why So Pale and Wan," and "Love's Clock." Places Suckling's work in its literary context.

Miner, Earl. *The Cavalier Mode from Jonson to Cotton*. Princeton, N.J.: Princeton University Press, 1971. Though he disapproves of Suckling the man, Miner often finds in him the poetic embodiment of Cavalier love poetry. In fact, Miner believes the "battle of the sexes" cliché was first given Cavalier expression in Suckling's "A Soldier" and "Loves Siege."

Skelton, Robin. *Cavalier Poets*. London: Longmans, Green, 1960. Skelton devotes one chapter of his monograph to Suckling's poetry, which he finds self-conscious and heavily influenced by John Donne. Much of the chapter is devoted to an appreciation of Suckling's "A Ballad upon a Wedding."

Squires, Charles L. *Sir John Suckling*. Boston: Twayne, 1978. Although Squires covers Suckling's life, plays, poems, prose, and literary reputation, he also provides careful readings of several poems, and his criticism of the four plays is detailed. Suckling emerges as the spokesman for the Cavalier era. Supplemented by a chronology and an annotated select bibliography.

Summer, Joseph H. *The Heirs of Donne and Jonson*. Oxford, England: Oxford University Press, 1970. Summers considers Suckling as an exemplar of the gentleman at court and finds in his verse debts to Ben Jonson and John Donne. Treating the narrative voice in poetry, Summers makes interesting distinctions between the Donne originals and the Suckling responses, particularly in the cases of "The Indifferent" and "Love's Deity," which are answered in Suckling's Sonnets II and III.

HENRY HOWARD, EARL OF SURREY

Born: Hunsdon, England; 1517
Died: London, England; January 19, 1547

Principal poetry

An excellent Epitaffe of syr Thomas Wyat, 1542; *The Fourth Boke of Virgill*, 1554 (translation); *Certain Bokes of Virgiles Aenaeis*, 1557 (translation); *Songes and Sonettes*, 1557 (also known as *Tottel's Miscellany*); *The Poems of Henry Howard, Earl of Surrey*, 1920, 1928 (Frederick Morgan Padelford, editor).

Other literary forms

Henry Howard, Earl of Surrey, did not contribute to English literature with any other form besides poetry. His poetic innovations, however, helped to refine and stabilize English poetry.

Achievements

As a translator and original poet, Surrey prepared the way for a number of important developments in English poetry. His translations and paraphrases are not slavishly literal; they are re-creations of classical and Continental works in terms meaningful to Englishmen. He naturalized several literary forms—the sonnet, elegy, epigram, and satire—and showed English poets what could be done with various stanzas, metrical patterns, and rhyme schemes, including terza rima, ottava rima, and poulter's measure. He invented the English or Shakespearean sonnet (three quatrains and a couplet) and set another precedent by using the form for subjects other than love. His poems exerted considerable influence, for they circulated in manuscript for some time before they were printed. Forty of them appear in *Songes and Sonettes* (better known as *Tottel's Miscellany*), a collection of more than 270 works which saw nine editions by 1587 and did much to establish iambic meter in English poetry. Surrey shares with Sir Thomas Wyatt the distinction of having introduced the Petrarchan mode of amatory verse in England.

His innovations in poetic diction and prosody have had more lasting significance. Surrey refined English poetry of aureate diction, the archaic and ornate language cultivated by fifteenth century writers. His elegant diction formed the basis of poetic expression until well into the eighteenth century.

His greatest achievement is his demonstration of the versatility and naturalness in English of the iambic pentameter line. Surrey invented blank verse, which later poets brought to maturity. The metrical regularity of much of his rhymed verse (a regularity perhaps enhanced by Tottel's editor) had a stabilizing effect on English prosody, which had long been in a chaotic state. In *The Arte of English Poesie* (1589), George Puttenham hailed Wyatt and Surrey as "the first reformers of our English meetre and stile," for they "pollished our rude & homely maner of vulgar Poesie." Until the present century Surrey's smoothness was generally preferred to Wyatt's rougher versification.

Surrey's essential quality, a concern with style, informed his poetry, his life, and the Tudor court of which he was a brilliant representative. Consistently as a poet and frequently as a courtier he epitomized learning and grace; for his countrymen he was an exemplar of culture.

Biography

Henry Howard, styled Earl of Surrey from 1524, was the eldest son of Thomas Howard, third Duke of Norfolk. The elder Howard, one of the most powerful leaders of the old nobility, saw to it that his heir received an excellent education. At the age of twelve, Surrey was translating Latin, French, Italian, and Spanish and practicing martial skills. He was selected as the companion of Henry Fitzroy, Henry VIII's illegitimate son who had been created Duke of Richmond. The youths, both proud, impetuous, and insecure, were settled at Windsor in the spring of 1530. Surrey was married in 1532 to Lady Frances de Vere; the couple began living together a few years later, and he was evidently devoted to her for the rest of his life.

Surrey and Richmond accompanied the King to France in the autumn of 1532. The young men resided with the French court, then dominated by Italian culture, for most of the following year. Surrey acquired courtly graces and probably became acquainted with the work of Luigi Alamanni, a Florentine writer of unrhymed verse. Shortly after Surrey and Richmond returned to the English court, the King's son married Surrey's sister Mary.

In 1540, Surrey was appointed steward of the University of Cambridge in recognition of his scholarship. Having also distinguished himself in martial games, in 1541 he was made Knight of the Garter. His military education was completed when he was sent to observe the King's continental wars. The first English artistocrat to be a man of letters, statesman, and soldier, the handsome and spirited Earl was esteemed as a model courtier. During his final seven years, he was occupied with courtly, military, and domestic matters, finding time to write only when he was out of favor with Henry VIII or otherwise in trouble.

Early in 1543, Surrey, Thomas Clere, Thomas Wyatt the Younger, and another young man indulged in disorderly behavior which led to the Earl's brief imprisonment in the Fleet. Still in the King's good graces, he spent most of the next three years serving in France and building an elegant, costly house in the classical style. As Marshal of the Field and commander of Boulogne, he proved to be a competent officer who did not hesitate to risk his own life. He was wounded while leading a courageous assault on Montreuil. After a defeat in a minor skirmish, he was recalled in the spring of 1546.

By that time he had made enemies who were intent on destroying him. He was imprisoned for threatening a courtier who had called Norfolk morally unfit to be regent during the minority of the King's son, Edward. Making much of Surrey's pride in his Plantagenet ancestry, his enemies built a case that he intended to seize power. His request to be allowed to confront his chief accuser in single combat—characteristic of his effort to live by the chivalric code of a vanishing era—was denied. His sister Mary and certain supposed friends testified against him. Maintaining his innocence, Surrey forcefully defended himself and reviled his enemies during an eight-hour trial for treason; but, like many others whom the Tudors considered dangerous or expendable, he was condemned and beheaded on Tower Hill.

Analysis

An aristocrat with a humanistic education, Henry Howard, Earl of Surrey, considered literature a pleasant diversion. As a member of the Tudor court, he was encouraged to display his learning, wit, and eloquence by writing love poems and translating continental and classical works. The poet who cultivated an elegant style was admired and imitated by his peers. Poetry was not considered a medium for self-expression. In the production of literature, as in other polite activities, there were conventions to be observed. Even the works that seem to have grown out of Surrey's personal experience also have roots in classical, Christian, Italian, or native traditions. Surrey is classical in his concern for balance, decorum, fluency, and restraint. These attributes are evident throughout his work—the amatory lyrics, elegies, didactic verses, translations, and biblical paraphrases.

He produced more than two dozen amatory poems. A number of these owe something to Petrarch and other continental poets. The Petrarchan qualities of his work, as well as that of his successors, should not be exaggerated, however, for Tudor and Elizabethan poets were also influenced by native tradition and by rhetorical treatises which encouraged the equating of elegance and excellence. Contemporaries admired the fluency and eloquence which made Surrey, like Petrarch, a worthy model. His sonnet beginning "From Tuscan cam my ladies worthi race," recognized in his own time as polite verse, engendered the romantic legend that he served the Fair Geraldine (Elizabeth Fitzgerald, b. 1528?), but his love poems are now recognized as literary exercises of a type common in Renaissance poetry.

Surrey's courtly lovers complain of wounds; they freeze and burn, sigh, weep, and despair—yet continue to serve Love. Representative of this mode is "Love that doth raine and live within my thought,"one of his five translations or adaptations of sonnets by Petrarch. The poem develops from a military conceit: the speaker's mind and heart are held captive by Love, whose colors are often displayed in his face. When the desired lady frowns, Love retreats to the heart and hides there, leaving the unoffending servant alone, "with shamfast looke," to suffer for his lord's sake. Uninterested in the moral aspects of this situation, Surrey makes nothing of the paradox of Love as conqueror and coward. He does not suggest the lover's ambivalence or explore the lady's motives. Wyatt, whose translation of the same sonnet begins "The longe love, that in my thought doeth harbor," indicates (as Petrarch does) that the lady asks her admirer to become a better man. Surrey's speaker, taught only to "love and suffre paine," gallantly concludes, "Sweet is the death that taketh end by love." The point is not that Surrey's sonnet should be more like Wyatt's but that in this poem and in many of his lyrics Surrey seems less concerned with the complexity of an experience than with his manner of presenting it. Most of the lines are smooth and regularly iambic, although there are five initial trochees. The poem's matter is carefully accommodated to its form. The first quatrain deals with Love, the second with the lady, and the third with the lover's plight. His resolve is summarized in the couplet: despite his undeserved suffering, he will be loyal. The sonnet is balanced and graceful, pleasing by virtue of its musical qualities and intellectual conceit.

Some of the longer poems do portray the emotions of courtly lovers. The speaker in "When sommer toke in hand the winter to assail" observes (as several of Surrey's lovers do) that nature is renewed in spring, while he alone continues to be weak and hopeless. Casting off his despondency, he curses and defies Love. Then, realizing the gravity of his offense, he asks forgiveness and is told by the god that he can atone only by greater suffering. Now "undone for ever more," he offers himself as a "miror" for all lovers: "Strive not with love, for if ye do, it will ye thus befall." Lacking the discipline of the sonnet form, this poem in poulter's measure seems to sprawl. Surrey's amatory verse is generally most successful when he focuses on a relatively simple situation or emotion. "When sommer toke in hand the winter to assail," not his best work, is representative in showing his familiarity with native poetry: it echoes Geoffrey Chaucer's *Troilus and Criseyde* (1382) and describes nature in a manner characteristic of English poets. In seven other love poems, Surrey describes nature in sympathy with or in contrast to the lover's condition.

At a time when most amatory verse was written from the male perspective, Surrey assumed a woman's voice in three of his lyrics. The speaker in "Gyrtt in my giltlesse gowne" defends herself against a charge of craftiness pressed by a male courtier in a companion poem beginning "Wrapt in my carelesse cloke." Accused of encouraging men she does not care for, the lady compares herself to Susanna, who was slandered by corrupt elders. Remarking that her critic himself practices a crafty strategy—trying to ignite a woman's passion by feigning indifference—she asserts that she, like her prototype, will be protected against lust and lies. This pair of poems, if disappointing because Surrey has chosen not to probe more deeply into the behavior and emotions generated by the game of courtly love, demonstrates the poet's skill in presenting a speaker in a clearly defined setting or situation. His finest lyrics may fairly be called dramatic.

Two other monologues, "O happy dames, that may embrace" and "Good ladies, ye that have your pleasure in exyle," are spoken by women lamenting the absence of their beloved lords. They may have been written for Surrey's wife while he was directing the siege of Boulogne. Long separations troubled him, but his requests to the Privy Council for permission to bring his family to France were denied. After an exordium urging her female audience to "mourne with [her] awhyle," the narrator of "Good ladies" describes tormenting dreams of her "sweete lorde" in danger and at play with "his lytle sonne" (Thomas Howard, oldest of the Surreys' five children, was born in 1536). The immediate occasion for this poem, however personal, is consciously literary: the lady, a sorrowful "wight," burns like a courtly lover when her lord is absent, comforted only by the expectation of his return and reflection that "I feele by sower, how sweete is felt the more" (the sweet-sour antithesis was a favorite with courtly poets). Despite the insistent iambic meter characteristic of poulter's measure, one can almost hear a voice delivering these lines. In the best of his love poetry, Surrey makes new wholes of traditional elements.

His elegiac poems reflect his background in rhetoric. Paying tribute to individuals, he would persuade his readers to become more virtuous men and women. "Wyatt resteth here, that quick could never rest," the first of his works to be published, devotes more attention to praise of Wyatt than to lament and consolation. Using the figure of *partitio* (division into parts), he anatomizes the physique of this complete man in order to display his virtues—prudence, integrity, eloquence, justice, courage. Having devoted eight quatrains to praise, Surrey proceeds to the lament—the dead man is "lost" to those he might have inspired—with a consolation at the thought that his spirit is now in heaven. He implies that God has removed "this jewel" in order to punish a nation blind to his worth. In so coupling praise and dispraise, Surrey follows a precedent set by classical rhetoricians. He again eulogized Wyatt in two sonnets, "Dyvers thy death do dyversely bemoan" and "In the rude age," both attacking Wyatt's enemies. The former devotes a quatrain to each of two kinds of mourners, hypocrites who only seem to grieve and malefactors who "Weape envyous teares heer [his] fame so good." In the sestet, he sets himself apart: *he* feels the loss of so admirable a man. Here, as in a number of his sonnets, Surrey achieves a harmony of form and content. There is no evidence that he knew Wyatt personally. His tributes to the older courtier are essentially public performances, but they convey admiration and regret and offer a stinging rebuke to courtiers who do not come up to Wyatt's standard.

Many sixteenth century poets wrote elegies for public figures; more than twenty appear in *Tottel's Miscellany*. Surrey, as indicated above, was familiar with the literary tribute. In "Norfolk sprang thee," an epitaph for his squire Thomas Clere (d. 1545), he uses some of the conventions of epideictic poetry to express esteem, as well as grief, for the dead. Developed according to the biographical method of praise (seen also in "From Tuscan cam my ladies worthi race"), the sonnet specifies Clere's origins and personal relationships; it traces his career from his birth in Norfolk to his mortal wound at Montreuil—incurred while saving Surrey's life—to his burial in the Howards' chapel at Lambeth. By "placing" Clere geographically and within the contexts of chivalric and human relationships, Surrey immortalizes a brave and noble person. He has succeeded in writing a fresh, even personal poem while observing literary and rhetorical conventions.

Personal feeling and experience certainly went into "So crewell prison," a lament for Richmond (d. 1536) and the poet's youthful fellowship with him at Windsor—ironically, the place of his confinement as a penalty for having struck Edward Seymour. Subtly alluding to the *ubi sunt* tradition, he mentions remembered places, events, and activities—green and graveled courts, dewy meadows, woods, brightly dressed ladies, dances, games, chivalric competition, shared laughter and confidences, promises made and kept—as he does so, conveying his sense of loss. He praises, and longs for, not only his friend but also the irrecoverable past. Of Richmond's soul he says nothing. His consolation, if so it may be called, is that the loss of his companion lessens the pain of his loss of freedom. "So crewell prison," perhaps Surrey's best poem is at once conventional and personal.

Taught to regard the courtier as a counselor, he wrote a few explicitly didactic pieces. His sonnet about Sardanapulus, "Th' Assyryans king, in peas with fowle desyre," portrays a lustful, cowardly ruler. Such depravity, Surrey implies, endangers virtue itself. The poem may allude to the King, who had executed two Howard queens. (Surrey witnessed Anne Boleyn's trial and Catherine Howard's execution.) The degenerate monarch in Surrey's sonnet, however, bears few resemblances to Henry VIII, who had often shown his regard for Norfolk's heir and Richmond's closest friend. John Gower, John Lydgate, and other poets had also told the story of Sardanapulus as a "mirror" for princes. Surrey's "Laid in my quyett bedd" draws upon Horace's *Ars Poetica* (13-8 B.C) and First Satire (35 B.C.). The aged narrator, after surveying the ages of man, remarks that people young and old always wish to change their estate; he concludes that boyhood is the happiest time, though youths will not realize this truth before they become decrepit. Like certain of the love poems, "Laid in my quyett bedd" illustrates Surrey's dramatic ability.

The mock-heroic "London, hast thou accused me" was probably written while Surrey was imprisoned for harassing and brawling with some citizens and breaking windows with a stonebow. As C. W. Jentoft points out, the satirist, presenting himself as a God-sent "scourge for synn," seems to be delivering an oration. "Thy wyndowes had don me no spight," he explains; his purpose was to awaken Londoners secretly engaged in deadly sins to their peril. Appropriating the structure of the classical oration, he becomes, in effect, not the defendant but the prosecutor of a modern Babylon. The peroration, fortified with scriptural phrasings, warns of divine judgment.

Surrey's translations also reflect the young aristocrat's classical and humanistic education. He translated two poems advocating the golden mean—a Horatian ode and an epigram by Martial. In the former ("Of thy lyfe, Thomas") he imitates the terseness of the original. "Marshall, the thinges for to attayne," the first English translation of that work, is also remarkably concise. His intention to re-create in English the style of a Latin poet is evident in his translations of the second and fourth books of the *Aeneid*. He did not attempt to reproduce Vergil's unrhymed hexameters in English alexandrines (as Richard Stanyhurst was to do) or to translate them into rhymed couplets (as the Scottish poet Gawin Douglas had done). Familiar with the decasyllabic line of Chaucer and other native poets and the *verso sciolto* (unrhymed verse) of sixteenth century Italy, he devised blank verse, the form that was to be refined by Christopher Marlowe, William Shakespeare, and John Milton.

Textual scholars have encountered several problems in studying Surrey's translation of the *Aeneid*. His manuscripts are not extant, and all printed versions appeared after his death. The work may have been undertaken as early as 1538 or as late as 1544; in the light of his service at court and in France, it seems likely that the translation was done intermittently. Modern scholars now favor an early period of composition, which would make this translation prior to many of Surrey's other works and help to account for their refined, decorous style.

Another issue is the relationship of Surrey's work to the *Eneados* of Gawin Douglas (1474?-1522), whose translation had circulated widely in manuscript during Surrey's youth. According to Florence Ridley, "In more than 40 percent of his lines Surrey's wording was noticeably influenced by that of Douglas" (*The "Aeneid" of Henry Howard, Earl of Surrey*, 1963). In Book Four, perhaps completed later than Book Two, Surrey borrowed from Douglas less frequently. There is other evidence that his style was maturing and becoming more flexible: more frequent run-ons, feminine endings, pauses within the line, and metrical variations.

The distinctive qualities of Surrey's translation are largely owing to his imitation of Vergil's style. A young humanist working in an immature language and using a new form, Surrey was trying, as Italian translators had done, to re-create in the vernacular his Latin master's compactness, restraint, and stateliness. He did not always succeed. Generally avoiding both prosaic and aureate vocabulary, he uses relatively formal diction. To a modern reader accustomed to the blank verse developed by later poets, the iambic meter is so regular as to be somewhat monotonous. By means of patterned assonance, consonance, and internal rhyme, as well as the placement of caesuras, he has achieved a flowing movement which approximates Vergilian verse paragraphs. Phonetic effects often pleasing in themselves heighten emotional intensity and help to establish the phrase, not the line, as the poetic unit. It is not surprising, then, that Thomas Warton called Surrey England's first classical poet. Imitation led to innovation, the creation of a form for English heroic poetry. Even though blank verse did not come into general use until late in the sixteenth century, Surrey's achievement remains monumental.

The paraphrases of Ecclesiastes 1-5 and Psalms 55, 73, and 88, Surrey's most nearly autobiographical works, portray the "slipper state" of life in the Tudor court. Probably written during his final imprisonment in late 1546, they speak of vanity and vexation of spirit and cry out against vicious enemies, treacherous friends, and a tyrant who drinks the blood of innocents. Like Wyatt, whose penitential psalms he admired, he used Joannes Campensis' Latin paraphrases which had been published in 1532. Surrey's translations are free, amplifying and at times departing from the Vulgate and Campensis, as in this line from his version of Ecclesiastes 2: "By princely acts [such as the pursuit of pleasure and building of fine houses] strave I still to make my fame indure." Although his background was Catholic, these poems express Protestant sentiments.

In his versions of Psalms 73 and 88 he speaks of God's "elect" and "chosen," apparently placing himself in that company. While praying for forgiveness in Psalm 73, he notes that his foes are going unscathed and asks why he is "scourged still, that no offence have doon." Psalm 55 calls for divine help as he faces death and exulting enemies; at the end of this unpolished, perhaps unfinished poem, Surrey completely departs from his printed sources to inveigh against wolfish adversaries. The time to live was almost past, but it was not yet the time to keep silence. Like the other biblical paraphrases, this work has chiefly biographical interest. Expecting imminent execution, Surrey was still experimenting with prosody: Psalm 55 is the one poem in this group to be written in unrhymed hexameters rather than poulter's measure. Even in his last works, the poet is generally detached and self-effacing. Surrey's greatest legacy to English poets is a concern for fluent, graceful expression.

Mary De Jong

Bibliography

Casady, Edwin. *Henry Howard, Earl of Surrey.* New York: Modern Language Association of America, 1938. While Casady's book is essentially a biography of Surrey, it contains a twenty-page appendix that evaluates Surrey's "contribution to English literature." Casady acknowledges Surrey's debt to Sir Thomas Wyatt but claims that Surrey created a fresh poetic diction and experimented with new metrical forms. Provides an overview of Surrey's verse but does not analyze any poem in depth.

Lever, J. W. *The Elizabethan Love Sonnet.* 1956. Reprint. London: Methuen, 1978. Through a comparison of Surrey's love poems with their Petrarchan originals, Lever demonstrates Surrey's experimentation and use of sensory images. For Lever, the experimental early love poems are inferior to the later poems addressed to a noble lady, Sir Thomas Wyatt, a comrade, and Henry VIII.

Mazzaro, Jerome. *Transformations in the Renaissance English Lyric.* Ithaca, N.Y.: Cornell University Press, 1970. Mazzaro regards Surrey's poetry as completing the process of humanizing the lyric, of preferring the literal to the metaphorical, and of describing a natural rather than a moral world. He finds "When Raging Love" modern in its logical framework and in its emphasis on linear development rather than repetition.

Spearing, A. C. *Medieval to Renaissance in English Poetry.* Cambridge, England: Cambridge University Press, 1985. After discussing Renaissance classicism in Surrey's poetry, Spearing proceeds to extended analyses of three poems: two epitaphs on Sir Thomas Wyatt and "So crewell prison," the poem about Surrey's imprisonment at Windsor.

Thomson, Patricia. "Wyatt and Surrey." In *English Poetry and Prose, 1540-1674*, edited by Christopher Ricks. London: Barrie & Jenkins, 1970. Reprint. New York: Peter Bedrick Books, 1987. Thomson first compares Sir Thomas Wyatt and Surrey to John Skelton, whose poetry was primarily late medieval, then discusses Surrey and particularly Wyatt as inheritors of the Petrarchan tradition. Contains a fairly extensive discussion of Surrey's translation of the *Aeneid*.

MAY SWENSON

Born: Logan, Utah; May 28, 1919
Died: Ocean View, Delaware; December 4, 1989

Principal poetry

Another Animal: Poems, 1954; *A Cage of Spines*, 1958; *To Mix with Time: New and Selected Poems*, 1963; *Half Sun Half Sleep*, 1967; *Iconographs*, 1970; *Windows and Stones: Selected Poems by Tomas Tranströmer*, 1972 (translation, with Leif Sjöberg); *New and Selected Things Taking Place*, 1978; *In Other Words*, 1987.

Other literary forms

May Swenson's forays away from poetry included short fiction, drama, and criticism. A number of her short stories have appeared in magazines and anthologies. A play, *The Floor*, was produced in New York in 1966 and published a year later. Her best-known critical essay, "The Experience of Poetry in a Scientific Age," appeared in *Poets on Poetry* (1966). She also wrote the introduction to the 1962 Collier edition of Edgar Lee Masters' *Spoon River Anthology*.

Three books for young people have expanded the audience for Swenson's poetry. *Poems to Solve* (1966) and *More Poems to Solve* (1971) are selections of riddle poems taken from her other books. For still younger children there is *The Guess and Spell Coloring Book* (1976). Many poets owe a heavy debt to their childhoods, and few have discharged that debt more gratefully or delightfully. As a child, Swenson learned from her immigrant parents the language that she would later render into English in *Windows and Stones: Selected Poems by Tomas Tranströmer* (1972), a translation (with Leif Sjöberg) for which she won the International Poetry Forum Translation Medal. She recorded her own poems on both the Folkways and the Caedmon labels.

Achievements

As traditional as she was inventive, as alliteratively Anglo-Saxon as she was typographically contemporary, Swenson was well respected among twentieth century American poets. Her thirty-five-year career was an ongoing celebration of language wed to life-as-it-is. Her sharp-eyed curiosity led her to address a broader and more diverse range of subjects than did many of her contemporaries; she was rural and urban, scientific and mythic, innocent and worldly, and, sometimes, even literary; and she could be any number of these within the same poem. Once she fixed her attention on something, she had a remarkable gift for letting that object of her curiosity find its voice and for allowing the poem to determine its own form. No poet wrote more perceptively or persuasively about birds—or about astronauts.

Swenson was a member of the National Institute of Arts and Letters and a chancellor of the Academy of American Poets. She was awarded grants and fellowships by a number of agencies and organizations, including the Ford, Rockefeller, and Guggenheim Foundations, and the National Endowment for the Arts. In 1968, she won the Shelley Memorial Award, and in 1981, she shared with fellow poet Howard Nemerov the prestigious Bollingen Prize in Poetry, in recognition of her collection *New and Selected Things Taking Place.* She has, as well, served as a judge for the Lamont Award of the Academy of American Poets and for the National Book Awards. Her frequent readings and visiting professorships at a number of colleges and universities have further enhanced her contribution to American letters.

Biography

The daughter of Swedish immigrants, May Swenson grew up in Logan, Utah, a small college town. Her parents had left behind both their native land and their Lutheran faith to follow the teachings of the Mormon Church, which Swenson came to reject in spite of (or perhaps because of) her strict upbringing among the Latter-day Saints. As the oldest daughter in a large family, she learned early to value solitude, and at the age of thirteen, alone with her father's typewriter, she pecked out with two fingers a short piece she had written. When she looked at the resultant shape of the words on the page, she said, "This is a poem"; her life's work had begun.

Swenson's father taught woodworking and carpentry at Utah State University, which at the time was known as Utah State Agricultural College. Swenson studied English and art there and received her B.A. degree in 1939. She then worked as a reporter for a Salt Lake City newspaper; but after about a year, she made her break with home and family and moved to New York's Greenwich Village. Before gaining recognition as a poet, she worked at a variety of office jobs and, after a few years, began publishing in various magazines, including *Poetry* and *The New Yorker.* In 1954, a selection of her poems was chosen to appear with the work of two other poets (Harry Duncan and Murray Noss) in the first volume of Scribner's *Poets of Today* series. Within the next few years, she began the round of fellowships, residencies, and visiting professorships that sustained her for the rest of her career. Among her more notable positions and appointments were the editorship of New Directions Press, 1959-1966; positions as poet-in-residence at Purdue University, 1966-1967, at the University of North Carolina at Greensboro, 1968-1969 and 1975, at Lethbridge University in the Canadian province of Alberta, 1970, and at the University of California at Riverside, 1973; she also held a position on the staff of the Bread Loaf Writers' Conference, 1976. In addition, she spent time at the Yaddo and MacDowell colonies, sojourned in Europe, and traveled widely in the United States, giving readings and teaching. From 1970 until her death in 1989, Swenson and her longtime friend and companion, Rozanne Knudson, made their home in what Swenson called an "Adirondack shack" in Sea Cliff, New York, on Long Island Sound.

Analysis

In his introduction to Volume I of the *Poets of Today* series, John Hall Wheelock assessed the task of the contemporary poet as one of rediscovery and revelation, and in which a world gone stale must be renewed: "A poem gives the world back to the maker of the poem, in all its original strangeness, the shock of its first surprise. It is capable of doing the same for the rest of us." That volume included May Swenson's first book-length collection of poems, *Another Animal.* In the thirty-five years to follow, no voice in contemporary poetry showed more commitment to that task of poetic revelation and renewal. Although she was often spoken of as a nature poet, Swenson was as adept at celebrating the skyline of Brooklyn as a quiet wood. She was equally at home with astronauts and angels, with swans and subways. If she could bring her senses to bear upon a subject, it was the stuff of poetry.

Swenson's verse can be classified as poetry of the senses—especially of and for the eye. A good starting point for a consideration of her work is "Horses in Central Park," a celebration of light, color and texture: "Colors of horses like leaves or stones/ or wealthy textures/ liquors of light." A horse is not, at first glance, very much like a leaf or a stone, but Swenson always looks past that first glance to something more. The alliteration in the third line is only a mild example of her wordplay, which ranges from pure Anglo-Saxon to latter-day E. E. Cummings. Everything works together; the poem introduces a liquid tone, the sense suggests intoxication. What follows is no mere catalog of horses, but the play of light and words put through their paces. There is an autumnal truth, a lean horse the color of "sere October," fall cantering through fall. The procession continues, as "mole-gray back" and a "dappled haunch" pass by, along with "fox-red bay/ and buckskin blond as wheat." The reader takes in all the richness of the harvest and of October's light, distilled into the colors and liquid movements of horses. One need only witness the "Sober chestnut burnished/ by his sweat/ to veined and glowing oak" to let one's eyes at last convince the mind of what it may have shied away from at the poem's opening. Not only does this comparison work, of horse to oak leaf; it could not be better. This effortless rhetoric of the senses distinguishes Swenson's verse. One cannot believe everything one sees or hears, she seems to say, but one had better believe *in* it.

Swenson's verse is variously described as fierce, fresh, inquisitive, innovative, and sensuous. Her frequent experimentation with the physical appearance of her poems, however, has caused such adjectives to alight in the wrong places. Though she had dealt from the start in unorthodox punctuations, spacings, and typographic arrangements, Swenson's experiments in this direction culminated in *Iconographs.* This collection of shaped poems—"image-writing," as she described them—is mistakenly referred to by some as concrete poetry. Swenson makes it clear in an afterword that the poems were all finished down to the last word before being arranged into shapes that would enhance the words. In visual terms, the poems are the paintings, the shapes only frames. Thus, a poem on a José de Rivera mobile twists and turns on the page. In a poem called "The Blue Bottle," the words outline the shape of a bottle; in "How Everything Happens," a poem written after close observation of how ocean waves gather, break, and recede, the lines of the poem gather, break, and recede in a visual variation on the poem's message. Such devices are certainly consistent with Swenson's belief that words are, among other things, objects, and that a poem is itself an object, to be encountered by the eye and its companion senses, not merely by the intellect. These shaped poems are innovative enough in their appearance before they are even read, but it is not in their shapes that they succeed as poetry. When these or any of Swenson's poems succeed it is because of an absolute sureness of touch and rightness of language.

Her images are at times startling, but they work upon the senses and emotions in such a way that readers cannot help giving in to their aptness and inevitability. In "The Garden at St. John's," a mother caresses her baby, whose hair is "as soft as soft/ as down as the down in the wingpits of angels." Any momentary hesitation over "wingpits" is lulled by the enchanting repetition of "soft" and "down," and the image rings, or rather, whispers, true. "Water Picture," the upside-down world reflected in the surface of a pond would seem to be a conventional enough idea for a poem, but Swenson is not so interested in *ideas* as in *things*, and it is, indeed, the *thing* that finds expression here. Everyone has gazed into still water and watched the reflections, but when, in this poem, "A flag/ wags like a fishhook/ down there in the sky," when a swan bends to the surface to "kiss herself," and the "tree-limbs tangle, the bridge/ folds like a fan," one is *there* with a powerful immediacy.

Again and again Swenson affirmed that the wonders of the world are too good merely to be described or talked about. They must be shared as directly as possible. Her mode of sharing experience was to involve herself completely in an experience, to "live into" the experience in order to express it. Thus, there is much more to poetry than the mere recording or labeling of experience. Some of Swenson's most successful poems came out of the avoidance of simply giving a name to an object. Many of these are her "riddling" poems, in which the object shared is never named, but only hinted at. As one might expect, the images are heavily sensory, most often visual. One of her best known riddle poems is "By Morning":

> Some for everyone
> plenty

and more coming
Fresh   dainty   airily arriving
everywhere at once.

As with most of Swenson's riddles, the clues reveal rather than obscure their answer. One need not read far into this particular poem to realize that it is about snow, but the real charm of the poem lies much deeper than the simple solution of the riddle. Systems of imagery are at work as "a gracious fleece" that spreads "like youth   like wheat/ over the city." "Fleece" is picked up several lines down in the prediction that "Streets will be   fields/ cars be fumbling sheep." "Youth" and "wheat" resolve themselves together at the poem's conclusion: "A deep bright harvest will be seeded/ in a night/ By morning we'll be   children/ feeding on manna/ a new loaf on every doorsill." The avoidance of any explicit reference to snow is part of the poem's success, but the real strength of the piece is in the same rightness of expression that Swenson's work so consistently displays, right down to the use of extra space between certain words to vary the tempo, and, at times, the sense of a line.

In her work of "living into" the world, Swenson explored one territory which many poets have avoided—science. She wrote poems on electronic sound patterns and on the DNA molecule, as well as a number of poems on America's space program. To one who can derive so much wonder from the ordinary and familiar, the astronaut is a wonderful figure, though not solemnly so. In "August 19, Pad 19," the astronaut waits in his cramped capsule, "Positioned for either breech birth/ or urn burial," anticipating the liftoff that will drag him "backward through 121 sunsets." Just before the mission is aborted on account of weather, he puts himself into an unheroic perspective:

Never so impotent, so important.
So naked, wrapped, equipped, and immobile,
cared for by 5000 nurses.
Let them siphon my urine to the nearest star.

The treatment is more playful than disrespectful. The fun is not at the astronaut's experience; on the contrary, he knows to what extent he is to be admired, to what extent to be pitied, yet asks for neither admiration nor pity. He is no longer so distant from humanity as he might have seemed in space, umbilicaled, "belted and bolted in" ten stories above the pad. As he gazes through the capsule's tiny window seeing "innocent drops of rain" and "Lightning's golden sneer," the reader can sneer right back with him; the same things that ruin simple Sunday picnics ruin his splendid plans as well.

To say Swenson strives for variety in her work would not be quite accurate. Her variety comes naturally; more often than not it comes from within a poem. Once a poem has found its form, discovered its voice, and appeared in print, she rarely revises. An apparent exception to this rule is the selection of formerly shaped poems which appear in *New and Selected Things Taking Place*, minus their iconographic frames. Probably this indicates that, having done as much as she cared to do with the iconographic poem, she chose to second-guess herself and present some of these in more conventional configurations. A thorough study of this recent and comprehensive collection reveals something else. Since her early work, Swenson has moved toward more conventional form in her poems; certainly her punctuation has grown less experimental. Behind her newer verses is a mature poet, more aware than ever of her considerable strengths and less willing to divert the reader's attention in any way from what she does best. One of the finest poems of her later years is "October." It speaks in hard, clear images of growing older gracefully. In one of the poem's seven sections:

> I sit with braided fingers
> and closed eyes
> in a span of late sunlight.
> The spokes are closing.
> It is fall: warm milk of light,
> though from an aging breast.

Here, many years after the dappled light of "Horses in Central Park," light keeps its liquid quality but is less intoxicating, a more nourishing, comforting distillate. In this "warm milk" of a later, mellower light, the watcher is moved to something like prayer, in spite of herself.

Swenson was not an intensely *literary* poet, conscious of working in a particular tradition. Certainly any poet who addressed herself so fully to "the thing" could be expected to feel a special kinship with such writers as Marianne Moore and Elizabeth Bishop. Swenson acknowledged that kinship, as well as a special feeling for another master of wordplay, E. E. Cummings. There are, as well, poets whom she considered "healthy to read," and they are rather a mixed bag—Theodore Roethke, Gerard Manley Hopkins, Emily Dickinson, Walt Whitman, and among Swenson's contemporaries, Richard Wilbur, Anthony Hecht, Anne Sexton, and James Merrill, but this is no matter of influence or imitation. Swenson acknowledged as much affinity with such visual artists as Georgia O'Keeffe and Marcel Duchamp as with any literary artist. The poetry of others rarely moves her to song, and "literary" poems are rare among her works. Typically, a poem on Robert Frost, "R. F. at Bread Loaf His Hand Against a Tree," avoids the temptation to indulge in literary assessment and instead addresses Frost as part of the literal scene: "Companions he and the cross/ grained bark. . . ." What might have been, in other hands, literary history in verse is rendered instead into an exuberant portrait in wordplay. For purposes of inspiration, Swenson was less likely to look to literature than to the newspaper, the zoo, *Scientific American*, a walk in the woods, or a ride on the subway.

In this regard, Swenson's last volume of poems, *In Other Words*, is of a piece with her earlier work. Here are plenty of examples of Swenson's gift for discovering poetry taking place in unexpected places—a hospital blood test; the consignment of Charlie McCarthy, perhaps history's most famous ventriloquist's dummy, to the Smithsonian after the death of Edgar Bergen; a magazine ad for a digital watch. In Swenson's hands, all are the stuff of poetry.

A package received in the mail prompts "A Thank-You Letter." For the package? No, for "the wonderful cord 174″ long" that bound the package. The poem ends with the narrator's cat entangled in the string, "having a wonderful puzzle-playtime." The narrator admits,

> . . . I haven't yet
>
> taken the sturdy paper off your package.
> I hardly feel I want to. The gift has been
> given! For which, thank you ever so much.

The process in this poem in many ways encapsulates Swenson's approach to poetry as a whole: Swenson's approach is eclectic in the very best sense, for "eclectic" means, at its root, not "to throw together" but "to pick out."

Because she picked and chose so well, because she was so much a part of the experiences that she made into poetry, and because her poems are so resistant to paraphrase and explication, her works are their own best commentary. "A Navajo Blanket" is a sort of guided tour of one of the "Eye-dazzlers the Indians weave." Having worked in from the edges over paths of brilliant colors,

> You can sleep at the center,
> attended by Sun that never fades, by Moon
> that cools. Then, slipping free of zigzag and
> hypnotic diamond, find your way out
> by the spirit trail, a faint Green thread that
> secretly crosses the border, where your mind
> is rinsed and returned to you like a white cup.

No matter what colors she worked in, what patterns she wove, Swenson was always careful to include that "faint Green thread" that was her perpetual wonder at things as they are. By following that thread, the reader can embrace the world, a world clean and new, good to look upon, good to hold.

Richard A. Eichwald

Other major works
PLAY: *The Floor*, 1966.

NONFICTION: *The Contemporary Poet as Artist and Critic*, 1964; "The Experience of Poetry in a Scientific Age" in *Poets on Poetry*, 1966.

CHILDREN'S LITERATURE: *Poems to Solve*, 1966; *More Poems to Solve*, 1971; *The Guess and Spell Coloring Book*, 1976.

Bibliography

Gould, Jean. *Modern American Women Poets.* New York: Dodd, Mead, 1984. Gould's volume of literary biographies contains the single most complete account of Swenson's life. It includes details of her childhood, the influence—or lack of influence—of her parents' Mormon faith, and her associations with other writers, especially Robert Frost and Elizabeth Bishop. Gould also explores Swenson's longtime relationship with teacher and children's author Rozanne Knudson.

Hammond, Karla. "An Interview with May Swenson: July 14, 1978." *Parnassus: Poetry in Review* 7 (Fall/Winter, 1978): 60-75. In this piece, Swenson talks in some detail on a range of subjects, from her childhood and education to her writing habits, her approach to poetry, and her admiration for such poets as Elizabeth Bishop and E. E. Cummings. Throughout, she illustrates the discussion with examples from her work.

Howard, Richard. *Alone with America.* New York: Atheneum, 1969. This book-length study of modern American poets includes a chapter on Swenson, "Turned Back to the Wild by Love." Howard provides a fine, detailed study of Swenson's poetics and technique, illustrated by dozens of examples from her early poems.

Salter, Mary Jo. "No Other Words." *The New Republic* 201 (March 7, 1988): 40-41. This review of Swenson's last volume of poems, *In Other Words*, offers a brief but perceptive discussion of Swenson's poetic strengths and limitations. Salter compares her work to that of poets as diverse as Elizabeth Bishop, Gerard Manley Hopkins, and George Herbert.

Stanford, Ann. "May Swenson: The Art of Perceiving." *The Southern Review* 5 (Winter, 1969): 58-75. This essay treats Swenson as a master of observation and perception. Through numerous examples—drawn mostly from the poet's nature poems—Stanford explores Swenson's ability to surprise and delight the reader by observing the world from unexpected angles, or by simply noticing and recording the all-too-easily overlooked detail.

JONATHAN SWIFT

Born: Dublin, Ireland; November 30, 1667
Died: Dublin, Ireland; October 19, 1745

Principal poetry
"Verses wrote in a Lady's Ivory Table-Book," 1698(?); "Mrs. Harris' Petition," 1701; "A Description of the Morning," 1709; "A Description of a City Shower," 1710; "Mary the Cook-Maid's Letter to Dr. Sheridan," 1718; "Phillis: Or, The Progress of Love," 1719; "The Progress of Beauty," 1719-1720; "The Progress of Poetry," 1720; "The Progress of Marriage," 1721-1722; "A Satirical Elegy on the Death of a late Famous General," 1722; *Cadenus and Vanessa*, 1726; "Mad Mullinix and Timothy," 1728; "The Lady's Dressing Room," 1730; *Verses on the Death of Dr. Swift*, 1731; "The Day of Judgement," 1731; "A Beautiful Young Nymph Going to Bed," 1731; "Strephon and Chloe," 1731; "Cassinus and Peter," 1731; "A Love Song in the Modern Taste," 1733; "An Epistle to a Lady," 1733; *On Poetry: A Rapsody*, 1733; "A Character, Panegyric, and Description of the Legion Club," 1736; *The Poems of Jonathan Swift*, 1937, 1958 (Harold Williams, editor, 3 volumes).

Other literary forms
Jonathan Swift's major satires in prose are *A Tale of a Tub* (1704) and *Gulliver's Travels* (originally entitled *Travels into Several Remote Nations of the World . . . by Lemuel Gulliver*, 1726); both are included in the most useful general collection, *The Prose Works of Jonathan Swift* (1939-1968, Herbert Davis, editor, 14 volumes); but *"A Tale of a Tub" to Which Is Added "The Battle of the Books" and the "Mechanical Operation of the Spirit"* (1958, A. C. Guthkelch and D. Nichol Smith, editors) is also notable. Swift is also master of the short satiric treatise, as evidenced by *An Argument Against Abolishing Christianity* (1708) and *A Modest Proposal for Preventing the Children of Poor People of Ireland from Being a Burden to Their Parents* (1729). Noteworthy as well are his comical satires in prose, best exemplified by the "Bickerstaff" pamphlets against Partridge the Almanac-Maker (such as *Predictions for the Year 1708*, 1708; *The Accomplishment of the First of Mr. Bickerstaff's Predictions*, 1708; and *A Vindication of Isaac Bickerstaff, Esq.*, 1709). Swift's major political diatribes are included in *The Drapier's Letters to the People of Ireland* (1935); other notable political writings include his contributions to *The Examiner* (1710-1711); and the treatise termed *The Conduct of the Allies* (1711). The letters are assembled in *The Correspondence of Jonathan Swift* (1963-1965, Harold Williams, editor, 5 volumes). Equally interesting is his chatty and informal *Journal to Stella* (1766, 1768).

Achievements
By common consent, Swift is perhaps the greatest satirist who ever lived.

His prose creation *A Tale of a Tub* is clearly one of the densest and richest satires ever composed. His terse mock-treatise *A Modest Proposal* is considered the most brilliant short prose satire in the English language. The long pseudonarrative of his later years, *Gulliver's Travels*, is acknowledged to be his masterpiece.

For this very mastery, Swift was in his time considerably dreaded and feared. In his case, the pen *was* mightier than the sword, and politicians trembled and dunces quavered at his power. In many instances, his satire could instantly shade into invective, and Swift wrote many powerful tirades against individuals whom he openly named, reducing them to impotence by powerful mockery and public scorn. At one time, he was the most important political writer for the ruling Tory party; his essays, projects, and analyses were a potent force in the halls of government.

Yet all was not terror, violence, and indecorum. In addition to his nasty side—his "serious air"—he could, as Alexander Pope acknowledged, praising him in *The Dunciad* (1728-1743), take his rightful place as a great comedian; he could "laugh and shake in Rab'lais' easy chair." Swift was terribly potent precisely because he could be so terribly funny. He was an absolute master at writing little idiotic mock-solemn invitations to dinner, in composing virtually pig-Latin poetry, in donning masks and voices and assuming the roles of others. He will be remembered as the imitator of the voices of dunces: the perplexed but grandly complacent "Modern" hack writer of *A Tale of a Tub*; the utterly self-satisfied Isaac Bickerstaff (the Astrologer who could See Into and Predict the Future); the ceaselessly chattering poor female servant, Frances Harris; the quintessential public-defender M. B.; the "Patriot" Drapier; and the tautological and ever-to-be-befooled Lemuel Gulliver.

Finally, Swift was a poet of considerable skill. He deprecated his verse; he preferred throughout his career the jog-trot of the octosyllabic line, deliberately avoiding the heroic couplet that was in his day the reigning poetic form. He chose to treat "low" topics and paltry occasions in his verse, and he was ever fond of coarseness: many of his poems take up nearly unmentionable topics—particularly excrement. For such reasons, Swift was for long not taken seriously as a poet; the staid Victorians, for example, found in him nothing of the Arnoldian "high seriousness" and grim cheerfulness that heralded and endorsed progress. Currently, however, there is a renewed interest in Swift's poetry; a flurry of studies is annually appearing; and in this realm too, Jonathan Swift is coming to occupy his rightful—and rightfully very high—place.

Biography

Jonathan Swift, as Louis Bredvold has observed, was the "greatest genius" among the Augustan wits, and even more clearly "one of the most absorbing and enigmatic personalities in literature." He was a man of brute talent with

the pen, a man with remarkable intensity and drive, yet one who was fre-
quently alienated and rebuffed. Of English parentage, Swift was born in 1667
in Dublin, seven months after his father's death. In straitened circumstances,
Swift was reared in Ireland. His father had settled there at the time of the
Restoration of Charles II (1660); his paternal grandfather had been an
Anglican minister in England. Swift and his mother were dependent upon a
relatively well-to-do uncle, who did see to young Jonathan's education at
Kilkenny Grammar School (at that time, the best in the land). Swift's mother,
Abigail, returned to England to live; Swift remained in Ireland, and subse-
quently, with the help of his uncle, attended Trinity College, Dublin.

Going to England in 1689, Swift obtained a secretaryship under Sir William
Temple at Moor Park in Surrey, where he resided with few interruptions for
some ten years. Temple had been a major diplomat, an ambassador to The
Hague, and a wise conservative who had even arranged for the future King
William's marriage. Twice refusing to become Secretary of State, he had at
last retired with dignity and honor to a rural plot. At the least, Swift could
anticipate great instruction and "connections," but he never did realize any
actual preferment from this affiliation. It was also at Moor Park that Swift
met "Stella" (Esther Johnson), the eight-year-old daughter of Sir William's
housekeeper; a compelling and intimate relationship (still not fully fathomed
or explained) developed over the years between the two, which led to Stella's
following Swift to Ireland and living close to him for the remainder of her
life. Neither ever married. In 1694 Swift became an Anglican priest in Dublin,
with a remote parish in the isolated countryside at Kilroot. Nevertheless,
Swift stayed mostly at Moor Park in England until Temple's death in 1699,
whereupon he accepted the chaplaincy to the Earl of Berkeley, who was
settling in Ireland as Lord Justice. Still, preferment and advancement eluded
the young man.

After several false starts in literature, Swift found his true voice—in prose
and in verse—as a satirist. He wrote many short, incisive poems in the early
years of the new century, and a prose masterpiece, *A Tale of a Tub*, appeared
in 1704. The next decade was perhaps the most crucial in his career, for Swift
helped the Tories gain office after a lengthy absence, and he became their
chief spokesman, apologist, and potent political satirist (1710-1714). His power
and success in London were inordinate; he did not lack glory. During this
period Swift held court with the brightest of the Tory wits in the so-called
Scriblerus Club (the most famous of its kind in literary history), which included
such distinguished authors as Alexander Pope, Dr. John Arbuthnot, Matthew
Prior, and John Gay.

Ireland, however, could not be avoided for long. Swift had held (though
as an absentee) a post as minister to the parish of Laracor in Ireland, and the
most he could extract from his political allies (he had every reason to expect
more) was the Deanship of St. Patrick's in Dublin. Moreover, there were

other reasons for disillusionment: the Tory leaders had taken to squabbling among themselves, and their authority became precarious. Unable to patch up this rift, Swift sadly withdrew from London. The Tories fell resoundingly from power in 1714, with the sudden death of Queen Anne. There were immediate political repercussions: a Whig government even went so far as to seek to imprison the Tory leadership. Swift had already retired—for safety and out of necessity—to Ireland. He would seldom again be able to return.

After a period of quiet adjustment to the catastrophe which brought him to exile (1714-1720), Swift finally came to terms with his destiny and entered upon a great creative period. From 1719 on he wrote a great deal of poetry, and produced his prose masterpieces, *Gulliver's Travels* in 1726 and *A Modest Proposal* in 1729. His great period culminated with *Verses on the Death of Dr. Swift* (1731) and *On Poetry: A Rapsody* (1733).

In his old age, Swift was kept busy with cathedral affairs, with overseeing an extensive edition of his "Collected Works" being printed by George Faulkner in Dublin throughout the 1730's, and with polishing old works that he had not previously brought to fruition. His health—never too hardy— commenced rapidly to decline. After what is believed to have been a crippling stroke in 1742, Swift was declared incompetent, and others were assigned by a court to handle his affairs. He died in October, 1745, and was buried in St. Patrick's Cathedral. As a final touch of satiric bravado, Swift in his will left his little wealth for the establishment of a "hospital" or asylum for incurables— both fools and madmen. Jonathan Swift, if he had had the last word, would have implied that among mankind, there are fools and knaves—and little else.

Analysis

In 1689 Jonathan Swift, at twenty-two, came to Moor Park to serve as secretary under Sir William Temple. It was to be Swift's brush with gentility, polite learning, and aristocracy, and it served him well. As a raw, aspiring man of letters, the youthful Swift hoped to make his name as a serious poet, and in this period he composed a series of rather maudlin and certainly pedestrian poems that sought to soar in the panegyric strain, Pindaric odes in the manner of Abraham Cowley (and of John Dryden in his youth): polite but plodding celebrations and praises—to King William after the Battle of the Boyne ("Ode to the King," 1690-1691), to a supposedly Learned Organization ("Ode to the Athenian Society," 1692), to Dr. William Sancroft, to the successful Irish playwright William Congreve, and two effusions to Sir William Temple himself (all in 1692 and 1693). Like many young beginners, he was rather excessively enamored of his own productions ("I am overfond of my own writings . . . and I find when I writt what pleases me I am Cowley to my self and can read it a hundred times over," he tells a relative in a letter of May 3, 1692), but by 1693 even Swift himself recognized the hopeless nature of this stiflingly formal and elevated gentlemanly verse, for he broke off rudely in the midst of his second Ode to Temple and renounced such a Muse forever.

Certainly, *politesse* and officious, gaudy, and Cavalier verse (already a mode passing out of date since the Restoration in 1660) were never to be Swift's *forte*, yet even in these formal pieces there are some sparks and signs of the later Swift, for he could not restrain periodic outbursts of an inborn satiric temper as in "Ode to the Athenian Society":

> *She seems a Medly of all Ages*
> With a huge Fardingal to swell her Fustian Stuff,
> A new Comode, a *Top-knot*, and a Ruff,
> Her Face patch't o'er with *Modern Pedantry*,
> With a long sweeping Train
> Of Comments and Disputes, ridiculous and vain,
> *All of old Cut with a new Dye.* . . .

And in a rather strained posture—even for a satirist—he let himself boast of *"My hate, whose lash just heaven has long decreed/ Shall on a day make sin and folly bleed . . ."* ("To Mr. Congreve"). In his poem to Congreve, in fact, he had recommended that the writer should *"Beat not the dirty paths where vulgar feet have trod,/ But give the vigorous fancy room."*

Within a year Swift would take his own advice and relinquish oppressive formal structures and grand studied compliments. Indeed, throughout the remainder of his career as a poet, Swift purposely eschewed all hints of genteel elegance, polite praise, or formal density. Thereafter, his verse was rough, chatty, and colloquial, deliberately informal, low in diction and in subject— scrupulously out of the beaten track of the faddish mode in verse, the heroic couplet. For the rest of his life, Swift's poetry took its measure instead from the witty, learned, and coyly antipoetic practices of Samuel Butler's *Hudibras* (1663-1678), making use of the almost sing-song, Mother Goose-like octosyllabic couplet, pedestrian subjects, far-fetched rhymes, and coarse mien. In addition, Swift never indulged in the longer epical modes so much in favor in his day; his poems remained prosaic and short.

Hence, in the next extant verse of Swift to appear ("Verses wrote in a Lady's Ivory Table-Book"), the new mode is almost fully formulated and matured. He mocks the typical empty-headed young lady whose hall guestbook is entirely scribbled over (by suitors and herself as well) with the muck of self-regard and of shallow tastes, flirtatious clichés, and torpid vanities; such "Brains Issue" the poet considers "Excrement"—and real gentlemen are warned to avoid such a tart:

> Whoe're expects to hold his part
> In such a Book and such a Heart,

> If he be Wealthy and a Fool
> Is in all Points the fittest Tool,
> Of whom it may be justly said,
> He's a Gold Pencil tipt with Lead.

A number of strategies in operation here are certainly worthy of note, for they remained Swift's hallmarks throughout his career. First, Swift owes many of his themes to the Restoration and its stage themes of fops, seducers, and fashionable lovers; a frequent topic of his art is the idle, frivolous, vacant, and flirtatious city maiden and her mindless, posturing fop or "gallant." Swift endows these conventional and even humdrum subjects with venomous sting: such a woman is, in his imagery, no better than a whore, a prostitute of fashion, and her suitors are portrayed as perverse and impotent whoremasters: "tools" "tipt with Lead."

Swift's poetry transforms the polite inanities of social intercourse into monstrosities. His poetry gains all the more telling force precisely because of its seemingly innocuous outer clothing; bobbing along in quaint, informal four-footed lines, and immersed in chatty diction, the verse promises to be no more than light and witty. Yet the images soon transform such poetry into a species of savagery. Swift once mildly observed in one of his poems that "*Swift* had the Sin of Wit no venial Crime," and that "Humour, and Mirth, had Place in all he writ. . . ." It is true that Wit and Mirth are featured dramatically in virtually all Swift's creations, but let no reader be lulled into expectations of mild pleasure and repose, for the Dean's poetry often turns wit and humor deliberately sour.

A good example of this transformation may be observed in an early lampoon, "The Description of a Salamander," a deliberate cold-blooded attack on Baron Cutts the warrior, who had been nicknamed the "Salamander." In the poem, Cutts is metamorphosized into a salamander and reptile. Swift savors setting up the analogy, and does so with painstaking nicety:

> . . . should some Nymph who ne'er was cruel,
> Like *Carleton* cheap or fam'd *Duruel*,
> Receive the Filth which he ejects,
> She soon would find, the same Effects,
> Her tainted Carcase to pursue,
> As from the *Salamander's* Spue;
> A dismal shedding of her Locks
> And, if no Leprosy, a Pox.

Although this is an early effort, there is no doubt that Swift is adept at being ruthlessly unkind: words such as *cheap*, *Filth*, *Spue*, and *Pox* are staccato-like Anglo-Saxon monosyllables, and only seemingly simplistic. What is more, they are amassed with furious delectation and vigor. Yet the poem remains tightly contained, purporting throughout to be a calm, disinterested argument, a scientific demonstration, a precise comparison. Swift's robustness arises precisely because he can interfuse the careful language of reasoning with the gross irrationality of nightmarish visions of infectious and loathsome vice and disease.

Needless to say, a number of Swift's poems are less vicious, but there is always in them a certain flickering spark that implies imminent combustion. A number of his early poems are deliberate imitations or paraphrases of Horace, and others follow Ovid in telling a far-fetched story. Swift learns much from both of these classical authors about the manipulation of animal imagery, about the handling of diverse tones, and above all about sophistication: the juggling with diction, the juxtaposition of high and low styles, and the sly use of irony and indirection. Behind these deft usages is the potential adder and spike of the Swiftian assault.

Two companion pieces in this early period are almost universally admired: "A Description of the Morning" and "A Description of a City Shower." Both are studied presentations, ironic, quiet, and steady, while they also demonstrate another of Swift's strengths: parody. The two poems are species of City Pastoral, a mock-form that laughs at the fad of writing polite bucolic pieces about some never-never land of innocent shepherds and of the happy life in a pristine garden. Swift simply moves eclogues and idylls heavy-handedly indoors—and into the reeking, overcrowded, dirty London of the eighteenth century. The result (a frequent strategy in much of Swift's verse) is polite Vergilian verse that is overcome by gross content: thieving swains, whorish nymphs, and maids and apprentices too lazy to do any work.

Swift likes nothing better than to puncture civilization's postures, to divulge what Henry Fielding called *affectation*, and to blast holes in a nation's language of hypocrisy, concealment, euphemism, and deceit. Such uncovering can take the form of exposé: polite, tedious love-verse that is merely a tissue of clichés is rigorously parodied and exposed by hilarious ineptitudes of language ("A Love Song in the Modern Taste"), or a gross physical deformity is laid bare as a "modern nymph" disrobes and reveals herself to be in the last stages of disintegration from syphilis ("A Beautiful Young Nymph Going to Bed"). Swift would argue that false and impure language is exactly as viciously deceptive as ulcerous and pox-ridden physical reality. Both are instances of man-made corruption. With satiric glee, Jonathan Swift loves to call a spade a spade, or to paint a running sore in technicolor.

Swift is not always savage, cunning, or voracious. Some of his most pleasant verse remains Horatian, and plays quieter games. An early piece, "Mrs. Harris' Petition," reveals his mastery of mimicry; he assumes the voice and exact intonations of a middle-aged busybody servant who has lost her purse—and considers that event the greatest cataclysm since The Flood. (For a similar tone of voice, consult "Mary the Cook-Maid's Letter to Dr. Sheridan"). One of his longest poems in the early years, *Cadenus and Vanessa* is a masterpiece of coy indirection; one Esther Vanhomrigh had indiscreetly pursued the older Dr. Swift with some heat and passion: a polite and circuitous allegorical tale is used to cool her down and warn her off.

Swift is at times at his most elegant (if such a term may be applied to his hobble-footed, four-stressed, grossly rhymed lines) in a number of poems over the years (1719-1727) to Stella. These are usually poems on slight topics, birthday celebrations, or graver reflections in the later years upon her growing illness. They are always light and bantering in style, polite yet quaintly back-handed with compliments, and sometimes almost insulting. Swift was a master not only of the direct attack but also of ironic indirection, and, following Vincent Voiture, he loved what he called *raillery*—a kind of bantering jest that paid compliments by seeming complaints and mock- or near-insults. A good example would be lines from "On Stella's Birth-day 1719":

> STELLA this Day is thirty four,
> (We shan't dispute a Year or more)
> However Stella, be not troubled,
> Although thy Size and Years are doubled,
> Since first I saw Thee at Sixteen
> The brightest Virgin on the Green,
> So little is thy Form declin'd
> Made up so largely in thy Mind.

The jesting continues until that last line, and so do the whimsical inaccuracies: Stella was *not* thirty-four (but older), and Swift had *not* first met her when she was sixteen (more likely at eight); she is obviously invited to wince at the trite phrases about *bright Virgins*, *lofty queens*, *village greens*, and *sweet sixteens*, for these are the pabulum of most pedestrian Muses (even today they thrive in popular lyrics and Hallmark cards). Finally, there is the innuendo about her girth—so paradoxically multiplied but nevertheless "So little . . . declin'd." Swift could not resist in some way speaking the truth. Much of his verse is of this seriocomic, semiprivate nature (and includes epigrams, puns, some pig-Latin, invitations to dinner, verse epistles, windowpane scribblings, and merest notes), but all of it has a certain effervescence—and the Stella poems are surely the most accomplished in this vein.

Another body of poems, like the verse attacking Lord Cutts, consists of savage political invectives, bred of the heat and animosity of factions, contentions, and parties. Some of the most acerb include a potent libel against Richard Tighe in "Mad Mullinix and Timothy," a most vicious portrayal of the Duke of Marlborough, the renowned Whig general ("A Satirical Elegy on the Death of a late Famous General"), and, in his strongest poem of this type, a savage libelous attack upon the Irish Parliament, in "A Character, Panegyric, and Description of the Legion Club," which indicts the group as a crowd of mad demoniacs. One of the most artful of these politically tinged poems incorporates themes about similar corruptions in the arts: *On Poetry: A Rapsody*. Like Pope's *Peri-Bathos: Or, The Art of Sinking in Poetry* (1727), this poem purports to be a manual of instruction, a how-to handbook guiding one who seeks to become a degenerate modern-day political hanger-on and hack writer. The final implication is that most men are already so degraded, abject, and profligate that there ought to be no one, really, who needs such "helpful" advice. That is exactly Swift's point: the so-called Age of Reason is in reality decimated and dissolute, the last, the Fifth or Iron Age of Vice (in Hesiod's terms): the final stage of the creation's decline. Like Juvenal before him, Swift the satirist found it expedient to assume the worst about man's propensity for deterioration and debasement.

Perhaps Swift's most renowned poems are his most shocking; they defame women, employ scatology, and have often been considered "obscene" and even "unprintable." They use the typical Swiftian ploy of jolting the reader into paying attention by using paradoxes and coarse language, and they include in their number some of Swift's best verse. On the borderline in this category are such fine poems as "The Progress of Marriage" and "Phillis: Or, The Progress of Love," poems that speak in the crassest terms of ill-matched marriages, and which frankly wage battle against the trifling romantic slogans that presume that "true-love" and "feelings" and "good intentions" and "high hopes" will win out against all practical odds. Rather grimly, Swift shows— in gruesome detail—the fate of such marriages.

The most blatantly offensive of the scatalogical poems include "The Lady's Dressing Room," "A Beautiful Young Nymph Going to Bed," "Strephon and Chloe," and "Cassinus and Peter." Every one of these poems mocks the "double standard" that allows men to be most coarse in their everyday affairs and yet somehow naïve about the single topic of women (whom they place upon pedestals in the tradition of courtly love). This self-deception leads inevitably to disillusionment, misery, and the destruction of lives, just as it has made for sheaves of tedious, lackluster love poetry. In Swift's poems, rather dirty modern urban swains are baldly confronted with nymphs who defecate and stink (as do all people) and who in extreme cases are coming apart with syphilis and gonorrhea. The bane of Venus, in short, is that she is fetid and venereal. As a consequence of such a confrontation, the knavish and foolish men in these poems usually run mad—precisely as Gulliver does when he encounters man-as-Yahoo. The lesson applies as well to these dubious Lovers as it does to Gulliver: they are so easily unhinged because their minds never were screwed very well together; they have trained themselves—and society has trained them—to ignore or distort reality, to set up screens and shields and ideals—clouds of obfuscation that cut one off from everyday physical reality. Swift implies that if such men shut out actuality, they deserve the manure and laughter he heaps rather furiously upon them. These verses deserve more consideration than they usually receive.

Swift's most fruitful years span the period from 1730 to 1733, and special notice should be given to his masterpiece, the 484-line *Verses on the Death of Dr. Swift*. In it, the Dean chooses to defend a rather nasty maxim by François La Rouchefoucauld asserting that adversities befalling our friends do not necessarily displease us. Here is a sterling opportunity to expose human perversity, and Swift rises to the occasion. He points out amicably that all people like to get ahead of their acquaintances, and especially of their friends. Then he commences to use a marvelous example to "prove" his case: the occasion of his own demise. Sure enough, as Swift would have it, all of his friends in some way gloat over his passing. Even more curiously, enemies actually lament the Dean's death! Before the poem is through, it is paradoxically worked out that only men "indifferent," absolute strangers, can ever fairly assess one's merits or judge one's worth.

There is a further stickler that the reader should grasp in the thorny thicket of ironies infesting Swift's delightful poem: *all* men do in some way indulge in self-aggrandizement; men naturally exalt their ego over others, and do not mind in the least treading upon toes (or heads) in their implacable urge to ascend. The last touch of irony includes even Dean Swift, who was so curiously "generous" in consenting hypothetically to "sacrifice" his own life so that he might win this argument. That is the very point: Swift, like the rest of mankind, will stop at nothing to salve his ego or to engineer a victory—even the most trifling triumph in a debate. Men will sacrifice friends, relatives, and even twist and convert enemies, so that they might, in Swift's fond phrase, "lie uppermost." Men are engendered in heaps; it is each one's voracious inclination to climb to the top. Thus stands one of Swift's most pleasing (and yet vexing) conundrums.

For some two hundred years, Swift's poetry was seldom taken very seriously; it was, after all, not in the mainstream of the poetry of his own day, and much of it was crass and vulgar in the bargain. Swift himself had contributed to this downplaying of his talents, typically paying himself a left-handed compliment: his verse, he reports in a prose addendum to a poem ("A Left-handed Letter to Dr. Sheridan," 1718), is slight, for he composes with his "Left Hand, [when he] was in great Haste, and the other Hand was employed at the same Time in writing some Letters of Business." More and more often, however, recent criticism has been coming to take that self-deprecation with a grain of salt. The truth is that Swift's poetry is both dexterous *and* sinister—full of easy grace as well as of two-fisted power. His poems are disturbing yet pleasing, and growing numbers of readers are acknowledging that vexation and that pleasure. Perhaps the oppressive reality of warfare, terrorism, and recession has suggested that Swift and La Rochefoucauld came close to putting humanity in its place.

John R. Clark

Other major works

FICTION: *A Tale of a Tub*, 1704; *Gulliver's Travels*, 1726 (originally entitled *Travels into Several Remote Nations of the World . . . by Lemuel Gulliver*).

NONFICTION: *A Discourse of the Contests and Dissensions Between the Nobles and the Commons in Athens and Rome*, 1701; *The Battle of the Books*, 1704; *The Accomplishment of the First of Mr. Bickerstaff's Predictions*, 1708; *An Argument Against Abolishing Christianity*, 1708; *Predictions for the Year 1708*, 1708; *A Project for the Advancement of Religion, and the Reformation of Manners*, 1709; *A Vindication of Isaac Bickerstaff*, Esq., 1709; *The Conduct of the Allies*, 1711; *A Proposal for Correcting, Improving and Ascertaining the English Tongue*, 1712; *The Public Spirit of the Whigs*, 1714; *A Letter to the Shop-Keepers*, 1724; *A Letter to Mr. Harding the Printer*, 1724; *A Letter to the Whole People of Ireland*, 1724; *A Letter to . . . Viscount Moleworth*, 1724; *Some Observations upon a Paper*, 1724; *The Drapier's Letters and Other Works*, 1724-1725; *A Modest Proposal for Preventing the Children of Poor People of Ireland from Being a Burden to Their Parents*, 1729; *Journal to Stella*, 1766, 1768; *Letters to a Very Young Lady on Her Marriage*, 1797; *The Drapier's Letters to the People of Ireland*, 1935; *The Correspondence of Jonathan Swift*, 1963-1965 (Harold Williams, editor, 5 volumes).

MISCELLANEOUS: *Miscellanies in Prose and Verse*, 1711; *Miscellanies*, 1727-1723 (by Swift, Alexander Pope, and Other members of the Scriblerus Club, 4 volumes); *A Complete Collection of Genteel and Ingenious Conversation*, 1738; *The Prose Works of Jonathan Swift*, 1939-1968 (Herbert Davis, editor, 14 volumes); *Directions to Servants in General . . .* , 1745; *"A Tale of a Tub" to Which Is Added "The Battle of the Books" and the "Mechanical Operation of the Spirit,"* 1958 (A. C. Guthkelch and D. Nichol Smith, editors).

Bibliography

Hunting, Robert. *Jonathan Swift*. Boston: Twayne, 1989. While primarily useful as a source for biographical information, this volume does contain much insightful, if general, analysis of Swift's art. One chapter is devoted entirely to *Gullivers Travels*. Supplemented by a chronology, notes and references, a select bibliography, and an index.

Milic, Louis Tonko. *A Quantitative Approach to the Style of Jonathan Swift*. The Hague: Mouton, 1967. A detailed and quantitative analysis of the language Swift uses in his art, including analysis of such linguistic components as word patterns and frequency. Complemented by a list of tables and figures, a bibliography, an index, and an appendix.

Price, Martin. *Swift's Rhetorical Art: A Study in Structure and Meaning*. Hamden, Conn.: Archon Books, 1963. In this fascinating work, Price examines Swift's work in terms of rhetorical structures and especially in terms of persuasion. The author provides an introduction to the history of rhetoric as persuasion, then examines most of Swift's major novels. Supplemented by a general index.

Rembert, James A. W. *Swift and the Dialectical Tradition.* New York: St. Martin's Press, 1988. This scholarly work analyzes Swift in terms of the rhetorical tradition. After giving a brief history of the tradition, beginning with classical rhetoric, Rembert traces Swift's utilization of various rhetorical strategies. Includes a select bibliography and an index.

Rosenheim, Edward W. *Swift and the Satirist's Art.* Chicago: University of Chicago Press, 1963. In this useful study, Rosenheim first defines satire, then analyzes much of Swift's work in terms of that definition. Specific and comprehensive attention is given to *A Tale of a Tub.* Supplemented by an index.

ALGERNON CHARLES SWINBURNE

Born: London, England; April 5, 1837
Died: Putney, England; April 10, 1909

Principal poetry

Poems and Ballads, 1866; *A Song of Italy*, 1867; *Ode on the Proclamation of the French Republic*, 1870; *Songs Before Sunrise*, 1871; *Songs of Two Nations*, 1875; *Poems and Ballads: Second Series*, 1878; *Songs of the Springtides*, 1880; *The Heptalogia*, 1880; *Tristram of Lyonesse and Other Poems*, 1882; *A Century of Roundels*, 1883; *A Midsummer Holiday and Other Poems*, 1884; *Gathered Songs*, 1887; *Poems and Ballads: Third Series*, 1889; *Astrophel and Other Poems*, 1894; *The Tale of Balen*, 1896; *A Channel Passage and Other Poems*, 1904; *Posthumous Poems*, 1917; *Rondeaux Parisiens*, 1917; *Ballads of the English Border*, 1925.

Other literary forms

The most learned and versatile of all the Victorian poets, Algernon Charles Swinburne tried his hand with varying degrees of success at virtually every literary form available to him. He sought to make his mark as a dramatist and novelist as well as a poet and in the course of his career he published twelve complete plays excluding juvenilia and fragments. They are all tragedies written predominately in blank verse. *Atalanta in Calydon* (1865) and *Erechtheus* (1876) are based on the Greek model. *Chastelard* (1865), *Bothwell* (1874), and *Mary Stuart* (1881) constitute a trilogy that harks back in spirit and style to Swinburne's beloved Elizabethan period. *The Sisters* (1892) is his only play with a nineteenth century English setting. He wrote two semi-autobiographical novels, *Love's Cross-Currents* (1901; serialized as *A Year's Letters* in 1877) and the fragmentary *Lesbia Brandon* (1952), not published until many years after his death. The first makes use of the eighteenth century epistolary form, while the second adopts the omniscient point of view. Swinburne projected a collection of short prose tales on the model of Boccaccio to which he gave the title *Triameron*. He left a list of nineteen titles but only four tales have survived: "Dead Love," "The Portrait," "Queen Fredegond," and "The Marriage of Mona Lisa." In addition to numerous critical articles written for newspapers and periodicals, Swinburne left behind sixteen volumes of literary criticism, dating from 1866 when *Byron* was published to the posthumous *Contemporaries of Shakespeare*, which appeared in 1919. *William Blake: A Critical Essay* (1868), *Essays and Studies* (1875), *A Study of Shakespeare* (1880) and *Miscellanies* (1886) are the most significant of this body of material. He was also a voluminous letter writer. Cecil Lang has collected more than two thousand of Swinburne's letters in his six-volume edition.

Achievements

Swinburne comes closest of all the Victorians to being a Renaissance man. John Ruskin said that he could write as well in Greek, Latin, Italian, and French as he could in English. He wrote two burlesques entirely in French, a novel entitled *La Fille du Policeman* and a play, *La Soeur de la Reine*, of which only two acts are known to have survived. Swinburne was intimately familiar with five great literatures. Only John Milton among the English poets exceeded him in knowledge. Swinburne was a great parodist and translator, a prolific and fascinating letter writer, a novelist, and a voluminous dramatist and critic. His *The Heptalogia*, in addition to the well-known parody of Alfred, Lord Tennyson—"The Higher Pantheism in a Nut Shell"—contains a devastating parody of himself, the "Nephilidia," and fiendishly clever parodies of the Brownings, Coventry Patmore, "Owen Meredith," and Dante Gabriel Rossetti. Cecil Lang in his introduction to his edition of Swinburne's letters comments that Swinburne's ability to absorb the manner and reproduce the mannerisms of his targets constitutes "a miracle of 'negative capability.'" The same could be said of his border ballads, which seem more authentic than imitative or derivative. "Lord Scales," "Burd Margaret," and "The Worm of Spindlestonheugh" capture the form and essence of the early ballad as well as any modern poems.

According to Cecil Lang, Swinburne as a translator "could have ranked with the great masters." Passages from Greek and Latin poets appear in his works as well as selections from nineteenth century Italian and French writers. His only sustained translations are of François Villon, and some of them are masterpieces. His "Ballad of the Lords of Old Time" and "Ballad of the Women of Paris" capture the spirit of Villon's original poems as closely as it is possible for translations to do, and as English translations they are equaled only by Dante Gabriel Rossetti's "Ballad of Dead Ladies." Swinburne's failure to translate Villon's *The Great Testament* (1461), must be counted as a great loss to literature.

As a novelist Swinburne was the only certified aristocrat of the period to write fiction about the aristocracy. *Love's Cross-Currents* and *Lesbia Brandon*, in the words of Edmund Wilson, introduce us to "a world in which the eager enjoyment of a glorious out-of-door life of riding and swimming and boating is combined with adultery, incest, enthusiastic flagellations and quiet homosexuality" (*The Novels of A. C. Swinburne*). Wilson regards *Love's Cross-Currents* as almost a neglected masterpiece. *Lesbia Brandon* contains passages of superb description, strong characterization, and convincing dialogue. Both works suggest that Swinburne had at least the potential of being a significant novelist. Unfortunately, these novels are the most neglected of his major writings.

Although Swinburne's reputation is based primarily on his poetry, it was as the author of *Atalanta in Calydon* that he first gained fame. This little-read play is best remembered today for its choruses, which are often included in anthology collections of Swinburne, but it is a genuine *tour de force*: a treatment in English, on the model of Greek tragedy, of a famous myth which had not been used before as the subject of a play. It is widely regarded by critics as the finest Greek tragedy in English, although the concentration of Milton's *Samson Agonistes* (1671) is closer to the Greek tragedians than the diffuse blank verse of Swinburne's work. About *Erechtheus*, Swinburne's other experiment with Greek drama, David G. Riede writes in his *Swinburne: A Study of Romantic Mythmaking* that it "is a masterpiece in all respects— it is unrivaled as a re-creation of the Greek spirit and drama, nearly untouchable as a sustained lyric effusion, astounding in its metrical variety, dazzling in its metaphoric representation, and even remarkable in its philosophical import. . . ." Unfortunately, this play today is even less read than *Atalanta in Calydon*. Swinburne's trilogy on Mary Stuart was deeply researched and created over a period of many years, but it is entirely unsuited for the theater. *Bothwell* alone has well over fifty characters and the epic length of its five acts illustrates Swinburne's disregard for the contemporary stage. *Chastelard* is the easiest of the trilogy to read, but the extent of its preoccupation with sexual passion has prevented it from being as widely appreciated as its artistry warrants. *Mary Stuart* is given high marks by T. Earl Welby in his *A Study of Swinburne* for transforming prose matter into poetry, but Welby concludes that it "inspires respect rather than enthusiasm." Of Swinburne's other plays it should perhaps be said that *Marino Faliero* compares favorably with Byron's treatment of the same subject, *The Duke of Gandia* displays the powerful concentration of style of which Swinburne was capable, and *The Sisters* provides a fascinating insight into Swinburne's strange sexual proclivities.

As a critic, Swinburne's contributions are more substantial. At his best he is capable of judicious insights expressed in fine prose, while at his worst his strong feelings lead to idiosyncratic pronouncements and his prose style is baroque to the point of opacity. Swinburne left behind no innovations of critical approach and no permanent principles of judgment. Critical theory did not particularly interest him. Although he is the most cosmopolitan of the Victorian critics, his attentions are directed almost exclusively to literature or in some few cases to painting. Unlike Matthew Arnold, he does not travel in the broader ranges of society and religion. Swinburne's strength as a critic rests in his abiding love of literature and his genuine respect for those who made permanent contributions. This most aristocratic of English writers created in his mind an aristocracy of genius which included not only William Shakespeare and Victor Hugo, whom he revered to the point of idolatry, but also such writers as François Villon, William Blake, Robert Burns, and Charles Baudelaire. He had a special affinity for those writers who cut across the grain of convention. His *William Blake: A Critical Essay* is immensely original, charting new paths through the wilderness of the Prophetic Books and repairing years of neglect of this poet. If the insights now appear dated, certain passages have retained the freshness of great poetry.

It was as a poet that Swinburne made his most memorable and lasting contributions to literature. The seventeen volumes of poetry he published in his lifetime, exclusive of volumes printed only for private circulation, constitute a remarkable feat of creative exuberance even in an age as prolific as the Victorian. His early poetry is sometimes characterized by such rhetorical excess that the figures of speech call attention to themselves rather than enforce wider meanings. Such uncontrolled use of rhetoric is especially pronounced in the lengthy *A Song of Italy* and in the sadomasochistic poems of the first series of *Poems and Ballads*. As he matured as a poet, Swinburne came to exercise greater imaginative control over his materials, and his finest poems display a masterful command of the resources of language to create visions of striking beauty. "A Forsaken Garden" and "Ave Atque Vale," Swinburne's magnificent elegy on Baudelaire, clearly illustrate that rhetorical richness held in check by imaginative restraint which is characteristic of Swinburne at his best. A similar progressive mellowing of subject matter is evident in Swinburne's poetry. The violent denunciations of traditional Christianity and the preoccupation with various forms of sexual perversion that mark so much of Swinburne's early work disappear from the middle and later poetry, just as the melancholy hedonism of the early poems gives place to optimistic declarations about the triumph of freedom in the political poems and to a kind of quiet stoicism in the more personal ones. That said, it should be remembered that variety of subject matter and form remains the hallmark of Swinburne's huge body of poetry and easy generalizations about it must be regarded with suspicion.

Biography

Algernon Charles Swinburne was born in London on April 5, 1837. His family on both sides was aristocratic, the Swinburnes being clearly traceable to the time of Charles I and the Ashburnhams dating back before the Norman Conquest. As the eldest of six children, Swinburne had an active childhood, spent mainly at the family seat on the Isle of Wight with regular visits to another family house in Northumberland. The contrasting beauty of these diverse parts of England left a lasting impression on Swinburne, who as a child displayed an almost Wordsworthian responsiveness to nature. He early developed a passion for the sea, which is reflected in much of his poetry.

From the beginning Swinburne was surrounded by books and fine paintings. His mother, Lady Jane, introduced him to a wide range of literature, including the Bible, William Shakespeare, Sir Walter Scott, Charles Dickens, Dante, and Molière. She also taught her son French and Italian, laying the foundation for his cosmopolitanism. In April of 1849 Swinburne entered Eton College. In the four years he spent there he received a thorough grounding in Greek and Latin poetry and some acquaintance with the French and Italian classics. He acquired independently a remarkable knowledge of English literature. He was especially attracted to the Elizabethan dramatists, an interest that would remain constant for the remainder of his life. *The Unhappy Revenge*, a blood-curdling fragment in the manner of Cyril Tourneur and John Webster, dates from about 1849. His earliest poem to survive, "The Triumph of Gloriana," was a school exercise to commemorate a visit by Queen Victoria and Prince Albert to Eton on June 4, 1851. Its stiff heroic couplets give no clue of the direction Swinburne's genius was to take.

Although his academic record at Eton was good, it was decided in August of 1853 for reasons that are not entirely clear that he would not return, much to the surprise of his classmates. Instead, he would receive private tutoring for his entrance into Oxford, where his family expected him to pursue a degree leading to a legal or ecclesiastical career. Swinburne's patriotism was fired when he learned of Balaklava in the fall of 1854 and he wished to enter the army, but his father, Admiral Charles Henry Swinburne, would not permit it, perhaps because of his son's frailty. After a summer trip to Germany in the company of an uncle, Swinburne entered Balliol College, Oxford, on January 23, 1856.

At Oxford, Swinburne fell under the influence of John Nichol, the guiding spirit of Old Mortality, a small group of student intellectuals to which Swinburne belonged. Nichol, who was to remain a lifelong friend, undermined Swinburne's religious faith and confirmed him in political republicanism. It was under Nichol's influence that Swinburne wrote the "Ode to Mazzini" and became a devotee of the Italian patriot. Later, Swinburne was to be an outspoken advocate of Italian Unity. Most of Swinburne's future political poems were either to espouse Liberty and Freedom or castigate Tyranny in equally fervent language. Percy Bysshe Shelley may have become the main spiritual presence in Swinburne's political poetry, but it was Nichol who first directed Swinburne's thought along republican lines.

Another major influence on Swinburne at Oxford was the Pre-Raphaelite Brotherhood. In 1857 he met Dante Gabriel Rossetti, William Morris, and Edward Burne-Jones and immediately fell under their spell. Morris' poems, particularly "The Defence of Guenevere," influenced Swinburne profoundly. Shortly after meeting Morris he began *Queen Yseult*, and until 1860 his poems are, in the words of Georges Lafourcade, "a long self-imposed grind, a series of prosodic exercises" (*Swinburne: A Literary Biography*). One such exercise was *Laugh and Lie Down*, an Elizabethan pastiche written in 1858-1859, the sadomasochistic elements of which anticipate Swinburne's discovery of the writings of the Marquis de Sade in 1861. In 1860, because of his preoccupation with poetry and his irregular habits, which were cause for increasing concern, Swinburne encountered serious academic difficulties at Oxford, and he left without taking a degree.

In the spring of 1861, after a visit to France and Italy, Swinburne settled in London determined to make his mark as a poet. Shortly before, he had published *The Queen-Mother. Rosamond. Two Plays,* plays which did nothing to establish his reputation. His father had reluctantly agreed to a literary career for his son and settled upon him a small allowance. Swinburne quickly resumed his relations with the Pre-Raphaelites, developing a close friendship with Rossetti which was to last until 1872. He also made friends with such notable figures as Richard Burton, the explorer, and Simeon Solomon, the painter, and throughout the decade lived a bohemian life marked by increasingly severe alcoholic debauches from which he was repeatedly rescued by his father. In 1862 an affair with Jane Faulkner, the only serious love of his life, ended unhappily, causing him to write "The Triumph of Time," one of his finest poems. About this time he also wrote an autobiographical novel, *A Year's Letters,* which appeared under the pseudonym of "Mrs. Horace Manners" in 1877. Also to 1862 belongs "Laus Veneris," his first poem to crystallize many of the themes of the first series of *Poems and Ballads*: the apotheosis of female beauty, the celebration of eroticism, the wish for death, the defiance of God, and the damnation of Christianity as a religion of restraint. Along with poetry, Swinburne wrote a number of critical reviews in the early 1860's including favorable articles on Charles Baudelaire's *Les Fleurs du Mal* (1857, *Flowers of Evil*) and George Meredith's *Modern Love* (1862). In spite of all these efforts, serious recognition continued to elude Swinburne until *Atalanta in Calydon* was published, at his father's expense, in 1865. The reviews were all but unanimously enthusiastic. Swinburne was at last established in the front ranks of Victorian poets. His triumph was marred only by the fact that Walter Savage Landor, whom he had visited in Florence the year before to dedicate the then unfinished work, had died. Also in 1865 appeared *Chastelard,* the first part of a dramatic trilogy on Mary Stuart. The next year saw the publication of *Poems and Ballads* (first series), which scandalized the reading public. The volume was widely condemned by the reviewers as immoral, heretical, and insincere. Swinburne, never one to take criticism calmly, replied in kind with *Notes on Poems and Reviews.* After *Poems and Ballads,* Swinburne's drinking grew worse and in 1867 he had an affair with the scandalous Adah Isaac Menkin, which was the talk of London society. Swinburne's image as the *enfant terrible* of the Victorian Period was firmly established. Yet throughout this period of storm and stress Swinburne was able to do some of his best work. After several years of writing and revising, *William Blake: A Critical Essay* made its appearance in 1868, as did "Ave Atque Vale," the serenely beautiful elegy on Baudelaire. According to Lafourcade, these two works bring an end to the Pre-Raphaelite and Art-for-Art's-Sake phases of Swinburne's poetic growth.

In London on March 20, 1867, Swinburne met Giuseppe Mazzini, whom he had idolized since his Oxford days, and his political consciousness was intensified. He gave up writing his erotic novel, *Lesbia Brandon,* and for the next three years devoted his efforts to writing poems on political and social themes. A visit to France in the summer of 1869 confirmed his hatred of Napoleon III, which he recorded in several scathing sonnets. Swinburne's renewed interest in world affairs came to a head in 1871 with the publication of *Songs Before Sunrise*. This volume marks a dramatic shift in the direction of Swinburne's poetry. The private eroticism of *Poems and Ballads* had given way to public denunciations of political and religious repression and Shelleyan prophecies of the triumph of freedom.

After the publication of *Songs Before Sunrise* Swinburne began to dissipate more than ever and yet his output throughout the decade was prodigious. In the 1870's his poetry becomes quieter in tone and more melancholy and introspective. The second series of *Poems and Ballads* is tinged with a stoical acceptance of the impermanence of youth and love which is absent from the first. *Bothwell*, the most impressive work of his dramatic trilogy, appeared in 1874, followed by *Erechtheus* in 1876. In the 1870's Swinburne turned increasingly to criticism. His *Essays and Studies*, which contains discerning appreciations of several contemporaries, was published in 1875. From 1875 to 1880 he worked on *A Study of Shakespeare*. Always contentious, he became increasingly involved in quarrels of various kinds. His attack on Ralph Waldo Emerson in the form of a public letter was occasioned by an unfavorable remark that Emerson allegedly made about him to the press. He attacked George Eliot in his *A Note on Charlotte Brontë* (1877) and was involved in a protracted dispute with F. J. Furnival, the Shakespearean scholar, on ideological grounds. He wrote a brilliant parody of Tennyson and revised earlier ones on the Brownings, all published in *The Heptalogia* in 1880.

After his father's death in 1877 Swinburne's health broke. Through much of 1878 he was bedridden from dissipation, and the decade that began with his expulsion from the Arts Club ended with the poet prostrate in his disordered London chambers near death from alcoholism. His friend and legal adviser, Theodore Watts (later Watts-Dunton), rescued him, and for the last thirty years of his life Swinburne lived at Watts's home, "The Pines," in Putney. Watts severely restricted Swinburne's social contacts, but he did accompany him to Paris in 1882 for his meeting with Victor Hugo, whom Swinburne had revered for so long. This was to be his last visit to the Continent. During his years at "The Pines" Swinburne contributed well over two hundred articles to newspapers and periodicals and published more than twenty volumes. *Mary Stuart* was published in 1881, finally completing the dramatic trilogy conceived years before. Swinburne's early interest in Arthurian materials was revived and *Tristram of Lyonesse and Other Poems* appeared in 1882 and *The Tale of Balen* in 1896. He also continued to write political poems, directed largely against Russia abroad and William Gladstone and Charles Parnell at home. His aristocratic background never allowed him to regard the liberal prime minister as anything other than a dangerous radical. He opposed Home Rule as fiercely as earlier he had advocated the liberation of Italy. He ended as a republican who was opposed to democracy.

Having outlived most of his friends and all of his family except for one sister, Swinburne died at "The Pines" on April 10, 1909. He was buried in Bonchurch Churchyard on the Isle of Wight. Theodore Watts-Dunton, true to the poet's request, would not permit the Burial of the Dead to be read over the grave.

Analysis

The body of Algernon Charles Swinburne's poetry is so vast and varied that it is difficult to generalize about it. Swinburne wrote poetry for more than sixty years and in that time he treated an enormous variety of subjects and employed many poetic forms and meters. He wrote English and Italian sonnets, elegies, odes, lyrics, dramatic monologues, ballads, and romances; and he experimented with the *rondeau*, the *ballade*, and the *sestina*. Much of this poetry is marked by a strong lyricism and a self-conscious, formal use of such rhetorical devices as alliteration, assonance, repetition, personification, and synecdoche. Swinburne's brilliant self-parody, "Nephilidia," hardly exaggerates the excessive rhetoric of some of his earlier poems. The early *A Song of Italy* would have more effectively conveyed its extreme republican sentiments had it been more restrained. As it is, content is too often lost in verbiage, leading a reviewer for *The Athenaeum* to remark that "hardly any literary bantling has been shrouded in a thicker veil of indefinite phrases." A favorite technique of Swinburne is to reiterate a poem's theme in a profusion of changing images until a clear line of development is lost. "The Triumph of Time" is an example. Here the stanzas can be rearranged without loss of effect. This poem does not so much develop as accrete. Clearly a large part of its greatness rests in its music. As much as any other poet, Swinburne needs to be read aloud. The diffuse lyricism of Swinburne is the opposite of the closely knit structures of John Donne and is akin to the poetry of Walt Whitman.

Nowhere is this diffuseness more clearly visible than in those poems of the first series of *Poems and Ballads* which proved so shocking to Victorian sensibilities: "Anactoria," "Laus Veneris," "Dolores," "Faustine," and "Felise." Although they all exhibit technical virtuosity, these poems are too long and their compulsive repetition of sadomasochistic eroticism grows tiresome. Poems that celebrate the pleasures and pains of sexual love are most successful when the language is sufficiently sensuous to convey the immediacy of the experience—Ovid's *Amores* comes to mind—and it is ironic that Swinburne's sensual poems in this early volume fall somewhat flat because they are not sensuous enough. Faustine and Dolores fail to come to life, just as the unnamed speakers, reveling in the pains of love, remain only a voice. One feels that the dramatic form is ill-chosen. Swinburne tells us in his *Notes on Poems and Reviews* that in "Dolores" he strove "to express that transient state of spirit through which a man may be supposed to pass, foiled in love and weary of loving, but not yet in sight of rest; seeking refuge in those 'violent delights' which 'have violent ends,' in fierce and frank sensualities which at least profess to be no more than they are." This is a legitimate purpose for a poem, but it is not realized in these early works.

Still, this volume cannot be dismissed too lightly. Swinburne wrote it partly to shock and partly to accomplish what he attributed to Charles Baudelaire's *Flowers of Evil*: the transformation of ugliness into beauty, immorality into morality by the sheer power of the imagination. He certainly succeeded in shocking, and at times he was able to invest desperate and dark thoughts with a languorous beauty of sound, as in these lines from "The Garden of Proserpine":

> I am tired of tears and laughter,
> And men that laugh and weep;
> Of what may come hereafter
> For men that sow to reap:
> I am weary of days and hours,
> Blown buds of barren flowers,
> Desires and dreams and powers
> And everything but sleep.

This is quintessential early Swinburne. Nothing had been heard in English poetry quite like it. For all their defects, the longer dramatic poems in the first series of *Poems and Ballads* expanded the boundaries of the subject matter of English poetry in much the way that Whitman did for American poetry. In the shorter lyrics, such as "A Leave-taking," "Rococo," and "A Match," Swinburne created a note of elusive melancholy that had not been heard before. "Madonna Mia," one of the most exquisitely beautiful lyrics in the language, by itself compensates for the flawed longer poems and ends on a more hopeful note than the other poems of the volume.

In Swinburne's next volume of poems, *Songs Before Sunrise*, the Femme Fatale is replaced by the goddess Freedom; the earlier obsession with flagellation is sublimated into a more acceptable form of violence—namely, the overthrow of tyranny; and the desperate hedonism of the "Hymn to Proserpine" gives way to the militant humanism of the "Hymn of Man." "A little while and we die; shall life not thrive as it may?" is changed to "Men perish, but man shall endure; lives die, but the life is not dead." The doctrine of Art for Art's Sake evaporates in these poems of social concern as the influence of Victor Hugo and Giuseppe Mazzini replaces that of Baudelaire and Marquis de Sade. With the exception of "Before a Crucifix," a powerful attack on the Roman Catholic Church for self-aggrandizement in a suffering world, the poems of *Songs Before Sunrise* are aggressive, forward-looking accounts of the defeat of oppression and the triumph of liberty. "Hertha" affirms the immortality of man—"In the buds of your lives is the sap of my leaves; ye shall live and not die"—and asserts that "the morning of manhood is risen, and the shadowless soul is in sight." This philosophical poem ends, in words that echo Percy Bysshe Shelley's *Prometheus Unbound* (1820), with a revelation of the death of God and the birth of "love, the beloved Republic, that feeds upon freedom and lives." The other philosophical poems of *Songs Before Sunrise*, the "Hymn of Man," similarly asserts the immortality of the race and proclaims the demise of God, who in the figure of Christ is imaged as a tyrant: "By the spirit he ruled as his slave is he slain who was mighty to slay/ And the stone that is sealed on his grave he shall rise not and roll not away." The poem concludes with a striking perversion of Scripture, a characteristic technique of Swinburne:

> Thou art smitten, thou God, thou art smitten; thy death is upon thee, O Lord.
> And the love-song of earth as thou diest resounds through the wind of her wings—
> Glory to Man in the highest! for Man is the master of things.

The other poems of this volume are more closely related to the events of the day. "Super Flumina Babylonis" celebrates the release of Italy from bondage in imagery that recalls the resurrection of Christ. The open tomb, the folded graveclothes, the "deathless face" all figure in this interesting poem that sings out, "Death only dies." In "Quia Multum Amavit," France, shackled by tyranny, is personified as a harlot who has been false to liberty. She has become "A ruin where satyrs dance/ A garden wasted for beasts to crawl and brawl in." The poem ends with France prostrate before the spirit of Freedom, who speaks to her as Christ spoke to the sinful woman in the Pharisee's house, in a tone of forgiveness.

Although Swinburne's later political poems continued to attack tyranny abroad, especially in Russia, the emphasis in them shifted to England. In *A Channel Passage and Other Poems*, Swinburne's last volume of poetry published in his lifetime, the poems having to do with political subjects tend to reflect Swinburne's insularity. Poems such as "The Centenary of the Battle of the Nile," "Trafalgar Day," and "Cromwell's Statue" celebrate glorious moments of England's past in language of chauvinistic hyperbole, while others such as "The Commonweal: A Song for Unionists," "The Question," and "The Transvaal" counsel the severest measures against England's enemies, who, be they Irish or Boers, are invariably depicted as the "cowardliest hounds that ever lapped/ Blood" or "dogs, agape with jaws afoam." These poems lack the rhetorical richness of *Songs Before Sunrise*, suggesting that in the twilight of his career Swinburne's strength lay not in contention but in the peaceful lyricism that informs "The Lake of Gaube" and "In a Rosary," the finest of the poems in this volume.

With the publication in 1878 of *Poems and Ballads: Second Series*, Swinburne reached the height of his powers as a poet. The unhealthy eroticism and hysterical denunciations of Christianity have disappeared. The language is altogether more restrained and there is a greater harmony of form and substance. The major themes are the impermanence of love and the inevitability of death. The predominant mood is elegiac, but the despair of "Hymn to Proserpine" has been replaced by the resignation of "At Parting," and a few of the poems hold out some hope of personal immortality, although on this subject Swinburne's private beliefs are never made clear.

In "A Forsaken Garden," one of the loveliest of Swinburne's poems, the landscape as dry as "the heart of a dead man" serves as an emblem for "lovers none ever will know/ Whose eyes went seaward a hundred sleeping/ Years ago." "Love deep as the sea as a rose must wither" and lovers now living must follow those who have gone before. The poem concludes that the forsaken garden is now beyond further change until the world itself ends, and there with the ghosts of bygone lovers "As a god self-slain on his own strange altar/ Death lies dead." This mood-piece manages to convey through the effective use of detail and tight control of rhetoric a landscape more vividly realized than is to be found in Swinburne's earlier poems. "A Vision of Spring in Winter" displays an equally rich texture of natural description brought into focus by a restrained imagination. In this lovely poem Swinburne bids farewell to youth. The poet tells the spirit of Spring, "I would not bid thee, though I might, give back/ One good thing youth has given and borne away." The loves and hopes of youth "Lie deeper than the sea" and Spring could not restore them even if the poet wished for their return. The poem ends on a wistful note: "But flowers thou may'st and winds, and hours of ease/ And all its April to the world thou may'st/ Give back, and half my April back to me."

Virtually all of the elegies in this remarkable volume merit special mention. In "Inferiae," a poem of simple and quiet beauty, Swinburne pays tribute to his father, who has just died; and in words whose marmoreal quality recalls Landor, the poet who earlier had proclaimed the death of God expresses hope of immortality. "In Memory of Barry Cornwall" opens with a marvelous picture of a kind of Socratic paradise "where the singers whose names are deathless/ One with another make music unheard of men." "To the beautiful veiled bright world where the glad ghosts meet" has gone "Barry Cornwall." Although Time has taken him and other poets from us, the poem affirms that he shall not take away "the flower of their souls," nor will "the lips lack song for ever that now lack breath." The elegy on Baudelaire, "Ave Atque Vale," was written soon after the publication of the first series of *Poems and Ballads*, but it is closer in language and tone to this volume, where it properly appears. Swinburne's deep affection for the dead French poet is felt throughout, and the resonant poignance created by the sibilance and dark vowels of the majestic stanzas and accentuated by the speaker's apostrophe of Baudelaire as *brother* helps make this one of the great elegies of English poetry. It conveys more sincerity than either "Lycidas" or "Adonais" and it is more tender than

"Thyrsis." After paying tribute to Baudelaire's genius—"Thou sawest, in thine old singing season, brother/ Secrets and sorrows unbeheld of us"—the poem affirms that even though he is "far too far for wings of words to follow," his poetry lives on. Remembering that everyone will one day meet death as the poet has, the poem concludes with a profound serenity.

There is no such serenity in "Fragment on Death," one of Swinburne's masterful translations of François Villon. Here death is depicted in all its medieval horror. This and the other translations, particularly the "Ballad of the Women of Paris," provide a contrast to the poems already discussed, but not so shocking a one as the four sonnets attacking Russia, which appear completely out of place in this volume.

After the second series of *Poems and Ballads*, Swinburne continued to publish poems for twenty-six years in a continuing variety of subject matter and form. The Arthurian romances *Tristram of Lyonesse and Other Poems* and *The Tale of Balen*, while containing passages of undisputed power and beauty, suggest that Swinburne's forte as a poet was not in extended narration. The many poems about babies in *A Century of Roundels* reveal a mature tenderness that one would not have expected from the author of *Songs Before Sunrise*. There are beautiful passages in *Songs of the Springtides*. The second series of *Poems and Ballads*, however, remain the pinnacle of Swinburne's achievement as a poet, and if he had written no more poetry after 1878, his reputation would have been essentially unchanged.

Robert G. Blake

Other major works

LONG FICTION: *Love's Cross-Currents*, 1901 (serialized as *A Year's Letters* in 1877); *Lesbia Brandon*, 1952.

PLAYS: *The Queen-Mother. Rosamond. Two Plays*, 1860; *Atalanta in Calydon*, 1865; *Chastelard*, 1865; *Bothwell*, 1874; *Erechtheus*, 1876; *Mary Stuart*, 1881; *Marino Faliero*, 1885; *Locrine*, 1887; *The Sisters*, 1892; *Rosamund, Queen of the Lombards*, 1899; *The Duke of Gandia*, 1908.

NONFICTION: *Byron*, 1866; *Notes on Poems and Reviews*, 1866; *William Blake: A Critical Essay*, 1868; *Under the Microscope*, 1872; *George Chapman*, 1875; *Essays and Studies*, 1875; *A Note on Charlotte Brontë*, 1877; *A Study of Shakespeare*, 1880; *Miscellanies*, 1886; *A Study of Victor Hugo*, 1886; *A Study of Ben Jonson*, 1889; *Studies in Prose and Poetry*, 1894; *The Age of Shakespeare*, 1908; *Three Plays of Shakespeare*, 1909; *Shakespeare*, 1909; *Contemporaries of Shakespeare*, 1919.

MISCELLANEOUS: *The Complete Works of Algernon Charles Swinburne*, 1925-1927 (20 volumes; reprinted 1968).

Bibliography

Harrison, Antony H. *Swinburne's Medievalism: A Study in Victorian Love*

Poetry. Baton Rouge: Louisiana State University Press, 1988. Although most of this book deals with Swinburne's poetic dramas, the chapter on *Poems and Ballads*, "Historicity and Erotic Aestheticism," provides an illuminating discussion of the influence of "historicist, erotic, and formal concerns" on several of Swinburne's most famous medieval lyrics.

Hyder, Clyde K., ed. *Swinburne: The Critical Heritage.* New York: Barnes & Noble Books, 1970. This volume in the Critical Heritage series charts the reception and evolving evaluation of Swinburne's work to 1920. Authors from Henry Brooks Adams to Sir Max Beerbohm state their opinions, ranging from amusement to damnation. Notable omissions are T. S. Eliot and Ezra Pound. The controversy over *Poems and Ballads* is well represented. The introduction provides an excellent overview.

Louis, Margot Kathleen. *Swinburne and His Gods: The Roots and Growth of an Agnostic Poetry.* Montreal: McGill-Queen's University Press, 1990. An intelligent investigation of the importance of Swinburne's "religious polemics." The use of "demonic parody" and whore goddesses in the early works is compared to the biblical sources. The alternative mythologies of later works are also discussed and related, in an appendix, to the myth-making of William Blake. Includes an extensive bibliography.

McGann, Jerome J. *Swinburne: An Experiment in Criticism.* Chicago: University of Chicago Press, 1972. This "experiment in criticism" uses historical, psychological, and textual approaches in the form of an imaginative dialogue among five people acquainted with Swinburne. While claiming to offer "nothing definitive" in the way of literary analysis, it nevertheless offers a wealth of insights. Its "earnest self-parody" suggests "the absurd limits of analytic knowledge."

Peters, Robert L. *The Crowns of Apollo: Swinburne's Principles of Literature and Art.* Detroit: Wayne State University Press, 1965. An examination of Swinburne's prose that discovers the foundations of Swinburne's poetry. In addition to Swinburne's reactions against the didactic and moral aims of art, Peters explores the importance of detail to Victorian aesthetics and the notion of "gathering form" in Swinburne's poetics. Numerous plates illustrate the relevance of Swinburne's theories to the visual arts.

Riede, David G. *Swinburne: A Study of Romantic Mythmaking.* Charlottesville: University Press of Virginia, 1978. A study in influence in the best sense, Riede's book sees Swinburne's poetry attempting to resolve certain conflicted projects of the Romantics, choosing William Blake's myth over his Christian mysticism, George Gordon, Lord Byron's heroic stance over his posing, William Wordsworth and Samuel Taylor Coleridge's humanism over their divinely informed pantheism, and Percy Bysshe Shelley's myth-making over his skepticism.

Thomas, Donald. *Swinburne: The Poet in His World.* New York: Oxford University Press, 1979. This biography takes Swinburne as a "child of his time," despite his reputation as "the figurehead of rebellion and modernity in literature." Thomas' coolheaded discussion of the poet's sadomasochism, alcoholism, and atheism allows him to discuss the relation between Swinburne's life and letters without hysteria and with great insight.

ALLEN TATE

Born: Winchester, Kentucky; November 19, 1899
Died: Nashville, Tennessee; February 9, 1979

Principal poetry

The Golden Mean and Other Poems, 1923 (with Ridley Wills); *Mr. Pope and Other Poems*, 1928; *Poems: 1928-1931*, 1932; *The Mediterranean and Other Poems*, 1936; *Selected Poems*, 1937; *The Winter Sea*, 1944; *Poems: 1920-1945*, 1947; *Poems: 1922-1947*, 1948; *Poems*, 1960; *The Swimmers and Other Selected Poems*, 1971; *Collected Poems: 1919-1976*, 1977.

Other literary forms

Although Allen Tate earned his literary reputation as a poet, the majority of his published work is prose. He is well known as an essayist, having published nine books of essays and contributed essays to a number of anthologies, including the Agrarian manifesto *I'll Take My Stand* (1930). His other nonfiction works include two biographies, *Stonewall Jackson: The Good Soldier* (1928) and *Jefferson Davis: His Rise and Fall* (1929). He also published a critically acclaimed novel, *The Fathers* (1938), set during the Civil War. Tate also worked as an editor and a translator, editing poetry anthologies and other literary works and translating some of the works of Charles Baudelaire and various classical poets. Each of these works demonstrates at least one of Tate's three major concerns: poetry, history, and the state of modern culture.

Achievements

Much of Tate's popular reputation as a poet rests on a single poem, "Ode to the Confederate Dead," written before he was twenty-six years old. It brought its author considerable fame both in America and abroad, but unfortunately it "typecast" him. Tate later wrote poems that were perhaps better and certainly ideologically different, but he was and still is so strongly identified with that work that his later poetry was for the most part neglected.

If the public saw him as a one-poem poet, however, he fared better at the hands of critics. He received a number of honors, including many honorary degrees; perhaps his most outstanding award was the National Medal for Literature in 1976. He also received the Bollingen Prize for Poetry in 1956, the Brandeis University Medal for Poetry in 1961, and the Gold Medal of the Dante Society of Florence in 1962. He was elected to both the American Academy of Arts and Letters in 1964 and the American Academy of Arts and Sciences in 1965. His *Collected Poems: 1919-1976* was awarded the Lenore Marshall Prize for Poetry in 1978.

Tate was one of the most widely known of the Agrarian/Fugitive poets. While some of his themes, techniques, and concerns were similar to those of his Southern colleagues, unlike some of them, he was not labeled (and subsequently dismissed) as a "regional" poet. Tate was as popular and as comfortable in the literary circles of New York and Europe as he was in that of his Vanderbilt associates, and his poetry demonstrates that Southern concerns are universal concerns as well.

Biography

John Orley Allen Tate was born in Winchester, Kentucky, the third son of John Orley and Eleanor Varnell Tate. His early life foreshadowed the gypsy-like wanderings of his later years; because of his father's various business interests, the family moved frequently. These moves resulted in Tate's rather sketchy education. As a teenager, he wrote a few poems, but his real love was music. He studied the violin under excellent teachers at the Cincinnati Conservatory of Music, but left when his teachers concluded that, while he had some talent, he had no exceptional gift for music.

Tate, his musical ambitions thwarted, was accepted at Vanderbilt University and entered in 1918. He had no particular interest in literature when his college career began. He was, however, strongly influenced by some of his teachers, especially Walter Clyde Curry. The medieval and Renaissance scholar lent him books, encouraged him to write poetry, and introduced him to John Crowe Ransom, with whom he later also studied. Under the influence of these two gifted teachers, Tate joined Vanderbilt's Calumet Club, a literary society whose membership also included Donald Davidson. Davidson invited Tate to participate in a discussion group which evolved into the Fugitives. Tate was an eager participant in this group of teachers and students and contributed many poems to its literary journal, *The Fugitive*. He was graduated from Vanderbilt in 1923 after having taken a year off from his studies because of poor health; his diploma was dated 1922, so that technically he was graduated "with his class." In his last year at Vanderbilt, he met Robert Penn Warren, a sixteen-year-old sophomore, who became his lifelong friend.

Tate had envisioned New York as the literary mecca of America, and he visited the city in 1924. He met Hart Crane, whose work he admired, as well as other authors. Upon his return, he visited the Warrens and there he met Caroline Gordon, the first of his three wives. After their marriage, they moved to New York, where Tate worked as an editor and continued to contribute to *The Fugitive* until it ceased publication in 1925. The Tates remained in New York until 1930, except for two years spent abroad on a Guggenheim Fellowship; then they moved back to Tennessee.

In Tennessee, Tate was able to enjoy the company of almost all of his old friends again. From this "reunion" arose the Agrarian movement. In 1934, Tate, seriously in debt, turned to college teaching. He taught at a number of colleges, but not until 1951 was he offered a tenured position, at the University of Minnesota, where he taught until his retirement in 1968. After his retirement, he returned to Sewanee, Tennessee.

Tate was a Southern poet in every sense of the term, but he was not limited to regional issues and popularity. His circle of literary friends included T. S. Eliot, Ford Madox Ford, and John Peale Bishop; his fame was international.

Analysis

Allen Tate's poetry has often been described as obscure; but while it is difficult and frequently misunderstood, it is not obscure. The difficulties in reading Tate's poems arise mainly from his allusions, many of which are classical.

A facet of Tate's poetry which is frequently misunderstood is his use of history as a theme. To Tate, a sense of history is no mere nostalgic longing for bygone glory. It is rather an understanding of those qualities of earlier cultures which made them human. In several poems, Tate expresses the belief that modern man has discarded too many of these qualities and thus has become less human. Tate does not suggest that man turn his back on modern culture and attempt to return to a more classical and simpler way of life, but he does seem to believe that modern technology and humanism are mutually exclusive. He is in favor of the creation of a new culture rather than the re-creation of an older one.

Tate's techniques as well as his themes are worthy of study. He rejected at first, but later acknowledged, the truism that form and content should be inextricably related, and he described free verse as a failure. His poems show an experimentation with many different forms. Also typical of Tate's poems is the use of unusual adjectives. "Ambitious November" and "brute curiosity of an angel's stare" (both from "Ode to the Confederate Dead") may be cited. These adjectives have the effect of capturing the attention of readers and forcing them to explore the images in order to understand them. A similar technique is his play of word upon word, frequently by exact repetition. Tate's poetry is also characterized by the use of concrete details to modify highly abstract language. Such details, sometimes consisting of single words only, are somewhat jarring to the reader, as they are no doubt meant to be. Finally, Tate can move easily from a formal, "scholarly" style to the use of highly sensuous diction, often within the same poem. He seems to be acutely aware of the tension that is produced by the contrast between Latinate and Anglo-Saxon vocabulary. He chooses the diction suited to his subject, with the language illustrating changes in imagery or tone.

Much attention has been focused on the effect other poets have had on Tate's poetic techniques and themes. His early poetry has been compared with that of his teacher and friend, John Crowe Ransom, while his later work is often compared to that of T. S. Eliot, whom Tate greatly admired. Tate was, however, writing such poetry before he had even read Eliot. In any case, the issue of anyone's "influence" on Tate is nebulous; certainly his work is not derivative, whatever the generalized debt he may owe Ransom, Eliot, and other writers with whose work he was familiar.

A good introduction to Tate's poetry is "The Mediterranean," a poem which displays many of his techniques and concerns. In fact, this poem appears as the first item in each of his collections (except *Collected Poems: 1919-1976*, which is arranged in order of first publication); it is considered to be one of the best of his shorter pieces. The poem begins with a Latin motto, which, as usual, Tate neither identifies nor translates. The motto comes from the first book of the *Aeneid* (c. 29-19 B.C.) and in the original reads "Quem das finem, rex magne, laborum?" ("What limit, great king, do you place on their labors?") Tate changes "laborum" to "dolorum" (pain, either physical or mental, but here probably mental). This motto should indicate to the reader that a knowledge of the *Aeneid* is necessary to an understanding of the poem. Indeed, a reader without a great deal of knowledge of the *Aeneid* would probably overlook or not understand many of Tate's allusions to it. The poem is, first of all, dramatic; it can be read simply as a description of the dramatic setting. Beneath this surface, however, is the reference, maintained throughout the poem, to the events in the *Aeneid*, as well as a commentary on the modern human condition by contrast with the past.

The dramatic situation of the poem is simple: a group of people are on a boat trip, a sort of party. The speaker is a member of that group. The voyage of Aeneas is recalled by the speaker, setting up what seems to be an unlikely parallel, although many a weekend sailor may imagine himself to be a Columbus, a Magellan—or even an Aeneas.

In the first stanza, the setting is described. It is a long bay surrounded by a cliff, similar to the bay on which Aeneas landed in Italy. The cliff, called the "peaked margin of antiquity's delay," serves as a symbol of the border between the past and present. Time is an important element here, and the first image illustrates Tate's belief that a difficult barrier exists between the past and present. This idea is developed throughout the poem by means of a contrast between the mythical past, represented by the heroic Aeneas, and the monotonous present, represented by the modern sailors who are attempting to retreat into antiquity. They themselves, however, as symbols of modern man, have made that return impossible.

The third stanza contains an important allusion to the *Aeneid* which continues to develop the contrast between the past and present. The speaker says that the party "made feast and in our secret need/ Devoured the very plates Aeneas bore." The reference is to the third book of the *Aeneid*, in which the harpies place a curse on Aeneas and his men: Aeneas will not find the land he is searching for until he and his men have become desperate enough to eat the plates they are carrying. The terms of the curse are fulfilled when the men eat wheat cakes on which they have placed food, thus signaling that they have arrived at their destination. The modern sailors parody this fulfillment of the curse on Aeneas; they too are "cursed" and are seeking another land.

The image is repeated in the fourth and fifth stanzas, emphasizing the idea of the removal of a curse.

The curse is explored in the last four stanzas; a question indicates what the curse is: "What prophecy of eaten plates could landless/ Wanderers fulfill by the ancient sea?" By sailing on the "ancient sea" and recalling Aeneas, the wanderers have established some contact with the past, but the contact is incomplete and ephemeral. Tate tells the reader why this is so in stanza 6: it is modern man's "lust for power" which has been his undoing. His final, strong image is that of a land of plenty in which what should be a bountiful harvest is left to "rot on the vine." This is the land, he reminds the reader, where he was born; one needs not seek a foreign land to regain the qualities of a great culture.

A somewhat similar theme is treated in Tate's best-known poem, "Ode to the Confederate Dead." The title of the poem is somewhat misleading, since the poem is not an ode, or public celebration, to the dead Confederate soldiers. The speaker is a modern man who must face the fact of his isolation, which becomes evident to him through his reflection on the various symbols in the poem, most significant of which is the cemetery where he stands. The speaker is not characterized; in fact, his lack of individuality is an important element in the poem.

Like many of Tate's other poems, "Ode to the Confederate Dead" contains striking diction. He makes use of unusual adjectives, oxymorons, and other techniques and figures, letting the reader know immediately that the poem is not a conventional glorification of the men who fought and died for the Confederacy. Tate's vision is broader than that, and his theme is more universal.

The first section contains a great deal of nature imagery, the speaker personifying nature in an almost Romantic fashion. It is interesting to note, however, that he describes the wind as whirring, a sound associated with machinery rather than nature. This section also contains an extended image of piles of fallen leaves; the month is, as is made explicit in the next section, November. The deadness of the leaves is emphasized, drawing a parallel between the leaves and the soldiers.

In the second section, the speaker focuses his attention on the graves. The graves, like the men who lie in them, have been unable to withstand the effects of time. The stone angels on the graves have been stained, chipped, and even broken. This section also reveals that the speaker sees the dead soldiers as having lost their individual identities; they have become merely the "Confederate dead," a group of people from whom time has removed all sense of individuality. The speaker sympathizes with such a loss, for he feels that he has been similarly imposed on by modern culture.

The third and fourth sections emphasize this sense of loss. The speaker feels that modern man is ineffectual; he has "waited for the angry resolution/

Of those desires that should be yours tomorrow." Modern man has praise for the dead Confederate soldiers, he says, but does not see that the dead soldiers were "hurried beyond decision" to their deaths.

The last sections of the poem contain a question. How, the speaker asks, should people commemorate the dead soldiers? He refers again to their anonymity and uses the word "chivalry," an idea he has merely suggested before. "Chivalry" connotes high ideals and historical tradition, but the tradition died because its followers failed to put its ideals into practice. The speaker has no desire to recapture the past of the dead soldiers; it seems to him no better than the present, which, by the end of the poem, he has come to accept.

The speaker in "Ode to the Confederate Dead" is a philosopher, but he is also a solipsist, believing that the self is the only reality. This flaw, the belief only in self, is a failing that Tate seems to feel is typical of modern man. Thus the theme is similar to that of "The Mediterranean," as well as others of Tate's poems. The concerns of modern man, he suggests, are petty, somehow not human. There is, however, no resolution to the problem; the tone is despairing. Several critics have pointed out that "Ode to the Confederate Dead" is "dark," containing none of the images of light of which Tate was so fond. The speaker seems truly doomed by his inability to see beyond himself.

The problems and failings of modern man also dominate "Seasons of the Soul," considered by many critics to be the best of Tate's later poetry. The poem is dedicated to John Peale Bishop, Tate's friend and a poet for whom he had great respect. The two men occasionally wrote companion poems and frequently helped and criticized each other's work. Following the dedication in the poem, there is an epigraph, which, like the motto in "The Mediterranean," is neither identified nor translated (it is from Dante's *Inferno*). In the lines quoted, the speaker says that he reached up and broke a branch from a thorn tree, which cried out asking, "Why have you torn me apart?" Imprisoned inside the tree is the soul of a man, presumably a man who has died by suicide. The punishment fits the crime; the soul which denied its human form has been given a nonhuman exterior in which to spend eternity. The epigraph is significant in three ways. First, Dante in this part (Canto XIII) of the *Inferno* is describing the punishment of the violent, and Tate feels that violence is another of modern man's great flaws. Second, there is the suggestion that modern man, in denying his humanity, has damned himself to a fate similar to that of suicide. Finally, the epigraph alerts the reader to the presence of allusions to Dante in the poem.

"Seasons of the Soul" is divided into four sections named for each of the seasons, and critics disagree on their significance in the poem. Some have seen a correspondence between the seasons and the elements, while others argue that the seasons represent the recurring obsessions of man. The idea of the unending rotation of the seasons is emphasized in several places. Three of the sections, "Summer," "Winter," and "Spring," begin similarly with an invocation, a technique associated with the epic tradition. The epic poets asked in their invocations for help in treating their subjects adequately, for they wrote of great deeds far beyond their own capabilities. They sought to go beyond their own limitations through the aid of the muse, who represented the epic tradition. In "Seasons of the Soul," Tate's use of the invocation is ironic, since a major element in the poem is man's search for salvation through some source outside himself, a search which is futile. The one section which has no invocation is "Autumn." The most likely explanation for this omission, according to George Hemphill in *Allen Tate* (1964), is that this section is devoted to the obsessions of man as solipsist. Since solipsistic man is unable to accept anything but himself as reality (and, by extension, as significant), he would not feel the need to invoke the aid of any muse or god.

The seasons are presented in sequence, beginning with summer. By choosing thus to begin the poem, Tate indicates that he is not using the four seasons in the traditional manner to represent the four ages of man; using the seasons in that manner would necessitate beginning with spring. In fact, most critics have noticed a logical progression in the poem from season to season and have pointed out that much of its meaning is lost if the reader attempts to begin reading the sequence at some section other than "Summer." The sequence is representative of man's development; to return to Hemphill's interpretation of the poem's sections, "Summer" concerns man as activist or politician, "Autumn" concerns him as solipsist, "Winter" concerns him as a sexual being, and "Spring" concerns him as a religious being. These concerns are similar to the seasons in their unrelenting reoccurrence.

In "Summer," Tate is concerned with the effects of political activity, especially war, on man's humanity, and he once again denounces whatever leads to dehumanization. The poem refers to World War II and the occupation of "Green France," a basically agrarian culture, by the "caterpillar feet" of Germany's technical culture. Here Tate's view of war is that of a true conscientious objector; he seems to feel that no war is justified, since the effect of violence on man's soul is so devastating as to render every victory Pyrrhic.

The season of the second part of the poem is autumn, the season of "Ode to the Confederate Dead." The speaker, often identified as the poet, relates a dream he had of falling down a well into a house. He tries to leave the house, but what appears to be the front door is a false door. His parents are in the house, but they do not recognize him. The speaker seems to have wandered (or, more accurately, fallen) into a hell especially designed for him since it fulfills his worst fear, that of the loss of his own identity. In losing his identity, the solipsist loses all. He has been damned by his inability to transcend himself, like the speaker in "Ode to the Confederate Dead." Once again Tate warns of the dangers of modern man's egocentricity.

While a logical link exists between the first and second sections of the poem, some critics have been unable to see such a transition between the second and third sections. Since the third is about sex, apparently that is the retreat of the speaker from his personal hell. He looks for comfort and perhaps even salvation in sex, for he begins with an invocation to Venus, goddess of love. He asks her to return to the sea, from which she came; this impossible act, the speaker feels, is preferable to modern religion in which God is seen as dried up, no longer bearing the wounds of Christ which represent man's salvation. God is as dead to modern man as the sea-gods, such as Neptune, are. Unlike these gods, Venus is still alive as far as modern man is concerned. Tate, however, uses images of coldness and violence to describe modern man's sexual feelings. The shark is a symbol of man's sexual "perversion." This section ends with a return to the section of the *Inferno* from which the epigraph comes. The speaker breaks a branch from a tree and hears the blood of a suicide speak to him as it drips on him from the tree. The blood tells him that it is the blood of men who have killed themselves because of love's deceit. The reference to blood is reminiscent of all the water imagery used throughout this section. The blood imagery further reminds the reader that this section deals with the heart, whereas the previous section deals with the mind and the first section with the tension between the mind and heart. There clearly is no salvation through sex for modern man.

The final section deals with religion; man, having found no help elsewhere, turns to Christianity. The invocation is to spring, described as "irritable"—reminiscent of T. S. Eliot's description of April as "the cruelest month" in *The Waste Land* (1922). Spring is irritable because it is unable to stay and settle down. In the second stanza the speaker recalls his childhood innocence, which refused to acknowledge the reality of death but was amused, rather, by the "ancient pun" which equated death and orgasm.

In the fourth stanza Tate suggests that man can find peace only when he accepts the idea of death. Although this concept is Christian, the imagery is pagan, with references to Plato's cave and Sisyphus' rock. Tate moves from this thought into the specific mother imagery of the last two stanzas. The first mother has been identified as St. Monica, mother of St. Augustine of Hippo. According to legend, St. Monica was a difficult mother, insisting that her son become a Christian. The early images of death as a gentle, loving "mother of silences" are continued through the reference to St. Monica, a stern mother who led her son to the salvation of Christianity, and the nameless mother of the last stanza. In this final stanza Tate raises a question which he does not answer: Is death a "kindness"? Certainly the orthodox view of Christianity insists that man turn his eyes toward heaven where a "better life" awaits him. Tate, however, is a rather unorthodox Christian and in this poem is still trying to come to terms with religious questions.

Throughout these three rather similar poems, as well as in others, Tate's major concern is the state of modern culture and modern man. He is a kind of prophet, warning man of the consequences of his way of life. In some of his works he offers remedies for man's dilemmas, although he does not hesitate to blame him for being the cause of his own problems. Tate's poems will no doubt be read in the future as a fairly accurate record of the concerns of twentieth century man. Read in the chronological order in which they appear in *Collected Poems: 1919-1976*, they further serve as a record of the spiritual development of Tate himself, a poet of considerable talent and vision.

Claire Clements Morton

Other major works

LONG FICTION: *The Fathers*, 1938.

NONFICTION: *Stonewall Jackson: The Good Soldier*, 1928; *Jefferson Davis: His Rise and Fall*, 1929; *Reactionary Essays on Poetry and Ideas*, 1936; *Reason in Madness, Critical Essays*, 1941; *On the Limits of Poetry, Selected Essays 1928-1948*, 1948; *The Hovering Fly and Other Essays*, 1949; *The Forlorn Demon: Didactic and Critical Essays*, 1953; *The Man of Letters in the Modern World: Selected Essays, 1928-1955*, 1955; *Collected Essays*, 1959; *Essays of Four Decades*, 1968; *The Poetry Reviews of Allen Tate, 1924-1944*, 1983.

Bibliography

Bishop, Ferman. *Allen Tate*. Twayne United States Authors series. New York: Twayne, 1967. Though composed while Tate was still writing, Bishop's book offers a good survey of his life and work up to that point; Tate's final years didn't change much. Includes a chronology, detailed notes and references, and a select bibliography.

Dupree, Robert S. *Allen Tate and the Augustinian Imagination: A Study of the Poetry*. Baton Rouge: Louisiana State University Press, 1983. Dupree has accomplished here the most thorough traversal of Tate's poetry to date, but he does confine his attention to the poetry. His approach is methodical and comprehensive, disclosing ingenious insights. Since poetry was Tate's central concern, what Dupree discovers here carries over to other aspects of his work. Includes an index, a bibliography, and notes.

Meiners, P. K. *Everything to Be Endured: An Essay on Robert Lowell and Modern Poetry*. Columbia: University of Missouri Press, 1970. Although not primarily concerned with Tate, this eighty-nine-page essay reveals much about him and his impact on mid-twentieth century poetry. Because it offers no bibliography, its usefulness is limited, but some of the insights into Tate remain unsurpassed.

Squires, Radcliffe. *Allen Tate: A Literary Biography*. New York: Bobbs-Merrill, 1971. Also written before Tate's death, this book is primarily a writing biography—that is, it considers the life of the writer with reference to his writings. The telling benefits from the personal acquaintance of Squires with Tate. Contains much anecdotal material, a bibliography, indexes, and notes.

_____, ed. *Allen Tate and His Work: Critical Evaluations.* Minneapolis: University of Minnesota Press, 1972. Squires here assembles essays on all phases of Tate's writing, editing, teaching, and life, including several by Tate's associates in the Agrarian movement, especially John Crowe Ransom and Donald Davidson. Cleanth Brooks, Howard Nemerov, and Louis D. Rubin, Jr. are also represented. Contains a complete bibliography.

Stewart, John Lincoln. *The Burden of Time: The Fugitives and the Agrarians.* Princeton, N.J.: Princeton University Press, 1965. This valuable study focuses more on the intellectual movements associated with Tate than on Tate himself. Since, however, these movements formed a large part of his life, they are revealing. Includes substantial comments on both poetry and criticism, and the coverage is thorough and deep. Complemented by footnotes and a bibliography.

JAMES TATE

Born: Kansas City, Missouri; December 8, 1943

Principal poetry
The Lost Pilot, 1967; *The Oblivion Ha-Ha,* 1970; *Hints to Pilgrims,* 1971, 1982; *Absences: New Poems,* 1972; *Viper Jazz,* 1976; *Riven Doggeries,* 1979; *Constant Defender,* 1983; *Reckoner,* 1986; *Distance from Loved Ones,* 1990.

Other literary forms
James Tate's *Hottentot Ossuary* (1974) is a collection of short stories; he wrote *Lucky Darryl* (1977), a novel, with Bill Knott.

Achievements
James Tate came onto the literary scene at the age of twenty-three, when his first full-length manuscript of poems, *The Lost Pilot,* was published in the Yale Younger Poets Series—a prestigious competition run by Yale University Press, which has introduced many of the finest American poets at the start of their careers. The poetry world took notice of this young prodigy of verse and has continued to be astonished by Tate's prolific output. Seventeen other works, long and short, appeared in the next five years. Tate became editor of the *Dickinson Review* in 1967 and has also served as an associate editor at Pym-Randall Press and Barn Dream Press (small presses located in Cambridge, Massachusetts) and as a consultant to the Coordinating Council of Literary Magazines. For two years running, in 1968 and 1969, and again in 1980, he received writing fellowships from the National Endowment for the Arts; he won a National Institute of Arts and Letters Award in 1974, followed two years later by a Guggenheim Fellowship. In 1972, he was the Phi Beta Kappa poet at Brown University.

Tate has established himself as a formidable exponent of literary surrealism of a peculiarly American kind. His work has garnered the praise of many academic critics and journal reviewers; his poetry has appeared across the gamut of magazines in North America and England and has influenced the style of many young writers.

Biography
James Tate was born in Kansas City, Missouri, in 1943. He began college study at the University of Missouri in Columbia and finished his B.A. at Kansas State College in Pittsburg, Kansas, in 1965. He entered the Writers Workshop at the University of Iowa and received an M.F.A. in poetry in 1967. From 1966 onward, Tate has taught creative writing and literature courses, first at the University of Iowa (1966-1967), followed by short stints at the University of California at Berkeley (1967-1968), Columbia University (1969-1971),

and Emerson College in Boston, where he was poet-in-residence in 1970-1971. He joined the regular teaching faculty at the University of Massachusetts at Amherst in 1971 and has remained there except for short periods of residence in Sweden, Ireland, and Spain.

Analysis

There are two kinds of poets in the world: those who grow with age and alter style, outlook, and argument over the years, and those who burst onto the scene fully fledged and polish what is in essence an unchanging perception of life throughout their careers. James Tate is of the second sort; his stunning appearance in his first major book, *The Lost Pilot*, set the pattern for all he would write over the succeeding decades. The poetry of *Distance from Loved Ones* is a richer, denser, more masterful execution of the style and themes he set for himself as a young man.

Variation for Tate is a subtle thing; beneath the variances of style and diction lies a core of subjects and emotions that are constant in his poetry: loss of relations, the quixotic world of appearances, a violent underworld of emotion waiting to erupt through the crevices of the mundane. The central theme running throughout Tate's canon is the desire to shatter superficial experience, to break through the sterility of suburban life and drown it in erotic passion. His characters languish from unfulfilled longings; the objects he contemplates are all prisoners of definition and stereotype; life is a desert of routine expectation waiting to blow up from the forces of liberated imagination, whimsy, outrage, and humor.

Tate joins a long line of Midwestern writers who fought in their writing against the domestic tedium of their region. Theodore Dreiser set the pattern of the rebellious Midwestern writer in his novels about youths trapped in the social coils of work, poverty, and loveless marriages; Sherwood Anderson paved the way of modernist writers through his depictions of the sterile sanity of small-town life in his novel *Winesburg, Ohio* (1947). F. Scott Fitzgerald and Ernest Hemingway explored the unrealizable dreams of their characters, who had escaped only partway from their families and bleak pasts. Poets of the Midwest, including T. S. Eliot, Ezra Pound, and Carl Sandburg, emphasized realistic detail in their unflinching reports of what had gone wrong in American society in their time.

The Lost Pilot joins this tradition of harsh assessments of Midwestern life; the argument itself is a rather somber account of a young man's loneliness, despair, and feelings of isolation. "The End of the Line," from the middle section of the book, is emblematic of the themes treated in the poems. "We plan our love's rejuvenation/ one last time," the speaker comments, but the jaunty tone of the piece breaks down as he admits that the relationship has gone sour for good. The poems acutely examine the meaning of relationships, the risk of loving someone, the desolation at losing a father or lover through unexplained accident or fatal whim. This instability lying at the heart of emotion makes everything else around him equally shimmering and unreal.

Tate's use of surrealist language, the dreamy, irrational figures and images that define his view of things, is derived from European and South American writing of the twentieth century. The original motives of surrealism sprang from the devastations of war and the corruption of the state. For Tate, though, the corruption lies somewhere else: in the incapacity of human beings to face their dilemmas honestly, to admit that the heart is wild, immoral, anarchic, or that life is essentially a reality beyond the grasp of moral principles. For Tate, the American situation is the opposite of war-torn Europe or politically corrupt South America. The American scene is *too* stable, too ordered and domesticated; underneath the neat appearances of reality lies a universe of chaotic energies waiting to spring back. To that degree, one may casually link Tate's vision to the horrific suspense of Stephen King's novels or to the wounded idealism of Tom Wolfe and Hunter Thompson. In each of these writers lives a certain purity of taste for the natural world, and for the lost values of a pastoral and Edenic past which modernity has outraged and insulted.

To love in Tate's poetry is to tap into this hidden volcano of impacted irrationality, to tease its powers awake. Most often, his lovers quake at the first sign of wilderness in their emotions and drift back to the safety of their homely, selfish worlds. To fall in love is to touch nature directly, and to break through to the other side of reality. This sentiment is expressed at the close of *The Lost Pilot* when Tate writes, "I am falling, falling/ falling in love, and desire to leave this place." The place he desires to leave is that parched desert of convention where all of his characters languish.

The poetry of this first collection generates a kind of philosophical earthquake in its brief descriptions, debunking the moral fictions of an ordered life through the riotous outpouring of illogical imagery. This is a poetry of emotional purgings, of discreet, Janovian primal screams into the bedroom mirror.

The Lost Pilot is grounded by its title poem, an elegy combining a son's wit, fantasy, and tears over the death of his father in World War II. The phrase itself is instructive; a pilot is one who finds his way through dark skies. The father as lost pilot compounds the son's forlornness; here is a father who has disappeared, a guide without compass who leaves his son behind in a dull, seemingly trackless void. The reader learns in the poem that the son keeps an annual vigil and looks up to see his father orbiting overhead—a curious, droll, and yet appropriate image for the son's grief. Another poem, written to his mother, commemorates Father's Day in an ironic reference to the missing father. A careful look at all the poems reveals the image of the missing father in each of them: He haunts the world as a peculiar absence of love, as when lovers leave the poet, or emotion goes rank and sour.

In the closing poem, "Today I Am Falling," even the title suggests something of Tate's humor in poetry: the falling has no object, but in the text the reader finds that the falling is toward love, which in turn leads only to the desire to escape. The place the speaker is trying to reach is a "sodium pentothal landscape," a place of lost memories aroused by the intravenous intake of a "truth serum" once used in psychotherapy. That landscape lies behind repression and emotional stagnation, its "bud about to break open." The trembling surface of Tate's language here and elsewhere is that effort to break through the false appearance of things, the dull veneer of human convention concealing passion and the energy of nature.

Yet for a poet trying to break through, the early poems are terse, carefully worked miniatures that technically belie their purpose. Tate prefers a short, three-line stanza as his measure, with a varying line of between five and six syllables, usually end-stopped—that is, punctuated with a comma-length pause, or ended with a period. The flow of speech often requires enjambment, the running through of one line to the next, but not in the free-verse fashion of breaking lines arbitrarily at prepositions, adjectives, and nouns after the manner of prose. Instead, Tate makes sure his phrases are well-defined rhythmically before cutting to the next line. If he carries the rhythm through to the next line, or allows it to leap over a stanza break, usually he has found some emphatic word to terminate the line before he does so.

The poems on the page look slightly cramped and compressed, as if the thinking were squeezed down to an essence of protest. The poetry written by Tate's contemporaries is expansive, even sprawling by comparison. Few poets took the medium to these limits of compression, and when they did, they were freer with the pattern of line and accent. One may speculate that Tate's statements are intended as whispers in tight places—quick, emergency pleas to the reader or to himself. However they are intended, the language is uniformly limpid, purified, the hesitation revised out of each smoothly cresting phrase. There is high finish in the wording and phrasing, which may at times work against the sense of emotional torment Tate wants to convey.

Thumbing through the pages of *The Lost Pilot*, one is struck by the contradiction between polished execution and troubled content. The move in poetry after 1945 was to incorporate into the linguistic and prosodic structure of the poem the *movement* of emotion tracked by the meaning of words. The poem should come apart in sympathy with, or in representation of, the emotional disarray of the speaker, and the language of the poem should involve the detritus of spent or erupting emotion in its configuration. Distillation of language down to an essence was in some ways a Christian aesthetic carried over into "closed" or traditional poetics—a sense of language as having a spiritual inner text which the poet pared down to achieve communication with the soul. The throwing up of verbal dross and trivia into the language stream of lyric after 1945 was an effort to join "soul music" with the blunt, earthy matter of nature; hence the languorous and wayward course of much lyric energy in the postmodern era. In Tate, however, and in a contingent of "Southern" male poets who came of age with him, one finds uniformly tidy and balanced typographical structures that avoid technical deformation.

Tate's aesthetic tradition, which includes Wallace Stevens, Robert Frost, the European Symbolists, and the Deep Image movement of Robert Bly and James Wright, rejected a "projective" aesthetic that would incorporate the turmoil of mind into the finished artwork. That distinction between content and execution may have proved over the years to be confining to the range of Tate's subject matter and stylistic virtuosity. There is the hint of a technical repression of feeling in this mode of terse lyric, of funneling into sparse and smoothly patterned verses the chaos of longing and rage intended by the poems. The risk one takes in keeping to this method of writing is that emotional diversity may be diluted by the repetition of lyric forms.

Through the succession of Tate's later books, the poem does not change its technical strategy except to grow in size: Stanza and line are fleshed out, articulation is fuller and more sonorous, and rhythm has greater sweep, but the poet set his stylistic signature in *The Lost Pilot*, and the rules he gave himself were essentially unalterable thereafter. The burden on readers is to pay keen attention to content against a background of similar, even uniform measures, to make out with sympathetic attention the varying inner world that has been systematized in repetitive lyrical patterns. The burden on Tate is to risk everything on the line itself, to dazzle, compel, and sweep away the reader on the force of an image, a powerful phrase, the stunning resolution of a whole poem on a single word.

In *The Oblivion Ha-Ha*, a three-stanza poem, "The Pet Deer," works on the principle of the single line holding the poem aloft. Stanza 1 is purely functional exposition, given in limpid phrases; stanza 2 sets up the conflict implied in the deer's realizing that is a kind of centaur in love with a human girl; stanza 3 builds slowly toward the closing line, revealing that the girl is unaware of "what/ the deer dreams or desires." Here repression is located in an animal, a deft reversal of Tate's usual argument. The girl is placid, lovely, unaffected in her sexual allure; the deer is the captive soul unable to break out and satisfy desire.

The poem hangs by the thread of its final line along with the touches in several other phrases, but in sum, it works on the plainness of its exposition, its setup of an incident, which it transforms by a single lyric thrust of insight. This is Symbolist methodology given an American stamp by Tate's withholding the intellectual and ideological motives of the lyric act. In Symbolist poetry almost any incident will reveal the poet's own psyche, which he will have expressed referentially through an object, animal, or character.

The deer is, by the twists of psychic projection in this poem, the poet himself, the girl a combination of lovers longed for and lost. The art of the poem is to raise the ordinary theme of repression and longing to a degree of generality that turns experience into fable, myth, or even allegory. Too broad a stroke, and the delicate suggestibility of language collapses; too little said, and the poem remains a mere fragment of thought without affect.

"Here is my heart,/ I don't know what to do with it," Tate writes in another poem, "Plea Based on a Sentence from a Letter Received by the Indiana State Welfare Department." The line expresses succinctly the theme of *The Oblivion Ha-Ha*. The title has confused critics; it is usually taken to mean a kind of maniacal laughter in the face of a bitter world. But a secondary definition of "ha-ha" is a garden enclosure, usually of hedge or earthwork, separating one small planting bed from surrounding ground. In early Roman gardens, a raised inner court often supported a small statue of Adonis, a chthonic god of fertility; in modern times, gazebos and small terraces take the same role as the Adonis mound. Curiously, the garden meaning of the word, derived from French, bears the same hyphen as the first meaning. Tate's conceit may be that one laughs helplessly at sight of the enclosed Eden, thus doubling the meanings into one trope.

That inner garden reserve, perhaps, is the point of the title, an inner garden that is shut in or inaccessibly remote and psychological, but rooted in the familiar world of human senses. The oblivion ha-ha is the soul, the secret inner self in its own mound of earth, which the poems try to capture.

In "The Salute," a man dreams about a black widow whom he loves; yet he "completely misunderstood" her "little language." The secret soul is located on one side or another of broken relationships; lovers who try to reach across the distance confront either the sorrows of the deer or the suicidal love of this dreamer, willing to mate with a spider who kills her lovers. "Nobody gets what he wants," Tate writes in a later poem, "Consumed," which closes on this characteristic remark about a lover, "You are the stranger/ who gets stranger by the hour." Another poem on parents, "Leaving Mother Waiting for Father," returns to the theme of loss, with the speaker leaving his doll-like, decrepit mother leaning against a hotel, as he goes off into the world an adult orphan.

In every case, Tate creates a portrait of an isolated heart longing for relation and failing to achieve it. The world that denies love to his characters is superficially intact, but beneath appearance it festers with neurotic passion and chaos. Is it any wonder, therefore, that his next book would be called *Absences*? In it, Tate experiments with a looser style; prose poems appear in section 3, while long poems occupy section 2. The title poem and "Cycle of Dust" are sequential works that have more diffuse imagery and lack the point of surprise perfected in the short lyric.

The interesting turn in *Absences* is in the image making itself; it focuses on characters who dismantle themselves, or try to disappear, in their blind effort to cross over to the "other" side of reality. These figures do not quite make it; they practice escaping from the blind literalism of things but end up dismantling only their defined selves. They do not reach Paradise. The shift to decomposing this part of reality marks Tate's decision to alter the lyric path he was on. From here onward, Tate drops the Edenic or pastoral ideal altogether and concentrates instead on exploding the empirical world of sense and definition. Experience itself will be his target.

Put another way, in *Absences* and beyond, one half of the metaphoric principle of his poetry drops away, the ideal and hidden dimension of vision. What remains is the imploding and decaying half of reality, the objects metaphor dwells on to hint at possibilities in the dream world. There are only the objects themselves now, deformed, fragmentary, increasingly meaningless as the stuff of lyric. More and more, Tate will imply the end of such language: There is still the need to escape, to break out of reality into the other world, but references to the other world by image or suggestion are rare. His poems dwell on the disappearance of reality itself, its decomposition into fantasy and paradox. In "Harm Alarm," the second poem of *Absences*, a man fearfully examines his street, decides that all harm lies "in a cradle/ across the ocean," and resumes his walk after observing that his "other" self should "just about awake now" as the source of that harm. The divided self splits evenly between dream and waking, serene emptiness and conflictual, wounded life. Pain abounds as the defining attribute of consciousness; the pin functions as a motif in a number of these poems.

There is little or no plot, and no organization to narrate the flow of language. The poems accumulate around the thematic abstraction of reality's own breakup. That means that individual lines and sentences have the burden of forming the book. Reading Tate, one looks for lines, images, and stunning metaphors as the point of poetry. There is no structural principle embodying language or visionary argument. Tate's assumption is that reality is dead, and the surreal lyric depicts that through its own formlessness and its occasional glimpses into magic through a phrase or word. Another position would hold that the poem itself is an object of nature, an expression of creative principles. Tate's metaphysic, however, is still linked with the Christian view that meaning derives from a spiritual source outside of nature. These poems, strange and irrational as they are, are secularized forms of prayer, beseeching an "outside" for grace and succor.

These matters are summed up in "Wait for Me," when he writes, "A dream of life a dream of birth/ a dream of moving/ from one world into another// All night dismantling the synapses/ unplugging the veins and arteries." The rest of the poem is about the dissolving self, the fading consciousness, as the reader continues to watch, in this world, with him. The tone is not far removed from the self-abnegating fervor of the medieval martyr, whose longing to purify life and join God are merely the extreme of Tate's lyrics of self-abandonment. "I hear a laugh swim up/ from the part of myself/ I've killed," he writes in "Delicate Riders," in which the reader sees that it is the spiritual self that has died out in the contemporary desert of materialism. "I who have no home have no destination either," he writes in "The Boy." "One bone against another,/ I carve what I carve/ to be rid of myself by morning/ by deep dreams disintegrated."

Tate's feud with reality is that it has no soul; it is the broken world of modern, spiritless philosophy. What remains is the memory of soul in magical lyricism, which surveys the fallen world and discovers fading glimmers of spirit in paradox, accidental juxtaposition, chaotic series, and the like.

This mordant perspective on the world is the subject of his next major book, *Viper Jazz*, published in the Wesleyan Poetry Program series (Wesleyan University Press) in 1976. In it Tate reins in the experimentalism of *Absences* and writes in short, stanzaic lyrics and prose poems on the theme of "worlds refused by worlds." A man goes crazy with his obsessions in "Many Problems," his suffering soul dying on "the boneyard of vegetables/ the whole world is built on." In "Read the Great Poets," the couch allows "the spirit to leave/ the broken body and wander at will" through "this great dull life."

In "Blank-Stare Encounter," the speaker blurts out a new imperative, "I want to start a new religion," but the dead world's "blank stare drags me along." The point is, however, that no "new religion" is forthcoming from Tate. Midway through *Viper Jazz* one begins to feel a withdrawal from that premise and the setting in of a reductive new attitude that is partly resignation and partly a return to the chattier, amusing voice of early lyrics. There is a quality here of stand-up comedian, the one-liner gag writer who keeps his audience off balance by surrealist turns.

From *Viper Jazz* to the following book, *Riven Doggeries*, one notes with misgivings a certain carelessness in the work; the language is flimsy, form is lazily sketched in, and poems turn on anecdote and coincidence, sometimes without the clinching phrase to energize them. The theme for much of *Riven Doggeries* is travel, both actual and mind-travel, the feverish transport into and out of reality as the locus of mere existence. By now it is obvious that there is no Paradise opening through the mist; instead, Tate's style hardens into a parody of the real world, a burlesque of the poet's daily life on which the shreds of a previous idealism still cling. "We are all members/ of Nature's alphabet. But we wanted more," he writes in "Nature Poem: Demanding Stiff Sentences," a pun-laced and well-crafted lyric tucked into the middle of the book. Yet such reminders of his romantic principles do not make up for his lax writing.

As a sign that the verse poem may be wearing out here, Tate turns increasingly to the prose poem as miniature short story and frame for the fantasized speech he is using. In "Missionwork," part 3 of *Riven Doggeries*, the language is dense and humorous again, and self-mocking. "It's a sickness, this desire to fly," he notes. Here too the ideal slips away in a dozen forms, from fireflies to dogs—the dog is an essential motif of the absconding spirit throughout the book, the "rivening" of the title.

The prose poem, used here with skill, crept into poetry and has become a standard form in the American repertoire. Beginning with the French poet Charles Baudelaire's *Petits Poèmes en prose*, 1869 (also known as *Le Spleen de Paris; Paris Spleen* 1869), an early experiment in the mode, poets have discovered its use as a form of fantasizing meditation, but without the rhythmic intimacy or precision required in verse. Prose is borderless, a more "submerged" form of writing in that line breaks and phrasings are no longer functions of intense feeling or ideation. A poet's prose makes the presumption of being literal, often somber self-analysis, just as fantasy and the absurd slowly decompose the argument. The trick is to construct an elaborate ruse of confidentiality that is undone the moment the next improbable detail is sprung on the reader's belief, crushing it. Some writers, including Tate and his friend Charles Simic, compound the irony by going past the point of disbelief to reestablish partial credibility.

Both books show Tate trying to find ways to open the poem, to spread out its intricate patterns and create more space for rambling monologue and humorous asides. Tate's efforts are directed at colloquializing his verse speech, which begins to take effect in *Constant Defender*, published in 1983. Here a well-balanced fantasy mixes with verse compression, though the clinching phrase is often muted in the process. The dialectic between spiritual ideals and the morbidity of the real take subtler form, as in "Tall Trees by Still Waters," where "the actual world was pretending again,/ no, not pretending, imagining an episode/ of unbelievable cruelty, involving invalids."

The self of these poems is more harried, beaten down, and Kafkaesque than in previous books. One detects the wearing down of the idealist in such poetry, intimated in the title—the wearying vigilance of the "constant defender" of his beliefs. The theme running throughout is of abandoned houses to which the speaker returns forlornly, disillusioned once more at cruelty and indifference. In "Tell Them   Was Here," the "I" being left blank, the poem ends, "Started to leave,// turned, scratched out my name—/ then wrote it back again." A darker look at self occurs in "Lousy in Center Field," a wonderful poem with dazzling imagery that remarks, "I'm frozen once again/ in an attitude of unfortunate/ interior crumbling mouseholes." He is the ballplayer who has lost all interest in catching the ball, which flies over him in a cobwebbed sky.

The landscape is filling up with the dead souls of the modern city. This theme, though tentative and sketchy in *Constant Defender*, becomes pronounced in Tate's later books: *Reckoner*, published in 1986, and *Distance from Loved Ones*, which appeared in 1990. Both continue the breezier, conversational style that set in with *Constant Defender.* The poems work as accumulations of one-line observations, some pithy, some empty, with here and there a humorous turn or a startling image to enliven the pace of what is often tedious aggregates of lines. One poem flows into the next in these books, in which a manic speaker seems desperate to keep up his chatter against a growing sense of loss in his life.

Reckoner mixes prose poems and lyric or narrative verse; the tone shifts slightly from one to the other, but Tate has turned his attention away from the formality and finish of individual poems to the sense of words running together across boundaries to create a metatextual whole. The poems no longer hold up as unique, intricately structured maps of thought; their titles and shapes on the page maintain a certain ghost of formality over which the content leaps. The resulting flow of commentary creates the impression of a speaker's feverish avoidance of some impending tragedy. Even the humor is shrill, worn out, the emotions exhausted by frenetic articulation. The jokes and grotesque exaggeration have an almost menacing insistence; the reader has come upon their formulas many times before in Tate.

Many of the poems open on the same frenetic tempo, with fully punctuated sentences lined up as stanzas, as in "The Flithering Ignominy of Baba Ganoosh," which begins,

> He played the bongo drums and dated infant actresses.
> His signature still glitters in all the most exhausted hotels.
> He has positive contempt for rain, for chattering.
> His sofa was designed by a butcher.

This is the sort of *schtick* Henny Youngman made famous, the one-liner that waits for guffaws or the drummer's rim shot in the background. A pace of this kind wears out humor and begins arousing other emotions by its drugged repetition. Poem after poem renounces the minutiae of the waking world, as some other, darker voice hints that the underlying hidden world has sealed itself for good. The speaker is someone left behind, unable to imagine the possibility of regaining what he somewhere calls the "parallel world." "I've been feeling so cooped up in this hotel," begins a prose poem, "Magazines," where banter goes on for a page without resolution, without argument, without premise even, but for this dejection that pervades all of *Reckoner.*

In *Distance from Loved Ones*, the pace does not slacken, but the theme of universal death gathers emphasis and becomes a central motif, with many references to death, the dying, the already deceased who are memories of the speakers. There are now "citizens of the deep," as the speaker remarks in the opening poem, "Quabbin Reservoir," while he alone kills time along the shore as the last of the living voices. Other ghosts are portrayed, as in "Peggy in the Twilight," who "spent half of each day trying to wake up, and/ the other half preparing for sleep."

Tate's characters in *Distance from Loved Ones* keep lonely vigils among the dead; their voices have turned to memory. Many of the poems are variations on the elegy, the very form with which *The Lost Pilot* began. The poems' characters, variations on that youthful speaker who awaited his father's orbital return each birthday, live futile, empty lives waiting to join the dead around them. They have no purpose in life; their only defense against remorse is their disjunctive humor, their ability to disconnect the tedious logic of their world and playfully deconstruct their own identities.

In "How Happy We Were," one of these loners notes that his vision of eternity included "a few of the little angels/ whose sole job it is to fake weeping for people like us." Crowds in America practice "dead mall worship," he writes in "Beaucoup Vets," and in "Anatomy," a beautiful girl studies anatomy and continually cries. The others "know she is dying inside." In "Taxidermy," "Everything is dead anyway." In a sense, the death of the father in Tate's first book has spread out over his many books to encompass the world; the memory of the dead father created a glimmering afterlife Tate never could bring into sharp focus or make the basis of a sustaining vision. His poetry began as elegy and has built a vast edifice of language to exhaust the content of that emotion.

Paul Christensen

Other major works

LONG FICTION: *Lucky Darryl*, 1977 (with Bill Knott).
SHORT FICTION: *Hottentot's Ossuary*, 1974.

Bibliography

Garden, Stephen. "James Tate." In *American Poets Since World War II*, edited by Donald J. Greiner. Vol. 5 in *Dictionary of Literary Biography*. Detroit: Gale Research, 1980. A general commentary on Tate's early poetry to *The Oblivion Ha-Ha*.

Levis, Larry. "Eden and My Generation." In *Conversant Essays: Contemporary Poets on Poetry*, edited by James McCorkle. Detroit: Wayne State University Press, 1990. A broad-ranging survey of the lines and forces of contemporary poetry, in which James Tate is located, and of its major theme in the loss of Eden.

Rosen, R. D. "James Tate and Sidney Goldfarb and the Inexhaustible Nature of the Murmur." In *American Poetry Since 1960: Some Critical Perspectives*, edited by Robert B. Shaw. Cheshire, Eng.: Carcanet Press, 1973. Argues that both Tate and Goldfarb belong to a generation that uses poetry to escape from the postwar age; their writing, notes Rosen, is that of moral outlaws.

EDWARD TAYLOR

Born: Near Sketchley, Leicestershire, England; c. 1645
Died: Westfield, Massachusetts; June 24, 1729

Principal poetry

The Poetical Works of Edward Taylor, 1939 (Thomas H. Johnson, editor); *The Poems of Edward Taylor,* 1960 (Donald E. Stanford, editor); *A Transcript of Edward Taylor's Metrical History of Christianity,* 1962 (Donald E. Stanford, editor); *Edward Taylor's Minor Poetry,* 1981 (Thomas M. Davis and Virginia L. Davis, editors; volume 3 of *The Unpublished Writings of Edward Taylor,* 1981).

Other literary forms

Edward Taylor is best known today for his poetry. To his congregation at Westfield, Massachusetts, however, he was far better known for his sermons. He did apparently write the moral sequence of thirty-five poems, "God's Determinations," as a guide for members of his congregation, who were unable to assure themselves that they had achieved the state of grace. Even so, the Westfield minister did not intend that his poems should ever be published. There is some indication, however, that he did plan to publish some of his sermons, particularly those gathered together by Norman S. Grabo as *Edward Taylor's Treatise Concerning the Lord's Supper* (1966); these eight sermons attack Solomon Stoddard's liberal position regarding the admission of persons to the Eucharist who were not always certain they possessed the gift of God's grace.

The fourteen sermons collected, again by Grabo, as Edward Taylor's *Christographia* (1962) deal with two major issues: first that the "blessed Theanthropie," God's son united with man in the body of Jesus of Nazareth, was a necessary condition created by God to redeem the elect among mankind; and, second, that this God-man constitutes the perfect model after whom each of the saints should construct his life. These fourteen sermons correspond precisely in subject matter to poems forty-two through fifty-six of the "Preparatory Meditations," Second Series. All of these published sermons are necessary reading for serious students of Taylor's poetry; they reveal his public attitudes toward many issues with which he grapples in his private poetry. In 1981, there appeared a three-volume set, *The Unpublished Writings of Edward Taylor* (Thomas M. Davis and Virginia L. Davis, editors), which includes Taylor's church records, minor poems, and additional sermons.

In 1977, an extensive holograph manuscript of thirty-six sermons, dating from 1693 to 1706, was unearthed in Lincoln, Nebraska. These as yet unpublished sermons treat "types": events, persons, or things in the Old Testament which represent or shadow forth similar events, persons (particularly Jesus of Nazareth), or things in the New Testament. Taylor's *Diary* has been published (1964, F. Murphy, editor); he kept this record during his journey to New England and until he located, after graduation from Harvard in 1671, at Westfield. The style of the *Diary* is candid and immediate; one almost shares with Taylor his vividly described seasickness.

Achievements

For today's readers, Taylor's finest achievement is his poetry. Those of his own time, however, remembered Taylor for his accomplishments as minister and physician to the Westfield, Massachusetts, community. In his edition of Taylor's poems, Thomas H. Johnson lists an inventory of the poet's library that includes the titles of several now arcane books on surgery and alchemy. Appropriately enough, the vocabulary of Taylor's medical practice often makes its way into his poetry.

Perhaps it was this professional versatility that enabled Taylor to construct elaborate metaphysical conceits with such agility. His poems can bear comparison to the work of John Donne, George Herbert, and Andrew Marvell. Indeed, Taylor's best poems are among the finest composed by an American.

Biography

The details of Edward Taylor's life are not abundant. He was born in or near Sketchley, Leicestershire, England, probably in the year 1645. He may have attended the University of Cambridge or one of the dissenting academies, for when he was admitted to Harvard in 1668, he was given advanced standing. It is certain that he early began training for the ministry. He had been brought to New England by the Act of Uniformity of Charles II; passed in 1662, this law required all schoolmasters (Taylor may have served in that capacity at Bagworth, Leicestershire) and ministers to take an oath of allegiance to the Anglican church. Of course, Taylor's religious orthodoxy in the Puritan mode of worship prevented him, in good conscience, from taking the oath.

Taylor records his voyage across the Atlantic with vivid precision in his *Diary*. Even before his ship could get away from the British Isles, it was beset by a "violent storm" that filled the forcastle of the ship "ankle-deep" with water and so bathed the mate that "the water ran out of the waist of his breeches." Although the young man often found himself subdued by the constant rocking of the vessel, he was particularly taken with the life he discovered in the sea; he describes more than ten different types of fishes and several kinds of "sea fowl." On a few occasions he and the crew spotted different kinds of driftwood. One such event held a pleasant surprise for them. Upon finding "a piece of white fir-wood full of barnacles, which are things like dew-worm skins about two inches long hanging to the wood," they learned that the other end housed a species of shellfish, so "we had a dish of them." Toward the end of the journey as the vessel approached land, Taylor saw his first fireflies: "About eight I saw a flying creature like a spark of red fire (about the bigness of an bumble bee) fly by the side of the ship; and presently after, there flew another by. The men said they were fireflies." The poet's fascination with nature continued in later years, as poems such as "Upon a Spider Catching a Fly" and "Upon a Wasp Chilled with Cold" attest.

The *Diary* also records his admission to Harvard, some humorous incidents that occurred there, and his calling after graduation in 1671, to minister to the congregation at Westfield, Massachusetts. While he was at Harvard, he roomed with Samuel Sewall, author of the famous *Diary* (1878-1882) and the judge at the Salem witch trials. In later years, Sewall names Taylor some fourteen times in the *Diary* and records in a letter that it was Taylor who induced him to attend Harvard. During his student days, the future minister of Westfield served as college Butler, a position of responsibility which, however, did not prevent him from becoming involved in some youthful acts of relatively innocuous consequence. He took his calling to the ministry of the Westfield congregation, however, very seriously; in his *Diary* he records his doubts about his suitability as a minister. This sincere examination of his conscience before God establishes for the first time in Taylor's known writings the pattern that prevails in his private, poetic "Meditations," Series One and Two.

On November 5, 1674, after courting her through letters and verse, Taylor married Elizabeth Fitch of Norwich, Connecticut. The first Mrs. Taylor died some fifteen years later, having given birth to eight children. Taylor recorded his grief in one of his most moving poems, "A Funerall Poem upon the Death of My Ever Endeared and Tender Wife." In 1692, at the age of about fifty, the Westfield minister was married again, to Ruth Wyllys of Hartford, who bore him six more children and who survived him by about six months. Taylor's ministry of almost sixty years was a fruitful one. While bearing the responsibility of meeting his congregation's medical as well as spiritual needs, Taylor wrote his "Preparatory Meditations," attacked Solomon Stoddard's "liberalism" (Stoddard, who attended Taylor's ordination on August 27, 1679, had served as Harvard's first librarian during Taylor's attendance at the college), received an M.A. degree from Harvard in 1720, and visited Samuel Sewall, whom he solicited on one occasion (in 1691) to supervise the apprenticeship of one of his sons to a shopkeeper at Ipswich. Taylor died on June 24, 1729, a much-loved and revered divine whose tombstone records that as a "Venerable, Learned, and Pious Pastor" he "had served God and his Generation Faithfully."

Analysis

At the time when English poetry, following the lead of John Dryden, was moving into a century of neoclassicism, Edward Taylor was writing verse in the Metaphysical mode of John Donne, characterized by complex syntax, striking conceits, and intimate direct address: most of Taylor's poems are addressed to God. In addition to his Metaphysical style, of primary interest to today's readers of Taylor's poetry are his propensity to employ the meditative technique, his practice of coordinating private poetic meditation with public sermon, his perhaps unexpected but nevertheless felicitous use of classical allusions, and his attention to the function of the fancy or the imagination in the poetic process.

"Huswifery," perhaps Taylor's most famous poem, also displays one of his most eloquent conceits. As did most Puritans of his time, Taylor often found evidence of God's providence in the quotidian. In "Huswifery," he discovers God's purpose for the poet's public ministry in his wife's spinning wheel, perdurable symbol of America's pioneer struggle. The poem begins with this arresting plea, "Make me, O Lord, Thy spinning wheel complete." The poet then develops this conceit in a logical fashion, first according to ingenious analogies drawn between the various components of the spinning wheel and second by focusing on the machine's product, clothing. That which holds the fibers of wool to be spun, the distaff, becomes "Thy holy word"; the flyers that twist the fibers into thread (or yarn) represent the poet's religious emotions; and the spool that collects the thread embodies his soul. Extending the spinning wheel conceit a bit further, the poet next asserts that the loom on which the threads are woven into cloth serves, like a minister of God's message, as the instrument for delivering His message to those in need (his congregation). The clothes prepared in this fashion should then become the minister's apparel, displaying God's "shine" and revealing that he is "clothed in holy robes for glory."

Another poem that employs conceits with equal success is Taylor's "Meditation Thirty-Nine" (First Series). This longer poem develops two conceits: sin as poison, and Jesus of Nazareth as "the sinner's advocate" or defense attorney before God. The inspiration for this meditation is I John 2:1 "If any man sin, we have an advocate with the Father, Jesus Christ the righteous." Taylor opens the poem with the exclamation: "My sin! My sin, My God, these cursed dregs,/ Green, yellow, blue streaked poison." These "Bubs [pustules] hatched in nature's nest on serpents' eggs" act in his soul like poisons in his stomach and "set his soul acramp." He alone cannot conquer then, "cannot them destroy." Alone and unassisted without God's help, these "Black imps . . . snap, bite, drag to bring/ And pitch me headlong hell's dread whirlpool in." By delaying the preposition "in" until the end of the line, Taylor startles his readers, thereby focusing attention on his wretched predicament as sinner. To be sure, Taylor's intention, since he wrote these poems as private meditations with God, in preparation for the administration of the Eucharist, was not to appeal to an audience schooled in the Metaphysical style. Such recognition does not, however, lessen the certainty that his intention is most definitely to appeal to an even more critical audience, his God, whose attention he does indeed want to capture and hold.

At this most critical point in his acknowledgment of his fallen state, the poet catches a glimpse of "a twinkling ray of hope," Christ as advocate; for him, then, "a door is ope." With this introduction of an advocate, Taylor begins to build his legal conceit. The sight of the advocate first engenders a promise of release from his pain. Temporary joy is replaced by a renewed sense of guilt, however, as he realizes that all his advocate has to work with is "the state/ The case is in." That is, if the case his advocate pleads before God, the final judge, is short of merit, then judgment may still go against him. As Taylor puts it, if the case is bad: "it's bad in plaint." He continues by observing, "My papers do contain no pleas that do/ Secure me from, but knock me down to, woe." Again the poet wrenches the syntax, but again for the same reason. Despite the "ray of hope," he fears that the gravity of his "Black imps" may yet doom him to hellfire. As before, his purpose is to focus on his apparently hopeless condition. His reason then begins to instruct him. Even though the biblical text causes him to recall his past sins while also promising him a defense attorney before God, he concludes, without benefit of understanding, "I have no plea mine advocate to give." He is forced to cry out, "What now?" His reason teaches him that his advocate is unique; as God's only Son, He has sacrificed His human body to provide the believing and worthy sinner the gift of redemption. These "dear bought arguments" are "good pleas" indeed. Following this grasp of his reason which informs him that the "ray of hope" is constant and true, the poet asks "What shall I do, my Lord?" How can he act or conduct his life so "that I/ May have Thee plead my case?" He exercises his will and decides to "fee" or pay his lawyer "With faith, repentence, and obediently" give the efforts of his ministry to fighting against the commission of "satanic sins" among his parishioners. This unique agreement between lawyer and client obliges the lawyer "My sins [to] make Thine," while at the same time it emboldens the client, the poet, "Thy pleas [to] make mine hereby."

The agreement is struck, then; "Thou wilt me save; I will thee celebrate." Taylor intends, however, not merely to celebrate his advocate through his works "'gainst satanic sins," but he desires intensely that "my rough feet shall Thy smooth praises sing." This intense desire to please God in return for God's love freely given, the eros-*agape* motif, pervades Taylor's meditative poetry. The ababcc rhyme scheme, which Taylor adopts for all of his meditations, serves a purpose beyond that ordinarily expected; the final words of each line are "I," "advocate" (the noun), "hereby," "celebrate," "within," and "Sing." With slight rearrangement, these words make this fitting statement: I hereby celebrate [my] advocate within song. Thus Taylor accomplishes his end both directly and implicitly. In doing so, he well fulfills John Calvin's dictum in *The Institutes of the Christian Religion* (1536) that "We recommend the voice and singing as a support of speech [in the worship service], where accompanying love [that is] pure of spirit."

The process that governs this poem's construction is that of the meditation, an intellectual exercise codified by St. Ignatius Loyola in his *Spiritual Exercises* (1548) and passed on to Taylor probably through the widely circulated and immensely popular (among Puritans) *The Saints' Everlasting Rest* (1650), written by one of the seventeenth century's foremost Puritan authorities on meditation, Richard Baxter. While this mental process or guide to philosophical contemplation was implicitly understood from pre-Christian days (see the entry, *meditatio* in Charlton T. Lewis and Charles Short's *A Latin Dictionary*, 1879), Loyola's *Spiritual Exercises* did much to make commonplace this process which uses the mental faculties of memory, understanding, and will. As the poem itself illustrates, the memory of the one engaged in meditation is jogged or aroused, usually by some biblical text; the understanding or reason of the meditator then grapples with the significance of this memory recalled in conjunction with the biblical text; and, finally, the meditator's grasp of the significance of text and memory lead him to pledge to serve God with the new understanding he has acquired. The biblical text, "If any man sin, we have an advocate with the Father, Jesus Christ the righteous," causes the poet to remember his own poisonous sins, and to recall his redeemer, but also to fear that his sins may weigh too heavily against him in the balance of God's justice. His understanding then reassures him that Christ, having bought his sins in His human sacrifice, is a formidable advocate in his behalf and that the strength of his belief will give His advocate all the "surety" he will need. The knowledge of God's gift of His only Son so overwhelms the poet or meditator that he pledges to serve Him in both deeds and poetry.

Taylor adopts this basic mode of construction in many of his meditations, as a brief examination of "Meditation Eight" (First Series) affirms. This poem derives its inspiration from another biblical text, John 6:51, part of which is "I am the living bread which came down from heaven." This text moves the poet to conjure up a vision in which he is looking up toward heaven, trying to discover how man can ever have "pecked the fruit forbad" and consequently have "lost . . . the golden days" and fallen into "celestial famine sore." What is man to do now? How can he regain paradise? His reason informs him that, alone and without God's help, this earth "cannot yield thee/ here the smallest crumb" of that living bread. According to the poem, the only way out of this barren mortality is by way of "The purest wheat in heaven, His dear—dear Son." The fallen sinner must "eat thy fill of this, thy God's white loaf." If one exercises his will and chooses to eat this "soul bread," then "thou shalt never die." Once again scripture provokes memory, which in turn stimulates the understanding, which finally brings about a resolve of the will.

One can easily see how this meditative process accords well with preparation and resolve to administer God's word with as much intensity and expression as a sincere and gifted pastor can muster. Investigation among those sermons

with which scholars are able to align specific meditative poems proves rewarding indeed. All the fourteen sermons of the *Christographia*, for example,
correspond exactly to the "Meditations" (Second Series), forty-two through
fifty-six. The examination of but one such pair, sermon and poem, serves the
present purpose. Both "Meditation Fifty-Six" and the fourteenth sermon of
the *Christographia* collection are based on the same biblical text, John 15:24:
"Had I not done amongst them the works, that none other man hath done,
they had not had Sin." This final sermon of the series marks the culmination
of Taylor's analysis of the "blessed Theanthropie," his explanation for the
person of God's divine Son. In this concluding homily, the minister attempts
to establish that no works of men or of nature (since God is the Author of
both) surpass the works of God or His Son; God, therefore, commands the
devotion of His believers.

The sermon opens with the observation that the white blossom of the clove
tree, when "turned to be green, . . . yields the pleasentest [sic] Smell in the
World." The minister uses this clove blossom imagery as a structural device
by means of which, when he returns to it at the sermon's conclusion, he unifies
his text, for the flower which exudes the most pleasant order predicts the
closing corollary that the works of Christ are "the Sweetest Roses, and brightest flowers of his own Excellency." This flower imagery does not, however,
play a significant structural role in the poem. The poet delays this sensuous
appeal to smell until the thirteenth line. Preceding the poem's "White-green'd
blossoms" are evocations of other senses, including the sight of his "Damask
Web of Velvet Verse" that the poet offers in humility to God, and the taste
of "Fruits so sweete that grow/ On the trees of righteousness." This explication of the senses follows rather closely Loyola's recommendation given in
some of his *Spiritual Exercises* (see, for example, the First Week, Fifth
Exercise); Taylor, therefore, here conforms, whether consciously or not, to
Loyola's famous codification of the meditative process. The purpose of the
sermon, however, is clearly not meditation but utilitarian and effective communication of the doctrine, which the minister articulates as follows: "That
Christ's works were so excellent, that never any did the like thereto."

Throughout both sermon and poem, the author expands upon the Tree of
Life metaphor, which appears first in Genesis. In the popular *The Figures or
Types of the Old Testament* (1683), a copy of which Taylor owned and annotated, Samuel Mather, whose nephew was one of Taylor's classmates at Harvard, explains that "the Tree of Life in Paradise was a Type of Christ." This
Old Testament Tree of Life, which was located in the center of Eden, "shadows forth" or prefigures Christ in the New Testament. When Adam and Eve
were cast out of Paradise, they were denied the gift of God's grace available
to them from the eating of the fruit of this Tree; according to Christian
understanding of the Adamic myth, it then became necessary for Christ to
come into the world of men in order to restore this "fruit" of God's grace;

that is, to redeem fallen men. Understandably, Taylor often refers to this myth in his poems and sermons, but he does so with particular intensity in this sermon and this poem. The minister tells his parishioners that "his [Christ's] Works are his rich Ornaments," while the poet extolls Christ as "a Tree of Perfect nature trim" whose branches "doe out/ shine the sun."

This "Tree of Perfect nature" produces, in the poem, fruits of this perfection which he identifies as God's gift of grace. The minister is also, of course, much interested in the question of grace, but he does not regale his congregation with conceits spun about the Tree of Life; rather, with attention to practicality, he emphasizes "Christ's works mediatoriall" [sic] which translate "the Soule from a State of Sin, and a Sinfull life, into a State of holiness." Underscoring this distinction between the poem's richness of imagery and the sermon's concentration on the delivery of practical doctrine are their respective descriptions of Christ. While the sermon calls Christ "the brightness of his Fathers Glory," the poem more extravagantly describes him as one whose "fruits adorne/ Thyselfe, and Works, more shining than the morn" and as one whose "Flowers more sweet than spice/ Bende down to us."

The sweet flowers of Christ's works, says the minister, far exceed "Kingly Performances." Kings and rulers of the temporal world "ofttimes build their Palaces in oppression." The minister does not expand his case to include the naming of specific illustrations. The poet, however, provides rich examples of worldly power. Indeed, he names Psammetichos' huge labyrinth, supposed to have been built by Daedalus; the Roman emperor Titus (A.D. 40-81), and his Colosseum; Nero's Golden Palace; and other symbols of temporal power. Whereas the poet heaps up specific cases of earthly artifice and thereby poignantly contrasts God's works and man's most ambitious constructions, the minister, more simply concerned with the transience of earthy mortality, explains how man's buildings, no matter how magnificent, "are but of Clayy natures."

The minister is also disposed to contrast the egalitarian nature of the laws of God, which apply to all men equally, with the laws of kings that "are like Copwebs that catch little flies, but are Snapt in pieces by the greater." This web imagery occurs in the poem, but in a quite different context. As noted above, the poet sees his verse as "A Damask Web of Velvet," hardly as an ensnaring "copweb." It is possible, however, that the labyrinthine image of Psammetichos' maze conjured up in the mind of the minister the image of man's laws seen as oppressive "copwebs." It should be observed, nevertheless, that at this point as at others, poems and sermon are not always in exact agreement.

The conclusion of Taylor's sermon is the more interesting precisely because it does not appear to agree fully with the poem. In the poem, Taylor prays that his God will "Adorn my Life well with thy works": and will "make faire/ My Person with apparrell thou prepar'st." For, if he is so clothed, his

"Boughs," extending the Tree of Life conceit to himself, "shall loaded bee with fruits that spring/ Up from thy Works." Such a prayer reveals the preparation of a sincere minister about to deliver God's word to his flock. The minister, however, appears to rebuke the poet for his extravagance. In the sermon's conclusion, the minister declares that all the most excellent works of man in this world "are but dull drudgeries and lifeless painted cloaths compared to Christs." Of especial significance at this crucial point in the sermon's concluding lines, however, is the comparison that Taylor draws between man's works and those of God.

He cites the example of the famous Alexandrian painter, Apelles, who rebuked one of his students for overlaying a painting of Venus with gold; Apelles told the student that he had not created a beautiful representation, but simply a rich one. Taylor the poet has done precisely the same thing in his poem; he has decorated God's word with elaborate images and drawn out conceits, but he has expressed the hope that God will adorn him in a similar fashion. The minister determinedly concludes that men's works are "of no worth." "Ours are Worth nothing," the minister says "without he puts . . . the Worthiness of his on them." To be sure, the poet is as devoted to God as the minister is, and has carefully sought God's assistance in the construction of his poem. Nevertheless, the minister, who has written a much less "adorned" sermon, appears to admonish the poet, as well as his congregation, not to forget that the "clothes" he would wear both in the poem and in the sermon are worn with God's benevolence. What appears to be reticence on the part of the poet here was full-blown trepidation at an earlier point in Taylor's poetic career. The twenty-first meditation of the First Series (1686) displays this fear in unmistakable candor: "Yet I feare/ To say a Syllable [as poet] lest at thy day [Judgment Day]/ I be presented for my Tattling here."

In his Introduction to his edition of *Christographia*, Norman S. Grabo concludes, as others have, that Taylor's "sermons seem to explicate the poems." This observation is no less true of "Meditation Fifty-Six" and "Sermon Fourteen." More appears to be at work, however, in this pair. The medium of the poem, with its possibilities for elaborate tropes and figures, together with the poem's condition of privacy, allows Taylor to pursue his personal devotion to God with virtually limitless zeal; indeed, knowing that his heavenly audience, God, will hardly misconstrue his motives but that his earthly audience, the members of his congregation, very well may, Taylor the poet can, his earlier trepidation notwithstanding, express himself with more candor and fervor than Taylor the minister can. As a result, his meditations are always richer and more passionate than his often somber and always sober sermons. Two other factors that characterize his poetry corroborate this assumption: his use of classical allusions and the manner in which he describes the function of the imagination in the poetic process.

As is the case of the Apelles allusion, Taylor uses classical allusions in his sermons as exempla or as instructional illustrations for the benefit of his parishioners. In his poems, his application of them is quite predictably more figurative. Wholly unexpectedly, however, is the fact that Taylor applies references to classical paganism in contexts that are usually positive or favorable. For example, in the long series of thirty-five poems, "Gods Determinations," the poet seems to revel in drawing implied allusions to Greek mythology when describing God's creation of the world in the first poem of the sequence. The poet asks, "Who blew the Bellows of his Furnace Vast?"—doubtless a reference to Hephaestus, Greek god of the hearth and metalworking. Surely Atlas stands beneath the line: "Where stand the Pillars upon which it stands?"

This engaging use of classical references usually gives way to a more serious and often more complex application. In the seventy-ninth meditation of the Second Series, for example, Taylor, contrary to the expected and even prescribed convention, extends the practice of typology to classical mythology. The poet's practice here is of particular significance since it points toward the nineteenth century emphasis on symbolism to be found in the works of such American writers as Herman Melville and Nathaniel Hawthorne. The text for this meditation is Canticles 2:16; "My beloved is mine and I am his." Since the Puritans (and many others) interpreted this entire book, which contains some of the most sensuous and sensual poetry in the Bible, as an allegory of man's relation to God, one might conclude that the subject of this poem must be the analogy between sexual love (eros) and God's unconditional, unselfish love for man (*agape*).

With that expectation, one may find the first four lines of the poem somewhat puzzling: "Had I Promethius' filching Ferula [fennel]/ Filld with its sacred theft the stoln Fire:/ To animate my Fancy lodg'd in clay,/ Pandora's Box would peps [pelt] the theft with ire." Knowledge of the Greek myth of Prometheus, who stole fire from the gods and gave it to man, helps to explain what is happening in these lines. Prometheus was seen by the ancients as a truly heroic champion of mankind, as Aeschylus' tragedy *Prometheus Bound* illustrates. As a consequence of Prometheus' defiance, however, Zeus sent Pandora, whom he forced to bring to man the infamous box of woes and tribulations. Zeus forbade Pandora to open the box, but knowing her to be inveterately curious, he also knew that her opening of the box would merely be a matter of time. Now the typology may be made clear. Taylor has obviously rejected the Prometheus myth as insufficient to animate his "Fancy lodg'd in clay"; that is, to set his imagination into motion so that he can compose a meditation appropriate to his devotion to God. The stanza's final lines, however, do suggest to him the source suitable for the kind and degree of inspiration he requires: "But if thy Love, My Lord, shall animate/ My Clay with holy fire, 'twill flame in State."

The Prometheus myth fails to give him the necessary inspiration, not because it is pagan, but because, in Taylor's conception here, it is typological of the Adamic myth (of man's fall from grace). Prometheus, like Satan, defies Zeus, or God, and Pandora, a type of Eve, manifests the unfortunate trait of curiosity that causes her to disobey Zeus, just as Eve's curiosity prompts her to disobey God and to yield to Satan's temptation to eat of the Tree of Knowledge (of good and evil). Although Taylor's complex typology here is aesthetically pleasing, it is surprising, since Samuel Mather had cautioned against such a practice. In *The Figures or Types of the Old Testament*, which, it will be recalled, the poet owned and annotated, Mather unequivocally states, "It is not safe to make any thing a type meerly upon our own fansies and imaginations; it is *Gods* Perogative to make *Types*." Here Taylor clearly exceeds the limitations that his Puritan compatriots would impose upon him. Perhaps Taylor recognized this quality in his poetry and such recognition led to his request that his poems not be published.

At any rate, as the investigation of the Prometheus myth suggests, the drawing out of typologies that are not God's is not the only practice for which Taylor could have received censure had his poems appeared in print. As Taylor's lines and Mather's dictum suggest, the poet is here "guilty" of indulging himself with the making of inventions of his own imagination. Whereas his attitude toward the use of classical allusions is unguarded, particularly in his poetry—he simply uses such references when he feels moved by the demands of the verse to do so, often creating rich and satisfying lines—such is not the case with his management of the imagination. Toward this essentially aesthetic idea, Taylor sometimes appears to be ambivalent. Certainly Mather's injunction against its use offers a partial explanation of Taylor's ambivalence. Earlier in the seventeenth century, William Perkins, renowned patriarch of English Puritanism, wrote *A Treatise of Mans Imaginations* (1607) in which he calls the imagination a "corrupt fountaine." He arrives at this conclusion from Genesis 8:21, "the imaginacion of mans heart is evil even from his youth" (from the Geneva Bible). In one of his *Christographia* sermons, Taylor himself espouses a similar position when he admonishes his congregation not to be deluded by "Fictitious imaginations" which "indeed are the Efficacy of Errors."

Regarding his attitude toward the imagination, Taylor the poet contradicts Taylor the minister. Unlike the minister who refers to the imagination only twice in his published sermons (both times in a negative context), the poet cites "fancy," "Phansy," or some other form of this word (as verb or adjective) forty-six times in his published poetry. He never uses the synonym "imagination" in his poetry, probably preferring the disyllabic "fancy" to the pentasyllabic synonym for purposes of rhythm. When he cites "fancy" and its various spellings and forms, he does so in a manner that establishes a readily discernible pattern. When the word occurs at the beginning of a poem, always in a meditation, it is invariably used within the positive context of serving the poet as a necessary tool for setting poesies into motion. When "fancy" appears somewhere internally within a poem, however, as it does twice in the perhaps publicly recited "Gods Determinations," the concept usually identifies the imperfect human attempt to construe points of Puritan theology; these imperfect attempts to interpret theological or doctrinal matters without dependence upon the truly regenerate heart (informed by the gift of God's grace) always conclude incorrectly.

In the "Second Ranke Accused" from the "Gods Determinations" series, for example, the poet-minister threatens that those captured by God's justice, the so-called regenerate, may not be regenerate if their hearts are not filled with the "sweet perfume" of God's grace; if such is not the case, "Your Faith's a Phancy," and therefore untrue. In those poems that begin with the concept of the fancy, however, the poet applies it to the initiation of his meditative process. It is Taylor's recognition of the necessary role of the imagination in the writing of exalted verse (in his case, his most impassioned "talks" with God) that most interests today's readers. Of great significance, then, is the fact that the poet identifies the essential role of the imagination in the "Prologue" to the "Preparatory Meditations." Here he describes himself as but a "Crumb of Dust which is design'd/ To make my Pen unto thy Praise alone." Immediately following this exercise in self-deprecation, however, he writes: "And my dull Phancy I would gladly grinde/ Unto an Edge of Zion Precious Stone." At one point in the Second Series meditations, the poet asks God's angels to "Make me a pen thereof that best will write./ Lende me your fancy, and Angellick skill/ To treate this theme, more rich than Rubies bright." Another of the same series opens with this enthusiastic line: "I fain would have a rich, fine Phansy ripe." Finally, the discussion of the Prometheus typology that begins the seventy-ninth meditation of this series establishes that, although the subject of the entire poem is the eros-*agape* theme, the poem's first problem is to discover the difference between man's myths, which served ancient poets such as Vergil, Catullus, and Ovid for poetic inspiration, and God's Word, which, finally, can alone animate the poetic process of this believer's "Fancy lodg'd in clay."

There can be little doubt, then, that, despite injunctions against the allegedly "evil" fruits of this mental faculty, Taylor the private poet found it a necessary tool for colloquies with his God. A possible explanation for this contradiction between private poet and public minister (who was also author of "Gods Determinations") may be offered by observing that Loyola had prescribed, in his *Spiritual Exercises*, the use of the imagination as requisite to begin the process of meditation. The exercitant must place himself in the proper frame of mind for meditation by picturing to himself events in the life of Christ or biblical history or occurrences in his own life that prompt him to recognize the need for spiritual colloquy. Later in his own century, Baxter appears somewhat to mollify Perkins' attitude toward this mental faculty when he advises, in *The Saints' Everlasting Rest*, that the person engaged in meditation should focus his mental attention on the joys of heaven by getting "the liveliest Picture of them in thy minde that thou canst." At the same time, nevertheless, it should be observed that, in *A Treatise Concerning Religious Affections* (1746), Jonathan Edwards, some seventeen years after Taylor's death, summarily condemns this faculty as that means by which the devil produces evil thoughts in the soul; as the Great Awakener puts it, "it must be only by the imagination that Satan has access to the soul, to tempt and delude it."

Taylor's consistent acknowledgment of the power of the imagination should make him appealing to contemporary students of American literature. At a time when attitudes toward the imagination were, for the most part, hostile (recall Alexander Pope's line from *An Essay on Man*, 1733-1734, "Imagination plies her dang'rous art," II, 143), Taylor identified the concept as a paramount significance to poesies, anticipating Samuel Taylor Coleridge's analysis of imagination in *Biographia Literaria* (1817).

John C. Shields

Other major works

NONFICTION: *Diary*, 1964 (F. Murphy, editor).

RELIGIOUS WRITINGS: *Christographia*, 1962 (Norman S. Grabo, editor); *Edward Taylor's Treatise Concerning the Lord's Supper*, 1966 (Norman S. Grabo, editor).

MISCELLANEOUS: *The Unpublished Writings of Edward Taylor*, 1981 (Thomas M. Davis and Virginia L. Davis, editors; 3 volumes).

Bibliography

Gatta, John. *Gracious Laughter: The Meditative Wit of Edward Taylor*. Columbia: University of Missouri Press, 1989. Gatta is an insightful expositor of Taylor's poetry, citing his "peculiar blend of verbal wit, meditative earnestness, and comic exuberance" as an index of his "singularity as a sacred artist." Gatta has opened up a new avenue of inquiry into Taylor's acknowledged supremacy as a Colonial poet, positing his wit as the bridge between his theology and his poetics. In addition, Gatta's bibliography provides the most comprehensive source of primary and secondary sources available.

Grabo, Norman. *Edward Taylor*. Rev. ed. Boston: Twayne, 1988. This updated version of an earlier biocritical introduction to Taylor's life and work remains the single best source of explication of Taylor's aesthetic and theological influences. Grabo believes Taylor "operates within a mystical tradition without being a mystic," and thus explains how Taylor is able to marry his reasoned Calvinism to an aesthetic imagination to embrace the infinite in words.

Keller, Karl. *The Example of Edward Taylor.* Amherst: University of Massachusetts Press, 1975. A groundbreaking biocritical work of Taylor's poetry. Keller argues convincingly that Taylor must be viewed as a Christian humanist and calls for—and achieves—a reevaluation of Taylor as Colonial America's foremost poet and aesthetician.

Rowe, Karen E. *Saint and Sinner: Edward Taylor's Typology and the Poetics of Meditation.* Cambridge, England: Cambridge University Press, 1986. Rowe notes, as no other Taylor scholar has previously, the relationship between Puritan typology—its use of Old Testament narratives as a guide to the meaning of the mundane devotional life of Colonial believers—and its role in Taylor's craftsmanship as a poet. Offers appendices that exhaustively examine the relationship between individual Taylor poems and their sources in sermons prepared for congregational consumption. According to Rowe, Taylor sought—and achieved—a transcendent language for expressing the infinite in the finite.

Scheick, William. *The Will and the Word: The Poetry of Edward Taylor.* Athens: University of Georgia Press, 1974. Scheick's primary focus here is on Taylor's "Preparatory Meditations," a close reading and explication of his Lord's Supper poems. His thesis is that Taylor derives his aesthetic vision and his theological virtue from the works of Saint Augustine.

Stanford, Donald. *Edward Taylor.* Minneapolis: University of Minnesota Press, 1965. This early pamphlet in the University of Minnesota series is still an incisive introduction to Taylor's poetics and, in particular, his personal version of Milton's *Paradise Lost*, "God's Determinations." Stanford hits his target consistently and elucidates Taylor's opposition to the heretical view of the Lord's Supper propounded by his Colonial adversary, Richard Henry Stoddard.

SARA TEASDALE

Born: St. Louis, Missouri; August 8, 1884
Died: New York, New York; January 29, 1933

Principal poetry

Sonnets to Duse and Other Poems, 1907; *Helen of Troy and Other Poems*, 1911; *Rivers to the Sea*, 1915; *Love Songs*, 1917; *Flame and Shadow*, 1920; *Dark of the Moon*, 1926; *Stars To-Night: Verses New and Old for Boys and Girls*, 1930; *Strange Victory*, 1933; *The Collected Poems of Sara Teasdale*, 1937.

Other literary forms

Sara Teasdale attempted drama in a one-act play, *On the Tower*, which appeared in *Helen of Troy and Other Poems*. She began a biography of Christina Rossetti, her favorite woman poet, in 1931, but never completed it. Finally, Teasdale edited two anthologies: *The Answering Voice: One Hundred Love Lyrics by Women* (1917) and *Rainbow Gold: Poems Old and New Selected for Boys and Girls* (1922).

Achievements

Teasdale is remembered as a lyric poet. She was one of the most widely read poets in America in the years before her death in 1933. Her later collections, *Flame and Shadow*, *Dark of the Moon*, and *Strange Victory* are considered her best. Her collection *Love Songs* went through five editions in 1917, and she was awarded a five-hundred-dollar prize, the forerunner of the Pulitzer Prize, by Columbia University.

Biography

A line of Sara Teasdale's poetry aptly describes her early life: "I was the flower amid a toiling world." Teasdale grew up in a sheltered atmosphere of reading, painting, and music, and literary interests became a large part of her life at an early age. Because of her frail health, she had fewer activities than the average child and was doted upon by her middle-aged, wealthy parents. She was the youngest of four children of Mary Elizabeth Willard and John Warren Teasdale.

Teasdale's family, Puritanical and devout, embraced the ideals of a New England education brought to St. Louis, Missouri, by T. S. Eliot's grandfather, the Reverend William Greenleaf Eliot, who founded the Mary Institute for girls. Born in St. Louis, she attended the Mary Institute and later Hosman Hall, from 1898 to 1903, and the intellectual and social influence of these schools was strong. She did translations of Heinrich Heine, her first poetic influence, and she began writing poetry as a schoolgirl. Her contributions to the *Wheel*, a monthly magazine published by herself and her friends, the "Potters," 1904-1907, just after high school, revealed her early talent for lyrics, songs, and sonnets.

Teasdale had a gift for friendship. She formed strong and lasting friendships with some of the most interesting writers of her generation, many of them living in St. Louis, which in the late nineteenth and early twentieth centuries was an intellectual hub. Her friends among fellow-poets included John Myers O'Hara, John Wheelock, Orrick Johns, Amy Lowell, Joyce Kilmer, and Vachel Lindsay. Her friendships with women were strong and she remained close to some of the "Potters," including Grace and Willamina Parish, Caroline Risque, and Vine Colby, as well as having special friendships with Marion Cummings, Marguerite Wilkinson, and Margaret Conklin. The latter was a young woman whom she met at the Connecticut College for Women who was a faithful companion at the end of her life.

Teasdale will be remembered as the woman who rebuffed Vachel Lindsay's offer of marriage. To Lindsay, Teasdale was a "jewel-girl" and he immortalized his love for her in his poem "The Chinese Nightingale." Teasdale, though fond of Lindsay and cherishing their friendship, had quite a different "angle" on life. Lindsay was usually penniless, full of vitality and energy, a man of the soil in life and in his poetry; Teasdale was used to a life of luxury, easily sapped of energy, and desirous of seclusion. She married a man of her own class and background who would take care of her; she and Ernst Filsinger, an expert on international trade, were married on December 14, 1914, and the early years of their marriage were happy. They lived in New York City, which Teasdale captured in several of her poems in *Helen of Troy and Other Poems* and *Rivers to the Sea*.

In the late 1920's, Teasdale decided to leave her husband because of his constant traveling and preoccupation with business. She took a painful trip to Reno and secured a divorce while Filsinger was in South America. After that, she became more and more reclusive and her health worsened. Like Alice James, she renounced full participation in life, using her ill-health as a weapon. She began a biography of Christina Rossetti in 1931 but was not able to complete it. Greatly affected by her friend Marguerite Wilkinson's drowning, her divorce from Filsinger, and Lindsay's suicide in 1931, and suffering from the aftereffects of an attack of pneumonia, Teasdale was found submerged in a bathtub, dead from an overdose of barbiturates, in New York City, in 1933.

Analysis

Sara Teasdale is distinguished as a lyric poet who evokes moods related to romantic love, the beauty of nature, and death. The substance of much of her early poetry is longing and dreams, and the image of the fantasy lover is virtually omnipresent: a lover who is elusive and disembodied, like the male figures in the work of the lonely Emily Brontë.

A major theme, a concomitant of the fantasy lover image in Teasdale's poetry, is delight in restraint and renunciation, "the kiss ungiven and long desired." This delight in restraint has its origins in four strands of Teasdale's life and reading that interweave in her poetry: the Romantic tradition of John Keats, Percy Bysshe Shelley, A. C. Swinburne, and, later, Christina Rossetti; her devout Puritan background; her ill-health, which separated her from full participation in life and led her to imagine rather than to participate in experience; and the role of women in the early twentieth century. This delight in the unattainable is evident in her early poems, such as "The Look," one of her most widely reprinted poems: "Strephon's kiss was lost in jest,/ Robins's lost in play/ But the kiss in Colin's eyes/ Haunts me night and day." Though long an admirer of Eleonora Duse, it is said that when she had the opportunity actually to see Duse dance, she chose not to. It was very typical of Teasdale; the *idea* of Duse's art was enough for her.

This theme of renunciation in her life and poetry is related to her religious background. Though religious sentiment was never overtly expressed in her poetry, she followed a strict moral code all her life. Her official biographer, Margaret Haley Carpenter, notes that Teasdale was never tempted to enter the bohemian life-style of some of her contemporaries even though Teasdale herself noted that the Puritan and the pagan warred within her. She remained a sensitive, shy, orderly, restrained woman throughout her life, and this reticence is reflected in her poetry. Except for "kisses," "looks," and "voices," the physical body is not present in her poetry, even though much of it deals with romantic love.

In the experience of Nature, unlike the experience of love, there is a sense of Teasdale's presence and participation. Her joy in the beauty of nature, particularly the sea and the stars, is embodied in many of her most successful poems. Her early poems reveal this delight—not quite the animal "appetite" found in William Wordsworth, but a direct and simple emotion that continues to charm the reader. Her nature poems are like gem-cut lockets holding precious snippets of experience; not surprisingly, they were intriguing to the Japanese, who have translated many of them. She, in turn, loved the *idea* of Japan and said of Japanese writing, "When I look at those vertical lines, they remind me of wisteria blooms."

In her later poetry, *Flame and Shadow*, *Dark of the Moon*, and *Strange Victory*, however, the beauty and simplicity of nature turn into a kind of terror related to death, as in "The Sea Wind":

> In the dead of night when the sky is deep
> The wind comes awaking me out of sleep—
> Why does it always bring to me
> The far-off, terrible call of the sea?

The death of Teasdale's mother and her older brother, George, in 1924, transformed her perspective and a new somberness and awareness of death entered her poetry. Her later verse expresses the attitude, ripened toward the end of her life, of one who is self-sufficient and possesses one's soul in silence, as in "The Solitary":

> My heart has grown rich with the passing of years,
>   I have less need now than when I was young
> To share myself with every comer
>   Or shape my thoughts into words with my tongue.

Teasdale's use of simple, unaffected language, easily accessible to readers, together with her interest in presenting the feminine experience of love, links her with her contemporaries. In her anthology *The Answering Voice: One Hundred Love Lyrics by Women*, she notes that sincere love poems by women are rare in England and America in the nineteenth century; in making her selections, she "avoided poems in which the poet dramatized a man's feelings rather than her own." Although the modern reader may feel that Teasdale's fantasy lovers, her denial of the body, and her frail romantic moods do not go far enough in representing the subtleties and complexities of women's relationships with men, she must be acknowledged to be a woman who found her voice.

Patricia Ondek Laurence

Other major works
   PLAY: *On the Tower*, 1911.
   ANTHOLOGIES: *The Answering Voice: One Hundred Love Lyrics by Women*, 1917; *Rainbow Gold: Poems Old and New Selected for Boys and Girls*, 1922.

Bibliography
Carpenter, Margaret Haley. *Sara Teasdale: A Biography*. New York: Schulte, 1960. An excellent, lengthy, and detailed biographical source. Eleven chapters are devoted to Teasdale's life, one chapter to her ancestry and early influences, and another to her work. Supplemented by a select bibliography and an index.
Drake, William. *Sara Teasdale: Woman and Poet*. San Francisco: Harper & Row, 1979. The definitive biographical source on Teasdale. Drake has done meticulous research and makes many valuable insights into Teasdale's life and work. Complemented by notes and an index.
_____. "Sara Teasdale's Quiet Rebellion Against the Midwest." *The Bulletin—Missouri Historical Society Bulletin* 36 (July, 1980): 221-227. A very interesting discussion of selected poems in terms of a negative Midwest cultural influence. Thought-provoking, though limited in scope.

Monroe, Harriet. *A Poet's Life.* New York: Macmillan, 1938. A useful survey of Teasdale's life and work by a close friend. It contains many fascinating recollections and is easy to read. Monroe makes frequent perceptive comments on Teasdale's poetic achievements. The work is useful primarily for anecdotal and biographical information. Supplemented by an index and a bibliography.

Schoen, Carol B. *Sara Teasdale.* Boston: Twayne, 1986. A fine, detailed, concise analysis of much of Teasdale's poetry, focusing on important themes and topics. Contains much specific discussion of Teasdale's poetry and biographical material that supplements the analysis. Includes a chronology, notes and references, a select bibliography, and an index.

ALFRED, LORD TENNYSON

Born: Somersby, England; August 6, 1809
Died: Near Haslemere, England; October 6, 1892

Principal poetry

Poems, Chiefly Lyrical, 1830; *Poems*, 1832 (imprinted 1833); *Poems*, 1842; *The Princess*, 1847; *In Memoriam*, 1850; *Maud and Other Poems*, 1855; *Idylls of the King*, 1859-1885; *Enoch Arden and Other Poems*, 1864; *The Holy Grail and Other Poems*, 1869 (imprinted 1870); *Gareth and Lynette*, 1872; *The Lover's Tale*, 1879; *Ballads and Other Poems*, 1880; *Tiresias and Other Poems*, 1885; *Locksley Hall Sixty Years After, Etc.*, 1886; *Demeter and Other Poems*, 1889; *The Death of Œnone and Other Poems*, 1892.

Other literary forms

Although Alfred, Lord Tennyson is best known today for his poetry, he wrote several dramatic works that were popular in his own day. His first play, *Queen Mary*, was published in 1875. From that time until his death he continued writing verse dramas: *Harold* (1876), *The Falcon* (1879), *The Cup* (1881), *Becket* (written in 1879, published in 1884), and *The Foresters* (1892). Most of these were staged very successfully. The renowned producer and actor Henry Irving starred opposite Ellen Terry in *The Cup*, which ran for more than 130 nights. Irving also produced *Becket* several times after Tennyson's death, achieving success in both England and America. Generally speaking, however, his contemporaries' judgment that Tennyson was a greater poet than a dramatist has been confirmed by modern critics. Tennyson's only prose composition was also a play, *The Promise of May* (1882); it was not well received by theatergoers. Although he published no criticism in his lifetime, Tennyson, like most of his contemporaries, expressed his critical opinions of his own and others' works in his conversations and in numerous letters. Hallam Tennyson's two-volume *Alfred, Lord Tennyson: A Memoir* (1897) of his father prints many of these documents, and preserves as well many of Tennyson's conversations and remarks about literature.

Achievements

During his lifetime Tennyson attracted a popular following seldom achieved by any poet in any age. While his first four volumes received little favorable attention, the publication of *In Memoriam* in 1850 brought him overnight fame, and his subsequent works were all best-sellers. His Victorian contemporaries liked all forms of his poetry: over sixty thousand copies of *In Memoriam* were sold in the first few months after publication; ten thousand copies of the Arthurian tales entitled *Idylls of the King* sold in the first week after publication in 1859, and the remainder of the first edition shortly there-after; and the first edition, sixty thousand copies, of his volume of narrative poems and lyrics, *Enoch Arden and Other Poems* (1864) sold out shortly af-ter it was published. His popularity continued until his death; twenty thou-sand copies of *Demeter and Other Poems* (1889) were sold before publica-tion. Readers found in Tennyson's poetry excitement, sentiment, and moral solace; his works were a lighthouse in a stormy sea of social and moral un-certainty. Many turned to Tennyson as a teacher, seeing in his works a wis-dom not available in churches, schools, or public institutions.

Perhaps because he was so popular in his own day, Tennyson became the primary target for scores of critics of the two generations that followed. Critics of the post-World War I era condemned Tennyson for pandering to public demands that poetry be "uplifting," that it contain a moral for public con-sumption, and that it avoid controversial subjects. During the years between the World Wars, it became fashionable to speak of "the two Tennysons"; critics condemned the public poet who preached jingoism and offered moral platitudes in works such as *Maud* and *Idylls of the King*, yet found much of value in the private poet, a morbid, introverted person whose achievement lay in his lyrics, with their private symbolism developed to express personal anxieties and frustrations.

Critics writing since World War II have generally been more appreciative of the entire canon of Tennyson's poetry. Following the lead of Sir Charles Tennyson, whose sympathetic yet scholarly biography of his grandfather re-kindled interest in Tennyson as a serious poet both in his public and private roles, scholars have reexamined *In Memoriam*, *Idylls of the King*, *The Princess*, and *Maud* and found them to be works of considerable artistic merit. "Ulysses" is regarded as a significant short poem; *Idylls of the King* has been called one of the truly great long poems of the language; and *In Memoriam* is considered one of the world's great elegies.

Biography

Alfred Tennyson was born at Somersby in the Lincolnshire district of England on August 6, 1809, the fourth of twelve children. His father, the Reverend George Tennyson, was a brooding, melancholic man, whose life-long bitterness—inspired by his having been disinherited in favor of a younger brother—manifested itself in his behavior toward his family. Alfred was spared much of his father's wrath, however, because George Tennyson ap-parently recognized his fourth son's special brilliance and took pains to tutor him in history, science, and literature. Tennyson spent five years at Louth Grammar School (1815-1820), then returned home to continue his studies under his father's personal guidance.

Tennyson began writing poetry at an early age; at eight he was imitating James Thomson, at twelve he was writing romances in the manner of Sir

Walter Scott. In 1827, the year he entered Trinity College, Cambridge, he and his brother Charles published *Poems by Two Brothers*.

At Cambridge, Tennyson was an undisciplined student. He was well received by his fellow students, however, and in 1829 he was elected a member of the Apostles, a club devoted to intellectual inquiry. Through this association he met Arthur Henry Hallam, who was to figure prominently in his life. In 1829, Tennyson won the Chancellor's medal for his poem "Timbuctoo," and in 1830 he published *Poems, Chiefly Lyrical*. In March 1831, George Tennyson died, and shortly afterwards Tennyson left Cambridge without a degree.

Tennyson's 1832 volume, *Poems*, like his earlier one, was treated rather roughly by reviewers. Their comments, coupled with the death of Hallam in 1833, caused him to avoid publication for ten years. Hallam's death was an especially severe blow to Tennyson. Hallam had been engaged to Tennyson's sister, and the two men had become very close friends. The poet suffered prolonged fits of depression after receiving the news of Hallam's death. Eventually, however, he was able to transform his grief into a series of lyrics which he published in 1850, entitling the elegy *In Memoriam A. H. H.*

During the years between Hallam's death and the publication of *In Memoriam*, Tennyson was far from inactive. He lived with his mother and other members of his family, assisting in their moves from Somersby to Tunbridge Wells, then to Boxley. During these years he spent time in London, Cornwall, Ireland, and Switzerland, gathering material for his poems. In 1834, he fell in love with Rosa Baring, and when that relationship cooled, he lighted upon Emily Sellwood, whose sister had married his brother Charles. Tennyson had no real means of supporting a family at that time, so he was forced to wait fourteen years to marry. He returned to publishing in 1842, issuing a two-volume set entitled simply *Poems*; it contained both new materials and revisions of previously published poems. In 1847, he published *The Princess*, a long narrative exploring the roles of men and women in modern society.

Months after *In Memoriam* appeared in May 1850, Tennyson's fortunes rose meteorically. In June of that year he married Emily Sellwood. In November, he was named poet laureate, succeeding the recently deceased Wordsworth. During his forty-two years as laureate, he wrote numerous poems commemorating various public events, among them some of his more famous works, including "Ode on the Death of the Duke of Wellington" (1852) and "The Charge of the Light Brigade" (1854). He came to be lionized by the British public, and even the Royal Family made numerous personal requests for him to commemorate events of importance.

The decade of the 1850's was a productive and important one. In 1855 Tennyson published *Maud and Other Poems*; in 1859 he brought out a volume containing the first four Arthurian stories that would be joined by eight others during the next twenty-five years to form *Idylls of the King*.

The Tennysons' first child was stillborn, but in 1852 Hallam Tennyson was born. The family moved to Farringford on the Isle of Wight in 1853. The following year a second son, Lionel, was born.

The remainder of Tennyson's life can be characterized as personally stable but artistically tumultuous. During the 1860's, 1870's, and 1880's, several collections of his poems were issued. The poet added eight new volumes to his growing list of works. Beginning in the mid-1870's, Tennyson turned to drama, writing several successful plays and taking great interest in the details of their production. In 1886 his son Lionel died while returning from India. His elder son, Hallam, remained with the poet, serving as a kind of secretary and executor. In the early months of 1892, Tennyson's health began to fail, and he died in bed in October of that year, his hand resting on a volume of Shakespeare.

Analysis

Always praised for his ability to create musical lyrics, Tennyson is now recognized as a master of a number of verse forms and a thinker who brooded deeply over the problems of his age, attempting to capture these problems and deal with them in his poetry. He is also credited with being one of the few poets whose works demonstrate a real assimilation of the poetic tradition that preceded him. His poems reflect an insight into the crises of his own age, as well as an appreciation of problems that have faced all men, especially the problems of death, loss, and nostalgic yearning for a more stable world.

Early works such as "The Palace of Art" and "The Two Voices" are clear examples of the kind of poem for which Tennyson traditionally has been acclaimed. In each, the poet presents a sensitive person who faces a crisis and is forced to choose between radical alternatives. In "The Palace of Art," the speaker must choose between self-indulgence in a world of artistic beauty and commitment to a life of service; in "The Two Voices," the speaker's choice is either to escape the harsh realities of an oppressive world through suicide, or to continue living with only the faintest glimmer of hope. Tennyson's highly regarded classical poem "The Lotos-Eaters" explores the same themes. For his subject, the poet drew on the incident in the *Odyssey* (c. 800 B.C.) in which Odysseus' men disembark in the paradisiacal land of the lotus-eaters and fall under the enchantment of the lotus fruit. The poem is also influenced by Edmund Spenser's *The Faerie Queene* (1590, 1596), where the figure of Despair argues for the same kind of languid repose that the mariners sing of in "The Lotos-Eaters." Tennyson uses all his powers of description and his special command of the language to select words and phrases whose tonal qualities and connotative meanings strongly suggest the sense of repose and stasis. The musical quality of the poem is enhanced by the meter, the effectiveness of caesura and enjambment, and the varying line-lengths used throughout, especially the extensive use of long lines broken by numerous caesuras near the end of the lyric. "The Lotos-Eaters," a combination of narrative and choric song, describes the arrival of the mariners in a land that appears to be perpetually "afternoon," where "all things always seemed the same." Here the "wild-eyed melancholy Lotos-eaters" bring to the travelers the food that will dull their desire to continue on to Ithaca. Having partaken of the fruit of the lotus, the mariners begin to think of their homeland as merely a dream, too distant a goal, no longer worth striving for. As they lie on the beach, one suggests that they "return no more," and the others quickly take up the chant; their choric song, in eight sections, makes up the remainder of the poem. In the song, the mariners review the many hardships they have faced and the many more that await them if they continue their journey. About them they see that "all things have rest"; they ask "Why should we toil alone?" Rather than continue, they beg to be given "long rest or death, dark death, or dreamful ease." The poem's final statement is an exhortation to "rest, ye brother mariners, we will not wander more." It is unwise, however, to assume that the mariners' decision to opt for "dreamful ease" over a life of "toil" is Tennyson's own position. Rather, "The Lotos-Eaters" explores, from only one perspective, the dilemma of commitment versus retreat. The poet treats the same theme in many other poems in which the speaker takes a decidedly different view.

Tennyson's complex treatment of this theme of commitment to ideals can be seen in one of his most famous shorter works, "Ulysses." This poem also exemplifies numerous other characteristics common to much of Tennyson's poetry, particularly his use of irony. Indeed, in "Ulysses" the reader can see the glimmerings of the essentially ironic poetic form that emerged during the nineteenth century made popular by Robert Browning—the dramatic monologue. "Ulysses" is a poem inspired by Tennyson's personal experiences; yet in the poem Tennyson transforms his experiences into a work of art that speaks of an issue that concerns all men. In "Ulysses," Tennyson is both typically Victorian and still a poet for all times. The call to action at the end of the poem and the emphasis on each man's "work" was no doubt appealing to the poet's contemporaries. In the twentieth century, under the scrutiny of critics more aware of the subtleties of Tennyson's ironic vision, the poem provides pleasure for its refusal to yield to a simplistic reading.

In "Ulysses" the reader discovers how Tennyson uses the poetic tradition, especially the legacy of classical and Renaissance poets. Like "The Lotos-Eaters," "Ulysses" is based in part on Homer's *Odyssey*. The classical epic is not the only source, however, for by the poet's own admission the poem owes much to the portrait of Ulysses in Dante's *Inferno*. In Dante's poem, Ulysses is found in hell, condemned as a deceiver for having led his men away from Ithaca in search of vain glories. That Tennyson chose to draw his own hero from sources that present such radically different views of Ulysses suggests that he wanted to create an ironic tension in his own work. In the *Inferno*, Ulysses tells Dante that, unable to remain at home, he was compelled by wanderlust to set forth in search of new adventures. The spirit of Homer's unconquerable quester is captured in Tennyson's poem, but Dante's condemned spirit is always there to remind the reader that there may be dangers in pursuing the ideal at the expense of other considerations.

When one first reads "Ulysses" one can easily be swept along by the apparent vigor of the hero's argument. His description of life in his native Ithaca, where he is "matched with an aged wife," forced to "meet and dole/ Unequal laws" in a land whose people he regards as "savage," makes it easy for the reader to understand Ulysses' wish to return to a life of seafaring adventure. Among these people, Ulysses is not appreciated for the adventures that have caused him to "become a name" throughout the Mediterranean world. His experiences have become absorbed into the very fiber of his being; he reflects that "I am a part of all that I have met." Small wonder that the confines of his island home seem to imprison him! He realizes that his many exploits are only doorways to future experiences, an "arch" beyond which "gleams/ That untravelled world" he has yet to see. At home he finds himself becoming "dull," like a weapon left to "rust unburnished."

Realizing that he can no longer be happy as ruler in such a land, Ulysses declares that he will leave his "sceptre and the isle" to his son Telemachus, a man more capable and more patient than his father when operating in the "sphere/ Of common duties." Ulysses recognizes that he and his son are different—"He works his work, I mine"—and it is best for all if each man follow his own destiny. This difference is easy for the modern reader to accept, as it suggests a truism about human nature that those imbued with the Romantic desire for self-fulfillment find immediately palatable.

Having passed on his kingship to his son, Ulysses turns to the companions who have "toiled, and wrought, and thought" with him, and calls them to one last voyage. As night draws near, he urges them to embark once more in the ship that will carry them to lands where "some work of noble note, may yet be done." "'Tis not too late," he exhorts them, "to seek a newer world." His purpose is to "sail beyond the sunset" until he dies. The unextinguishable spirit of adventure, burning still in the heart of this old warrior, is summed up best in the closing lines, where he proclaims to those who accompany him that, although they are no longer young, they can still be men of "heroic hearts," "strong in will,/ To strive, to seek, to find, and not to yield."

Because the poem was composed shortly after the death of Tennyson's friend Arthur Henry Hallam, some critics have seen "Ulysses" as a statement of the poet's personal commitment to continue living and writing even after suffering a great personal tragedy that seemed to have robbed life of its meaning. Looking at himself as an old man who had been deprived of the spark of adventure and facing a fast-approaching death of his creative self, Tennyson chose to continue living and working. Only through an active commitment to life itself could he hope one day to see "the great Achilles," here meant to represent Hallam. Such a biographical interpretation is supported by Tennyson's comment, preserved in Hallam Tennyson's *Alfred, Lord Tennyson: A Memoir*, that "Ulysses" expressed his "feeling about the need of going forward, and braving the struggle of life" after Hallam's death.

The biographical interpretation can be supported in part by a close reading of the text. The resounding note of optimism, at least on the surface of the poem, is apparent. All of the images associated with life on the isle of Ithaca suggest dullness, a kind of death-in-life. Tennyson displays his mastery of the single line in his withering description of the people of Ithaca; ten monosyllables capture the essence of those whom Ulysses has come to despise: they "hoard, and sleep, and feed, and know not me." Here is avarice, indolence, a suggestion of animal satisfaction with physical ease, and, most important, a lack of appreciation for the man who has raised himself from the multitude and won fame through bravery, cleverness, and other distinctly human qualities. Similarly, Tennyson has Ulysses describe the life of wandering and the yearning for further adventures in most appealing terms, both sensual and intellectual. Ulysses' is a "hungry heart"; he wishes to "drink/ Life to the lees," having previously "drunk delight of battle with my peers." In a single phrase borrowed from Homer, Tennyson's Ulysses recalls the great struggle in which he first won fame, far away from home on the "ringing plains of windy Troy." The excitement of battle serves as a counterpoint to the dullness of life in Ithaca. The hero's excitement is captured in his final exhortation, in which the poet once again resorts to a line of monosyllables that bombard the reader in staccato fashion: "To strive, to seek, to find, and not to yield." Active verbs call the mariners to action and the reader to acceptance of the hero's decision.

Despite the stirring note of optimism in this final line, however, the poem cannot be accepted simply as another example of strident Victorian rhetoric aimed at encouraging one to have faith in oneself and one's God and press on in the face of uncertainties. In fact, when the uncertainties in the poem are considered carefully, the reader begins to see another side of the aged hero. Ulysses is certain of his boredom with having to govern the "savage race" and of the resentment he harbors toward them because they fail to honor him for his past exploits. What Ulysses will substitute for his present life, and what good he will accomplish in leaving Ithaca, is not at all clear. Some notable work "may yet be done," but he cannot be certain that his new wanderings will lead to anything but death: "It may be that the gulfs will wash us down," he cautions. Of course, he and his mariners may "touch the Happy Isles" where they will be reunited with "the great Achilles," but the chance of such a reunion is at best tenuous. In fact, such a desire implies a kind of death wish, since Achilles has departed this life for Elysium.

One may sympathize with Ulysses, seeing that his present life is unfulfilling, and agree that pursuing tenuous goals is better than stagnating. At this point, though, one must recall that the dreary condition on Ithaca is not related by the poet as factual, but rather is described by Ulysses himself. Since the poem is dramatic in nature, only the hero's own word provides a touchstone for judging things as they really are, and it is possible that Ulysses' view is jaundiced. One must consider, too, that Tennyson draws not only from Homer but also from Dante for his portrait of Ulysses; the Dantean quality of the hero cannot be overlooked, and in the *Inferno* Ulysses is found in hell, having led his mariners to their doom. In the version of the *Inferno* that Tennyson probably read, that by H. F. Cary (1805), Ulysses tells Dante that no familial feelings could overcome the "zeal" he had to explore the world, a feeling that he calls "man's evil and his virtue." Tennyson's Ulysses may also be a victim of this curse and blessing. Despite his pronounced enthusiasm for a life of heroic adventure, Ulysses may in fact merely be running away from his responsibilities. If the reader recalls from the *Odyssey* the hero's struggles to return to his wife and son, Ulysses' behavior in Tennyson's poem must appear a little suspect. The beloved and faithful Penelope is now scorned as an "aged wife." Telemachus, although praised for his sagacity and patience, is still not of the heroic mold.

A word of caution is in order here. In the past, critics have been quick to call Ulysses' description of his son a thinly disguised piece of sarcasm, but this reading smuggles twentieth century notions into a nineteenth century context. Words such as "blameless" and "decent" were not terms of disapprobation in the nineteenth century, nor would Tennyson have been denigrating Telemachus by pointing out that he worked best in the sphere of "common duties." In fact, in his other poetry and in the writings preserved in Hallam Tennyson's *Alfred, Lord Tennyson: A Memoir*, Tennyson clearly had great respect for men and women who served society at the expense of personal gratification. Precisely because the duties that Ulysses turns over to Telemachus are ones that Tennyson and his contemporaries considered important for the continuation of ordered society, Ulysses' decision to abdicate them makes his motives questionable. It is at least possible to see that behind the hero's rhetoric lies a clever scheme to convince his listeners, and the reader, that his actions are motivated by the highest intentions, when in fact he is abandoning a job he finds distasteful and difficult in order to pursue a life-style he finds more gratifying. Such a possibility makes it difficult to see Ulysses as a hero; rather, he appears to be an irresponsible villain for whom Tennyson and the critical reader can have little sympathy. That Tennyson would have held such a man in low regard is evident from his own remarks; as recorded in Hallam Tennyson's *Alfred, Lord Tennyson: A Memoir*, he once told a young aspirant to university life that a man "should embark on his career in the spirit of selfless and adventurous heroism and should develop his true self by not shirking responsibility."

In the light of this ambiguity, it is easy to construe Ulysses' real decision as an affirmation not of life but of death, and to see his desire to journey forth again as a kind of death-wish. Whether one adopts such a reading depends largely on the way one views the tone of the final segments of the poem, in which Ulysses states publicly his reasons for undertaking such a voyage. If this public harangue is merely a rhetorical pose intended to win over skeptical followers so that they will man the hero's ship on this futile journey, then "Ulysses" is a poem of deceit and despair, a warning to the reader of the hypnotic power of such rhetoric to sway listeners into a mood of naïve optimism. On the other hand, if one is convinced of the hero's sincerity in his call to strive, seek, find, and not yield, one cannot help considering "Ulysses" another of the many poems in which Tennyson offers hope and support to his fellow Victorians, tempering such optimism with the notion that one can never be absolutely certain whether the journey through life will lead to paradise or merely to death, adrift on an angry sea.

The dilemma may never be solved satisfactorily, for in "Ulysses," Tennyson is experimenting with a relatively new poetic form, the dramatic monologue, in which ambiguity and ironic distance are characteristic. Although "Ulysses" does not possess all the formal qualities of the dramatic monologue, it does contain the essentials. Situation and action are inferred only from the speech of the main character, and the reader's assessment of motives rests on his estimation of the character of the speaker. The hero's exhortation is intended not only to be heard by his fellow mariners but also to be overheard by the reader; one feels compelled to judge the merits of the hero's philosophy. What one brings to the poem—knowledge of the *Odyssey* or *The Divine Comedy*, or of Tennyson's life—may help to determine whether one should accept or reject Ulysses' call. In any case, the act of choosing demanded by the poem forces one to make a moral commitment of some kind. The need for making such judgments, and the complexities involved in making them, are matters which concern Tennyson in all of his poetry. The ambiguity of the poem is intentional, reflecting the dilemmas faced in the real world by Tennyson and his readers.

The same concerns that one finds in Tennyson's shorter compositions, such as "Ulysses," are also reflected in the poet's longer works. Tennyson wrote four long poems: *The Princess*, *In Memoriam*, *Maud*, and *Idylls of the King*. None of these is typical of traditional narrative poetry, and in several ways they anticipate the long poems of the twentieth century. All four are fragmented in some way; none tells a single story from a consistent perspective. *The Princess* is the most tightly constructed of Tennyson's long poems. In this medley a group of seven young men and women each create part of a tale about a Princess who has removed herself from the world of men to establish a college for women. Princess Ida and the Prince who comes to "rescue" her and win her love are the products not of a single creator but of seven, as each young person participating in the game adds to both story line and character development. As a result, the poem is actually two stories—that of the Princess whose tale is created by the young people, and that of the young people who are themselves very like the characters they create. Throughout the poem songs are interspersed to serve as counterpoint to the narrative and to highlight major themes.

Maud is also a medley. Here, however, the variation is in the verse form, and the fragmentary structure mirrors the nature of the hero, a man poised on the edge of disaster and dementia.

Idylls of the King, Tennyson's Arthurian poem, consists of twelve separate pieces tied together by the overarching structure provided by the legend itself—the rise and fall of Arthur and his Round Table. Within this framework individual idylls remain relatively self-contained units. The poet's examination of the downfall of a society that abandons its ideals is carried forward through an intricate patterning of repeated images and parallel scenes.

Tennyson's most fragmented long poem is the one for which he is best remembered and most praised. *In Memoriam* is a collection of more than 130 lyrics, composed by the poet over seventeen years and finally pieced together to record his reaction to the death of his dearest friend. Rather than being a continuous narrative, *In Memoriam* is a loosely assembled collage that, when read as a whole, reflects the varied emotions that one man experiences when prompted by the death of a loved one to face the reality of death and change in the world and the possibilities for life after death. Like "Ulysses," the poem is inspired by Tennyson's personal grief, yet it uses this personal experience as a touchstone for examining an issue that plagued all men of his era: man's ability to cling to faith in God and an afterlife in the face of the challenges of the new science.

The "I" of *In Memoriam* is not always to be identified with the poet himself; rather, as Tennyson himself said, the speaker is sometimes "the voice of the human race speaking thro' him [that is, the poet]." Nine years before Darwin published *Origin of Species*, Tennyson was questioning the value of the individual human life in the light of scientific discoveries proving that whole species of animals that once roamed the earth had long ago become extinct. In the much-anthologized middle section of *In Memoriam*, Tennyson's narrator observes of nature, "So careful of the type she seems,/ So careless of the single life," only to cry despairingly in the next lyric,

> "So careful of the type?" but no.
> From scarpéd cliff and quarried stone
> She cries, "A thousand types are gone:
> I care for nothing, all shall go."

Here is the "Nature, red in tooth and claw" that men of Tennyson's age, nurtured on faith in a benevolent God, found impossible to comprehend.

Tennyson sees his personal dilemma over the loss of Hallam and the larger problem involving the conflict between the biblical account of creation and scientific discoveries as essentially similar. The speaker of *In Memoriam* passes through several emotional stages: from grief and despair over his loss; to doubt, which presumes that all is not lost in death; to hope, based not solely on blind trust but also on "intuition," man's sense that a higher Person exists to guide his life and the life of nature itself; to, finally, faith, an acceptance of the notion of immortality and permanence even in the face of changes in nature that the speaker cannot deny. In the poem, Tennyson's friend Hallam becomes a symbol of a "higher Race," a harbinger of a better life, one sent to earth ahead of his time to offer hope to all men that the changes and impermanences of life exhibit not chaos but rather a divine pattern of progress, a movement toward God himself. In terms that anticipate the twentieth century theologian and mystic, Pierre Teilhard de Chardin, Tennyson concludes his elegy with a tribute to his friend who appeared on earth "ere the times were ripe," and who now lives with the beneficent God who guides this process of evolution, "who ever lives and loves,/ One God, one law, one element,/ And one far-off divine event,/ To which the whole creation moves."

The note of optimism at the end of *In Memoriam* is achieved only after a great deal of agonizing doubt. In fact, T. S. Eliot believed that the strength of Tennyson's elegy lay not in its final affirmation of faith, but rather in the quality of its doubt. The fragmentary nature of the poem allows Tennyson to explore that doubt with much greater range and intensity than would a more typical narrative structure. For example, Section LX begins with two lines that refer directly to the speaker's grief over his lost friend: "He past; a soul of nobler tone:/ My spirit loved and loves him yet." The remaining fourteen lines, however, are an extended simile, in which the speaker compares his grief to the feelings of a young girl for a boy who is above her in social status. The girl's "heart is set/ On one whose rank exceeds her own." Seeing the young man "mixing with his proper sphere," and recognizing "the baseness of her lot," the girl experiences jealousy, without knowing what she should be jealous of, and envy of those who are fortunate enough to be near her beloved. She goes about her life in the "little village" that "looks forlorn" to her, feeling that her days are "narrow" as she performs her common household chores in "that dark house where she was born." From her friends she receives no pity (they "tease her" daily), and she is left alone at night to realize the impossibility of ever achieving the union she desires: "How vain am I," she weeps, "How should he love a thing so low?"

The link to the larger themes of the poem, the speaker's grief over the loss of his friend, is found most obviously in the lyric's opening lines. Once that link is established, the parallels between the feelings of the speaker and the young girl he describes in the remaining lines become apparent at numerous points. The different "spheres" in which the girl and her beloved live represent the difference the speaker sees between himself and his friend, whom he calls elsewhere the "herald of a higher race." The "little village" is the speaker's world, into which the dead friend will no longer come. The most important image used to link this lyric with the other sections of *In Memoriam* is the "dark house" in which the girl must pass her days. That image, first appearing in Section VII when the speaker stands before his friend's house in London shortly after learning that his friend has died, recurs in several other sections and always suggests the loss the speaker feels at his friend's death.

Section LX, then, is typical of many lyrics that Tennyson pieced together to form *In Memoriam*. In it, the speaker's grief, inexpressible in its magnitude, is made realizable by comparison with feelings that immediately touch the reader. One develops a sense of the speaker's loss, and his friend's greatness, through the process of empathetic association with more familiar feelings of loss and pain experienced in the sphere of everyday life. Similarly, when the speaker begins to understand that the loss of his friend should not be cause for despair, but rather for joy, that joy is transmitted to the reader by associating the speaker's feelings with traditional symbols of happiness—the three Christmas seasons that form important structural links within *In Memoriam* and the wedding celebration that closes the poem. The celebration of the wedding is a most appropriate close for this poem: the union of two lives to form a single unit from which new life will spring mirrors man's ultimate union with God, "To which the whole creation moves."

Laurence W. Mazzeno

Other major works

PLAYS: *Queen Mary*, 1875; *Harold*, 1876; *The Falcon*, 1879; *The Cup*, 1881; *The Promise of May*, 1882; *Becket*, 1883; *The Foresters*, 1892; *The Devil and the Lady*, 1930 (unfinished).

NONFICTION: *The Letters of Alfred Lord Tennyson, Volume 1: 1821-1850*, 1981 (Cecil Y. Lang and Edgar F. Shannon, editors).

MISCELLANEOUS: *The Works of Tennyson*, 1907-1908 (9 volumes; Hallam, Lord Tennyson, editor).

Bibliography

Buckley, Jerome Hamilton. *Tennyson: The Growth of a Poet*. Cambridge, Mass.: Harvard University Press, 1961. The first major favorable treatment of the poet following decades of disparagement, organized as a critical biography. Buckley examines Tennyson's growing awareness of his vocation as a poet and provides a critical assessment of all the major poetry. This is the first study to make extensive use of unpublished manuscripts; it is especially valuable for its discussion of Tennyson's major Arthurian poem, *Idylls of the King*.

Culler, A. Dwight. *The Poetry of Tennyson*. New Haven, Conn.: Yale University Press, 1977. A comprehensive examination of Tennyson's poetic corpus, focusing on ways the poet exemplifies Victorian concerns, especially those dealing with the notion of apocalypse. Culler avoids biographical criticism, opting instead to show how the poet mirrors his age. The discussion of earlier poems and of some of those not normally given serious attention (such as the English idylls and the civic poems) is particularly valuable.

Hair, Donald S. *Domestic and Heroic in Tennyson's Poetry*. Toronto: University of Toronto Press, 1981. Hair explores a central concern of all Tennyson's poetry: the importance of the family as a center of values. In examining the major poems and several minor pieces, Hair shows how heroic qualities emerge from domestic situations and are linked to domestic values. The final section on *Idylls of the King* provides an extended discussion of Tennyson's method of elevating domestic values to heroic status.

Jordan, Elaine. *Alfred Tennyson*. Cambridge, England: Cambridge University Press, 1988. Jordan devotes individual chapters to the English idyls, the dramatic monologues, and the major poems (*The Princess*, *In Memoriam*, *Maud*, and *Idylls of the King*) to illustrate her thesis that Tennyson was intensely interested in gender issues and was ambivalent regarding the validity of patriarchal methods of governing society.

Martin, Robert Bernard. *Tennyson: The Unquiet Heart*. New York: Oxford University Press, 1980. This critical biography attempts to get behind the public mask created by the poet and his family in order to explore the psychological tensions out of which Tennyson's greatest poetry came. Includes important supplementary material on the Tennyson family and an excellent select bibliography.

Tucker, Herbert F. *Tennyson and the Doom of Romanticism*. Cambridge, Mass.: Harvard University Press, 1988. Focusing on the poems written during the first half of the poet's career, Tucker traces the influence of the poetic tradition, especially the Romantic poets, on Tennyson before he became his country's laureate and in the years immediately following his rise to fame after the publication of *In Memoriam*. Contains an exceptionally good bibliography.

DYLAN THOMAS

Born: Swansea, Wales; October 27, 1914
Died: New York, New York; November 9, 1953

Principal poetry

18 Poems, 1934; *Twenty-five Poems*, 1936; *The Map of Love*, 1939; *New Poems*, 1943; *Deaths and Entrances*, 1946; *Twenty-six Poems*, 1950; *In Country Sleep*, 1952; *Collected Poems, 1934-1952*, 1952; *The Poems of Dylan Thomas*, 1971 (Daniel Jones, editor).

Other literary forms

Dylan Thomas wrote one novel, *The Death of the King's Canary* (1976), in collaboration with John Davenport. His stories and collections of stories include the very popular, essentially autobiographical, *Portrait of the Artist as a Young Dog* (1940) and many posthumous publications. Scripts include the extremely popular *Under Milk Wood* (1954); *The Doctor and the Devils* (1953), which has been translated into German, Czech, and Spanish and was republished with four additional scripts in 1966; and *Quite Early One Morning* (1954), which has variant English and American versions. Thomas' letters are rich with biographical materials and critical insights. There are three important collections: *Letters to Vernon Watkins* (1957), written to, and edited by, Vernon Watkins, his friend and fellow poet; *Selected Letters of Dylan Thomas* (1966), edited by Constantine FitzGibbon, his "official" biographer; and *Twelve More Letters by Dylan Thomas* (1969), a limited edition supplemental to the FitzGibbon collection. Many other articles, poems, letters, scripts, and stories are widely scattered in manuscripts, anthologies, newspapers, and magazines. Whether a complete bibliography, much less an inclusive edition, of Thomas' work can ever be made is an open question. J. Alexander Rolph's *Dylan Thomas: A Bibliography* (1956) and Ralph Maud's *Dylan Thomas in Print: A Bibliographical History* (1970) are important efforts in this direction.

Achievements

Whatever else may be said about Thomas' poetry, it had the qualities needed to bring its author to the attention of the English-speaking world by the time he was twenty-two years old. Whether it was simply his tone, his subject matter, or a bit of both, Thomas' poems elicited a marked response in readers caught in a fierce economic depression. In any immediate sense, the poems were not optimistic; they sang of no golden age in the offing. Instead, mildly outrageous in subject matter and language, defiant of the ugly processes of life and death, and apparently even more defiant of conventional poetic forms, they seemed to project a knowledge of the inner workings of the universe denied to other mortals but toughly shared. Small wonder, then, that Thomas gained a hearing as poet and seer in the literary world and among general readers. While the first impact of *18 Poems* was slight, *Twenty-five Poems* established Thomas as a writer to be reckoned with. The book generated several critical questions. Did the world have a new John Keats on its hands, a poet who came almost at once to literary maturity and whose works would be permanent; or was Thomas simply a minor poet who had struck a rich topical vein which would soon be exhausted; or was he, worst of all, as seemed to some most likely, a mere wordmonger whose obscure rantings would soon become mere curiosities, interesting, if at all, only to literary historians? Nearly five decades after *18 Poems*, Thomas has been firmly established as a true poet, but discussion of the ultimate value of his poetry continues. What is clear is that he had a strong hold on the public imagination for roughly two decades and, during that time, helped to shape the idea of what poetry is or can aspire to be.

Biography

Dylan Marlais Thomas is firmly identified in many minds as the Welsh poet par excellence, as the voice of modern Wales speaking in the bardic tradition of *The Mabinogion* (c. twelfth and thirteenth centuries) and in the Renaissance tradition of William Shakespeare's mystic, Owen Glendower. In fact, Thomas' poetry is scarcely Welsh at all. G. S. Fraser, in his excellent critical biography, *Dylan Thomas* (1965), points out that Thomas loved Wales without being especially Welsh. Jacob Korg remarked in his biography, *Dylan Thomas* (1965), that Thomas' life and times have only a limited relevance to his poetry, and what influence there is, is transformed into a personal inner world. "Fern Hill," "Over Sir John's Hill," and a few other poems are set in the countryside and seashore that Thomas knew, and "Hold Hand, These Ancient Minutes in the Cuckoo's Month" speaks accurately of the brutality of the Welsh winter and spring, but rarely does Thomas' poetry treat in any serious way either the real or mythical history and countryside of Wales, the realities of the depressed industrial Wales he knew as an adolescent, or the postwar Wales he returned to after the horrors of the London bombing or the triumph of the American tours. The rough and intimate life of the family and village he treats so graphically in other genres seems to lie outside his idea of poetic fitness.

Thomas was born and reared in Swansea, in southern Wales, east by a few miles from Carmarthen and its environs, Fern Hill and Laugharne, which were to play such an important part in his personal life. Swansea, urban and industrial, contrasts strongly with the idyllic Carmarthenshire. Thomas' immediate family consisted of his father, David John Thomas; his mother, Florence Thomas (née Williams); and an older sister, Nancy. He was liberally supplied with aunts, uncles, and cousins of all sorts, and shared the usual family closeness of the Welsh, though his wife, Caitlin, recorded in *Leftover Life to Kill* (1957) that he tried hard but unsuccessfully to free himself from its puritanical background.

Thomas' paternal grandfather was, among a number of other vocations, a poet, not especially distinguished, who took for himself the bardic name "Gwilym Marles." "Gwilym" is William and "Marles" was taken from the Welsh stream Marlais, which, in its proper spelling, later became Thomas' middle name. Thomas' father had poetic ambitions of his own and was determined that his son should have his chance to become a poet. Disappointed in his hope for a distinguished career in education, he had settled with some lasting bitterness for a schoolmastership in the south of Wales. Thomas' poem "Do Not Go Gentle into That Good Night" furnishes some measure of his bitterness at his father's lingering death from cancer, and of the son's reciprocation of the father's love.

Thomas' school days were unusual only in that he began to write poetry early. His close friend in grammar school was Daniel Jones, who was later to edit *The Poems of Dylan Thomas*. They wrote more than two hundred poems together, each contributing alternate lines—Jones odd, Thomas even.

Thomas left school in 1931 and worked until 1932 for the *South Wales Daily Post*. The period of his most intense activity as a poet had already begun in 1930 and was to extend to 1934. Daniel Jones calculated that during this period Thomas' output was four times greater than that of the last nineteen years of his life. Ralph Maud has edited the four so-called "Buffalo Notebooks," which contain working drafts of Thomas' poems from 1930 to August, 1933—except for the period of July, 1932, to January, 1933—publishing them, with other manuscript material, in *Poet in the Making: The Notebooks of Dylan Thomas* (1968). Maud has observed that Thomas came to think of these poems as a sort of mine of early drafts and drew upon them, generally with some revision, for a number of poems in *Twenty-five Poems*; he continued to do so until the notebooks were purchased in 1941 for what is now the Lockwood Memorial Library of the State University of New York at Buffalo.

Thomas' last two years in Swansea, 1932 to 1934, foreshadowed the importance of the theater in his life. Bill Read, in his too-lightly regarded biography, *The Days of Dylan Thomas* (1964), traces an active interest in acting and playwriting while Thomas was still in school, then details Thomas' journeyman experience in a community theater group, the Mumbles Stage Society. By all accounts, Thomas rapidly became a competent actor, but the bohemianism which was to mar his personal life had already become established and caused his expulsion from the group.

In 1933, Thomas began to place poems in British papers and magazines which had more than local circulation. In September, 1933, he began a correspondence with the future novelist Pamela Hanford Johnson, who eventually married another novelist, C. P. Snow. The correspondence ripened into a friendship, which in turn became a love affair after visits in 1934. In November, Thomas moved to London, the center of his activities until 1937.

18 Poems appeared in December, 1934. Although the book caused hardly a ripple, when it was followed in 1936 by *Twenty-five Poems*, Thomas' reputation was established, helped not a little when the book was received by the prestigious poet Edith Sitwell.

Twenty-five Poems contains a rich trove of some of Thomas' best work. The sonnet sequence "Altarwise by Owl-Light," for example, has still not been exhausted by critical study. The sequence is generally viewed as containing the elements which make Thomas' poetry at once difficult and rewarding: religious, overtly Christian, motifs; packed metaphor and imagery, some of it traditional, some of it esoteric in various ways; high style mixed with colloquial phrasing; and the always-present theme of life-and-death as a process centered around, informed by, and powered through, sexuality.

Perhaps the central event of Thomas' personal life was his meeting with Caitlin Macnamara at a London pub party in April, 1936. The daughter of the eccentric Yvonne Majolier and Francis Macnamara, Caitlin was immediately drawn to Thomas and the affair quickly became serious. By all accounts, Caitlin's temperament was as mercurial as Thomas' own. After a trip together to Cornwall, they married on July 11, 1937, in Penzance, without any visible means of support or any moral support from Thomas' family. They lived at first in Hampshire, southwest of London, with Caitlin's mother. It was a relatively happy and carefree time.

In the fall of 1938, Thomas and his wife moved to Wales, living at first with Thomas' parents, then alone in Laugharne, where their first son, Llewelyn, was born in January, 1939. In August, *The Map of Love* was published, complete with Augustus John's portrait of Thomas. This book contains a number of more or less surrealistic stories plus sixteen poems. In spite of the celebrated episode of Thomas' participation in the Surrealist Exhibition of June 26, 1936, where he read poetry and passed around a cup of strong tea, the notion that Thomas was at any time a surrealist writer has been thoroughly exploded. G. S. Fraser argued that *The Map of Love* generated the New Apocalypse movement, later the New Romanticism, which was, in turn, superficially influenced by Surrealism and Dadaism. H. H. Kleinman, in *The Religious Sonnets of Dylan Thomas* (1963), argued that Thomas could not have been a Surrealist because he was essentially nonliterary as a reader. Earlier than either, Marshall Stearns, in "Unsex the Skeleton: Notes on the Poetry of Thomas" (1944), placed a high value on Thomas' poetry because of its originality and because of the influence it had on the Apocalypse group, specifically Henry Treese, G. S. Fraser, and J. F. Hendry. When Richard Church, a Dent publishing company official, objected to some of Thomas' poems as surrealistic, Thomas rejected the charge and described Surrealism as a "pernicious experiment" which was beneath him, adding that "every

line of his poetry was to be understood by the reader thinking and feeling."
In any case, the book was well received and contained at least two outstanding poems, the brittle elegy "After the Funeral (In Memory of Ann Jones)" and the splendid compact birthday piece, "Twenty-Four Years."

On September 3, 1939, Great Britain declared war against Nazi Germany, beginning a struggle from which the world as Thomas had known it would never reemerge. During the relatively quiet early stages, before the German drives in the spring of 1940 which led first to the evacuation of Dunkirk and then to the surrender of France, Thomas registered shock about the war and determined not to be involved in it. Called up for military service in April, just after *Portrait of the Artist as a Young Dog* was published, he was found unfit for service. In June, he moved to an artist's colony in the Cotswolds and thence to London in the fall. There began a long period of poverty and writing scenarios for war documentaries, an occupation which may have been emotionally damaging, but which also stood him in good stead as preparation for later participation in filmmaking. His personal life continued to be on the windy side of bohemianism, especially during the periods when Caitlin was in Wales. On March 3, 1943, his daughter Aeron was born while Caitlin was still in London. The Thomases were to have no more children until their second son, Colm, was born in Carmarthen on July 24, 1949, just over four years before his father's death.

The war years saw only a single slim volume of poetry produced, *New Poems*. Included in this book were several poems of first importance: "And Death Shall Have No Dominion," "The Marriage of a Virgin," "The Hunchback in the Park," the long and controversial "Ballad of the Long-Legged Bait," "Once Below a Time," "Deaths and Entrances," and one of his few war poems, "Among Those Killed in the Dawn Raid Was a Man Aged One Hundred." In spite of the title, the poems were not "new"; they were drawn from earlier publication in scattered periodicals.

In the spring of 1945, the European phase of the war was finished and the Thomases returned once more to Wales, settling this time in New Quay on the western coast and moving from there to Oxford in 1946, and finally, in the spring of 1949, to the Boat House in Laugharne, with which Thomas is, perhaps, most often associated. He produced one book of poetry during this period, *Deaths and Entrances*. Meanwhile, he was busy writing and acting for the British Broadcasting Corporation, writing filmscripts, and traveling abroad to Italy, Czechoslovakia, and, finally, America, on the first of four tours.

In August, 1950, after his return from America, *Twenty-six Poems* was published. This limited edition, printed by hand in Italy, signed by Thomas, and in all ways a pretentious production, signaled a new sort of arrival. Rather a large number of people were now willing to pay handsomely for the status conferred by owning a copy of a limited edition of his work.

The American tours were triumphs for Thomas. He appears to have basked in the adoration of American society and academic groups. From the detailed accounts of his mentor, John Malcolm Brinnin, recorded in his biographical *Dylan Thomas in America: An Intimate Journal* (1955), Thomas worked very hard while at the same time continuing to behave in off-hours in the feckless manner for which he was now notorious.

Even so, in February, 1952, a second handsome edition appeared, the six poems of *In Country Sleep*. This book was almost immediately eclipsed by the publication in November of Thomas' most important book, *Collected Poems, 1934-1952*. Again, the format was impressive and the edition included a number of specially bound copies. This volume includes nearly all of Thomas' poetry and forms the point of departure for any serious study of his work.

While the fourth American tour was under way, Thomas was taken ill in New York, lapsed into a coma, and died on November 9, 1953. He was buried on November 24 in St. Martin's Churchyard, Laugharne, Wales.

Analysis

Three poems will serve to illustrate, provisionally, the range in theme and technique of Dylan Thomas' poetry: "And Death Shall Have No Dominion," "Altarwise by Owl-Light," and "Over Sir John's Hill." All three deal with the life-in-death theme which permeates Thomas' work. The first is a very early poem, rather clear and personal in its statement; the second, consisting of ten sonnets treated as a single entity, involves a great deal of Christian material, though it is not incontrovertibly a Christian poem and presents many problems of analysis and interpretation; the third is a "Welsh" poem inasmuch as it is set in Wales and may well spring from Welsh folk material. While the middle poem is considered to be difficult, the last is sequentially clear in its narrative progression, panorama of images, and vivid descriptions.

"And Death Shall Have No Dominion" appears in the "Buffalo Notebooks" dated April, 1933, and was published in *The New English Weekly* on May 18, 1933, and in *Collected Poems, 1934-1952*. It consists of three stanzas, each beginning and ending with the phrase "And death shall have no dominion." The rhythm is based on a four-stress count with enough variations to intrigue the serious prosodist. These may involve eccentric massing of stresses, as in the title line, or stressing or not stressing the same word in a single line, as in "When their bones are picked clean and the clean bones gone." Aside from the title-refrain, the poem does not lend itself to simple syllable count, though lines two and six consistently have eight syllables and line five has nine. The other four lines are more or less irregular. For the most part, the lines tend to fall irregularly into the iambic and anapestic patterns common to English versification. Alliteration runs throughout the poem. End-rhyme, assonance, and consonance also play a part in the sound pattern. Lines two and three of the second stanza, for example, substitute alliteration for end-rhyme with "windily" and "way," while "way" is assonant with "break" in line five. Moreover, "windily" is assonant with the first word of the following line, "twisting," which, in turn, is assonant with both words of the phrase "sinews give." More alliteration is found in line three in "lying long," and "lying" echoes "windings" in line two. Such intricacy of sound patterning is the rule in Thomas' poetry.

This rhythmical music contributes much to the readability and understanding of the poem. Prosed, the first stanza says little more than that human beings will die in many ways and places and their bodies will return to the elements and be scattered. The elements, however, will live again because love will continue its purpose of regeneration, and death will not rule life. Of course, prosing cannot indicate the cosmic triumph of "They shall have stars at elbow and foot." The second paragraph works with images of sea-death and of torture, and plays on the paradox that the broken will remain whole. The third stanza picks up a minor theme of madness and couples it with a wasteland setting. In spite of madness, in spite of burial and dissolution, the poem insists that something will continue to hammer the elements into life until the sun itself breaks down. Again, the prosing gives little notion of the desolation evoked by "Where blew a flower may a flower no more/ Lift its head to the blows of the rain."

In an essay in the *Explicator* (1956), Thomas E. Connolly professed to see both Christian and Platonic elements in the poem and suggested the influence of Percy Bysshe Shelley's *Adonais* (1821) and John Milton's "Lycidas" (1645) as well. The Christian note is at best vague, while the breaking down of the sun and the persistence with which the elements return to the flesh instead of to the godhead seems clearly enough to refute Platonism. Whatever the merits of the *Adonais* identification may be, Thomas' resources would be poor indeed if he had to depend on "Lycidas" for sea-drowning imagery. On the other hand, Korg agrees with Connolly's identification of St. Paul's Epistle to the Romans as the source of the title-refrain and the language indicating that the dead in the sea will rise again. Korg rejects the idea that the lines Christianize the poem and sees them, instead, as part of a "more generalized mysticism."

"Altarwise by Owl-Light" is a much more difficult and controversial poem. The first seven of its ten sonnets were published in *Life and Letters Today* (1935) and the last three were published at various times during 1936 in *Contemporary Poetry and Prose*. They were printed later as a sequence in *Twenty-five Poems*.

The poems comprising "Altarwise by Owl-Light" are traditional sonnets mainly inasmuch as they have fourteen lines each; they do not follow the rhyme scheme of either the English or the Italian form. In fact, their rhyme is of the incidental and varied pattern characteristic of so much of Thomas' poetry. Terminal sounds are patterned, but hardly enough so to be considered formalized. The rhythm is equally irregular. Most lines contain five stressed syllables, many of them iambic, but that the overall pattern is dominated by iambs is doubtful. Even so, the poems are recognizable as variants of the twentieth century sonnet.

Elder Olson, in *The Poetry of Dylan Thomas* (1954), developed what must be by far the most intricate analysis of the poems' symbolism. He assembled charts to demonstrate that the poems are based on astrology, basically Herculean in identity. Although Olson's interpretation has been rejected for the most part by other critics, it hardly merits Jones's curt dismissal as "ludicrously complex decipherment." On a different tack, Bernard Knieger, in an essay in the *Explicator* (1956), offered an interpretation to counter a rather muddled one by R. N. Maud earlier in the same periodical. Knieger defined the themes of "Altarwise by Owl-Light" as being simultaneously Christian and sexual. E. H. Essig, again in the *Explicator* (1958), built on Olson's and Knieger's interpretations to demonstrate a fully Christian poetry. In 1965, G. S. Fraser rejected Olson's position out of hand and joined David Daiches in the opinion, expressed in *College English* (1954), that, although splendid in parts, the sonnets are, as wholes, "oppressive and congested." At the same time, he declared that the sonnets "are important because they announce the current orthodox Christian feeling . . . which was henceforth increasingly to dominate Thomas' work in poetry." The opinion is interesting in the face of Thomas' remark, reported by J. M. Brinnin in an article in the *Atlantic Monthly* (1955), that he now intended to write "poems in praise of God's world by a man who doesn't believe in God." Daniel Jones, perhaps, deserves the last word. He argued that "Altarwise by Owl-Light" could be termed "absolute poetry," held together, not by ordinary logic, but by a pattern of words and images joined by a common relationship with such things as "sex, birth, death, Christian and pagan religion and ritual." He saw the poem as "sustained by a single metaphor" and as beyond translation into other words or thoughts. Like Fraser, he saw the poem marking a change in Thomas' poetry, but unlike Fraser, he saw it as moving away from the extravagant expression of the earlier work and toward economy.

It is clear that "Altarwise by Owl-Light" demonstrates Thomas' concern for the life-death paradox taken on the grandest scale and illuminated, at least in part, by the Christian mythos. Also helpful is the understanding that the persona of the poems is a universalized character who is at once himself and the Christ who dies, and who is also all the human beings who have ever died and who will ever die. With their insistence upon the mysteries of life in death, mercy in destruction, God in man, the sonnets are quintessentially Thomas.

"Over Sir John's Hill" first appeared in *Botteghe Oscure* in 1949 and was later included in the *Collected Poems, 1934-1952*. Daniel Jones pointed out that the poem was written during Thomas' residence at Laugharne. The area of "Sir John's Hill" borders an estuary east of the outlet of the River Towy, a semiwilderness area supporting many wildfowl and birds of prey. The poem, then, reflects a setting which was intimately familiar to Thomas; even so, except for the place-names, the setting could be nearly any waste area in the world where land and a large body of water meet.

Jones's detailed study of the prosody of "Over Sir John's Hill" is interesting. He has noted the varied but exact patterning of the long and short lines based on a syllabic count, the longest line containing fifteen syllables, the shortest containing only one; lines of either thirteen and fourteen syllables, or four to six syllables are the most common line lengths. Jones also observed that the poem's four stanzas have a rhyme pattern of aabbccbxdadxx, a, b, c, and d being either full-rhymes or half-rhymes, and x indicating alliteration with first-syllable assonance. Jones considered the verse form to be representative of Thomas' work at its best and most mature. While he conceded that such intricacy is open to the charge of artificiality and that syllabic verse tends to be "easily overcome by the natural patterns of the English language, based upon combinations of weak and strong stresses," he argued that all artists must work within "self-imposed discipline."

While "Over Sir John's Hill" exists on many levels, it can be approached quite usefully from the point of view of allegory. Allegory works by having each actor's part function on several levels simultaneously in a linear story. The trick is to see that each actor functions differently, though interrelatedly, in several stories at once. Thus, an actor may be a bird, functioning as a bird, and a bird functioning as a mortal man, and a man functioning as an immortal soul, all at the same time. Put another way, one actor plays three parts in three stories, all fully coherent, in the telling of one tale. In "Over Sir John's Hill," there is a persona who narrates the action, observes it, and participates in it. The "young Aesop fabling" watches the drama of bird life and bird death on the estuary shortly before sunset. On the literal level, the persona watches while a hawk, during last light, is destroying sparrows. A fishing heron watches and grieves and the grief is echoed by the "tear" of the river. The bird life then settles down, an owl hoots, and the persona hears the sound of the river in the willows just before the plunge of night.

On the ethical level, "Over Sir John's Hill" is a grim sort of parody of the legal system and of institutionalized religion. The birds and the countryside echo human behavior. The hill itself represents a judge who has, on evidence which is never presented in the poem, reached a verdict of condemnation; thus, he is sitting with the symbol of the death sentence on his head, the "black cap of jackdaws." That the cap is formed of jackdaws is instructive. The jackdaw's habit of playing jokes on people is reflected in the term "gulled birds," which Thomas may have picked up from his interest in Jacobean tragedy. "Gulled," in that context, means "fooled" and here functions to undercut the quality of human justice. As jackdaws are also minor carrion birds, their use as a "black cap" heightens the grim note. The hawk represents the executioner, as is indicated by the adjective "tyburn," an allusion to the Tyburn Tree or Tyburn Elms, a thirteenth century place of execution on the River Tybourne and later the slang name for the gallows built near the site of London's Marble Arch. The identification is intensified by an immediate reference to "wrestle of elms" and the "noosed" hawk. The law, it would seem, chooses its victims at random, and the victims themselves are by nature young and silly, foredoomed and courting death. They sing "dilly dilly, come let us die," and are described by the persona and the heron as "led-astray birds." The saintly heron, at the ethical level, stands for the church, which observes the workings of human justice without protest, though it grieves for the victims. The heron, like the church, continues to carry on its own business in spite of the mundane horrors about it. On the ethical level, then, society is formal, filled with sorrow but not with mercy, and its conceptions of justice, death, and divinity are at once structured and casual.

The divine level is still more disquieting. The persona regards nature in an old-fashioned way, his words couched in fresh metaphor, as he describes nature as the Book in which divinity can be read. He opens "the leaves of water" and reads psalms there, and in a shell he reads "death." He and the heron-church ask for God's mercy, the God who, in silence, observes the sparrow's "hail," a term implying not only the sparrows' song of praise but also the numbers in which their dead bodies pelt the earth. If the God of the poem is more merciful than the indifferent hill-judge, the poem does not say so. Of salvation and an afterlife there is no affirmation; the "lunge of night" seems dreadfully final, not Thomas' more usual affirmation of a circular process in which death is the entrance to life, in which life is repeated rather than translated to a divine realm. It may be that, after the war, Thomas was no longer able to see the cycle of nature as an endlessly repeating pattern. If "Over Sir John's Hill" is in fact a celebration, it is an unusually dark one, even for Thomas.

In placing Thomas as a poet, Howard Nemerov's conclusion, expressed in *The Kenyon Review* (1953), that "he has written a few beautiful poems" furnishes a good point of departure. In a way, that is the best that can be said for any poet, even the greatest. David Daiches, who denied a place of greatness to Thomas in his essay in *College English* (1954), said that "it is enough that he wrote some poems that the world will not willingly let die." Richard A. Werry, again in *College English* (1955), allowed Thomas' poetry greater depth than is generally granted, suggesting that at least a half dozen of his poems will last out the twentieth century. This is rather faint praise. Even if Thomas' poetry comes down to no more than that, a few lasting poems, still, to have caught the imagination and the spirit, if not fully the understanding, of the people who endured the Depression and World War II, to have embodied in his poetry a fearless, if bitter, search for reality and a limited hope in a world bereft of its traditional theological certainties, is no mean feat. This much, at least, Thomas achieved.

B. G. Knepper

Other major works

LONG FICTION: *The Death of the King's Canary*, 1976 (with John Davenport).

SHORT FICTION: *Portrait of the Artist as a Young Dog*, 1940; *Selected Writings of Dylan Thomas*, 1946; *A Child's Christmas in Wales*, 1954; *Adventures in the Skin Trade and Other Stories*, 1955; *A Prospect of the Sea and Other Stories*, 1955; *Early Prose Writings*, 1971; *The Followers*, 1976; *The Collected Stories*, 1984.

PLAYS: *Under Milk Wood*, 1954.

SCREENPLAYS: *Three Weird Sisters*, 1948 (with Louise Birt and David Evans); *No Room at the Inn*, 1948 (with Ivan Foxwell); *The Doctor and the Devils*, 1953; *The Beach at Falesá*, 1963; *Twenty Years A'Growing*, 1964; *Rebecca's Daughters*, 1965; *Me and My Bike*, 1965.

RADIO PLAYS: *Quite Early One Morning*, 1944; *The Londoner*, 1946; *Return Journey*, 1947; *Quite Early One Morning*, 1954; (twenty-two radio plays).

NONFICTION: *Letters to Vernon Watkins*, 1957 (Vernon Watkins, editor); *Selected Letters of Dylan Thomas*, 1966 (Constantine FitzGibbon, editor); *Poet in the Making: The Notebooks of Dylan Thomas*, 1968 (Ralph Maud, editor) *Twelve More Letters by Dylan Thomas*, 1969 (Constantine FitzGibbon, editor).

MISCELLANEOUS: *"The Doctor and the Devils" and Other Scripts*, 1966 (two screenplays and one radio play).

Bibliography

Davies, Walford. *Dylan Thomas*. Philadelphia: Open University Press, 1986. A biography and an introduction are followed by several chapters on the poems: poems on poetry, early poetry, comparisons of early and late poems, "Fern Hill," and the last poems. The final chapter attempts to put Thomas' work in context and to draw some conclusions regarding the poet in relationship to society, his style, and the way he uses language. Good notes contain bibliographical references.

Ferris, Paul. *Dylan Thomas*. New York: Dial Press, 1977. This excellent biography contains new material found in American archives and also those of the British Broadcasting Corporation. Ferris interviewed more than two hundred people who either knew Thomas or worked with him. He attempts to separate the facts from the legendary reputation of Thomas. This book elaborates on, and enhances, the "approved" biography by Constantine FitzGibbon (*The Life of Dylan Thomas*, 1965), the personal memoirs by Caitlin Thomas (*Leftover Life to Kill*, 1957), and John Malcolm Brinnin (*Dylan Thomas in America*, 1955).

Kleinman, Hyman H. *The Religious Sonnets of Dylan Thomas: A Study in Imagery and Meaning*. Berkeley: University of California Press, 1963. Analyzes the religious sonnets in sequence seeing them as a development from uncertainty to an affirmation of spiritual faith. Detailed explications give a close analysis of the imagery which is drawn from sources as varied as the medieval mystery plays, English poetry, myth, seventeenth century sermons, and movies. A short but fine study of the work, not the man.

Korg, Jacob. *Dylan Thomas*. New York: Twayne, 1965. A general discussion of Thomas and his work ("The Rhetoric of Mysticism") begins this study. Readings and analyses of two early collections, *18 Poems* and *Twenty-five Poems*, are followed by discussions of the later poems, fiction, and the dramatic works. Thomas is characterized throughout as a mystic with a romantic and mythic disposition. Korg explores the dichotomy between Thomas' sophisticated style and his often "barbaric" subject matter. Includes a chronology, a biographical sketch, notes and references, and a somewhat dated select bibliography. An excellent survey for the student.

Olson, Elder. *The Poetry of Dylan Thomas*. Chicago: University of Chicago Press, 1954. This book examines Thomas' original use of language and proposes an interesting and provocative point of view: that he was basically a symbolist writer concerned with a "nightmare universe"—particularly up to his later poems. A bibliography by William H. Huff is appended.

Sinclair, Andrew. *Dylan Thomas: No Man More Magical*. New York: Holt, Rinehart and Winston, 1975. This study examines Thomas' Welsh heritage and characterizes "the finest lyric poet of his age" as essentially a Welsh bard and minstrel. The text describes the life and artistic development of this contradictory poet and his quest for a "sweet final resolution of the soul." Published in England under the title *Dylan Thomas: Poet of His People*.

Tindall, William York. *A Reader's Guide to Dylan Thomas*. New York: Farrar, Straus & Giroux, 1963. This book is a poem-by-poem explication of Thomas' *Collected Poems, 1934-1952*. The author follows a development of themes and aesthetics from the dark early poems to the brighter poems later in the collection. An excellent guide for students, this survey includes an introductory essay examining Thomas' reputation and investigating the political, religious, surrealistic, Freudian, and Welsh elements in his work.

EDWARD THOMAS

Born: London, England; March 3, 1878
Died: Arras, France; April 9, 1917

Principal poetry
Six Poems, 1916; *Poems*, 1917; *Last Poems*, 1918; *Collected Poems*, 1920, 1928, 1979.

Other literary forms

Although Edward Thomas is remembered today as a poet, throughout his working life he supported himself and his family by writing various sorts of prose. He always considered himself to be a writer, and the lasting tragedy of his life was that he never seemed able, until the outbreak of World War I, to buy enough time to devote himself to the art of writing as he obviously wished to do.

Ironically, the war in which he died also provided him with the structured, organized environment and the freedom from financial anxiety which enabled him to produce the work which has secured his reputation.

His entire prose opus runs to nearly forty volumes, most of which were published during his lifetime. The titles cover a variety of subjects. It is also possible to see what a remarkable volume of work he produced in the years 1911 to 1912, a productivity which culminated, after nine published works, in a breakdown in 1912.

Although the prose work of Thomas is often dismissed as being unimportant, it is obvious from merely reading the titles where his main interests lay. Themes of nature and of the British countryside predominate, together with literary criticism.

In fact, Thomas was a remarkably perceptive literary critic. He was among the first reviewers to appreciate the work of Robert Frost, and he also recognized Ezra Pound's achievement in *Personae* (1909), which he reviewed in its first year of publication. When he began to write, he was heavily influenced by Walter Pater's code of aesthetics, his love of rhetoric, and his formality. He was later to have to work hard to rid his prose of those features, which he recognized as being alien to his own poetic voice.

Achievements

In his poetry, Thomas succeeded in realizing two ambitions, which another poet of nature set out as his aims more than a century earlier. In the Preface to the *Lyrical Ballads* (1800), William Wordsworth stated that his intent in writing poetry was "to exalt and transfigure the natural and the common," and also to redefine the status of the poet so that he would become "a man speaking to men." Wordsworth's poetry received both acclaim and abuse when it first appeared, and formed an expectation of poetry which continued until the end of the nineteenth century. By that time, the Aesthetic movement had come to the fore, and poetry was well on its way, at the outbreak of World War I, toward suffocating itself with overblown rhetoric.

Thomas is not generally regarded as a war poet, being discussed more often in conjunction with Thomas Hardy and Walter de la Mare than with Wilfred Owen, Siegfried Sassoon, and Isaac Rosenberg. By combining his acute perceptions of both nature and political events, however, Thomas produced poetry in which evocations of place and detailed descriptions of nature become a metaphor for man's spiritual state. F. R. Leavis, writing in *New Bearings in English Poetry* (1932) made this observation: "He was exquisitely sincere and sensitive, and he succeeded in expressing in poetry a representative modern sensibility. It was an achievement of a very rare order, and he has not yet had the recognition he deserves." Today, Thomas' poetry is widely known, and he has become almost an Establishment figure in the literature of the early twentieth century. Yet it is a measure of his achievement that in returning to his slender *Collected Poems*, it is always possible to be stimulated and surprised by his work.

Biography

Edward Philip Thomas was born in London, the eldest of six boys. Both of his parents were Welsh, and Thomas always had an affinity with the Principality, spending much time there during his childhood, although the landscapes of his poetry are predominantly those of the south of England. Thomas' father was a stern, unyielding man who had risen by his own efforts to a social position far above that which might be expected from his poor background. Having succeeded in elevating himself, he was naturally very ambitious for his eldest son, and Thomas received an excellent education, attending St. Paul's school, Hammersmith (as a contemporary of G. K. Chesterton and E. C. Bentley, among others), and going on from there to Jesus College, Oxford.

Shortly before going to Oxford, Thomas met Helen Noble; it was one of the momentous events in his life. Both he and Helen had very advanced ideas for their time; they were already lovers while Thomas was still an undergraduate. They discussed their future lives together, and how they would bring up their children in accordance with Richard Jeffries' theories of freedom and the open-air life. Helen herself said, "We hated the thought of a legal contract. We felt our love was all the bond there ought to be, and that if that failed it was immoral to be bound together. We wanted our union to be free and spontaneous." In the spring of 1899, Helen discovered that she was pregnant and was rather appalled to discover that Edward himself, as well as her friends in the bohemian community in which she lived, thought that they should be married. Helen's family were shocked to learn of Helen's pregnancy, insisting on a hurried marriage and refusing to help the young couple in any way. Thomas' family was more sympathetic, allowing Helen to live with them and helping Thomas while he worked toward his degree.

Once he was graduated, the need to earn money to support his family became pressing, and, determined not to become submerged in the drudgery of an office job, Thomas solicited work from publishers. Until the time that he joined the Artists' Rifles, Thomas was to support himself and his family by writing. They were always poor, and he often reproached himself bitterly because he had no regular source of income.

Writing became a chore to him, something to be done merely for the sake of the money. In 1912, he suffered a breakdown brought on by overwork. At about that time, also, he met Robert Frost and formed a close friendship with the American poet. Thomas was among the first to appreciate Frost's poetry, and Frost encouraged Thomas to try his hand at writing poetry himself; Thomas gradually gained confidence in his ability to say what he wanted in poetry. When he was killed by a bombshell in the spring of 1917, what might have become a considerable voice in English poetry was tragically silenced.

Analysis

Perhaps the most notable feature of Edward Thomas' poetry, which strikes the reader immediately, is its characteristic quietness of tone and its unassertive, gentle quality. He is primarily a poet of the country, but through his descriptions of the English landscape, impressionistic and minutely observed, he also attempts to delineate some of the features of his own inner landscape.

As may be seen from the titles of the many books of prose that he wrote before beginning to write poetry at the behest of Robert Frost, he was always deeply interested in nature and the land. Many of the fleeting observations in his poetry are drawn from his notebooks, in which he recorded such things as the first appearance of a spring blossom and the first sightings of various species of birds. In his prose, as opposed to the notebooks, his style was highly rhetorical, so that the keen observations which make his poetry so effective are lost in a plethora of adjectival excess. In one of his reviews he wrote that "The important thing is not that a thing should be small, but that it should be intense and capable of unconsciously symbolic significance." In his poetry, by the acuity of his observation and the spareness and tautness of his language, he certainly achieves remarkable—if low-key—intensity. He also achieves, in his best work, an unforced symbolic resonance.

"As the Team's Head-Brass" is one of Thomas' most impressive achievements; at first reading, it may appear to be only an account of a rural dialogue between the poet and a man plowing a field. It begins with a reference to the plowman, and to some lovers who are seen disappearing into the wood behind the field being plowed. The lovers are not directly relevant to the substance of the poem, but they are an important detail. The poem begins and ends with a reference to them, and although they are in no sense representative of a Lawrentian "life-force," their presence in the poem does suggest the triumph of life and love over death and destruction. The very mention of the lovers reinforces the image of the plow horses "narrowing a yellow square of charlock"—that is, destroying the (living) weeds, that *better* life may grow.

"If we could see all all might seem good" says the plowman, and this seems to be Thomas' contention in this poem. The writing throughout is highly controlled, the structure of the poem reinforced with alliteration and internal rhyme—seeming to owe something to Gerard Manley Hopkins and ultimately even to the Welsh *cynghanedd* form, with the use of "fallen/fallow/plough/narrowing/yellow/charlock" all in four lines, and then later in the same opening section, "word/weather/war/scraping/share/screwed/furrow." Writing about Thomas in *New Bearings in English Poetry* (1932), F. R. Leavis observes that "we become aware of the inner life which the sensory impressions are notation for." This is particularly true of "As the Team's Head-Brass." The closing lines bring the whole poem together most succinctly—the lovers, forgotten since the opening lines, emerge from the wood; the horses begin to plow a new furrow; "for the last time I watched" says Thomas, and the reader must pause here to ask whether he means "for the last time on this particular occasion" or "for the last time ever." All the conversation in the poem has been about war, and in the last two lines come the words "crumble/topple/stumble," which, although used ostensibly with reference to the horses and the soil, may equally be taken to refer back to the fallen tree upon which the poet is sitting, the plowman's workmate who has been killed in the war, the changing state of society, and the relentless passage of time.

This poem is not typical of Thomas' work, however, for it is longer and much more detailed and elaborate than most of his poems. More typical of his work are poems like "Tall Nettles" and "Adlestrop," which evoke the moment without attempting to do more than capture the unique quality of one particular place or one particular moment in time. "Adlestrop" is a poem much anthologized, and much appreciated by those who love the English countryside. It has been described as the most famous of modern "place" poems, and yet it also seems to conjure up an almost sexual tension (perhaps by the use of the words "lonely fair"?) of a kind which is often implicit in such hot summer days. This is a sense of the poem which the contemporary poet Dannie Abse has obviously found, for he has written a poem entitled "Not Adlestrop," in which the unspecified lady actually makes an appearance in a train going in the opposite direction. Abse's poem is something of a literary joke, but it does pinpoint an element of unresolved sexual tension in several of Thomas' poems.

For example, "Some Eyes Condemn," "Celandine," and "The Unknown" all seem to be worlds away in mood from "And You, Helen," a poem written for his wife. The poignant "No One So Much As You," a kind of apologia for an imperfectly reciprocated love, was written for Mary Elizabeth Thomas, the poet's mother, although it has often been mistaken for a love poem to his wife. In either case it would seem that familiarity did not necessarily increase Thomas' love for his family—in fact, it was obvious, both from his despairing reaction to the news of Helen's second pregnancy and from his well-documented impatience with domestic life—that distance and mystery were important elements of attraction for him. Perhaps fortunately for all concerned, Thomas' dissatisfactions and unfulfilled longings seem to have made up only a very small part of his nature. Having come to poetry late, he wastes little time in cataloging regrets for what he might have been and concentrates mainly on what he was able to do best—that is, to capture his own impressions of English rural life and country landscapes and combine them in poetry with various insights into his own personality.

It would not be possible to offer a succinct analysis of Edward Thomas' poetry without referring to his deeply felt patriotism. In her excellent book *Edward Thomas: A Poet for His Country* (1978), Jan Marsh describes an incident which occurred soon after Thomas enlisted in the British Army, although he was in fact over the usual age limit for enlistment. A friend asked the poet what he thought he was fighting for; Thomas bent down and picked up a pinch of earth and, letting it crumble through his fingers, answered, "Literally, for this."

This is the predominant impression which the reader carries away from an encounter with Thomas' poetry, for here is a sensitive, educated man who, despite his cultivation, is deeply attuned to the land. This affinity is particularly clear in the country people who inhabit Thomas' poetry, for they are always portrayed as being part of a long and noble tradition of rural life. Thomas does not romanticize his vision: he portrays the cruelties of nature as well as its beauties. A recurring image in his poetry is that of the gamekeeper's board, hung with trophies in an attempt to discourage other predators. Perhaps because he makes an honest attempt to describe the reality of country life without attempting to gloss over or soften its less attractive aspects, he succeeds superbly. Since his death, when his poetry was scarcely known, Thomas' work has become steadily more popular, so that today he is known as one of England's finest nature poets.

Vivien Stableford

Other major works

NONFICTION: *The Woodland Life,* 1897; *Horae Solitariae,* 1902; *Oxford,* 1903; *Rose Acre Papers,* 1904; *Beautiful Wales,* 1905; *The Heart of England,* 1906; *Richard Jeffries,* 1909; *The South Country,* 1909; *Rest and Unrest,* 1910; *Rose Acre Papers,* 1910; *Feminine Influence on the Poets,* 1910; *Windsor Castle,* 1910; *The Isle of Wight,* 1911; *Light and Twilight,* 1911; *Maurice Maeterlinck,*

1911; *Celtic Stories*, 1911; *The Tenth Muse*, 1911; *Algernon Charles Swinburne*, 1912; *George Borrow: The Man and His Books*, 1912; *Lafcadio Hearn*, 1912; *Norse Tales*, 1912; *The Icknield Way*, 1913; *The Happy-Go-Lucky Morgans*, 1913; *The Country*, 1913; *Walter Pater*, 1913; *In Pursuit of Spring*, 1914; *The Life of the Duke of Marlborough*, 1915; *A Literary Pilgrim in England*, 1917; *Cloud Castle and Other Papers*, 1922; *Essays of Today and Yesterday*, 1926; *Chosen Essays*, 1926; *The Last Sheaf*, 1928; *The Childhood of Edward Thomas*, 1938; *The Prose of Edward Thomas*, 1948 (Roland Gant, editor).

CHILDREN'S LITERATURE: *Four-and-Twenty-Blackbirds*, 1915.

Bibliography

Gant, Roland, ed. *Edward Thomas on the Countryside*. London: Faber & Faber, 1977. Traces the evolution of both the prose and poetry of Thomas as he matured as a writer. An interesting introduction sets forth the background and pastoral influences on him as an individual and on his works categorized by groups.

Kirkham, Michael. *The Imagination of Edward Thomas*. Cambridge, England: Cambridge University Press, 1986. Kirkham ignores chronology as he explores Thomas' imagination by identifying the characteristic style that is evidenced in his poetry. Augmented with a solid bibliography and an index, this book is extremely helpful for an in-depth study of Thomas.

Marsh, Jan. *Edward Thomas: A Poet for His Country*. New York: Barnes & Noble Books, 1978. Marsh pursues the image of Thomas as a melancholic who used his poetry and prose to "paint" landscapes celebrating the English countryside. His natural and unobtrusive style illustrates the vital English life in which he fervently believed.

Motion, Andrew. *The Poetry of Edward Thomas*. London: Routledge & Kegan Paul, 1980. Motion approaches Thomas' poetry as drawing from the Georgian tradition while anticipating the arrival of the Modernists in content and in form. Motion examines the subtle style of Thomas and introduces him as an evolutionary poet.

Smith, Stan. *Edward Thomas*. London: Faber & Faber, 1986. Thomas is considered in this book as the "quintessential English poet," whose devotion to the rural countryside is reflected in his poetry. Several critical approaches are presented, and the selected bibliography is helpful.

Thomas, R. George. *Edward Thomas: A Portrait*. Oxford, England: Clarendon Press, 1985. This book provides rare insight into the life and work of Edward Thomas by making use of letters, memoirs, and personal papers. Biographical in nature, and supported by an excellent bibliography, the book gives a solid foundation for the study of his prose and poetry.

HENRY DAVID THOREAU

Born: Concord, Massachusetts; July 12, 1817
Died: Concord, Massachusetts; May 6, 1862

Principal poetry
   Poems of Nature, 1895; *Collected Poems of Henry David Thoreau*, 1943, 1964 (Carl Bode, editor).

Other literary forms
   Henry David Thoreau published two books during his lifetime: *A Week on the Concord and Merrimack Rivers* (1849) and *Walden* (1854). Three additional books edited by his sister Sophia and his friend William Ellery Channing were published soon after his death: a collection of his travel essays entitled *Excursions* (1863), *The Maine Woods* (1864), and *Cape Cod* (1864). During his lifetime Thoreau also published essays in various periodicals. They were generally of three kinds: travel essays such as "A Yankee in Canada," nature essays such as "Walking," and social and political essays such as "Life Without Principle" and "Civil Disobedience." Those essays are collected in the standard "Walden" edition of Thoreau's complete writings, and the best of them are generally available today in paperback collections. Thoreau also dabbled in translations and occasionally published in *The Dial* his translations of Greek and Roman poetry. Perhaps Thoreau's greatest literary work, however, is his journal, which he kept throughout most of his adult life and most of which is available in the last fourteen volumes of the "Walden" edition of his collected writings. A portion of the journal from 1840 to 1841 was omitted from the collected writings but was later edited and published by Perry Miller in *Consciousness in Concord* (1858). Also not included in the collected writings were portions of the journal dealing with Thoreau's first trip to Maine and portions which Thoreau himself cut out for use in his books. The Princeton University Press brought together Thoreau's journals in a more unified way in *Journal*, a two-volume edition published in 1981 and 1984.

Achievements
   During his own lifetime, Thoreau met with only modest literary success. His early poems and essays published in *The Dial* were well-known and appreciated in transcendentalist circles but were generally unknown to popular audiences. As a lecturer, his talks were appreciated by the most liberal of his audiences but were generally found to be obscure or even dangerous by more conservative listeners. Thus, he had brief spurts of popularity as a lecturer, particularly in 1859 to 1860, but was not generally popular on the lecture circuit. His first book, *A Week on the Concord and Merrimack Rivers*, was published in 1849 at his own expense in an edition of one thousand copies.

It met with very little success; only 294 copies were sold or given away, while the remaining copies were finally shipped four years later to Thoreau himself, who sarcastically remarked in his journal, "I have now a library of nearly nine hundred volumes, over seven hundred of which I wrote myself: Is it not well that the author should behold the fruits of his labor?" Although *A Week on the Concord and Merrimack Rivers* carried an advertisement of the forthcoming publication of *Walden*, the failure of the first book prompted Thoreau to withhold publication of the later one until he could feel more certain of its success. After much revision, Thoreau published *Walden* in 1854. It met with generally favorable reviews and good sales, over seventeen hundred copies of an edition of two thousand being sold in the first year. By 1859 it was out of print, but it was reissued in a second edition shortly after Thoreau's death. *Walden* won Thoreau some fame with general audiences and created a small but devoted number of disciples who would occasionally visit Thoreau in Concord or send him complimentary copies of books. After the success of *Walden*, Thoreau found it easier to publish his essays in the more popular periodicals, such as *Putnam's Magazine* and the *Atlantic Monthly*. In his last years he also acquired some notoriety as an abolitionist through his impassioned lectures and essays on John Brown.

Thoreau's literary reputation has risen steadily since his death, his writings appealing primarily to two very different kinds of readers: those who see him as an escapist nature writer and those who see him as a political radical. As Michael Meyer suggests, his advice to people to simplify their lives and return to an appreciation of nature has had especially strong appeal in times of economic difficulty such as the 1920's and 1930's, and it has also served to cushion criticism of Thoreau in times such as the 1940's, when his political views seemed unpatriotic. Today it is probably still his nature writing that appeals to most readers. His social and political views, particularly his concept of passive resistance expressed in his essay "Civil Disobedience," have periodically made their influence felt in the actions of major social and political reformers such as Mahatma Gandhi and Martin Luther King. Thoreau's popularity peaked in the 1960's when his nature writing and his political views simultaneously found an audience of young American rebels advocating retreat from urban ugliness and materialism and passive resistance to an unpopular war. Since the 1960's his popularity has subsided somewhat, but he continues to be widely read, and his place among the great writers of American literature seems secure.

Biography

Henry David Thoreau (christened David Henry Thoreau) was born in Concord, Massachusetts, on July 12, 1817, the third of four children of John and Cynthia Thoreau. His father was a quiet man whose seeming lack of ambition had led to a series of unsuccessful attempts to establish himself as a shopkeeper prior to his finally establishing a very successful pencil factory in Concord. His mother was an outgoing, talkative woman who took in boarders to supplement the family's income. Both parents were fond of nature and could often be seen taking the children picnicking in the Concord woods.

Thoreau received a good grammar school education at the Concord Academy and seems to have had an essentially pleasant and typical boyhood. He attended Harvard College from 1833 to 1837, taking time out during his junior year to recuperate from a prolonged illness and to supplement his income by teaching for several months in Canton, Massachusetts. Upon being graduated near the top of his class, he took a teaching job in the Concord public schools, but after a few weeks he resigned in protest over the school board's insistence that he use corporal punishment to discipline his students. Unable to find another position, Thoreau opened a private school of his own and was eventually joined by his older brother John. John's cheerful disposition together with Henry's high academic standards made the school very successful until it was closed in 1841 because of John's prolonged illness.

During these years as a teacher, Thoreau traveled to Maine, took, with his brother, the famous excursion on the Concord and Merrimack rivers which eventually became the subject of his first book, delivered his first lecture, and published his first essay and his first poetry in *The Dial*. Through one of his students, Edmund Sewall (whom he praises in one of his best-known poems, "Lately, Alas, I Knew a Gentle Boy") he met Ellen Sewall, the only woman to whom he seems to have been romantically attracted in any serious way. Ellen seems to have been the subject or recipient of a number of Thoreau's poems of 1839 and 1840, but his brother John was the more forward of the two in courting Ellen, and it was after John's proposal to Ellen had failed that Henry also proposed, only to be rejected as John had been.

After the closing of the school, Thoreau was invited to live with Ralph Waldo Emerson's family as a handyman; he stayed two years, during which time he continued to contribute to, and occasionally help Emerson edit, *The Dial*. In 1842, his brother John died suddenly of a tetanus infection, leaving Thoreau so devastated that he himself briefly exhibited psychosomatic symptoms of the disease. The following year, a brief stint as a tutor to William Emerson's family on Staten Island confirmed his prejudice against cities, so he returned to Concord, where in 1844 he and a companion accidentally set fire to the Concord Woods, thus earning some rather long-lasting ill will from some of his neighbors and some long-lasting damage to his reputation as a woodsman.

For several years, Thoreau had contemplated buying a house and some land of his own, but in 1845 he settled for permission from Emerson to use some land near Walden Pond to build his own cabin. He built a one-room cabin and moved in on July 4, thus declaring his intention to be free to work on his writing and on a personal experiment in economic self-reliance. He continued to use the cabin as his main residence for two years, during which time he wrote *A Week on the Concord and Merrimack Rivers* and much of *Walden*, raised beans, took a trip to the Maine Woods, and spent his famous night in the Concord jail for nonpayment of taxes. An invitation from Emerson to spend another year as a resident handyman finally prompted him to leave the pond in the fall of 1847, but he left with little regret, because, as he says in *Walden*, "I had several more lives to live, and I could not spare any more time for that one." The fruits of his stay at the pond finally began to appear in 1849, when *A Week on the Concord and Merrimack Rivers* and his essay on "Resistance to Civil Government" (later renamed "Civil Disobedience") were both published.

Throughout the 1840's, Thoreau had become increasingly interested in the natural sciences, and he began to spend much time gathering and measuring specimens, often at the expense of his writing, so that by 1851 he had reason to complain in his journal, "I feel that the character of my knowledge is from year to year becoming more distinct and scientific; that, in exchange for views as wide as heaven's scope, I am being narrowed down to the field of the microscope." His scientific and mechanical abilities had benefits for the family's pencil-making business, however, because in 1843 he had developed a more effective means of securing the graphite in the pencils and was later to improve the quality of pencils still further. Throughout his life he main-tained of necessity an interest in the family business, although he seldom enjoyed having to take active part in it. His aversion to the routine of regular employment also applied to his surveying talents, which were called on by his neighbors increasingly after 1850. Although by 1851 Thoreau seems to have felt that life was passing him by without his having been able to achieve his goals, the publication of *Walden* in 1854 revived his self-esteem when the book sold well and brought a small but devoted group of admirers.

Throughout the 1850's Thoreau made several excursions to Canada, the Maine Woods, and Cape Cod which culminated in travel essays in popular periodicals. He also traveled to New Jersey and to Brooklyn, where he met Walt Whitman, with whom he was favorably impressed. Thoreau's admiration for Whitman's raw genius was surpassed only by his admiration for John Brown, the abolitionist, whom he first met in 1857 and whose cause he vig-orously supported in lectures and published essays.

In 1860, Thoreau caught a bad cold which eventually developed into tuber-culosis. Advised to seek a different climate, Thoreau took a trip to Minnesota in 1861, a trip which provided him with some brief glimpses of "uncivilized" Indians but with no relief from his illness. After returning to Concord, his health continued to deteriorate, and he died at home on May 6, 1862.

Analysis

For Henry David Thoreau, the value of poetry lay not primarily in the poem itself, but in the act of writing the poem and in that act's influence on the poet's life. The importance of poetry to the poet is, as he says in *A Week on the Concord and Merrimack Rivers*, in "what he has become through his work." Since for the transcendentalists life was superior to art, Thoreau could assert that "My life has been the poem I would have writ,/ But I could not both live and utter it." No art form could surpass God's act of creating nature or man's act of shaping his own life. In his journal for 1840, Thoreau suggests that the best an artist can hope for is to equal nature, not to surpass her. The poet's job is to publish nature's truth accurately, and thus at times, verse seemed to him to be the best vehicle for publicizing nature because of its greater precision. By the mid-1840's, however, he had mostly abandoned verse and concluded that "Great prose, of equal elevation, commands our respect more than great verse, since it implies a more permanent and level height. . . . The poet often only makes an irruption . . . but the prose writer has conquered . . . and settled colonies." In 1851 he found it necessary to warn himself to beware "of youthful poetry, which is impotent." Another problem with poetry was that it was too artificial. One could not capture in words the rhythms of the wind or the birds. He found that "the music now runs before and then behind the sense, but is never coincident with it." One could make music, or one could make sense; Thoreau eventually preferred the latter.

Because of this ambiguous attitude toward the value of verse (he eventually came to speak of both good verse and good prose as "poetry"), Thoreau's poetry is seldom first-rate, and even at its best it does not rival that of such contemporaries as Emily Dickinson and Walt Whitman. Nevertheless, it is of significance to the modern reader, first, because it demonstrates vividly the problems that American poets faced in freeing themselves artistically from European influences, and second, because it provides some fresh insights, not available as fully in his prose, into some of the deepest problems of Thoreau's life, especially his attempts to cope with the problems of love and friendship and of his own role as an artist.

Thoreau could never quite free himself from imitating the great poets he admired to find a voice of his own. He mined his expert knowledge of Greek and Latin to write epigrams or odes (essentially Horatian in form) such as "Let Such Pure Hate Still Underprop," which is also reminiscent of the seventeenth century Metaphysical poets in its use of paradox. Indeed, it is the Metaphysicals to whom Thoreau seems to have turned most often as muses for his own poetry: the paradoxes, introspection, and elaborate conceits of John Donne or Andrew Marvell. At other times one can find in Thoreau's verse the loose rhythms of John Skelton's near-doggerel dimeter, as in "The Old Marlborough Road," or the more graceful tetrameter couplets, which are Thoreau's most frequently used form and which, as critic Henry Wells suggests, can also be traced to the Metaphysicals. Finally, Thoreau frequently employs the three-part structure and tight stanza form of George Herbert's meditations. The stanza form of "I Am a Parcel of Vain Strivings Tied," for example, is clearly modeled on Herbert, while a poem such as "The Poet's Delay" has, as H. Grant Sampson suggests, the three-part meditative structure which moves from a particular scene in nature to the poet's awareness of the scene's wider implications, and finally to the poet's recognition of the scene's specific spiritual meaning for him.

Although Thoreau most frequently looked to the past for poetic models, he did admire some of the Romantic poets of his own day, particularly William Wordsworth. Thoreau's "I Knew a Man by Sight," for example, portrays a typical Wordsworthian rustic wanderer, while in Thoreau's unfortunate attempt at rhyme in the lines "Late in a wilderness/ I shared his mess" readers also see the glaring difference in poetic skill between the two poets. In "My Books I'd Fain Cast Off, I Cannot Read," Thoreau expresses a view of the superiority of nature to books, very much like that in Wordsworth's "Expostulation and Reply." In several other poems he seems to echo Wordsworth's theories of human development. In "Manhood," for example, Thoreau presents the same view of the child as father of the man that Wordsworth presents in "Ode: Intimations of Immortality." In "Music," he also presents a view of man's loss of youthful faculties and of compensation for that loss with adult wisdom similar to that presented by Wordsworth in "Lines Composed a Few Miles Above Tintern Abbey" and in *The Prelude* (1850).

From this unlikely mixture of classical, Metaphysical, and Romantic influences, Thoreau apparently hoped to create a poetry which would express his own love of paradox, introspection, and nature, while creating a style both stately and rugged, at once elevated and natural. The task was, as Thoreau himself came to realize, impossible. It is also interesting to note, however, that Thoreau seems not to have looked to his own countrymen, except perhaps Ralph Waldo Emerson, for models. His diction and rhythms are most frequently traceable to European influence, and when he attempts to break free of that influence, he usually meets with only modest success or complete failure.

Because Thoreau's prose is generally more effective than his poetry, when he deals with a topic in both genres the poetry is generally valuable primarily as a gloss on the prose. In "Wait Not Till Slaves Pronounce the Word," for example, Thoreau reminds the reader that slavery is as much a state of mind as an external condition: "Think not the tyrant sits afar/ In your own breasts ye have/ The District of Columbia/ And power to free the Slave." His statement in *Walden*, however, makes the same point more powerfully: "It is hard to have a Southern overseer; it is worse to have a Northern one; but worst of all when you are the slave driver of yourself." Some of Thoreau's nature poems do present some fresh minor insights into Thoreau's view of nature, but those poems which are of most value and interest in their own right are those which shed autobiographical light on some of his personal dilemmas either unexpressed or not expressed as well in his prose, particularly his attempt to find an ideal friendship and his attempt to meet the artistic goals he set for himself.

Thoreau's ideal of friendship, expressed most fully in the "Wednesday" chapter of *A Week on the Concord and Merrimack Rivers*, is typically transcendentalist in its insistence on paradox in human relationships. To Thoreau, friends were to be united with one another and yet separate. They were to love one another's strengths while at the same time hating one another's weaknesses, to be committed to one another and yet be free, to express their love and yet remain silent. They were to be equal, and yet he insists that only a friendship contracted with one's superior is worthwhile. Friendship, as he suggests in a manuscript poem entitled "Friendship," was to combine truth, beauty, and goodness in a platonic spiritual oneness, symbolized in the poem by two oak trees which barely touch above the ground but which are inseparably intertwined in their roots. Although he tends to over-intellectualize this concept of friendship, Thoreau was quite in earnest in seeking it in his friends, especially after his college years when he was trying to define his own identity through those he cared about. The person who perhaps came closest to being the soulmate whom Thoreau sought was his brother John. Unfortunately, as is often the case with affection for relatives, Thoreau found that he could seldom express his love for John adequately. When John died, his only outlet was to pour out his affection in his writings by dedicating his first book to him and by writing a gently moving poem, "Brother Where Dost Thou Dwell."

Others who for a time seemed to realize his ideal were Edmund Sewall (one of his students) and Edmund's sister, Ellen. To Edmund, Thoreau wrote one of his best poems, "Lately, Alas, I Knew a Gentle Boy." In this poem, Edmund Sewall is described as one who effortlessly wins the love of all around him by his quiet virtue. Mutual respect between the poet and the boy leads them both to keep their love unexpressed, however, and they paradoxically find themselves "less acquainted than when first we met." The friendship thus slips away without being overtly expressed, and the poet is left to cherish only "that virtue which he is." Although this poem certainly has androgynous qualities and is sometimes used to suggest a youthful homosexuality in Thoreau, it seems wiser to take it for what it more obviously is: one of the clearest and most moving of Thoreau's expressions of the joys and frustrations of Platonic love. His poems to Edmund's sister, Ellen, are similarly Platonic in tone. In one poem ("Love"), for example, he describes himself and Ellen as a "double star" revolving "about one center." In "The Breeze's Invitation," he adds a pastoral touch, describing himself and Ellen as a carefree king and queen of a "peaceful little green." In such poems, the reader sees a Thoreau who, beneath the Platonic and pastoral conventions, is a young man earnestly seeking affection—a young man much more vulnerable than the didactic prose philosophizer of *A Week on the Concord and Merrimack Rivers* or the self-confident chanticleer in *Walden*.

That same human vulnerability is also the most striking quality of those poems that deal with Thoreau's artistic goals. Aside from his journals, it is in his poems that Thoreau most fully reveals his artistic hopes and disappointments. Those hopes were a typically romantic mixture of active achievement and passive reception. On the one hand, as he suggests in "The Hero," a man must contribute something new to his world; he must, as he says in *Walden*, "affect the quality of the day." On the other hand, he can achieve such results only if he is receptive to the inspiration of God through nature. Such inspiration at its most powerful culminates in the sort of mystical experience described by Thoreau in his poem "The Bluebirds," in which he describes his feelings as if "the heavens were all around,/ And the earth was all below" and as if he were a "waking thought-/ A something I hardly knew."

Such mystical experiences were the crucial source of the poet's action, whether in writing or in deeds; thus, as Paul O. Williams has demonstrated, much of Thoreau's poetry deals directly or indirectly with the subject of inspiration. The fullest and clearest treatment of the theme is in "Inspiration," a poem in which he describes having occasionally felt a godlike sensitivity to the world so powerful that he felt thoroughly reborn and ready to "fathom hell or climb to heaven." The poet's predicament, however, was that such pure inspiration could seldom be translated untainted into action, and it is this predicament which is at the heart of several of his best poems. In "Light-Winged Smoke, Icarian Bird," one of the most often reprinted and discussed of his poems, he cryptically describes himself as a flame and his poetry as the smoke which he sends heavenward to God. Unfortunately, as the smoke rises to God, it also blots out the truth of God's sun and negates the poet's purpose of clarifying that truth. Thoreau's point here, as Eberhard Alsen convincingly argues, is that even the "clear flame" of the poet is not pure enough to avoid misrepresenting God's truths. That sense of the human artist's limitations in a world of infinite wonder sometimes led Thoreau to feel that his life was being wasted, as in "The Poet's Delay," in which he expresses his fear that while nature's seasons progress into autumn and bear fruit, his own "spring does not begin." Elsewhere, however, as in "I Am a Parcel of Vain Strivings Tied," he consoles himself with a sacrificial satisfaction that his own failures will allow others to be more fruitful. If he is a parcel of picked flowers unable to produce further beauty, at least the other flowers can bloom more beautifully because his have been thinned out of the garden.

In such poems as these, one realizes that Thoreau sensed early what is quite clear when one surveys the body of his poetry: that verse was not the best vehicle for his thoughts but that it freed him to make his prose more powerful. He would have to wait until the publication of *Walden* to feel that the slow-paced seasons of his artistic life had truly begun to bear fruit. Nevertheless, his poetry served him both as a valuable testing ground for his ideas and as an outlet for some of his deepest private problems. It is also worth the modern reader's time because it provides an occasional peek behind the persona of his prose works and because it helps in understanding the dilemma of the Romantic artist, attempting to convey the ideal while being hindered by the very real limitations of human language—a problem which confronts many twentieth century poets as well.

Richard J. Schneider

Other major works
NONFICTION: *A Week on the Concord and Merrimack Rivers*, 1849; *Walden*, 1854; *Excursions*, 1863; *The Maine Woods*, 1864; *Cape Cod*, 1864; *The Writings of Henry David Thoreau*, 1906.

Bibliography
Harding, Walter. *The Days of Henry Thoreau*. New York: Alfred A. Knopf, 1965. This fine scholarly biography has not been surpassed and remains a model for readability. Harding places the poetry insightfully in the pattern of Thoreau's life. Complete with illustrations, a bibliographical note, and a thorough index.

Harding, Walter, and Michael Meyer. *The New Thoreau Handbook*. New York: New York University Press, 1980. This updated version of a standard basic reference on Thoreau is generally the first source to be consulted for help. Contains a considerable amount of factual information about the writings and the writer, arranged for easy access. Chronologies, indexes, and cross-references increase its usefulness.

Howarth, William. *The Book of Concord: Thoreau's Life as a Writer*. New York: Viking Press, 1982. Howarth presents a writer's biography, paying particular attention to the relationship between the life and the writings and showing exactly how the work evolved. Includes a list of sources, an index, notes, and a number of drawings.

Richardson, Robert D. *Henry Thoreau: A Life of the Mind*. Berkeley: University of California Press, 1986. This outstanding study focuses primarily on the development of Thoreau's leading themes and the formulation of his working philosophy. Richardson offers unusually clear accounts of some of the writer's complex theories. Provides helpful notes, a bibliography, and an index.

Shugard, Alan. *American Poetry: The Puritans Through Walt Whitman*. Boston: Twayne, 1988. Contains both informative introductory sketches and a running account of the evolution of American poetry. Shugard's account of Thoreau is brief but just. Includes extensive notes and references and a useful bibliography.

Thoreau, Henry David. *Henry David Thoreau: Collected Poems.* Edited by
Carl Bode. Enl. ed. Baltimore: The Johns Hopkins University Press, 1964.
Contains all the poetry Thoreau is known to have written—a surprisingly
large number, considering that he did not consider himself to be a poet.
Provides an excellent thirteen-page introduction, sixty-eight pages of textual introduction and notes, forty-four pages of commentary, and sound indexes.

Waggoner, Hyatt H. *American Poets: From the Puritans to the Present.* New
York: Houghton Mifflin, 1968. This volume is one of the most comprehensive and detailed histories of American poetry available. Waggoner is the
established authority in the field. He gives Thoreau appropriate space and
a sympathetic treatment. An appendix, detailed notes, an extensive bibliography, and a good index supplement the volume.

CHARLES TOMLINSON

Born: Stoke-on-Trent, Staffordshire, England; January 8, 1927

Principal poetry

Relations and Contraries, 1951; *The Necklace*, 1955, 1966; *Seeing Is Believing*, 1958; *A Peopled Landscape*, 1963; *American Scenes and Other Poems*, 1966; *The Way of a World*, 1969; *Written on Water*, 1972; *The Way In and Other Poems*, 1974; *The Shaft*, 1978; *Selected Poems 1951-1974*, 1978; *The Flood*, 1981; *Airborn/Hijos del Aire*, 1981 (with Octavio Paz); *Notes from New York and Other Poems*, 1984; *The Return*, 1987.

Other literary forms

Charles Tomlinson has published much work of translation, including *Versions from Fyodor Tyutchev, 1803-1873* (1960, with Henry Gifford), *Castilian Ilexes: Versions from Antonio Machado, 1875-1939* (1963, with Henry Gifford), and *Ten Versions from "Trilce" by César Vallejo* (1970, with Henry Gifford). In addition, he edited *The Oxford Book of Verse in English Translation* (1980). From among Tomlinson's many published essays of commentary and criticism, the most significant longer ones are *The Poem as Initiation* (1967), *Some Americans: A Personal Record* (1981), and *Poetry and Metamorphosis* (1983). *Marianne Moore: A Collection of Critical Essays* (1969) and *William Carlos Williams: A Critical Anthology* (1972), two volumes that he edited, are also important in Tomlinson's career.

Achievements

Tomlinson is generally recognized as a major English poet of the postmodernist era. His work in traditional forms with conservative themes has set him apart from "apocalyptic" poets such as Dylan Thomas, as well as from the poets of "the Movement," such as Philip Larkin. Tomlinson, a successful painter, has achieved recognition for his style of precise vision in poetry, and he has been often noticed as a seminal force in bringing the work of William Carlos Williams and other American writers to the serious attention of British poets and critics.

His achievements in poetry (as well as in painting) have won Tomlinson many awards and honors, including the Bess Hokin Prize for Poetry in 1956, a traveling fellowship from the Institute of International Education in 1959-1960, the Levinson Prize for Poetry in 1960, the Frank O'Hara Prize in 1968, election as Fellow of the Royal Society of Literature in 1974, an honorary doctorate in literature at Colgate University in 1981, and the Wilbur Award for Poetry in 1982.

Biography

Born in the English Midlands into a lower-class family, Tomlinson was restless to escape the confinements of a mining community. The political conservatism of his father, Alfred Tomlinson, an estate agent's clerk, had a strong influence on the development of young Tomlinson's sensibility. Tomlinson attended Queen's College, University of Cambridge, from 1945 to 1948; while there he studied under Donald Davie, who became a lifelong friend and colleague. After receiving his degree, Tomlinson was married to Brenda Raybould. They moved to London, where Tomlinson taught in an elementary school and worked at his painting. In 1951 he published his first collection of poems.

In 1951-1952 he traveled in Italy, where he worked briefly as private secretary to Percy Lubbock. While in Italy he gradually abandoned his painting in favor of composing poems. Returning to London, he earned an M.A. from London University in 1954. In 1956 he took a position as lecturer in English poetry at the University of Bristol.

Tomlinson's next volume of poetry, *Seeing Is Believing*, attracted the attention of several American critics. In 1959 he fulfilled a long-held wish to meet William Carlos Williams, whom he visited in Rutherford, New Jersey. On the same trip to the United States, made possible by a fellowship, he also visited Yvor Winters in California. Before returning home, he visited Marianne Moore in Brooklyn, New York, and returned for a second visit with Williams in New Jersey.

With Henry Gifford he published the first of several joint projects of translation, *Versions from Fyodor Tyutchev*, in 1960. Tomlinson was invited to serve as visiting professor at the University of New Mexico in 1962-1963. During this year he met two persons who would prove to be very important for his career, the "objectivist" poets Louis Zukofsky and George Oppen. He was introduced to other young American writers, Robert Duncan and Robert Creeley, and he visited the painter Georgia O'Keefe at her home in New Mexico.

His poems collected for *A Peopled Landscape* in 1963 showed how important William Carlos Williams had become for Tomlinson's style. After a reading tour of New York State for the Academy of American Poets, in 1967 he went back to Italy, where he met Ezra Pound and also Octavio Paz, who would become a valued friend.

Returning to the United States as Olive B. O'Connor Professor of Literature at Colgate University, Tomlinson delivered the Phi Beta Kappa lecture, which was published as *The Poem as Initiation*. He continued to travel in the United States and Europe, lecturing and working on his translations, from 1969 to 1971. Tomlinson's painting and poetry were brought together in *Words and Images* in 1972, and some of his poems were set to music by Stephen Strawley and recorded by Jane Manning in 1974. After another reading tour in the United States, his poetry and graphics were collected by the Arts Council of Great Britain as an exhibition at Hayward Gallery in 1978 in London and then toured Great Britain until 1981. Although Tomlinson did not cease his international traveling, his graphic work continued to bring him more recognition to match his reputation as a poet.

In 1982 he received the prestigious Wilbur Award for Poetry and delivered the Clark Lectures at Cambridge, titled "Poetry and Metamorphosis." Some of his poems were again set to music, in a song cycle that was performed in Belgium in 1985. The next year Keele University held an exhibit, "Charles Tomlinson: A Celebration," of his books, manuscripts, photographs, and graphics, and then established an archive of his poetry recorded for commercial issue on audio cassettes. Also in the 1980's Tomlinson published a selection of his poems in French and Italian, served as visiting professor at McMaster University, Canada, and delivered the Edmund Blunden Lecture in Hong Kong. He has frequently given interviews from his home near Bristol, where he continued to serve the university as reader and then professor in English poetry.

Analysis

Throughout his career, Charles Tomlinson has used his arts of poetry and painting to challenge nature's objectivity with the shaping powers of human (subjective) imagination. He has spoken of the invitation to make meaning out of apparent meaninglessness, by discovering that "chance" rhymes with "dance," and that "chance" interrupts and enlivens the deadening effects of certitude. Therefore, in volume after volume Tomlinson tests the proposition expressed by the title of his third collection, *Seeing Is Believing.* At first, this seems to limit one's imaginative capacity (to believe) to the outlines of things in sight, to the exteriors of being. Gradually, however, it becomes clear that Tomlinson's aesthetic detachment is an illusion of objectivity, that his art warms with the energies of combating objects in natural settings, negotiating space for culture and ritual, and rescuing values from history to compensate for anger at what humankind threatens to waste through ignorance and brutality.

The only poem that Tomlinson chose to rescue from his first collection, *Relations and Contraries*, to include in his *Collected Poems* is one simply entitled "Poem." Short though it is, "Poem" suggests a major interest of the early poetry: it describes a sequence of sounds heard by an "unstopped ear" from a winter scene of activity, including horses' hooves making "an arabesque on space/ A dotted line in sound." This containment of space with sound, to make "space vibrate," is an effort that Tomlinson's next volume, *The Necklace*, continues to make, as in "Aesthetic," where "reality is to be sought . . . in space made articulate." Imagination uses language to establish an order of things, set firmly in their own world, though subject to human play, as in "Nine Variations in a Chinese Winter Setting."

This last poem takes its title from one by Wallace Stevens, the American poet whose work was an early important influence on Tomlinson. That influence continued to show in the third collection, *Seeing Is Believing*, which uses the painter's experience to capture an essential artistic attitude toward objects or acts in space. Thus "Object in a Setting" achieves the sense of being in a piece of glass that resists all efforts "to wish it a more human image," and "Paring the Apple" illustrates the beauty of art that forces "a recognition" of its charm even from those who look for a more "human" art in portraits. Still, the paring is an act of "human gesture," which compels its own recognition that art requires the human to be, and so all art is essentially a human endeavor. The poem, "A Meditation on John Constable," is art re-creating art: a poem about a painter making a painting. The title reinforces the very human essence of the artistic process: meditating about a human being who is an artist.

This is even more clear in those poems of *Seeing Is Believing* that occur as the consequence of visits to places. Although "At Holwell Farm" seeks to capture the "brightness" of air that is gathered "within the stone" of the farm's wall and buildings, it moves to a gentle observation that it is a "dwelling/ Rooted in more than earth," guarding an "Eden image." "On the Hall at Stowey" records a visit to a deserted house, allowed to fall into ruin while the fields about it continue to be fruitful and well attended. The poet is angry that five centuries of culture have fallen into decay here, where once pride of tradition was boldly beautiful. What humanity bestowed upon the objective space of nature, humanity has taken away through the objective distancing of time.

A Peopled Landscape takes the concerns of place and time more warmly into more poems, as in "Harvest Festival: At Ozleworth." The poet notices the ironic juxtaposition of remnants from both Roman and Christian history in the market scene of this country village: a harvest festival of pagan origins is conducted beneath the stone arch of a Christian church, to deepen the scene of space with the complexities of history. Working with juxtapositions of this kind, Tomlinson uses his return from a trip to the United States to observe differences between modern and traditional values in "Return to Hinton," where he lovingly catalogs the details of his home, whose "qualities/ are like the land/ —inherited." These are contrasted with life in a "rich and nervous land" where "locality's mere grist/ to build." This poem uses the three-layered verse form of Tomlinson's American model William Carlos Williams; the preference for the American style of poetry is a complication of the poem's theme, which admits its complicity in the process of modern detachment from traditional "farm-bred certainties." This same sense of separateness from tradition, along with a yearning to enjoy the pleasures of the past, is a strong element of "The Farmer's Wife" in the same volume.

The impact and importance of American experience are dramatized by the title of Tomlinson's next volume, *American Scenes and Other Poems*, which nevertheless includes poems not immediately referring to American scenes or settings, such as "A Given Grace." This is one of Tomlinson's most discussed poems, partly because it continues to show the influence of Stevens as well as that of Williams and Moore. It does not use the three-layered form, but it establishes an imagist posture associated with the Americans. The title, deliberately tautological, derives from the beauty of "two cups" set on a mahogany table; the "grace" given is a power of evocation from form to imagination, aptly recorded as the poem itself.

In "The Hill" a woman gives grace to the poet's perception. She climbs a hill, making it yield to her human pressure and take its shape of meaning from her presence. A more explicitly American scene is exploited in "The Cavern," which recounts a descent that begins as a tourist's jaunt but ends as a press toward "a deeper dark" where the self discovers its "unnameable and shaping home." The poem works with gentle irony as it works out the myth of Theseus exploring the labyrinth: it acquires additional force if the final discovery of the self in its "shaping home" also suggests that the self is the minotaur as well as, or instead of, the heroic Theseus. Yet there is further irony here, since the poem derives from Tomlinson's travels through the American Southwest, where he records a discovery about his deepest self (repeating the experience of his predecessor D. H. Lawrence). This self-discovery is repeated in other poems, such as "Idyll," which describes how the poet is drawn by the creative contrasts of quiet Washington Square in the heart of loud, bustling San Francisco. Here is not a desert cavern, but there is nevertheless a similar sense of self renewed by its identity in distance: a boy reading (beneath the lintel of a church upon which is carved a verse from Dante) draws the poet into a sympathetic identification as universal reader, for whom the message of the Square is a "poised quiescence, pause and possibility."

One of Tomlinson's most acclaimed volumes is *The Way of a World*, which includes the lovely "Swimming Chenango Lake," a poem about establishing an artful relationship between human subjectivity and nature's objectivity. It sympathetically observes the poise of a swimmer, who has paused in a quiescent moment to study possibilities before leaping into an autumn lake. The swimmer is like an artist, measuring the "geometry of water" before attempting to master it with his skill, but the swimmer is also all humanity participating in the challenging processes of all nature. In this poem Tomlinson has brought together many of his career's themes: aesthetic observation through detachment, cold reflectiveness, and human calculation. Like the swimmer, human beings "draw back" from the cold mercilessness of nature, even as they force a kind of "mercy" from it, making nature sustain the human experience.

In this volume Tomlinson demonstrates more decisively his strong distaste for extremism of all kinds, whether political or artistic, even though he has himself explored the use of American experimental aesthetic practices. His poem "Prometheus" is a strong work of imagination in which the poet listens to a radio broadcast of music by the Russian composer Aleksandr Scriabin; since there is a storm outside his house at the time, the poet can juxtapose the two events, artistic and natural, to each other. Because Scriabin's *Prometheus* is a work intended to help further the apocalypse of revolution, his music is examined as an exercise in political irony. This is made possible by the mockery of "static" in the radio's transmission during an electrical storm; the static is a figurative vehicle for the poet's mockery of art in the service of political propaganda. Music is the source of inspiration for another poem of the volume, "Night Transfigured," which derives from a work by Arnold Schoenberg. This poem is a kind of conclusion to a three-poem sequence beginning with "Eden" and followed by "Adam," as the poet becomes a new Adam-artist transfiguring the night of modernism with his light of imagination.

Tomlinson includes in *The Way of a World* two interesting experiments of his art, "Skullshapes" and "To be Engraved on the Skull of a Cormorant." The former is one of the poet's several exercises in "prose poems," which escape rigid classification because they are not measured in verse but neither are they merely prose. "Skullshapes" is a meditation on the shapes of different kinds of skulls; these are shapes of nature that summon imagination to fill "recess and volume" and to trace the "lines of containment, lines of extension." This is what Tomlinson does with his short poem "To Be Engraved on the Skull of a Cormorant," in which he accepts nature's challenge to turn a space of death into a rhythm of living affirmation.

Tomlinson has said in interviews that he learned to be a poet by watching the water in canals running through his home village; the title of his collection *Written on Water* captures some of the feeling he has for that time of his childhood. Yet the title also carries other levels of meaning, including the interest a painter has in working with water (the source of life itself) and the chance an artist takes in any medium that his or her work will not last. From among the poems that focus on the element of water, "Mackinnon's Boat" is an idyllic review of a day's work of fishing, sometimes presented from the view of a dog that lies in the bow of the boat, seemingly eager for return to land. This poem echoes the theme of "Swimming Chenango Lake," with its passage through and over a medium of nature as a mastery of its force. This same move of transcendence by human art, via imagination, occurs in "Hawks," which negotiates the element of air in its metaphors of achieving a right relationship between contraries.

Several of his poems in *The Way In and Other Poems* have brought Tomlinson much appreciative critical attention, particularly the sequence that begins with "Under the Moon's Reign." Other poems, however, continue the nostalgic review of the past that has often been a manner of his writing. There is a sharper edge to some of these poems, as the poet's sorrow turns more often into anger at what modern life has done to traditional values and ancient landscapes. "The Way In" ironically notices two old people, like an ancient Adam and Eve, puttering about in the waste regions of the city where the poet drives to work. He may regret what humans have done to the landscape and he may deplore the empty lives the old couple seem to live, but he feels himself contributing to the devastation as he depresses the accelerator of his automobile. "Gladstone Street" and "At Stoke" take him back to scenes of his youth, where there is no improvement of an industrial wasteland and where the changes are few; still, it brings evidence that whatever the poet has accomplished, he owes much to his origin in that place of "grey-black." These poems of return and observation often follow the shape of experience drawn from driving. In "Night Ride," the poet sees well by artificial lighting but deplores the loss of vision to see the stars. Progress may make "our lights seem more beautiful than our lives," but it can also blacken the optimistic planners of the past, such as Josiah Wedgewood's utopian schemes in "Etruria Vale." Tomlinson dates the beginning of a new era for Great Britain from the end of World War II, which is marked in "Dates: Penkhull New Road." He sees it as a place that expresses a time: "Something had bitten a gap/ Out of the stretch we lived in." This is a commentary on postwar Great Britain as much as it is an observation about the physical disruption of a street in an English village.

Space for imagination to work across landscapes of special places can be found in revisiting scenes of youth and childhood, but it can also be discovered without leaving a present scene. This is the tactic of the four-poem sequence beginning with "Under the Moon's Reign." Moonlight transfigures the landscape to create a new world, after the *Götterdämmerung* of twilight's apocalypse; this is the closest Tomlinson can come to acceptance of extremism, and he does so in a tone of quiet irony. It is in such a moonlit terrain that "Foxes' Moon" is set, to allow an interruption of England's "pastoral" existence by an alien, intruding presence: the foxes who "go/ In their ravenous quiet"—utterly different modes of being for humanity to contemplate. The third poem, "The Dream," takes the speaker into a wider world of contemplation, where new spaces are made of cities within cities; dreams are the proportioning of sleep that "replenishes/ To stand reading with opened eyes/ The intricacies of the imagined spaces." No amount of dreaming, however, nor any amount of artful creation, can relieve the anguish and pain of one who stands over the "little ash" of a loved one, in "After a Death." Articulating the space of words does not assuage the burden of vision that feels "the imageless unnaming upper blue" of "this burial place" straddling a green hill.

Perhaps ends of things, ends of lives, establish important terms of definition, as Tomlinson writes more often on this theme. As he puts it in his prose-poem of this volume, "The Insistence of Things," there is an "insistence of things" that "face us with our own death, for they are so completely what we are not." Thus moonlight shows, as does the grim determination of the foxes' barking between dreams, that death is a function of "the insistence of things."

The hard outlines of those insistences can be observed in history as well as across the spaces of the present. *The Shaft* collects poems that drive a shaft through time as well as into the dark depths of the earth. Extremist leaders of the French Revolution are presented in "Charlotte Corday," "Marat Dead," and "For Danton," to show the insufficiency of lives devoted to desperate deeds. At the real center of being is a fecund darkness, as in the title poem, "The Shaft," which is a womblike cavity (reached through a "cervix of stone"); as one bends to enter, one feels "a vertigo that dropped through centuries." One cannot remain there for long; it is "a place of sacrifice," but it allows escape and rebirth, as there is a return to "the sun of an unfinished summer." One may draw upon the dark energies of being in one's quest for a way back into the realm of light, where work is to be done.

In both *The Flood* and *The Return* Tomlinson's poetry acquires more religious qualities, as he describes the renovating experience of fighting destruction from the very water that inspired his work as a poet and painter, and as he ritualizes his life to receive the gifts of loving human companions as well as coldly indifferent natural forces. "The Flood" describes how taken by surprise he was when the stream near his house broke its banks in a flood that swept through his stone wall and across the lower floor of his home; it shook his "trust in stone" and "awakened" his eyes to fresh perceptions of nature's force. That there is compensation from nature is celebrated in a poem that echoes William Wordsworth's "The Recompense," which follows the route of expectation of viewing a comet, being disappointed, and then discovering new energies from a moonrise to reward the efforts of unnourished hope. The same appreciation for compensations drives the imagination in "The Return," which prepares the poet for the return of his wife on a winter's journey after a time of separation from each other.

These volumes, *The Flood* and *The Return*, embody contrasting themes constant throughout Tomlinson's career as poet: the concern for values of historical culture that are threatened with annihilation and the opportunity for renewal that nature constantly offers to the human imagination. The poet refuses to be intimidated by apocalypses of nature or of history. Instead, he keeps his artist's eye alert for new objects to replenish his hunger for fresh experience to nourish his poetry and his painting.

Richard D. McGhee

Other major works

NONFICTION: *The Poem as Initiation*, 1967; *Some Americans: A Personal Record*, 1981; Isaac Rosenberg of Bristol, 1982; *Poetry and Metamorphosis*, 1983; *The Sense of the Past: Three Twentieth Century British Poets*, 1983.

EDITED TEXTS: *Marianne Moore: A Collection of Critical Essays*, 1969; *William Carlos Williams: A Critical Anthology*, 1972; *The Oxford Book of Verse in English Translation*, 1980.

TRANSLATIONS: *Versions from Fyodor Tyutchev, 1803-1873*, 1960 (with Henry Gifford); *Castilian Ilexes: Versions from Antonio Machado, 1875-1939*, 1963 (with Gifford); *Ten Versions from "Trilce" by César Vallejo*, 1970 (with Gifford).

MISCELLANEOUS: *Words and Images*, 1972; *In Black and White: The Graphics of Charles Tomlinson*, 1976; *Eden: Graphics and Poetry*, 1985.

Bibliography

Bedient, Calvin. "Charles Tomlinson." In *Eight Contemporary Poets.* London: Oxford University Press, 1974. This study argues that Tomlinson has a narrow range but rich style. A review of his main theme, measuring relationships, is initiated through comparisons with Wordsworth, Williams, and Stevens. Bedient analyzes poems that drain images of ego and poems of intense and severe meditation. Bibliography and notes are included.

Brown, Merle E. "Intuition vs. Perception: On Charles Tomlinson's 'Under the Moon's Reign.'" In *Double Lyric: Divisiveness and Communal Creative in Recent English Poetry.* New York: Columbia University Press, 1980. This essay analyzes "Under the Moon's Reign" to test a thesis that contemporary English poetry works through contradictory modes, passive but exact observation and an active subjectivity that shapes what is observed. Tomlinson's sequence shows depth and movement toward a grandeur of desolation in the final poem. Contains notes and an index.

John, Brian. *The World as Event: The Poetry of Charles Tomlinson.* Montreal: McGill-Queen's University Press, 1989. John says that Tomlinson's poetry creates a language of the senses, enlarges definitions, and pursues understanding of experience. His poems proceed as ceremonies of initiation toward an image of "Eden," explored in sometimes ironic ways while the poet aims to recover a bit of paradise after all. Included are a photograph, notes, a bibliography, and an index.

King, P. R. "Seeing and Believing: The Poetry of Charles Tomlinson." In *Nine Contemporary Poets: A Critical Introduction.* New York: Methuen, 1979. A substantial study, this essay presents Tomlinson's poetry as an independent endeavor in which the poet uses his painter's eye to search for a right relationship between people and places, time and history, to find delight in the act of seeing as the self adjusts to reality. There are notes, a bibliography, and an index.

O'Gorman, Kathleen, ed. *Charles Tomlinson: Man and Artist.* Columbia: University of Missouri Press, 1988. Eleven essays, two interviews, a poem, a chronology, and a foreword by Donald Davie cover Tomlinson's career. Six essays present different perspectives on his poetry, and two provide overviews of his development. Three essays study interrelationships of his painting and poetry. Features illustrations, a bibliography, and an index.

Watkins, Evan. "Charles Tomlinson: The Poetry of Experience." In *The Critical Act: Criticism and Community.* New Haven, Conn.: Yale University Press, 1978. Answers charges that Tomlinson's poetry is "anachronistic." Concentrating on poems from *The Way of a World* and the sequence beginning with "Under the Moon's Reign" in *The Way In*, Watkins applies theories from Harold Bloom to an appreciation of Tomlinson's work. Notes and index are included.

Weatherhead, A. Kingsley. "Charles Tomlinson." In *The British Dissonance: Essays on Ten Contemporary Poets.* Columbia: University of Missouri Press, 1983. This essay explores a question raised by Tomlinson, whether form is in objective reality or imposed by subjective perception. It also presents Tomlinson as a poet who bridges many of the divisions that separate contemporary poets and their themes. The volume includes notes, a bibliography, and an index.

JEAN TOOMER

Born: Washington, D.C.; December 26, 1894
Died: Doylestown, Pennsylvania; March 30, 1967

Principal poetry

"Banking Coal," in *Crisis*, 1922; *Cane*, 1923 (prose and poetry); "Blue Meridian," in *New American Caravan*, 1936; *The Wayward and the Seeking*, 1980 (Darwin T. Turner, editor, prose and poetry); *The Collected Poems of Jean Toomer*, 1988.

Other literary forms

Most of Jean Toomer's work was in genres other than poetry. His one published volume of creative writing, *Cane*, contains only fifteen poems, mostly short, and fourteen pieces which appear to be in prose. Yet, they are all informed with the poet's rather than the novelist's sensibility, and some of them are poems in all but line breaks, while all of them use assorted poetic devices either throughout or sporadically.

Toomer published several pieces of fiction after *Cane*, generally quite experimental inasmuch as they lacked plot, often included philosophical meditations, and indeed often worked more like poetry, with impressionistic scenes and descriptions and an emphasis on developing a theme through juxtaposition of sections rather than an overall sequence of action. Among these are "Winter on Earth" (*The Second American Caravan*, 1929), "Mr. Costyve Duditch" (*The Dial*, 1928), and "York Beach" (*New American Caravan*, 1929). The first two were collected in the posthumous volume *The Wayward and the Seeking*, edited by Darwin T. Turner, along with a previously unpublished story from 1930, "Withered Skin of Berries," which is more in the style of *Cane*, though much longer than most of the pieces in that book.

Toomer published one short, fragmentary play during his lifetime, "Balo," in Alain Locke's collection *Plays of Negro Life* (1927), and two of several other plays which he wrote in *The Wayward and the Seeking*.

Nonfiction predominates in Toomer's work, indicating his concerns with philosophical and spiritual goals, as in "Race Problems and Modern Society" (1929), "The Flavor of Man" (1949), and *Essentials: Definitions and Aphorisms* (privately printed in 1931, some of its aphorisms having been printed earlier in *The Dial* and *Crisis*, with many appearing much later in *The Wayward and the Seeking*). These aphorisms are occasionally poetic and certainly worthy of contemplation, but they might be stronger if incorporated into actual poems. Portions of several versions of Toomer's autobiography appear in *The Wayward and the Seeking*. The rest of his many unpublished works, including many poems, remain in the Toomer Collection of the Fisk University Library.

Achievements

Cane is one of the most memorable and appealing books in African-American literature, conveying a vivid sense of the life of southern blacks around 1920 (though little changed since the time of slavery) and showing clearly the conflicts between the feelings of black people and the desensitizing and spirit-diminishing urban life they found in the North. Yet *Cane* is significant not merely for its content but for its innovative form and style as well. Its combination of prose and verse, stories and poems, produces a unified impression, with poems foreshadowing or commenting on adjacent stories and the stories and sketches exploring a multitude of perspectives on black life, rural and urban.

Toomer's impressionistic style, his seductive but not mechanical rhythms, his brilliant imagery and figurative language, his manipulation of language to produce a wide range of emotional and literary effects, were refreshing to many black writers during and after the Harlem Renaissance of the 1920's. Instead of adhering strictly to traditional European models of form and meter (like that of his major black contemporaries Claude McKay and Countée Cullen) or the literary realism and straightforward narrative style of black fiction to that date, he joined the progression of revolutionary poets and fiction writers who were creating literary Modernism, from Walt Whitman on through James Joyce, D. H. Lawrence, Gertrude Stein, Sherwood Anderson, and T. S. Eliot, up to Toomer's friend and contemporary Hart Crane.

Very few of Toomer's other works come even close to the towering achievement of *Cane*, but its poems and poetic prose provided later writers a successful means of evoking the feel of the black experience. A reader can still sense echoes of its style in the evocative prose of novelist Toni Morrison.

Biography

Jean Toomer (born Eugene) spent most of his life resisting a specific racial label for himself. His childhood and youth were spent in white or racially mixed middle-class neighborhoods in Washington, and his parents were both light-skinned. Jean's father left shortly after his birth and his mother died after remarrying, so that the most potent adult influences on his life were his maternal grandparents, with whom he lived until his twenties. His grandfather, P. B. S. Pinchback, had been elected Lieutenant-Governor in Reconstruction Louisiana and served as Acting Governor in 1873. Toomer believed that his victory was helped by his announcement that he had black blood, although Toomer denied knowing whether it was true. One thing is clear: Pinchback had indeed served the Union cause in the "Corps d'Afrique."

Later in life Toomer denied that he was a Negro—an acceptable statement if one understands his definition of "Negro" as one who identifies solely with the black race, for he, with certainly a great deal of nonblack ancestry, saw himself as not white, either, but "American," a member of a new race which would unify the heretofore conflicting racial groups through a mixture of racial strains. The attainment of such an "American" race remained his goal throughout most of his life after *Cane*.

Toomer's education after high school was varied, from agriculture at the University of Wisconsin to the American College of Physical Training in Chicago. Rather than completing courses toward a formal degree, however, he pursued his own reading in literature and social issues while working at assorted jobs until he decided to devote all his efforts to writing.

The real nudge came in the form of a three-month stint as substitute principal of a school in a small Georgia town in the fall of 1921. He returned to Washington in November with material for a whole book. He published several poems and stories in assorted periodicals the following year and then gathered most of them and many new ones into a carefully structured book called *Cane*, published in 1923 by Boni and Liveright. The book caused a considerable stir among the influential white literati with whom he associated (such as Waldo Frank, Sherwood Anderson, and Hart Crane) and among black writers and intellectuals as well. Yet in its two printings (the second in 1927) it sold fewer than a thousand copies.

That same year, Toomer met the Russian mystic George Gurdjieff and embraced his philosophy of higher consciousness. After studying with him in France, Toomer returned to spread his teachings in America. A ten-month marriage to a white poet, Margery Latimer, ended with her death in childbirth in 1932. Two years later he married another white woman, Marjorie Content, and spent the rest of his life with her. This period in Toomer's life was largely devoted to self-improvement for himself and others, as he lectured and continued to write primarily philosophical and spiritually oriented work. He continued to publish some literary works until 1936, when his career came virtually to an end, despite attempts to have other works published. He became a Quaker and maintained no further identity with the black race, dying in 1967 largely forgotten.

Analysis

Jean Toomer was the writer of one book; no matter how often the phrase is used to disparage him, it cannot be denied. Beyond *Cane*, his only other works of value are the long poem "Blue Meridian," a small amount of short fiction, and his autobiographical writings. His plays, most of his other poetry, and his nonfiction are negligible. Yet even had he written only *Cane*, he would always be remembered as a major African-American author—and primarily as a poet.

Cane is an eccentric book, experimental and unclassifiable in its combination of poems and what is technically prose—pieces which are generally developed as short stories (somewhat like those of Anderson or Joyce) but are occasionally "mere" sketches, sometimes prose-poems without plot, encompassing no more than a few pages and conveying impressionistically the sense of a person's spirit. Some of the pieces approach drama, with conversation printed like dialogue, setting described as meticulously as for a stage designer, and action presented in the present tense.

Yet, whether prose, drama, or verse, all is imbued with a poet's sensibility: precise depiction of details using all the senses vividly, a rhythmic quality without slavish adherence to metrics, a sensitivity to words, phrasing, variations of theme, a fine ear for sound, and a polished sense of organic structure. Few books, whether prose or verse, have less of the prosaic than this one, which can put readers in an almost unabated state of intensity and exaltation, drawing them in by language, sound, rhythm, and form.

Toomer's purpose in this work is to embody what he sees as the dying folk-spirit of the South by depicting the lives of its people and re-creating their feelings through language and rhythm. *Cane* achieves a vivid sense of the sensuality of its women, the alternating anguish and joy of life in the South, the toughness and beauty of the land of Georgia. These themes appear primarily in the first third of the book; the second third moves North into the city, where blacks from the South have difficulty fitting into the white-dominated social patterns while retaining roots in the South; in the final third, Ralph Kabnis, a Northern black man, comes South and the focus is on his conflict with the South, looking ahead to William Faulkner's *Absalom, Absalom!* (1936) and Quentin Compson's climactic cry "I don't hate the South!" Throughout the book, Toomer shows both attraction to the South and a sense of holding back from it—on the part of a narrator in the first third, of Kabnis in the last third, and of assorted Northern-based characters in the middle third, who are losing touch with their black roots. The book, however, is hardly a glorification of the way of life of Southern blacks: Kabnis notes that things are not so bad as the North thinks; yet the South still hosts an occasional lynching, as Toomer several times reminds his readers. Still, Toomer appreciates a vitality in Southern blacks which disappears when they are removed from the land, a process that Toomer views as unfortunately inevitable in the modern world.

To create this sense of vitality and closeness to the land and the natural world, Toomer uses a vast array of references to nature—the pines, the canefields, the sky at dusk, the red soil—as images themselves, as similes or metaphors in connection with his characters, or as recurring leitmotifs in the operatic development of his sketches. He uses rhythm and repetition to engage the reader in the immediacy of these sensory experiences. A close analysis of one of his pieces—"Karintha," the opening sketch in *Cane*—will illustrate Toomer's typical methods.

Like other pieces in the book, "Karintha" opens with an epigraph, a song-like refrain of four lines which recurs throughout the sketch as a unifying device. The first of four paragraphs of varying lengths then introduces Karintha as a child, summing her up in the first sentence, which is poetically accretive rather than prosaically structured; the final adjective cluster echoes words from the epigraph's refrain. Two sentences in parallel construction follow, dealing with the actions the old men and the young men take with her, followed by two sentences in response to these, describing their respective feelings about her. The final sentence sums up the paragraph and "this interest of the male," with a metaphoric interpretation of it and a note of foreboding.

The second paragraph re-creates her girlhood in terms of concrete actions and images: visual (color, shape, light), auditory (sounds of feet, voice, silence), kinetic (running, wind), tactile (stoning the cows, touching the earth). It sums up her sexual nature as well and ends with two sentences referring to the wishes of the old and young men from the first paragraph, regarding Karintha as she matures. Before Karintha is shown as a woman, the refrain of the epigraph is repeated, the first three lines each being cut by a few words. The new rhythm creates a pace appropriately faster than the wondering, more meditative earlier version.

The third paragraph makes assorted references to the subject matter and phrasing of earlier paragraphs. Repetitions of actual sentences and phrases and of sentence structure (in a series of short sentences showing what young men do for Karintha) evoke the sense of poetry, as does the second half of the paragraph, which, through indirection, reveals Karintha's murder of her infant. The birth is presented as a kind of emotionless miracle unconnected wtih Karintha herself, while the scene is given sensory richness. Juxtaposed, after ellipses, is the description of a nearby sawmill, its smoldering sawdust pile, and the heaviness of the smoke after Karintha's return. Ending this paragraph is a short song that someone makes up about smoke rising to "take my soul to Jesus," an unconsciously appropriate elegy for the unwanted baby.

The final paragraph begins as the third did—"Karintha is a woman"—and then echoes the last sentence of the first paragraph: "Men do not know that the soul of her was a growing thing ripened too soon." Toomer then suggests her unbreachable remoteness from men; the last sentence recalls the first in this sketch, describing her at twenty in the phrases used to describe her as a child. After a last repetition of her name, followed by ellipses, comes a repetition of the epigraph, followed by an ominous repetition of its last two words, "Goes down," and then more ellipses, hinting at the inevitable descent and defeat of this beautiful, vital creature, brought to maturity too soon through misuse by men.

Though printed as prose, this piece is essentially poetic; the outer details of Karintha's life are merely hinted, but Toomer's poetic prose gives a full sense of Karintha's person and appeal through the precise sensory details of the second paragraph, the recurring patterns of the old and young men's responses to her, and the use of songs as commentary. The echoes and repetitions of images and phrases act as leitmotifs, and Toomer's careful arrangement of them gives the piece a satisfying structure and a strong sense of Karintha's doom, trapped in an unchanging pattern.

Such leitmotifs, along with vivid imagery and sentence patterns that are short, repeated, often fragmentary, are used throughout the prose pieces of *Cane* in place of rhyme and meter and line division to produce the quality of poetry. Indeed, many of these pieces (including "Rhobert," "Calling Jesus," "Seventh Street") must be read, like "Karintha," more as poetry than as fiction.

In the pieces clearly printed as poetry, Toomer is less experimental. Many of his poems use orthodox rhyme schemes and meters that a Henry Wadsworth Longfellow or James Russell Lowell would approve. Yet scarce as the poems in *Cane* are, they cover a variety of forms that few single books of poetry display. "Song of the Son," for example, is skillfully rhymed, beautifully evoking in five stanzas of flowing iambic pentameter the Southern music which the poet is trying to capture in literature—as he says in this poem, before it vanishes. There are poems of rhymed couplets and brief pieces such as the Imagists might produce. There is a "Cotton Song," such as the work songs that slaves or free but poor farmhands might sing. There is much free verse, notably in "Harvest Song." Toomer's choices are not arbitrary; they suit the moods and subjects of their respective poems, conveying the spectrum of feelings that the writer wishes to present, from joy and exaltation to bitterness and despair.

Toomer also varies style and tone, as well as form, to suit theme and mood. Grim and laconic irony flavors "Conversion," as the African succumbs to "a white-faced sardonic god." "Georgia Dusk" offers lush images both of Southern life and of the African past (a recurring motif throughout the book). "Portrait in Georgia," with its short free-verse lines, reads like a catalog of bodily parts, such as an auctioneer would have prepared. Each is described through images of Southern white violence: "lyncher's rope," "fagots," "scars," "blisters," "the ash of black flesh after flame." This poem makes no explicit statement, but the juxtaposition of human parts with these images, presented so simply and concisely, evokes a subtle sense of horror and sets up an appropriately ominous mood for the following story, "Blood-Burning Moon," which ends with an actual lynching. However attractive may be the Georgia of pines, red soil, sweet-smelling cane, and beauteous dusks, Toomer insists on reminding his reader of the dangers there as well, even without explicit condemnation of the bigoted whites or the oppressive social system. Toomer works by indirection, but without diminished effect.

A similarly strong but quite different effect is achieved in "Harvest Song," which presents a field worker suffering at the end of a long day from chill, hunger, thirst, and fatigue. Each poetic "line" is made up of one or more sentences and takes up between one and five lines of print on the page. These sentences are generally short, simple statements that the speaker can barely utter, and they are often repeated, emphasizing his basic human needs, which remain unsatisfied. Toomer's words may not be those that the worker would actually use, but they mirror his thoughts closely, just as the prose pieces of *Cane* give a clear sense of their characters' minds and lives without using their actual language. The simple sentences and their repetition give an accurate sense of the worker's numbness. The poem's last long line (five sentences) is a more exalted outburst, though still despairing: the harvester beats his soft palms against the stubble in his field, causing himself pain that takes away his awareness of hunger, as the last sentence makes shockingly clear. "Harvest Song" indeed! The speaker hardly feels like singing with his throat parched from thirst; and what he harvests for himself means only more pain. Through the use of first-person narration and a simple style, Toomer evokes not pity for the poor worker, not an external look as in Edwin Markham's "The Man with the Hoe," but rather an empathy from within, allowing the reader to participate fully in the experience.

Too often, unfortunately, Toomer's later poetry drops the effective devices used in *Cane* and becomes didactic, explicitly philosophical, lacking *Cane*'s brilliantly realized images of concrete reality or its sharp, often startling metaphors. Toomer was mightily inspired by his few months in Georgia, and his sojourn even affected his interpretations of his own more familiar Washington and New York life; but after he had said what he had to say about the South, and the North in relation to the South, he seems to have exhausted his inspiration, except for his more "universal" themes, with only a little sense of poetry left, to be used in "Blue Meridian" and his stories "Winter on Earth" and "Withered Skin of Berries." The latter story returned Toomer to the lyrical style and poetic sense of structure of the *Cane* stories, but for the most part, Toomer preferred to ignore stylistic and literary matters and chose to express his spiritual and philosophical beliefs, largely influenced by George Gurdjieff's teachings, urging a regeneration of humanity that would eliminate the differences imposed by racial and other categories and bring people closer to God, one another, and the natural world.

This is the point that he makes explicitly in his last major work, the long poem "Blue Meridian," first published in full in *New American Caravan* (1936) after a selection from an earlier version had appeared in *Adelphi* and *Pagany*. A further revised version is printed in Langston Hughes and Arna Bontemps' anthology *The Poetry of the Negro, 1746-1949* (1949), which places more emphasis on God and more clearly reveals Toomer's notion of the transformed America. A few of the more minor revisions are for the better. This is the version published in *The Wayward and the Seeking*, with some incidental changes.

"Blue Meridian" follows a structure much like that of Whitman's longer poems, such as "Passage to India" or "Crossing Brooklyn Ferry," with recurring phrases or stanzas, often significantly altered. While it is not divided into individual sections, as Eliot's *The Waste Land* (1922) and Crane's *The Bridge* (1930) are—nor does it use the range of poetic forms of which Eliot and Crane availed themselves—it nevertheless follows those poems in being an examination and criticism of the twentieth century world, achieving a multifaceted view by varying tone and form.

Written largely in a hortatory, exalted style in an effort to invoke Toomer's higher spiritual goals for a better world and an unified humankind, "Blue Meridian" explores the past and current conditions of America. The European, African, and red races are presented in appropriate images—even stereotypes—each being shown as incomplete. Toomer's goal, as in much of his prose, is to achieve a new race beyond individual racial identities, a "universal human being" to be called the "blue meridian," the highest stage of development beyond white and black, beyond divisions of East and West, of religion, race, class, sex, and occupational classification, and transcending the materialism of a commercial culture and the private concerns of individuals. The message is not so different from Whitman's, except for greater criticism of modern business and the insistence on the mingling of the races.

Racial themes and the black experience are missing from Toomer's later poems—and even some of his earlier ones, such as "Banking Coal" (*Crisis*, 1922). He was living with a white wife, quite isolated from the African-American literary world, or from any literary world at all. Certainly one should not say that a black writer (even one with so little black ancestry as Toomer) should write only on black themes, but any writer should write out of direct experience; too much of Toomer's poetry aside from *Cane* is vague and didactic, too intentionally "universal," too generally spiritualized, and essentially prosaic, like his aphorisms, which lack the bite of Ralph Waldo Emerson's.

Unfortunately, Toomer's vocabulary in this later poetry—including "Blue Meridian"—too often emulates that of Whitman at his most inflated moments, even when Toomer has a true poetic idea, as in "The Lost Dancer," which opens: "Spatial depths of being survive/ The birth to death recurrences. . . ." It is not so much the Latinate vocabulary, which Toomer's great contemporaries Crane and Stevens also used, but rather that, while they made much of the orotund, sensual sounds and suggestiveness of Latinate words, Toomer's word-choices are flat and vague, words made familiar through bombastic social-science jargon. Whereas the *Cane* poems stand out particularly for the vitality of their imagery, the apt metaphors and similes in "Face" and "Portrait in Georgia," the richness of language and sensory detail in "Song of the Son" and "Georgia Dusk," the harshness of the concrete nouns, verbs, and adjectives in "Harvest Song," images in the later poetry are greatly minimized. Here Toomer abandons the exalted Romantic eloquence of "Song of the Son," the verbal and emotional starkness of "Harvest Song," in favor of making philosophical statements.

At his best, Toomer was a brilliant artist in words, a sensitive portrayer of the life he lived and observed, as well as a sincere and concerned member of the human race. *Cane* will forever keep his name alive and arouse an interest in his other work, however inferior most of it has turned out to be. The musical quality of his best poetry and prose will be admired, not for its mere beauty but for its aptness to its subjects: the beauty and appeal as well as the tragedy of the life of the South.

Scott Giantvalley

Other major works

FICTION: *Cane*, 1923 (prose and poetry); "Mr. Costyve Duditch," in *The Dial*, 1928; "York Beach," in *New American Caravan*, 1929; *The Wayward and the Seeking*, 1980 (Darwin T. Turner, editor, prose and poetry).

PLAY: "Balo," in Alain Locke's *Plays of Negro Life*, 1927.

NONFICTION: "Winter on Earth," in *The Second American Caravan*, 1929; "Race Problems and Modern Society," 1929; *Essentials: Definitions and Aphorisms*, 1931; "The Flavor of Man," 1949.

Bibliography

Benson, Joseph, and Mabel Mayle Dillard. *Jean Toomer*. Boston: Twayne, 1980. The first book-length study of Toomer, this volume is an excellent introduction to Toomer's life, work, and place in American literature. After a biographical chapter, the book examines Toomer's novel *Cane* and representative later works. The fine bibliography includes unpublished works by Toomer and an annotated list of secondary sources.

Byrd, Rudolph P. "Jean Toomer and the Writers of the Harlem Renaissance: Was He There with Them?" In *The Harlem Renaissance: Revaluations*, edited by Amritjit Singh, William S. Shiver, and Stanley Brodwin. New York: Garland, 1989. In this article, Byrd argues that Toomer should not be considered part of the Harlem Renaissance because he was not in Harlem for many of the Renaissance's most important years, he did not associate himself with other Harlem writers, and he refused to be labeled as a "Negro" writer.

Durham, Frank, ed. *The Merrill Studies in "Cane."* Columbus, Ohio: Charles E. Merrill, 1971. This volume is a collection of documents that reveal the history of Toomer's most important work, his novel *Cane*. Includes biographical essays, contemporary and more recent introductions to the novel, contemporary reviews, and critical essays. Interestingly, the authors of the reviews and critical pieces are labeled as black or white writers.

Kerman, Cynthia Earl, and Richard Eldridge. *The Lives of Jean Toomer: A Hunger for Wholeness*. Baton Rouge: Louisiana State University Press, 1987. One of the most comprehensive biographies of Toomer yet written, this volume traces in careful detail how the writer was influenced by his unstable childhood, his fascination with mysticism, and his brief career among the literary elite of the 1920's. Includes a chronology, nearly thirty illustrations, and an extensive bibliography.

McKay, Nellie Y. *Jean Toomer, Artist: A Study of His Literary Life and Work, 1894-1936*. Chapel Hill: University of North Carolina Press, 1984. Primarily a literary analysis, this book examines Toomer's major published works, especially *Cane*, and places them in the contexts of American and African-American literature. The relationship between Toomer's work and his life is also examined, drawing heavily on his autobiographical writings.

O'Daniel, Therman B., ed. *Jean Toomer: A Critical Evaluation*. Washington, D.C.: Howard University Press, 1988. This large volume contains forty-six essays and an extensive bibliography. The essays are arranged thematically, and cover Toomer's life; his work as novelist, short-story writer, poet, and playwright; his friendships with other writers; religious and male-female themes; and various interpretations of *Cane*. An excellent and accessible collection.

THOMAS TRAHERNE

Born: Herefordshire, England; c. 1637
Died: Teddington, England; October, 1674

Principal poetry
  A Serious and Patheticall Contemplation of the Mercies of God, 1699 (better known as *Thanksgivings*); *The Poetical Works of Thomas Traherne*, 1903; *Traherne's Poems of Felicity*, 1910.

Other literary forms
  Thomas Traherne's reputation is based primarily on his religious works, both in poetry and prose. His treatises include *Roman Forgeries* (1673); *Christian Ethicks* (1675); and the meditation *Centuries of Meditations* (1908).

Achievements
  Traherne is usually categorized with the seventeenth century Metaphysical poets, although his poetry lacks the quality of wit that characterizes John Donne's and George Herbert's. His poetry is religious and philosophical and bears closest comparison with that of Henry Vaughan, to whom it was attributed when first discovered in a London bookstall in 1896. Plato is the ultimate source of Traherne's thinking, both in verse and prose, and his works demonstrate his reading of many other writers in the Platonic tradition, including St. Augustine, St. Bonaventure, Marsilio Ficino, Pico della Mivandola, and the Cambridge Platonists. Scholars have generally judged Traherne to be more interested in philosophy than poetry. Perhaps as a consequence, his prose works have received more critical attention than his poetry, especially *Centuries of Meditations*, a devotional work in the Anglican tradition of Lancelot Andrewes and Donne. *Christian Ethicks*, published the year after Traherne's death, was the only systematic treatise intended for the educated English layman to appear in the thirty years following the Restoration. Because of the attention he paid to infant and childhood experiences and the importance he ascribed to them in the development of an understanding of divinity, Traherne has been suspected of the Pelagian heresy (which denies the doctrine of original sin). His name is frequently linked with such Romantic poets as William Blake and William Wordsworth, who also praised childhood innocence as the state in which humans are most closely in touch with the eternal.

Biography
  The few bits of information known about Thomas Traherne's life come principally from John Aubrey's *Miscellanies* (1696), which reveals that Traherne was twice visited by apparitions, and from Anthony à Wood's *Athenae Oxoniensus* (1691-1692), where he is identified as a son of John Traherne, a shoemaker who was related to Philip Traherne, twice mayor of Hereford.

Traherne also had a brother Philip, who revised and edited some of his poems. Traherne was educated at Brasenose College, Oxford, where he took his B.A. degree on October 13, 1656. He was ordained and, on December 30, 1657, was appointed to the Rectory at Credenhill, County Hereford. While at Credenhill, Traherne became spiritual adviser to Mrs. Susanna Hopton. She had become a Roman Catholic after the execution of Charles I but rejoined the Church of England after the Restoration and became the center of a religious society for which Traherne wrote *Centuries of Meditations*. Mrs. Hopton's niece married Traherne's brother Philip. Traherne returned to Oxford to take his M.A. on November 6, 1661, and his B.D. on December 11, 1669. In 1667, he became chaplain to Sir Orlando Bridgman, Keeper of the Seals in the Restoration. Traherne's death occurred three months after his patron's, and he was buried beneath the reading desk in the church at Teddington on October 10, 1674. *Roman Forgeries*, the equivalent of a modern B.D. thesis, was his only work published in his lifetime, although he was preparing *Christian Ethicks* for publication at the time of his death. There may yet be more works of Traherne to be discovered, for as recently as 1964 a manuscript called "Select Meditations," also organized by "centuries," came to light and was established as Traherne's.

Analysis

Modern readers first encountered Thomas Traherne as a poet, and the publication of his poems fortuitously coincided with the renewed interest in the seventeenth century poets signaled by H. J. C. Grierson's 1912 edition of John Donne. Although Traherne was not included in Grierson's famous 1921 anthology of Metaphysical poetry, he has always been categorized with those poets, although in the second rank. Traherne might be surprised to find himself among the ranks of the poets at all, for his verse, at least as much of it as has been discovered, comprises only a portion of his known writings, and there is reason to believe that he placed more importance on two of his prose works, *Christian Ethicks* and *Centuries of Meditations*. Thematically, and even stylistically, his poetry is of a piece with his prose, which deserves some consideration here, both for the light it throws on his poetry and for its own sake.

Widely and deeply read, intellectually eclectic, and religiously heterodox, Traherne reminds one of John Milton, whom he preceded in death by less than a month. Both were modernists, sharing in the new humanist emphasis of their era. Traherne, however, found a place in the established Church, something that the great Puritan poet would have found impossible. Traherne lacked the genius that made Milton an original, and readers of the younger poet are always conscious of his debts to thinkers and writers greater than he. He copied into his Commonplace Book from those whom he especially admired, many of whom are in the Platonic tradition, such as Hermes Trismegistus, whose *Divine Pymander* Traherne copied in its 1657 English translation, and Henry More, the Cambridge Platonist, from whose *Divine Dialogues* (1668) Traherne copied extracts. Another unpublished manuscript (British Museum Manuscript Burney 126) is known informally as the Ficino Notebook because it consists of extracts from Ficino's Latin epitomes and translations of Plato. It also contains a long Latin life of Socrates and an otherwise unidentified work entitled "Stoicismus Christianus."

Traherne's writings are almost exclusively religious, and the influence of Plato, without whom Christianity would be a very different religion, is therefore unsurprising. What is surprising is Traherne's apparent acceptance of Platonic doctrines usually rejected by the Christian Fathers, such as the doctrine of the soul's preexistence, and his modification of other doctrines, such as the traditional Platonic opposition of the material and spiritual worlds, from their usual adaptation to Christian dogma. Hints of the soul's memory of an existence previous to the earthly one is one of the motifs in Traherne's poetry that reminds readers of the Romantic poets, especially Wordsworth of the "Ode: Intimations of Immortality from Recollections of Early Childhood." Were it not for the fact that Traherne's work was not discovered until nearly fifty years after Wordsworth's death, scholars would doubtless have searched for the Trahernian influence on him. In *Centuries of Meditations*, 3.2, Traherne marvels, "Is it not strange that an infant should be heir of the whole world, and see those mysteries which the books of the learned never unfold?" His exaltation of infancy and childhood in particular makes him seem a precursor of the Romantic movement. Like Wordsworth, Traherne values childhood innocence because the "Infant-Ey," as he says in a poem of that title, "Things doth see/ Ev'n like unto the Deity." Attributing such power to the child requires, as he paradoxically says, "a learned and a Happy Ignorance" and is one of the indications that Traherne believed in the preexistence of the soul. Although he never expressly states such a belief, it can be inferred from his writings, particularly *Centuries of Meditations* and *Christian Ethicks*, where he discusses other aspects of Neoplatonic mysticism.

On the other hand, Traherne rejects the traditional Platonic preference for the ideal world over the real. In fact, as Carol Marks has noted in "Traherne and Cambridge Platonism" (1966), Traherne holds that the spiritual world is enhanced by its physical actualization. Another way in which Traherne departs from strict Platonism is in his conception of time and eternity. For Platonic philosophers, as Richard Jordan points out in *The Temple of Eternity* (1972), time is the earthly, mortal image of eternity, but for Traherne, this is part of eternity, just as the physical world is part of God's unified creation. Here again, Traherne is reacting against the medieval emphasis on the opposition between this world and the next, finding instead a reconciliation.

His reaction to the Aristotelian dichotomies of the Scholastic philosophers is one of the affinities between Traherne and the Cambridge Platonists. He also shared their distaste for the Calvinist preoccupation with original sin and, like them, focused on man's potential, through the exercise of reason, to achieve happiness. In fact, as more than one scholar has suggested, Traherne's theology may have been Pelagian; his heavy stress on the power of childhood innocence almost requires a denial of the doctrine of original sin. Patrick Grant asserts in *The Transformation of Sin* (1974) that Traherne's theology is indebted to St. Irenaeus, one of the pre-Nicene Fathers to whom the Cambridge Platonists also looked for a method whereby pagan philosophy could be incorporated into Christianity. Stanley Stewart in *The Expanded Voice* (1970) finds Traherne aligned with the Arminians at Oxford who struck a balance between Pelagian "secularism" and Calvinistic determinism. Traherne's emphasis on man's potential for creation, which man shares with God, and his slight attention to sin, certainly distinguish him from Donne and Herbert. Traherne's accommodation of less traditional religious views probably was one of the factors that earned for him the position as chaplain to Bridgman, who allied himself overtly with the Latitudinarian cause and, before Traherne, had employed a Latitudinarian divine.

Traherne's approach to theology was essentially exploratory, searching for truth rather than dogma. "Let it be your Care to dive to the Bottom of true Religion, and not suffer your Eyes to be Dazled with its Superficial Appearance," he wrote in *Christian Ethicks*. That attitude is evident in *Roman Forgeries*, a polemic with the ostensible purpose of indicting the Roman church for its flagrant forgeries of documents and falsification of historical facts. Stewart's book sets the work in the rhetorical context of the anti-Papist tracts of the late Tudor and Stuart dynasties, but goes on to argue the preeminent influence of a 1611 work by Dr. Thomas James lengthily entitled *A Treatise of the Corruption of Scripture, Councels, and Fathers, by the Prelats, Pastors, and Pillars of the Church of Rome for Maintenance of Popery and Irreligion*. Like James, Traherne's purpose is less to vent anti-Catholic vitriol, although *Roman Forgeries* observes convention in that regard, than to reexamine, scientifically, texts condemned as false, with an eye toward religious certainty.

Renaissance Platonists, such as those at Cambridge and such as Traherne, asserted that man was the bond of the universe, the link between the spiritual and the material, between the Creation and the Creator; that belief probably accounts for the self-centered quality of much of Traherne's work, especially *Centuries of Meditations*. The notion of man as microcosm is found in many places, but a probable source for Traherne is Pico's *Oratio de hominis dignitate* (1486, *Oration on the Dignity of Man*), which he especially praised. For Pico and others, when man was created in the image of God, he was also made the quintessence of the universe. Thus, although Traherne's philosophy of life seems rather self-centered, as more than one critic has pointed out, it is possible that he was using himself as microcosmic man. Stewart finds that the *Centuries of Meditations* is a self-centered work and yet not egotistic; rather,

Traherne indulges in "a process of perfect narcissism," for in self-love one finds the beginning of love of the universe, created by God.

Despite Traherne's identification as a poet, scholarly attention has concentrated on *Centuries of Meditations*, particularly in the years since the publication of Louis Martz's two studies, *The Poetry of Meditation* (1954) and, especially, *The Paradise Within* (1964), in which Martz places *Centuries of Meditations* in the tradition of the Augustinian meditative exercise. Much of Traherne's writing, including his poetry, derives from that tradition, including *Meditations on the Six Days of the Creation* (1717) and an unpublished work, *The Church's Year-Book*. The century was an established subgenre of the Anglican manual of meditation. Earlier examples include Thomas Wilson's *Theological Rules* (1615), organized in four centuries, and Alexander Ross's *A Centurie of Divine Meditations* (1646). Traherne's work is divided into five centuries, all except the fifth containing one hundred short meditations. Since the fifth century ends with the tenth meditation followed by the numeral "11," scholars have felt obliged to ponder whether the work is unfinished or whether perhaps Traherne purposely ended abruptly so that the reader (or perhaps his patron, Susanna Hopton), having become adept at meditation through studying the first four centuries, could complete the fifth meditation for himself on the forty-eight blank pages remaining in the manuscript. Such a fanciful explanation, the ultimate in self-effacement in an otherwise self-centered work, seems unlikely. Martz feels "a sense of completion" after the tenth meditation in Century Five, and says, mystically, that "the conclusion lies in the eloquent silence of those blank pages." Indeed, Traherne was not unaware of the importance of silence for the mystic, as his poem "Silence" demonstrates. "A quiet Silent Person may possess/ All that is Great or High in Blessedness," the poem begins. This poem, however, is followed in the Dobell Folio by other poems, not blank pages.

The most influential discussion of the source of the *Centuries of Meditations* is by Louis Martz, who sees it as an Anglican adaptation of the Augustinian meditative mode, particularly as exemplified by St. Bonaventure's *Itinerarium Mentis in Deum* (1259, *Journey of the Mind to God*). Martz finds a basis for Traherne's optimism in Augustine's discussion of the power of the human mind in *De Trinitate* (397-401, *On the Trinity*), and he identifies the *Centuries of Meditations* as a "confessional" work, moving through the three stages of confession of sin, confession of praise, and confession of faith that Augustine's *Confessions* (397-401) moves through. Traherne's five-part division mirrors St. Bonaventure's *Itinerarium*. Bonaventure's journey opens with a Preparation, corresponding to Traherne's first century. Traherne prepares for the meditative exercise by meditating on the cross and by introducing one of his most important images, Adam in Paradise. The central sections of Bonaventure's work set forth the Threefold Way to God, which is accomplished by Traherne's three central centuries. Traherne begins his contemplative journey autobiographically, drawing in Centuries Two and Three on personal experience in this world, taken as a mirror of the divine world. In the fourth century, he leaves personal experience behind and attempts to discuss the divine principles themselves. Bonaventure's *Itinerarium* closes with a Repose, which corresponds to Traherne's fifth century.

Most subsequent commentators on the *Centuries of Meditations* pay homage to Martz, even when they disagree with him. Isabel MacCaffrey suggests in an appreciative review of Martz's book that Traherne's plan was not simply Augustinian but Ignatian ("The Meditative Paradigm," 1965), an idea that gains support from the knowledge that Traherne used an English translation of a meditative work by a Spanish Jesuit in the composition of the *Thanksgivings* and especially in the *Meditations on the Six Days of the Creation* and in *The Church's Year-Book*. Gerard Cox, who calls the application of Bonaventure and Augustine to Traherne "highly questionable," argues instead that the *Centuries of Meditations* is organized according to Platonic principles derived from the Cambridge Platonists Theophilus Gale and Benjamin Whichcote ("Traherne's *Centuries*: A Platonic Devotion of 'Divine Philosophy,'" in *Modern Philology*, 1971). Cox, however, undercuts his own discussion by conceding that the Platonic organizing principle "is not sufficiently in control" so that the *Centuries of Meditations* has often seemed "a haphazard collection of meditations." Jordan argues for a three-part structure for the work, each part devoted, respectively, to the world, the individual soul, and God, and points out that in his promised discussion of the attributes of God, Traherne never mentions love, which he had discussed in relation to the other two topics. Century Five, then, Jordan suggests, must have been intended as a meditation on God's love. Although his three-part division of a work divided by its author into five parts seems strained, his explanation for the incomplete state of the fifth century is reasonable. Stewart dismisses all attempts to find or impose an order on the work as symptomatic of modern unresponsiveness "to literary experiences not based on novelistic assumptions about beginning, middle, and end," and claims that the *Centuries of Meditations* proceeds by accretion.

Stewart claims that basically the same principle underlies the organization of *Christian Ethicks*, a collection of Baconian essays on various virtues, theological and moral. While each chapter does proceed in the exploratory fashion of Francis Bacon's essays, and while each one is self-contained, so that there is no particular necessity to the organization of most of the book—indeed the discussion of the cardinal virtues justice and prudence is interrupted by the discussion of the theological virtues, faith, hope, charity, and (Traherne's addition) repentance—Traherne nevertheless sees the whole as governed by a general purpose, as his Preface "To the Reader" makes clear. One tradition from which *Christian Ethicks* derives is the gentleman's handbook, which instructed Renaissance men in the attainment of the various virtues required of a gentleman. Traherne's handbook, however, will be different. He will not treat the virtues "in the ordinary way," he says, as that has already been done; rather, he seeks "to satisfie the Curious and Unbelieving Soul, concerning the reality, force, and efficacy of *Vertue*" as a means to Felicity. As Carol Marks says in the general introduction to the 1968 edition of *Christian Ethicks*, the work is distinguished by "persuasive emotion, rather than intellectual originality." Rhetorically speaking, "persuasive emotion" is an aim ascribed by seventeenth century rhetoricians to poetry, and indeed the work may be compared with *The Faerie Queene* (1590, 1596), whose end was also "to fashion a gentleman." Traherne echoes, as well, Milton's purpose in *Paradise Lost* (1667) when he says, "You may easily discern that my Design is to reconcile Men to GOD."

Edmund Spenser claimed that the virtues celebrated by his poem were such "as Aristotle hath devised," and Carol Marks asserts that ethical textbooks in seventeenth century England all derived from the *Nicomachean Ethics* (unknown). Traherne's organizational plan, however, as outlined in the Preface, is not really Aristotelian. He divides human history into four parts, according to the "estates" of Innocence, Misery, Grace, and Glory, and assigns to each its appropriate virtues. He emphasizes in his Preface his reluctance to speak of vice, claiming to be completely occupied with the discussion of virtues. The arduous *via negativa* through the circles of Hell was not for him. Rather, as Anne Ridler says in the Introduction to her edition of the poems, Traherne is a "master of the Affirmative Way."

Traherne's Platonism and Neoplatonic mysticism and his interests in meditation and ethical instruction recur throughout his poetry, and, indeed, there are occasional poems scattered among the prose works already discussed. The only poems published before the twentieth century are those known as the *Thanksgivings*, nine psalmlike poems praising God's creation. Traherne's other lyrics are in two different manuscripts known as the Dobell Folio, named for the bookseller who first identified the author, and *Traherne's Poems of Felicity*, a group of poems selected and transcribed by Traherne's brother Philip, who also edited them very heavily, as duplicate poems from the Dobell Folio demonstrate. He smoothed out rhythms, mended defective rhymes, regularized stanza forms, and made the expression "plainer" by substituting the literal for the metaphorical. Two versions of a line from one of Traherne's best-known poems, "Wonder," demonstrate Philip's method. In the Dobell Folio version, the line is "The Streets were pav'd with golden Stones." In *Traherne's Poems of Felicity*, only one word is changed, but it is a significant one: "The Streets seem'd paved with Golden Stones." Philip has changed the metaphor into a simile, making the line safer, less bold. The Dobell Folio comprises thirty-seven poems. All but six are also in *Traherne's Poems of Felicity*. The latter manuscript is, however, the only source for thirty-eight of its sixty-one poems. Because of the extensiveness of Philip's emendations to the poems also contained in the Dobell Folio, the textual accuracy of the poems for which Philip's version is the only source is clearly unreliable.

The Dobell Folio is a holograph, so it is likely that the poems in it were arranged in their present order by the author. The general plan seems to be man's spiritual biography from infancy to maturity. The opening poem is appropriately entitled "The Salutation," although it is not a greeting to the reader, but the child's greeting to life. Childhood innocence, especially as it resembles the state of Adam in Paradise, is the subject of the first four poems. The next six, from "The Preparative" to "The Approach," concern ways of coming to know God, chiefly through appreciation of his works, a theme which recurs throughout the poems and is frequently expressed by catalogs of God's works. Traherne's reading of philosophers and theologians is everywhere apparent, most obtrusively in a poem called "The Anticipation" employing technical terminology from the Aristotelian tradition to exploit the paradox that God is at once the end, the means, and the cause of natural law. The titles of the last eight poems in the sequence reveal Traherne's Christianized Platonism. There are four, entitled, respectively, "Love," "Blisse," "Desire," and "Goodnesse," among which are interposed four poems, each entitled "Thoughts." Love and desire, according to Platonic doctrine, are the forces that motivate man to seek bliss and goodness, and thoughts are the means, the "Engines of Felicitie," to use one of his rare Metaphysical conceits. Thoughts are the means to a mystical apprehension of God, as quotations from "Thoughts: III" and "Thoughts: IV" exemplify: "Thoughts are the Angels which we send abroad,/ To visit all the Parts of Gods Abode." They are "the Wings on which the Soul doth flie."

His emphasis on "thoughts" in these poems is another reminder of Traherne's familiarity with the meditative tradition; John Malcolm Wallace has argued in "Thomas Traherne and the Structure of Meditation" (1958) that the poems of the Dobell Folio constitute a five-part meditation in the Augustinian-Jesuit tradition, as described by Martz. Whether such a process was the poet's intention cannot be proved. More recently, A. L. Clements in *The Mystical Poetry of Thomas Traherne* (1969) has interpreted the Dobell Folio using a somewhat simpler three-part framework. He sees the poems moving from childlike innocence, through fallen adult experience, to blessed felicity, the traditional Christian life-pilgrimage. Scholars seem to agree, in any case, that the manuscript is a patterned work of art and not simply a random collection of poems.

The same cannot be said about *Traherne's Poems of Felicity*. There can be little doubt of Traherne's authorship of all the poems of the manuscript, for they express the same themes and exhibit the same stylistic features as those in the holograph manuscript. Nevertheless, it cannot be said with certainty that choice lines are not Philip's revisions.

Stylistically, Traherne's poetry has never received much critical approbation, although some recent critics have argued that New Critical tenets have made it impossible for twentieth century readers to appreciate Traherne. Two primary characteristics of his poetic—his heavy reliance on abstractions and his frequent catalogs of, for example, God's creations do not make for vivid verse. Yet his relative avoidance of imagery is deliberate, as the well-known poem on his poetic, "The Author to the Critical Peruser," attests. Traherne specifically rejects "curling Metaphors" in favor of "naked Truth." It may be, as some sympathetic scholars have thought, that his style represents his attempt to transcend imagistic language in an effort to apprehend Platonic ideas, but he is a difficult poet to enjoy for readers who have learned to admire concrete diction and sensual imagery. Such imagery as he does use is often biblical and Christian—images of light, fire, water, mirrors, and, from the Neoplatonic tradition, the eye and the circle. Like other contemporary Christian poets, he makes frequent use of paradoxes, a figure fundamental to Christian theology. One particularly striking hyperbolic, oxymoronic example is "Heavenly Avarice," which he uses to describe "Desire" in the poem of that title. Paradoxes, like abstractions, are part of his effort to raise the mind to the level where apparent opposites are seen to be one.

In English literary history, Traherne is himself something of a paradox. He has achieved a reputation as a poet, and yet his best work was done in prose. As a thinker, he did not achieve anything new, and yet his work demonstrates more consistently than any of the other Metaphysical poets that he was a serious student of philosophy and religion. He was a sort of quiet rebel, remaining in the established church and yet fearlessly examining, and sometimes abandoning, its doctrines. Traherne was not unique; he was very much a man of the Renaissance and Reformation; yet, to study him is to achieve a new insight into the intellectual life of seventeenth century England.

John Thomson

Other major works

RELIGIOUS WRITINGS: *Roman Forgeries*, 1673; *Christian Ethicks*, 1675; *A Serious and Patheticall Contemplation of the Mercies of God*, 1699; *Meditations on the Six Days of the Creation*, 1717; *Centuries of Meditations*, 1908.

Bibliography

Clements, A. L. *The Mystical Poetry of Thomas Traherne.* Cambridge, Mass.: Harvard University Press, 1969. Clements reviews Traherne's criticism, discusses the Christian contemplative tradition that provided the content for his writing, outlines the literary criticism found in his poetry, and provides separate chapters on the threefold spiritual process of innocence, fall, and redemption. Contains extended analyses on the poems "My Spirit" and "The Preparative."

Day, Malcolm M. *Thomas Traherne*. Boston: Twayne, 1982. Day's study of Traherne's meditations and poems focuses on his use of abstraction, paradox, and repetition to evoke in his readers a sight of eternity unlike the childlike vision earlier critics described in his work. Day provides a biographical chapter, thoughtful analyses of Traherne's work, a chronology, and an annotated select bibliography.

De Neef, A. Leigh. *Traherne in Dialogue: Heidegger, Lacan, and Derrida*. Durham, N.C.: Duke University Press, 1988. De Neef's study investigates the applicability to Traherne's work of three popular theories, with their themes of being, psychic identity, desire, and "the discursive economy of supplementarity." May prove relatively inaccessible to nonspecialists, but provides an interesting discussion of current literary theory, especially the new historicism, although it contains few extended analyses of Traherne's literary work.

Grant, Patrick: *The Transformation of Sin: Studies in Donne, Herbert, Vaughan, and Traherne*. Montreal: McGill-Queen's University, 1974. Using Traherne's early *Roman Forgeries* to establish Traherne's interest in Saint Irenaeus, Grant uses Irenaean beliefs in man's potential to be godlike to reconcile two disparate threads—the Augustinian theodicy of guilt and the optimism in the Cambridge Platonists and hermeticism—in Henry Vaughan's work and particularly his prose.

Martz, Louis L. *The Paradise Within: Studies in Vaughan, Traherne, and Milton*. New Haven, Conn.: Yale University Press, 1964. In a lengthy essay, Martz uses the Augustinian meditative tradition, as reflected in St. Bonaventure's *Intinerarium* (journey), to analyze Traherne's *Centuries of Meditations*. According to Martz, Traherne believed that Adam's original creative power still exists in man and that man's duty is to restore the paradise that Christ's sacrifice made possible. In an appendix, Martz discusses the Osborn manuscript, an early draft of Traherne's "Select Meditations."

Stewart, Stanley. *The Expanded Voice: The Art of Thomas Traherne*. San Marino, Calif.: Huntington Library, 1970. Although the bulk of his book is devoted to Traherne's prose, Stewart does devote two chapters to the poetry, which is discussed in the context of a literary tradition. Contains two extensive readings of Traherne's poems, "The Preparative" and the lesser known "Shadows in the Water."

Wade, Gladys Irene. *Thomas Traherne*. Princeton, N.J.: Princeton University Press, 1944. Reprint. New York: Octagon Books, 1969. Wade's book is the first modern scholarly treatment of Traherne's life and work (her book is divided equally between the two). In addition to individual chapters devoted to Henry Vaughan's major literary publications, Wade discusses Traherne as a Christian, a Platonist, and a mystic, and provides a bibliography of Traherne's criticism.

FREDERICK GODDARD TUCKERMAN

Born: Boston, Massachusetts; February 4, 1821
Died: Greenfield, Massachusetts; May 9, 1873

Principal poetry

Poems, 1860; *The Sonnets of Frederick Goddard Tuckerman*, 1931 (Witter Bynner, editor); *The Complete Poems of Frederick Goddard Tuckerman*, 1965 (N. Scott Momaday, editor).

Other literary forms

Although Frederick Goddard Tuckerman, like Henry David Thoreau, was an accomplished naturalist who kept a journal, and although during his lifetime he published observations of astronomical and meteorological phenomena, he is recognized primarily today for his poetry.

Achievements

Following almost complete obscurity during the late 1800's, Tuckerman has received considerable acclaim from modern critics and writers. In 1931 Witter Bynner ranked his sonnets "with the noblest in the language." Yvor Winters, in 1965, placed him with Emily Dickinson and Jones Very as "the three most remarkable American poets of the nineteenth century." Galway Kinnell, at a 1981 reading in Kansas City, Missouri, called Tuckerman the equal of Walt Whitman, Stephen Crane, and Dickinson. These judgments have, to some extent, been validated by the inclusion of Tuckerman's verse in recent anthologies. Although Tuckerman published only one book of poems, in 1860, his current critical recognition—particularly for his sonnets—is high. Not only is he praised for the quality of his verse, but he is also seen as an important figure opposing the mainstream of nineteenth century American Romanticism.

Biography

Frederick Goddard Tuckerman was born on February 4, 1821, in Boston, the youngest son of Edward and Sophia (May) Tuckerman. The poet's father was a partner in the Boston firm of Tuckerman, Rogers and Cushing, Wholesalers and Importers; he died in 1842, leaving an ample inheritance. Frederick—named for F. W. Goddard (a kinsman whose accidental death in 1820 while crossing the Lake of Zurich was the subject of an elegy by his traveling companion, William Wordsworth)—prepared for college at the private school of Bishop John Henry Hopkins and at the Boston Latin School. He entered Harvard with the class of 1841, but eye trouble forced him to leave college for a time. Later, he entered the law school, was graduated in 1842, and, after reading law in the office of Edward D. Schier, was admitted to the Suffolk bar in 1844. In 1847, he moved from Boston to Greenfield, in western Massachusetts. On June 17, 1847, he married Hannah Lucinda Jones, daughter of David S. Jones of Greenfield. They had three children: Edward, Anna, and Frederick. At Greenfield, Tuckerman abandoned the practice of law and lived a life of relative seclusion and retirement. He studied botany and astronomy, and he wrote poetry. Twice he traveled abroad. On the first of these excursions, in 1851, he met Alfred, Lord Tennyson. During the second visit, in 1855, he was Tennyson's guest at Farringford, the Isle of Wight. The friendship between the two men appears to have been cordial. Tuckerman wrote to his brother Edward, "At parting Mr. Tennyson gave me the original ms. of 'Locksley Hall,' a favour of which I may be justly proud, as he says he has never done such a thing in his life before, for anybody."

Several of Tuckerman's poems first appeared in *The Living Age*, *Putnam's*, and *The Atlantic Monthly*. In 1854, he had prepared a manuscript version of a book of poems. It is possible that he carried this manuscript with him when he visited Tennyson in 1855. In 1857, within a week after the birth of their third child, Hannah Tuckerman died. His wife's death caused Tuckerman to become even more withdrawn from the public. It was not until 1860 that the poems in the 1854 manuscript were printed, privately, by Ticknor and Fields of Boston. The volume was reprinted twice in America, in 1864 and 1869; there was also an English edition in 1863. Tuckerman sent complimentary copies of the 1860 *Poems* to an impressive list of his contemporaries: in addition to William Gladstone, the list included Ralph Waldo Emerson, Nathaniel Hawthorne, Henry Wadsworth Longfellow, William Cullen Bryant, and Jones Very (who had been his tutor, briefly, at Harvard). Thereafter, although he continued to write (his last sonnet sequence was written in 1872), he apparently made no further effort to gain public recognition. Tuckerman died Friday, May 9, 1873, at his boarding place, the American House, in Greenfield.

Analysis

Frederick Goddard Tuckerman's career as a poet illustrates a typical pattern in American letters: honored by some recognition during his lifetime, he received virtually no critical attention until 1931, when his poetry was rediscovered, reexamined, and placed back on the reading lists of American scholars. This critical revival—like that of the Metaphysical school of poetry or that of the poetry of Robert Browning—has been sustained primarily in the academic world. With this pattern in mind, it is difficult to arrive at an objective evaluation of Tuckerman's work. Contemporaries such as Ralph Waldo Emerson, Nathaniel Hawthorne, and Henry Wadsworth Longfellow gave his poetry careful praise. Emerson was most enthusiastic, commenting favorably on Tuckerman's "love of native flowers, the skill to name them and delight in words that are melodies. . . ." Hawthorne judged the 1860 volume of poems to be "A remarkable one," but he cautioned:

> I question whether the poems will obtain a very early or wide acceptance from the public . . . because their merit does not lie upon the surface, but must be looked for with faith and sympathy, and a kind of insight as when you look into a carbuncle to discover its hidden fire.

Longfellow assured Tuckerman that he had a "very favorable" opinion of the poems, but, like Hawthorne, he warned that "external success with the world" might be something quite different from "internal success."

Tuckerman's "Rhotruda," which Emerson singled out for praise, is a good example of the kind of narrative poetry that won Tuckerman the cautious approval of his contemporaries. The poem, set in the time of Charlemagne, is about two lovers, Rhotruda and Eginardus. Visiting Rhotruda after curfew one night, Eginardus is trapped by a snowstorm; he cannot return to his room across the courtyard because the snow would reveal his footsteps. Rhotruda carries him on her shoulders so that only her footsteps mark the snow. Charlemagne, however, has seen the act. The next morning, he confronts the lovers with the truth. Instead of sentencing Eginardus to death, however, he orders the two lovers to marry. The final image of the poem is vividly expressed:

> . . . Like a picture framed in battle-pikes
> And bristling swords, it hangs before our view—
> The palace court white with the fallen snow,
> The good king leaning out into the night,
> And Rhotruda bearing Eginard on her back.

It is Tuckerman's unconventional sonnets, however, rather than his more traditional Tennysonian narratives, that have won for him his current recognition. Witter Bynner, in his appreciative introduction to the sonnets, sounded the keynote in Tuckerman's revival by recognizing in his work a style "as modern as any twentieth century sonneteer." He defended Tuckerman's liberties with metrics and rhyme schemes, asserting: "He was as tenderly conscious of his form as was ever any maker of the sonnet. Instead of bungling or staling the sonnet-form, he renewed it and, moulding it to his emotion, made it inevitable." Bynner also praised the intellectual honesty that Tuckerman brought to his work: "Never did a man write poetry more straightly to himself—with nothing fictitious. He is isolated in an intense integrity toward nature, toward his own mind, and toward the unknown God."

Sonnet X, in the fourth series of sonnets (from *The Complete Poems of Frederick Goddard Tuckerman*), dated 1860-1872, illustrates the qualities of Tuckerman's poetry that Bynner most admired. The first eight lines are marked by uneven metrics; one line has thirteen syllables. The rhyme scheme begins as a traditional Italian sonnet but skews itself into a curiously distorted

figure: abba, cdeedc, fggf. In substance, the sonnet seems to follow the traditional Italian form: question, followed by answer. The question, however,
is multiple: the listener is asked whether he has seen "reversed the prophet's
miracle" (the worm that takes on the appearance of a twig), or whether he
has wondered at the "craft that makes/ The twirling spider at once invisible,"
or "heard the singing sand," or "ever plucked the little chick-wintergreen
star/ And tasted the sour of its leaf?" The answer is both mysterious and
promising:

> . . . Then come
> With me betimes, and I will show thee more
> Than these, of nature's secrecies the least:
> In the first morning, overcast and chill,
> And in the day's young sunshine, seeking still
> For earliest flowers and gathering to the east.

N. Scott Momaday, in his Introduction to *The Complete Poems of Frederick
Goddard Tuckerman*, continued in the direction initiated by Bynner. Momaday called Tuckerman's view of nature "noticeably different than that which
predominates in the literature of his time and place," noting: "Where Emerson
found realized in nature the transcendent spirit of the universe, Tuckerman
saw only a various and inscrutable mask." Momaday characterized Tuckerman
as a poet who kept "the stage properties of contemporary Romantic literature"
but defined the Romantic sense of isolation "in terms of intellectual honesty
rather than self-reliance"; who celebrated "fact" rather than "sentiment";
who trained his attention "upon the surfaces rather than the symbols of his
world."

"Tuckerman," Momaday wrote, "was a man who made herbariums. . . .
His poems are remarkable, point-blank descriptions of nature; they are filled
with small, precise, and whole things: purring bees and vervain spikes, shives
and amaryllis, wind flowers and stramony." Even in the sentimental "Refrigerium," this gift for description is evident. The poem, in three stanzas of
seven lines each, is a lament for a lost love, "lying/ In a slumber sweet and
cold." The specific details—the natural objects and furnishings of earth's vast
"refrigerium"—are, however, presented with a naturalist's objectivity and
accuracy: "Let the slow rain come and bring/ Brake and stargrass, speedwell,
harebell,/ All the fulness of the spring. . . ." In many ways, the specificity of
details contributes to the sentiment. The speaker notes, for example, how
graves have run together in "the blending earth," the stones even being linked
together by spiderwebs.

Winters, in the foreword to *The Complete Poems of Frederick Goddard
Tuckerman*, sees in Tuckerman a modern sensibility that rivals that of the
French Symbolists with its structure of "controlled association." "The Cricket,"
not published until 1950, illustrates what Winters most admires about Tucker-

man's verse: imagery, combined with abstract statement sufficient to support a theme "of some intellectual scope." The poem, in five sections, is an ode (in the tradition of the "great odes" of John Dryden, Thomas Gray, John Keats, and William Wordsworth). In the first section, the poet invokes as his muse "a little cooing cricket." In section two, the speaker describes, with concrete, vivid detail, the sleepy afternoon; by the end of the day, the cricket muse has multiplied: "From tingling tassle, blade, and sheath,/ Rising from nets of river vines,/ Winrows and ricks . . ./Rising and falling like the sea,/ Acres of cricks!" In section three, the significance of the poet's choice of muse is made clear: the cricket is both celebrant of sunshine and "bringer of all things dark." In section four, the speaker recalls the classical role of the cricket as a singer of grief. In section five, the speaker brings together the themes of the preceding sections: praise, change, life, death. The poem concludes with a stoical celebration of the limited possibilities that life offers: "Rejoice! rejoice! whilst yet the hours exist—/ Rejoice or mourn, and let the world swing on/ Unmoved by cricket song of thee or me."

Tuckerman's present reputation seems to be based on two characteristics: the close observation of nature—of facts rather than symbols—that placed him in opposition to his contemporaries; and a concern with the metaphysical enigma of life that gives his poetry a peculiarly modern tension and pessimism. Some critics have seen this latter quality as "a kind of chronic melancholy which for the most part appears to be indulgence." Others, however—particularly Momaday—value Tuckerman's poetry for both its artistic and its intellectual opposition to the mainstream of American Romanticism.

Robert C. Jones

Bibliography

Donoghue, Denis. *Connoisseurs of Chaos: Ideas of Order in Modern American Poetry*. 2d ed. New York: Columbia University Press, 1984. This wide-ranging study devotes a valuable chapter to recurrent oppositional themes in Tuckerman's poetry: public and private, human and natural, physical and metaphysical, and truth and ambiguity. Also offers brief but insightful comparisons of Tuckerman to other modern poets such as Emily Dickinson, T. S. Eliot, William Empson, Wallace Stevens, and Walt Whitman.

England, Eugene. *Beyond Romanticism: Tuckerman's Life and Poetry*. Albany: State University of New York Press, 1991. A combined biography and critical study, and the best source for information about Tuckerman. Written by the foremost expert on the poet, the book examines how Tuckerman was molded by, and yet reacted against, Romanticism. Includes extensive readings of individual poems, an index, and an exhaustive bibliography.

_____. "Tuckerman and Tennyson: 'Two Friends . . . on Either Side the Atlantic.' " *New England Quarterly* 57 (June, 1984): 225-239. This important essay explores how Tuckerman's poetry was strongly influenced by his friendship with Alfred, Lord Tennyson. The first half examines letters between the two men, while the second half demonstrates how, through his close study of the English poet, Tuckerman moved beyond him as a model and established his own unique poetic identity.

Golden, Samuel. *Frederick Goddard Tuckerman.* New York: Twayne, 1966. This widely available book provides basic information about Tuckerman's life and several insightful readings of his poems. Some of Golden's biographical reconstructions, however, are based too fully on Tuckerman's sonnets and not fully enough on other kinds of historical materials. For a more accurate biography, students should consult Eugene England's *Beyond Romanticism: Tuckerman's Life and Poetry.*

Momaday, N. Scott. "The Heretical Cricket." *The Southern Review* 3 (January, 1967): 43-50. This brief, well-written study focuses on "The Cricket," considered by many critics to be Tuckerman's most important poem. Arguing that this ode is essentially anti-Romantic, Momaday compares "The Cricket" to William Cullen Bryant's "Thanatopsis" and finds the former more modernistic because it accepts death intellectually without sublimating it as a longed-for communion with nature.

Winters, Yvor. Foreword to *The Complete Poems of Frederick Goddard Tuckerman.* New York: Oxford University Press, 1965. Although it is overly polemical, this short essay argues intriguingly that Tuckerman should not be placed uncritically in the New England poetic tradition, but rather that he fits more understandably in the tradition of French symbolism and is especially close to the sensibilities of the French poet Paul Verlaine.

LOUIS UNTERMEYER

Born: New York, New York; October 1, 1885
Died: Newton, Connecticut; December 18, 1977

Principal poetry
The Younger Quire, 1910; *First Love*, 1911; *Challenge*, 1914; . . . *and Other Poets*, 1916; *These Times*, 1917; *Including Horace*, 1919; *The New Adam*, 1920; *Heavens*, 1922; *Roast Leviathan*, 1923; *Collected Parodies*, 1926; *Poems*, 1927 (with Richard Untermeyer); *Burning Bush*, 1928; *Adirondack Cycle*, 1929; *Food and Drink*, 1932; *First Words Before Spring*, 1933; *Selected Poems and Parodies*, 1935; *Long Feud: Selected Poems*, 1962.

Other literary forms
Louis Untermeyer's poetry represents only a fraction of his total work. He put his name on well over a hundred books, ranging from *The Kitten Who Barked* (1962, a children's story) to *A Treasury of Ribaldry* (1956), and from his historical novel *Moses* (1928) to *A Century of Candymaking, 1837-1947* (1947). Most of his effort, however, went into four areas: anthologies of poetry, criticism, biography, and children's literature. His chief anthologies were *Modern American Poetry* (1919, 1962), *Modern British Poetry* (1920, 1962), and *A Treasury of Great Poems* (1942, 1955). He broke new ground in criticism with *The New Era in American Poetry* (1919, 1971) and provided a useful literary reappraisal in *American Poetry from the Beginning to Whitman* (1931). His early textbook *Poetry: Its Understanding and Enjoyment* (1934, with Carter Davidson) paved the way for Cleanth Brooks and Robert Penn Warren's *Understanding Poetry* (1938) and a host of others. Although Untermeyer published one massive analytical biography, *Heinrich Heine: Paradox and Poet* (1937), he was better known for the biographical essays in *Makers of the Modern World* (1955) and *Lives of the Poets* (1959). Untermeyer's contributions to children's literature include collections of poetry such as *This Singing World* (1926) and *Stars to Steer By* (1941), as well as many stories and collections of stories—among them, *Chip: My Life and Times* (1933), *The Donkey of God* (winner of the 1932 Italian Enit Award for a book on Italy by a non-Italian), *The Last Pirate: Tales from the Gilbert and Sullivan Operas* (1934), and *The Golden Treasury of Children's Literature* (1959, with Byrna Untermeyer).

Achievements
Louis Untermeyer exerted a shaping influence on modern American poetry. That influence, however, did not derive from his own voluminous verse. Indeed, Untermeyer has not been greatly honored as a poet. His verse has escaped the scrutiny of modern scholars and his work was never awarded a

Pulitzer Prize. Moreover, Untermeyer seemed to regret his poetic profligacy and lamented that "too many facile lines of praise and protest" had filled his volumes. In *Long Feud*, he trimmed the canon of poems he cared to preserve to a spartan 118 pages.

If Untermeyer's impact as a poet was limited, his impact as a critic, critical biographer, and anthologist was almost limitless. He has been described as Robert Frost's Boswell, but he really ought to be seen as a twentieth century version of James Boswell and Samuel Johnson combined. Through appreciative reviews, loving editorial labors, and reverent selections in his anthologies, Untermeyer was able to do more for Frost than Boswell ever did for Johnson. Moreover, Untermeyer's engaging *Lives of the Poets* is a worthy sequel to Johnson's biographical sketches and is massively supplemented by the scientific, political, and literary biographies in his *Makers of the Modern World*.

Although Untermeyer modestly understated his contribution to Frost's success, Frost himself was quick to acknowledge it, saying publicly, "Sometimes I think I am a figment of Louis' imagination." Indeed, in an article for the Chicago *Evening Post* on April 23, 1915, Untermeyer became the first reviewer in America to praise Frost's *North of Boston* (1914). He was the second scholar to praise Frost's poetry in a book, *The New Era in American Poetry*, and he was among the first to include Frost in an anthology.

As the friendship between the two poets strengthened, Untermeyer's advocacy continued. Every new edition of *Modern American Poetry* included more poems by Frost, who wrote appreciatively to his friend in 1941, "I look on [the anthology] as having done more to spread my poetry than any one other thing." Untermeyer continued to write warm reviews of Frost's poetry; he became Frost's earliest biographer; and he published the first volume of Frost's letters and conversations. In 1943, Untermeyer made himself "somewhat unpleasant" with his fellow judges on the Pulitzer Poetry Jury by insisting in a minority report that the year's prize should be awarded to *A Witness Tree*, making Frost the only author ever to win four Pulitzer Prizes.

What Untermeyer did massively for Frost, he did less passionately but just as selflessly for many other poets. *The New Era in American Poetry* devoted whole chapters to Vachel Lindsay, Carl Sandburg, Edwin Arlington Robinson, Amy Lowell, Edgar Lee Masters, and Ezra Pound, while also giving prominence to Sara Teasdale, Hilda Doolittle, Stephen Vincent Benét, and William Rose Benét. His ten editions of *Modern American Poetry* and nine editions of *Modern British Poetry* helped to win recognition and popularity for three generations of young poets. His service for nearly a quarter century as chairman of the Pulitzer Poetry Jury allowed him to assist the careers of Mark Van Doren, both Benéts, Karl Shapiro, Robert Lowell, W. H. Auden, Peter Viereck, Gwendolyn Brooks, Carl Sandburg, Marianne Moore, Archibald MacLeish, Theodore Roethke, Wallace Stevens, Elizabeth Bishop, Richard Wilbur, Robert Penn Warren, Stanley Kunitz, W. D. Snodgrass, Phyllis

McGinley, and William Carlos Williams. He served as Merrill Moore's literary adviser during Moore's life, and he was a faithful literary executor after Moore's death.

In brief, through poems, lectures, reviews, anthologies, and personal services, Untermeyer did more than any of his contemporaries to win a popular audience for modern poetry.

Biography

Louis Untermeyer was born in 1885 into a well-to-do family of German-Jewish jewelers. His formal education ended at fifteen when he refused to return to high school and discovered that Columbia University would not admit him without passing marks in algebra and geometry. He then worked in the family jewelry business while establishing his career as a poet and literary jack-of-all-trades. His literary successes allowed him to devote less and less time to the jewelry business until he formally resigned at the age of thirty-seven.

Untermeyer eventually moved away from New York City and bought Stony Water, a 160-acre farm in the Adirondacks that became the setting for some of his finest lyrics. Although he continued to earn his living through writing and lecturing, he made a brief stab at commercial farming, raising Hampshire pigs and Jersey cows, tapping maples, harvesting apples, and marketing Stony Water preserves. In his autobiography *Bygones* (1965), Untermeyer compared his situation with that of the gentleman farmer who celebrated the first anniversary of his venture into dairy farming by proposing a toast: "Friends," he said, "you will notice that there are two shaped bottles on the table. One shape contains champagne; the other contains milk. Help yourself to them carefully; they cost the same per quart."

The outbreak of World War II brought Untermeyer back to the city. He joined the Office of War Information, where he worked with Howard Fast, Santha Rama Rau, and the film director John Houseman. Later, as editor of the Armed Services Editions, Untermeyer oversaw the republication of forty works of literature a month. By the end of the war, he had helped to deliver some 122,000,000 books into the hands of America's servicemen.

When the war ended, Untermeyer wished to remain in a salaried position for a variety of reasons, not the least of which was the expense associated with his growing contingent of ex-wives. He accepted a position with Decca Records directing their efforts to sell recordings of plays and poetry. In 1950, he became a celebrity as one of the original panelists on CBS-TV's *What's My Line?* McCarthyism was, however, frothing and unfettered in the early 1950's, and Untermeyer became its victim, not because of communist sympathies on his part, but because nearly forty years earlier he had published a book entitled *Challenge* (criticized at the time for too lavish praise of democracy) and worked on a liberal magazine called *The Masses*. The baseless hostility of the self-appointed censors was sufficiently rabid that Untermeyer was forced from the show and even from public life.

He retreated to the Connecticut countryside where he soon became intimate with Arthur Miller, Van Wyck Brooks, Robert Penn Warren, Malcolm Cowley, and actress Margaret Sullavan. Untermeyer's complete repatriation did not come until 1961, when he was honored by being chosen Consultant in Poetry to the Library of Congress. During the next two years, he was twice asked by the State Department to serve as a literary ambassador, giving lectures in India and Japan. In 1963, Untermeyer returned to his home in Connecticut, where he wrote his memoirs, published books for children, and continued to update his anthologies until his death on December 18, 1977.

The love of poetry demonstrated in Untermeyer's anthologies was in large part a love of passion, and for him a life of emotion was not a vicarious ideal only. In life, particularly in married life, Untermeyer experienced every variation of happiness, heartache, and humorous complexity. In all, he was married six times and divorced five times by a total of four women. In 1907, he married his first wife, the respected poet Jean Starr; he divorced her sixteen years later in Mexico and remarried her shortly thereafter in New Jersey (*not* New York, since state law there held that he had always remained married to Jean). These complications led Louis to wonder "which state was the state of matrimony" and whether he "might be committing bigamy by illegally marrying the same wife twice." Virginia, his second wife, married Louis in Mexico in 1923, became pregnant in Switzerland, delivered a baby in London, and divorced Louis (who had returned to Jean) in Missouri—all within a period of two years. Esther, the third wife and a lawyer, helped Louis to obtain a second Mexican divorce from Jean—this time by mail. Esther then married Louis in 1933 in a ceremony performed, appropriately, by a professional comedian. Louis and Esther lived together in contentment for a number of years before they gradually drifted apart. At sixty-two, Untermeyer divorced Esther in Mexico to marry his fourth wife, Byrna. When Esther learned of the divorce, she sued, alleging that Louis' Mexican divorce from Jean had been valid, while his Mexican divorce from her was not. The somewhat bemused judge ruled that Untermeyer had never been married to Esther or Virginia, was not married to Byrna, and remained legally tied to Jean from whom he had been separated for more than twenty years. Untermeyer subsequently persuaded Jean to divorce him in Nevada (their third divorce) so that he could marry Byrna a second time and live legally with the woman he loved.

Despite his fondness for children, Untermeyer was generally too busy to take much part in rearing his own sons. Richard, his son by his first wife, hanged himself at the age of nineteen. His second son, John, was reared by Virginia, who rarely allowed Louis to see the child. His adopted sons, Lawrence and Joseph, were reared less by Untermeyer than by his caretakers at

Stony Water.

Analysis

The qualities of mind and temperament that made Louis Untermeyer such a superb anthologist kept him from attaining the same level of excellence in his poetry. He was too appreciative of the moods, approaches, and words of others—too prone to imitation and parody. He was rarely able to find his own voice; or rather, his *own* voice was often the mockingbird's, wryly reproducing the songs of others. Moreover, the virtues of his impressionistic criticism—directness and clarity—were poetic vices in a period of Empsonian ambiguity.

Untermeyer's poems fall into five broad categories: parodies; modern recreations of religious or mythological events; adaptations of another poet's spirit, tone, or verse form; idealistic exhortations concerning social consciousness; and a few entirely new creations. Thus, Untermeyer's poems range from the overtly imitative to the mildly innovative. They vary widely in subject and style, but are unified by romanticism undercut with irony. This romanticism was a fundamental part of Untermeyer's personality. It guided him as he exuberantly collected belongings, friends, experiences, passions, and poems.

The instincts of a romantic collector were evident throughout Untermeyer's life. His earliest memories were of the "colorful mélange" of assorted portraits, porcelains, and petit-point cushions that littered his parents' home. During reveries before a Dutch landscape or a jeweled bird, Untermeyer's mind turned to fantasy, while his taste was tutored by delight in the diversity of the family's collections. His love of fantasy led him to read, as he put it, "a hodge-podge of everything I could lay my mind on": *The Arabian Nights' Entertainments* (c. 1450), the Rover Boys, *The Three Musketeers* (1844), *The Rime of the Ancient Mariner* (1798), Jean de La Fontaine's *Fables* (1668, 1673-1679, 1694), Alfred, Lord Tennyson's *Idylls of the King* (1859-1885), Dante's *Inferno*, and so on. This eclectic but diverting reading in bed by night naturally reduced Untermeyer to mediocrity in school by day. He found the classroom too limiting and controlled in its approach to life and learning.

Thus, at the age of seventeen, Untermeyer entered the family jewelry business—the first in what was to become the startlingly diverse collection of his occupations. Yet, even the jewelry business was too mundane for Louis. He devoted long afternoons to the unfinished verses he kept concealed in his desk beneath production reports and packets of gemstones. In the evenings he wrote poems and reviews, for which he found a ready market. His earliest collection of poems, *First Love*, was a vanity press edition subsidized by his father, but its sales quickly offset the cost of publication. His next volume, *Challenge*, was picked up by the Century Company, and Untermeyer's germinating poetic career obtained a firm roothold.

The dual careers of poet and businessman were insufficient to quench

Untermeyer's romantic thirst for experience. He used his contacts in the literary world to help him to his third career as a magazine editor. He first obtained a position as a contributing editor to *The Masses*, where he made friends of such prominent left-wing personalities as Max Eastman and John Reed. He then became one of the founding editors of *The Seven Arts*, a short-lived (1916-1917) literary magazine that published pieces by Sherwood Anderson, D. H. Lawrence, Carl Sandburg, Robert Frost, Eugene O'Neill, Vachel Lindsay, and John Dewey. From 1918 to 1924, he was a contributing editor to the *Liberator*, from 1934 to 1937 he was poetry editor of the *American Mercury*, and for many years he wrote a weekly column for the *Saturday Review* (until 1952, *The Saturday Review of Literature*).

In 1919, Untermeyer collected and revised a number of his impressionistic reviews and published them in *The New Era in American Poetry*. When Alfred Harcourt decided to bring out an anthology of modern American poetry, Untermeyer was the logical editor. *Modern American Poetry* was followed in the next year by *Modern British Poetry*. Thus, Untermeyer, who had already been a success as a jeweler, poet, and magazine editor, now assumed the role of anthologist. It was the right task for a man who, by his own confession, had "the mind of a magpie" and who collected stamps, flowers, pictures of actresses in cigarette packs, cats (both living and artificial), careers, and wives. This multiplicity of interests continued to shape Untermeyer's life. In subsequent years, he became a gentleman farmer, publisher, record producer, and television celebrity. Despite these varied careers, Untermeyer always felt most at home at his desk. There, he wrote, "I am doing what I am supposed to do: fulfilling my function whether I write in the role of biographer, storyteller, editor of anthologies, impressionistic critic, or, occasionally, poet." The order of those activities says much about Untermeyer's own priorities and poetic self-image.

For a collector who wished to be a poet, parody was the natural literary mode. Indeed, Untermeyer's first booklet, *The Younger Quire*, was a parody of *The Younger Choir*, an anthology of youthful poets (including Untermeyer) that was introduced and lavishly praised by Edwin Markham. Untermeyer's parody came to exactly twenty-four pages (one quire) and included a series of "back-of-the-hand tributes" combining "simulated innocence and real malice." He continued to write burlesques throughout his long career, publishing them in . . . *and Other Poets*, *Including Horace*, *Collected Parodies*, and *Selected Poems and Parodies*.

Parody is, however, parasitic, and Untermeyer was too thoughtful and creative to remain locked into such a limited style. In another large group of poems, the penchant for parody is reined in as Untermeyer re-creates a religious, mythological, or literary event from a modern perspective. In "Eve Speaks," for example, Eve asks God to pause before judging her. She argues that Eden was a place for child's play and angelic calm but not a place for

Adam who, being neither child nor angel, was formed to struggle and create. Untermeyer implies that eating the fruit of the tree of knowledge was essential to human fulfillment and that God had been wrong to forbid it. Thus, the poem is a typical statement of Untermeyer's philosophy of life. He implies that the Judeo-Christian religions have distorted the old myths in an effort to impose order and morality. For Untermeyer, the romantic collector, life is only truly lived through struggle, passion, sexuality, creation, and experience. All of these were to be gained only through knowledge, the forbidden fruit.

Untermeyer's romantic sensuality led him to fill his poems with descriptions of almost Keatsian opulence and vividness. The terrors of Judgment Day, for example, are suggested by phenomena: "trampling winds," "stark and cowering skies," "the red flame" of God's anger licking up worlds, the stars falling "in a golden rain." Here, the pathetic fallacy, which often mars other descriptions by Untermeyer, becomes an effective indication of God's fearful power; before his wrath, the elements, too, cringe and flee. By standing unterrified amid such fury, Eve immediately wins the reader's respect, just as her boldness in questioning God's judgment had piqued the reader's interest. As she begins to explain herself, her description of Paradise is traditional except for the contemptuousness of the occasional reference to its "drowsy luxury" and "glittering hours." Such descriptive phrases prepare the reader to see Eden as Eve saw it, a place where Man and Woman are treated like children, "swaddled with ease" and "lulled with . . . softest dreams." The circling night-bird "out beyond the wood," the "broadening stream," and the distant hills become symbols of freedom, symbols of the unknown. Eve learns that individuality can be obtained only through rebellion, that knowledge must be reached through uncertainty, and that creation grows out of struggle. She eats of the fruit of sensual knowledge, as Untermeyer would have all men and women do.

Untermeyer makes other particularly interesting attempts to modernize religious mythology in "Sic Semper," "God's Youth," and "Burning Bush." The first of these looks at the myth of the Fall from another perspective. In "Eve Speaks," Untermeyer had made no mention of Satan; Eve's revolt grew out of her understanding of Adam's human needs. In "Sic Semper," Untermeyer brilliantly and economically overturns the traditional view of Satan. The fallen angel becomes "the Light-Bringer, Fire-Scatterer"—man's benefactor and not his foe. Lucifer and Prometheus become one, bringing light to minds in darkness. Then, in a horrifying betrayal, man—knowing too well the future costs of truth, wisdom, and love—puts Lucifer in hell.

Similarly, "God's Youth" is a delightful reconception of deity. The God of the Old Testament is himself old—bored by the unchanging march of years and the "yawning seasons." During the Creation, Untermeyer insists, "God was young and blithe and whimsical," letting loose his desires and filling the earth with "fancies, wild and frank." During the Creation, then, the child-god lived as Untermeyer would have the man-child continue to live.

"Burning Bush" is by far the most sacrilegious of Untermeyer's biblical re-creations. The poem's title is an allusion to Exodus 3:2 in which the angel of the Lord appears to Moses in the form of a burning bush. Through imagery that is intentionally indirect and metaphoric, Untermeyer transforms the burning bush into a sexual symbol. In the still of the night "runners of the flame" fill the "narrowest veins," and in "an agony of Love" bodies burn but are not consumed. The biblical voice of God becomes the ecstatic cries of the lovers that later give way to "the still, small voice" of contentment in the postcoital quiet. The sexual act, which is itself "knowledge," passion, creation, and experience, becomes a metaphor for the presence of God, who *still* speaks to man through the burning bush. Through this metaphor, the poem becomes a twelve-line exposition of Untermeyer's temperament and philosophy of life.

The poems in the third category of Untermeyer's verse all involve emulation. Many of them reflect the spirit and sometimes the words of the favorite poets of Untermeyer's youth: Robert Herrick, Heinrich Heine, A. E. Housman, Thomas Hardy, and Horace. They tend to be witty, ironic, and sensuous. They frequently deal with the traditional subject matter of romantic poetry—love, spring, snow, dawn, sunset, birdsongs, the moon, and the stars—but Untermeyer is well aware that these poetic topics can often become substitutes for real passions. The romanticism of many of these poems is, therefore, undercut by irony; in others—"Georgian Anthology" and "Portrait of a Poet," for example—Untermeyer is openly scornful of formalized, passionless romanticism. For this reason, Untermeyer classified himself (along with John Crowe Ransom, Robert Lowell, and Richard Wilbur) as a romantic ironist, but given his devotion to passion, struggle, and creativity, one can question the sincerity of much of the irony. One feels that Untermeyer's scorn of the romantic posturing of others is itself a form of romantic posturing.

On the whole, these are Untermeyer's least successful poems. Untermeyer *was* a romantic and therefore became a romantic ironist only with difficulty. Moreover, most of the poems give one the impression of having been written before and better by others. A typical example is "Fairmount Cemetery," a poem in Housman's style. The speaker looks back on the cemetery, his first trysting spot, and remembers his extravagant claims that "love is all that saves"; meanwhile, the dead men lie "Chuckling in their graves." The cemetery setting is too obviously a contrivance, the claims of the lover are overblown and unrealistic, and the concluding commentary of the dead injects a crude blatancy. The only part of Untermeyer's personality that shows up in "Fairmount Cemetery" is the collector's love of varied poetic styles.

A smaller, but far better, group of poems was written in imitation of Frost's understated style. As in Frost's best lyrics, an understanding of life's tragic possibilities emerges through the speaker's recollection of an occurrence in nature. "Nightmare by Day," for example, begins with a setting and even a verse form that are nearly identical to Frost's in "Dust of Snow." In search of peace, the speaker has walked alone far into the woods until there are no more tracks in the snow. Something in front of him, glimpsed but not yet recognized, makes his "pulses freeze," and, as he watches, a trail of blood begins to grow, spreading as it melts the snow. The mystery of this image of death in a place of peaceful isolation disturbs the speaker so that ever after he himself awaits the sudden blow and the red droplets on the snow.

The impact of this terrifying incident is augmented by the plain diction and the stark imagery. Ninety-eight of the poem's 110 words are monosyllables; the average sentence contains only nine words; the only colors are white, black, and red; the only objects are the snow, the speaker, the trees, the trail of blood, and one "chuckling crow." Yet, upon reflection, the incident itself is both mysterious and premonitory, just as the simple, unforced verse reveals, upon reflection, the technical difficulty of densely rhymed iambic dimeter.

If the poem has a weakness, it is in the improbability of the events described. At its best, Frost's lyric poetry grows out of an ordinary occurrence. That is not the case in "Nightmare by Day." Here, the ultimate situation is extraordinary. The blood is very fresh, but there has been no sign of a bleeding animal or of a hunter, and no sound of gunfire. These are not insuperable difficulties, of course; hawks and owls, for example, hunt silently and leave no trail. Untermeyer is, however, less interested in the incident as a natural phenomenon than as a symbol of sudden, unpredictable violence and impending death. Hence, he makes no effort to explain the ominous scene. Nevertheless, the odd congruence of events, the dreamlike improbability, demands recognition, and Untermeyer *does* recognize it, calling the entire incident a "dream" in the final stanza. The poem's title, however, "Nightmare by Day," emphasizes that the events have been real, and the nightmarish reality of this waking dream contributes largely to its impact.

An equally good imitation of Frost's style is found in "The Scraping of the Scythe." The poem grows out of the contrasts between two sounds: the song of the bluebird and the screech of the sharpening scythe. The one is a song of leisure, the other a sound of labor; the one pleasurable, the other painful; the one the call of summer, the other the call of fall. As the speaker notes, when the two fill the air at once, one need not hear the words, "To know what had transpired." The sharpening of the scythe is an omen of colder weather to come and a symbol of inevitable death. Thus, in order *not* to hear that sound, the speaker never allows his own fields to be cut, but the reader knows that nothing can postpone the fall—and the speaker does, too.

The success of these poems arises at least in part from the fact that they are compatible with Untermeyer's outlook on life. If death is unavoidable and unpredictable, then it makes all the more sense to live fully, freely, and passionately. As much as Untermeyer admired Frost and Frost's poetry, he could not wholly endorse the somber pessimism embodied in Frost's style or the conservatism of Frost's personality. For a more compatible political and emotional outlook, Untermeyer occasionally turned to William Blake, whose radical politics and unconventional piety were much closer to his own views. Hence, Untermeyer's religious re-creations make many of the same points that Blake did in his poems objecting to those who would bind "with briars [his] joys and desires."

Sometimes Blake's influence on Untermeyer gives rise to weak imitation, as in "Envy," a poem in the manner of Blake's "The Clod and the Pebble," which pits the rooted willow against the meandering brook in a debate about life-styles; a poem such as "Glad Day (After a Color Print by Blake)," however, grows out of inspiration more than out of imitation. This paean to daylight is pure Untermeyer—lover of generosity, confidence, sensuality, clarity, and joy. Like "Eve Speaks," this poem excels in its descriptions, particularly in the personification of day, which becomes a naked body, free, outgiving, and rejoicing. Hence, as before, the pathetic fallacy is made tolerable because it is a "given," a part of Blake's drawing that Untermeyer must accept and explain.

Thus, Untermeyer's parodies, re-creations, and imitations derive from, and play upon, his strengths as a collector and a romantic, appreciative reader. The two final groupings are more original. One group of poems is largely hortatory. They include some of Untermeyer's most widely known pieces— "Caliban in the Coal Mines," "Prayer," and "On the Birth of a Child." They are light verse suitable for communicating their overt moral and political messages, but too blatantly propagandizing to qualify as significant poems. The best that can be said is that in them Untermeyer remains true to himself. Particularly in "Prayer," he speaks from the heart as he asks to remain "ever insurgent," "more daring than devout," "filled with a buoyant doubt," and wide-eyed and sensual while cognizant of others' misery. His final prayer, that of a thoroughgoing romantic, is to remain at the end of life "still unsatisfied."

If the last group of Untermeyer's poems is derivative at all, it owes its inspiration to Walt Whitman. In a style all his own, Untermeyer attempts to describe common aspects of the contemporary world, often striving to see mundane things with a childlike wonder and a romantic imagination. The poems' titles identify their unconventional subjects: "In the Subway," "To a Vine-Clad Telegraph Pole," "A Side Street," "Boy and Tadpoles," "Food and Drink," "Hairdressing," "Hands," "Portrait of a Child," "Portrait of a Dead Horse," "Portrait of a Machine," and so on. In these poems, Untermeyer eschews both the subject matter of romantic poetry and the introspective approach of most modern verse. The poem "Still Life" is both an example of Untermeyer's approach and an explanation of it. Like Untermeyer's poems, a still-life painting portrays things, "A bowl of fruit upon a piece of silk," but it also conveys emotions through the choice of color and form. The still life contains no direct autobiography, but the artist's "voice so full of vehement life" can still be "heard." In the same way, Untermeyer's poems about modern life convey his perspective without descending into private symbolism, autobiographical digressions, or Freudian associations.

"Coal Fire" is a good example of what can be achieved through such verse. The poem explains to a child why fire comes out of coal. In doing so, it uses poetic devices that particularly appeal to children, yet it uses those devices with a mastery that should delight adults. The actual content of the poem is, however, entirely mundane; coal is the remnant of ancient trees. To interest the child, Untermeyer personifies parts of these trees, putting them in situations with which a child could empathize. Like children, each leaf must be "taught the right/ Way to drink light." Each twig must "learn/ How to catch flame and yet not burn." Each branch must grow strong on this "diet of heat." Simultaneously, Untermeyer develops a series of delightful paradoxes. The dead black coal was once a living green net. Before there was any running thing to ensnare, this net snared the sun. Paradoxically, the leaves "drink light," catch flame without burning, and eat heat. Finally, the poem's heavy alliteration and frequent rhyme heighten the delight, especially since the alliteration and the rhyme so frequently emphasize key words: "these . . . were trees," "to learn . . . not burn," "branch and . . . bough began," "to eat . . . of heat," and so on. More important, however, this lucid examination of coal-fire subtly describes the burning coal as though the light within it were passion imprisoned. The intensity of the verse increases as the fire fingers the air, grows bolder, twists free, consumes the imprisoning coal, "leaps, is done,/ And goes back to the sun." There is nothing allegorical in the poem, but a reader would have to be curiously insensitive not to recognize in it Untermeyer's love of freedom, light, and passion.

In 1955, when Untermeyer had already lived his biblically allotted three score years and ten, he was selected Phi Beta Kappa poet by Harvard University. For a man who had virtually ceased composing poetry twenty years earlier, it was a rare opportunity to pronounce dispassionate judgment upon his long and extraordinarily varied career. The poem he wrote, "A Displaced Orpheus," did just that. In it, Orpheus awakens after a long silence to discover that he has lost the knack of moving mountains and assuaging lions. He attends a series of universities to relearn the lost art and produces sterile stanzas in the manner of W. H. Auden, T. S. Eliot, and William Empson. Although Untermeyer intended these parodies to illustrate the deficiencies of much modern poetry, they also illustrate the limitations of his own imitative approach to composition. Thus, Orpheus' situation becomes Untermeyer's. Time has stripped him of his reputation, and his failures have cost him the woman he loves. All that remains is the desire to struggle, the urge to create. Only when he retrieves his "still unbroken lute" and sings for "that last listener, himself," does he rediscover his power. The birds and beasts gather about him, the trees bow down, and his woman looks upon him with "rediscovering eyes."

One could wish that Untermeyer had taken Orpheus' lesson more truly to heart and that he had sung for himself more often, but perhaps then the passionate collector would only have delighted himself with more parodies. Songs coming out of the soul often have a hard and bitter birth. All but a few are stillborn. In "Eve Speaks," "Nightmare by Day," "Coal Fire," "A Displaced Orpheus," and a handful of others, Untermeyer produced more healthy offspring than most poets do. Posterity should be grateful.

Jeffrey D. Hoeper

Other major works

FICTION: *Moses*, 1928; *The Wonderful Adventures of Paul Bunyan*, 1945.

NONFICTION: *The New Era in American Poetry*, 1919, 1971; *American Poetry from the Beginning to Whitman*, 1931; *Poetry: Its Understanding and Enjoyment*, 1934 (with Carter Davidson); *Heinrich Heine: Paradox and Poet*, 1937; *From Another World*, 1939; *A Century of Candymaking, 1837-1947*, 1947; *Makers of the Modern World*, 1955; *Lives of the Poets*, 1959; *The Letters of Robert Frost and Louis Untermeyer*, 1963; *Bygones*, 1965.

ANTHOLOGIES: *Modern American Poetry*, 1919, 1962; *Modern British Poetry*, 1920, 1962; *A Treasury of Great Poems*, 1942, 1955.

CHILDREN'S LITERATURE: *This Singing World*, 1926; *The Donkey of God*, 1932; *Chip: My Life and Times*, 1933; *The Last Pirate: Tales from the Gilbert and Sullivan Operas*, 1934; *Stars to Steer By*, 1941; *The Golden Treasury of Children's Literature*, 1959 (with Byrna Untermeyer); *The Kitten Who Barked*, 1962.

HUMOROUS WRITING: *A Treasury of Ribaldry*, 1956.

Bibliography

Frost, Robert, and Louis Untermeyer. *The Letters of Robert Frost to Louis Untermeyer.* New York: Holt, Rinehart and Winston, 1963. The most valuable collection of Frost's letters to Untermeyer in a correspondence that lasted almost fifty years. The letters are remarkably edited.

Harcourt, Brace. *Sixteen Authors: Brief Histories, Together with Lists of Their Respective Works.* New York: Author, 1926. Offers short histories of sixteen authors and their works, including Sinclair Lewis, Carl Sandburg, Virginia Woolf, and Untermeyer. The entry on Untermeyer provides a fine assessment of Untermeyer's poetry and poetic development. Contains illustrations and a bibliography.

Lowell, Amy. "A Poet of the Present." *Poetry* 11 (December, 1917): 157-164. This review of Untermeyer's early verse volume, *These Times*, turns out to be a lovely appreciation of the young poet.

Pound, Ezra. *EP to LU: Nine Letters Written to Louis Untermeyer by Ezra Pound.* Edited by J. A. Robbins. Bloomington: Indiana University Press, 1963. A fine collection of letters written by Pound to Untermeyer. Useful as a source of information on Pound's perception of Untermeyer.

Untermeyer, Louis. *Bygones: The Recollections of Louis Untermeyer.* New York: Harcourt, Brace & World, 1965. The second of Untermeyer's reminiscences in which the eighty-year-old looks back on his life. Where the earlier "autobiography" was about other people, this one is primarily, and self-consciously so, about the author. It is a very personal volume focusing on the highlights of Untermeyer's career, including excellent chapters on the McCarthy years, his tenure at the Library of Congress, and his travels.

_____. *From Another World: The Autobiography of Louis Untermeyer.* New York: Harcourt, Brace, 1939. Untermeyer's first attempt at autobiography is devoted to anecdotes and comments on the author's friends and acquaintances among the literary community. It is significant in that it sheds light on the American renaissance which began before World War I. Untermeyer passes judgements, comments on works and relationships, and tells stories and jokes. In general he deals only with the surfaces of events and encounters and does not explore any issue in great depth. His style and energy are as vivid as the range of his acquaintances is impressive.

JOHN UPDIKE

Born: Shillington, Pennsylvania; March 18, 1932

Principal poetry

The Carpentered Hen and Other Tame Creatures, 1958; *Telephone Poles and Other Poems*, 1963; *Verse*, 1965; *Dog's Death*, 1965; *The Angels*, 1968; *Bath After Sailing*, 1968; *Midpoint and Other Poems*, 1969; *Seventy Poems*, 1972; *Six Poems*, 1973; *Query*, 1974; *Cunts (Upon Receiving the Swingers Life Club Membership Solicitation)*, 1974; *Tossing and Turning*, 1977; *Sixteen Sonnets*, 1979; *An Oddly Lovely Day Alone*, 1979; *Five Poems*, 1980; *Jester's Dozen*, 1984; *Facing Nature*, 1985.

Other literary forms

A prolific writer in all genres, John Updike is known chiefly as a novelist. His major works have been best-sellers and have won significant critical acclaim both from reviewers for highbrow publications and from academics. Among his most noted novels are *The Centaur* (1963), *Couples* (1968), and the four novels depicting the life of Harry "Rabbit" Angstrom: *Rabbit, Run* (1960), *Rabbit Redux* (1971), *Rabbit Is Rich* (1981), and *Rabbit at Rest* (1990). He is also an accomplished and respected writer of short stories, of which he has published several volumes, and a first-rate critic and essayist.

Achievements

Updike has achieved his fame largely through his novels. These works, and his growing collection of prose essays and reviews, have earned for him a reputation as one of America's leading literary voices. His poetry, on the other hand, has brought only modest acclaim. Many critics consider him only a dilettante in this genre, a show-off who is clearly skilled in handling poetic forms both traditional and modern. Since much of his work is gentle satire and light verse, he is often accused of lacking substance. Updike's record of publication for individual poems, however, belies that judgment to some degree. His poems have appeared in such journals as *The New Yorker* and *The Atlantic*, and even in *Scientific American*. As with much of his prose, Updike has shown an ability to deal in verse with a wide variety of experiences, making both the commonplace and the abstruse immediately accessible to his readers.

Biography

Born March 18, 1932, John Hoyer Updike grew up during the Depression in Shillington, Pennsylvania, and in the farming country outside this Northeastern town. His father was a mathematics teacher, his mother an intelligent, well-read woman who encouraged her son's reading. The Updikes lived with

John's grandparents during the novelist's earliest years; many of the boy's memories of life in that household have found their way into his fiction and poetry. A good student in high school, Updike went to Harvard in 1950 on a full scholarship. There, while majoring in English, he edited the *Lampoon* and entertained visions of becoming a commercial cartoonist. While still a student at Harvard in 1953, Updike married Mary Pennington, an art student at Radcliffe. The following year, he was graduated summa cum laude.

Updike's own artistic talent was further fostered by a year's study at the Ruskin School of Drawing and Fine Art in Oxford, England, immediately following graduation. There, his first child, Elizabeth, was born. She was to be followed in the next six years by three others: David (1957), Michael (1959), and Miranda (1960).

Updike's desire to achieve fame through the visual arts was put aside in 1955, when he received an offer to join the staff of *The New Yorker*, to which he had sold his first story the year before. His full-time association with the magazine ended in 1957, however, when he took the daring step of becoming an independent writer, moving his family to Ipswich, Massachusetts, and establishing an office there. His first book, a collection of poems titled *The Carpentered Hen and Other Tame Creatures*, appeared in 1958.

The publication of two novels, *The Poorhouse Fair* (1959) and *Rabbit, Run*, brought Updike both critical and popular acclaim. For *The Centaur*, he received the National Book Award in 1964 and in the same year was elected to the National Institute of Arts and Letters. These were but the first of many honors.

Though a resident of New England continuously after 1957, Updike frequently traveled abroad. His first important trip was in 1964-1965, when he visited the Soviet Union, Romania, Bulgaria, and Czechoslovakia as a member of the U.S.S.R.-United States Cultural Exchange Program. In 1973, he served as a Fulbright lecturer in Africa. From his experiences in these countries, Updike brought back a wealth of materials that allowed him to expand his repertoire of characters beyond New England and Pennsylvania to include two of his most memorable creations: the middle-aged Jewish novelist Henry Bech and the African ruler Hakim Ellelou.

Updike and his family remained residents of Ipswich until 1974, when John and Mary were divorced. Shortly after the breakup of his marriage, Updike moved to Boston, then to Georgetown, Massachusetts. In 1977, he married Martha Bernhard, a divorcée whom he had known when both lived in Ipswich. Even during this period of personal difficulty, Updike's volume of writings poured forth unabated, and he went on to display both skill and versatility in a variety of literary genres.

Analysis

An appropriate starting point for an analysis of John Updike's poetry is

Charles T. Samuels' summary remark in his brief study of the writer: "In verse," Samuels notes, Updike "frequently exploits the familiar," often simply "as an occasion to display his talent for comic rhyme." What strikes the reader immediately about Updike's poems is his heavy reliance on everyday experience, whether autobiographical or generic, and the way he manipulates language to achieve distinctive, often unusual and amusing, rhyming and rhythmical patterns. Reviewers of individual volumes of Updike's work have not always been convinced, however, that this kind of rhetorical gamesmanship has offered sufficient compensation for a body of works that are, in fact, intellectually lightweight when compared to the serious fiction that Updike has produced during the past two decades. As a result, the serious student of Updike's poetry is faced with examining the work in a critical vacuum, or in the constant context of his fiction.

One can see, though, that Updike's poetry demonstrates his ability to work deftly within a variety of forms, turning them to his own purposes. His published poems include sonnets, free verse modeled on that of Walt Whitman and contemporary figures, Spenserian stanzas, elegiac quatrains, extended commentary in heroic couplets, and works that follow (at times almost slavishly) other poetic conventions. More often than not, the forms are used in parody, as are the manifold rhyme schemes that remind one of the cantos of Lord Byron's *Don Juan* (1819-1824) in their variety and in their reliance on sight rhyme or colloquial pronunciation for effect. For example, in "Agatha Christie and Beatrix Potter," Updike closes his short, humorous comparison of these authors (whose works he sees as essentially similar) with a couplet of praise for having given readers "cozy scares and chases/ That end with innocence acquitted—/ Except for Cotton-tail, who did it." Similarly, in a light limerick poking fun at young Swedish scholars, he opens with the couplet: "There was a young student of Lund/ Whose -erstanding was not always und."

Like many contemporary poets, Updike also relies on the appearance of the poem on the page for effect. In poems such as "Typical Optical," he prints various lines in different type styles and sizes to make his point: As one gets older, one's vision (literally) changes, and what one could see at close range as a child becomes blurred to more mature eyes. As a result, when Updike says that the novels of Marcel Proust and the poetry of John Donne "Recede from my ken in/ Their eight-point Granjon," he emphasizes the problem by printing the phrase "eight-point Granjon" in the type face and size to which it refers. Then, in his closing remark that his "old eyeballs" can now "enfold/ No print any finer/ Than sans-serif bold," he prints the final phrase in sans-serif type and has the final word in bold print. Similarly, the lines of the poem "Pendulum" are printed beneath the title at angles resembling the swinging of a pendulum on a clock, and individual words in the poem "Letter Slot" are arranged on the page to suggest letters falling through a mail slot onto the floor.

The reader often laughs at such tricks, but the poetry cannot be judged first-rate simply for the author's ability to manipulate both the language and the conventions of the tradition in which he works. As a consequence, Updike is too often dismissed as a dilettante in this field. A close examination of his published volumes, however, reveals that the author himself is careful to distinguish between "poetry" and "light verse." Much of what Updike calls "light verse" is simply poetic exercise, intended to highlight the wonderful ability of language to evoke amusement and thought in both reader and writer. Often the impetus for such poetry comes from the world around Updike: newspaper accounts, books that are popular best-sellers, visits he has made to various places where the benign incongruities of life manifest themselves to him. Poems such as "V. B. Nimble, V. B. Quick" may not offer substantial food for thought: The genesis of the poem—an entry in the British Broadcasting Corporation's *Radio Times* that "V. B. Wigglesworth, F.R.S., Quick Professor of Biology" will speak on an upcoming program—triggers in Updike's mind a humorous comparison with the hero of the nursery rhyme "Jack Be Nimble, Jack Be Quick," and the resultant verse about a frenetic scientist dashing off experiments and hurrying off to talk about them provides momentary pleasure to readers without trying to make a serious observation about the world of science. This poem, and many others like it in the Updike canon, are simply offered as tidbits to evoke humor and sympathy in an otherwise somber world.

Because Updike is so facile at handling the many demands facing the poet, it is easy to overlook the serious nature of much of his output. A substantial number of his poems are attempts to examine the significance of his own life's experiences and to explore questions of importance to contemporary society. As in his fiction, Updike is especially concerned with the place of religion in the modern world, and often, beneath the surface playfulness, one can see the poet grappling with complex moral and philosophical issues. He is also a careful student of the literary tradition he has inherited, and his attempts to examine the place of literature as an interpreter of experience often find their way into his poems.

The way in which Updike combines the comic and the serious is illustrated quite well in his poem "Love Sonnet." Its title suggests its subject, but the content is at first glance enigmatic. The opening line, "In Love's rubber armor I come to you," is followed by a string of letters printed down the page, as if they were the endings of lines which have been omitted: "b/ oo/ b./ c,/ d/ c/ d:/ e/ f—/ e/ f./ g/ g." The form of the sonnet has thus been preserved (the "oo" sound of the third line rhyming with the "you" at the end of the first line), but the content is absent. Adding simultaneously to the confusion and to the humor is the overt sexual implication of the only full line: One cannot mistake the literal meaning of the proposition. Nevertheless, a closer look at the poem, especially in the light of the literary tradition which it seems to parody, suggests that there may in fact be serious purpose here. Traditionally, sonnets have been poems about love. While their content has varied, the form itself has usually suggested to readers the kind of interpretation the poet expects. One looks for the words in a sonnet to be metaphors describing the way in which a speaker feels about his beloved. In this poem, however, the process is reversed. The overt reference to physical lovemaking is the metaphor: "Love's rubber armor" is the sonnet form itself, an elastic medium in which the lover, working within conventions—and protected by them—is able to "come to" his beloved and display both his wit and his devotion. In this way, then, Updike is making a comment on the literary tradition: The sonnet form has both strengths and weaknesses; its conventions provide a way to ensure that meaning is conveyed, but limit the extent to which the writer may put the form to use without risking misinterpretation. Appearing at first to be a risqué comic piece about a subject much talked of and trivialized in Updike's own society, "Love Sonnet" emerges as a serious statement about the nature of poetry itself.

The special strengths and weaknesses of Updike as a poet can be seen in those poems which he presents to the world as "poems" rather than verses. In these he is often franker in discussions of sex, and the explicit language may offend some readers. No subject seems sacred, yet it is precisely the concern Updike has for sacred things in human life that leads him to write graphically about human relationships. From his study of everyday occurrences, Updike tries to isolate that which is important for man, to show how man constructs meaning from the disparate events of his own life.

The most extended example of Updike's use of individual events to make statements about universals occurs in his long autobiographical poem "Midpoint." Published as the centerpiece of Updike's 1969 volume of poetry, *Midpoint and Other Poems*, "Midpoint" is a collage of text, drawings, and photographs that traces the poet's life from infancy to its midpoint, as Updike reaches age thirty-six. Though the poem has been dismissed by some critics as "quirky," Updike himself insists that in it he demonstrates what is for him an artistic credo, a search for "the reality behind the immediately apparent." In "Midpoint," Updike reveals himself to be a believer in "pointillism" as both technique and philosophy: "Praise Pointillism, Calculus and all/ That turn the world infinitesimal." Like Whitman in *Leaves of Grass* (1855), Updike takes his own life as an example of the human condition, finding in it something of value to share with other men.

"Midpoint" consists of five cantos, four of which are modeled closely on writers of the past. Each is preceded by a short "argument" reminiscent of that provided by John Milton in *Paradise Lost* (1667), in which Updike provides the reader with clues to the action of the canto. In the first, in stanzas reminiscent of those in Dante's *The Divine Comedy* (c. 1320), Updike reviews his childhood and his growing awareness of himself as a discrete entity in the universe. An only child, he comes to see himself as the center of that universe, a point around which the world revolves. Though to sing of himself (an allusion to Whitman) is "all wrong," he has no choice since he has no other subject so appropriate or about which he knows so much. The second canto consists exclusively of photographs: Updike as baby and young child, his parents, himself as a teenager, himself and his wife, their first child. These are printed with varying degrees of sharpness: Some appear crisply defined, some are little more than a blur of dots on the page. This intentional shifting of focus carries out graphically the theme Updike expresses in the "argument" that he prints at the beginning of the canto: "Distance improves vision." In a sense, the action in this canto repeats that of the first, but from another perspective: The reader sees what he has just read about.

The third canto, composed in Spenserian stanzas, is titled "The Dance of the Solids." Based on Updike's readings in *Scientific American*, it presents in verse a view of the way the universe is constructed. The bonding of atomic particles into larger and larger structures eventually "yield[s],/ In Units growing visible, the World we wield!" It would be easy to lose sight of the poet's purpose in these most ingenious iambic pentameter lines. Updike uses the language of science, and even mathematical formulas, with exceptional precision to present his argument. For example, in explaining what happens when a solid is heated, he writes: "$T = 3Nk$ is much too neat." The stanzas are not simply virtuoso performances; in them, Updike provides an analogy for examining the human condition. Just as the visible world is composed of subatomic particles combined in meaningful ways, so are men's lives simply the ordered and meaningful arrangements of individual incidents. To understand the meaning, one must first isolate and describe the incident.

The fourth canto, "The Play of Memory," contains text, line drawings, and close-ups from the photographs that appear in canto 2. The text is modeled on Whitman's poetic technique of free verse. In this section of the poem, Updike explores his marriage and the role sex plays in shaping human lives. The final canto, written in couplets that suggest the method of Alexander Pope in *An Essay on Man* (1733-1734), is a review of the modern scene in which Updike the poet finds himself. In it, he offers advice, alternately serious and satiric, for living. In the fashion of Arthur Hugh Clough in "The Last Decalogue," a parody of the Ten Commandments, Updike admonishes his readers: "Don't kill; or if you must, while killing grieve"; "Doubt not; that is, until you can't believe"; "Don't covet Mrs. X; or if you do,/ Make sure, before you leap, she covets you." As in the third canto, readers may become so enraptured with the wise witticisms and the deft handling of poetic form that they lose the sense of the canto's place within the poem. In fact, the poem has prompted more than one reader to wonder, as did the reviewer for *Library Journal* in 1970, what Updike was "up to" in "Midpoint."

If, however, one accepts what Updike himself has said about "Midpoint," that in it he attempts to explain his own attitudes about his life and art, one can see the poem as a kind of poetic credo, a systematic statement about the poet's acceptance of his role as poet. The many references to other artists and the conscious use of recognizable forms associated with specific poets and poems suggest that Updike is using his own life to make a statement about the way art is created. In fact, in the closing lines of the fifth canto, he observes, "The time is gone, when *Pope* could ladle Wit/ In couplet droplets, and decanter it." No longer can *"Wordsworth's* sweet brooding" or *"Tennyson's* unease" be effective as vehicles for explaining the human condition. The world is now a sad and perhaps an absurd place, and art has followed suit by offering those who come to it only "blank explosions and a hostile smile." Updike, who has accepted the notion of the absurd from modern theologians who have pointed out that faith cannot be rational even if it is essential, offers this poem as an ironic, sometimes comic, and sometimes highly personal and hence prejudicial view of the world. For Updike, autobiography has become metaphor, because only by viewing the world through others' eyes can individuals hope to understand something of the significance of their own predicament. Similarly, as he has used the events of his own life to make a statement about life itself, Updike uses the forms of his predecessors to make a statement about the efficacy of art in the modern world.

Updike's art, especially his poetry, is thus intentionally enigmatic, because it contains a discoverable but not self-evident truth. The surface finish, whether comic, ironic, or sexually explicit, is often simply the bait to lure readers into the world of the poem. Once there, Updike asks his readers to look closely at their own lives, often challenging them to be as introspective about themselves as he is about his own experiences. In that way, he hopes to help others make sense of a world that he believes is essentially good and in which good men can prosper.

Laurence W. Mazzeno

Other major works

LONG FICTION: *The Poorhouse Fair*, 1959; *Rabbit, Run*, 1960; *The Centaur*, 1963; *Of the Farm*, 1965; *Couples*, 1968; *Bech: A Book*, 1970; *Rabbit Redux*, 1971; *A Month of Sundays*, 1975; *Marry Me: A Romance*, 1976; *The Coup*, 1978; *Rabbit Is Rich*, 1981; *The Witches of Eastwick*, 1984; *Roger's Version*, 1986; *S.*, 1988; *Rabbit at Rest*, 1990.

SHORT FICTION: *The Same Door*, 1959; *Pigeon Feathers*, 1962; *Olinger Stories: A Selection*, 1964; *The Music School*, 1966; *Museums and Women and Other Stories*, 1972; *Too Far to Go: The Maples Stories*, 1979; *Problems and Other Stories*, 1979; *Three Illuminations in the Life of an American Author*, 1979; *The Chaste Planet*, 1980; *The Beloved*, 1982; *Bech Is Back*, 1982; *Trust Me*, 1987.

PLAYS: *Three Texts from Early Ipswich: A Pageant*, 1964; *Buchanan Dying*, 1974.

NONFICTION: *Assorted Prose*, 1965; *Picked-Up Pieces*, 1975; *Hugging the Shore: Essays and Criticism*, 1983; *Just Looking: Essays on Art*, 1989; *Self-Consciousness*, 1989.

Bibliography

Detweiler, John. *John Updike*. Boston: Twayne, 1972. This study attempts to demonstrate the qualities of irony and self-consciousness inherent in Updike's work. Proceeding chronologically, the author omits specific study of the poems, but the background work on Updike is important for a thorough reading of his verse. Includes a brief chronology, notes and references, and a select bibliography.

Greiner, Donald J. *The Other Updike: Poems/Short Stories/Prose/Play*. Athens: Ohio University Press, 1981. This analysis shows a growing concern with mortality and loss in the works of Updike. The author proposes that as a poet, Updike is primarily concerned with shaping the power of language. He traces his development from light verse to "spiritual confusion." Particular attention is paid to the development of themes and techniques. This is the best study of Updike's poetic output. Supplemented by a detailed chronology.

MacNaughton, William R., ed. *Critical Essays on John Updike*. Boston: G. K. Hall, 1982. The introduction to this volume gives an extremely useful survey of Updike's scholarship in English—from bibliographies and biographies to criticism and scholarship—reviewed in clumps of years (1958-1966, 1967-1974, 1975-1980). Each section looks at Updike's output, then reviews books, general articles, and articles on specific works. The preface has exhaustive notes that include bibliographical references. The body of the volume contains sixteen reviews of Updike's work and sixteen critical essays, none, unfortunately, on the poetry.

Rao, G. Nageswara, ed. *The Laurel Bough: Essays Presented in Honour of Professor M. V. Rama Sarma*. Bombay: Blackie and Son, 1983. This collection contains an essay entitled "The Novelist as Poet: John Updike" by S. P. Appasamy. A reading of the poems with extensive quotations gives an excellent, though brief, analysis of Updike's verse. The author deals with the roots of Updike's Christianity and sees the beginnings of the artist that came to be.

Samuels, Charles T. *John Updike*. Minneapolis: University of Minnesota Press, 1969. This taut, forty-three page pamphlet is a critical study inspired by Samuels' 1968 *The Paris Review* interview with Updike. Samuels looks at the author's work thematically and makes some early references to the poetry. Contains a bibliography.

Vargo, Edward P. *Rainstorms and Fire: Ritual in the Novels of John Updike*.

Port Washington, N.Y.: Kennikat Press, 1973. This examination of the novels shows them to be a "powerful indictment of the spiritual shallowness of contemporary America." Vargo looks at Updike's use of ritual through pattern, myth, and celebration and offers a system through which a reader can approach Updike's verse. This study is heavily influenced by a Christian reading of Updike.

MARK VAN DOREN

Born: Hope, Illinois; June 13, 1894
Died: Torrington, Connecticut; December 10, 1972

Principal poetry

Spring Thunder and Other Poems, 1924; *7 P.M. and Other Poems*, 1926; *Now the Sky and Other Poems*, 1928; *Jonathan Gentry*, 1931; *A Winter Diary and Other Poems*, 1935; *The Last Look and Other Poems*, 1937; *Collected Poems 1922-1938*, 1939; *The Mayfield Deer*, 1941; *Our Lady Peace and Other War Poems*, 1942; *The Seven Sleepers and Other Poems*, 1944; *The Country Year*, 1946; *The Careless Clock: Poems about Children in the Family*, 1947; *New Poems*, 1948; *Humanity Unlimited: Twelve Sonnets*, 1950; *In That Far Land*, 1951; *Mortal Summer*, 1953; *Spring Birth, and Other Poems*, 1953; *Selected Poems*, 1954; *Morning Worship*, 1960; *Collected and New Poems 1924-1963*, 1963; *The Narrative Poems*, 1964; *That Shining Place: New Poems*, 1969; *Good Morning: Last Poems*, 1973.

Other literary forms

In addition to poetry, Mark Van Doren also wrote drama, fiction, and various nonfiction works. Two of his plays, *The Last Days of Lincoln* (1959) and *Never, Never Ask His Name* (1966), were produced in 1961 and 1965, respectively. The latter was published in *Three Plays*, together with two unproduced plays, *A Little Night Music* and *The Weekend That Was*. His works of fiction include the novels *The Transients* (1935), *Windless Cabins* (1940), *Tilda* (1943), and *Home with Hazel* (1957), as well as several books of short stories that were eventually published in three volumes as *Collected Stories* (1962-1968). Van Doren also wrote three books of children's fiction.

Van Doren's nonfiction works include *The Autobiography of Mark Van Doren* (1958) and critical and biographical works on various authors. He also did a great deal of editorial work, including anthologies and critical editions of works of fiction and nonfiction. The authors with whom he dealt critically include John Dryden, Henry David Thoreau, William Shakespeare, and Nathaniel Hawthorne.

Achievements

One of Van Doren's most impressive achievements is the sheer volume of his work; he was the author of fifty-six and the editor of twenty-three books. He was honored with the Pulitzer Prize in 1940 for his *Collected Poems 1922-1938*. His other awards include Columbia University's Alexander Hamilton Medal in 1959, the Hale Award in 1960, the Huntington Hartford Creative Award in 1962, and the Emerson-Thoreau Award in 1963. He also received many honorary degrees. In addition to formal awards, Van Doren's poetry won praise for its craftsmanship from other better-known poets, including Robert Frost, Allen Tate, and T. S. Eliot.

Biography

Mark Albert Van Doren, the son of Dr. Charles Lucius Van Doren and Dora Ann Butz, was born on his parents' farm near Hope, Illinois, and lived there for the first six years of his life. Then Van Doren's parents moved with him and his four brothers to the university town of Urbana, Illinois, where Dr. Van Doren had planned to retire but instead continued to practice medicine.

Van Doren attended the University of Illinois at Urbana, as his well-known older brother Carl had done. Both men were strongly influenced by Stuart Sherman, an English professor, and Mark was also taught by Leonard Bloomfield, the linguist, then a young instructor of German. Van Doren received his bachelor's degree in 1914 and entered the university's graduate program in English. A course with Sherman in nineteenth century prose writers introduced Van Doren to the writings of Thoreau, the subject of his master's thesis, which was published in 1916. He received his master's degree in 1915.

Mark Van Doren again followed his brother Carl's footsteps, going in 1915 to study at Columbia University, where Carl had studied and where, at the time, he was teaching English. Carl helped to guide his brother's doctoral studies and even suggested the topic of Mark's dissertation, Dryden's poetry. Van Doren's academic career was interrupted in 1917 by World War I. His army career, during which he never left the United States, consisted mainly of paperwork and ended with the armistice in 1918.

At the beginning of 1919 Van Doren returned to New York to continue work on his dissertation. He was awarded a fellowship to study abroad in 1920 and spent the year in London and Paris, finishing his dissertation in London and receiving his degree upon his return home. His dissertation, like his master's thesis, was published. He spent the summer of 1920 serving as literary editor of *The Nation*, replacing Carl, who wanted some free time to devote to other literary projects; he began teaching at Columbia in the fall of 1920. Planning to teach for only a short time, he in fact remained at Columbia until his retirement in 1959. He also lectured regularly at St. John's College in Annapolis, Maryland, from 1937 to 1957, and in 1963 he came out of retirement to accept a visiting professorship at Harvard University.

In 1922 Van Doren married Dorothy Graffe, with whom he had worked on *The Nation*. They had two sons, Charles and John, and lived in New York and on a farm in Cornwall, Connecticut.

In addition to his teaching and writing, Van Doren also resumed work on *The Nation*. He served as literary editor from 1924 to 1928 and as film critic from 1935 to 1938, as well as being a frequent contributor in the period between those two positions. As literary editor, he published the works of then unknown poets such as Robert Graves, Hart Crane, and Allen Tate. *The Nation* was virtually a Van Doren family publication, with Carl, his first wife Irita, and Mark and his wife all serving in various editorial positions.

Another of Van Doren's professional activities was his participation in a radio program called "Invitation to Learning" from 1940 to 1942. This weekly CBS program consisted of the discussion each week of a great literary work. For a year the panel members were Van Doren, his friend Allen Tate, and Huntington Cairns. Van Doren also spent seven weeks reading Nathaniel Hawthorne's *The Scarlet Letter* (1850) fifteen minutes a day, for a CBS radio broadcast.

In 1953 Van Doren was semiretired from Columbia. He spent most of his time writing and traveling with his wife, the author of numerous books, including a biography of her husband. Six years later, at the age of sixty-five, Van Doren retired completely from college teaching. He continued to write until his death in 1972.

Analysis

Although Mark Van Doren wrote more than one thousand poems, critics have not responded commensurately. Very few critics have seriously treated Van Doren's poetry, although other poets have praised it and almost no one has made unfavorable comments about it. More than one critic has suggested that the volume of the work has discouraged criticism. Since Van Doren wrote many good poems but none which have been singled out for special merit, a comprehensive study of his work would be a lengthy task. Van Doren's subject matter and style also vary so widely that choosing "representative" poems for study is virtually impossible. Finally, and most significantly, his poems can generally be grasped at first reading by any reader; unlike some of his contemporaries, Van Doren did not write poems requiring extensive annotation in order to be understood by the average reader. His poetry is therefore much more accessible than the work of many other modern poets, making the critic's work as interpreter for the most part unnecessary.

Despite the variety of Van Doren's poetry, some common themes do emerge. He frequently wrote about family and friends, love, death, animals, and nature—familiar "poetic" topics treated in a traditional manner. His imagery may be effective but is not startling or brilliant; his diction is precise but not unusual. His love for New England in general and his Connecticut farm in particular has caused critics to compare him with Robert Frost. Van Doren has also been compared with various other poets, from John Dryden to Edwin Arlington Robinson, but, as Allen Tate observed, any traces of other poets are blended to create a unique body of poetry. Taken as a whole, Van Doren's poetry is "like" no one else's. It is highly personal in that it is centered around the events, people, concerns, and literature he knew well.

Some of Van Doren's poetry deals with typically American subjects. "A

Winter Diary," one of his longest poems, is a fictitious verse diary of a winter spent on his Connecticut farm. The poem is written in heroic couplets, the form which Dryden popularized in his poetic dramas. At the beginning of the poem, the speaker explains the reason for its being written: after a "certain winter" had ended, he wanted to record his many memories of it because he felt they were already beginning to fade.

Those memories begin with the end of the summer, when the speaker and his family see their neighbors, who have spent the summer in the country, returning to town. In previous years the speaker has joined in this exodus, but this time he is staying in the country and looking forward to the solitude that fall will bring. The poem records the memories and thoughts of the speaker through the winter to the beginning of spring. The events described in the poem are commonplace—a snowfall, family meals, games—but they are magnified by the joy and the sense of newness that the speaker feels. The winter, with its country solitude, has brought peace to him, and for once the spring represents an unwelcome intrusion. The poem, with its personal, "homey" tone, had much popular appeal and was admired by critics as well.

Another of Van Doren's poems, "The Sage in the Sierra," is also rather typically American. Its subtitle is "Emerson: 1871" and the speaker in the poem is Ralph Waldo Emerson himself. By 1871, Emerson had already written everything he was to write; speaking in the poem, he says that "they," a pronoun which in this poem is neither given nor requires an antecedent, are disappointed; they pity him because he is no longer writing. They want him to write, and they assume that he would if he could. Emerson, however, does not want to be seen or to see himself merely as the hand that holds the pen; from the Sierra and a Concord brook he has learned the power and importance of silence and is for the time being content, like them, simply to exist. In his youth, he says, his mind was a forest and he felt the need to capture every bird in words. Now that he is older, his mind is still a forest but he is content with only watching the birds. Even storms, emotional as well as actual, pass over him with little effect.

He compares the "pure fire" of his present life to the "smoke" of his writing, which has obscured his experiences rather than making them clearer to him. In his writing, he says, he attempted to give the world truth and knowledge. He suggests that his youthful arrogance was greater than his own knowledge at the time, and that having since then experienced what he had previously written about, he no longer feels the need to serve as the world's teacher. The poem ends with the statement that he wishes to be left alone to live his life quietly, for he refuses to help others experience life at the expense of his own. The poem is sensitive in its portrayal of Emerson and imaginative in its argument: Emerson stopped writing by choice, not because of the decline of his abilities. Van Doren uses Emerson as a representative of all creative artists, whom he sees here as sacrificing their own lives for their art and for mankind.

Van Doren uses a more traditional theme in "Now the Sky." This poem is echoed in a section of "A Winter Diary" that uses the same astronomical imagery. The speaker, gazing at the stars on a calm night, asks himself a rather trite question: For how many years have men done what I am doing now? The stars are often seen as a symbol of eternity, since they existed before man and have outlasted centuries of men who have looked at them. The speaker sees the constellations first in these historical terms, but he says that modern man has knowledge that the earlier stargazers did not possess. Man once saw the constellations, he says, as pictures drawn on the sky, but modern man "knows" that this view is incorrect. Man looked upon the stars as a sort of nightly drama, with the characters interacting and heralding the arrival of each new season. The speaker says that the sky was like a room to ancient man, which people entered and left in predictable fashion.

To modern man, however, the constellations hold neither drama nor mystery. Man has tamed the animals and forsaken the heroes of the constellations through his scientific knowledge. He still has a "game" to play, however— the game of pretending that "the board was never lost," that man has kept the civilizing influence of earlier, less scientific ages. In its theme, the poem is more "modern" than much of Van Doren's poetry.

Van Doren's thirty-two sonnets are traditional and Shakespearean in form and similar to Renaissance sonnet sequences in subject matter, particularly to Edmund Spenser's *Amoretti* (1595). The thoughts expressed in the sonnets are neither original nor remarkable, but Van Doren's diction, in its clarity and simplicity, never descends to triteness. Like "A Winter's Diary," these sonnets show Van Doren's interest in traditional poetic forms that other modern poets had largely abandoned.

A complete study of Van Doren's poetry reveals no poetic innovations or surprises; it is the work of a competent poet and careful craftsman. Several critics have accurately applied the term "lucidity" to his work. Even his most complex poems are not obscure, although they were written at a time in which obscurity in poetry often seemed to be considered more of a virtue than a flaw.

The most admirable quality of Van Doren's poetry, says Richard Howard in his foreword to *Good Morning: Last Poems*, is his insistence that each poem be the first poem, as he says in "The First Poem." This insistence probably accounts for the breadth of his poetry, for he approached each new poem as if it possessed not only newness but also primacy, and he regarded the poetry of others in the same manner as he regarded his own. At the same time, he acknowledged his debt to the many English lyric poets who preceded him and whose tradition he helped to continue.

Claire Clements Morton

Other major works

LONG FICTION: *The Transients*, 1935; *Windless Cabins*, 1940; *Tilda*, 1943; *Home with Hazel*, 1957.

SHORT FICTION: *Collected Stories*, 1962-1968.

PLAYS: *The Last Days of Lincoln*, 1959 (produced in 1961); *Three Plays*, 1966 (includes *Never, Never Ask His Name*, produced in 1965).

NONFICTION: *Henry David Thoreau*, 1916 (Master's thesis); *The Poetry of John Dryden*, 1920 (dissertation); *Shakespeare*, 1939; *Private Reader*, 1942; *Liberal Education*, 1942; *Noble Voice*, 1946; *The Autobiography of Mark Van Doren*, 1958; *The Professor and I*, 1958; *The Essays of Mark Van Doren*, 1980.

CHILDREN'S LITERATURE: *Dick and Tom: Tales of Two Ponies*, 1931; *Dick and Tom in Town*, 1932; *The Transparent Tree*, 1940.

Bibliography

Claire, William, ed. *The Essays of Mark Van Doren, 1942-1972*. Westport, Conn.: Greenwood Press, 1980. Although the emphasis here is on Van Doren's work as a critic, the introduction by Claire provides useful information on Van Doren's poetry and prose, discussing his early influences and development as a writer. Notes that Van Doren's critical approach was consistent with his position as a poet, namely that a poet "made statements and gave opinions as a professional on the theory that a civilized audience existed to hear them."

Hendrick, George, ed. *The Selected Letters of Mark Van Doren*. Baton Rouge: Louisiana State University Press, 1987. These letters, arranged chronologically, give insight into the literary and cultural world in which Van Doren lived. The introduction, although brief, provides some useful details about his poetry, such as his early influences and what other writers and critics thought of him.

Quartermain, Peter, ed. *American Poets, 1880-1945*. Vol. 45 in *Dictionary of Literary Biography*. Detroit: Gale Research, 1986. The entry on Van Doren is useful to the beginning reader, with its biographical sketch and listing of published works. The critical commentary mentions his more spiritual orientation in the later poems, such as *Morning Worship* and *Good Morning: Last Poems*.

Southworth, James G. *More Modern American Poets*. Freeport, N.Y.: Books for Libraries Press, 1954. An interesting, in-depth critique of Van Doren that is sympathetic to his earlier works—citing him as a poet of "keen perception and sensitivity"—but that says he falls short in his later works. Southworth says, simply, that Van Doren writes too much and recommends that the poet look beyond "structural form to that of significant form."

Young, Marguerite. "Mark Van Doren: A Poet in an Age of Defoliation." *Voyages*, Winter, 1970, 60-62. Young explores the shadow quality in Van

Doren's poems, citing "Like Son" ("the people are intangible"), "Uncle Roger" (the poet tells of the *memory* of a train), and "Old Whitey" (a horse with noiseless hooves). Discusses Van Doren's use of imagery, particularly his ability to elevate images into a state of divinity. A thoughtful review, complex in its explanation of the deeper reaches of Van Doren's work.

MONA VAN DUYN

Born: Waterloo, Iowa; May 9, 1921

Principal poetry

Valentines to the Wide World, 1959; *A Time of Bees*, 1964; *To See, To Take*, 1970; *Bedtime Stories*, 1972; *Merciful Disguises*, 1973; *Letters from a Father and Other Poems*, 1982; *Near Changes: Poems*, 1990.

Other literary forms

Two short stories by Mona Van Duyn were published in *The Kenyon Review* in the 1940's. She has published reviews and criticism in *College English*, *American Prefaces*, and many literary magazines.

Achievements

One of the few poets today who succeed in incorporating a contemporary sensibility within tight and traditional forms, Van Duyn did not receive appropriate recognition until she won the Bollingen Prize in 1969-1970 and her book *To See, To Take* received the National Book Award in 1971. She had, however, won several prizes previous to those—the Eunice Tietjens Award, the Harriet Monroe Award from *Poetry*, the Helen Bullis Award from *Poetry Northwest*, the Hart Crane Memorial Award from American Weave Press, and first prize in the Borestone Mountain Awards Volume of 1968. She was one of the first five American poets to be awarded a grant from the National Endowment for the Arts. In 1972-1973 she held a Guggenheim Fellowship. The Loines Prize from the National Institute of Arts and Letters was given to her in 1976, and in 1980 she received the ten-thousand-dollar Fellowship of the Academy of American Poets. Both Cornell College and Washington University, where she taught for many years, have awarded her honorary doctorates.

Although she is not a prolific writer, she has always been known and admired by her peers. Her poems have been highly praised by poet-critics as diverse as Carolyn Kizer, Richard Howard, and James Dickey. The critic David Kalstone spoke of her work as manifesting "a whole life *grasped*, in the most urgent and rewarding sense of the word." The domestic world, as tightly enclosed as her chosen forms, is the most frequent source of her poetic content. She has said, "I find my richest hunting ground for poems in that place where the undomesticated feelings, snapping and snarling, run round the domestic ring." Her achievement is that she makes the most of this material, shining so bright a light on subdued and quotidian events that their poignant and lasting aspects are revealed. She achieves her effects by hard work, revising each poem extensively. "What I try to do," she has stated, "is move readers' minds and feelings simultaneously with a structure which is intense and formal. If beauty means integrity, then a poem should be beautiful."

Biography

Born in Waterloo, Iowa, in 1921, Mona Van Duyn began her career by being class poet in the first grade in Eldora, Iowa, where her father ran a service station, a cigar store, and a soda fountain. She wrote poems throughout childhood and adolescence, then studied writing at Iowa State Teachers College and the State University of Iowa. She met her husband, Jarvis Thurston, now Professor of English at Washington University, while they were students. They were married on August 31, 1943.

In 1947, they founded and became coeditors of the magazine *Perspective, a Quarterly of Literature*, in whose pages were introduced such poets as W. S. Merwin and W. D. Snodgrass and other writers of stature. Van Duyn was instructor in English at the State University of Iowa in 1945, and at the University of Louisville from 1946 to 1950. From 1950 to 1967 she was lecturer in English at Washington University, St. Louis, and has since taught at the Salzburg Seminar in American Studies, at Bread Loaf, and at various other writers' workshops throughout the United States. Her first collection, *Valentines to the Wide World*, came out in 1959 in a fine art edition from Cummington Press, illustrated with prints by Fred Becker. Her next collection, *A Time of Bees*, was published by he University of North Carolina in its paperback series in 1964. Atheneum published *To See, To Take* in 1970, *Merciful Disguises*—her collected poems although not designated as such—in 1973, and *Letters from a Father and Other Poems* in 1982. In 1950 Van Duyn and her husband settled in St. Louis, where they have formed the nucleus of a strong literary community including the poets Donald Finkel, Constance Urdang, and Howard Nemerov, and the novelists William Gass and Stanley Elkin.

Analysis

In an epigraph to one of her poems, Mona Van Duyn cites Norman O. Brown: "Freud says that ideas are libidinal cathexes, that is to say, acts of love." For Van Duyn also, ideas are acts of love. Hers is a poetry shaped around the impact of ideas on one who is in love with them. To write poetry is, for her, to engage in an act of love. To write poetry is to make real the world which, although it exists externally, becomes known only when the mind's projections play over it. The life from which she writes is the life of the mind; there are few overtly dramatic events in her poetry. Her mind is excited by language—hence the frequent literary references in her poems—but it is also excited by what is not-mind, everyday accidental happenings, intense emotions, whatever is irrational, recalcitrant, and unyielding to intellectual analysis or explanation. Her poems burst out of the tension between these polarities, the poem itself—often self-reflexive—being the only method she can find to maintain truth and sanity.

A kind of poetic manifesto appears in an early poem, the second "Valentines to the Wide World" in the volume of that title, in which Van Duyn describes her dislike of panoramic scenes because they are too abstract; the vast view of nature provides only a useless exhilaration. She finds "the poem" more useful because its pressure breaks through the surface of experience and because it is specific. "It starts with the creature/ and stays there." This "pressure of speech," even if it is painful or akin to madness, is still what makes her appreciate her life, feeling that to spend it "on such old premises is a privilege." In the third "valentine" she sees the beauty of the world as "merciless and intemperate," as a "rage" which one must temper with "love and art, which are compassionate."

Compassion is an outstanding characteristic of Van Duyn's poetry, both as motive and expression, and yet it is manifested through a wrestling with intellectual questions and an urge to apply her knowledge. Van Duyn's long lines are particularly suitable for expressing discursive thought. Love and beauty are traditional themes of Romantic poets, but in Van Duyn they are united with an affinity for the forms and emphases of literary classicism reminiscent of the eighteenth century, with its bent toward philosophizing in poetry and its allegiance to strict and rhyming forms, especially the heroic couplet.

A classic philosophical problem therefore arises for Van Duyn in her early poems—the split between mind and body. In "From Yellow Lake: An Interval," she expresses discontent with her body as an impediment to overcoming the separateness she feels. The language of the poem has theological undertones: the beetles are "black as our disgrace," a reference to human sin and evil. Crows flying overhead become her dark thoughts, feeding upon "my mind, dear carrion." The poet sees each creature as an analogue of something human—the turtle is "flat as our fate" and the pike's "fierce faith" hooks him fatally on the fisherman's lure. Having a modern mind, the poet cannot find any theological answer to her questioning of the meaning of the creation that painfully yet beautifully surrounds her. The poem supplies the only resolution: summer has warmed her but she must go back to "the wintry work of living," that is, the life of the mind of an ordinary human being, and "conspire in the nailing, brutal and indoors,/ that pounds to the poem's shape a summer's metaphors." The notion of original sin has here been given a new twist: the animal body is "innocent," a parable or metaphor, a natural "given," and the summer is the warmth of love, whereas the mind is that which creates separation, which construes evil and perversely invents the forms of pain. The mind, even if separated from the natural world, is still the only thing she has to work with. Only the poem—actually the process of making a work of art—

can heal the split between mind and body, winter and summer, pain and love, by creating reality through metaphor.

In Part I of "To My Godson, on His Christening," Van Duyn continues in a mildly theological context to ponder her awareness of human imperfection (the classical definition of original sin) which not even the poet's artistic effort can completely escape. Here "metaphors" are in effect charitable deeds, "beautiful doors" out of the walled-up room of existence that is everyone's fated life. In Part II, a lexicon is the poet's gift to the baby, to help him learn words, since his world will not come into existence until he can name it—that is, use language, the way God made the world by speaking the Word, the *Logos*. This remnant of Christian thought fades into the background as, in Part III, the poet's mind concentrates on the uniqueness and transitoriness of each individual and of the species. This recognition nevertheless provides a "feast of awareness" and pleasure in the new life that is the positive aspect of the transitory; the reader is reminded that both dying and being born continue constantly. Being born means coming into a world of pain, but also into a circle of other people who, like the poet, will oversee the child and care for him. This caring, whether religiously motivated or not, reveals the charity and generosity that is Van Duyn's most characteristic and attractive attitude throughout her work.

Charity, of course, is a synonym for compassionate love, and love in Van Duyn is a reiterated word and theme. The word "love" appears in all but three of the poems in *A Time of Bees*, the collection that followed *Valentines to the Wide World*. She does not abandon the theme of poetry, but here unites it with the theme of love in the long poem, "An Essay on Criticism," a tour de force in couplets that echoes Alexander Pope's eighteenth century poem of the same title and also explores the aesthetics of its day, leavening this subject matter with contemporary sensibility, idiom, and wit.

In the frame of this poem, the poet, about to open and cook a package of dehydrated onion soup, is interrupted by the arrival of a friend, a young girl who has fallen in love and has discovered "how love is like a poem." In the dialogue that follows, many famous critical theories of poetry are cited and explored. The girl in love speaks first. She clutches the poet's arm "like the Mariner," an allusion to Samuel Taylor Coleridge's *The Rime of the Ancient Mariner* (1798) which the poet employs to join an intense, even obsessed, Romantic view of poetry in one embrace with the classic love of intellect and rationality.

After the girl leaves, the poet continues to talk to herself as if gripping "a theoretical Wedding Guest"—Coleridge again—and to grapple inwardly and intellectually with various aspects of the interaction between life and art. She takes the side of the poem, "for I believe in art's process of working through otherness to recognition/ and in its power that comes from acceptance, and not imposition." At this point she finds tears falling into her onion soup, but onions did not cause them; the thought of love did. The poem has to be completed in a human reader's heart. In the complex punning of the last line—tears as "essay" (attempt)—life is asserted to be victorious over art, but poem-making is plainly what maintains their intricate and fruitful balance.

In Van Duyn's next volume, *To See, To Take*, published in 1970, she endeavored to step away from autobiographical reference and to elucidate her concerns by adopting the technique of the persona. In "Eros to Howard Nemerov," for example, she speaks through the traditional personification of love, the Greek god, who is addressing the representative modern American poet with a humorous eye turned on the posturings and vagaries of hippie love in the 1960's. Van Duyn's observant eye and sense of humor lead her directly to satire in "Billings and Cooings from 'The Berkeley Barb,'" a satire still *à propos* now that "personal" want ads have become institutionalized. Many Van Duyn poems begin with newspaper quotations as epigraphs, a method she uses to initiate subtle and accurate political and social commentary; by this device she avoids obvious or propagandistic rhetoric that often mars overtly "political" poetry.

Van Duyn cannot be said to be entirely apolitical, but her focus is always personal. Personal love, individual consciousness of passing time is what she stresses. The theme of the passage of time emerges particularly in this volume in two memorial poems, "The Creation" and "A Day in Late October." In "The Creation" Van Duyn mourns a friend's death; as art is a metaphor for life, she sees the friend's life as having been taken away as a pencil drawing is erased. "A Day in Late October," written after the death of Randall Jarrell, asserts the primacy of death, life's inseparable companion, over art—the art of poetry—by means of an extraordinary divagation for this poet: she breaks out of the poetic form altogether and falls back on prose, which is a kind of death of poetry, to express "what cannot be imagined: your death, my death." Death and the passing of time cannot fail to reinvoke a sense of the preciousness of love; the word "love" is repeated as often in this collection as in the previous one.

Despite her adoption of the persona to avoid excessive "personality," two fine poems in this volume spring from autobiography, a mode in which she has both sharpened her technical skills and widened her attitude of appreciation. "Postcards from Cape Split" show her gift for straightforward description of the natural world. The facts of the place where she is vacationing in Maine carry their own intrinsic symbolic weight, so simply stating them is enough. The central motif of "Postcards from Cape Split" is abundance—unearned richness exemplified by hillsides covered with heliotrope, the sea surrounding the house whose interior mirrors the sea, a plethora of villages and shops, generous neighbors, flourishing vegetable gardens. The poet is dazzled and appreciative: "The world blooms and we all bend and bring/ from ground and sea and mind its handsome harvests." The mind remains a primary locus, but the emphasis here is on contentment and gratitude; the world's unasked for generosity is indispensable.

The second autobiographical poem, "Remedies, Maladies, Reasons" strikes quite a different note, although its power also stems from a straightforward statement of facts—the facts of Van Duyn's childhood. It is a record of her mother's acts and speeches that imposed on the child a view of herself as weak, ill, and in danger of dying. The record is brutal and nauseating; it continues in the mother's letters describing her own symptoms simply quoted in her own words, so overwhelming a body-hatred and self-hatred that it is miraculous that the poet survived it. The word "remedies" in the title has a heavily ironic ring, but by the time the poem ends, it has taken another turn of meaning: implicitly the act of making a poem from these horrors relieves them. It provides a remedy by evoking the sight of her mother as an attractive woman and as the mother the child wanted, who came in the night when called and defended the child against her felt enemy, sickness. The poem's last line—"Do you think I don't know how love hallucinates?"—constructs a complex balance, reasserting that love still exists but has maintained itself internally by a costly distortion of external fact. Without overtly referring to poetry as an aid, this poem is a remarkable testimony to the capacity of shaped language to restore a sane perspective and to enable one's mind to open to revision of memory, an act of love that is analogous to revision of the language of a poem.

If vision and revision are the loving acts which give rise to the making of a poem, the poem itself is the "merciful disguise of metaphor" which masks the horror and brutality of the world, making it possible for humans to live with its limitations. The most stringent and widespread personal limitation that love undertakes culturally is marriage. Marriage is to love what the heroic couplet is to poetry. Van Duyn has chosen—or has found herself unable to escape from—both rigors. In her first volume she explored marriage as "the politics of love" in the wryly witty, rather lighthearted poem "Toward a Definition of Marriage." At the end of her third book appears the tough-minded, occasionally viciously clear-eyed poem "Marriage, with Beasts" in which one feels that the imagery of animals in a zoo, Swiftian in its satiric accuracy, hardly qualifies as "merciful disguise." It is pitiless exposé.

Marital combat is elevated to a cosmic mythic vision of antagonistic masculine and feminine principles in the previously unpublished poem "A View" in the last section of *Merciful Disguises*. The "you" and the "I" of the poem are driving through Colorado. The mountain with its "evergreen masculinity" is obliviously and continuously ascendant over the depleted "mined-out" female earth. The ending is covertly linked with marriage: the "you," the car's driver, male by cultural definition as well as presumably in fact, asks the "I" how she is, and she says that she is "admiring the scenery, and am O.K."

The "view" of the title is a pun indicating "opinion" as well as landscape; it is the closest that Van Duyn's poetry—always centered on a woman's consciousness—comes to embodying a feminist perspective as it presents a seemingly unbridgeable gap between the man's state of well-being and the woman's unending state of struggle and exhaustion.

By the time of the publication of *Letters from a Father and Other Poems* in 1982, the poet is far better than merely self-deprecatingly "O.K." The complexity of her relationship with her parents resolved itself in the gentleness and forgiveness that came with their deaths in 1980 within three months of each other. The title poem, "Letters from a Father," is a foreshadowing of those deaths as well as a revival and revision of the poet's childhood memories. This poem's power comes from its almost verbatim quotation of her father's words, a technique that verifies the poet's loving ability to give herself and her art wholly to someone else. She thereby redeems both the sad intractable fact of death and also the self-entangled contemporary language of poetry, which badly needs a reminder that it must have reference to something outside itself.

In the poem "The Stream," about the death of her mother, the poet returns to her original and perennial concern, love, and, in an extended metaphor, sees love as a narrow stream running below ground, held down, unseen, but finally finding its way up until it is visible. This vision of the stream of love also suggests the stream of time flowing toward death, a flow echoed by the long flowing line whose form—the couplet with slant end-rhyme, Van Duyn's favorite—seems to constitute the same sort of facilitating obstacle that the rock and earth present to the underground stream of water. That water rises higher in a narrow tube is a physical fact; thus love rises under "the dense pressure of thwarted needs, the replay/ of old misreadings." Her mother's death has brought the stream of love to light, revealing to her "the welling water—to which I add these tears."

The tears and the poem, as in the earlier but different context of "An Essay on Criticism," join in felicitous confluence. The stringent form, when one gives in to it, is what produces genuine depth and maturation in life as well as in art. Van Duyn's development as a poet has been steady and straightforward, even relentlessly undeviating, without sudden switches of style or experimental or uncertain phases. She has never gone back on her commitment to work with tight forms, to deal with the world's pain, and to remain in love with the world despite its worst. Her poem "Since You Asked Me . . ." answers the question which must have been put to her a number of times: Why do you use rhyme and measure, since these are so old-fashioned and out of date? She says that she uses rhyme "to say I love you to language" and to combat the current linguistic sloppiness of "'y'know?' and 'Wow!'" She uses measure because it is "not just style but lifestyle."

Her manifesto is also a call to arms: she urges other poets to have "an almost religious/ regard for un-with-it truth." While love has always been her concern, as with the Romantic poets, she never neglects the classicist's need to take moral responsibility for the world, a responsibility that is not only compatible with art and creativity but also the whole motive for the artist's undertaking. The medium, rhyme, is "a challenge to chaos *hurled./* Why use it? Why, simply/ to save the world." That commitment—to save the world—is the fullest anyone can make. Mona Van Duyn's pledge to that goal has made her one of the most distinguished and accomplished contemporary poets, honored and honorable.

Jane Augustine

Bibliography
Augustine, Jane. "Mona Van Duyn." In *Contemporary Poets*, edited by James Vinson and D. L. Kirkpatrick. 4th ed. New York: St. Martin's Press, 1985. Augustine provides a short but glowing analysis of Van Duyn's poetry. She calls Van Duyn an "excellent poet" whose work deserves "to find a larger audience." Includes a primary bibliography. A good introduction.
Grim, Jessica. Review of *Near Changes: Poems*, by Mona Van Duyn. *Library Journal* 115 (March 15, 1990): 94. Grim calls Van Duyn's collection "reflective in a refreshingly straightforward way." Grim affirms that Van Duyn continues to address domestic themes, from the deep love developed through a long marriage to a trip to the grocery store.
Jones, Debra G. "Mona Van Duyn." In *Contemporary Authors*, edited by Deborah A. Straub. Vol 7. New Revision series. Detroit: Gale Research, 1982. Contains a short resumé of Van Duyn's career, as well as the author's analysis of her work. Jones states that Van Duyn writes about life, love, and marriage, and that she feels that art and love justify the pain of life. The article also contains a 1981 interview by Jean W. Ross.
Ludvigson, Susan. "Mona Van Duyn." In *American Poets Since World War 2*, edited by Donald J. Greiner. Vol. 5 in *Dictionary of Literary Biography*. Detroit: Gale Research, 1980. Ludvigson offers a short biography of Van Duyn and an analysis of her major poems. The author praises Van Duyn, saying that her poems mix domestic situations with unusual and sophisticated insights. A wonderful introduction to the poet.
Moss, Howard. *The Poet's Story.* New York: Macmillan, 1973. Moss collects the short stories of twenty writers who are much better known for their poetry. In this collection, Moss includes Van Duyn's short story "The Bell." Interesting, for it demonstrates Van Duyn's versatility as a writer.

HENRY VAUGHAN

Born: Newton-on-Usk, Wales; April 17, 1622
Died: Llansantffraed, Wales; April 23, 1695

Principal poetry

Poems, 1646; *Silex Scintillans,* Parts I and II, 1650, 1655; *Olor Iscanus,* 1651; *Thalia Rediviva,* 1678; *The Secular Poems of Henry Vaughan,* 1958 (E. L. Marilla, editor); *The Complete Poetry of Henry Vaughan,* 1964 (French Fogle, editor).

Other literary forms

Henry Vaughan, whose religious poetry reflects the influence of John Donne and George Herbert, published translations of several religious and medical treatises.

Achievements

Vaughan is usually grouped with the "Metaphysical" poets, anthologized particularly with John Donne, George Herbert, Richard Crashaw, and Andrew Marvell. While there is some justification for this association, in Vaughan's instance it has resulted in a somewhat too-narrow estimation of his work and its historical context. In the "Metaphysical" collections, to be sure, Vaughan has been represented by some of his best poems, such as "Regeneration," "The World," or "Affliction," drawn from *Silex Scintillans.* These works, however, have often been grouped in contrast with the lyrics from Herbert's *The Temple* (1633). Invariably Vaughan has been admired only as a lesser foil to his great predecessor; while admittedly Vaughan had his great moments, he lacked the sustained intensity of Herbert. Moreover, Vaughan's gracious preface to the 1655 edition of *Silex Scintillans* shows much regard for the creator of *The Temple.* Given such authority, it is not surprising that Vaughan's modern reputation, emerging in the "Metaphysical" revival of the twentieth century, has been overshadowed by the accomplishments of George Herbert.

Fortunately, recent scholarship has begun to redress the imbalances concerning Vaughan with thorough study of his work and his milieu. By his own admission, Vaughan lived "when religious controversy had split the English people into factions: I lived among the furious conflicts of Church and State" ("Ad Posteros" in *Olor Iscanus*). His was the time that saw a people indict, condemn, and execute its monarch in the name of religious fervor and political expedience. His was the time that saw the final vestiges of ancient families' power supplanted by parliamentary prerogatives of a potent middle class. Vaughan defined his place outside the struggle in order to take part in it as conservator of the Anglican-Royalist cause, a defender of the British Church in poetry and prose tied closely to the attitudes and values of pagan and Christian pastoral literature. Moreover, in his own Welsh countryside and lineage, Vaughan found the touchstone for his conservatorship, an analogue of the self-imposed exiles of early Church fathers who took refuge from the conflicts and hazards of the world.

Biography

Henry Vaughan was one of twins born to Thomas and Denise Vaughan in 1622, ten years after a union that brought the elder Vaughan into possession of house and lands at Trenewydd (Newton-on-Usk). The father of the poet apparently had no calling except that of a gentleman, and in later life he seems to have been fond of suing and being sued by his relatives. The Vaughan family had resided in the Brecknock region of Wales for generations and traced their line back to David ap Llwellen, known as "Davey Gam," who was knighted and slain at the Battle of Agincourt in 1415. The poet's twin, also named Thomas, obtained a greater measure of fame in his own lifetime than Henry did. He was a philosopher of the occult sciences who at one point engaged in a pamphlet war with the noted Cambridge Platonist writer, Henry More. He settled near Oxford and died in 1666. Contemporary scholars have suggested that the elaborate pastoral eclogue, *Daphnis*, appearing in *Thalia Rediviva*, was the poet's farewell to his twin.

As befit the heirs of a minor country gentleman, the twins began their formal studies about 1632 with the Rector of Llangatock, Matthew Herbert, continuing until 1638. The poet recalls that Herbert, "Though one man . . . gave me double treasure: learning and love." Following this tutelage, the twins were sent off to Jesus College, Oxford. They were seventeen; they had grown up steeped in Welsh language and culture. While the record of Thomas Vaughan's matriculation at Jesus College survives, no similar record exists for the poet. He apparently remained in Oxford until 1640, when he set forth to London with the intention of studying law. Shortly after his arrival, the King's favorite, the Earl of Stafford, and Archbishop Laud were indicted. Stafford was executed by a reluctant monarch in the following May. Perhaps at this time Vaughan began translating Juvenal's tenth satire on the vanity of human wishes. While at London, Vaughan began his poetic "apprenticeship," steeping himself in the writings of Ben Jonson and his Cavalier followers such as Thomas Randolph. These efforts were published in the *Poems* of 1646. One imagines the young Henry Vaughan's brief tenure in London as preparation for a respectable civic life, perhaps dividing his time between the city and the Welsh countryside. It was not to be.

In the summer of 1642, the first Civil War erupted; Henry Vaughan hastened to Wales. There he accepted the post of secretary to the Chief Justice of the Great Sessions, Sir Marmaduke Lloyd, probably retaining it until 1645. At the same time, Vaughan courted Catherine Wise, the daughter of a Warwickshire family. The "Amoret" poems in the 1646 volume were probably written and arranged in honor of his courtship and subsequent marriage to her. With the outbreak of the second Civil War, Vaughan left the service of the law to join the Royalist army.

The appearance of the first part of *Silex Scintillans* in 1650, arguably the finest volume of poetry published by anyone in the years of the Interregnum, was unspectacular. Not until 1655, when he added additional poems and a revealing preface, did Henry Vaughan provide posterity with the ill-conceived notion of his religious "conversion." Of all the facts concerning Henry Vaughan's life, no nonevent is as important as the "conversion." It was invented in the nineteenth century by the Reverend H. F. Lyte, who edited the first publication of Vaughan's work since the poet's lifetime. Lyte took remarks in the 1655 Preface concerning Vaughan's illness as a metaphor for a spiritual malaise cured by a heavy dose of Protestant piety. As a result of Lyte's homily, Vaughan's secular poetry suffered absolute neglect until the mid-twentieth century. *Silex Scintillans* was considered artistic proof of a conversion because it is Vaughan's best, most sustained work. A more accurate reading of what happened to Henry Vaughan was that he matured, as a man and as an artist. He found his unique voice in the urgency of the moment, in the defeat of his religious and political party, in the example of Herbert's poetry, in the pastoralism of passages in the Bible, in the whole tradition of finding the virtuous life in rural surroundings.

One senses, throughout his mature work, Vaughan's urgent defense of the values of simplicity and rural piety tempered from within by resolve. Vaughan included translations of Boethius and Casimir Sarbiewski in *Olor Iscanus*. They offer a pattern of stoic acceptance of this world's reversals by seeking virtue in retirement. Retirement, as Vaughan sees it, is not passive, however. It is a conscious choice. Thus, his allusions to illness in his Preface to *Silex Scintillans* must be regarded within the larger context of his discovery of Herbert's poems and his condemnation of trifling, uncommitted poetry. Vaughan was always an Anglican and a Royalist. He did not convert: he simply found his way to fight back. From the remove of the country, Vaughan discovered a role for himself in a strife-torn society more potent than that of soldier or solicitor: as a poetic defender of God and king.

No doubt other events contributed to Vaughan's recognition of his poetic mission, including the death of a younger brother, William, in 1648, and of his first wife Catherine five years later. He married her sister Elizabeth in 1655, the same year that a translation of Henry Nollius' *Hermetical Physick* appeared. By then Vaughan had elected medicine as a new career. That he continued to write verse is evidenced by the dates of poems in Vaughan's final collection, *Thalia Rediviva*. Thalia is the Muse of pastoral poetry. Vaughan continued to see himself in terms of the rural tradition of poetry because he found there a synthesis of images, metaphors, and implied or explicit values that harmonized with his religious and political beliefs. He continued to practice medicine, according to one contemporary account, as late as autumn, 1694. When he died the following spring, he was buried overlooking the countryside he so long celebrated, in the churchyard of the faith he so vehemently defended, his stone reciting his link to the Silures, the ancient Welsh tribe from which he took his epithet, "The Silurist," by which he was often known.

Analysis

Henry Vaughan's first collection, *Poems*, is very derivative; in it can be found borrowings from Donne, Jonson, William Habington, William Cartwright, and others. It contains only thirteen poems in addition to the translation of Juvenal. Seven poems are written to Amoret, believed to idealize the poet's courtship of Catherine Wise, ranging from standard situations of thwarted and indifferent love to this sanguine couplet in "To Amoret Weeping": "Yet whilst Content, and Love we joyntly vye,/ We have a blessing which no gold can buye." Perhaps in "Upon the Priorie Grove, His Usuall Retirement," Vaughan best captures the promise of love accepted and courtship rewarded even by eternal love:

> So there again, thou 'lt see us move
> In our first Innocence, and Love:
> And in thy shades, as now, so then
> Wee'le kisse, and smile, and walke again.

The lines move with the easy assurance of one who has studied the verses of the urbane Tribe of Ben. That other favorite sport of the Tribe—after wooing—was drink, and in "*A Rhapsodie*, Occasionally written upon a meeting with some friends at the Globe Taverne, . . ." one sees the poet best known for his devout poems celebrating with youthful fervor all the pleasures of the grape and rendering a graphic slice of London street life. Though imitative, this little volume possesses its own charm. Perhaps it points to the urbane legal career that Vaughan might have pursued had not the conflicts of church and state driven him elsewhere.

The poet of *Olor Iscanus* is a different man, one who has returned from the city to the country, one who has seen the face of war and defeat. Nowhere in his writing does Vaughan reject the materials of his poetic apprenticeship in London: he favors, even in his religious lyrics, smooth and graceful couplets where they are appropriate. This volume contains various occasional poems and elegies expressing Vaughan's disgust with the defeat of the Royalists by Cromwell's armies and the new order of Puritan piety. The leading poem, "To the River *Isca*," ends with a plea for freedom and safety, the river's banks "redeem'd from all disorders!" The real current pulling this river—underscoring the quality of *Olor Iscanus* which prompted its author to delay publication—is a growing resolve to sustain one's friends and one's sanity by choosing rural simplicity. The idea of this country fortitude is expressed in many ways. For example, the Cavalier invitation poem, "To my worthy friend, *Master T. Lewes*," opens with an evocation of nature "Opprest with snow," its rivers "All bound up in an *Icie Coat.*" The speaker in the poem asks his friend to pass the harsh time away and, like nature itself, preserve the old pattern for reorder:

> Let us meet then! and while this world
> In wild *Excentricks* now is hurld,
> Keep wee, like nature, the same *Key*,
> And walk in our forefathers way.

In the elegy for Lady Elizabeth, daughter of the late Charles I, Vaughan offers this metaphor: "Thou seem'st a Rose-bud born in *Snow*,/ A flowre of purpose sprung to bow/ To headless tempests, and the rage/ Of an Incensed, stormie Age." Then, too, in *Olor Iscanus*, Vaughan includes his own translations from Boethius' *The Consolation of Philosophy* (523) and the Horatian Odes of the seventeenth century Polish writer Casimir Sarbiewski. In these, the "country shades" are the seat of refuge in an uncertain world, the residence of virtue, and the best route to blessedness. Moreover, affixed to the volume are three prose adaptations and translations by Vaughan: *Of the Benefit Wee may get by our Enemies*, after Plutarch; *Of the Diseases of the Mind and the Body*, after Maximum Tirius; and *The Praise and Happiness of the Countrie-Life*, after Antonio de Guevera. In this last, Vaughan renders one passage: "*Pietie and Religion* may be better Cherish'd and preserved in the Country than any where else."

The themes of humility, patience, and Christian stoicism abound in *Olor Iscanus* in many ways, frequently enveloped in singular works praising life in the country. The literary landscape of pastoral melds with Vaughan's Welsh countryside. For Vaughan the enforced move back to the country ultimately became a boon; his retirement from a "world gone mad" (his words) was no capitulation, but a pattern for endurance. It would especially preserve and sustain the Anglican faith that two civil wars had challenged. In Vaughan's greatest work, *Silex Scintillans*, the choices that Vaughan made for himself are expressed, defended, and celebrated in varied, often brilliant ways.

New readers of *Silex Scintillans* ("The Flashing Flint") owe it to themselves and to Vaughan to consider it a "whole book" containing engaging individual lyrics; in this way its thematic, emotional, and Imagistic patterns and cross references will become apparent. The first part contains seventy-seven lyrics; it was entered in the Stationers' Register on March 28, 1650, and includes the anonymous engraving dramatizing the title. Fifty-seven lyrics were added for the 1655 edition, including a preface. The first part appears to be the more intense, many of the poems finding Vaughan reconstructing the moment of spiritual illumination. The second part finds Vaughan extending the implications of the first. Above all, though, the whole of *Silex Scintillans* promotes the active life of the spirit, the contemplative life of natural, rural solitude.

Some of the primary characteristics of Vaughan's poetry are prominently displayed in *Silex Scintillans*. First, there is the influence of the Welsh language and Welsh verse. Welsh is highly assonant; consider these lines from the opening poem, "Regeneration": "Yet *it* was frost w*i*th*in*/ And surly w*i*nds/ Blasted my *i*nfant buds, and s*i*nne/ L*i*ke clouds eccl*i*ps'd my m*i*nd." The *dyfalu*, or layering of comparison upon comparison, is a technique of Welsh verse which Vaughan brings to his English verse. A second characteristic is Vaughan's use of Scripture. For example, the idea of spiritual espousal which informs the Song of Solomon is brought forward to the poet's own time and place. "Hark! how his *winds* have chang'd their *note*,/ And with warm *whispers call* thee out" ("The Revival") recalls the Song of Solomon 2:11-12. In "The Dawning" Vaughan imagines the last day of mankind and incorporates the language of the biblical Last Judgment into the cycle of a natural day. Will man's judge come at night, asks the poet, or "shal these early, fragrant hours/ Unlock thy bowres? . . ./ That with thy glory doth best chime,/ All now are stirring, ev'ry field/ Ful hymns doth yield."

Vaughan adapts and extends scriptural symbols and situations to his own particular spiritual crisis and resolution less doctrinally than poetically. In this practice, Vaughan follows Herbert, surely another important influence, especially in *Silex Scintillans*. Nearly sixty poems use a word or phrase important to *The Temple*; some borrowings are direct responses, as in the concluding lines of "The Proffer," recalling Herbert's "The Size." Sometimes the response is direct; Vaughan's "The Match" responds to Herbert's "The Proffer." Herbert provided Vaughan with an example of what the best poetry does, both instructing the reader and communicating one's own particular vision. This is Vaughan's greatest debt to Herbert, and it prompts his praise for the author of *The Temple* in the Preface to *Silex Scintillans*. Further, Vaughan emulates Herbert's book of unified lyrics, but the overall structure of *The Temple*—governed by church architecture and by the church calendar—is transformed in Vaughan to The Temple of Nature, with its own rhythms and purposes.

The Temple of Nature, God's "second" book, is alive with divinity. The Welsh have traditionally imagined themselves to be in communication with the elements, with flora and fauna; in Vaughan the tradition is enhanced by Hermetic philosophy, which maintained that the sensible world was made by God to see God in it. The poet no doubt knew the work of his brother Thomas, one of the leading Hermetic voices of the time. Henry Vaughan adapts concepts from Hermeticism (as in the lyric based on Romans 8:19), and also borrows from its vocabulary: beam, balsam, commerce, essence, exhalations, keys, ties, sympathies occur throughout *Silex Scintillans*, lending force to a poetic vision already imbued with natural energy. "Observe God in his works," Vaughan writes in "Rules and Lessons," noting that one cannot miss "his Praise; Each *tree, herb, flowre*/ Are shadows of his wisedome, and his *Pow'r*."

Vaughan is no pre-Romantic nature lover, however, as some early commentators have suggested. Rather, *Silex Scintillans* often relies on metaphors of active husbandry and rural contemplation drawn from the twin streams of pagan and biblical pastoral. Many of the lyrics mourn the loss of simplicity and primitive holiness; others confirm the validity of retirement; still others extend the notion of husbandry to cultivating a paradise within as a means of recovering the lost past. Drawing upon the Cavalier poets' technique of suggesting pastoral values and perspective by including certain details or references to pastoral poems, such as sheep, cots, or cells, Vaughan intensifies and varies these themes. Moreover, he crosses from secular traditions of rural poetry to sacred ones. "The Shepheards"—a nativity poem—is one fine example of Vaughan's ability to conflate biblical pastoralism asserting the birth of Christ with "literary" conventions regarding shepherds.

Several poems illuminating these important themes in *Silex Scintillans* are "Religion," "The Brittish Church," "Issac's Marriage," and "The Retreate" (loss of simplicity associated with the primitive church); "Corruption," "Vanity of Spirit," "Misery," "Content," and "Jesus Weeping" (the validity of retirement); "The Resolve," "Love, and Discipline," "The Seed Growing Secretly," "Righteousness," and "Retirement" (cultivating one's own paradise within). These are, of course, not the only lyrics articulating these themes, nor are these themes "keys" to all of the poems of *Silex Scintillans* but Vaughan's treatment of them suggests a reaffirmation of the self-sufficiency celebrated in his secular work and devotional prose. In his finest volume of poems, however, this strategy for prevailing against unfortunate turns of religion and politics rests upon a heartfelt knowledge that even the best human efforts must be tempered by divine love.

Vaughan's last collection of poems, *Thalia Rediviva*, was subtitled "The Pass-times and Diversions of a Countrey-Muse," as if to reiterate his regional link with the Welsh countryside. The John Williams who wrote the dedicatory epistle for the collection was probably Prebendary of Saint David's, who within two years became Archdeacon of Cardigan. He was probably responsible for soliciting the commendatory poems printed at the front of the volume. That Vaughan gave his endorsement to this Restoration issue of new lyrics is borne out by the fact that he takes pains to mention it to his cousin John Aubrey, author of *Brief Lives* (1898) in an autobiographical letter written June 15, 1673. Moreover, when it finally appeared, the poet probably was already planning to republish *Olor Iscanus*. Thus, though his great volume of verse was public reading for more than two decades, Vaughan had not repudiated his other work.

Nor would he have much to apologize for, since many of the finest lyrics in this miscellany are religious, extending pastoral and retirement motifs from *Silex Scintillans*: "Retirement," "The Nativity," "The True Christmas," "The Bee," and "To the pious memorie of C.W. . . . ." Moreover, *Thalia Rediviva* contains numerous topical poems and translations, many presumably written after *Silex Scintillans*. The most elaborate of these pieces is a formal pastoral eclogue, an elegy presumably written to honor the poet's twin, Thomas. It is Vaughan's most overt treatment of literary pastoral; it closes on a note that ties its matter to the diurnal rhythms of the world, but one can recognize in it the spirit of *Silex Scintillans*: "While feral birds send forth unpleasant notes,/ And night (the Nurse of thoughts,) sad thoughts promotes./ But Joy will yet come with the morning-light,/ Though sadly now we bid good night!" Though not moving in the dramatic fashion of *Silex Scintillans* through a reconstruction of the moment and impact of divine illumination, the poems of *Thalia Rediviva* nevertheless offer further confirmation of Henry Vaughan's self-appointed place in the literature of his age.

Kenneth Friedenreich

Other major works

NONFICTION: *Hermetical Physick*, 1655 (translation); *The Chymists Key to Open and to Shut*, 1657 (translation).

MISCELLANEOUS: *The Works of Henry Vaughan*, 1914, 1957 (L. C. Martin, editor).

Bibliography

Calhoun, Thomas O. *Henry Vaughan: The Achievement of "Silex Scintillans."* Newark: University of Delaware Press, 1981. Calhoun claims that *Silex Scintillans* is in the tradition of lyric sequences that originated with Petrarch's *Le Rime*. After outlining that tradition, Calhoun examines the revisions in *Silex Scintillans* in terms of biographical details, historical events, and stylistic concerns. Of particular interest is his discussion of the influence of hermetic medicine. "Regeneration," and "Resurrection and Immortality" receive lengthy analysis.

Durr, R. A. *On the Mystical Poetry of Henry Vaughan.* Cambridge, Mass.: Harvard University Press, 1962. After reviewing standard Vaughan topics— conversion, relationship to George Herbert, childhood motif—Durr identifies three major metaphors in Vaughan's work: the growth of the lily, the dark journey, and the spiritual espousal. Contains exhaustive readings of three poems, "Regeneration," "The Proffer," and "The Night," as well as appendices concerning the "divine spark," the Book of the Creation, and mysticism.

Friedenreich, Kenneth. *Henry Vaughan.* Boston: Twayne, 1978. Friedenreich discusses three characteristics of Vaughan's style—the Welsh language, the Bible, and Hermetic philosophy—and illustrates their impact on Vaughan's work. *Olor Iscanus, Silex Scintillans,* and the major prose receive the bulk of the attention. Includes lengthy analyses of individual poems, a chronology, and a select annotated bibliography.

Garner, Ross. *Henry Vaughan: Experience and the Tradition.* Chicago: University of Chicago Press, 1959. Garner devotes separate chapters to Vaughan's spiritual quest ("Ishmael" becomes Vaughan), Hermeticism, nature poetry (with references to William Wordsworth), and religious poetry. Of particular interest is Garner's discussion of Vaughan's poetry in terms of E. M. W. Tillyard's five characteristics of the Elizabethan Age. Garner's index unfortunately does not include individual poems by Vaughan.

Post, Jonathan F. S. *Henry Vaughan: The Unfolding Vision.* Princeton, N.J.: Princeton University Press, 1982. Post, who divides his emphasis between Vaughan's secular and religious poems, declares the heart of his study is *Silex Scintillans.* Although he covers many of Vaughan's poems, some— among them "The Night" and "Regeneration"—receive lengthy analysis. Contains a general index, as well as an index to Vaughan's poems.

Rudrum, Alan, ed. *Essential Articles for the Study of Henry Vaughan.* Hamden, Conn.: Archon Books, 1987. Rudrum has reprinted twenty-one articles, only two of which are excerpts from books on Vaughan. He provides readers with a ready access to major Vaughan scholars analyzing individual poems such as "The Night" and "Regeneration," as well as discussing Vaughan's subjects such as nature, infancy, Hermeticism, and mysticism.

Simmonds, James D. *Masques of God: Form and Theme in the Poetry of Henry Vaughan.* Pittsburgh: University of Pittsburgh, 1972. Simmonds, unlike most Vaughan critics, stresses Vaughan's secular poetry, which he relates to Ben Jonson's ideas about the well-ordered poem. Both the love poetry and the satires are discussed in depth, and the book concludes with an illuminating treatment of the "bed-grave" image in Vaughan's poetry. Contains a bibliography and appendices concerning Vaughan's illness, the identity of Amoret, and profane literature.

PETER VIERECK

Born: New York, New York; August 5, 1916

Principal poetry

Terror and Decorum: Poems, 1940-1948, 1948; *Strike Through the Mask!*, 1950; *The First Morning*, 1952; *The Persimmon Tree*, 1956; *The Tree Witch: A Poem and a Play (First of All a Poem)*, 1961; *New and Selected Poems*, 1967; *Archer in the Marrow*, 1987.

Other literary forms

Metapolitics: From the Romantics to Hitler (1941) is a criticism of nineteenth century Romanticism, which Peter Viereck argues lies at the base of Nazism. Viereck has also written several volumes defending his variety of political conservatism, including *Conservatism Revisited: The Revolt Against Revolt, 1815-1949* (1949), *Shame and Glory of the Intellectuals* (1953), and *The Unadjusted Man* (1956).

Achievements

Since the 1940's, Viereck has won wide recognition for his poetry, which follows the style he calls Manhattan classicism. His poetry emphasizes form and rhyme and displays remarkably effective wordplay. He places great stress upon morality and uses his verse to defend the humanist values he professes. Critics sometimes accuse him of being overly didactic, but many consider him a major American poet. Viereck has received a Guggenheim Fellowship for his poetry and won the Pulitzer Prize for Poetry in 1949.

Biography

Peter Viereck was born in New York City on August 5, 1916. He achieved remarkable scholastic success in his college years and was graduated from Harvard University summa cum laude in 1937. After attending the University of Oxford on a fellowship, he returned to Harvard, where he received his M.A. and Ph.D. in European history.

Parallel with Viereck's rise in the academic world, a more dramatic story was taking place. Viereck's father, George Sylvester Viereck, was a noted journalist and author whose circle of friends included Sigmund Freud, H. L. Mencken, and Kaiser Wilhelm II. He had temporarily lost popularity during World War I, since his sympathy for Germany put him at odds with the policy of the United States. The decade of the 1920's, however, was characterized by disillusionment with American participation in the war, and Viereck was to a large extent restored to favor.

Adolf Hitler's rise to power in January, 1933, changed the picture once more. It soon became evident that Viereck was not prepared to abandon his sympathy for Germany. He became an apologist for Hitler (indeed a paid agent of the Reich), and almost all of his friends deserted him. During World War II, he was arrested and tried for sedition.

Peter Viereck broke with his father and has rarely mentioned him in his writing. Perhaps as a reaction against the senior Viereck, much of his activity as a historian has concentrated on analyzing the rise of the Nazis to power.

After completing his military service in World War II, Viereck taught at several universities. He soon settled permanently at Mount Holyoke College in Vermont. To Viereck, academic life is not a detached pursuit of knowledge but rather a way of coming to grips with current problems. He developed an unusual variety of conservatism and has written several books explaining and defending it. Although his books have been widely reviewed, few American conservatives count themselves as his followers.

Viereck's reputation rests principally on his work as a poet; collections of his poetry have won for him considerable attention and admiration. Although respected by most critics as a presence in American poetry, he has not been especially influential on other poets.

Analysis

Peter Viereck has been remarkably consistent in adhering to certain principles throughout his career as a poet. Together, these principles make up the "Manhattan classicism" mentioned earlier; understanding them is crucial for anyone who wishes to read him.

Deeply affected by the rise of Nazism and communism in the twentieth century, Viereck has asked one fundamental question throughout his career: how did these nefarious systems arise and maintain themselves? In part the answer lies in the particular historical circumstances of each case. In Viereck's opinion, a deeper and more general cause underlies the events that preoccupy most historians. Romanticism is the culprit; it is Viereck's principal aim in both his poetry and his prose to expose and combat this artistic movement.

His conclusion at once raises a further question: what does Viereck mean by Romanticism? He has chiefly in mind the uncontrolled display of emotion. Romantic artists such as Richard Wagner thought that their superiority to the ordinary run of men entitled them to disregard moral restraint in their work. What counted was that artists express themselves fully, and they need answer to no one but themselves. This approach has had disastrous consequences when extended from art to politics. Viereck rejects the notion that what is true in art can be false in politics and holds that since the ignoring of moral restraint has been disastrous in politics, it must be halted at its artistic source.

Rather than be the expression of the artist's unbridled feelings, a poem should illustrate "humanist values." Viereck does not intend anything controversial by this phrase; he has in mind the ordinary moral virtues. Although interested in religion, he does not require poets to adhere to Christianity or any other creed; he himself is not a believer.

It may appear so far that much fuss has been made over very little. After all, few poets see themselves as Nietzschean immoralists. Yet Viereck does not think it sufficient for poets to accept morality in their lives or even to avoid contradicting its rules in their poetry. He maintains that poets have the duty to defend and explain moral principles in their work. His didactic notion of proper poetry has been rejected by most of his contemporaries, though some poets, most notably Yvor Winters, profess a similar view.

Viereck carried the point one step further. A writer should not only defend correct morality but must also assail those writers who set themselves against its unyielding requirements. To Viereck the main twentieth century example of the betrayal of artistic responsibility has been Ezra Pound. Pound's devotion to the Fascist regime of Benito Mussolini is in Viereck's opinion the logical outcome of his poetic principles. Pound's main work, the voluminous *The Cantos* (1970), advocates a repellent political and ethical position—and this suffices to discredit it as outstanding poetry. So great is Viereck's distaste for Pound that some mention of him surfaces in nearly everything Viereck writes.

The requirements of humanist values extend beyond content. Many twentieth century poets have curtailed or abandoned altogether the use of meter and rhyme. To Viereck this betokens the lack of discipline that is the core of Romanticism. His own poetry is almost always written in standard metrical form and displays to the full his talent for rhyme.

These principles were fully evident in Viereck's first published verse collection, *Terror and Decorum*. The first poem in the book, "Poem," exemplifies Viereck's artistic credo. In part influenced by Charles-Pierre Baudelaire and T. S. Eliot, Viereck views the poet as the guardian of language, with the responsibility to maintain a tight control over language; if this task is not attended to, "lush adverbs" and other uncontrolled parts of speech may get out of hand. True to his own principles, Viereck wrote "Poet" in strict iambic pentameter, his favorite poetic form.

"Poet" displays the tensions and paradoxes of Viereck's position. Although Romanticism is anathema, the exalted view of the poet he professes here is a key doctrine of the great Romantics. Like Percy Bysshe Shelley, to whom poets are the unacknowledged legislators of humankind, Viereck considers the poet to be a monarch. Through poets' control of language, they can dominate the politics of their time. Further, although "Poet" calls for restraint, it itself is characterized by elaborate metaphor and personification.

The reader might so far have the impression that Viereck is a grim Savonarola, incapable of humor. This is decidedly not the case; indeed, one of Viereck's chief weapons in his struggle against disorder is satire. He also indulges in ordinary wit; in one notable instance, he constructs a long poem from the World War II slogan "Kilroy was here."

Although "Kilroy" treats the slogan humorously, it soon becomes apparent that Viereck has a serious message to expound. The anonymous soldier who writes "Kilroy was here" wherever he goes symbolizes the adventurer, and Viereck compares him to Ulysses, Orestes, and, in the poem's climax, God. Kilroy displays the spirit of free individualism that Viereck holds to be the proper human attitude. Unsure of what, if anything, is the ultimate basis of the world and of values, the individual must make his or her own way.

"Kilroy," like "Poet," shows Viereck's love-hate relation with Romanticism. The adventurer is a stock figure of Romanticism, but the supposed anti-Romantic Viereck devotes the poem to praise and advocacy of him. The tension in Viereck's position extends to the poem's style. Viereck defends strict adherence to form, but "Kilroy" is an unusual mix of genres. It begins as a humorous poem but shifts to a serious expression of Viereck's ethics and metaphysics. It does not follow from the presence of dissonances in his work that Viereck is a bad poet. His efforts to maintain a system of belief against certain contrary tendencies in his personality add to his poems' interest.

Like that of any other good poet, Viereck's work is not all of a piece. As his career developed, his verse tended to become more lyrical. A good example of his lyrical style is "Arethusa, the First Morning," which appeared in *The First Morning*. Arethusa was a sea nymph changed by Artemis into a spring. The poem pictures the former nymph wondering what has happened to her. Viereck uses her perplexity to introduce a meditation about the stages of life and the nature of consciousness. What, if anything, can one really know?

Viereck has no answer to this question. Rather, his response is that human beings cannot have any knowledge of what lies behind the world that appears to them. Specifically, there is no reason to think that life has any meaning beyond what individuals can give it. There is no life beyond death, and human beings do not fit into a cosmic scheme of things.

The annihilation of death fills Viereck with dread. This reaction is present in other works besides "Arethusa." What ought one's response to be? When a doe steps into the spring, Arethusa feels a kinship with her and a sympathy for all nature. Viereck suggests that the experience of the unity of the world can help humankind deal with the fear of death, to the extent that anything can do so. The attitudes displayed in "Arethusa" are of great importance to Viereck; perhaps anxious that readers not forget them, he included another version of the poem, entitled "River," in *New and Selected Poems*. The new version drops the mythological references but retains the message of the original.

As always, Viereck finds enemies of correct doctrine to combat; in *The First Morning*, it is New Criticism that is the target of his wrath. He assails this style of criticism in a section of the book called "Irreverences," which consists of a series of short rhyming verses, written in a mocking style; "1912-1952, Full Cycle" is probably the poem in this group that most effectively conveys his thought.

Viereck's mockery was motivated by much more than personal rivalry or the fact that the New Critics did not care for his verse and rarely if ever discussed it. He thought that their views were inimical to sound art. They contended that a poem was an artifact that ought to be studied apart from the intentions of the author, which at best were a matter of conjecture. The historical background of the poem was also irrelevant: history and criticism were separate disciplines that ought not to be mixed.

To Viereck these views were merely a variant of the Romantic artist's betrayal of moral responsibility. Adherence to them would prevent poets and critics from teaching the very lessons Viereck thought it most urgent to convey. If a poem was a self-contained entity, it could not at the same time be an instrument for teaching virtue. Small wonder that Viereck believed himself justified in using every literary weapon at his command against New Critics such as Allen Tate. Satire was his chosen instrument in "Irreverences," but to a large extent his project backfired. Many of the volume's reviewers failed to see the serious purpose behind his work, and the book was not very favorably received.

"Nostalgia," a poem included in *The Persimmon Tree*, enables the reader to come to a fuller understanding of Viereck's ideas. The poem depicts God, who has absented Himself from the world for eight thousand years, deciding to return to earth for a surprise visit. Instead of receiving a warm welcome from His creation, he is recognized by no one; he is no longer worshiped. The poem makes evident that for Viereck God, if He exists at all, has no benevolent intentions or even much interest in human beings. He is an arbitrary and capricious power, and people must make their way without Him.

"Nostalgia" illustrates another tension in Viereck's position. Many people who lack religious belief think that morality can be built on nonreligious foundations. The questions "Does God exist?" and "What are the foundations of morality?" are to philosophers such as David Hume and John Stuart Mill distinct and independent. Viereck is not entirely in their camp. The reader senses that Viereck's absence of faith makes him doubt the basis of morals as well. When he insists on upholding the virtues and condemns poets who fail to do so, he is in part suppressing his fear that morality is in fact without basis.

Another part of Viereck's philosophy comes to expression in *The Tree Witch.* This is both a poem and a play, but only the former will be discussed here. The work has an unusual theme. An old tree has been cut down to make room for an eight-lane highway, and some "fifty-year old children" separate a dryad from the tree and chain it in a garage. The poem features alternating lines by the human beings and the dryad. (A dryad is a tree spirit; talking trees are featured in *Terror and Decorum* and are a trademark of Viereck's poetry.)

Viereck's sympathies are clearly on the dryad's side. The men who imprison her claim to be acting for her welfare, but they are enemies of nature. By taking her away from the tree, they (along with those who have cut down the tree) kill her.

Viereck uses this bizarre account to symbolize the struggle between nature and technology which he thinks characteristic of the twentieth century. Machines, once built, have a dynamic of their own that leads people to fall victim to these supposed tools. People increasingly subordinate themselves to machines; labor has become monotonous and overly rapid.

True value lies in harmony with nature, which must be respected for its own sake rather than viewed as raw material for the creation of tools. Technology out of control returns Viereck to a theme prominent early in his career. He views it as a central element to the rise of Nazism and communism. The correct attitude toward nature is an essential part of the humanist values Viereck defends.

Here once more Viereck is led into paradox. The defense of nature against all-powerful machines is a mainstay of Romanticism. Many of the persons Viereck is most concerned to attack for their political follies are fervent proponents of this view. The philosopher Martin Heidegger, whom Viereck attacks as a Nazi in *Metapolitics*, made warnings about the imminent takeover of the world by technology a key theme of his teaching. For a professed anti-Romantic, Viereck adopts a large number of Romantic positions.

Viereck issued his longest continuous work in 1987—*Archer in the Marrow*. This is an epic poem composed in "cycles" on which Viereck worked for twenty years. The work depicts a three-way conversation between God, the man He has created, and contemporary humankind. The theme of the epic is whether human beings are "things" determined by outside forces or, on the contrary, have the power to control their own fate and surpass themselves.

Viereck presents God as anxious to keep human beings under His thumb. Human beings cannot withstand the divine power, but they have an ally who gives them a fighting chance in the struggle for autonomy. God is afraid of Eve or Aphrodite, whose feminine nature symbolizes attunement with nature. Eve rarely appears directly in the poem, and her views and characteristics must be pieced together from the lines of the other characters. In spite of her elusiveness, she is humankind's best chance for salvation. Viereck, apparently worried that readers might not get the message, includes in the book a commentary explaining his poem.

Throughout his career, Viereck has defended a clearly expressed set of values. He has braved the perils of nonconformity, since didactic poetry is out of fashion. Much more than a preacher in verse, Viereck is a gifted literary artist who has devoted his poetic talents to conveying a message he thinks of vital concern. The tensions in his views show that he has had to struggle against himself to keep his poetry under the firm control he thinks proper.

Bill Delaney

Other major works

NONFICTION: *Metapolitics: From the Romantics to Hitler*, 1941; *Conservatism Revisited: The Revolt Against Revolt, 1815-1949*, 1949; *Shame and Glory of the Intellectuals*, 1953; *The Unadjusted Man*, 1956.

Bibliography

Ciardi, John. "Peter Viereck: The Poet and the Form." *University of Kansas City Review* 15 (Summer, 1949): 297-302. This early article remains one of the best analyses of Viereck's work. (A handicap for those who wish to study Viereck is that he has received little detailed attention in books.) Ciardi gives a carefully balanced treatment of Viereck's ideas and techniques. As a poet himself hostile to modernism, Ciardi sympathizes with Viereck's negative view of Pound.

Dickey, James. Review of *The Tree Witch*. *Sewanee Review* 70 (Summer, 1962): 484-503. Dickey, a poet himself, emphasizes that Viereck is a poet who wishes to instruct readers about the nature of human beings. He praises Viereck's technical resourcefulness and his creative use of language. Viereck has a strong and courageous personality, which unmistakably emerges in his verse. He ranks as an important American poet.

Hénault, Marie. *Peter Viereck*. New York: Twayne, 1969. A rare book-length study of Viereck's work. It gives a relatively comprehensive account of Viereck's poetry and prose to the date of publication, although some of the poetry is not discussed. Hénault is very favorable to Viereck and defends him against negative reviewers.

Rossiter, Clinton. *Conservatism in America*. New York: Vintage Books, 1962. Essential for understanding Viereck's political and ethical ideas. Rossiter notes the importance of moderation for Viereck. Undue expression of emotion is to be avoided, both in politics and in literature. Rossiter brings out the unity of Viereck's prose and poetry: all of his works aim to convey his firmly held beliefs.

Viereck, Peter. "Form in Poetry." In *Archer in the Marrow*. New York: W. W. Norton, 1987. Here Viereck offers an account of his own poetic principles. He analyzes several of his poems to show their structure, contrasts his poetic theories with those of other critics, and mounts one more assault against Ezra Pound and his modernist allies.

JOSÉ GARCÍA VILLA

Born: Manila, Philippines; August 5, 1914

Principal poetry

Many Voices, 1939; *Poems by Doveglion*, 1941; *Have Come, Am Here*, 1942; *Volume Two*, 1949; *Selected Poems and New*, 1958; *Poems 55*, 1962; *Poems in Praise of Love*, 1962.

Other literary forms

In 1929, José García Villa edited the first comprehensive anthology of Filipino short stories in English, for the *Philippines Free Press*. The earliest published volume of his own work was also a collection of stories, *Footnote to Youth: Tales of the Philippines and Others*, released by Scribner's in 1933. Many of these tales had appeared earlier in *Clay*, the mimeographed literary magazine which he founded at the University of New Mexico and which first drew the attention of Edward O'Brien. *The Best American Short Stories of 1932*, in fact, was dedicated to Villa by O'Brien, whose introduction included Villa "among the half-dozen short story writers in America who count" and compared him with one of O'Brien's earlier discoveries, Sherwood Anderson. Even as O'Brien was prophesying a career for Villa as novelist, however, the young writer had already turned his attention exclusively to poetry. The stories, therefore, retain their interest chiefly as preliminaries to attitudes and techniques associated with Villa's poems.

A third of the twenty-one stories in *Footnote to Youth* are semiautobiographical portraits of a hermit-protagonist suffering self-imposed isolation in the Philippines, New Mexico, and New York City. There is a repetitive pattern of rejected illegitimate children, either unwanted or inadequately cared for; of antagonism between fathers and grown sons; of the protagonist's alienation from those with whom he is, only temporarily, most intimate; of a love-hate identification with José Rizal, martyred hero of the 1896 Revolution, as a father-image whose own paternity is clouded; of rejection in courtship and marriage; of self-importance recovered through sentimentalized identification with the suffering Christ, the god mocked and misunderstood.

This sense of recoil from hurt is conveyed in Villa's stories principally through antinarrative devices. In some cases, the paragraphs are numbered and condensed, so that typographically they resemble stanzas in a poem. Nor is incident allowed to flow into incident. O'Brien wrote of Villa's combining "a native sensuousness of perception and impression" with the "traditionally Spanish expression of passionate feeling in classical reticence of form." More likely, however, the compartmentalization of the narrative indicates the aftermath of a series of unhappy encounters between a sensitive personality and an insensitive world unprepared to give him the recognition he deserves. The stories dazzle with color, their principal emotion being intensely lyrical.

Achievements

As a self-exile from the Philippines for decades, Villa has earned awards and a reputation in both the Western and Asian worlds. In the United States, he has been the recipient of a Guggenheim Fellowship, an American Academy of Arts and Letters Award, a Bollingen Fellowship, and a Rockefeller grant. In Greenwich Village during the 1940's and 1950's he was considered a "regular," as a member of the New Directions avant-garde. In Great Britain his reputation also flourished, as a result of Edith Sitwell's high praise of his "great and perfectly original work." Gradually such distinction, coming from overseas, influenced his countrymen at home. Although there were complaints that he did not write about subjects identifiably Filipino, and that he did not write with the folk simplicity of Carlos Bulosan's *New Yorker* tales of sweet-sour satire, an entire generation of college-educated Filipinos began not only to envy his success but also to emulate his sophistication and inventiveness. The prominence given him by this growing cult assisted in securing for him a Pro Patria Award, in 1961, and a Cultural Heritage Award in 1962. In 1973, he became the first Filipino writer in English to be declared a National Artist, with a government pension for life.

Biography

José García Villa once insisted that "Biography I have none and shall have none. All my Pure shall beggar and defy biography." He was requiring that his identity be sought exclusively in his poems, his purer self. For most of his life he has maintained just such distances, shunning intimacies.

Whenever he has boasted that his physician-father was chief of staff for General Aguinaldo during the Revolution of 1896, he has identified himself less with the healer, in that figure, than with the power of the prototypical rebel. In fact he strenuously resisted his father's attempt to make a doctor of him. At the University of the Philippines he turned instead to the study of law, whose logic and case-history specifics he also soon found too constraining. He was temporarily suspended from college in June, 1929, for having written "Man Songs," a poem too sexually explicit for the times and the authorities. In that same year, for his story "Mir-i-Nisa," a fable of native courtship, he became the first recipient of an award in what was to become a distinguished annual contest in the *Philippines Free Press*. Because he felt unappreciated by his father and inadequately recognized by his fellow Filipinos, he spent the prize money taking himself into exile in America. He was determined to be answerable only to himself.

In 1932, he received a B.A. from the University of New Mexico, where his literary magazine *Clay* published the first work (a poem) by William Saroyan, the early writings of William March, David Cornel de Jong, and others, as well as many of his own short stories. These attracted the attention of Edward O'Brien, who dedicated *The Best American Short Stories of 1932* to Villa and placed eleven of his tales on that year's list of distinctive stories. Elated, Villa went to New York City, taking *Clay* with him, the magazine that O'Brien declared to be the prospective rival of Whit and Hallie Burnett's *Story* magazine. Although Villa had difficulty finding salaried work during the Great Depression and claimed that he was discriminated against because of his nationality, in 1933 Scribner's published his collection of stories, *Footnote to Youth*, dedicated to O'Brien, who wrote an introduction to the volume. In 1939, his first book of poems, *Many Voices*, appeared in Manila; in 1940 it won honorable mention in the Commonwealth Literary Contest. The following year, *Poems by Doveglion* was published in Manila and *Have Come, Am Here* in the United States in 1942. The latter was in close contention for the Pulitzer Prize. Befriended by Mark Van Doren, he pursued graduate studies at Columbia on a partial scholarship from that university and another from the Commonwealth of the Philippines. As an avocation, he painted geometric portraits in the cubist mode and hung them in his apartment next to several by E. E. Cummings.

By 1942, he was working for the Philippine embassy in Washington, D.C., clipping newspaper stories of the battles on Bataan and Corregidor. His mind, however, was less on his clerical duties than on his own writing. When he was refused a raise because he typed so slowly, Villa exclaimed, "What do you take me for, a mechanic?" He returned to New York at once and married Rosemarie Lamb, by whom he later had two sons. In 1949, he published *Volume Two*, the book which introduced his experimental "comma poems." He became an associate editor with New Directions, as well as with the Harvard *Wake* for special issues on Marianne Moore and Cummings. His poems have consistently appeared in American and world anthologies since the 1940's. In 1958, a largely retrospective work, *Selected Poems and New*, was released. He taught poetry workshops at both the City College of New York and the School for Social Research. In various ways he was also attached to the Philippine Mission to the United Nations until he was declared a National Artist in 1973.

Analysis

Both his admirers and his detractors agree on the essential inwardness of José García Villa's poetry. For the latter, this is a symptom of narcissism hardly useful to the urgent needs of a newly independent nation. For the former, it is a sign of a transcendent mysticism whose universality should be given priority over nationalism. The poet himself has declared that he is not at all interested in externals, "nor in the contemporary scene, but in *essence*." His dominant concern is not description but metaphysics, a penetration of the inner maze of man's identity within the entire "mystery of creation."

The poems themselves, however, often suggest something less than such perfection and therefore something more exciting: purification-in-process, the sensual nature in man struggling to survive transfiguration. The body strains to avoid emasculation even as the spirit ascends. Consequently, the flesh seems glorified, although not in any ordinary spiritual manner which would diminish the splendor of the sense. Edith Sitwell, in her Preface to *The American Genius* (1951), refers to this paradox as an expression of "absolute sensation," mingling a "strange luminosity" with a "strange darkness." Villa himself best epitomizes the blinding heat of this attempted fusion by repeatedly adopting the persona/pseudonym "Doveglion": a composite Dove-eagle-lion.

Even the ordinary early poems, replete with piety and puppy love and first gathered in *Many Voices*, then in *Poems by Doveglion*, occasionally manage to move the imagination toward the outermost limits of language, a crafted inarticulateness conveying the inexpressible. When he was seventeen, Villa could compare the nipple on the coconut with a maiden's breast, and drink from each; but later lyrics match God and genius, both suffering "The ache of the unfound love" and, in their lonely perfection, left contending for primacy with each other. For Villa, these maturer poems are also the first attempts to create by wordplay, combining "brilliance and/ consecration." A romantic vocabulary emerges, repeated like a code or incantation: star, wind, birds, roses, tigers, dark parts, the sun, doves, the divine. More experimentally, he inverts phrases and therefore logic, in expectation of profound meaning beyond the rational. He writes, "Tomorrow is very past/ As yesterday is so future" and "Your profundity is very light./ My lightness is very profound." Above all, he is trying to "announce me": "I am most of all, most." The defiant rebel who is his own cause begins to be apparent in these poems published in the Philippines.

Even as *Many Voices* and *Poems by Doveglion* were going to press, however, his experiments had taken a quantum leap forward. When Sylvia Townsend Warner came to New York in 1939 as Britain's delegate to the Third Congress of American Writers, she was astounded by the verses being prepared for *Have Come, Am Here*, which included the best of Villa's previous work and much more. It was two years later that the book reached the hands of Sitwell, whose eyes fell on the poem "My most. My most. O my lost!," a brief litany of the protagonist's "terrible Accost" with God; she was moved by its "ineffable beauty." The volume is a mixture of adoring love lyrics and joyous, combative rivalry with God. To convey their "strange luminosity," she felt compelled to make comparisons with the religious ecstasies of William Blake and Jakob Boehme, as well as with such other mystics as St. Catherine of Genoa and Meister Eckhart.

It was a matter of special pride for Villa to note that in six of his poems he introduced a wholly new method of rhyming which he called "reversed consonance." As he explains it, "a rhyme for *near* would be *run, green, reign*," with the initial *n-r* combination reversed in each instance. Such a rhyme, of course, is visible if the reader has been forewarned; but even then the ear can hardly notice the event. Still, the device is one more variation among Villa's many attempts, through decreation and reassemblage, to penetrate the energy fields of convention and release explosive forces from the very "depths of Being," as Sitwell puts it. Much more interesting, however, and more successful than reversed consonance in satisfying this quest for fire is the inexorable forward force of both his love lyrics and his "divine poems." Occasionally these poems are indistinguishable from one another because the protagonist addresses both his beloved and his God with the same possessive, mastering rhetoric: "Between God's eyelashes I look at you,/ Contend with the Lord to love you. . . ." At times in compulsive narcissism the protagonist even treats them as mirrors for himself, then briefly relents, guiltily considering himself to be Lucifer or Judas. Such interplays of ambiguity are made inevitable by the poems' brevity and density, the constant ellipses and startling juxtapositions: oranges and giraffes, pigeons and watermelons, yellow strawberries, "pink monks eating blue raisins," the crucified Christ as peacock, the wind shining and sun blowing.

Sometimes in these poems one can recognize the synaesthesia of the French symbolists, E. E. Cummings' curtailments of standard grammar, Blakean nature as divine emblems, or the equivalent of cubist/surrealist transformations of reality. Mostly, however, Villa is an original. One senses in him a compelling inner necessity to prove that purity proceeds from the proper combination of what are normally considered impurities. His is the rebel's revenge against mediocrity. a Promethean ascent-in-force to regain godhead. Fellow poet Rolando Tinio, in *Brown Heritage* (1967), says that Villa "speaks of God becoming Man and concludes that Man has become God." Villa's countrymen have grudgingly accepted his preeminence abroad. Villa, however, has always thought of himself as too exceptional to be a representative Filipino. He would not live in the shadow of his wealthy father in the Philippines; at best he could make a desperate living in New York during the Depression and World War II. Emotionally homeless, he fortified his exile by offering in his poetry a protagonist both essential and universal. For Villa that meant a rejection of common codes and orders, a rising above all local circumstances. *Have Come, Am Here* reflects this profound need for self-justification.

Resounding critical acclaim for these poems came instantly, from Sitwell, Richard Eberhart, Horace Gregory, Marianne Moore, and well over a dozen world anthologists. For them, Villa's poetry is as cryptic as a Zen *koan* and therefore as rewarding as any other religious meditation, the very dislocation of syntax soliciting a revelation. Still others, entranced by their initial experience of *Have Come, Am Here,* have reported that later readings show a tendency in Villa toward formula that is too facile, as if, were any poem shaken hard enough, its words would finally form another, by the laws of chance and permutation. The poetic vocabulary is not only too romantic for pragmatic readers, but it is also rather impoverished because it is more repetitive than resonant. Similarly, these poems, whether sacred or profane, ultimately manifest the same basic love for a self more praised than explored. Readers accustomed to tangible substance and foreseeable consequences are troubled by an incandescence that, for them, blinds more than it illuminates.

The same polarity of reaction occurred with the appearance of the "comma poems" in *Volume Two.* Between each word in these poems Villa placed an unspaced comma, "regulating the poem's density and time movement." His intent was to control the pace of each poem's progress with measured dignity. The effect resembles musical notation, although Villa preferred to compare the technique with Georges Seurat's pointillism. Unlike reversed consonance, this innovative device does indeed add "visual distinction." It cannot, however, rescue such verses as Villa's "Caprices" or most of his aphorisms; it can only make them seem pretentious. Some of the new "divine poems," nevertheless, are among the author's best, their dynamics rising from the mystery of things seen in mid-metamorphosis: for example, "The,bright,Centipede" beginning its stampede from "What,celestial,province!" Villa's quarrels with his co-Creator ("My dark hero") also manage a magnificence which can pass beyond self-celebration. There is as much visionary quickening in the image of "God,dancing,on,phosphorescent,toes,/ Among,the,strawberries" as in the inscrutable Lion carrying "God,the,Dark,Corpse!" down Jacob's ladder. In poems as powerful as these, the commas seem like sacerdotal vestments woven from metallic mesh. In lesser poems, however, the commas serve merely as a façade to conceal or decorate an inner vacuousness. A few poems, in fact, have been rescued from his earliest volumes and have merely been rehabilitated through use of this fresh overlay.

More serious questions than those raised by *Volume Two*'s unevenness have been directed toward Villa's continuing reliance on a small cluster of romantic terms whose effect is reduced as their possible combinations approach exhaustion. Furthermore, the prolonged role of rebel has led Villa to virtual self-imitation in the steady use of reversals, negatives, and reductives. The "not-face" and "un-ears" of his earlier lyrics become an established pattern later: "In,my,undream,of,death,/I,unspoke,the,Word"; "the,Holy,/ Unghost—"; "Unnight,/ Me"; "In,not,getting,there,is,perfect,Arrival"; "The, clock,was,not,a,clock"; "May,spring,from,*Un*—,/ Light. . . ." By substitution, strange, suggestive equations can emerge ("Myself,as,Absence,discoverer,/ Myself,as,Presence,searcher"); but so can codes so manneristic that others can imitate them successfully ("Yesterday,I,awoke,today"; gold blackbirds; blue-eyed trees). Two different kinds of innocence are offered: that of the true visionary breaking through the barriers of ordinary reality to a tranquillity beyond words and worry; and that of the mindless child playing at anagrams with alphabet blocks (as the poet himself much earlier playfully signed himself "O. Sevilla").

Much mirroring is bound to occur in a poet who is less God-driven, as Richard Eberhart claims Villa is, than obsessed with the trinity of his own godhead (Poet, Word, and Poem), as Tinio suggests. Within those confinements, intensity has to compensate for lack of variety; and critics of all persuasions admit that, at his best, Villa does brilliantly manage that irresistible tenacity, that sense of seizure, even if at the expense of the subject's being its sole object. Dismissing nakedness for the sake of translucent nudity, he comes to sacrifice more and more the sensate body of other persons to exclamations on his own exultant sensibility. That habit limits the plausibility of comparisons which Villa offers between his own work and the paintings of Georges Seurat or Pablo Picasso. Seurat, understanding the optics of his day, provides in each canvas the subjective process of atomized vision and the objective configurations of person, place, and thing which that process projects. Picasso, similarly, even in a hundred portraits of the same model, admits and conveys the realization of plenitude, of multiple perspectives, as both perceiver and perceived undergo subtle alterations in time, angle of vision, psychological attitude, degree of rapport, and the like.

That no such plenitude, no such endless surprise has been available to Villa became clear with the publication of *Selected Poems and New*. There are several noteworthy new comma poems in this collection, though no startling innovations within that general usage. "Xalome," "And,if,Theseus—then, Minotaur," "Death and Dylan Thomas," and "The Anchored Angel" at least offer ponderous objects for contemplation which, unlike his aphorisms, his lighthearted cries over the blue-eyed bird in a tree, and "A Valentine for Edith Sitwell," appropriate with ease the pace provided by the commas. Such objects also warrant the invitation to meditation which Villa's associational techniques offer in the best of his poems.

By far the larger part of the previously unpublished section of this volume is devoted to forty-eight "adaptations," conversions of other people's prose into poems. His sources are Rainer Maria Rilke's letters, Simone Weil's notebooks, André Gide's journals, and book reviews and letters to the editors of *Time* and *Life*. No word of his own is interjected into the originals, although "to achieve the tightness of verse" he omits occasional "connectives and extra adjectives." In several cases, borrowing from the visual arts, Villa offers what he calls collages: the original lines of a *Life* magazine caption, for example, rearranged in their sequence; or portions from two different sections of a book brought together. Many of these adaptations have received critical praise, particularly as they show a masterful control of musical phrasing, in a variety of tempos and turns that indicate once more the limitations of the comma as a single musical measure. The value of the adaptations naturally depends so heavily on the intrinsic merit of the originals—Franz Kafka, Henry Miller, William Carlos Williams—that one might have expected the application of this kind of craft to others' work as an early stage of apprenticeship. The adaptations lack, for example, the degree of participation-beyond-translation visible in Robert Lowell's volume of "collaborations," *Imitations* (1961); nor have they generated any insights or techniques, as did Ezra Pound's experience with free translations from Provençal poetry which allowed him, in his *Cantos*, to adapt documents from American history as well as selected phrases and ideograms from the Italian and the Chinese.

Since *Selected Poems and New*, Villa's effort seems to have been devoted less to improving his reputation than to maintaining it, particularly in the Philippines. A number of chapbooks appeared in Manila, in 1962, reprinting portions of his earlier writing, to reestablish himself in his native land. This latter-day identification with a culture which finds no specific presence in his poems and from which he remains geographically remote seems rather anomalous, but there are Filipinos who think he has performed better ambassadorial service than many foreign affairs officers. Villa's egocentric poetry is at the opposite extreme from the Filipino's sense of togetherness (*bayanihan*) or the family extended through ritual kinship. His role as rebel is not incongruous, however, if viewed from his people's long history of oppression as a Spanish colony; the Philippine Revolution of 1896, which briefly established a republic whose rejection by the United States caused the Philippine-American War, 1899 to 1902; the Commonwealth years, during which Filipinos had to prove their superiority in order to be considered equals; the guerrilla years of World War II; and the strains of political but not quite economic independence thereafter.

Whether he intends it or not, Villa reinforces the feeling of those Filipinos who demand that they be defined by their own mores and folkways; his "unsonment" poems can be taken as collective resentment of paternalism, however benevolent, proferred by former colonial powers. Even the seeming blasphemy of certain "divine poems" resembles the hybrid religious observances among Asia's only Christian people, once resentful of Spanish religious orders that served as arms of overseas administrations. The nationalists can understand in Villa their defiance and aspiration, the right to self-determination, the refusal to be humiliated by anyone. For these various reasons, Villa continues to be ranked highest among an increasing number of distinguished Filipino poets.

Leonard R. Casper

Other major works

SHORT FICTION: *Philippine Short Stories*, 1929 (editor); *Footnote to Youth:*

Tales of the Philippines and Others, 1933; *Selected Stories,* 1962; *The Portable Villa,* 1962; *The Essential Villa,* 1965.

NONFICTION: *A Celebration for Edith Sitwell,* 1946 (editor).

Bibliography

Abad, Gemino H. "The Self as Genius and God as Peacock: A Study of 'Mysticism' in José García Villa's Poetry." *University College Journal* 8 (1964): 172-185. After a thoughtful analysis of symbolism and theme, Abad concludes that Villa, despite external appearances, is not in the Metaphysical tradition of Western literature. Abad focuses on such important symbols as skull, rose, and fire, and such important themes as the Catholic dogma of hypostasis.

Casper, Leonard. *New Writing from the Philippines: A Critique and Anthology.* Syracuse, N.Y.: Syracuse University Press, 1966. The section on Villa in this book is indispensable, not only because it comes from the foremost critic of Philippine literature but also because it puts into proper perspective the achievement of a poet and short-story writer who was lauded too much and too soon.

Demetillo, Ricaredo. *The Authentic Voice of Poetry.* Diliman: University of the Philippines, Office of Research Coordination, 1962. The chapter on Villa not only establishes historical context but also does an excellent job of establishing his place in Philippine literature and of delineating his strengths and weaknesses, concluding that Villa is a second-rate poet.

Grow, L. M. "José García Villa: The Poetry of Calibration." *World Literature Written in English* 27 (Autumn, 1987): 326-344. This article contends that Villa is usually revered for the wrong reasons. He is hampered by moral earnestness and thus does not make the fullest use of his lyric gifts, which are visible in spectacular opening lines.

Meredith, William. "Second Verse, Same as the First." *Poetry* 75 (February, 1950): 290-295. This short study concentrates on the famous "comma poems." It is ideal for students because it cites and analyzes complete poems as examples. Meredith's verdict is that only the playful poems are successful experiments in punctuation and diction.

Santos, Bienvenido N. "José García Villa in Exile." In *Philippine Harvest: An Anthology of Filipino Writing in English,* edited by Maximo Ramos and Florentino B. Valeros. Manila: E. F. David, 1953. Although a bit more difficult to find than some other studies, this article is worth the effort needed to locate it. Written by one of the great Filipino authors, the article is an exceptionally close-up biographical sketch, which incidentally reveals Santos as much as it reveals Villa.

Tinio, Rolando S. "Villa's Values: Or, The Poet You Cannot Always Make Out, or Succeed in Liking Once You Are Able To." In *Brown Heritage: Essays on Philippine Cultural Tradition and Literature,* edited by Antonio G.

Manuud. Quezon City: Ateneo de Manila University Press, 1967. In spite
of the rather unfortunate choice of title, Tinio has done sound scholarship
here, up to the standard of the rest of the contents of this massive, but
landmark, volume. A must for any student of Philippine life or letters.
The title is self-explanatory.

DAVID WAGONER

Born: Massillon, Ohio; June 5, 1926

Principal poetry

Dry Sun, Dry Wind, 1953; *A Place to Stand*, 1958; *Poems*, 1959; *The Nesting Ground*, 1963; *Staying Alive*, 1966; *New and Selected Poems*, 1969; *Working Against Time*, 1970; *Riverbed*, 1972; *Sleeping in the Woods*, 1974; *A Guide to Dungeness Spit*, 1975; *Collected Poems 1956-1976*, 1976; *Travelling Light*, 1976; *Who Shall Be the Sun?*, 1978; *In Broken Country*, 1979; *Landfall*, 1981; *First Light*, 1983; *Through the Forest: New and Selected Poems, 1977-1987*, 1987.

Other literary forms

Best known as a poet and novelist, David Wagoner has written plays—*An Eye for an Eye for an Eye* was produced in Seattle in 1973—as well as short fiction and essays. He edited and wrote the introduction to *Straw for the Fire: From the Notebooks of Theodore Roethke, 1943-1963* (1972).

Achievements

It is possible that Wagoner will be best remembered as one of the finest "nature" and "regional" poets of twentieth century America, and as one who has been instrumental in generating renewed interest in Native American lore. To categorize him so narrowly, however, does disservice to his versatility, and to the breadth of his talent and interests. Publishing steadily since the early 1950's, Wagoner has created a body of work that impresses not only for the number of volumes produced, but also for their quality. His novels have been praised for their energy and humor and in many cases for the immediacy of their Old West atmosphere. He received a Ford Fellowship for drama (1964), but it is as a poet that he has been most often honored: with a Guggenheim Fellowship (1956), a National Institute of Arts and Letters Grant (1967), a National Endowment for the Arts Grant (1969). *Poetry* has awarded him its Morton Dauwen Zabel Prize (1967), its Oscar Blumenthal Prize (1974), and its Eunice Tietjens Memorial Prize (1971). *Sleeping in the Woods* and *Collected Poems 1956-1976* were nominated for National Book Awards, and *In Broken Country* for an American Book Award. Wagoner was elected a chancellor of the Academy of American Poets in 1978, succeeding Robert Lowell. In 1991, he was awarded the $25,000 Ruth Lilly Poetry Prize.

Despite these accomplishments, and despite the fact that his poems appear regularly in mass-circulation magazines such as *The New Yorker* and *The Atlantic Monthly*, as well as the literary quarterlies, Wagoner is generally conceded to be among the most under-appreciated of American poets. With the exception of "Staying Alive," few of his works are included in major poetry anthologies. There are several possible explanations for this. First, he lives in Seattle and has chosen as his primary subject matter the land and people of the Pacific Northwest—thus giving rise to the dismissive "regional" label. It is also possible that some of his own best qualities may work against him. His subject matter is anything but trendy; the reader searches his poems in vain for Vietnam, the Cold War, civil unrest, the sexual revolution, drugs, The Rolling Stones, or Watergate. The only explicit social comment one is likely to find is contained in a half dozen or so poems addressing the Weyerhaeuser Company, a logging firm, and its practice of clear-cutting three-mile swaths of virgin forest.

Perhaps the major problem, as X. J. Kennedy suggests, is Wagoner's very "readability." Much of his poetry seems, at least on first encounter, curiously unpoetic, even prosy. His unpretentious language and casual, conversational tone frequently combine with his sense of humor to create a deceptively simple surface for his complex and serious ideas. This simplicity does make the work accessible; on the other hand, it may actually encourage the casual or first-time reader to dismiss Wagoner's work as lightweight.

Even in his most alienated and melancholy early poems, Wagoner's wit continually asserts itself. He is fond of puns, palindromes, and other forms of wordplay, and makes frequent use of colloquialisms, folk sayings, clichés, non sequiturs, and other lunacies of ordinary speech, often twisting words or phrases in such a way that they take on startling new meanings. Still, it is not as a semantic magician that Wagoner should be remembered; there are not a great many "quotable" lines—in the sense of the exquisite image of dazzling insight to be isolated for admiration out of context—in his work. Wagoner is at least as much philosopher as poet, and his poems, effective as they are when looked at individually, together take on cumulative power and meaning. Outwardly dissimilar poems are often interrelated below the surface to a marked degree. The result is a coherent, explicitly delineated philosophy, a "way" of life based on acceptance, self-reliance, and a profound reverence for the natural world.

Biography
David Russell Wagoner was born on June 5, 1926, in Massillon, Ohio, and was reared in Whiting, Indiana, the son of a steelworker. After receiving his B.A. degree from Pennsylvania State University in 1947, and his M.A. from Indiana University two years later, Wagoner began his teaching career at DePauw University, returning after a year to Pennsylvania State University. During this time, he was deeply influenced by Theodore Roethke, with whom he had studied as an undergraduate. In 1954, Roethke was instrumental in Wagoner's move to the University of Washington, where he is now Professor of English. X. J. Kennedy has speculated that perhaps "the most valuable

service Roethke ever performed for Wagoner was to bring him to the Pacific Northwest and expose him to rain forests"—and to the culture of the Northwest Coast and Plateau Indians, one might add. Not only has Wagoner made use in his own poems of specific Native American myths and legends, but he has also absorbed the Indians' animistic spiritualism into his own philosophy. In the author's note to *Who Shall Be the Sun?*, he explains that Indians "did not place themselves above their organic and inorganic companions on earth but recognized with awe that they shared the planet as equals." Wagoner finds this equality "admirable and worthy of imitation," as much of his poetry indicates.

When not teaching, Wagoner has worked as a railroad section hand, a park policeman, and a short-order cook. He is a member of the Society of American Magicians. For many years he has served as editor of *Poetry Northwest*.

Analysis

Those who insist on calling David Wagoner a regional or nature poet are certainly correct, to a point. From his earliest collection on, his work has amply indicated a sensitivity to the landscape around him. Later poems, in particular, have been praised for their descriptive qualities. The same can be said of many writers, but the use to which Wagoner has put his rain forests, mountains, rivers, and coastlines, is uniquely his own. His wilderness, with its unsentimental, uncompromising beauty, serves on one level as a conventional metaphor: the landscape, physical and spiritual, through which one travels on one's life journey. Rather than seeing rocks, trees, and animals, however, as separate entities to be reacted to—climbed over, caught and eaten, run from—Wagoner views the natural world as the medium through which humans can best learn to know themselves. Put another way, if one can accept one's place as a part of the ongoing natural processes of life, death, decay, and rebirth, one begins to "see things whole." It is this sense of wholeness, this appreciation for the interrelatedness of all the "organic and inorganic companions on earth" to which Wagoner invites his reader, as if to a feast.

The way to this ideal state involves an apparent paradox: in order to find oneself, one must first lose oneself, shedding the subject/object, mind/body, spirit/intellect dualities typical of "rational" Western thought. In "Staying Alive," a traveler lost in the woods is faced not only with problems of physical survival but also with "the problem of recognition," by anyone or anything external that might be looking for him, as well as recognition of his own true nature. Unable to make contact with others, the traveler is advised that "You should have a mirror/ With a tiny hole in the back . . ." that will reflect the sun and flash messages, that will reflect one's familiar physical image and that, because of the aperture, will also allow one to see through one's physical self to the wholeness of the surrounding natural world.

It is clear that, in Wagoner's view, modern industrial society has created too many wastelands and polluted waterways, and more than enough fragmented citizens such as "The Man from the Top of the Mind," with "the light bulb screwed into his head,/ The vacuum tube of his sex, the electric eye." This gleaming creature of pure intellect can "Bump through our mazes like a genius rat" but is incapable of any human emotion except destructive rage. On every level, it would appear, one has become estranged—from oneself, from others and from one's environment. In place of this fragmentation and alienation, Wagoner offers synthesis: the ability to see and experience things whole. In a remarkable series of poems, he not only extends the offer but also provides an explicit, step-by-step guide—a Scout's Handbook or survival manual for the reader to follow.

Although these "Handbook" poems span several volumes (from *Staying Alive* through *In Broken Country*), they are best read as a single group. All are similar in language and tone; all address an unnamed "you," offering advice for coping with problems that might arise on a wilderness trip. Should one find oneself lost, one need only remember that "Staying alive . . . is a matter of calming down." Further poems instruct one on what to do when "Breaking Camp," or "Meeting a Bear" ("try your meekest behavior,/ . . . eyes downcast"), even after "Being Shot" ("if you haven't fallen involuntarily, you may/ Volunteer now . . ."). In each case, "you," the reader, are put in touch—in most cases both literally and figuratively—with something that has previously seemed foreign or outside the realm of ordinary human experience. In other words, lack of sensitivity to natural processes results in estrangement and isolation. By becoming more receptive, and perhaps less "top of the mind" rational, one allows for the possibility of "rescue" in the form of new understanding.

Frequently, since they typically involve a stripping away of the ego, these new insights prove to be humbling. Traveling "From Here to There," one can see the destination easily, while the distance deceives and one is confused by mirages: "Water put out like fire, . . . flying islands,/ The unbalancing act of mountains upside down." The problem of recognition resurfaces; nothing is what it seems. There is nothing to do but keep slogging: "One Damn Thing After Another," until finally, having "shrugged off most illusions" you "find yourself" in a place "where nothing is the matter/ . . . asking one more lesson." Still harder to accept are the lessons that teach acquiescence in mortality; lessons that teach that even a violent death is as much a part of the life process as birth. In "Being Shot," one finds oneself helpless on the forest floor, "study[ing]/ At first hand . . . the symptoms of shock." With Wagoner's open and accepting life view, death is as natural and therefore as necessary as birth, and "To burrow deep, for a deep winter," as "Staying Alive" advises, will result, come spring, in a renewal of some kind, if only because—should one not survive—one's decaying body will provide nutrients with which to feed other forms of life.

A series of poems in the final section of *In Broken Country* provide a guide to survival in the desert rather than the forest. Similar in tone and intent to the earlier "Handbook" poems, these divert from "The Right Direction" past "The Point of No Return," where ". . . from here on/ It will take more courage to turn than to keep going." The process is what matters.

The "you" in these poems is never identified. There is a strong sense that the reader is being addressed directly, as if he or she has enrolled in an Outward Bound course and is receiving a curious mix of practical and cryptic last-minute advice before setting out on a solo adventure. There is also a sense of the poet talking to himself, working his own way both from the industrialized northern Indiana of his youth to the rain forests of Washington, and, in a parallel journey, from a sense of alienation to one of harmony. In *Dry Sun, Dry Wind*, Wagoner's first collection, his affinity with nature is already apparent, but no real contact seems possible. The poet remains isolated, seeing about him images of destruction ("sun carries death to leaves"), decay and uncertainty ("last year's gully is this year's hill"). Time flies; memory is unable to delay it. The natural environment, blighted though it is, is "Too much to breathe, think, see" ("Warning"). In the early poems, the relationship between man and nature—or man and anything or anyone else—was generally one of conflict, an ongoing struggle for control resulting in disillusionment: a war, rather than a reconciliation, of opposites. "Progress" was often best achieved through violence to the land, and the stillness that in later works will open the way to enlightenment has precisely the opposite effect in early poems such as "Lull." Recognition, and, by extension, synthesis, is possible only when "the wind hums or wheels," creating movement, a kind of artificial life.

It is perhaps significant that none of the poems from this first volume has been included in any subsequent collection. The suggestion is that Wagoner quickly moved beyond these early efforts, struggling with his own problem of recognition as he searched for a true voice of his own. The major themes are there, often apparent only in their negative aspects, as, for example, the fragmentation and conflict that will yield in later poems to synthesis. In addition, there is at least one poem that deserves reading on its own merit.

"Sam the Aerialist" is "sick of walking." He wants to fly. Like the poet, like the trickster of Native American myth, like dreamers everywhere, he hungers for the impossible and yearns to exceed his natural bounds. In this, Sam is like most of the human race. His crime is not so much his desire to fly as it is his attitude, which is aggressive, self-serving, exploitative: Sam has a "lust for air" that is anything but properly reverent. The birds, therefore, instead of sharing their secrets with him, "have kept/ Far from his mind." "Birds are evil," Sam concludes,

> they fly
> Against the wind. How many have I pulled
> Apart . . .
> To learn the secret?

Sam learns by destroying. He lacks the empathy that could move him toward true understanding, and he remains isolated, cut off from his own nature as well as that around him.

Although he is never again referred to by name, there is a sense in which Sam the Aerialist's presence is felt throughout Wagoner's later poetry. He represents a kind of high-technology Everyman; his failings are the failings of society at large. He makes a stubborn but useful pupil. If such a one can absorb the early wisdom of "The Nesting Ground," that sometimes standing still will gain one more than flight; if he can follow where the "Handbook" poems lead and lose himself in the discovery that there is a bottom as well as a top to his mind, then perhaps all is not lost. Certainly, there is an aspect of Sam in the "you" to whom the "Handbook" poems speak.

Another step beyond specific survival lore in Wagoner's progress from alienation to harmony is represented by several groups of poems based on the mythology of the Northwest Coast and the Plateau Indians. Wagoner's interest in Native American culture is longstanding. "Talking to the Forest," included in *Staying Alive*, responds to a Skagit tribesman's statement: "When we can understand animals, we will know the change is halfway. When we can talk to the forest, we will know the change has come." In *Riverbed*, "Old Man, Old Man" teaches that "Every secret is as near as your fingers." It was in the 1974 collection *Sleeping in the Woods*, however, that the pivotal group, "Seven Songs for an Old Voice," first appeared. This Voice, still singing the ancient animisitic wisdom as reverently as it did in the days before the Iron People (whites) arrived, offers hymns equally to Fire, which keeps enemies away, and to the Maker of Nightmares, who "eat[s] my sleep for . . . food." Other songs address death, the soul leaving the body and returning to it, and the First People, nonhumans who became rocks, animals, plants, and water when they learned of the coming of mankind. No matter what the subject, the tone is one of acceptance and awe. Death is part of life. Terrifying as they are, nightmares are not to be denied. The Voice promises to "drink what you bring me in my broken skull,/ The bitter water which once was sweet as morning."

These Seven Songs are included in *Who Shall Be the Sun?* along with other previously collected poems, new groups of "Songs for the Dream-Catchers," "Songs of Only-One," "Songs of He-Catches-Nothing," and two groups of Myths and Legends—one each from the Plateau and Northwest Coast Indian tribes. Wagoner explains in his Author's Note that the Myths and Legends are retellings of existing stories. The Songs are original works, but Wagoner stresses his debt to the Indians' spirit if not their words.

As Robert K. Cording points out, these Indian-lore poems allow Wagoner to blend several hitherto separate themes. For the Native American, the interrelationship of man and nature has traditionally been a given, as has a belief in the power of various religious and quasireligious rituals and practices that non-Indians might call magic. Magic, as a motif, appears fairly frequently in Wagoner's earlier work; in this collection, human beings "magically" converse with the spirits of the First People in the trees above them and the dust beneath their feet. It is not only the First People who are capable of such transformations. Animals can take on human shapes; humans too can put on different skins. In certain situations the dead can return to earth and the living can cross in safety to the land of the dead. Magic here is more than sleight-of-hand and an Indian's dreams are tools more powerful than the technology of Sam the Aerialist, as the title poem shows. "Who Shall Be the Sun?" the People ask, and despite his apparent lack of suitability for the job, Snake's ability to dream, coupled with his seemly modesty, allows him to succeed where the assertive, egocentric Raven, Hawk, and Coyote (who can merely think) have failed.

"Who Shall Be the Sun?" and other poems in the Myth and Legend sections are written in a language that closely echoes the cadences of English prose translations of Indian legends with which the reader may be familiar. The song groups are distinct from one another, the tone and rhythm consistent with each singer's personality and the subject addressed. It should be noted that although the pervading attitude is one of reverence and peace, not all of these poems present such a harmonious picture. Coyote and Raven, classic tricksters, are as likely to cause harm with their pranks as they are to improve the lot of those they purport to help, as the Indian culture, like any other, has always had its share of misfits, liars, and thieves. There is disease, madness, and death, of course, as well as someone called Only-One, who, half-blinded by the beak of an injured heron he had attempted to heal, sees only halves of things. Scarred by smallpox, neither truly dead nor truly alive, Only-One is an isolated soul. He dances with Dead Man, and the half-girl he takes for his bride turns out to be the bird that blinded him.

Following *Who Shall Be the Sun?*, Wagoner returned to a more characteristic range of subjects. *In Broken Country* mixes poems about love, childhood memories, parents, poets (including a lovely elegy to Roethke), bums, and prisoners (Wagoner himself included). A dozen desert "Handbook" poems are preceded by a series of self-parodying mock-"Handbook" entries. *Landfall* also covers a broad range, although a particularly strong unifying cord runs throughout. A number of the most moving poems are about making contact with one's past, not merely in the sense of looking back and remembering, but in trying for reconciliation with aspects of one's life that may have caused one pain. Over the years, Wagoner has written poems about his father—puttering around the house, building a wall—a pleasant-seeming man, drained by his job in the steel mill. A certain edgy ambivalence of tone in these poems has kept the elder Wagoner an insubstantial figure. "My Father's Garden" changes this, introducing the reader to a man who picked "flowers" for his family: "small gears and cogwheels/ With teeth like petals," found in the scrapheap he passed on his way to work, work which "melted" his mind to the point that all he retained of an education in the classics was enough Latin and Greek for crossword puzzles. Paired with this is "My Father's Ghost," an extraordinary piece based on a Midwestern folk saying and reminiscent in tone of the Indian songs. Having performed the proper rituals, the poet should be able to see his father's spirit; but the charms do not work. The room stays empty. It is necessary to "imagine him," then; "and dream him/ Returning unarmed, unharmed. Words, words. I hold/ My father's ghost in my arms in his dark doorway."

The final section, " A Sea Change," describes a journey with no destination, in which the poet and his wife leave forest, desert, and marsh behind and head out to sea. This sea voyage is more explicitly psychological than the "Handbook" poems, but here, too, reconciliations take place. The travelers must come to terms with the unfamiliar element to which they have entrusted their lives; in doing so, they will discover that it is not so foreign as they thought. They must overcome their dread of the dimly seen monsters coiling in the depths. In doing so, they discover that the monsters never break through the "mirror" of the water's surface— suggesting, perhaps, that to accept one's demons as the Old Voice singer accepted nightmares and death is to rob them of much of their power. In contrast to Wagoner's explicitly instructive poems, the Sea Change group does not explain precisely by what means these primal fears are to be overcome or how other changes are to be brought about. At journey's end, "Landfall," the two travelers simply come "wallowing" ashore like their "hesitant helpless curious ancestors," having somehow been in touch with a past too dim for memory or rational understanding. On feet that "keep believing/ In the sea," they regain firm ground, asking, "Have we come home? Is this where we were born? . . . this place/ Where, again, we must learn to walk?"

Wagoner's own answer to this would be yes, over and over again, on all ground and in all weather, backward, on our hands, on water, and on air. Getting there means starting over; starting over means rebirth, renewal, a second chance to see things whole. In many ways, this is just what Wagoner has been doing throughout his career.

Sara McAulay

Other major works

LONG FICTION: *The Man in the Middle*, 1954, 1955; *Money, Money, Money,* 1955; *Rock*, 1958; *The Escape Artist*, 1965; *Baby, Come On Inside*, 1968; *Where*

Is My Wandering Boy Tonight?, 1970; *The Road to Many a Wonder*, 1974; *Tracker*, 1975; *Whole Hog*, 1976; *The Hanging Garden*, 1980.

PLAY: *An Eye for an Eye for an Eye*, 1973.

NONFICTION: "Introduction," in *Straw for the Fire: From the Notebooks of Theodore Roethke, 1943-1963*, 1972 (edited).

Bibliography

Boyers, Robert. "The Poetry of David Wagoner." *The Kenyon Review* 32 (Spring, 1970): 176-181. An appreciative review noting that *Staying Alive* marks a turning point in Wagoner's development. Boyers states that from now on, Wagoner could claim to be a major figure in contemporary American poetry.

Lieberman, Laurence. *Unassigned Frequencies: American Poetry in Review, 1964-1977.* Urbana: University of Illinois Press, 1977. The article on Wagoner, "David Wagoner: The Cold Speech of the Earth," looks at how this poet maps out a topography through his choice of words and images. Compares the later poems with the earlier ones and cites the same imagination but with greater depth of vision. Offers strong, in-depth criticism of *Collected Poems 1956-1976* and places Wagoner in the company of Walt Whitman, Robert Frost, Edgar Lee Masters, and William Stafford.

O'Connell, Nicholas. *At the Field's End: Interviews with Twenty Pacific Northwest Writers.* Seattle: Madrona, 1987. The interviewer explores with Wagoner the subjects of his poems and how he has re-created the Northwest landscape on paper. Examines the structure and sense of rhythm in his poems. Of particular note is a discussion of *Who Shall Be the Sun?*, a collection of poems that Wagoner read aloud to the Blackfeet tribe and for which he received much praise.

Pinsker, Sanford. *Three Pacific Northwest Poets: William Stafford, Richard Hugo, and David Wagoner.* Boston: Twayne, 1987. A useful and insightful introduction to Wagoner's poems, analyzing his choice of themes and techniques. Contains critical commentary on all of his major poems. Notes that among Wagoner's strengths is his "sense of the dramatic."

Waggoner, Hyatt H. *American Visionary Poetry.* Baton Rouge: Louisiana State University Press, 1982. Chapter 7, "Traveling Light," explores Wagoner's identity as a visionary poet through his nature poems. Examines Wagoner's portrayal of the wilderness and how he guards himself in his poems. A sympathetic critique that praises Wagoner's volume, *The Nesting Ground.*

DIANE WAKOSKI

Born: Whittier, California; August 3, 1937

Principal poetry

Coins and Coffins, 1962; *Discrepancies and Apparitions*, 1966; *The George Washington Poems*, 1967; *Inside the Blood Factory*, 1968; *Greed*, 1968-1984 (13 parts); *The Moon Has a Complicated Geography*, 1969; *The Magellanic Clouds*, 1970; *The Motorcycle Betrayal Poems*, 1971; *Smudging*, 1972; *Dancing on the Grave of a Son of a Bitch*, 1973; *Looking for the King of Spain*, 1974; *Virtuoso Literature for Two and Four Hands*, 1975; *The Man Who Shook Hands*, 1978; *Cap of Darkness*, 1980; *The Magician's Feastletters*, 1982; *The Rings of Saturn*, 1986; *Medea the Sorceress*, 1990.

Other literary forms

Diane Wakoski wrote three critical essays that were published by Black Sparrow Press: "Form Is an Extension of Content" (1972), "Creating a Personal Mythology" (1975), and "Variations on a Theme" (1976). These essays, with other essays that had originally appeared in *American Poetry Review*, where she was a regular columnist between 1972 and 1974, and in her books of poetry, were reprinted in *Towards a New Poetry* (1979).

Achievements

More popular with poetry readers than with poetry critics, Wakoski has nevertheless carved a niche for herself in American poetry. A prolific writer (she has published some fifty books of poetry) and indefatigable reader of her own poetry, she has gained a following of readers who appreciate her intensely personal subject matter, her personal mythology, her structural use of digression and repetition, and her long narrative forms. Throughout her work the subject is herself, and the themes of loss, betrayal, and identity recur as she probes her relationships with others, most often father figures and lovers. Though her poems are read sympathetically by feminists, she is herself not political and rejects the notion that she can be identified with a particular ideology or school of poetry. Her work has brought her several awards, among them the Bread Loaf Robert Frost Fellowship and the Cassandra Foundation Award, as well as grants from such sources as the Guggenheim Foundation and the National Endowment for the Arts.

Her work, sometimes criticized for its perceived self-pity, actually uses loss or betrayal as the impetus for the speaker to work through different self-images and gender reversals to celebrate—usually with a trace of ironic self-awareness—beauty or the self, and, in effect, to solve the problem posed at the beginning of the poem.

Biography

Diane Wakoski was born in California in 1937 to parents who shaped not only her life but also her poetry. Shortly after her birth, her father, John Joseph Wakoski, reenlisted in the navy and made it his career. Her contact with the "Prince Charming" figure, as she describes him in an autobiographical account, was infrequent and unfulfilling, leaving her with a sense of loss she later explored in her poetry. Her relations with her mother were equally unsatisfying and stressful; by the time she left high school, Wakoski says, she found her mother, whom her father had divorced, a "burden." Speaking of her childhood, Wakoski claims that she was born into a "world of silence," that she was "surrounded by silent people." She was poor, emotionally isolated (she also had few friends), and—from her own point of view—physically unattractive. These factors surely relate to the fixation with male figures and subsequent betrayal in her poems and explain, to some extent, the compulsive need to analyze, to dissect, and to communicate at length in a prolific body of work.

The only positive reinforcement she received in high school was from sympathetic teachers who encouraged the development of her academic talents. She also discovered that she enjoyed performing for an audience. (This "exhibitionistic" tendency, as she has described it, is reflected in her poetry readings, which are very much "performances.") After graduation from high school, she passed up a scholarship to the University of California at Berkeley and attended Fullerton Junior College because she expected her high school sweetheart to enroll there as well. When he attended a different college and responded dutifully, not supportively, to the news of her pregnancy, she experienced a "betrayal," rejected his marriage proposal, and subsequently gave up her baby for adoption.

In the fall of 1956, after attending a poetry class at Whittier College, she enrolled at Berkeley, where she began writing poetry in earnest, publishing some of it in *Occident*, the campus literary magazine. Wakoski believes that her career was launched when her student poetry reading at the San Francisco Poetry Center resulted in another reading there, this time as a "real" poet. Before she left Berkeley she was pregnant again, this time by a fellow artist-musician with whom she later moved to New York; since marriage did not seem appropriate and both were career-minded, she again gave up her baby for adoption.

In New York, Wakoski continued to write poetry and give poetry readings, while she became acquainted with several established writers, one of whom, LeRoi Jones (later Amiri Baraka), published some of her poems in *Four Young Lady Poets* in 1962. *Coins and Coffins*, her first book of poems, was also published in 1962, but it was not until 1966, with the publication of *Discrepancies and Apparitions* by a major publishing house, Doubleday, that she became an established poet. In rapid succession she published two of her most important books, *The George Washington Poems* and *Inside the Blood Factory*, as well as the first four parts of *Greed*. During the late 1960's she also experienced a failed first marriage and a few failed romantic relationships, one of which produced the raw material for *The Motorcycle Betrayal Poems*, her most publicized collection of verse.

The 1970's were a productive decade for Wakoski, who averaged more than two books a year, maintained an almost frenetic pace with poetry readings, and gained at the University of Virginia the first of many academic posts as writer-in-residence. She also began a long-standing association with Black Sparrow Press, which has published many of her books. Of particular interest in this decade is the appearance of two collections of poetry concerning yet another mythological figure, the King of Spain. During this period she turned her attention to criticism, writing a regular column for *American Poetry Review* and publishing a collection of her criticism in *Towards a New Poetry*.

Wakoski's personal life continued to provide content for her verse: her second marriage ended in divorce in 1975. In 1977, however, she renewed her friendship with poet Robert Turney and was married to him in 1982. The 1980's also saw the completion of *Greed*, which she had begun in 1968, and other books of poetry, though her productivity decreased. Other significant publications included *The Rings of Saturn*, and *Medea the Sorceress*, two volumes that rework old themes and myths but also extend Wakoski's "universe," which is at once personal and all-inclusive.

Analysis

Since Diane Wakoski believes that "the poems in her published books give all the important information about her life," her life and her art are inextricably related. She states that the poem "must organically come out of the writer's life," that "all poems are letters," so personal in fact that she has been considered, though she rejects the term, a confessional poet. While most readers have been taught to distinguish between the author and the "speaker" of the poem, Wakoski is, and is not, author and speaker. She refers to real people and to real events in her life in detail that some critics find too personal as she works through a problem: "A poem is a way of solving a problem." For Wakoski, writing a poem is almost therapeutic; it is talking the problem out, not to a counselor or even to the reader, but to herself. She has said, "The purpose of the poem is to complete an act that can't be completed in real life"—a statement that does suggest that there are both reality and the poem, which is then the "completed" dream. As a pragmatist, she has learned to live with these two worlds.

Wakoski believes that once a poet has something to say, the content, he or she finds the appropriate form in which to express it. In her case, the narrative, rather than the lyric, mode is appropriate; free verse, digression, repetition, and oral music are other aspects of that form. She carves out a territory narrowly confined to self and then uses the universe (the moon, the rings of Saturn, Magellanic clouds), history (George Washington, the King of Spain), personal experience (the motorcycle betrayal poems), and literary feuds to create, in the manner of William Butler Yeats, her personal mythology. The mythology is, in turn, used to develop her themes: loss and acceptance, ugliness and beauty, loss of identity and the development of self; that is, the themes are dualistic and, significantly, susceptible to the resolution she achieves in the poem. For her, poetry is healing, not fragmenting.

Coins and Coffins, her first book of poetry, is dedicated to La Monte Young, the father of her second child and another in a series of lost loves. In this volume, she introduces the image of the lost lover, thereby creating her own personal mythology. "Justice Is Reason Enough" is a poem indebted to Yeats: "the great form and its beating wings" suggests "Leda and the Swan." The "form" in this poem, however, is that of her apocryphal twin brother, David, with whom she commits incest. She mourns her brother, "dead by his own hand," because of the justice that "balances the beauty in the world." Since beauty is mentioned in the last line of the poem, the final mood is one of acceptance and affirmation.

The missing lover is also the central figure of *Discrepancies and Apparitions,* which contains "Follow That Stagecoach," a poem that Wakoski regards as one of her best and most representative. Though the setting is ostensibly the West, with the archetypal sheriff and Dry Gulch Hollow, the hollow quickly becomes a river, the speaker, a swimmer in a black rubber skin-diving suit, and the tough Western sheriff, a homosexual authority figure. The opening lines of the poem, "The sense of disguise is a/ rattlesnake," suggest the poses and masks, even the genders, she and the lover-sheriff put on and discard as he fails her: "oh yes you are putting on your skin-diving suit very fast running to the/ ocean and slipping away from this girl who carries a loaded gun." The roles are reversed as she assigns herself the potency he lacks: his gun "wanders into/ hand," while her phallic gun is constantly with her. The poem ends with characteristic confidence: "So I'll write you a love poem if I want to. I'm a Westerner and/ not afraid/ of my shadow." The cliché cleverly alludes to the "shadow" as the alter ego, her second, masculine self; the lover, it is implied, rejects his own wholeness.

In *The George Washington Poems,* dedicated to her father and her husband, she continues to debunk the American hero, this time taking on "the father of my country" (a title that is given to one of the poems), the patriarchal political and militaristic establishment. In the twenty-three poems in the volume, "George Washington" appears in his historical roles as surveyor, tree chopper, general politician, and slaveowner; however, he also anachronistically appears as the speaker's confidant, absentee father, and (sometimes absentee) lover. When the first poem, "George Washington and the

Loss of His Teeth," begins with the image of "George's" (Wakoski refers irreverently to "George" throughout the poems) false teeth, Wakoski wittily and facetiously undercuts the historical image of male leadership in the United States.

In "The Father of My Country," Wakoski demonstrates both the extraordinary versatility of the "George Washington" figure and the way repetition, music, and digression provide structure. The first verse-paragraph develops the idea that "all fathers in Western civilization must have/ a military origin," that all authority figures have been the "general at one time or other," and concludes with Washington, "the rough military man," winning the hearts of his country. Often equating militancy and fatherhood and suggesting that it is the military that elicits American admiration, the speaker abruptly begins a digression about her father; yet the lengthy digression actually develops the father motif of the first verse-paragraph and examines the influence he has had on her life. Although his is a name she does not cherish because he early abandoned her, he has provided her with "military,/ militant" origins, made her a "maverick," and caused her failed relationships. Having thought her father handsome and having wondered why he left her, she is left with the idea of a Prince Charming at once desirable and unattainable. When she speaks of "Father who makes me know all men will leave me/ if I love them," she implies that all of her relationships are fated reenactments of childhood love betrayed.

At the end of the poem she declares that "George" has become her "father,/ in his 20th century naval uniform" and concludes with a chant, with repetitions and parallels, that expresses both her happiness and her uncertainty: "And I say the name to chant it. To sing it. To lace it around/ me like weaving cloth. Like a happy child on that shining afternoon/ in the palm-tree sunset her mother's trunk yielding treasures,/ I cry and/ cry,/ Father,/ Father,/ Father,/ have you really come home?"

Inside the Blood Factory, Wakoski's next major poetic work, also concerns George Washington and her absentee father, but in this volume her range of subject matter is much wider. There is Ludwig van Beethoven, who appears in later poems; a sequence concerning the Tarot deck; a man in a silver Ferrari; and images of Egypt—but pervading all is the sense of loss. In this volume the focus, as the title implies, is on physiological responses as these are expressed in visceral imagery. The speaker wants to think with the body, to accept and work with the dualities she finds in life and within herself.

Inside the Blood Factory also introduces another of Wakoski's recurring images, the moon, developed more extensively later in *The Moon Has a Complicated Geography* and *The Magellanic Clouds*. For Wakoski, the moon is the stereotypical image of the unfaithful woman, but it is also concrete woman breastfeeding her children, bathing, communicating with lovers, and menstruating. Wakoski insists on the physicality of the moon-woman who is related to the sun-lover, but who is also fiercely independent. She loves her lover but wants to be alone, desires intimacy ("wants to be in your wrist, a pulse") but does not want to be "in your house," a possession. (Possession becomes the focus for the ongoing thirteen parts of *Greed*.) When the question of infidelity arises, the speaker is more concerned with being faithful to herself than to her lover(s). In this poem ("3 of Swords—for dark men under the white moon" in the Tarot sequence) the moon-woman can be both submissive and independent, while the sun-lover both gives her love and indulges in his militaristic-phallic "sword play."

As is often the case in Wakoski's poetry, an image appears in one volume and then is developed in later volumes. Isis, a central figure in *The Magellanic Clouds*, is introduced in "The Ice Eagle" of *Inside the Blood Factory*. The Egyptian goddess-creator who is simultaneously mother and virgin, appears as the symbolic object of male fear: "the veiled woman, Isis mother, whom they fear to be greater than all else." Men prefer the surface, whether it be a woman's body or the eagle ice sculpture that melts in the punchbowl at a cocktail party; men fear what lies beneath the surface—the woman, the anima—in their nature.

The Magellanic Clouds looks back at earlier volumes in its reworking of George Washington and the moon figures, but it also looks ahead to the motorcycle betrayal figure and the King of Spain. Of Wakoski's many volumes of poetry, *The Magellanic Clouds* is perhaps the most violent as the speaker plumbs the depth of her pain. Nowhere is the imaging more violent than in the "Poems from the Impossible," a series of prose poems that contain references to gouged-out eyes, bleeding hands, and cut lips.

Isis, the Queen of the Night speaker, figures prominently in *The Magellanic Clouds*. In "Reaching Out with the Hands of the Sun," the speaker first describes the creative power of the masculine sun, cataloging a cornucopia of sweetmeats that ironically create "fat thighs" and a "puffy face" in a woman. The catalog then switches to the speaker's physical liabilities, ones that render her unbeautiful and unloved; with the "mask of a falcon," she has roamed the earth and observed the universal effect that beauty has on men. At the end of the poem the speaker reaches out to touch the "men/ with fire/ direct from the solar disk," but they betray their gifts by "brooding" and rejecting the hands proferred them.

In "The Queen of Night Walks Her Thin Dog," the speaker uses poetry, the "singing" that recurs in Whitmanesque lines, to penetrate the various veils that would separate her from "houses," perhaps bodies, in the night. The poem itself may be the key in the locked door that is either an entrance or an exit—at the end of the poem, "Entrance./ Exit./ The lips" suggests a sexual and poetic act. In the third poem, "The Prince of Darkness Passing Through This House," the speaker refers to the "Queen of Night's running barking dog" and to "this house," but the Prince of Darkness and the Queen of Night are merged like elemental fire and water. Like a Metaphysical poet, Wakoski suggests that the universe can be coalesced into their bodies ("our earlobes and eyelids") as they hold "live coals/ of commitment,/ of purpose,/ of love." This positive image, however, is undercut by the final image, "the power of fish/ living in strange waters," which implies that such a union may be possible only in a different world.

The last poem in the volume, "A Poem for My 32nd Birthday," provides a capsule summary of the speaker's images, themes, and relationships. In the course of the poem she associates a mechanic with a Doberman that bites, and then she becomes, in her anger, the Doberman as she seeks revenge on a lover who makes her happy while he destroys her with possessive eyes that penetrate the "fences" she has erected. After mentioning her father and her relatives, who have achieved "sound measure/ of love" ("sound measure" suggests substance but also a prosaic doling out of love), she turns to her mother, who threatens her with a long rifle that becomes a fishing pole with hooks that ensnare her. The speaker reverts to her "doberman" behavior, and, though she persists in maintaining "distance," she uses her poems and songs to achieve acceptance: "I felt alive./ I was glad for my jade memories."

In _The Motorcycle Betrayal Poems_, betrayal, always a theme in Wakoski's poetry, becomes the central focus; the motorcycle mechanic represents all the men who have betrayed her. The tone is at times humorous, so much so that the poems may not be taken seriously enough, but there is also a sense of desperation. These poems explore the different roles and images available to define identity, and the roles are not gender-bound. The speaker, who expresses her condition in images of isolation and entrapment, is fascinated with aggressive male roles, embodied in the motorcyclist. While she wryly admits that she is the "pink dress," she at times would like to reverse the roles; she is also aware, however, that the male roles do not satisfy her needs, do not mesh with her sexual identity. In this collection her identity is again developed in terms of lunar imagery, this time with reference to Diana, associated with the moon and the huntress, here of the sexual variety, and with the desert: both are lifeless, and both reflect the sterility of her life. The speaker does suggest, through the water imagery that pervades her poems, that this condition is not permanent, that her life can be sustained, but only through a man's love. Ultimately, the speaker is plagued with another duality: she desires what has persistently destroyed her.

The same contradictory feelings about men are reflected in the title poem of _Smudging_, a collection of verse that includes King of Spain poems, prose poems, two parts of _Greed_, and miscellaneous poems touching on recurrent themes, motifs, and myths. "Smudging," another of Wakoski's favorite poems, encapsulates many of the themes as it probes the divided self. There are two "parts" of the speaker, the part that searches "for the warmth of the smudge pot" and the "part of me that takes your hand confidently." That is, the speaker both believes that she has the warmth and fears that she lacks it. Like her mother, she must fear the "husband who left her alone for the salty ocean" (with associations of sterility and isolation); yet she, like the orange she metaphorically becomes, transcends this fear through "visions" and the roles she plays in her head—these make her "the golden orange every prince will fight/ to own."

With Wakoski, transcendence seems always transitory; each poem must solve a problem, often the same one, so that the speaker is often on a tightrope, performing a balancing act between fear and fulfillment. As the poem moves to its solution, the speaker continues to waver, as is the case in "Smudging." At the beginning of the poem, the speaker revels in warmth and luxuriance; she refers to amber, honey, music, and gold as she equates gold with "your house," perhaps also her lover's body, and affirms her love for him. Even before the change signaled by "but" occurs in the next line, she tempers the image: "the honeysuckle of an island" is not their world but "in my head," and the repetition of "your" rather than "our" suggests the nagging doubts that lead to memories of her childhood in Orange County. The fear of the laborers outside the house, the memory of the absentee father—she has left these behind as she finds love and warmth with her mechanic lover, whose warmth is suspect, however, because he "threw me out once/ for a whole year." Mechanically expert, he does not understand or appreciate her "running parts" and remains, despite their reunion, "the voices in those dark nights" of her childhood. She, on the other hand, has become the "hot metal," "the golden orange" that exists independently of him.

Dancing on the Grave of a Son of a Bitch is a bit of a departure from Wakoski's earlier poetry, although it is consistent in mythology and themes with the rest of her work. The title poem, dedicated to her motorcycle betrayer, the mechanic of "Smudging," reiterates past injustices and betrayals, but the speaker is more assured than vengeful. Despite the opening curse, "God damn it," and her acknowledgment that his leaving made her "as miserable/ as an earthworm with no earth," she not only has "crawled out of the ground," resurrecting herself, but also has learned to "sing new songs," to write new poems. She denies that hers is an angry statement, affirming instead that it is joyful, and her tone at the end of the poem is playful as she evokes the country singer's "for every time/ you done me wrong."

There is similar progression in the "Astronomer Poems" of the volume. As in earlier poems, she uses the moon/sun dichotomy, but there is more acceptance, assurance, and assertiveness as she explores these myths. In "Sun Gods Have Sun Spots," she not only suggests male-sun blemishes but also affirms her own divinity in a clever role reversal: "I am/ also a ruler of the sun." While "the sun has an angry face," the speaker in "The Mirror of a Day Chiming Marigold" still yearns for the poet or astronomer to study "my moon." Wakoski thus at least tentatively resolves two earlier themes, but she continues to develop the King of Spain figure, to refer to the "rings of Saturn," to include some Buddha poems and some prose fables, and to use chants as a means of conveying meaning and music. In her introduction to the book, she explains that she wishes readers to read the poems aloud, being "cognizant" of the chanted parts. Since Wakoski is a performing poet, the notion of chants, developed by Jerome Rothenberg, was almost inevitable, considering her interest in the piano (another theme for future development) and music. In fact, Wakoski uses chants, as in "Chants/Chance," to allow for different speakers within the poem.

Virtuoso Literature for Two and Four Hands, a relatively slender volume of poetry, not only alludes to Wakoski's fifteen years of piano study but also plays upon the keyboard-typewriter analogy to explore past relationships and her visionary life. Two of Wakoski's favorite poems, "The Story of Richard Maxfield" and "Driving Gloves," which are included in this volume, involve people she resembles, one a dead composer and artist and one a Greek scholar with a failed father, but the poems conclude with affirmations about the future. It is not Maxfield's suicide that disturbs the speaker; she is concerned with his "falling apart," the antithesis of his "well-organized" composing. The poem, despite the repetition of "fall apart," ends with her certainty "that just as I would never fall apart,/ I would also never jump out of a window." In the other poem, the speaker begins with familiar lamentations about her sad childhood and turns to genes and the idea of repeating a parent's failures. Noting that she, like her mother, wears driving gloves, she is terrified that she will be like her boring, unimaginative mother; Anne, like her unpublished novelist/ father, is a bad driver. Despite Anne's belief that "we're all like some parent/ or ancestor," the speaker tells Anne that "you learned to drive because you are not your father" and states that she wears gloves "because I like to wear them." Asserting that their lives are their own, she dismisses the past as "only something/ we have all lived/ through." This attitude seems a marked departure from earlier poems in which her life and behavior are attributed to her father's influence.

While *Waiting for the King of Spain* features staple Wakoski figures (George Washington, the motorcycle mechanic, the King of Spain), lunar imagery (one section consists of fifteen poems about an unseen lunar eclipse, and one is titled "Daughter Moon"), and the use of chants and prose poems, it also includes a number of short poems—a startling departure for Wakoski, who has often stated a preference for long narrative poems. As a whole, the poems continue the affirmative mood of *Virtuoso Literature for Two and Four Hands*. The King of Spain, the idealized lover who loves her "as you do not./ And as no man ever has," appears and reappears, the wearer of the "cap of darkness" (the title of a later collection), in stark contrast to the betrayers and the George Washington persona. Here, too, there is less emphasis on the masculine—sun imagery, though it appears, and more of a celebration of the moon imagery.

The two poems in the collection that Wakoski considers most illustrative of her critical principles are warm, accepting, flippant, and amusing. In "Ode to a Lebanese Crock of Olives" the speaker again refers to the body she regards as physically unattractive, but she accepts her "failed beach girl" status and stacks the deck metaphorically in favor of abundance ("the richness of burgundy,/ dark brown gravies") over the bland ("their tan fashionable body"). In fact, the "fashionable" (always a negative word for Wakoski) body provides the point of contrast to affirm Wakoski's own beauty: "Beauty is everywhere/ in contrasts and unities." This condemnation of thinness is extended to art and poetry in "To the Thin and Elegant Woman Who Resides Inside of Alix Nelson." For Wakoski, fullness is all: "Now is the time to love flesh." Renouncing the Weight Watchers and *Vogue* models of life and poetry, she argues for the unfettered fullness of "American drama" and the "substantial narrative." Wakoski declares, "My body is full of the juice of poetry," and concludes the poem with an amusing parody of the Lord's Prayer, ending with "Ah, men" (surely the source of the false doctrine of beauty).

The Man Who Shook Hands represents a point of departure for Wakoski, who seems in this volume to return to the anger, hostility, and bitterness of her earlier poems. The feelings of betrayal, here embodied in the figure of a man who merely shakes hands the morning after a one-night relationship, resurface as the speaker's quest for love is again unsuccessful. The speaker in "Running Men" is left with the "lesson" the departing lover "so gently taught in your kind final gesture,/ that stiff embrace." The sarcasm in "gently" and "kind" is not redeemed by her concluding statement that she lives "in her head" and that the only perfect bodies are in museums and in art. This realization prepares the reader for the last line of the volume: "How I hate my destiny."

Although the complete *Greed*, all thirteen parts, was published in 1984, parts of it were printed as early as 1968, and Wakoski has often included the parts in other collections of her poetry. It is bound by a single theme, even if greed is defined in such general terms that it can encompass almost everything. It is the failure to choose, the unwillingness to "give up one thing/ for another." Because the early parts were often published with other poems, they tend to reflect the same themes—concerns with parents, lovers, poetry—and to be written in a similar style. Of particular interest, however, given Wakoski's preference for narrative, is part 12, "The Greed to Be Fulfilled," which tends to be dramatic in form. What begins as a conversation between the speaker and George becomes a masque, "The Moon Loses Her Shoes," in which the actors are the stock figures of Wakoski mythology. The resolution of the poem for the speaker is the movement from emotional concerns to intellectual ones, a movement reflected in the poetry-music analogy developed in part 13.

. Wakoski's other later poetry suggests that she is reworking older themes while she incorporates new ones, which also relate to her own life. In *Cap of Darkness* and *The Magician's Feastletters* she explores the problem of aging in a culture that worships youth and consumption; this concern is consistent with the themes of *Virtuoso Literature for Two and Four Hands.* The later *Rings of Saturn*, with the symbolic piano and ring, and *Medea the Sorceress*, with its focus on mythology and woman as poet-visionary, reflect earlier poetry, but also reflect the changing emphasis, the movement from emotion to intellect, while it retains the subjectivity, as well as the desire for fulfillment, beauty, and truth, that characterizes the entire body of her work. Though often compared to Sylvia Plath, a comparison she destroys in part 9 of *Greed*, and often seen as squarely in the feminist mainstream, Diane Wakoski remains a unique and intensely personal voice in American poetry.

Thomas L. Erskine

Other major work
NONFICTION: *Towards a New Poetry*, 1979.

Bibliography

Gannon, Catherine, and Clayton Lein. "Diane Wakoski and the Language of Self." *San Jose Studies* 5 (Spring, 1979): 84-98. Focusing on *The Motorcycle Betrayal Poems*, Gannon and Lein discuss the betrayal motif in terms of the speaker's struggle for identity. In the poems the speaker uses the moon image to consider possible alternative images for herself, and in the last poem of the book she achieves a "richer comprehension of her being."

Lauter, Estella. *Women as Mythmakers: Poetry and Visual Art by Twentieth-century Women.* Bloomington: Indiana University Press, 1984. Lauter devotes one chapter to Wakoski's handling of moon imagery in several of the poet's books. Though she sometimes uses conventional woman-moon and man-sun associations, Wakoski reverses the stereotypes as she explores male-female relationships. There is also a related discussion of Isis and Diana as aspects of the speaker's personality.

Martin, Taffy Wynne. "Diane Wakoski's Personal Mythology: Dionysian Music, Created Presence." *Boundary 2: A Journal of Postmodern Literature* 10 (Fall, 1982): 155-172. According to Martin, Wakoski's sense of absence and lost love prompts desire, which in turn animates the poetry, giving it life. Martin also discusses Wakoski's mythmaking, her use of digression as structural device, and her use of musical repetition.

Ostriker, Alicia Luskin. *Stealing the Language: The Emergence of Women's Poetry in America.* Boston: Beacon Press, 1986. An outstanding history of women's poetry, Ostriker's book includes extended readings of some of Wakoski's works, especially *The George Washington Poems.* For the most part, Ostriker focuses on the divided self (the all-nothing and the strong-weak) in Wakoski's poetry and discusses the ways in which the poet's masks and disguises become flesh. There is an extensive bibliography concerning women's poetry.

Wakoski, Diane. Interview by Taffy Wynne Martin. *Dalhousie Review* 61 (Autumn, 1981): 476-496. In an excellent interview, Martin elicits detailed answers from Wakoski about a wide range of topics: part 10 of *Greed,* her relationships with her parents, the literary influences on her poetry, and her responses to many New American poets. Of particular interest is Wakoski's discussion of how memory functions as narrative and how it can structure a poem.

_____. "A Terrible War." Interview edited by Philip L. Gerber and Robert J. Gemmett. *The Far Point* 4 (1970): 44-55. In a conversation with members of the English faculty at the State University of New York at Brockport, Wakoski identifies the "terrible war" as the opposing public demands for an inspired genius who also must work in a Puritan culture. Wakoski also discusses "confessional poetry," her special imagery and its relationship to metaphor, and the theme of communication in her work.

_____. *Towards a New Poetry.* Ann Arbor: University of Michigan Press, 1980. The book includes not only Wakoski's criticism, much of which is commentary on her own poetry, but also five revealing interviews, only two of which had previously been published in major journals. In the introduction, Wakoski lists her "best" poems, the ones she believes illustrate her personal mythology, her use of image and digression, and the kind of music she thinks is important to contemporary poetry.

DEREK WALCOTT

Born: Castries, St. Lucia, West Indies; January 23, 1930

Principal poetry

Twenty-five Poems, 1948; *Poems,* 1951; *In a Green Night: Poems, 1948-1960,* 1962; *Selected Poems,* 1964; *The Castaway and Other Poems,* 1965; *The Gulf and Other Poems,* 1969; *Another Life,* 1973; *Sea Grapes,* 1976; *The Star-Apple Kingdom,* 1979; *The Fortunate Traveller,* 1981; *Midsummer,* 1984; *Collected Poems, 1948-1984,* 1986; *The Arkansas Testament,* 1987; *Omeros,* 1990.

Other literary forms

Derek Walcott has written several plays, published in *Dream on Monkey Mountain and Other Plays* (1970), *The Joker of Seville and O Babylon!: Two Plays* (1978), *Remembrance and Pantomime: Two Plays,* (1980), and *Three Plays* (1986).

Achievements

Walcott's work is infused with both a sacred sense of the writer's vocation and a passionate devotion to his island of birth, St. Lucia, and the entire Caribbean archipelago. A cultural dichotomy supplies the major tensions in his writing: he combines native French Creole and West Indian dialects with the formal, high structures of English poetry. His mystic sense of place and eruptive imagination are poised against a highly controlled metrical form. As a lyrical and epic poet he has managed to encompass history, culture, and autobiography with an intensely aesthetic and steadily ironic vision. Walcott is arguably a major poet in his ability to dramatize the myths of his social and personal life, to balance his urgent moral concerns with the ideal of a highly polished, powerfully dense art, and to cope with the cultural isolation to which his mixed blood sadly condemns him.

The Dream of Monkey Mountain, his most highly lauded play, won the 1971 Obie Award. He received the *Los Angeles Times Book Review* poetry prize in 1986 for *Collected Poems.* In 1972 the University of the West Indies awarded him an honorary doctorate of letters.

Biography

Derek Alton Walcott was born in Castries, the capital of St. Lucia, to a civil servant, Warwick, and a mother, Alix, who headed a Methodist grammar school. St. Lucia is a volcanic island of 238 square miles in the Lesser Antilles, halfway between French Martinique to the north and English St. Vincent to the southeast. It was discovered by Christopher Columbus in 1502, then contested for generations by the French and British, until the latter gained legal control in 1803, to yield their colonial hold only in 1959. Yet the Gallic influence remains, insofar as the population of about 100,000, largely of black African descent, speaks a Creole patois.

Since Walcott is descended from a white grandfather and black grandmother on both sides of his family, he has found himself ineluctably suspended between loyalties, resentments, fears, and fantasies. He has referred in essays to a schizophrenic boyhood, split between two lives: the interior pull toward poetry and the exterior push toward the world of action, as well as the raw spontaneity of his native argot opposed to the syntactical sinews of formal English. Inescapably, he has been both victim and victor of his divided culture, a kind of Caribbean Orestes who shuttles between the legends and folklore of his upbringing and the formal traditions of the cosmopolitan West. In his work Walcott has made much of the bridging geography of the West Indies, since they link Columbus and Crusoe, Africa and America, slavery and colonialism, exploitation and emancipation. Curiously, he even compartmentalizes his writing, stressing oral tales and folk language in his plays while suffusing most of his poems with an Elizabethan richness and Miltonic dignity of diction.

In *Another Life* Walcott has rendered an autobiographical narrative of his childhood and early career. This long narrative poem unfolds the evolution of a poet who will always consider himself "the divided child." At school he was taught European art, history, and literature, but his mother insisted on connecting him to the Africa-based culture of the black St. Lucian majority. A landscape painter and teacher, Harry Simmons, and a drawing and drinking friend, Dunstan St. Omer, sought to fashion him in their images. Walcott discovered, however, that "I lived in a different gift,/ its element metaphor" and abandoned the canvas for the printed page.

In part 3, "A Simple Flame," he falls in love with Anna, but her golden body cannot long compete with his passion for poetry,

> which hoped that their two bodies could be made
> one body of immortal metaphor.
> The hand she held already had betrayed
> them by its longing for describing her.

He mythicizes his Anna, dissolving her into all the literary Annas he has adored: Eugene O'Neill's Anna Christie, Leo Tolstoy's Anna Karenina, and the great modern Russian poet Anna Akhmatova. He leaves for study abroad.

In part 4, "The Estranging Sea," he returns home, "one life, one marriage later" (to Fay Moston, from 1954 to 1959). He encounters Dunstan, called "Gregorias," and finds him alcoholic, unable to hold a job, painting poorly, failing even at suicide. He learns that Harry Simmons *has* killed himself, with his body lying undiscovered for two days. Walcott then scathingly denounces ill-wishers who condemn their promising artists to an early grave.

He finds comfort and hope in the sea, wishes a peaceful rest to his friends and loves, and dedicates himself to literature, his fury spent:

> for what else is there
> but books, books and the sea,
> verandahs and the pages of the sea,
> to write of the wind and the memory of wind-whipped hair
> in the sun, the colour of fire?

Walcott made his debut as a writer in 1948, with *Twenty-Five Poems*, privately printed at Barbados with a two-hundred-dollar loan from his mother and hawked by the author through the streets of Castries. In 1951 he released his second collection, *Poems*, while studying at the Mona campus of the University of the West Indies. During the 1950's he taught at secondary schools and colleges in St. Lucia, Grenada, and Jamaica. In 1958 he moved to Trinidad and there founded, in 1959, the Trinidad Theatre Workshop, with which he remained associated as both playwright and director until 1976, seeking to blend Shakespearean drama and calypso music, Bertolt Brecht's stage craft with West Indian folk legends. Crucial in his development as a dramatist were several months he spent in New York City in 1958, studying under José Quintero on a Rockefeller grant, learning how to incorporate songs and dances into a dramatic text.

For many years Walcott has divided his time between a home in Trinidad and teaching positions in the United States, including visiting professorships at Columbia, Harvard, and Boston universities. His career has been both prolific and versatile, not only as poet and playwright but also as producer, set designer, painter, critic, and cultural commentator. He is married, for the third time, to Norline Metivier, and has one son from his first marriage and two daughters from his second.

Analysis

Derek Walcott's first important volume of verse, *In a Green Night: Poems, 1948-1960*, was a landmark in the history of West Indian poetry, breaking with exotic native traditions of shallow romanticism and inflated rhetorical abstractions. In such entries as "A Far Cry from Africa," "Ruins of a Great House," and "Two Poems on the Passing of an Empire," he began to confront the complex personal fate that would dominate all of his work—his identity as a transplanted African in an English-organized society. In "A Far Cry from Africa" he concludes,

> I who am poisoned with the blood of both,
> Where shall I turn, divided to the vein?
> I who have cursed
> The drunken officer of British rule, how choose
> Between this Africa and the English tongue I love?

Betray them both, or give back what they give?
How can I face such slaughter and be cool?
How can I turn from Africa and live?

Using the English tongue he loves does not preclude Walcott's outrage at the degradation to which the British Empire has subjected his people, "the abuse/ of ignorance by Bible and by sword." He calls "Hawkins, Walter Raleigh, Drake,/ Ancestral murderers and poets." Yet this rage-filled poem ends on a note of compassion, as the speaker recalls that England was also once an exploited colony subject to "bitter faction." The heart dictates anger, but the intelligence controls and mellows feelings, perceiving the complexity of human experience.

In the initial poem, "Prelude," the young poet looks down on his island and sees it beaten into proneness by indifferent tourists who regard it as insignificant. Yet he knows that his poetry is a means of transcending his land's triviality "in accurate iambics." He thus sets the stage and plot for his personal odyssey as an artist, which he would undertake over and over again in his career. With the duplicity of a guerrilla and the self-conscious stance of T. S. Eliot's J. Alfred Prufrock, he plans to "straighten my tie and fix important jaws,/ And note the living images/ Of flesh that saunter through the eye."

In the poem's concluding stanza, the speaker states that he is "in the middle of the journey through my life," as Dante was at the opening of his *Inferno* (c. 1320). He encounters the same animal as the Florentine poet—a leopard, symbolizing self-indulgence. Walcott thus merges his identity as an islander with his mission as a poet, his private self becoming a public metaphor for art's affirmation.

In "Origins" he composes a creation myth of his native place, finding in the cosmogonic conditions of his landscape a protean identity as an individual and an epic consciousness of his culture, akin to that of Walt Whitman and Pablo Neruda. The sonic boom of the first two lines—"The flowering breaker detonates its surf./ White bees hiss in the coral skull"—is reminiscent of the acoustical flamboyance present in such Hart Crane poems as "Voyages" and "O Carib Isle." The warm Caribbean waters become an amniotic bath for the poet, who sees himself as "an infant Moses" envisioning "Paradise as columns of lilies and wheat-headed angels." In sections 3 and 4 of his long poem Walcott pays homage to his island's language, laying out undulating strings of images in the manner of Aimé Césaire, another West Indian poet and dramatist, with the roll of surrealistic phrases imitating the roll of the surf.

In a Green Night exhibits Walcott's remarkable formal virtuosities. He can compose rhyming quatrains of iambic tetrameter, as in the title poem, or a traditional sonnet sequence, such as in "Tales of the Islands," that combines subtle metrical music with exuberant energy. He can chant like Dylan Thomas ("A City's Death by Fire"), be as astringent as W. H. Auden ("A Country

Club Romance"), or indulge in Creole language ("Parang"). Like Andrew
Marvell, whose Metaphysical poetry was an influential model for the early
Walcott, he is caught between the pull of passion and his awareness of its
futility.

In *The Castaway and Other Poems* Walcott's focus on the artist's role becomes more overt, as he describes the poet as the archetypal artist-in-exile,
thus a castaway, symbolizing also West Indians in general as historical discard from other cultures. He perceives the poet, paradoxically, as both the
detached observer of society and its centrally located, living emblem. Walcott adopts the protean Robinson Crusoe image for this purpose, dramatizing
him as Adam, Columbus, Daniel Defoe, even God, as the first inhabitant of
a second Paradise, as discoverer and ruler of the world he has made. He insists on a complex relationship between the creative, exploring artist and a
largely imperceptive community that tends to isolate and ignore him, yet that
the poet nonetheless persists in representing. Sometimes he finds art inadequate in trying to order inchoate life, as in "Crusoe's Island":

> Art is profane and pagan,
> The most it has revealed
> Is what a crippled Vulcan
> Beat on Achilles' shield.

The next collection, *The Gulf and Other Poems*, deepens the theme of isolation, with the poet extending his sense of alienation to the world of the
1960's: John Kennedy's and Che Guevara's killings ("The Gulf" and "Che"),
racial violence in the United States ("Blues"), the Vietnam War ("Postcards"),
the civil war in Nigeria ("Negatives"). The gulf, then, is everywhere, with
divisions mocking people's best efforts at unity, intimacy, order, harmony,
happiness. Despite his disappointments, Walcott employs the gulf image am-
bivalently. To be sure, it encompasses the moral wasteland that the world has
largely become; more optimistically, however, it stands for a healing awareness of separateness whereby the castaway, Crusoe-like artist understands his
identity and place in the world. In the last analysis, Walcott insists, it is the
poet's art that endures: "some mind must squat down howling in your dust,/
some hand must crawl and recollect your rubbish,/ someone must write your
poems." The poet's apartness does not, then, result in his total alienation—
he still commits his art to the world's experiences.

In *Another Life*, Walcott avoids self-centered egotism as he mythologizes
his island life, reimagining the *Iliad* (c. 800 B.C.) in the context of his own
land and culture and using the odyssey motif to sustain this long poem. He
even envisages his islanders as Homeric archetypes (Ajax, Cassandra, Helen,
and others), engaged in an intense quest for their national identity. The poet's
journey becomes a microcosm of the West Indian's, indeed the New World's,
search for wholeness, acceptance, and fulfillment. As the young Derek Walcott is taught by Gregorias, the peasant-painter-pal, he develops his talent—

though for letters rather than the visual arts—within the context of an artistic tradition that articulates the dreams and needs of his people. He ends the superbly sustained narrative by celebrating both the painter's and the poet's mission:

> Gregorias, listen, lit,
> we were the light of the world!
> We were blest with a virginal, unpainted world
> with Adam's task of giving things their names.

Sea Grapes is a quieter, more austere book than *Another Life*, a calm after the storm, with many of its poems elegiac, elegant, sparely constructed, sad. The prevailing mood of the volume is one of middle-aged acceptance, maturation, and resignation: "why does my gift already look over its shoulder/ for a shadow to fill the door/ and pass this very page into eclipse?" ("Preparing for Exile"). Again, Walcott rehearses the tensions of his divided heritage as a West Indian trying to accommodate his African instincts to the formalities and calculations of European modes. In the title poem he equates himself to the sea-wandering Odysseus, longing for Nausicaa while duty-bound for his home and family, torn between obsession and responsibility, and poignantly concludes, "The classics can console. But not enough." A five-part, long work, "Sainte Lucie," is a psalm to St. Lucia, mixing French Creole with English, vernacular speech with stately diction.

The Star-Apple Kingdom is a lyrical celebration, studded with vivid images. Its most ambitious poem, "The Schooner Flight," features a seaman-poet, Shabine, a fleeing castaway from his island; Shabine is clearly a Walcott double, with "Dutch, nigger and English" in him, so that "either I'm nobody, or I'm a nation." Shabine's ordeal is the allegory of Everyman. He loves his wife and children but also desires the beautiful Maria Concepcion. Like Odysseus, he encounters terrors and defeats them; unlike Odysseus, he often runs away from his duties rather than toward them. He does manage to escape a web of corruption and betrayal, however, and matures into a waterfront Isaiah whose vision embraces his people's history, learning to appreciate nature's simplicities, "satisfied/ if my hand gave voice to one people's grief."

The protagonist of "The Star-Apple Kingdom" is more sophisticated, satirical, and astute than Shabine, with his reflections more acerbic and cerebral. The poem begins as he peruses a photograph album dating from the Victorian era, featuring such subjects as "Herefords at Sunset in the Valley of the Wye." Then he ponders the miseries of blacks excluded from the joys of the plantation aristocracy, "their mouths in the locked jaw of a silent scream." A dream possesses him. In it he plunges into a nightmare procession of Caribbean injustices, both during and after the rule of colonialism. Awakening at dawn, he feels rejuvenated and serene. His eye falls on an elderly, black cleaning woman who now represents to him his people's strength and endurance, with a "creak of light" evoking the possibility of a better future for both her and them.

In *The Fortunate Traveller* Walcott largely removes his pulsating sensibility from his home turf, focusing on New England, Manhattan, the American South, Chicago, London, Wales, and Greece. In "Old New England" he apprentices himself to the American vernacular, sounding somewhat like Robert Lowell in such statements as "Old Glories flail/ the crosses of green farm boys back from 'Nam." Yet no one can successfully assume a new idiom overnight, and Walcott's pentameters usually retain their British, Yeatsian cadences:

> The crest of our conviction grows as loud
> as the spring oaks, rooted and reassured
> that God is meek but keeps a whistling sword.

Some of Walcott's many virtues are evident in this collection: He is deeply intelligent, keeps enlarging his range of styles and reach of subjects, has a fertile imagination, and often commands precise, sonorous eloquence. In "Hurucan" he compellingly summons the god of hurricanes, "havoc, reminder, ancestor," who stands allegorically for the world's oppressors. In "The Hotel Normandie Pool," he masters both his social topic and personal memories. At the pool Walcott imagines a fellow exile, Ovid, banished from Rome to a Black Sea port, facing the rigors of a harsher climate yet continuing to compose his verses, epitomizing the predicament of an educated colonial poet writing in the language of an empire.

The book's best poem is its last, "The Season of Phantasmal Peace." It begins at twilight, as migrating birds lift up the net of the shadows of the earth, causing a "passage of phantasmal light/ that not the narrowest shadow dared to sever." These singers unify the earth's various dialects and feel "something brighter than pity" for creatures that remain below, wingless, in their dark holes and houses. The birds close the poem by undertaking an act of brief charity, lifting their net above betrayals, follies, and furies. The poem thereby lifts whatever darkness exists for an instant of peace, constituting a transcendent surge of song beyond the implied darkness of the world's wars and hatreds.

Midsummer is a gathering of fifty-four poems, a number that corresponded to Walcott's age when the book was published. These lyric poems give the sense of their author noting his preoccupations during the course of a year. He equates midsummer with boredom, stasis, middle age, midcareer, and the harsh glare of self-examination, as he tries to fix the particular tone and texture of his inner life from one summer to the next. He turns ethnographer, chronicling hotel and motel life in Rome, Warwickshire, New York, Boston, and Chicago. Two-thirds of the sequence is set, however, in the tropics of

Central America and his Caribbean islands.

As always, Walcott is nowhere comfortably at home. In the West Indies, he sees that "our houses are one step from the gutter," with "the doors themselves usually no wider than coffins." Once more, he plays Odysseus-in-exile: "And this is the lot of all wanderers, this is their fate,/ that the more they wander, the more the world grows wide." Writing to a friend in Rome, he contrasts its ancient heritage with the Caribbean area's sand-weighted corals, its catacombs with "silver legions of mackerel." In Boston, he mocks the stale air of cobblestoned streets and Transcendentalist tradition, feeling self-consciously black amid New England's white spires, harbors, and filling stations, with pedestrians, moving like "pale fishes," staring at him as though he were a "black porpoise."

Unable to resolve his dilemma of perpetual uprooting, Walcott is graceful enough to parody his wanderings among cultures and his position as a prodigal son who cannot arrive at any home or rest. In "LI" he tells himself, half-mockingly, "You were distressed by your habitat, you shall not find peace/ till you and your origins reconcile; your jaw must droop/ and your knuckles scrape the ground of your native place."

In poem 27, Walcott sardonically describes the American impact on the West Indies, such as a chain-link fence separating a beach from a baseball field. "White, eager Cessnas" dot an airstrip in St. Thomas; fences separate villas and their beaches from illegal immigrants; "bulldozers jerk/ and gouge out a hill, but we all know that the dust/ is industrial and must be suffered." Even a pelican "coasts, with its engine off." No wonder that he feels "the fealty changing under my foot."

In 1986 Walcott's American publisher issued his *Collected Poems, 1948-1984*, a massive 516-page tome that included selections from all of his previous books and the entirety of *Another Life*. Critical reception was largely laudatory, particularly welcoming Walcott's lyrical gifts, the extraordinary variety of his styles and settings, the sensuous eloquence and freshness of his language, the intensity of his tone, and his talent for uniting power with delicacy. Some reviewers, however, complained of inflated rhetoric, a penchant for grandiose clichés, diction that is overly ornamental, and a tendency to propagandize at the expense of authentic feeling.

Walcott resumes his doomed search for a homeland in *The Arkansas Testament*. In the work's first section, "Here," he again inspects the society of his native island but finds only incomplete connections, fragmented friendships. In the moving "The Light of the World," set in a minibus in St. Lucia, the speaker segues from social intimacy to abandonment. He leaves the vehicle, concluding, "They went on in their transport, they left me on earth./ . . . / There was nothing they wanted, nothing I could give them but this thing I have called 'The Light of the World.'" The "light" is Walcott's talent for writing—to which his fellow passengers are largely oblivious.

In the "Elsewhere" section, the poet searches for fulfillment in other countries, praying "that the City may be just/ and humankind be kind." In the title poem, consisting of twenty-four segments of sixteen lines each, the speaker wanders from a motel in Fayetteville, Arkansas, to an all-night cafeteria, then returns to his motel, noting the exploitation of black Americans and calling the American flag "the stripes and the scars." His conclusion is, as usual with Walcott, bleak: "Bless . . . / these stains I cannot remove/ from the self-soiled heart."

Images of dislocation and disharmony pervade the book, inducing a melancholy mood. Walcott refers to the Sphinx, to sirens and satyrs—all of them half-human, half-animal. Doors are unhinged, telephone calls are unanswered, poetry goes unread; justice and mercy are usually unmet. *The Arkansas Testament* is a musical chant mourning the world's many woes.

Omeros is a colossal modern epic, Walcott's most ambitious achievement, which universalizes his persistent themes of displacement, isolation, exploitation, estrangement, exile, and self-division. He merges the island chain of his Caribbean with the Mediterranean island chain now called Greece, where the *Iliad* and *Odyssey* (c. 800 B.C.) are conventionally attributed to an Achaean bard, Homer, whose name is "Omeros" in modern Greek form. Omeros/ Homer makes several appearances in the poem, most frequently as Seven Seas, a poor, blind fisherman, but also as an African tribal singer and as a London bargeman, thus helping to internationalize this narrative of more than eight thousand lines.

The links between the ancient Greeks and modern Antilleans are plausible enough: Both societies were and are seafaring, and both inhabit islands rife with legends, ghosts, and natural spirits. Walcott takes an audacious gamble when he assumes that the Caribbean patois, with its linguistic uncertainties, is capable of occasionally declaiming in classically patterned verse; he uses three-line stanzas in a salute to Dante's *terza rima*. He safeguards his venture, however, by minimizing the Creole argot and having most of the action related by a patently autobiographical, polished narrator: a displaced poet living in Boston and Toronto, visiting the Great Plains and the sites of American Civil War battles and encountering Omeros in both London and St. Lucia.

Walcott likens his squabbling, scrounging fishermen to the ancient Greeks and Trojans, and projects Homeric counterparts in his modern Caribbean Helen, Achille, Hector, Circe, and Philoctete. Helen works as a housemaid in the home of Major and Mrs. Plunkett. As in Greek mythology, she is beautiful, proud, lazy, shallow, selfish, and magnetically irresistible to men. When she is fired by Mrs. Plunkett, she goes to work (occasionally) as a waitress, exciting the libidos of two fishermen friends, Hector and Achille. Walcott likens her to Judith and Susannah, Circe and Calypso, with her body creating a stirring drama out of every appearance.

Walcott's Hector differs drastically from Homer's, who had an ideal marriage to Andromache and was the Trojans' indispensable hero. This Hector abandons, at Helen's behest, his dignified but poorly paying work as a fisherman for the degrading but more lucrative job of taxiing tourists, hustling passengers at the wharf and airport. Paralleling Homer, Achille kills Hector in a fight over Helen, she settles down with him, and they will be parents to her expected child, sired by Hector.

The poem's focus expands further as it deals with Major Plunkett. At first he seems a stereotypical British colonial, with his "pensioned moustache" and Guinness-drinking taste. Walcott associates him, however, with not only the end of the Empire but also Montgomery's World War II victories in the Middle Eastern desert, and further with American Caucasian settlers displacing the Indians. Undertaking genealogical research, the major discovers an ancestor who took part in the victory of the British Navy's Admiral George Brydges Rodney over Admiral François-Joseph-Paul de Grasse's French fleet, acquiring St. Lucia as part of the British West Indies.

Then there is Philoctete, a fisherman disabled by a festering sore on his thigh. The link with the Greek myth is evident. Philoctetes, listed as one of the Greek Helen's many suitors, wanted to lead a flotilla of seven ships against Troy, but never reached it. Bitten on the foot by a snake on the island of Lemnos, he was ostracized by the other Achaean chieftains because the stench of his infected, rotting flesh nauseated them. Walcott's Philoctete is wounded by a rusty anchor and is also abandoned by his fellows while Achille undertakes a journey to Africa.

In the end, Philoctete is cured by a native healer and rejoins the island's fishing community. Yet the only cure Walcott offers is the palliative of his poem: "Like Philoctete's wound, this language carries its cure,/ its radiant affliction." *Omeros* holds much woe and desolation in its complex web, but Derek Walcott's epic is a magnificent feat of cultural interweaving.

Gerhard Brand

Other major works

PLAYS: *Dream on Monkey Mountain and Other Plays*, 1970; *The Joker of Seville and O Babylon!: Two Plays*, 1978; *Remembrance and Pantomime: Two Plays*, 1980; *Three Plays*, 1986.

Bibliography

Balakian, Peter. "The Poetry of Derek Walcott." *Poetry* 148 (June, 1986): 169-177. This sensitive, eloquently written article surveys Walcott's work from his earliest text through *Collected Poems, 1948-1984.* Balakian firmly declares Walcott a major modern poet, ranking him with William Butler Yeats, Rainer Maria Rilke, and Pablo Neruda.

Brown, Lloyd W. "The Personal Odyssey of Derek Walcott." In *West Indian Poetry*. Boston: Twayne, 1978. Brown studies the evolution of Walcott's career in four major collections: *In a Green Night, The Castaway and Other Poems, The Gulf and Other Poems,* and *Another Life*. A sensitive and learned analysis.

Dove, Rita. "Either I'm Nobody, Or I'm a Nation." *Parnassus: Poetry in Review* 14, no. 1 (1987): 49-76. Dove appraises Walcott's career from his earliest poems through *Collected Poems, 1948-1984,* with particularly illuminating interpretations of *Another Life* and *The Star-Apple Kingdom*. She concentrates on the poet's metrics and imagery, stressing his imaginative sea symbolism.

Hamner, Robert D. *Derek Walcott*. Boston: Twayne, 1981. Hamner conducts a thorough exploration of Walcott's plays, poems, and critical articles, ending with *The Star-Apple Kingdom*. His approach is extremely cautious: he will usually cite another author's analysis rather than risking his own. The text is supplemented by a selected bibliography of both primary and secondary sources and an index. Hamner does not annotate his secondary references.

Morris, Mervyn. "Derek Walcott." In *West Indian Literature*, edited by Bruce King. Hamden, Conn.: Archon Books, 1979. This incisive and succinctly worded chapter considers *Another Life, The Castaway and Other Poems, The Gulf and Other Poems,* and *Sea Grapes*. Morris makes a number of astute observations, but since he also deals with Walcott's early plays, considerations of space preclude extended analyses of the poetry collections.

EDMUND WALLER

Born: Hertfordshire, England; March 3, 1606
Died: Hall Barn, England; October 21, 1687

Principal poetry
Poems, 1645, 1664, 1686, ‹1690, 1693; "A Panegyrick to my Lord Protector," 1655; "A Poem on St. James' Park as lately improved by His Majesty," 1661; "Instructions to a Painter," 1666; *Divine Poems*, 1685; *The Second Part of Mr. Waller's Poems*, 1690.

Other literary forms
In 1664, Edmund Waller collaborated with Charles Sackville, the Earl of Dorset, Sir Charles Sedley, and several other young wits in translating Pierre Corneille's play, *Pompée* (c. 1642). He also had a hand in a Restoration adaptation of Francis Beaumont and John Fletcher's play *The Maid's Tragedy* (1610-1611); the revisions were printed in the second 1690 edition of the *Poems*. Three of Waller's speeches before the Short and Long Parliaments are reprinted by Elijah Fenton in *The Works of Edmund Waller, Esq., in Verse and Prose* (1729); extracts from speeches made in the Restoration parliaments can be found in Anchitell Grey's ten-volume *Debates of the House of Commons, from the Year 1667 to the Year 1694* (1763). Waller's extensive correspondence, both personal and political, has not been collected in any one edition.

Achievements
Although his poems were circulating in manuscript form from the late 1620's, Waller garnered little critical attention until nearly twenty years later. The discovery of his plot against parliament in 1643 pushed him into the political limelight; the publication of his poems in 1645 in four separate editions is in part attributable to the desire of the booksellers to capitalize on his public notoriety. The innovations of Waller's poetry—his peculiar style of classical allusion and his perfection of the heroic couplet—were fully appreciated only with the Restoration. As Francis Atterbury remarked in his "Preface to the Second Part of Mr. Waller's *Poems*" (1690), Waller stands "first in the list of refiners" of verse and ushers in the "Augustan age" of English poetry. John Dryden's comment in the "Preface to Walsh's Dialogue concerning Women"—"Unless he had written, none of us could write"— pays full tribute to Waller's role in charting the public mode so essential to Restoration and eighteenth century poetry. The Augustans continued to laud Waller; as late as 1766, the *Biographica Britannica* described him as "the most celebrated Lyric Poet that ever England produced."

With the Romantic reaction against neoclassical taste, Waller's reputation plummeted. Critics condemned his poetry as vacuous and artificial; doubts about the probity of his actions during the Civil War reinforced the aesthetic judgments. Elizabeth Barrett Browning's dismissal of Waller in *The Greek Christian Poets and the English Poets* (1863)—"He is feeble poetically, quite as surely as morally and politically"—exemplifies how biographical considerations distorted the critical picture. Edmund Gosse, the most important nineteenth century critic of Waller, savaged his subject in *From Shakespeare to Pope* (1885). Although Gosse argued that Waller's role in the rise of neoclassicism was lamentable, he did at least recognize that Waller had played a crucial role in that movement.

Despite the resurgence of interest in seventeenth century poetry led by Sir Herbert Grierson and T. S. Eliot early in the twentieth century, Waller's reputation continued to languish until the 1960's. Since then, several book-length studies and articles have examined the precise character and extent of Waller's influence on Augustan verse. Although no "Waller Revival" seems to be in the offing, his position in the history of English poetry now appears fairly secure. Future studies will probably focus on Waller's relation to other Caroline writers, an aspect of his work that still remains for the most part neglected.

Waller was certainly not the inventor of the heroic couplet, but he played a critical part in gaining its acceptance as the preferred verse form for neoclassical poetry. His style of classical allusion, singular in the 1620's and 1630's, provided the model for English poets of the succeeding century. Waller's innovations, however, were more valuable for public, political poetry than for meditative or amatory verse; Gosse's complaint that his technique proved deadly to eighteenth century lyric is more than a little justified. Waller's glory and his bane lie in his position as one of the truly transitional figures in English literature. Because he straddles the Renaissance and the Restoration, critics have been hard put to decide where to place him. As recent studies suggest, however, this transitional position renders Waller's works all the more important. The current interest in periodization will continue to make Waller the focus of critical scrutiny.

Biography

Edmund Waller was born on March 3, 1606, into a wealthy landowning family. John Hampden, the future parliamentary leader, was a maternal first cousin; Oliver Cromwell was a more distant kinsman. The death of Robert Waller in 1616 left his ten-year-old son the heir to an estate worth £3,500 per annum. Anne Waller, the poet's mother, sent him to Eton, and from there he proceeded to Cambridge. In 1620, he was admitted a Fellow-Commoner of King's College, but appears to have left without taking a degree. Waller may have represented Agmondesham, Buckinghamshire, in the Parliament of 1621;

it is certain that he sat for Ilchester in the Parliament of 1624 at the age of eighteen.

In July, 1631, Waller married Anne Bankes, the wealthy heiress of a London mercer, against the wishes of her guardians. The Court of Aldermen, which had jurisdiction over the wardship of Mistress Bankes, instituted proceedings against Waller in Star Chamber; only the personal intervention of King Charles I appeased the Aldermen and they dropped their suit upon payment of a fine by the young bridegroom. Anne Waller died in October, 1634, after bearing a son and a daughter.

Waller had begun writing verses at a young age. What is generally supposed to be his earliest poem, "On the danger of His Majesty (being Prince) escaped in the road at St. Andrews," was composed sometime during the late 1620's. A series of occasional poems on Charles I and Henrietta Maria constituted the bulk of Waller's literary production during the late 1620's and early 1630's. With his good friend George Morley, later Bishop of Winchester, the poet joined the philosophic and literary circle that Lucius Carey, Viscount Falkland, gathered about him at Great Tew. During this period Waller also became an intimate of Algernon Percy, who succeeded to the Earldom of Northumberland in 1632, and his sisters Lucy Hay, the Countess of Carlisle, and Dorothy Sidney, Countess of Leicester. Sometime after the death of his wife, Waller commenced a prolonged poetic courtship of Lady Leicester's daughter Dorothy, whom he celebrated under the name of Sacharissa (from the Latin *sacharum*, "sugar"). Many, though by no means all, of Waller's best-known lyrics are addressed to Lady Dorothy. It is questionable whether the Sidneys ever took Waller seriously as a suitor; in any event, with the marriage in July, 1639, of Lady Dorothy to Lord Spencer of Wormleighton, later created Earl of Sunderland, the poet was disappointed in his hopes. Waller and Lady Sunderland were frequent correspondents for the remainder of their lives. An anecdote relates that the pair met at the house of Lady Woburn after both had attained old age. The widowed Lady Sunderland asked, presumably in jest, "When, Mr. Waller, I wonder, will you write such beautiful verses to me again?" "When, Madam," replied the poet, "your ladyship is as young and handsome again."

With the political upheavals of the early 1640's, Waller entered upon the most active phase of his public career. He sat in the Short Parliament of 1640 as the member for Agmondesham; he was returned to the Long Parliament, which convened in November, 1640, for St. Ives. Waller at first aligned himself with the constitutional moderates who resisted the abuses of the royal prerogative, but as the temper of parliament grew more radical he increasingly took the side of the king. Waller played a prominent role in the attack on ship-money, of which his cousin Hampden was the most prominent opponent; his speech condemning what he considered an unlawful tax was immensely popular and reportedly sold twenty thousand copies in one day. On the other hand, Waller attacked the proposals to abolish the episcopacy, arguing that such tinkering with fundamental institutions would lead to the abolition of private property and undermine the bases of English society. With the outbreak of the Civil War in August, 1642, Waller remained in the parliamentary stronghold of London, but soon became embroiled in a scheme to end the conflict by delivering the city to the king. "Waller's Plot" was discovered in May, 1643, and its leaders arrested. Waller confessed all, an action that alienated him from many royalists; his brother-in-law, an accomplice in the plot, was hanged on the basis of Waller's testimony. Waller himself escaped execution by paying a fine of ten thousand pounds and reportedly spending three times that amount in bribes. After a year and a half in prison, the poet was released and banished to the Continent.

Waller spent the next six years in France and Italy. During that period, he married his second wife, Mary Bracey, and his poems were published, purportedly without his permission, in England. In 1651, Waller received a pardon from parliament and returned to England in January, 1652. He soon reached an accommodation with the Cromwell regime, and in 1665, published his famous "A Panegyrick to my Lord Protector." In the same year, he was appointed a Commissioner of Trade.

When the monarchy was later restored, Waller made the transition easily, he being among the first to greet the newly arrived Charles II with a poem entitled "Upon his Majesty's Happy Return." When Charles complained that this panegyric was inferior to that composed for Cromwell five years earlier, Waller made the celebrated reply, "Poets, Sir, succeed better in fiction than in truth." Waller's wit ensured his retention of a firm position at court during the reign of Charles and during that of his brother James II. The poet also continued to serve in parliament, steering a moderate course between the court and country parties and periodically reminding his colleagues of the importance of trade to England's greatness. He was a primary supporter of measures to extend religious toleration to Catholics and to Protestant dissenters.

Waller's second wife died in 1677, and soon afterward he retired to his home at Hall Barn, renowned for the woods and gardens that the poet had laid out himself. In his last years, Waller apparently underwent a religious conversion; rejecting his earlier works, he turned to composing hymns and meditations on spiritual themes. He died at Hall Barn on October 21, 1687, surrounded by his children and grandchildren, at the age of eighty-one.

Analysis

Edmund Waller's poetic corpus is singular in its homogeneity. Although his career spanned more than half a century, it is difficult to trace any stylistic development; as Samuel Johnson remarks in his "Life of Waller," "His versification was, in his first essay, such as it appears in his last performance."

What changes do appear in Waller's poetry are primarily thematic rather than technical and can be attributed to the demands of genre rather than to any maturation in style. An examination of several poems composed at different periods of Waller's life and for very different occasions demonstrates this uniformity and, at the same time, demonstrates the innovations that Waller brought to seventeenth century verse.

Waller's earliest poems are mainly panegyrics composed on Charles I and Henrietta Maria. In "Of His Majesty's receiving the news of the Duke of Buckingham's death," one of the best of these pieces, Waller charts the program that English poets would follow for the next century in celebrating the virtues of the Stuart monarchs. The assassination of George Villiers, Duke of Buckingham, in 1628 constituted a major blow, both political and emotional, to the young king. According to the Earl of Clarendon, Charles publicly received the news with exemplary calm. When a messenger interrupted the monarch at prayers to blurt out the report of Buckingham's death, Charles continued to pray without the least change of expression; only when the service was completed and his attendants dismissed did he give way to "much passion" and "abundance of tears." In his panegyric, Waller celebrates the king's public response to the assassination and suppresses the unedifying private sequel. Charles's refusal to suspend his household's devotions is viewed as an act of heroic piety:

> So earnest with thy God! can no new care,
> No sense of danger, interrupt thy prayer?
> The sacred wrestler, till a blessing given,
> Quits not his hold, but halting conquers Heaven.

The conceit of the "sacred wrestler," which implicitly identifies Charles with the biblical patriarch Jacob, emphasizes that it is only through exertion that the king masters his natural impulses of grief and fear. His outward composure proceeds from a tenacious courage rather than from any lack of feeling. The direct address of the first line and the succession of present tense active verbs inject the description with dramatic urgency. Although threatened by personal harm and lamed ("halting") by the loss of his chief minister, Charles struggles and triumphs. By subordinating his personal grief to a faith in divine providence, the king "conquers" no mere earthly kingdom, but heaven itself.

Waller provides a context for Charles's heroism by comparing his response to Buckingham's death with the behavior of Achilles and of David in similar circumstances. While Achilles reacts to the death of Patroclus with "frantic gesture," Charles maintains a princely serenity; while David "cursed the mountains" for the death of Jonathan, Charles prays. The English king represents the ideal Christian hero, of which David and Achilles were but imperfect types: his absolute self-control and religious faith crown those virtues that he shares with the heroes of biblical and classical antiquity.

Charles's composure in the face of adversity constitutes both the justification and the outward manifestation of his kingship. Waller's contemplation of Charles Stuart's simultaneous humanity and divinity explodes in a final burst of compliment:

> Such huge extremes inhabit thy great mind,
> Godlike, unmoved, and yet, like woman, kind!
> Which of the ancient poets had not brought
> Our Charles's pedigree from Heaven, and taught
> How some bright dame, compressed by mighty Jove,
> Produced this mixed Divinity and Love?

The poet's initial sympathy with the king in his effort to master his grief and fear gradually shades into an awed recognition of his godhead: dramatic struggle concludes in masquelike apotheosis.

Several aspects of Waller's technique in "Of His Majesty's receiving the news of the Duke of Buckingham's death" constitute innovations in Caroline verse. Although nearly every seventeenth century poet employed classical and biblical mythology in his work, Waller exploits this legacy in a new way; the detailed comparisons between Charles and Achilles and David anticipate the elaborate typological schemes used so effectively by poets such as John Dryden in *Absalom and Achitophel* (1681) or Alexander Pope in his Ethical Epistles. Accompanying this predilection for allusion is Waller's use of the extended simile and the Homeric epithet. All these devices derive from classical epic: by his own admission, Waller's early reading consisted mainly of Vergil, George Chapman's translation of Homer, and Edward Fairfax's translation of Torquato Tasso's *Gerusalemme Liberata* (1580-1581, *Jerusalem Delivered*).

More striking than the presence of sustained classical allusion, perhaps, is the regularity of Waller's verse. Of the nineteen couplets in the poem, all but one is closed; the individual lines are by and large end-stopped and the few instances of enjambment are not particularly dramatic. In short, Waller is using the heroic couplet with sophisticated ease in this poem of 1628-1629. Waller's sense of balance within individual lines is no less precise: rhetorical devices such as zeugma and chiasmus lend the poem an unmistakable Augustan ring.

The presence of these devices in panegyrics on the monarchs seems appropriate, but their translation to lyric is a surprising development. "Of the lady who can sleep when she pleases," for example, addresses the conventional amatory situation of the indifferent mistress and the love-harried suitor, but the classical frame of reference imparts an unwonted air of formality to the lover's plaint:

> No wonder sleep from careful lovers flies,

> To bathe himself in Sacharissa's eyes.
> As fair Astraea once from earth to heaven,
> By strife and loud impiety was driven;
> So with our plaints offended, and our tears,
> Wise Somnus to that paradise repairs.

In the remaining fourteen lines of the poem, Waller introduces yet another four deities and several more extended similes. Johnson notes with approval that Waller avoids Petrarchan and Metaphysical conceits and that his amorous verses "are less hyperbolical than those of some other poets. Waller is not always at the last gasp; he does not die of a frown, nor live upon a smile." Allusion, in fact, appears to fill the void left by Waller's abandonment of more traditional amatory conceits. The epic style brings with it an almost epic detachment; even when treating the most emotionally-charged situations or intimate passions, Waller maintains a tone of cool suavity. The seduction poem "To Phyllis," for example, opens dramatically—"Phyllis! why should we delay/ Pleasures shorter than the day?"—but the ensuing arguments are abstract, general, and lifeless. It is hard to imagine that a real woman or a real love is in question. After pointing out the insignificance of the past and the uncertainty of the future, Waller's speaker makes his climactic appeal: "For the joys we now may prove,/ Take advice of present love." It is instructive to compare the parallel plea made by the lover in Thomas Carew's nearly contemporary poem, "To A. L. Perswasions to love":

> Oh love me then, and now begin it,
> Let us not loose this present minute:
> For time and age will worke that wrack
> Which time or age shall ne're call backe.

Waller's poem is smooth and precise, but Carew's *suasoria* is more impassioned and psychologically sensitive. Carew here imparts an urgency to his request that Waller, for all his rhetorical skill, never quite musters.

Waller himself suggests the rationale behind his detachment in one of his best-known poems, "The story of Phoebus and Daphne, applied." The opening lines establish the parallel between the classical myth and the speaker's own love affair:

> Thyrsis, a youth of the inspired train,
> Fair Sacharissa loved, but loved in vain.
> Like Phoebus sung the no less amorous boy;
> Like Daphne she, as lovely, and as coy!

Her suitor's poetic gifts notwithstanding, Sacharissa refuses to yield. After a long chase, Thyrsis achieves a wholly unexpected prize:

> All but the nymph that should redress his wrong,

> Attend his passion, and approve his song.
> Like Phoebus thus, acquiring unsought praise,
> He catched at love, and filled his arm with bays.

The theory that poetry springs from a sublimated passion is hardly new, but the equanimity with which the speaker accepts his fate surprises the reader. Apparently no regret accompanies the loss of Sacharissa; as Warren Chernaik observes in *The Poetry of Limitation* (1968), "It is clear that Waller is happier with the poems (and the praise) then he would have been with the girl." Despite its frigid conclusion, "The story of Phoebus and Daphne, applied" contains a valid psychological insight. Amatory poetry is grounded in aspiration rather than in fulfillment; the pursuit of Sacharissa brings its own reward, though not the one for which the speaker had hoped. In "When he was at sea," however, Waller denies even this relation between poetry and love:

> Whilst I was free I wrote with high conceit,
> And love and beauty raised above their height;
> Love that bereaves us both of brain and heart,
> Sorrow and silence doth at once impart.

"Passion" is denied even a catalytic role in the composition of poetry; Waller's antithesis not only distinguishes between, but also absolutely opposes, the two realms of experience. In insisting upon this separation, Waller denies amatory verse any effective role in courtship. The love poem becomes a mere literary exercise. Viewed in the light of "When he was at sea," Waller's response when Charles II questioned the inferiority of his panegyric on the Restoration to that on Cromwell—"Poets, Sir, succeed better in fiction than in truth"—seems less a politic evasion than an accurate statement of his artistic principles.

Waller's avowed detachment from "passion," however, at times renders him an astute observer of amatory psychology. "Go, lovely rose," perhaps the most frequently anthologized of Waller's lyrics, revitalizes a traditional topos:

> Go, lovely Rose!
> Tell her that wastes her time and me
> That now she knows,
> When I resemble her to thee,
> How sweet and fair she seems to be.

The surprising yet apt zeugma of line 2 and the graceful intimation of mortality in the word "seems," which foreshadows the *carpe florem* admonition in the final stanza, exemplify the witty economy that the poet displays in his best work. In "To a fair lady, playing with a snake," Waller contemplates with bemused detachment the "innocence, and youth, which makes/ In Chloris' fancy such mistakes,/ To start at love, and play with snakes." A comic delicacy suffuses the treatment of the adolescent's simultaneous repulsion from and attraction to sexuality. "The fall" similarly integrates first love into the larger natural patterns of creation and decay. Waller's gentle eroticism and deft wit, sharpened by absolute rhetorical control, render his lyrics eminently memorable and eminently quotable.

With his return to England in 1655, Waller again resumed the public and political poetry that had been the object of his earliest work. In technique, "A Panegyrick to my Lord Protector" resembles the pieces written on Charles I in the 1620's and 1630's: the mixture of biblical and classical allusion, the typological mode, and the epic similes combine to heroicize Cromwell and legitimate his government. Waller's central conceit is an extended comparison between England and ancient Rome. As the death of Julius Caesar initiated a period of civil strife that ceased only with the emergence of Augustus, so Cromwell triumphs over the factious parliament that assumed control after the execution of Charles. Waller retains a certain sympathy for Charles, as the parallel with the great Caesar makes clear; but his major concern is with the new, imperialistic England that Cromwell strives to forge. "A Panegyrick to my Lord Protector" is a strong poem, but more a public performance than an investigation of the crisis in loyalties that Cromwell's rule provoked. It lacks the rich ambiguities in perspective that distinguish Andrew Marvell's poem on the same theme, "An Horatian Ode upon Cromwell's Return from Ireland."

Waller's willingness to pen panegyrics for both Cromwell and the Stuarts disgruntled royalists in his own day and gave him a reputation as a venal timeserver that has persisted into the twentieth century. It can be plausibly argued, however, that the poet's devotion is to England rather than to its rulers, and Waller was not alone in recognizing how Cromwell's capable rule quashed faction at home and raised the nation's prestige abroad. With the political chaos that succeeded Cromwell's death in 1658 and the emergence of Charles II as the one leader who could reunite Englishmen, Waller was quick to reassert his loyalties to the house of Stuart. The panegyrics that form the greatest part of Waller's Restoration poetry are, with a few exceptions, competent but undistinguished. "A Poem on St. James' Park as lately improved by His Majesty" is a panegyric *cum* topographical poem in the tradition of Sir John Denham's "Cooper's Hill." Drawing on the classical tradition of *concordia discors*, Waller presents the order of the park as a harmonious microcosm of the universal order. Structures in the landscape such as the Palace of Whitehall and Westminster Abbey assume a symbolic function, becoming reminders of the eternal values upon which England's greatness is based, whoever the ruler. The willingness to experiment with a new genre that Waller demonstrates in "A Poem on St. James' Park as lately improved by His Majesty" is also evinced by "Instructions to a Painter," a poem in which he "advises" an artist how to depict the British naval victory at Lowestoft in June, 1665. Waller's panegyric, which omits the less edifying details of the sea fight, elicited a series of satiric rejoinders that served to establish the "advice to a painter" trope as a standard motif in Restoration poetry.

The religious pieces of Waller's last years betray no flagging in poetic energy; as Atterbury remarks in his "Preface" to the 1690 *Poems*, "Were we to judge barely by the wording, we could not know what was wrote at twenty and what at fourscore." Perhaps the most moving passage of the religious poems is the final conceit in "Of the last verses in the book":

> The soul's dark cottage, battered and decayed,
> Lets in new light through chinks that time has made;
> Stronger by weakness, wiser men become,
> As they draw near to their eternal home.
> Leaving the old, both worlds at once they view,
> That stand upon the threshold of the new.

The fine image of the battered cottage in many ways sums up Waller's poetic career. Without forfeiting his basic values, Waller nevertheless learned to adjust to the shifting circumstances of seventeenth century England. Like "The Trimmer" popularized by George Savile, Marquess of Halifax, Waller retained an allegiance to moderation and balance in an age in which strong loyalties and excessive partisanship were the political and literary norm. Although his individual poems rarely achieve greatness, they are consistently witty, perceptive, and stylistically distinguished. The homogeneity of Waller's achievement, in fact, may be said to be his greatest triumph inasmuch as it provided one of the few fixed standards of excellence in a period of radical change. Waller's emphasis on balance and harmony, coupled with a willingness to incorporate new genres into his repertory, rendered him a fitting figure to usher in the new Augustan age.

Michael P. Parker

Other major works

PLAYS: *Pompey the Great* 1664 (translation); *The Maid's Tragedy*, 1690 (revised).

NONFICTION: *The Workes of Edmund Waller in This Parliament*, 1645; *Debates of the House of Commons from the Year 1667 to the Year 1694*, 1763 (ten volumes).

MISCELLANEOUS: *The Works of Edmund Waller, Esq., in Verse and Prose*, 1729 (Elijah Fenton, editor).

Bibliography

Chernaik, Warren L. *The Poetry of Limitation: A Study of Edmund Waller.* New Haven, Conn.: Yale University Press, 1968. Chernaik's book vividly depicts the political, cultural, and literary context in which Waller wrote his Cavalier lyric poetry, formal occasional poems, and heroic satire, but there are few extended analyses of his works. Contains a chapter accounting for the rise and fall of Waller's literary reputation.

Gilbert, Jack G. *Edmund Waller.* Boston: Twayne, 1979. Gilbert explores the complex relationship between Waller's political career and poetry, devotes separate chapters (with extended analyses of some poems) to the lyric and the political poems, and concludes by defining his view of art and fixing his position in English literature. Supplemented by a helpful chronology and an annotated select bibliography.

Miner, Earl. *The Cavalier Mode from Jonson to Cotton.* Princeton, N.J.: Princeton University Press, 1971. Miner utilizes Waller to demonstrate past Ben Jonson Cavalier motifs and provides lengthy analyses of "At Penshurst" and "A Poem on St. James' Park as lately improved by His Majesty," two topographical poems that express the social order that characterizes Cavalier poetry.

Piper, William Bowman. *The Heroic Couplet.* Cleveland: Case Western Reserve University, 1969. Provides an overall assessment of Waller's use of the heroic couplet from the early imperfections to the mature style reflected in "On St. James' Park." For Piper, however, Waller was not among the great poets, and he is compared unfavorably to Ben Jonson with respect to the Penshurst poems.

Richmond, H. M. "The Fate of Edmund Waller." In *Seventeenth-Century English Poetry: Modern Essays in Criticism,* edited by William R. Keast. Rev. ed. London: Oxford University Press, 1971. Richmond attributes Waller's decline in popularity and in literary merit to his faults as a person (his feigned madness, bribery, and informing to save his life), rather than to his poetic talents and the lack of the thought/feeling tension associated with the metaphysical poets.

Williamson, George. *The Proper Wit of Poetry.* Chicago: University of Chicago Press, 1961. Williamson discusses Waller's Restoration and Augustan wit in the poems "On a Girdle" and "The Story of Phoebus and Daphne, applied." For Williamson, Waller's use of myth as the chief source of his wit was unique among his contemporaries.

ROBERT PENN WARREN

Born: Guthrie, Kentucky; April 24, 1905
Died: Stratton, Vermont; September 15, 1989

Principal poetry

Thirty-Six Poems, 1935; *Eleven Poems on the Same Theme*, 1942; *Selected Poems 1923-1943*, 1944; *Brother to Dragons: A Tale in Verse and Voices*, 1953; *Promises: Poems 1954-1956*, 1957; *You, Emperors, and Others: Poems 1957-1960*, 1960; *Selected Poems: New and Old, 1923-1966*, 1966; *Incarnations: Poems 1966-1968*, 1968; *Audubon: A Vision*, 1969; *Or Else—Poem/Poems 1968-1974*, 1974; *Selected Poems 1923-1975*, 1976; *Now and Then: Poems 1976-1978*, 1978; *Being Here: Poetry 1977-1980*, 1980; *Rumor Verified: Poems 1979-1980*, 1981; *Chief Joseph of the Nez Percé*, 1983; *New and Selected Poems 1923-1985*, 1985.

Other literary forms

In an era when poets are often as renowned and influential as critics, Robert Penn Warren nevertheless stands out inasmuch as he achieved success on two creative fronts, having as great a critical reputation as a novelist as he has as a poet. This accomplishment is not limited to the production of one singular work or of a sporadic body of work; rather it is a sustained record of development and achievement spanning more than three decades. His fiction includes the novels *Night Rider* (1939), *At Heaven's Gate* (1943), *All the King's Men* (1946), *World Enough and Time: A Romantic Novel* (1950), *Band of Angels* (1955), *The Cave* (1959), *Wilderness: A Tale of the Civil War* (1961), and *Flood: A Romance of Our Time* (1964), and there is also a short-story collection, *The Circus in the Attic and Other Stories* (1947). There can be no doubt that *All the King's Men*, a highly fictionalized and richly wrought retelling of the rise and fall, by assassination, of the demagogic Louisiana governor Huey Long, has justifiably attained the status of an American classic; it is not only Warren's best novel but also his best-known work. The story of Willie Stark, the country-boy idealist who becomes far worse an exploiter of the public trust than the corrupt professional politicians he at first sets his heart and soul against, embodies many of Warren's most persistent themes, in particular the fumbling process self-definition becomes in a universe awry with irony and a world alive with betrayal and mendacity. Made into an Oscar-winning film, the novel was also very successfully adapted as a play by Warren in the 1950's.

Warren's considerable influence on the life of letters in twentieth century America was also exercised in a series of textbooks that he edited jointly with the noted critic Cleanth Brooks. The first, *An Approach to Literature* (1936), coedited as well by John Thibault Purser, was followed by *Understanding*

Poetry: An Anthology for College Students, edited by Warren and Brooks, in 1938, and *Understanding Fiction,* also edited by Warren and Brooks, in 1943. These texts utilized the practices (just then being formulated) of New Criticism, which encouraged a close attention to the literary text as a self-contained, self-referring statement. It is certain that several generations of readers have had their entire attitude toward literature and literary interpretation determined by Warren and Brooks's effort, either directly or through the influence of teachers and critics whose values were shaped by these landmark works.

Achievements

Robert Penn Warren was undoubtedly one of the most honored men of letters in American history. Among his numerous awards and honors were a 1936 Houghton-Mifflin Literary Fellowship for his first novel, *Night Rider;* Guggenheim fellowships for 1939-1940 and 1947-1948; and Pulitzer prizes for his novel *All the King's Men* (1947) and the poetry volume *Now and Then* (1979). (He was the only person to have won a Pulitzer for both fiction and poetry.) He also won the National Book Award for poetry with the volume *Promises* in 1958, the National Medal for Literature (1970), and the Presidential Medal of Freedom (1980). He was one of the first recipients of a so-called genius grant, a Prize Fellowship from the MacArthur Foundation, in 1981. In 1986 he was selected to be the first poet laureate of the United States, and he served in that distinguished capacity until age and ill health required him to resign the position in 1987.

Biography

Robert Penn Warren was born on April 24, 1905, amid the rolling hills of the tobacco country of southwestern Kentucky, in the town of Guthrie; he was the son of Robert Franklin Warren, a businessman, and Anna Ruth (Penn) Warren. He spent his boyhood there, and summers on his grandparents' farm in nearby Trigg County. Both grandfathers were Confederate veterans of the Civil War, and he was often regaled with firsthand accounts of battles and skirmishes with Union forces. The young Warren grew up wanting to be a sea captain, and after completing his secondary education in neighboring Clarksville, Tennessee, he did obtain an appointment to the United States Naval Academy at Annapolis.

A serious eye injury prevented his attending, however, and in 1920 Warren matriculated instead at Vanderbilt University in Nashville, set on becoming an electrical engineer. In his freshman English class, Warren's interest took a fateful turn as the young professor John Crowe Ransom and another, advanced student, Allen Tate, introduced him to the world of poetry. The two were at the center of a campus literary group called the Fugitives, and Warren began attending their meetings and soon was contributing to their bimonthly magazine, *The Fugitive*, which he edited in his senior year. Under the tutelage of Tate and Ransom, he became an intense student not only of earlier English poets, particularly the Elizabethans and such seventeenth century Metaphysical poets as John Donne and Andrew Marvell, but also of the contemporary schools that were emerging from the writings of older poets such as A. E. Housman and Thomas Hardy, as well as from the work of William Butler Yeats and T. S. Eliot.

Warren was graduated summa cum laude from Vanderbilt in 1925, taking a B.A. degree, and he continued his graduate studies at the University of California at Berkeley, from which he obtained an M.A. in 1927. He then enrolled in another year of graduate courses at Yale University and went on to spend two years as a Rhodes Scholar at the University of Oxford in England, which awarded him a B.Litt. degree in 1931.

While at Oxford, Warren completed his first published book, *John Brown: The Making of a Martyr* (1929), which took a rather callow, Southerner's view of the legendary hero of the abolitionist cause. When Paul Rosenberg, one of the editors of the *American Caravan* annual, invited him to submit a story, Warren "stumbled on" fiction writing, as he later recounted the incident. The result, "Prime Leaf," a story about labor troubles among tobacco growers back in his native Kentucky, would later find fuller expression in his first published novel, *Night Rider.*

Back in the United States, Warren joined the Agrarian movement, an informal confederation of many of his old Fugitive colleagues who were now espousing a return to agrarian, regional ideals in a Depression-ravaged America that was rapidly becoming more and more industrialized, urbanized, and, at least inasmuch as the images generated by popular culture were concerned, homogenized.

After teaching for a year as an assistant professor of English at Southwestern College in Memphis, he became, in 1931, an acting assistant professor of English at Vanderbilt. He remained there until 1934, when he moved on to accept a position at Louisiana State University in Baton Rouge. After promotion to associate professor in 1936, Warren took a full professorship at the University of Minnesota in 1942.

In 1935, while at Louisiana State, Warren had cofounded *Southern Review*, an influential journal with which he would remain until it folded in 1942. From 1938 to 1961, meanwhile, Warren served on the advisory board of another prestigious quarterly, *Kenyon Review.*

In 1930 Warren had married Emma Brescia, whom he divorced in 1951, shortly after accepting a position as professor of playwriting at the School of Drama of Yale University. On December 7, 1952, Warren married the writer Eleanor Clark, by whom he would father his two children, Rosanna, born in 1953, and Gabriel, born in 1955. Warren left his position with the drama school in 1956, but in 1961 he returned to New Haven, Connecticut, to rejoin the Yale faculty as a professor of English. From that time onward he made his home in nearby Fairfield and summered in Stratton, Vermont.

Warren continued his distinguished career as a teacher, poet, novelist, critic, editor, and lecturer virtually to the end of his long life. In February, 1986, the Librarian of Congress named him the first official poet laureate of the United States, a position he held until 1987. On September 15, 1989, the poet died at his summer home in Stratton. He was eighty-four years old.

Analysis

Robert Penn Warren was blessed twice over. He was a son of and grew up in a region of the country renowned for its love of the land and devotion to earthy folk wisdom and the art of storytelling. There was also a love of language, particularly the fustian spirit of the orator and the preacher, based on a deep, dark respect for the Word, orotund and oracular.

Added to that, however, Warren spent his formative years in a world that was making the transition from the comparative bucolic and optimistic sensibilities of the late nineteenth century to the frenzied, fearful, frenetic pace of the post-World War I 1920's. Poetry was being called into service by young people everywhere to try to explain what had happened, or at least give it manageable shape. T. S. Eliot's *The Waste Land* (1922) set the tone. At Vanderbilt among his fellow Fugitives, Warren was quickly put in touch with the new poetry that was emerging.

It is this combination of effects and influences that made Warren's poetry and gave it its vision. From the first, he hovered between the old and new— the mannered style, the modern flip; the natural scene, the symbolic backdrop; the open gesture, the hidden motive; original sin, the religion of humankind. This peculiar vantage point scored his vision, for it allowed him to know at first hand what his age was surrendering at the same time that it allowed him to question the motives for the surrender and the terms of the victory, the name of the enemy—or, better yet, his face.

Warren can bring the personal into the most profound metaphysical musings without blinking an eye or losing a beat, because finally the source of all vision, at least for Warren, is the darkest of selves at the heart of one's being, the unknown brother who shares not only one's bed but also one's body and makes, or so it seems, one's decisions. Self-discovery is Warren's trail, and the reader who follows it discovers that while it begins in coming to grips with the painful processes of caring in an uncaring world, it concludes in accepting caring as a moral obligation rather than merely a state of mind or soul. Like most twentieth century poets, Warren was really trying to reinvigorate the heroic ideal.

The early poem "To a Face in a Crowd" echoes the world-weary angst typical of the period, the 1920's, by rendering an urban apocalypse in the bleak, stark terms of lonely souls lost in vacant vistas, finding their meager consolations in passing strangers who may—or may not—be spiritual kindred with similar dreams and like despairs. It is night, and adjectives and nouns collide in a litany of pessimism and negativism: "lascivious," "lust," "bitter," "woe," "dolorous," "dim," "shroud." This vision is mitigated, however, by the markedly poetic tone of the language: "Brother, my brother, whither do you pass?/ Unto what hill at dawn, unto what glen. . . . ?" While there is hope, the speaker seems to be saying that the idyllic interlude is no longer a viable option; instead, "we must meet/ As weary nomads in this desert at last,/ Borne in the lost procession of these feet."

Among these early poems, "The Return: An Elegy" is by far the most successful effort, for in it Warren eschewed the derivative and imitative tone, mood, and theme of poems such as "To a Face in the Crowd" and found what time would prove to be the beginnings of his own voice and vision.

The setting is simple, though not at first easily discerned: in a Pullman as the train carries the speaker back home to the hills to attend his mother's funeral. Sentiment is kept at bay, almost with a vengeance, it might seem: "give me the nickels off your eyes/ . . . / then I could buy a pack of cigarettes." Only an occasional, italicized lapse into poeticized feeling—*"does my mother wake"*—among the details of the rugged mountain-country landscape that the speaker intersperses with his thoughts gives the sense that a profound emotional turmoil is seething beneath the modernist "flip": "Pines drip without motion/ The hairy boughs no longer shake/ Shaggy mist, crookbacked, ascends."

As the poem continues, however, the reader is gradually forced to realize that it is the tension between the speaker's grief and his desire not to sentimentalize his loss that give the poetry its incredible and peculiarly modern motive power: *"the old fox is dead/* what have I said." Thus, the speaker earns the right to lapse into the unabashed sentiment, at poem's end, of "this dark and swollen orchid of my sorrow."

This rare ability to combine the most enduring verbal expressions of human feelings with the most fleeting of contemporary realities and attitudes in a poetry that magically maintains its precarious balance between traditional poetic tone and style and the most ragged-edged and flippant of modern sensibilities continued to give Warren's work its own shape and direction as he expanded his range in the 1930's and 1940's. In "Pursuit," for example, his vision of the urban landscape has hardly improved, but it is peopled with three-dimensional emblems of a faltering, seeking humanity—"the hunchback on the corner," "that girl the other guests shun," "the little old lady in black." "Original Sin: A Short Story," meanwhile, places the reader in Omaha and the Harvard Yard and speaks of as cosmopolitan an image as "the abstract Jew," yet it ends its commentary on humanity's fated failings with country images of "the backyard and . . . an old horse cold in pasture."

So much is in keeping, of course, with the social and literary ideals that the original Fugitives formulated when they coalesced into the Agrarian movement. Their notion was that American democracy was not an urban but a rural phenomenon, forged by a link between the people and the land. In this regard, regionalism—the countryman's sense of place and of a devotion to his people—was not a pernicious thing but involved the very health of the nation, a health that the increasing pressures toward homogeneity of people and culture in sprawling urban centers could not only threaten but perhaps even destroy. Poets such as Warren became spokespersons both for that lost agrarian ideal and for the simple country folk forced by economic necessity into the anonymity of large cities, where they lived at the edge of squalor and struggled to maintain their small-town dignities.

Warren combines all these themes and concerns in "The Ballad of Billie Potts." As the speaker recounts the story of Big Billie, his wife, and their son, Little Billie, he mixes in long, parenthetical sections in which he seems to be addressing himself rather than the readers, urging himself to return— as if he could—to the life-styles of those hillbillies "in the section between the rivers," where they were poor by urban standards but rich in spirit, in faith in themselves, and in the power of familial love. In the lost idyll mode reminiscent of William Wordsworth's "The Ruined Cottage" and "Michael," the story of Little Billie's travails and his parents' despair when circumstances force the boy to leave "his Pappy in Old Kaintuck/ And [head] West to try his luck" is really a twentieth century throwback's yearnings for what were simpler and certainly more communal times. For him now there is only the endless urban tedium, the vacant, lonely sameness, maddeningly monotonous and vaguely threatening: "And the clock ticked all night long in the furnished room/ And would not stop/ And the *El*-train passed on the quarters with a whish like a terrible broom/ And would not stop."

Warren never ceased to contrast the earthiness of country values and country life with the mind-forged manacles that constrain the individual within the modern industrial landscape. At the heart of his vision, however, is a sense of the sad wasting of time and of love that mortality forces one constantly to consider. Clearly the problem is not "out there"; it is within us. The increasing urbanization of America is not the enemy, then, it is simply the latest battlefield—not the disease, but the symptom. The disease is life, and the ageless enemy is our insatiable need to try to make it make sense, to try to make it hurt less.

For Warren, then, one can hope only to keep oneself spiritually and emotionally—and painfully—alive in a world that tends undeniably toward death and decay. His villains become those who deny that life is hardship as much as those who visit hardships on others. Behind the indictment, though, there is always the lance of forgiveness, aimed as much at the heart of the speaker who dreads the pain of his feelings as much as at the iniquities that arouse it.

As the poet himself became a father and middle-aged, children rather than the lonely crowd figured more and more as the best emblems of the tragic core of the human condition, as well as of the human capacity to endure and transcend. The poetry consequently finds its locus more and more in personal experience, the day to day providing sufficient grist for the poet's thinking and feeling mill.

"The Child Next Door," from the prize-winning volume *Promises: Poems 1954-1956*, focuses not on the child "who is defective because the mother," burdened with seven already, "took a pill," but on an older sister, who is twelve and "beautiful like a saint," and who takes care of "the monster all day":

> I come, and her joy and triptych beauty and joy stir hate
> —Is it hate?—in my heart. Fool, doesn't she know that the process
> Is not that joyous or simple, to bless, or unbless,
> The malfeasance of nature or the filth of fate?

Warren's unstinting, almost embarrassing honesty as he records his feelings and attitudes, an honesty exercised in his poetry from as early as "The Return," gains him an edge of intimate moral ambiguity in this more mature poetry. The present poem concludes: "I think of your goldness, of joy, how empires grind, stars are hurled,/ I smile stiff, saying *ciao*, saying *ciao*, and think: this is the world." Whether that is the expression of a bitter resignation or a casual dismissal or a measure of joyful acceptance, the speaker will give no clue: "this is the world." Readers are left to measure the size of their own hearts and thereby experience both the pain of observing life too closely and, if they wish, the expiation of letting it go.

By now a cosmopolitan himself, Yale professor with an Oxford degree and summer home in Vermont, the boy who is father to the man did not forget the Kentucky hill-country source of his vision. In reminiscences such as "Country Burying (1919)," the autobiographical rather than symbolical and metaphysical seems to prevail, but there is still a telling tale. The poem is a requiem for all those lost "boy's afternoon[s]" when life was so present, even there amid tokens of death, and the mind more receptive, but the spirit would be somewhere else: "Why doesn't that fly stop buzzing—stop buzzing up there!" Apologies to Emily Dickinson aside, those were a boy's thoughts in 1919: in the poem they are some measure of the adult's remorse as he reached midcentury with the century. Now there is not only the pain of the present to endure; there is the pain of the past, its loss, as well.

This sense of remorse was never absent from Warren's poetry, but now it is outspoken and unremitting, and it becomes a major motivating factor in the later poetry. *Brother to Dragons*, a historical novel in verse written in the form of a play that the author calls a poem, is the apex of all Warren's previous pessimism, displaying little of his often-whimsical capacity to turn heel but not turn coat on caring too much for the human condition. In the largest sense, the poem is a severe indictment of the human animal. With some liberties but no real distortion of the facts, it recounts the tale of Lilburn Clarke, a Kentuckian who in the early nineteenth century brutally murdered a black slave over a trifling offense. Beyond the tragic scope of those facts, there was an even more tragic rub in Warren's view: Clarke was the nephew of Thomas Jefferson, himself a paradoxical figure who could pen the Declaration of Independence and still be a slaveholder, and who believed in the perfectibility of mankind.

Warren, who appears himself as a character in the poem by carrying on a pointed philosophical debate with Jefferson, used the bare bones of the story to call into question the worth, let alone the authenticity, of all human ideals. Still, in the lengthy monologue with which the poem concludes, he insists that despite this sorry record of human endeavor in the name of ideals that are always betrayed, "we must argue the necessity of virtue."

By the time the 1950's ended, Warren had established a new metier as a social commentator with an equally self-accusatory eye. In *You, Emperor, and Others*, the public and the private, the man and the child, the father and the son all find expression. "Man in the Street," with its singsong rhythms and nursery-rhyme, choruslike echoes, hits the gray flannel suits with their black knit ties and Brooks Brothers shirts not where they live but where they work, where each of them somehow makes accommodations with the vacuities of the corporate world. If it is a vision that virtually lends an air of nostalgic romance to an early poem such as "To a Face in the Crowd," "Mortmain" harks back to "The Return." It is the speaker's father who is dying now, but the irreverent flippancy of the earlier poem is not even there to be turned away from: "All things . . . // Were snatched from me, and I could not move,/ Naked in that black blast of his love." It is a poem in five parts, and in the last of those, "A Vision: Circa 1880," he imagines his father as a boy, "in patched britches and that idleness of boyhood/ Which asks nothing and is its own fulfillment." The poem ends with a turn to pure lyricism, without any reaching out to metaphysical solutions or conceits, merely the wholly verbal bounty of language giving life to dead time in images of a present, natural splendor.

Warren published seven additional volumes of poetry from 1960 to 1980, and the lyrical mode itself intensified into the speculative tone that he apparently could not abandon. Still, as he reminds the reader in the 1968 volume, *Incarnations*, "You think I am speaking in riddles./ But I am not, for// The world means only itself" ("Riddle in the Garden"). In *Audubon*, meanwhile, he asks, "What is love," and reminds the reader that "one name for it is knowledge," as if attempting to justify his lifelong preoccupation with trying to understand human beings and their place on earth and in the universe.

As the poet grew older, mortality became even more of an obsessive theme, and the issues of time past and time present, the poet now having a wealth of experience to draw upon, found even more expression in this new admixture of a metaphysical lyricism. In "Paradox," for example, from the "Can I See Arcturus from Where I Stand?" section of *Selected Poems, 1923-1975*, stargazer man is brought down to earth, or at least a sense of his limits, when he confronts a retelling of Zeno's paradox of the arrow and its unreachable goal. The natural simplicity and personal quality of the setting—a run on a beach that causes the speaker to recollect an earlier spirited chase—remove from the poem the bane of a *de profundis* that often intruded into Warren's most youthful metaphysical flights; the information is presented not as insight but as the sort of everyday truth any feeling, thinking person might draw from experience, should he or she care to. Indeed, the poem is finally a tender love lyric worthy, in its formal rhapsodic effect, of A. E. Housman:

> I saw, when your foot fulfilled its stride,
> How the sand, compressed, burst to silver light,
> But when I had reached that aureoled spot
> There was only another in further stride.

This bringing all vision down to earth is best exemplified in a late poem such as "Last Meeting." It is another hill-country recollection; the poet, now by all accounts elderly, recalls being back home once and meeting an elderly woman who had known him as a boy. Now she too is dead. "All's changed. The faces on the street/ Are changed. I'm rarely back. But once/ I tried to find her grave." He failed, he explains, but promises that he will yet succeed. Still, "It's nigh half a lifetime I haven't managed,/ But there must be enough time left for that." People's failures are little things, he seems to be saying toward the end of his creative life, and because Warren has done such an incredible job of exploring them in every other permutation throughout his long career, the reader should pay heed to the conclusions he reaches. People's failures, no matter how great, are little things; it is the burden of remorse they carry for them that is great.

Like Thomas Hart Benton, who painted the great vistas of Western deserts in his later years, Warren turns to the overlooked and the insignificant to find beauty and, in it, significances he may have missed. In "Arizona Midnight," "dimly I do see/ Against that darkness, lifting in blunt agony,/ The single great cactus." He strains to see the cactus; "it has/ its own necessary beauty." One must see through the apparent agony into the heart of the thing and seek out the beauty there, rather than pausing too long to reflect only on the tragic surface—which one can see only dimly, in any event.

It is no wonder, then, that one of Warren's last completed volumes was *Chief Joseph of the Nez Percé*. Here he returns to the tragic record that is the past, to betrayal and injustice and the bitter agony of exile despite one's having "done the right thing." Yet this time, in Joseph's enduring the arrogance of office and the proud man's contumely, Warren finds an emblem of triumph despite apparent defeat. Now he can see history not as irony, filled with the tragic remorse that looking back can bring, but as process and "sometimes, under/ The scrutinizing prism of Time,/ Triumphant." It seems to be the declaration of a total peace, and one cannot help but hear, as Warren surely must have hoped one would, echoing behind those words Chief Joseph's own: "I will fight no more forever."

A victory that is won against no odds is a sham. A victory that is won against life's own bitter truths is poetry. It certainly is Robert Penn Warren's.

Russell Elliott Murphy

Other major works

LONG FICTION: *Night Rider*, 1939; *At Heaven's Gate*, 1943; *All the King's Men*, 1946; *World Enough and Time: A Romantic Novel*, 1950; *Band of Angels*, 1955; *The Cave*, 1959; *Wilderness: A Tale of the Civil War*, 1961; *Flood: A Romance of Our Time*, 1964.

SHORT FICTION: *The Circus in the Attic and Other Stories*, 1947.

NONFICTION: *John Brown: The Making of a Martyr*, 1929.

EDITED TEXTS: *An Approach to Literature*, 1936 (with Cleanth Brooks and John Thibault Purser); *Understanding Poetry: An Anthology for College Students*, 1938 (with Brooks); *Understanding Fiction*, 1943 (with Brooks).

Bibliography

Bedient, Calvin. *In the Heart's Last Kingdom: Robert Penn Warren's Major Poetry.* Cambridge, Mass.: Harvard University Press, 1984. Bedient places Warren in the tradition of the poet-seeker who will know the truth at all costs.

Clark, William Bedford, ed. *Critical Essays on Robert Penn Warren.* Boston: G. K. Hall, 1981. The selection covers both the poetry and prose and includes twenty contemporary reviews, an interview, and eight in-depth articles. Among the authors are Malcolm Cowley, John Crowe Ransom, and Harold Bloom.

Justus, James H. *The Achievement of Robert Penn Warren.* Baton Rouge: Louisiana State University Press, 1981. A comprehensive and scholarly work, Justus sees Warren's major theme as a search for self-knowledge and examines the entire corpus, including the fiction and nonfiction prose as well as the poetry.

Walker, Michael. *Robert Penn Warren: A Vision Earned.* New York: Barnes & Noble, 1979. Walker's thesis is that Warren is best understood when he is examined as a regionalist, a Southern writer with outside interests. The book deals with the prose as well as the poetry.

Warren, Robert Penn. *Robert Penn Warren Talking: Interviews 1950-1978.* Edited by Floyd C. Watkins and John T. Hiers. New York: Random House, 1980. A collection of eighteen interviews conducted in a variety of modes and settings over a period of nearly thirty years, ranging from a session with students at Vanderbilt to a Bill Moyers transcript. Gives insights not only into Warren's thought and development during the period but also into the personality of the man as it emerges in the give-and-take of live discourse.

ISAAC WATTS

Born: Southampton, England; July 17, 1674
Died: London, England; November 25, 1748

Principal poetry

Horae Lyricae, 1706, 1709; *Hymns and Spiritual Songs*, 1707; *Divine and Moral Songs for Children*, 1715; *The Psalms of David*, 1719; *Reliquiae Juveniles: Miscellaneous Thoughts in Prose and Verse*, 1734.

Other literary forms

Isaac Watts's verse and prose is almost exclusively religious, although—as a practicing divine interested in the instruction of youth—he authored tracts that could be classified as pedagogical *and* theological. Foremost among these is a collection of prayers for little children entitled *The First Catechism*, 1692. This collection was followed by *The Art of Reading and Writing English*, 1721; *The Christian Doctrine of the Trinity*, 1722; *Logick: Or, The Right Use of Reason*, 1725; *An Essay Towards the Encouragement of Charity Schools*, 1728; *A Caveat Against Infidelity*, 1729; and his last work, *Useful and Important Questions Concerning Jesus, the Son of God*, 1746. Watts's *Sermons on Various Subjects*, in three volumes, appeared between 1721 and 1727.

Achievements

Watts, the Father of English hymnody, ranks as the highest among the Nonconformist writers of divine poetry during the eighteenth century. For more than a century he held the respect of those British and American Nonconformists who sought spiritual uplift from the worship services of their particular denominations. Although Watts established his literary reputation as a hymnodist, as a writer of divine odes for congregational worship, he saw himself as a poet, although one who later renounced poetry for the sake of edification. Among lower-class Christians, Watts sought to promote what he termed "pious entertainment," which, unfortunately, prevented him from achieving his potential as a pure literary artist. Indeed, on more than one occasion he felt the need to apologize for being so easily understood, for having written poetry that could be read without difficulty.

In addressing the simpler souls of the English-speaking world, Watts managed to fuse image with thought and emotion, attaining a level of intensity not often reached by his more learned Augustan colleagues. In so doing, he relieved the English hymn of considerable poetic excess—complex theology and imagery that, during the late seventeenth and early eighteenth centuries, were regarded as essential ingredients of divine poetry. Watts, however, recognized immediately the difference between the high aesthetic level of divine poetry and the practical regions in which congregational song had, out of necessity, to function. Thus, he set out to compose a body of verse representative of the vigorous human spirit. He aimed at poetry and song that applied the Gospels to the various experiences of life. He strived for clarity of language, simplicity of diction, and sympathy of understanding so that thousands of English worshipers, both within and without the religiosocial establishment, could lean upon his hymns as the natural expression of their own religious feelings.

Watts combined, in his hymnody, the soul of a poet and the conviction of a preacher. As a recognized cleric, he cast aside the theological mantle and reached down to the humblest of Christians, beckoning them to walk with God upon the high ground of Christian piety. Thus, he set a fashion and provided a model; for the last half of the eighteenth century, a whole school of hymnodists would continue his vitality and his directness. The key to Watts's legacy was the relationship of hymnody to literature. He stood as one of the few poets of the Augustan age who managed to preserve the spiritual enthusiasm of Protestant dissent and at the same time demonstrate that such enthusiasm could achieve some semblance of poetic expression. As both Independent divine and classical poet, he formed an obvious link between the zeal of the seventeenth century and the evangelical revival of George Whitefield and the Wesleys. Most important, that link—that transition—was built upon Watts's conviction that poetic and religious inspiration could be harnessed and combined by a person such as himself: a learned man, competently able to draw from tradition ideas congenial to his own times and his own temperament.

Biography

Isaac Watts was born at Southampton on July 17, 1674, the eldest of his father's nine children. Isaac Watts, senior, stood as a respected Nonconformist, one so serious about his essentially Puritan religious convictions that he served two prison terms rather than conform to the Establishment. After his release he maintained a successful boarding school at Southampton. Young Watts began his education under the direction of Reverend John Pinhorne, rector of All Saints church and headmaster of the Southampton Grammar School, who taught him Greek, Latin, and Hebrew. The boy's talent for learning and his taste for verse prompted citizens of the city to offer him a university education for eventual ordination into the Church of England. Of course he refused, which meant that he drifted, in 1690, toward the Nonconformist academy at Stoke Newington, London, under the care of Thomas Rowe, pastor of the Independent congregation at Girdler's Hall. Watts joined that congregation three years later.

In 1694, at the age of twenty, Watts left Rowe's academy and returned to Southampton. During this period he wrote the majority of hymns that would appear in *Hymns and Spiritual Songs*: "Behold the glories of the Lamb" was supposedly the first, composed in an attempt to elevate the standards of praise and prayer. Others followed, principally the results of requests from friends: "There is a land of pure delight" came from an uplifting experience upon viewing the scene across Southampton Water. Watts, however, returned to the district of Stoke Newington as tutor to the son of a prominent London Puritan, Sir John Hartropp. The tutor pursued his own investigations into theology and philosophy with the same intensity as his pupil, which may have been the principal reason for the eventual decline in his health.

In the meantime, Watts turned his attention from pedagogy to divinity. He preached his first sermon in 1698 and continued that activity for the next three years. Then, in 1702, he was ordained minister of the Independent congregation at Mark Lane, a pulpit that had been filled by such eminent Nonconformist orators as Joseph Caryl (1602-1673) and his successor, Dr. John Owen (1616-1683). Watts's congregation reflected the prominence and affluence of London Nonconformity, and the diminutive divine presided over it for the next ten years. In 1712, he became seriously ill with a fever, and his assistant, Samuel Price, assumed the role of copastor at the time when the congregation moved to another chapel just built in Bury Street. At that point, Sir Thomas Abney took the ailing Watts into his home, and he remained with the family until his death (Sir Thomas himself having died in 1722). Indeed, the *Divine and Moral Songs for Children* was written for and dedicated to Sir Thomas' daughters.

Because of his illness and general state of incapacity, there is really nothing to note concerning the last thirty-five years of Watts's life. He spent his days largely in study and in preparing his poetry and prose for publication. In 1728, Edinburgh University bestowed, unsolicited, the degree of Doctor of Divinity upon the poet, who died at Stoke Newington on November 25, 1748. He was buried at Bunhill Fields, the London resting place of Nonconformists, and a monument was erected to him in Westminster Abbey.

Analysis

Criticism of Isaac Watts's poetry has ranged from what could be termed "kind" to that which is obviously and totally negative. In his *Life of Watts* (1781), Samuel Johnson set the critical tone by complaining of the irregularity of his measures, his blank verse, and his insufficiently correspondent rhymes. As was his method, however, Johnson did find merit in Watts's smooth and easy lines and religiously pure thoughts, combined with ample piety and innocence. Still, the London sage wished for greater vigor in the hymnodist's verse. In the nineteenth century, critical commentators made sport of the sing-song patterns of Watts's children's hymns, while Lewis Carroll delighted in parodies of such pieces as "Let dogs delight to bark and bite," "'Tis the voice of the sluggard," and the "Busy bee." Such strokes secured for Watts the lasting reputation of an Independent minister who accomplished little, poetically, beyond penning stiff moral verses for little children in his spare moments.

Careful reading of the poet's prefaces to those collections intended for mature minds, however, reveals him to have been his own rather stern critic. As late as 1734, with his major poetry already published, Watts proclaimed (in *Reliquiae Juveniles*) that he had made no pretense to the name of poet, especially since the age and the nation had produced so many superior writers of verse. More than the mere conventional expression of humility, the statement leads directly to an examination of those "superior" souls steeped in classicism who helped Watts develop his poetic theories and practices. One, Mathias Casimir Sarbiewski (1594-1640)—although outside both Watts's age and his nation—demonstrated the advantages of a form, the ode, that he could easily adapt to congregational and private worship. The other, John Milton—like Watts a Nonconformist and a classicist—proved that blank verse could convey both meaning and elegance.

Sarbiewski—the Polish Jesuit, classical reviser of the breviary hymns under Pope Urban VIII, and known generally as the Christian Horace—wrote Latin odes and biblical paraphrases that became popular shortly after their publication in England in 1625 and 1628. Watts translated certain of those odes in his *Horae Lyricae* (both 1706 and 1709 editions); many other poets, both earlier and later, also translated some of Sarbiewski's works: among them were Henry Vaughan (in 1651), Sir Edward Sherburne (1651), the compilers of *Miscellany Poems and Translations by Oxford Hands* (1685), Thomas Browne (1707-1708), and John Hughes (1720). Even Samuel Taylor Coleridge translated Casimir's "Ad Lyram," but after the early nineteenth century little interest was expressed in the works of the Polish Jesuit. Watts probably discovered Casimir sometime between 1680 and 1690, when studying Latin at the Free School at Southampton under the tutelage of the Reverend John Pinhorne, rector of All Saints church. The earliest printed evidence of Casimir's influence appeared in Book II of *Horae Lyricae* in the form of an ode to Pinhorne, in which the young Watts thanked his schoolmaster for introducing him to the Latin poets, particularly Sarbiewski. The extravagant praise of Casimir and the translation of his poetry make it clear that Watts never really lost his schoolboy regard for that poet. In fact, in the Preface to the 1709 edition of *Horae Lyricae*, Watts admitted that he often added or deleted as many as ten or twenty lines in order to fit the original sense to his own design. Further, he apologized for not having been able to capture Casimir's force, exactness, and passion of expression.

Thirteen acknowledged translations and imitations of modern Latin appear throughout Watts's poems and hymns; ten of these come from Sarbiewski. The Casimir translations may be found in both the 1706 and 1709 editions of *Horae Lyricae*: "The fairest and only beloved," "Mutual love stronger than death," "Converse with Christ," "Forsaken yet helping," "Meditation in a

Grove," "Come, Lord Jesus," "Love to Christ present or absent," and the long narrative that received considerable praise from Robert Southey, "The Dacian Battle." In *Reliquiae Juveniles*, a collection of earlier poetry and prose, Watts included translations of "To Dorio" and "The Hebrew Poet." In the first piece, Watts reacted to what he termed the softness and the beauty of two four-line stanzas describing a lyric poet's first attempts on the "harp" and his introduction to the lyric form. He complained, however, of the difficulties of translation. "The Hebrew Poet" is very long—thirty four-line stanzas. Again, Watts notes the difficulty of accurate translation from the Old Testament Psalms: How does the translator Christianize the piece, yet at the same time retain the "Hebrew glory" and the quality of the original Latin ode? Early in the poem, he mentions "The Bard that climb'd to Cooper's-Hill," referring to Sir John Denham, who succeeded as a poet concerned with meditative and speculative subjects but who failed as a translator of the Psalms of David.

Despite his misgivings, Watts managed to do justice to Sarbiewski's Latin poetry. His study of Casimir and the practical exercise of translating his odes taught the Nonconformist poet to think in terms of higher Nature while praising God. Thus, his hymns challenged the Augustans to regard natural objects closely and with a certain degree of enjoyment, a characteristic found lacking in the vast majority of Watts's less pious contemporaries—principally John Sheffield, William Wycherley, Bishop Thomas Sprat, William Walsh, Bernard Mandeville, and, foremost among them, Jonathan Swift.

In his upbringing and training, and in his conception of the poet's purpose, certain tantalizing parallels exist between the early careers of Watts and John Milton. Milton died the same year that Watts was born. Both emerged from Puritan homes, having been exposed to the dominant literary and cultural traditions of their times. After classical educations (although Milton's was longer and perhaps more formal), both returned to their homes for further study, meditation, and work. As students, they both wrote Latin verse dedicated to their tutors: Milton's "Ad Thomas Iunium, Praeceptorem Suum" (1627) when he was nineteen, Watts's corresponding "Ad Reverendum Virum Dom. Johannem Pinhorne" (1694) at the age of twenty. Finally and more significantly, the two poets proclaimed the merits of biblical poetry and paraphrase; both determined that the poet's work was a divine mission, inspired by the love of God.

In an essay entitled "Of the Different Stops and Cadences in Blank Verse" (1734), Watts acknowledged his debt to Milton, a debt that may appear to counter the criticism of Dr. Johnson. He labeled Milton the esteemed parent and author of blank verse, of which *Paradise Lost* (1667) must stand as the noblest example. Milton, according to the Nonconformist hymnodist, assured his readers that true musical delight need not consist of rhyme, or even in the jingling sounds of like endings. Instead, that pleasure could easily be found in appropriate numbers, fit quantity of syllables, and the principal theme of the piece as it proceeds from one segment of a poem to another. Watts, however, must not be identified as an imitator of Milton or even as a follower; rather, his reliance upon Miltonic blank verse provided a sharp point of departure from the predominant form of the Augustan Age. He wrote blank verse when almost every other poet sped forward on the quick airs of the couplet. His particular blank verse, however, was indeed distinct from anything previously written in the form. It was neither epic, as was Milton's, nor dramatic, as was the verse of William Shakespeare and his successors. Instead, Watts's lines were lyrical and meditative blank verse, in the manner which William Cowper and then William Wordsworth would develop so brilliantly.

Watts acknowledged the superiority of Milton's verse to his own; nevertheless, he formulated five specific rules whereby the legacy of the great Puritan epic poet could be maintained but improved. Watts's criticism of Milton's blank verse began in *Horae Lyricae*, in which he declared that Milton's lengthy periods and parentheses ran him out of breath, while certain of his numbers seemed too harsh and uneasy. Watts refused to believe that roughness and obscurity added anything to the grandeur of a poem—even to an epic. Furthermore, he could not understand how archaisms, exoticisms, and "quaint uncouthness of speech" could be affected by poets merely for the sake of being labeled "Miltonian." Thus, instead of imitating Milton, Watts chose to experiment with his meter, producing in *Horae Lyricae* a combination of religious and poetic earnestness with great vividness and intensity.

Watts advanced his own theories of prosody, generally opposing the neoclassical traditions of the early eighteenth century—which may well be a major reason for his neglect today. In his *Reliquiae Juveniles*, Watts argued that a writer of verse should be attentive to the ear as well as to the eye. Challenging the dominance of the couplet, he complained that the form tended to end too abruptly and often without necessity. Such practice (he believed) produced poems that proceeded with excessive regularity; this uniformity, according to Watts, becomes tiresome and offensive to every sensitive ear. His criticism of the closed couplet, then, was tied to rhyme, punctuation, and general sentence sense, and he argued that poets often ended their couplets without being attentive to meaning.

In "Of the Different Stops and Cadences in Blank Verse," published in *Reliquiae Juveniles*, Watts set down five extremely exact rules (which he had followed in composing the majority of his congregational hymns) whereby the tiresome and offensive uniformity of the couplet could be avoided. First, he suggested that the poetic sentence be extended to between six and ten lines. Further, although he could identify at least ten places within a line where the sentence could end with the inclusion of a fixed stop, Watts cautioned against that stop occurring too early or too late. Third, he argued that two lines in succession ought not to appear in which the poet places a strong stop at the first or the ninth syllable. Most important to his argument was the rule that the final line in a poetic sentence or poetic paragraph should contain the sense of that passage, and that the next line should introduce a new scene, episode, or idea. Finally, Watts believed that every line should end with a short pause, which would provide respite, but not an end to the sense. In that fifth rule, the reader immediately sees Watts's concern for a poem in blank verse—a divine ode—that is to be written for or adapted to congregational worship.

Perhaps the most outstanding example of Watts's ability to apply his own rules to his own poetry is his most anthologized piece, "The Day of Judgment," from the 1706 edition of *Horae Lyricae.* In both content and form, those thirty-six lines have received more critical attention than any other Watts poem or hymn. Amy Reed, in relating "The Day of Judgment" to the various influences upon Thomas Gray's *An Elegy Written in a Country Churchyard* (1751), emphasizes Watt's skill in consistently offsetting the negative aspects of life: human vanity and the horrors of death and judgment. In their place, he introduced the thought of the saving power of Christ and the bliss of the righteous in heaven. Unfortunately, the lowest among the humble Christians who came into contact with Watts's poems relied only on their uncontrolled imaginations and saw only the gruesome elements of his Judgment Day: the fierce north wind, red lightning, bloody trumpets, and gaping waters quick to devour sinners. Another scholar, Enid Hammer, views the poem as a leap into the nineteenth century, believing it to be the link between the sapphics of Sir Philip Sidney and those of Robert Southey and Charles Lamb. Watts himself was so dedicated to the idea of the poem that he produced a prose version for the introduction to an essay, "Distant Thunder" (1734), another commentary on the theme of judgment.

Watts must be given credit for poetic and critical skills beyond a single poem on judgment or a single essay on the stops and cadences in blank verse. As a writer of religiously inspired odes and hymns for congregational worship, he stood almost alone, promoting the spiritual ardor of Protestant dissent. No doubt the eighteenth century reader and worshiper must have stood in awe at the wide range of that expression. Watts could, for example, strike fear into the hearts of children with his description of Hell (as in "Heaven and Hell"); he could ascend to heights of extreme tenderness (as in the well-known cradle hymn, "Hush, my dear, lie still and slumber"); he could visualize Eternity in the hand of the very God that made all men (as in his most noted hymn, "O God, our help in ages past").

Although he set out to Christianize the Old Testament Psalms and to make David speak as a Christian, Watts also needed to consider those eighteenth century Britons who would be his readers and his singers. Thus, in his hymns he saw clear parallels between Judea and Great Britain; historical events such as the gunpowder plot, the coming of William III and Mary to England, the end of the Stuarts and the accession of the Hanoverians, and the Jacobite uprisings, were occasions to set forth, poetically, clear lessons, sound political doctrine, and general thanksgiving. Watts had no real interest in limited or local occurrences; his primary focus was upon the larger issues that concerned, politically and intellectually, the citizens of a legitimate Christian nation. He limited his hymnody to the same three or four general areas: the weakness of man, the imperfections of society, the transience of human existence, and the hopes and fears of common creatures. Watts was nondenominational as long as he remained within those perimeters; he could rightfully claim that his hymns and psalm paraphrases held fast to the common denominators of universal Christianity.

Only relatively recently have scholars of hymnody, theology, and poetry been able to determine Watts's purpose as a hymnodist. In his three major hymn collections (*Horae Lyricae*, *Hymns and Spiritual Songs*, and the hymns for children) he developed a complete system of praise, a process by which persons at all stages of their lives could come together to express their feelings, experiences, and beliefs. Watts sought to make the divine ode representative of the individual worshiper's response to the word of God. *The Psalms of David* and the *Hymns and Spiritual Songs* became the poetical guidebooks by which the diverse denominations of British and American Nonconformity achieved fullness and directness of religious and ethical thought, especially during the eighteenth and early nineteenth centuries when authority and direction were lacking.

Despite the reception of Watts's hymns and psalms in England and America during the eighteenth and nineteenth centuries, the present age seems unwilling or unable to determine the poet's rightful place in British literary history. Although evangelical churchmen continue to hold him in esteem, his literary position is less secure. Nevertheless, few will challenge Watts's capabilities as a poet or his skills in prosody; all will accept him as an experimenter, willing to challenge the popular poetic forms of his era. Watts was a wise and discriminating theorist who developed rules of prosody patterned after the brightest lights of the seventeenth century. Despite his credentials, however, literary historians have not willingly allowed him to represent both English hymnody *and* English poetry. That is most unfortunate. Watts wrote verse that consciously explicated the doctrines of religious nonconformity and applied them to almost every facet of human experience. For that reason, the poems have not always been easily separated from the hymns, thus detracting from a full understanding of his verse. Watts intended a fusion between the poem and the congregational hymn, and a careful reading of his prose and poetry reveals his total concept of literature: he held it to be a repository wherein poetry and hymnody could eventually meet. Unfortunately, such a concept never has found a large audience, and Watts remains an Augustan poet of the second rank.

Samuel J. Rogal

Other major works
RELIGIOUS WRITINGS: *The First Catechism*, 1692; *The Art of Reading and Writing English*, 1721; *Sermons on Various Subjects*, 1721-1727 (3 volumes); *The Christian Doctrine of the Trinity*, 1722; *Logick: Or, The Right Use of Reason*, 1725; *An Essay Towards the Encouragement of Charity Schools*, 1728; *A Caveat against Infidelity*, 1729; *Useful and Important Questions Concerning Jesus, the Son of God*, 1746.

Bibliography
Adey, Lioney. *Class and Idol in the English Hymn*. Vancouver: University of British Columbia Press, 1987. This history of English hymnody places Watts's remarkable career in theological and historical perspectives while explaining the role hymns occupied in the church life of eighteenth century England. Adey's particular contribution is his argument that Watts's stern Calvinist upbringing determined his portrait of a Father God in his psalms and hymns. Adey's bibliography is a gold mine of primary sources related to Watts and the hymnody of his era.
Bailey, Albert Edward. *The Gospel in Hymns*. New York: Charles Scribner's Sons, 1950. A standard history of gospel hymnody places Watts at the center of the revolution in church music through his "rhymed theology." Bailey's extensive catalog of Watts's hymns, psalms, and poems is especially useful to researchers.
Benson, Louis Fitzgerald. *The English Hymn: Its Development and Use in Worship*. Richmond, Va.: John Knox Press, 1962. Benson presents a rather extensive analysis of Watts's religious poetry as he surveys English hymnody from its origins to the nineteenth century. Benson concludes that part of Watts's achievement consists in demonstrating the relationship between psalm paraphrase and actual poetry.
Escott, Harry. *Isaac Watts: Hymnographer*. London: Independent Press, 1962. In this biography, Escott uses biographical facts from Watts's life to underscore his critique of contemporary hymnology in his times and his body of poetic collections. Watts is seen here as a reformer and a precocious advocate of new theology of music for a generation of Protestant nonconformists.
Marshall, Madeleine F., and Janet Todd. *English Congregational Hymns in the Eighteenth Century*. Lexington: University Press of Kentucky, 1982. The authors find Watts's determination to redefine hymnography not only as setting Scripture to melody but also as the art of narrating the effect of Scripture on the life of individual Christians and his unique innovation to English church music. In a time of rationalistic Deism, Watts's poetry

sought to bring God the Father closer to human life as it is lived.

Sizes, Sandra A. *Gospel Hymns and Social Religion*. Philadelphia: Temple University Press, 1978. Sizes argues that Watts's hymns served as rallying anthems for his Nonconformist theological perspective. Her delineation of the effects of religious poetry and psalmody on social change in pre-Victorian England is particularly useful in understanding Watts's place in the evangelical reformation of his times.

Tanke, Susan S. *Make a Joyful Noise unto the Lord*. Athens: Ohio University Press, 1979. Tanke's thesis posits Watts as the father of modern hymnography who not only wrote hymns but also forged a system and theory behind their construction. Provides particular insight into the methodology Watts used in crafting several of his best known hymns.

PHILLIS WHEATLEY

Born: Gambia, Africa; 1753(?)
Died: Boston, Massachusetts; December 5, 1784

Principal poetry
Poems on Various Subjects, Religious and Moral, 1773; *The Poems of Phillis Wheatley,* 1966 (Julian Mason, editor).

Other literary forms
Phillis Wheatley's cultivation of the letter as a literary form is attested by her inclusion of the titles of several letters in each of her proposals for future volumes subsequent to the publication of her *Poems on Various Subjects, Religious and Moral* (1773). Regrettably, none of these proposals provoked enough response to secure publication of any new volumes. Scholars continue to discover both poems and letters that Wheatley names in these proposals. The letters mentioned in them are addressed to such noted persons as William Legge, Second Earl of Dartmouth; Selina Hastings, Countess of Huntingdon; Dr. Benjamin Rush; and George Washington. They display a graceful style and articulate some of Wheatley's strongest protestations in support of the cause of American independence and in condemnation of Christian hypocrisy regarding slavery.

Achievements
From the time of her first published piece to the present day, controversy has surrounded the life and work of America's first black poet, and only its second published woman poet, after Anne Bradstreet. Few poets of any age have been so scornfully maligned, so passionately defended, so fervently celebrated, and so patronizingly tolerated. Yet, during the years of her young adulthood, Wheatley was the toast of England and the Colonies. For years before she attempted to find a Boston publisher for her poems, she had published numerous elegies celebrating the deaths of many of the city's most prominent citizens. In 1770, she wrote her most famous and most often-reprinted elegy, on the death of "the voice of the Great Awakening," George Whitefield, chaplain to the Countess of Huntingdon, who was one of the leading benefactors of the Methodist evangelical movement in England and the Colonies.

Not finding Boston to be in sympathy with her 1772 proposal for a volume, Wheatley found substantial support the following year in the Countess of Huntingdon, whose interest had been stirred by the young poet's noble tribute to her chaplain. Subsequently, Wheatley was sent to London, ostensibly for her health; this trip curiously accords, however, with the very weeks that her book was being printed. It is likely that she proofread the galleys herself. At any rate, she was much sought after among the intellectual, literary set of London, and Sir Brook Watson, who was to become Lord Mayor of London within a year, presented her with a copy of John Milton's *Paradise Lost* (1667) in folio. The Earl of Dartmouth, who was at the time Secretary of State for the Colonies and President of the Board of Trade and Foreign Plantations, gave her a copy of Tobias Smollett's translation of *Don Quixote* (1755). Benjamin Franklin, to whom she would later inscribe her second book of poetry (never published), has even recorded that, while in London briefly, he called on Wheatley to see whether "there were any service I could do her."

In the opening pages of her 1773 volume appears a letter of authentication of Wheatley's authorship which is signed by still another of the signatories of the Declaration of Independence, John Hancock. Added to the list of attesters are other outstanding Bostonians, including Thomas Hutchinson, then Governor of Massachusetts, and James Bowdoin, one of the founders of Bowdoin College. Later, during the early months of the Revolution, Wheatley wrote a poem in praise of General Washington entitled "To His Excellency General Washington." As a result, she received an invitation to visit the General at his headquarters, and her poem was published by Tom Paine in *The Pennsylvania Magazine*. John Paul Jones, who also appreciated Wheatley's celebration of freedom, even asked one of his officers to secure him a copy of her *Poems*.

Nevertheless, she did not continue to enjoy such fame. A country ravaged by war has little time, finally, for poetry, and Wheatley regrettably, perhaps tragically, faced the rejection of two more proposals for a volume of new poems. Thwarted by the vicissitudes of war and poverty, Wheatley died from complications resulting from childbirth. Even so, her poetry has survived and is now considered to be among the best of its period produced in America or in England. It is just beginning to be recognized that, contrary to the opinion of those who would dispose of Wheatley as a mere imitator, she produced sophisticated, original poems whose creative theories of the imagination and the sublime anticipate the Romantic movement.

Biography

The known details of Phillis Wheatley's life are few. According to her master, John Wheatley of Boston, she "was brought from Africa to America in the Year 1761, between Seven and Eight Years of Age [sic]." Her parents were apparently sun-worshipers, for she is supposed to have recalled to her white captors that she remembered seeing her mother pouring out water to the sun every morning. If such be the case, it would help to explain why the sun is predominant as an image in her poetry.

Her life with the Wheatleys, John and Susanna and their two children, the twins Mary and Nathaniel, was probably not too demanding for one whose disposition toward asthma (brought on or no doubt exacerbated by the horrible "middle passage") greatly weakened her. The Wheatleys' son attended Harvard, so it is likely that Nathaniel served as the eager young girl's Latin tutor. At any rate, it is certain that Wheatley knew Latin well; her translation of the Niobe episode from Ovid's *Metamorphoses* (before A.D. 8), Book VI, displays a learned knowledge and appreciation of the Latin original. Wheatley's classical learning is evident throughout her poetry, which is thick with allusions to ancient historical and mythological figures.

The turning point of Wheatley's career, not only as an author but also as a human being, came when her *Poems on Various Subjects, Religious and Moral* was published in London in 1773. After she returned from England, having been recalled because of Susanna Wheatley's growing illness, she was manumitted sometime during September, 1773. It is probable that Wheatley was freed because of the severe censure that some English reviewers of her *Poems* had directed at the owners of a learned author who "still remained a slave." At this very point, however, the poet's fortunes began a slow decline. In 1778, at the height of the war and after the deaths of both John and Susanna Wheatley, she married John Peters, a black man of some learning who failed to rescue the poet from poverty.

Wheatley died alone and unattended in a hovel somewhere in the back streets of the Boston slums in 1784, truly an ignominious end for one who had enjoyed such favor. She was preceded in death by two of her children, as well as by the third to whom she had just given birth. She was at most only thirty-one years old. Given Wheatley's vision of the world "Oppress'd with woes, a painful endless train," it should not be surprising that her most frequently adopted poetic form is the elegy, in which she always celebrates death as the achievement of ultimate freedom—suggesting the thanatos-eros (desire for death) motif of Romanticism.

Analysis

In the past ten years, Phillis Wheatley has begun to receive the attention she deserves. George McMichael and others, editors of the influential two-volume *Anthology of American Literature* (1974, 1980), observe that she and Philip Freneau were "the most important poets" of America's Revolutionary War era. To be sure, one of the major subjects of her poetry is the American struggle for independence. Temporal freedom is not her only subject, however; she is also much concerned with the quest for spiritual freedom. Consequently, the elegy, in which she celebrates the Christian rewards of eternal life and absolute freedom after death, is her favorite poetic form. In addition, she delights in describing God's creation of nature's splendors and sometimes appears to enjoy the beauties of nature for their own sake and not simply as acts of God's providence. It is in her poem "On Imagination," however, that Wheatley waxes most eloquent; in this poem, perhaps her most important single work, she articulates a theory of the imagination which strikingly anticipates that of Samuel Taylor Coleridge. Indeed, Wheatley's affinities with Romanticism, which run throughout her poetry, may come to be seen as her surest claim to a place in literary history.

Such an approach to this early American poet contradicts the widespread critical view that Wheatley was a highly derivative poet, inextricably mired in the neoclassical tradition. Her preference for the heroic couplet, one of the hallmarks of neoclassicism, has deceived many into immediately classifying her as neoclassical. One must recall, however, that Lord Byron also had a passion for the couplet. Surely, then, one must not be satisfied with a cursory glance at Wheatley's adoption of the heroic couplet; one must go on to explore the content of her poetry.

Her political poems document major incidents of the American struggle for independence. In 1768, she wrote "To the King's Most Excellent Majesty on His Repealing the American Stamp Act." When it appeared, much revised, in *Poems on Various Subjects, Religious and Moral*, the poet diplomatically deleted the last two lines of the original, which read, "When wars came on [against George] the proudest rebel fled/ God thunder'd fury on their guilty head." By that time, the threat of the King's retaliation did not seem so forbidding nor the injustice of rebellion against him so grave.

"America," a poem probably written about the same time but published only recently, admonishes Britain to treat "americus," the British child, with more deference. According to the poem, the child, now a growing seat of "Liberty," is no mere adorer of an overwhelming "Majesty," but has acquired strength of his own: "Fearing his strength which she [Britain] undoubted knew/ She laid some taxes on her darling son." Recognizing her mistake, "great Britannia" promised to lift the burden, but the promise proved only "seeming Sympathy and Love." Now the Child "weeps afresh to feel this Iron chain." The urge to draw an analogy here between the poem's "Iron chain" and Wheatley's own predicament is irresistible; while America longs for its own independence, Wheatley no doubt yearns for hers.

The year 1770 marked the beginning of armed resistance against Britain. Wheatley chronicles such resistance in two poems, the second of which is now lost. The first, "On the Death of Mr. Snider Murder'd by Richardson," appeared initially along with "America." The poem tells how Ebenezer Richardson, an informer on American traders involved in circumventing British taxation, found his home surrounded on the evening of February 22, 1770, by an angry mob of colonial sympathizers. Much alarmed, Richardson emerged from his house armed with a musket and fired indiscriminately into the mob, killing the eleven- or twelve-year-old son of Snider, a poor German colonist. Wheatley calls young Christopher Snider, of whose death Richardson was later found guilty in a trial by jury, "the first martyr for the common good," rather than those men killed less than two weeks later in the Boston Massacre. The poem's fine closing couplet suggests that even those not in sympathy with the quest for freedom can grasp the nobility of that quest and are made indignant by its sacrifice: "With Secret rage fair freedom's foes beneath/ See in thy corse ev'n Majesty in Death."

Wheatley does not, however, ignore the Boston Massacre. In a proposal for a volume which was to have been published in Boston in 1772, she lists, among twenty-seven titles of poems (the 1773 volume had thirty-nine), "On the Affray in King Street, on the Evening of the 5th of March." This title, naming the time and place of the Massacre, suggests that the poet probably celebrated the martyrdom of Crispus Attucks, the first black to lose his life in the American struggle, along with the deaths of two whites. Regrettably, the poem has not yet been recovered. Even so, the title alone confirms Wheatley's continued recording of America's struggle for freedom. This concern shifted in tone from obedient praise for the British regime to supplicatory admonition and then to guarded defiance. Since she finally found a publisher not in Boston but in London, she prudently omitted "America" and the poems about Christopher Snider and the Boston Massacre from her 1773 volume.

She chose to include, however, a poem dedicated to the Earl of Dartmouth, who was appointed Secretary of State for the Colonies in August, 1772. In this poem, "To the Right Honourable William, Earl of Dartmouth, His Majesty's Principal Secretary of State for North America," she gives the Earl extravagant praise as one who will lay to rest "hatred faction." She knew of the Earl's reputation as a humanitarian through the London contacts of her mistress, Susanna. When the Earl proved to support oppressive British policies, the poet's expectations were not realized; within four years of the poem's date, America had declared its independence. Since her optimism was undaunted by foreknowledge, Wheatley wrote a poem which was even more laudatory than "To The King's Most Excellent Majesty on His Repealing the American Stamp Act." Perhaps she was not totally convinced, however; the poem contains some unusually bold passages for a colonist who is also both a woman and a slave.

For example, she remarks that, with Dartmouth's secretaryship, America need no longer "dread the iron chain,/ Which wanton *Tyranny* with lawless hand/ Had made, and with it meant t'enslave the land." Once again Wheatley uses the slave metaphor of the iron chain. Quite clearly she also accuses the Crown of "wanton *Tyranny*," which it had wielded illegally and with the basest of motives—to reduce the colonies to the inhuman condition of slave states. Here rebellious defiance, no longer guarded, is unmistakable; the tone matches that of The Declaration of Independence. It is a mystery how these lines could have gone unnoticed in the London reviews, all of them positive, of her 1773 volume. Perhaps the reviewers were too bedazzled by the "improbability" that a black woman could produce such a volume to take the content of her poetry seriously.

In this poem, Wheatley also presents a rare autobiographical portrait describing the manner in which she was taken from her native Africa. The manuscript version of this passage is more spontaneous and direct than the more formally correct one printed in the 1773 volume, and thus is closer to the poet's true feelings. It was "Seeming cruel fate" which snatched her "from Afric's fancy'd happy seat." Fate here is only apparently cruel, since her capture has enabled her to become a Christian; the young poet's piety resounds throughout her poetry and letters. Her days in her native land were, nevertheless, happy ones, and her abduction at the hands of ruthless slavers doubtless left behind inconsolable parents. Such a bitter memory of the circumstances of her abduction fully qualifies her to "deplore the day/ When Britons weep beneath Tyrannic sway"; the later version reads: "And can I then but pray/ Others may never feel tyrranic sway?" Besides toning down the diction, this passage alters her statement to a question and replaces "Britons" with the neutral "others." The question might suggest uncertainty, but it more probably reflects the author's polite deportment toward a London audience. Since, in the earlier version, she believed Dartmouth to be sympathetic with her cause, she had no reason to exercise deference toward him; she thought she could be frank. The shift from "Britons" to "others" provokes a more compelling explanation. In the fall of 1772, Wheatley could still think of herself as a British subject. Later, however, after rejoicing that the Earl's administration had given way to restive disillusionment, perhaps the poet was less certain about her citizenship.

Three years after the publication of her 1773 volume, Wheatley unabashedly celebrated the opposition to the "tyrannic sway" of Britain in "To His Excellency General Washington," newly appointed Commander-in-Chief of the Continental Army; the war of ideas had become one of arms. In this piece, which is more a paean to freedom than a eulogy to Washington, she describes freedom as "divinely fair,/ Olive and laurel bind her golden hair"; yet "She flashes dreadful in refulgent arms." The poet accents this image of martial glory with an epic simile, comparing the American forces to the power of the fierce king of the winds:

> As when Eolus heaven's fair face deforms,
> Enwrapp'd in tempest and a night of storms;
> Astonish'd ocean feels the wild uproar,
> The refluent surges beat the sounding shore.

For the young poet, America is now "The land of freedom's heaven-defended race!" While the eyes of the world's nations are fixed "on the scales,/ For in their hopes Columbia's arm prevails," the poet records Britain's regret over her loss: "Ah! cruel blindness to Columbia's state!/ Lament thy thirst of boundless power too late." The temper of this couplet is in keeping with Wheatley's earlier attitudes toward oppression. The piece closes as the poet urges Washington to pursue his objective with the knowledge that virtue is on his side. If he allows the fair goddess Freedom to be his guide, Washington will surely emerge not only as the leader of a victorious army but also as the head of the newly established state.

In Wheatley's last political poem, "freedom's heaven-defended race" has won its battle. Written in 1784 within a year after the Treaty of Paris, "Liberty and Peace" is a demonstrative celebration of American independence. British tyranny, the agent of American oppression, has now been taught to fear "americus" her child, "And new-born *Rome* shall give *Britannia* Law." Wheatley concludes this piece with two pleasing couplets in praise of America, whose future is assured by heaven's approval:

> Auspicious Heaven shall fill with favoring Gales,
> Where e'er *Columbia* spreads her swelling Sails:
> To every Realm shall *Peace* her Charms display,
> And Heavenly *Freedom* spread her golden Ray.

Personified as Peace and Freedom, Columbia (America) will act as a world emissary, an emanating force like the rays of the sun. In this last couplet, Wheatley has captured, perhaps for the first time in poetry, America's ideal mission to the rest of the world.

The fact that Wheatley so energetically proclaims America's success in the political arena certainly attests her sympathies—not with the neoclassic obsession never to challenge the established order nor to breach the rules of political and social decorum—but with the Romantic notion that a people who find themselves unable to accept a present, unsatisfactory government have the right to change that government, even if such a change can be accomplished only through armed revolt. The American Revolution against Britain was the first successful such revolt and was one of the sparks of the French Revolution. Wheatley's steadfast literary participation in the American Revolution clearly aligns her with such politically active English Romantic poets as Percy Bysshe Shelley and Lord Byron.

In her elegies, on the other hand, Wheatley displays her devotion to spiritual freedom. As do her political poems, her elegies exalt specific occasions, the deaths of people usually known to her within the social and religious community of the poet's Old South Congregational Church of Boston. As do her poems on political events, however, her elegies exceed the boundaries of occasional verse. The early, but most famous of her elegies, "On the Death of the Rev. Mr. George Whitefield, 1770," both illustrates the general structure in which she cast all seventeen of her extant elegies and indicates her recurring ideological concerns.

Wheatley's elegies conform for the most part to the Puritan funeral elegy. They include two major divisions: first comes the portrait, in which the poet pictures the life of the subject; then follows the exhortation, encouraging the reader to seek the heavenly rewards gained by the subject in death. The portrait usually comprises three biographical steps: vocation or conversion; sanctification, or evidence of good works; and glorification, or joyous treatment of the deceased's reception into heaven. Wheatley's elegy on Whitefield surprisingly opens with the glorification of the Great Awakener, already in heaven and occupying his "immortal throne." She celebrates the minister's conversion or vocation in an alliterative line as "The greatest gift that ev'n a God can give." Of course, she writes many lines describing the good works of a man wholly devoted to the winning of souls during the seven visits which he made to America during and after the period of the Great Awakening.

Whitefield died in Newburyport, Massachusetts, on September 30, 1770, having left Boston only a week or so before, where he had apparently lodged with the Wheatley family. Indeed, the young poet of sixteen or seventeen appears to recollect from personal experience when she observes that the minister "long'd to see *America* excel" and "charg'd its youth that ev'ry grace divine/ Should with full lustre in their conduct shine." She also seizes this opportunity to proclaim to the world Whitefield's assertion that even Africans would find Jesus of Nazareth an "*Impartial Saviour*." The poem closes with a ten-line exhortation to the living to aspire toward Whitefield's example: "Let ev'ry heart to this bright vision rise."

As one can see, Wheatley's elegies are not sad affairs; quite to the contrary, they enact joyful occasions after which deceased believers may hope to unite, as she states in "On the Death of the Rev. Dr. Sewell, 1769," with "Great God, incomprehensible, unknown/ By sense." Although man's senses may limit his firsthand acquaintance with God, these same senses do enable him to learn *about* God, especially about God's works in nature. The poem in the extant Wheatley canon which most pointedly addresses God's works in nature is "Thoughts on the Works of Providence." This poem of 131 lines opens with a ten-line invocation to the "Celestial muse," resembling Milton's heavenly muse of *Paradise Lost*.

Identifying God as the force behind planetary movement, she writes, "Ador'd [is] the God that whirls surrounding spheres" which rotate ceaselessly about "the monarch of the earth and skies." From this sublime image she moves to yet another: "'Let there be light,' he said: from his profound/ Old chaos heard and trembled at the sound." It should not go unremarked that Wheatley could, indeed, find much in nature to foster her belief, but little in the mundane world of ordinary men to sustain her spiritually. The frequency of nature imagery but the relative lack of scenes drawn from human society (with the exception of her political poems, and even these are occasions for abstract departures into the investigation of political ideologies) probably reflects the poet's insecurity and uncertainty about a world which first made her a slave and then gave her, at best, only second-class citizenship.

In "An Hymn to the Morning," one of her most lyrical poems, Wheatley interprets the morn (recall her mother's morning ritual of pouring out water to the rising sun) as the source of poetic afflatus or inspiration. The speaker of the poem, Wheatley herself, first perceives the light of the rising sun as a reflection in the eye of one of the "feather'd race." After she hears the song of the bird which welcomes the day, she turns to find the source of the melody and sees the bird "Dart the bright eye, and shake the painted plume." Here the poet captures with great precision the bird's rapid eye movement. The bird, archetypal symbol of poetic song, has received the dawn's warm rays which stimulate him to sing. When the poet turns to discover the source of melody, however, what she sees first is not Aurora, the dawning sun, but Aurora the stimulus of song reflected within the "bright eye" of the bird.

In the next stanza the poet identifies the dawn as the ultimate source of poetic inspiration when she remarks that the sun has awakened Calliope, here the personification of inspiration, while her sisters, the other muses, "fan the pleasing fire" of the stimulus to create. Hence both the song of the bird and the light reflected in its eye have instructed her to acknowledge the source of the bird's melody; for she aspires to sing with the same pleasing fire which animates the song of the bird. Like many of the Romantics who followed her, Wheatley perceives nature both as a means to know ultimate freedom and as an inspiration to create, to make art.

It is in her superlative poem, "On Imagination," however, that Wheatley most forcefully brings both aspirations, to know God and to create fine poetry, into clear focus. To the young black poet, the imagination was sufficiently important to demand from her pen a fifty-three line poem. The piece opens with this four-line apostrophe:

> Thy various works, imperial queen, we see,
> How bright their forms! how deck'd with pomp by thee!
> Thy wond'rous acts in beauteous order stand,
> And all attest how potent is thine hand.

Clearly, Wheatley's imagination is a regal presence in full control of her poetic world, a world in which her "wond'rous acts" of creation stand in harmony, capturing a "beauteous order." These acts themselves testify to the queen's creative power. Following a four-line invocation to the muse, however, the poet distinguishes the imagination from its subordinate fancy:

> Now, here, now there, the roving Fancy flies;
> Till some lov'd object strikes her wand'ring eyes,
> Whose silken fetters all the senses bind,
> And soft captivity involves the mind.

Unlike the controlled, harmonious imagination, the subordinate fancy flies about here and there, searching for some appropriate and desired object worthy of setting into motion the creative powers of her superior.

In "Thoughts on the Works of Providence," the poet describes the psychology of sleep in similar fashion. Having entered the world of dreams, the mind discovers a realm where "ideas range/ Licentious and unbounded o'er the plains/ Where Fancy's queen in giddy triumph reigns." Wheatley maintains that in sleep the imagination, once again "Fancy's queen," creates worlds which lack the "beauteous order" of the poet sitting before a writing desk; nevertheless, these dream worlds provoke memorable images. In "On Recollection" Wheatley describes the memory as the repository on which the mind draws to create its dreams. What may be "long-forgotten," the memory "calls from night" and "plays before the fancy's sight." By analogy, Wheatley maintains, the memory provides the poet "ample treasure" from her "secret stores" to create poetry: "in her pomp of images display'd,/ To the high-raptur'd poet gives her aid." "On Recollection" asserts a strong affinity between the poet's memory, analogous to the world of dreams, and the fancy, the associative faculty subordinate to the imagination. Recollection for Wheatley functions as the poet's storehouse of images, while the fancy channels the force of the imagination through its associative powers. Both the memory and the fancy, then, serve the imagination.

Wheatley's description of fancy and memory departs markedly from what eighteenth century aestheticians, including John Locke and Joseph Addison, generally understood as the imagination. The faculty of mind which they termed "imagination" Wheatley relegates to recollection (memory) and fancy. Her description of recollection and fancy closely parallels Coleridge's in the famous thirteenth chapter of *Biographia Literaria* (1817), where he states that fancy "is indeed no other than a mode of Memory emancipated from the order of time and space." Wheatley's identification of the fancy as roving "Now here, now there" whose movement is analogous to the dream state, where "ideas range/ Licentious and unbounded," certainly frees it from the limits of time and space. Coleridge further limits the fancy to the capacity of choice. "But equally with the ordinary memory," he insists, "the Fancy must receive all its materials ready made from the law of association." Like Coleridge's, Wheatley's fancy exercises choice by association as it finally settles upon "some lov'd object."

If fancy and memory are the imagination's subordinates, then how does the imagination function in the poet's creative process? Following her description of fancy in "On Imagination," Wheatley details the role the imagination plays in her poetry. According to her, the power of the imagination enables her to soar "through air to find the bright abode,/ Th' empyreal palace of the thund'ring God." The central focus of her poetry remains contemplation of God. Foreshadowing William Wordsworth's "winds that will be howling at all hours," Wheatley exclaims that on the wings of the imagination she "can surpass the wind/ And leave the rolling universe behind." In the realm of the imagination, the poet can "with new worlds amaze th' unbounded soul."

Immediately following this arresting line, Wheatley illustrates in a ten-line stanza the power of the imagination to create new worlds. Even though winter and the "frozen deeps"prevail in the real world, the imagination can take one out of unpleasant reality and build a pleasant, mythic world of fragrant flowers and verdant groves where "Fair Flora" spreads "her fragrant reign," where Sylvanus crowns the forest with leaves, and where "Show'rs may descend, and dews their gems disclose,/ And nectar sparkle on the blooming rose." Such is the power of imagination to promote poetic creation and to release one from an unsatisfactory world. Unfortunately, like reality's painful intrusion upon the delicate, unsustainable song of John Keats's immortal bird, gelid winter and its severe "northern tempests damp the rising fire," cut short the indulgence of her poetic world, and lamentably force Wheatley to end her short-lived lyric: "Cease then, my song, cease the unequal lay." Her lyric must end because no poet can indefinitely sustain a mythic world.

In her use of the imagination to create "new worlds," Wheatley's departure from eighteenth century theories of this faculty is radical and once again points toward Coleridge. Although she does not distinguish between "primary" and "secondary" imagination as he does, Wheatley nevertheless constructs a theory which approaches his "secondary" imagination. According to Coleridge, the secondary imagination, which attends the creative faculty, intensifies the primary imagination common to all men. Coleridge describes how the secondary imagination operates in this well-known passage: "It dissolves, diffuses, dissipates, in order to recreate;/ or where this process is rendered impossible, yet still at all/ events it struggles to idealize and to unify." In spite of the fact that Wheatley's attempt to dissolve, diffuse, and dissipate is assuredly more modest than Coleridge's "swift half-intermitted burst" in "Kubla Khan," she does, nevertheless, like the apocalyptic Romantics, idealize, unify, and shape a mythopoeic world. Proceeding in a systematic fashion, she first constructs a theory of a mental faculty which, when assisted by the associative fancy, builds, out of an act of the mind, a new world which does indeed stand in "beauteous order." This faculty, which she identifies as the imagination, she uses as a tool to achieve freedom, however momentary.

Wheatley was, then, an innovator who used the imagination as a means to transcend an unacceptable present and even to construct "new worlds [to] amaze the unbounded soul"; this practice, along with her celebration of death, her loyalty to the American struggle for political independence, and her consistent praise of nature, places her firmly in that flow of thought which culminated in nineteenth century Romanticism. Her diction may strike a modern audience as occasionally "got up" and stiff, and her reliance on the heroic couplet may appear outdated and worn, but the content of her poetry is innovative, refreshing, and even, for her times, revolutionary. She wrote during the pre-Revolutionary and Revolutionary War era in America, when little poetry of great merit was produced. Phillis Wheatley, laboring under the disadvantages of being not only a black slave but also a woman, nevertheless did find the time to depict that political struggle for freedom and to trace her personal battle for release. If one looks beyond the limitations of her sincere if dogmatic piety and her frequent dependence on what Wordsworth called poetic diction, one is sure to discover in her works a fine mind engaged in creating some of the best early American poetry.

John C. Shields

Bibliography

Jones, Jacqueline. "Anglo-American Racism and Phillis Wheatley's 'Sable Veil,' 'Length'ned Chain,' and 'Knitted Heart.' " In *Women in the Age of the American Revolution*, edited by Ronald Hoffman and Peter J. Albert. Charlottesville: University Press of Virginia, 1989. This sometimes difficult study includes fascinating biographical information and offers a close reading of dozens of poems. Jones delineates the importance of *Poems on Various Subjects, Religious and Moral* as an early commentary on slavery and on American female thought.

Richmond, Merle. *Phillis Wheatley*. American Women of Achievement series. New York: Chelsea House, 1988. Written for young adults, this biography is lively and informative. The dozens of illustrations include a portrait of Wheatley and a sample of her handwriting. Contains suggestions for further reading, a chronology, and an index.

Robinson, William H., ed. *Critical Essays on Phillis Wheatley*. Boston: G. K. Hall, 1982. This fascinating collection of sixty-five essays contains early comments and reviews, including several by Wheatley herself, important reprinted essays from 1834 to 1975, and five critical evaluations original to this book. An editor's introduction provides a biographical and critical overview. Supplemented by a chronology and an index.

_____. *Phillis Wheatley: A Bio-Bibliography*. Boston: G. K. Hall, 1981. After a brief biography and review of the critical reception, this volume presents an annotated list of representative writings about Wheatley from 1761 to 1979. Complemented by appendices reprinting and commenting on two of the poems and an extensive index.

_____. *Phillis Wheatley and Her Writings*. New York: Garland, 1984. This is by far the finest introduction to Wheatley by the preeminent Wheatley scholar. Presents a brief biography, the text of all the poems and surviving letters (several in facsimile) with an analysis, nine appendices providing background information, a bibliography, and an index.

WALT WHITMAN

Born: West Hills, New York; May 31, 1819
Died: Camden, New Jersey; March 26, 1892

Principal poetry

Leaves of Grass, 1855, 1856, 1860, 1867, 1871, 1876, 1881-1882, 1889, 1891-1892; *Drum-Taps*, 1865; *Passage to India*, 1871; *After All, Not to Create Only*, 1871; *As a Strong Bird on Pinions Free*, 1872; *Two Rivulets*, 1876; *November Boughs*, 1888; *Good-bye My Fancy*, 1891; *Complete Poetry and Selected Prose*, 1959 (James E. Miller, editor).

Other literary forms

Walt Whitman published several important essays and studies during his lifetime. *Democratic Vistas* (1871), *Memoranda During the War* (1875-1876), *Specimen Days and Collect* (1882-1883, autobiographical sketches), and the *Complete Prose Works* (1892) are the most significant. He also tried his hand at short fiction, collected in *The Half-Breed and Other Stories* (1927), and a novel, *Franklin Evans* (1842). Many of his letters and journals have appeared either in early editions or as parts of the New York University Press edition of *The Collected Writings of Walt Whitman* (1961-1984; 22 volumes).

Achievements

Whitman's stature rests largely on two major contributions to the literature of the United States. First, although detractors are numerous and the poet's organizing principle is sometimes blurred, *Leaves of Grass* stands as the most fully realized American epic poem. Written in the midst of natural grandeur and burgeoning materialism, Whitman's book traces the geographical, social, and spiritual contours of an expanding nation. It embraces the science and commercialism of industrial America while trying to direct these practical energies toward the "higher mind" of literature, culture, and the soul. In his Preface to the first edition of *Leaves of Grass*, Whitman referred to the United States itself as "essentially the greatest poem." He saw the self-esteem, sympathy, candor, and deathless attachment to freedom of the common people as "unrhymed poetry," which awaited the "gigantic and generous treatment worthy of it." *Leaves of Grass* was to be that treatment.

As James E. Miller points out in his edition of Whitman's *Complete Poetry and Selected Prose* (1959), the poet's second achievement was in language and poetic technique. Readers take for granted the modern American poet's emphasis on free verse and ordinary diction, forgetting Whitman's revolutionary impact. His free verse form departed from stanzaic patterns and regular lines, taking its power instead from individual, rolling, oratorical lines of cadenced speech. He subordinated traditional poetic techniques, such as alliteration, repetition, inversion, and conventional meter, to this expansive form. He also violated popular rules of poetic diction by extracting a rich vocabulary from foreign languages, science, opera, various trades, and the ordinary language of town and country. Finally, Whitman broke taboos with his extensive use of sexual imagery, incorporated not to titillate or shock, but to portray life in its wholeness. He determined to be the poet of procreation, to celebrate the elemental and primal life force that permeates man and nature. Thus, "forbidden voices" are unveiled, clarified, and transfigured by the poet's vision of their place in an organic universe.

Whitman himself said he wrote but "one or two indicative words for the future." He expected the "main things" from poets, orators, singers, and musicians to come. They would prove and define a national culture, thus justifying his faith in American democracy. These apologetic words, along with the early tendency to read Whitman as "untranslatable," or barbaric and undisciplined, long delayed his acceptance as one of America's greatest poets. In fact, if judged by the poet's own test of greatness, he is a failure, for he said the "proof of a poet is that his country absorbs him as affectionately as he has absorbed it." Whitman has not been absorbed by the common people to whom he paid tribute in his poetry. Today, however, with recognition from both the academic community and such twentieth century poets as Hart Crane, William Carlos Williams, Karl Shapiro, and Randall Jarrell, his *Leaves of Grass* has taken its place among the great masterworks of American literature.

Biography

Walt Whitman (christened Walter) was born in West Hills, Long Island on May 31, 1819. His mother, Louisa Van Velsor, was descended from a long line of New York Dutch farmers, and his father, Walter Whitman, was a Long Island farmer and carpenter. In 1823, the father moved his family to Brooklyn in search of work. One of nine children in an undistinguished family, Whitman received only a meager formal education between 1825 and 1830, when he turned to the printing trade for the next five years. At the age of seventeen he began teaching at various Long Island schools and continued to teach until he went to New York City to be a printer for the *New World* and a reporter for the *Democratic Review* in 1841. From then on, Whitman generally made a living at journalism. Besides reporting and freelance writing, he edited several Brooklyn newspapers, including the *Daily Eagle* (1846-1848), the *Freeman* (1848-1849), and the *Times* (1857-1859). Some of Whitman's experiences during this period influenced the poetry that seemed to burst into print in 1855. While in New York, Whitman frequented the opera and the public library, both of which furnished him with a sense of heritage, of connection with the bards and singers of the past. In 1848, Whitman met and was hired by a representative of the New Orleans *Crescent*. Although the job lasted only a few months, the journey by train, stagecoach, and steamboat through what Whitman always referred to as "inland America" certainly helped to stimulate his vision of the country's democratic future. Perhaps most obviously influential was Whitman's trade itself. His flair for action and vignette, as well as descriptive detail, surely was sharpened by his journalistic writing. The reporter's keen eye for the daily scene is everywhere evident in *Leaves of Grass*.

When the first edition of his poems appeared, Whitman received little money but some attention from reviewers. Included among the responses was a famous letter from Ralph Waldo Emerson, who praised Whitman for his brave thought and greeted him at the beginning of a great career. Whitman continued to write and edit, but was unemployed during the winter of 1859-1860, when he began to frequent Pfaff's bohemian restaurant. There he may have established the "manly love" relationships which inspired the "Calamus" poems of the 1860 edition of *Leaves of Grass*. Again, this third edition created a stir with readers, but the outbreak of the Civil War soon turned everyone's attention to more pressing matters. Whitman himself was too old for military service, but he did experience the war by caring for wounded soldiers in Washington, D.C., hospitals. While in Washington as a government clerk, Whitman witnessed Lincoln's second inauguration, mourned over the President's assassination in April, printed *Drum-Taps* in May, and later added to these Civil War lyrics a sequel, which contained "When Lilacs Last in the Dooryard Bloom'd."

The postwar years saw Whitman's reputation steadily increasing in England, thanks to William Rossetti's *Selections* in 1868, Algernon Swinburne's praise, and a long, admiring review of his work by Anne Gilchrist in 1870. In fact, Mrs. Gilchrist fell in love with the poet after reading *Leaves of Grass* and even moved to Philadelphia in 1876 to be near him, but her hopes of marrying Whitman died with her in 1885. Because of books by William D. O'Connor and John Burroughs, Whitman also became better known in America, but any satisfaction he may have derived from this recognition was tempered by two severe blows in 1873. He suffered a paralytic stroke in January, and his mother, to whom he was very devoted, died in May. Unable to work, Whitman returned to stay with his brother George at Camden, New Jersey, spending summers on a farm at Timber Creek.

Although Whitman recuperated sufficiently to take trips to New York or Boston, and even to Colorado and Canada in 1879-1880, he was never again to be the robust man he had so proudly described in early editions of *Leaves of Grass*. His declining years, however, gave him time to revise and establish the structure of his book. When the seventh edition of *Leaves of Grass* was published in Philadelphia in 1881, Whitman had achieved a total vision of his work. With the money from a Centennial edition (1876) and an occasional lecture on Lincoln, Whitman was able by 1884 to purchase a small house on Mickle Street in Camden, New Jersey. Although he was determined not to be "house-bound," a sunstroke in 1885 and a paralytic stroke in 1888 made him increasingly dependent on friends. He found especially gratifying the friendship of his secretary and companion, Horace Traubel, who recorded the poet's life and opinions during these last years. Despite the care of Traubel and several doctors and nurses, Whitman died of complications from a stroke on March 26, 1892.

Analysis

An approach to Walt Whitman's poetry profitably begins with the "Inscriptions" to *Leaves of Grass*, for these short, individual pieces introduce the main ideas and methods of Whitman's book. In general, they stake out the ground of what Miller has called the prototypical New World personality, a merging of the individual with the national and cosmic, or universal, selves. That democratic principles are at the root of Whitman's views becomes immediately clear in "One's-Self I Sing," the first poem in *Leaves of Grass*. Here, Whitman refers to the self as a "simple separate person," yet utters the "word Democratic, the word En-Masse." Citizens of America alternately assert their individuality—obey little, resist often—and yet see themselves as a brotherhood of the future, inextricably bound by the vision of a great new society of and for the masses. This encompassing vision requires a sense of "the Form complete," rejecting neither body nor soul, singing equally of the Female and Male, embracing both realistic, scientific, modern man and the infinite, eternal life of the spirit.

Whitman takes on various roles, or engages in what Raymond Cook calls "empathic identification" (*Walt Whitman Review*, 1964), to lead his readers to a fuller understanding of this democratic universal. In "Me Imperturbe," he is at ease as an element of nature, able to confront the accidents and rebuffs of life with the implacability of trees and animals. As he suggests in *Democratic Vistas*, the true idea of nature in all its power and glory must become fully restored and must furnish the "pervading atmosphere" to poems of American democracy. Whitman must also empathize with rational things— with humanity at large and in particular—so he constructs what sometimes seem to be endless catalogs of Americans at work and play. This technique appears in "I Hear America Singing," which essentially lists the varied carols of carpenter, boatman, shoemaker, wood-cutter, mother, and so on, all "singing what belongs to him or her and to none else" as they ply their trades. In longer poems, such as "Starting from Paumanok," Whitman extends his catalog to all the states of the Union. He intends to acknowledge contemporary lands, salute employments and cities large and small, and report heroism on land and sea from an American point of view. He marks down all of what constitutes unified life, including the body, sexual love, and comradeship, or "manly love." Finally, the poet must join the greatness of love and democracy to the greatness of religion. These programs expand to take up large parts of even longer poems, such as "Song of Myself" or to claim space of their own in sections of *Leaves of Grass*.

Whitman uses another technique to underscore the democratic principle of his art: he makes the reader a fellow poet, a "camerado" who joins hands with him to traverse the poetic landscape. In "To You," he sees the poet and reader as passing strangers who desire to speak to one another and urges that they do so. In "Song of the Open Road," Whitman travels the highways with his "delicious burdens" of men and women, calling them all to come forth and move forever forward, well armed to take their places in "the procession of souls along the grand roads of the universe." His view of the reader as fellow traveler and seer is especially clear in the closing lines of the poem:

> Camerado, I give you my hand!
> I give you my love more precious than money,
> I give you myself before preaching or law;
> Will you give me yourself? will you come travel with me?
> Shall we stick by each other as long as we live?

Finally, this comradeship means willingness to set out on one's own, for Whitman says in "Song of Myself" that the reader most honors his style "who learns under it to destroy the teacher." The questions one asks are one's own to puzzle out. The poet's role is to lead his reader up on a knoll, wash the gum from his eyes, and then let him become habituated to the "dazzle of light" that is the natural world. In other words, Whitman intends to help his reader become a "poet" of insight and perception and then release him to travel the public roads of a democratic nation.

This democratic unification of multiplicity, empathic identification, and comradeship exists in most of Whitman's poems. They do not depend on his growth as poet or thinker. Yet, in preparing to analyze representative poems from *Leaves of Grass*, it is helpful to establish a general plan for the various sections of the book. Whitman revised and reordered his poems until the 1881 edition, which established a form that was to remain essentially unchanged through succeeding editions. He merely annexed materials to the 1881 order until just before his death in 1892, then authorized the 1892 version for all future printings. Works originally published apart from *Leaves of Grass*, such as *Drum-Taps* or *Passage to India*, were eventually incorporated in the parent volume. Thus, an analysis of the best poems in five important sections of this final *Leaves of Grass* will help delineate Whitman's movement toward integration of self and nation, within his prescribed portals of birth and death.

"Song of Myself," Whitman's great lyric poem, exemplifies his democratic "programs" without diminishing the intense feeling that so startled his first readers. It successfully combines paeans to the individual, the nation, and life at large, including nature, sexuality, and death. Above all, "Song of Myself" is a poem of incessant motion, as though Whitman's energy is spontaneously bursting into lines. Even in the contemplative sections of the poem, when

Whitman leans and loafs at his ease observing a spear of summer grass, his senses of hearing, taste, and sight are working at fever pitch. In the opening section he calls himself "nature without check with original energy." Having once begun to speak, he hopes "to cease not till death." Whitman says that although others may talk of the beginning and the end, he finds his subject in the now—in the "urge and urge and urge" of the procreant world.

One method by which Whitman's energy escapes boundaries is the poet's ability to "become" other people and things. He will not be measured by time and space, nor by physical form. Rather, he effuses his flesh in eddies and drifts it in lacy jags, taking on new identities with every line. His opening lines show that he is speaking not of himself alone but of all selves. What he assumes, the reader shall assume; every atom of him, and therefore of the world, belongs to the reader as well. In Section 24, he represents himself as a "Kosmos," which contains multitudes and reconciles apparent opposites. He speaks the password and sign of democracy and accepts nothing which all cannot share. To stress this egalitarian vision, Whitman employs the catalog with skill and variety. Many parts of "Song of Myself" list or name characters, places, occupations, or experiences, but Section 33 most clearly shows the two major techniques that give these lists vitality. First, Whitman composes long single-sentence movements of action and description, which attempt to unify nature and civilization. The poet is alternately weeding his onion patch, hoeing, prospecting, hauling his boat down a shallow river, scaling mountains, walking paths, and speeding through space. He then follows each set of actions with a series of place lines, beginning with "where," "over," "at," or "upon," which unite farmhouses, hearth furnaces, hot-air balloons, or steamships with plants and animals of land and sea. Second, Whitman interrupts these long listings with more detailed vignettes, which show the "large hearts of heroes"—a sea captain, a hounded slave, a fireman trapped and broken under debris, an artillerist. Sections 34-36 then extend the narrative to tales of the Alamo and an old-time sea fight, vividly brough forth with sounds and dialogue. In each case, the poet becomes the hero and is actually in the scene to suffer or succeed.

This unchecked energy and empathy carry over into Whitman's ebullient imagery to help capture the physical power of human bodies in procreant motion. At one point Whitman calls himself "hankering, gross, mystical, nude." He finds no sweeter flesh than that which sticks to his own bones, or to the bones of others. Sexual imagery, including vividly suggestive descriptions of the male and female body, is central to the poem. Although the soul must take its equal place with the body, neither abasing itself before the other, Whitman's mystical union of soul and body is a sexual experience as well. He loves the hum of the soul's "valved voice" and remembers how, on a transparent summer morning, the soul settled its head athwart his hips and turned over on him. It parted the shirt from the poet's "bosom-bone," plunged its tongue to his "bare-stript heart," and reached until it felt his beard and held his feet. From this experience came peace and the knowledge that love is fundamental to a unified, continuous creation. Poetic metaphor, which identifies and binds hidden likenesses in nature, is therefore emblematic of the organic world. For example, in answering a child's question, "What is the grass?" the poet offers a series of metaphors that join human, natural, and spiritual impulses:

> I guess it must be the flag of my disposition, out
> of hopeful green stuff woven.
> Or I guess it is the handkerchief of the Lord,
> A scented gift and remembrancer designedly dropt,
> Bearing the owner's name someway in the corners, that we
> may see and remark, and say *Whose*?

The grass becomes hair from the breasts of young men, from the heads and beards of old people, or from offspring, and it "speaks" from under the faint red roofs of mouths. The smallest sprout shows that there is no death, for "nothing collapses," and to die is "luckier" than anyone had supposed. This excerpt from the well-known sixth section of "Song of Myself" illustrates how image-making signifies for Whitman a kind of triumph over death itself.

Because of its position near the beginning of *Leaves of Grass* and its encompassing of Whitman's major themes, "Song of Myself" is a foundation for the volume. The "self" in this poem is a replica of the nation as self, and its delineation in the cosmos is akin to the growth of the United States in the world. Without putting undue stress on this nationalistic interpretation, however, the reader can find many reasons to admire "Song of Myself." Its dynamic form, beauty of language, and psychological insights are sufficient to make Whitman a first-rate poet, even if he had written nothing else.

The passionate celebration of the self and of sexuality is Whitman's great revolutionary theme. In "Children of Adam" he is the procreative father of multitudes, a champion of heterosexual love and the "body electric." In "From Pent-Up Aching Rivers," he sings of the need for superb children, brought forth by the "muscular urge" of "stalwart loins." In "I Sing the Body Electric," he celebrates the perfection of well-made male and female bodies. Sections 5 and 9 are explicit descriptions of sexual intercourse and physical "apparatus," respectively. Whitman does not shy away from the fierce attraction of the female form, or the ebb and flow of "limitless limpid jets of love hot and enormous" that undulate into the willing and yielding "gates of the body." Because he sees the body as sacred, as imbued with divine power, he considers these enumerations to be poems of the soul as much as of the body. Indeed, "A Woman Waits for Me" specifically states that sex contains all—bodies and souls. Thus, the poet seeks warm-blooded and sufficient women to receive the pent-up rivers of himself, to start new sons and daughters fit for the great nation that will be these United States. The procreative urge operates on more than one level in "Children of Adam"—it is physical sex and birthing, the union of body and soul, and the metaphorical insemination of the poet's words and spirit into national life. In several ways, then, words are to become flesh. Try as some early Whitman apologists might to explain them away, raw sexual impulses are the driving force of these poems.

Whitman's contemporaries were shocked by the explicit sexual content of "Children of Adam," but modern readers and critics have been much more intrigued by the apparent homosexuality of "Calamus." Although it is ultimately impossible to say whether these poems reflect Whitman's homosexual associations in New York, it is obvious that comradeship extends here to both spiritual and physical contact between men. "In Paths Untrodden" states the poet's intention to sing of "manly attachment" or types of "athletic love," to celebrate the need of comrades. "Whoever You Are Holding Me Now in Hand" deepens the physical nature of this love, including the stealthy meeting of male friends in a wood, behind some rock in the open air, or on the beach of some quiet island. There the poet would permit the comrade's long-dwelling kiss upon the lips and a touch that would carry him eternally forth over land and sea. "These I Singing in Spring" refers to "him that tenderly loves me" and pledges the hardiest spears of grass, the calamus-root, to those who love as the poet himself is capable of loving. Finally, two of Whitman's best lyrics concern this robust but clandestine relationship. "I Saw in Louisiana a Live-Oak Growing" is a poignant contrast between the live oak's ability to "utter joyous leaves" while it stands in solitude, without companions, and the poet's inability to live without a friend or lover near. There is no mistaking the equally personal tone of "When I Heard at the Close of the Day," probably Whitman's finest "Calamus" poem. The plaudits of others are meaningless and unsatisfying, says Whitman, until he thinks of how his dear friend and lover is on his way to see him. When his friend arrives one evening, the hissing rustle of rolling waves becomes congratulatory and joyful. Once the one he loves most lies sleeping by him under the same cover, face inclined toward him in the autumn moonbeams and arm lightly lying around his breast, he is happy.

Other short poems in "Calamus," such as "For You O Democracy," "The Prairie Grass Dividing," or "A Promise to California," are less obviously personal. Rather, they extend passionate friendship between men to the larger ideal of democratic brotherhood. Just as procreative love has its metaphorical implications for the nation, so too does Whitman promise to make the continent indissoluble and cities inseparable, arms about each other's necks, with companionship and the "manly love of comrades." Still other poems move this comradeship into wider spans of space and time. "The Moment Yearning and Thoughtful" joins the poet with men of Europe and Asia in happy brotherhood, thus transcending national and continental boundaries. "The Base of

All Metaphysics" extends this principle through historical time, for the Greek, Germanic, and Christian systems all suggest that the attraction of friend to friend is the basis of civilization. The last poem in the "Calamus" section, "Full of Life Now," completes Whitman's panoramic view by carrying friendship into the future. His words communicate the compact, visible to readers of a century or any number of centuries hence. Each seeking the other past time's invisible boundaries, poet and reader are united physically through Whitman's poetry.

"Crossing Brooklyn Ferry" is the natural product of Whitman's idea that love and companionship will bind the world's peoples to one another. In a sense it gives the poet immortality through creation of a living artifact: the poem itself. Whitman stands motionless on a moving ferry, immersed in the stream of life and yet suspended in time through the existence of his words on the page. Consequently, he can say that neither time nor place nor distance matters, because he is with each reader and each fellow traveler in the future. He points out that hundreds of years hence others will enter the gates of the ferry and cross from shore to shore, will see the sun half an hour high and watch the seagulls floating in circles with motionless wings. Others will also watch the endless scallop-edged waves cresting and falling, as though they are experiencing the same moment as the poet, with the same mixture of joy and sorrow. Thus, Whitman confidently calls upon the "dumb ministers" of nature to keep up their ceaseless motion—to flow, fly, and frolic on—because they furnish their parts toward eternity and toward the soul.

Techniques match perfectly with these themes in "Crossing Brooklyn Ferry." Whitman's frequent repetition of the main images—sunrise and sunset, ebb and flow of the sea and river, seagulls oscillating in the sky—reinforces the belief in timeless, recurring human experience. Descriptions of schooners and steamers at work along the shore are among his most powerful evocations of color and sound. Finally, Whitman's employment of pronouns to mark a shift in the sharing of experiences also shows the poem's careful design. Whitman begins the poem with an "I" who looks at the scenes or crowds of people and calls to "you" who are among the crowds and readers of present and future. In Section 8, however, he reaches across generations to fuse himself and pour his meaning into the "you." At the end of this section, he and others have become "we," who understand and receive experience with free senses and love, united in the organic continuity of nature.

The short section of *Leaves of Grass* entitled "Sea-Drift" contains the first real signs of a more somber Whitman, who must come to terms with hardship, sorrow, and death. In one way, this resignation and accommodation follow the natural progression of the self from active, perhaps callow, youth to contemplative old age. They are also an outgrowth of Whitman's belief that life and death are a continuum, that life is a symphony of both sonatas and dirges, which the true poet of nature must capture fully on the page. Whereas in other poems the ocean often signifies birth and creation, with fish-shaped Paumanok (Manhattan) rising from the sea, in "Tears" it is the repository of sorrow. Its white shore lies in solitude, dark and desolate, holding a ghost or "shapeless lump" that cries streaming, sobbing tears. In "As I Ebb'd with the Ocean of Life," Whitman is distressed with himself for daring to "blab" so much without having the least idea who or what he really is. Nature darts upon the poet and stings him, because he has not understood anything and because no man ever can. He calls himself but a "trail of drift and debris," who has left his poems like "little wrecks" upon Paumanok's shores. Yet, he must continue to throw himself on the ocean of life, clinging to the breast of the land that is his father, and gathering from the moaning sea the "sobbing dirge of Nature." He believes the flow will return, but meanwhile he must wait and lie in drifts at his readers' feet.

"Out of the Cradle Endlessly Rocking" is a fuller, finally more optimistic, treatment of the poet's confrontation with loss. Commonly acknowledged as one of Whitman's finest works, this poem uses lyrical language and operatic structure to trace the origin of his poetic powers in the experience of death. Two "songs" unite with the whispering cry of the sea to communicate this experience to him. Central to the poem is Whitman's seaside reminiscence of a bird and his mate, who build and tend a nest of eggs. When the female fails to return one evening, never to appear again, the male becomes a solitary singer of his sorrows, whose notes are "translated" by the listening boy-poet. The bird's song is an aria of lonesome love, an outpouring carol of yearning, hope, and finally, death. As the boy absorbs the bird's song, his soul awakens in sympathy. From this moment forward, his destiny will be to perpetuate the bird's "cries of unsatisfied love." More important, though, Whitman must learn the truth that this phrase masks, must conquer "the word" that has caused the bird's cries:

> Whereto answering, the sea,
> Delaying not, hurrying not,
> Whisper'd me through the night, and very plainly before daybreak,
> Lisp'd to me the low and delicious word death,
> And again death, death, death, death.

Whitman then fuses the bird's song and his own with death, which the sea, "like some old crone rocking the cradle," has whispered to him. This final image of the sea as old crone soothing an infant underscores the central point of "Out of the Cradle Endlessly Rocking": old age and death are part of a natural flux. Against the threat of darkness, one must live and sing.

Like the tone of "Sea-Drift," darker hues permeate Whitman's Civil War lyrics. His experiences as a hospital worker in Washington, D.C. are clearly behind the sometimes wrenching imagery of *Drum-Taps*. As a wound dresser he saw the destruction of healthy young bodies and minds at first hand. These spectacles were in part a test of Whitman's own courage and comradeship, but they were also a test of the nation's ability to survive and grow. As Whitman says in "Long, Too Long America," the country had long traveled roads "all even and peaceful," learning only from joys and prosperity, but now it must face "crises of anguish" without recoiling and show the world what its "children enmasse really are." Many of the *Drum-Taps* lyrics show Whitman facing this reality, but "The Wound Dresser" is representative. The poet's persona is an old man who is called upon years after the Civil War to "paint the mightiest armies of earth," to tell what experience of the war stays with him latest and deepest. Although he mentions the long marches, rushing charges, and toils of battle, he does not dwell on soldiers' perils or soldiers' joys. Rather, he vividly describes the wounded and dying at battlegrounds, hospital tents, or roofed hospitals, as he goes with "hinged knees and steady hand to dress wounds." He does not recoil or give out at the sight of crushed heads, shattered throats, amputated stumps of hands and arms, the gnawing and putrid gangrenous foot or shoulder. Yet, within him rests a burning flame, the memory of youths suffering or dead.

Confronted with these horrors, Whitman had to find a way to surmount them, and that way was love. If there could be a positive quality in war, Whitman found it in the comradeship of common soldiers, who risked all for their fellows. In "As Toilsome I Wander'd Virginia's Woods," for example, Whitman discovers the grave of a soldier buried beneath a tree. Hastily dug on a retreat from battle, the grave is nevertheless marked by a sign: "Bold, cautious, true, and my loving comrade." That inscription remains with the poet through many changeful seasons and scenes to follow, as evidence of this brotherly love. Similarly, "Vigil Strange I Kept on the Field One Night" tells of a soldier who sees his comrade struck down in battle and returns to find him cold with death. He watches by him through "immortal and mystic hours" until, just as dawn is breaking, he folds the young man in a blanket and buries him in a rude-dug grave where he fell. This tale of tearless mourning perfectly evokes the loss caused by war. Eventually, Whitman finds some ritual significance in these deaths, as though they are atonement for those yet living. In "A Sight in Camp in the Daybreak Gray and Dim," he marks three covered forms on stretchers near a hospital tent. One by one he uncovers their faces. The first is an elderly man, gaunt and grim, but a comrade nevertheless. The second is a sweet boy "with cheeks yet blooming." When he exposes the third face, however, he finds it calm, of yellow-white ivory, and of indeterminable age. He sees in it the face of Christ himself, "dead and divine and brother of all." "Over the Carnage Rose Prophetic a Voice" suggests that these Christian sacrifices will finally lead to a united Columbia. Even though a thousand may have to "sternly immolate themselves for one," those who love one another shall become invincible, and "affection shall solve the problems of freedom." As in other sections of *Leaves of Grass*, Whitman believes the United States will be held together not by lawyers, paper agreements, or force of arms, but by the cohesive power of love and fellowship.

"When Lilacs Last in the Dooryard Bloom'd," another of Whitman's acknowledged masterpieces, repeats the process underlying *Drum-Taps*. The poet must come to terms with the loss of one he loves—in this case, the slain President Lincoln. Death and mourning must eventually give way to consolation and hope for the future. Cast in the form of a traditional elegy, the poem traces the processional of Lincoln's coffin across country, past the poet himself, to the President's final resting place. To objectify his emotional struggle between grief on the one hand and spiritual reconciliation with death on the other, Whitman employs several vivid symbols. The lilac blooming perennially, with its heart-shaped leaves, represents the poet's perpetual mourning and love. The "powerful fallen star," which now lies in a "harsh surrounding cloud" of black night, is Lincoln, fallen and shrouded in his coffin. The solitary hermit thrush that warbles "death's outlet song of life" from a secluded swamp is the soul or spiritual world. Initially, Whitman is held powerless by the death of his departing comrade. Although he can hear the bashful notes of the thrush and will come to understand them, he thinks only of showering the coffin with sprigs of lilac to commemorate his love for Lincoln. He must also warble his own song before he can absorb the bird's message of consolation. Eventually, as he sits amidst the teeming daily activities described in Section 14, he is struck by the "sacred knowledge of death," and the bird's carol thus becomes intelligible to him. Death is lovely, soothing, and delicate. It is a "strong deliveress" who comes to nestle the grateful body in her flood of bliss. Rapt with the charm of the bird's song, Whitman sees myriad battle-corpses in a vision—the debris of all the slain soldiers of the war—yet realizes that they are fully at rest and unsuffering. The power of this realization gives him strength to loose the hand of his comrade. An ever-blooming lilac now signifies renewal, just as death takes its rightful place as the harbinger of new life, the life of the eternal soul.

Whitman's deepening concern with matters of the spirit permeates the last sections of *Leaves of Grass*. Having passed the test of Civil War and having done his part to reunite the United States, Whitman turned his attention to America's place in the world and his own place in God's design. As he points out in "A Clear Midnight," he gives his last poems to the soul and its "free flight into the wordless," in order to ponder the themes he loves best: "Night, sleep, death and the stars." Such poems as "Chanting the Square Deific" and "A Noiseless Patient Spider" invoke either the general soul, the "Santa Spirita" that pervades all of created life, or the toils of individual souls, flinging out gossamer threads to connect themselves with this holy spirit.

In *A Reader's Guide to Walt Whitman* (1970), Gay Wilson Allen finds this late Whitman too often pathetically didactic and unpoetic, but he points out that the poet was still able to produce fine lyrics in his old age. One of these successful poems, "Passage to India," announces Whitman's intention to join modern science to fables and dreams of old, to weld past and future, and to show that the United States is but a "bridge" in the "vast rondure" of the world. Just as the Suez Canal connected Europe and Asia, Whitman says, America's transcontinental railroad ties the Eastern to the Western sea, thus verifying Columbus' dream. Beyond these material thoughts of exploration, however, lies the poet's realm of love and spirit. The poet is a "true son of God," who will soothe the hearts of restlessly exploring, never-happy humanity. He will link all human affections, justify the "cold, impassive, voiceless earth," and absolutely fuse nature and man. This fusion takes place not in the material world but in the swelling of the soul toward God, who is a mighty "centre of the true, the good, the loving." Passage to these superior universes transcends time and space and death. It is a "passage to more than India," through the deep waters that no mariner has traveled, and for which the poet must "risk the ship, ourselves and all."

Whitman also uses a seagoing metaphor for spiritual passage in "Prayer of Columbus," which is almost a continuation of "Passage to India." In the latter, Whitman aggressively flings himself into the active voyage toward God, but in "Prayer of Columbus" he is a "batter'd, wreck'd old man," willing to yield his ships to God and wait for the unknown end of all. He recounts his heroic deeds of exploration and attributes their inspiration to a message from the heavens that sped him on. Like Columbus, Whitman is "old, poor, and paralyzed," yet capable of one more effort to speak of the steady interior light that God has granted him. Finally, the works of the past fall away from him, and some divine hand reveals a scene of countless ships sailing on distant seas, from which "anthems in new tongues" salute and comfort him. This implied divine sanction for his life's work was consolation to an old poet, who, at his death in 1892, remained largely unaccepted and unrecognized by contemporary critics and historians.

The grand design of *Leaves of Grass* appears to trace self and nation neatly through sensuous youth, crises of maturity, and soul-searching old age. Although this philosophical or psychological reading of Whitman's work is certainly encouraged by the poet's tinkering with its structure, many fine lyrics do not fit into neat patterns, or even under topical headings. Whitman's reputation rests more on the startling freshness of his language, images, and democratic treatment of the common American citizen than on his success as epic bard. Common to all his poetry, however, are certain major themes: reconciliation of body and soul, purity and unity of physical nature, death as the "mother of beauty," and above all, comradeship or love, which binds and transcends all else. In fact, Whitman encouraged a complex comradeship with his readers to bind his work to future generations. He expected reading to be a gymnastic struggle and the reader to be a re-creator of the poem through imaginative interaction with the poet. Perhaps that is why he said in "So

Long" that *Leaves of Grass* was no book, for whoever touches his poetry "touches a man."

Perry D. Luckett

Other major works

LONG FICTION: *Franklin Evans*, 1842.

SHORT FICTION: *The Half-Breed and Other Stories*, 1927.

NONFICTION: *Democratic Vistas*, 1871; *Memoranda During the War*, 1875-1876; *Specimen Days and Collect*, 1882-1883; *Complete Prose Works*, 1892; *Calamus*, 1897 (letters, Richard M. Bucke, editor); *The Wound Dresser*, 1898 (Richard M. Bucke, editor); *Letters Written by Walt Whitman to His Mother, 1866-1872*, 1902 (Thomas B. Harned, editor); *An American Primer*, 1904; *Walt Whitman's Diary in Canada*, 1904 (William S. Kennedy, editor); *The Letters of Anne Gilchrist and Walt Whitman*, 1918 (Thomas B. Harned, editor).

MISCELLANEOUS: *The Collected Writings of Walt Whitman*, 1961-1984 (22 volumes).

Bibliography

Allen, Gay Wilson. *The Solitary Singer: A Critical Biography of Walt Whitman*. Rev. ed. New York: New York University Press, 1967. A careful, scholarly biography based on extensive archival sources—including manuscripts and letters—that attempts to treat Whitman's life in terms of the poet's work. A valuable study of his career, although superseded, in some respects, by the biographies of Justin Kaplan and Paul Zweig.

Gold, Arthur, ed. *Walt Whitman: A Collection of Criticism*. New York: McGraw Hill, 1974. Concentrates on academic criticism, on the poet's creative process, his literary reputation, his revisions of *Leaves of Grass*, and his vision of America in *Democratic Vistas*. A detailed chronology and a select, annotated bibliography make this collection a useful volume.

Kaplan, Justin. *Walt Whitman: A Life*. New York: Simon & Schuster, 1980. An elegant, deeply imagined biography that focuses on both Whitman and his times. Kaplan provides the fullest, most sensitive account of the poet's career, taking a chronological approach but managing to pinpoint and to highlight the most important phases of his subject's life. Kaplan's scholarship is impeccable.

Miller, James E., Jr. *Walt Whitman*. Rev. ed. Boston: Twayne, 1990. Miller concentrates on the development and structure of *Leaves of Grass*, its democratic "poetics," the major poems within it, "recurring images," "language and wit," and the "bardic voice." The first chapter and chronology provide a factual and analytical discussion of Whitman's biography, and Miller assesses the new criticism of the poet that has appeared since the original publication of his book in 1962. Supplemented by an annotated and updated bibliography.

Pearce, Roy Harvey, ed. *Whitman: A Collection of Critical Essays.* Englewood Cliffs, N.J.: Prentice-Hall, 1962. A comprehensive collection of criticism, including commentary by Ezra Pound and D. H. Lawrence, three articles on the structure of *Leaves of Grass*, and additional discussion of the poet's style and other works. Contains a chronology of important dates, an introductory overview of the critical literature on Whitman, and a useful, annotated bibliography.

Woodress, James, ed. *Critical Essays on Walt Whitman.* Boston: G. K. Hall, 1983. Divided into reviews and early reactions, essays and other forms of criticism, with an introduction surveying the history of Whitman criticism. This collection provides a good history of Whitman's place in American culture and an informative, if highly selective, view of scholarly treatments of his work. Contains an index.

Zweig, Paul. *Walt Whitman: The Making of a Poet.* New York: Basic Books, 1984. This volume is not a chronological biography but rather a biographical/critical meditation on Whitman's development as a poet. Zweig is steeped in the literature on Whitman and brilliantly explores how the "drab" journalist of the 1840's transformed himself into a major poet.

REED WHITTEMORE

Born: New Haven, Connecticut; September 11, 1919

Principal poetry

Heroes and Heroines, 1946; *An American Takes a Walk*, 1956; *The Self-Made Man*, 1959; *The Boy from Iowa*, 1961 (poetry and essays); *The Fascination of the Abomination*, 1963 (poetry, stories, and essays); *Poems, New and Selected*, 1967; *50 Poems 50*, 1970; *The Mother's Breast and the Father's House*, 1974; *The Feel of Rock: Poems of Three Decades*, 1982; *The Past, the Future, the Present: Poems Selected and New*, 1990.

Other literary forms

Reed Whittemore has published a smaller number of poems than the above list of books might suggest since most of his volumes of poetry include old poems from previous books. Only three of his volumes—*Heroes and Heroines*, *The Self-Made Man*, and *50 Poems 50*—consist entirely of new poems.

Whittemore has published many essays and reviews in magazines, most of them of a literary nature, but there are also essays on education, science, and television. *From Zero to Absolute* (1968) consists mainly of a series of lectures he gave on poetry at Beloit College in 1966. *The Poet as Journalist* (1976) is made up of the short pieces he wrote for *The New Republic* when he was the literary editor for that magazine. In his literary essays he often praises, with some qualifications, the early modern poets such as Ezra Pound and T. S. Eliot but is rather critical of most of his contemporaries, particularly the Beat poets, whom he has mocked in his satirical verse.

The publication of Whittemore's *William Carlos Williams: Poet from Jersey* (1975) was a surprising departure for this writer of short personal essays. The biography was criticized by some reviewers for being too casually written and for taking, at times, an irreverent attitude toward its subject, yet the book does give a clear and sympathetic portrait of Williams and, at the same time, punctures some of the more pretentious opinions of Williams and his disciples about free verse and other poetic matters.

Whittemore's biography of Williams has led him to two more books about the nature of biography: *Pure Lives: The Early Biographers* (1988) and *Whole Lives: Shapers of Modern Biography* (1990). These wide-ranging, erudite, and lively works trace biographical art from its beginnings (Plutarch, Aelfric) all the way to late twentieth century literary biographers (Richard Ellmann and Leon Edel). As in the Williams biography, Whittemore manages to combine his scholarly matter with a casual manner in interesting ways.

Achievements

The most striking characteristic of Whittemore's verse is its comedy. As

Howard Nemerov pointed out many years ago, Whittemore is not only witty (an admirable trait) but also funny (a suspect one). His most distinctive poems are those about serious subjects—the failure of belief, the difficulties of heroism, the search for the true self—that make intelligent statements while at the same time being very clever and humorous. Whittemore's emphasis on intelligence, moderation, and comedy makes him a rather unfashionable writer today, but these very qualities account for the success of his best poems.

Biography

Edward Reed Whittemore II was born in New Haven in 1919, being given the name of his physician father. He attended Yale, was graduated in 1941, went on to serve in the Army Air Force during World War II, and was discharged as a captain. He continued his education at Princeton after the war, although he never received an advanced degree. He married Helen Lundeen in 1952, and they had four children. He often depicts himself in his poetry as a middle-class figure, with middle-class burdens of family and job. Although his poetry is not of a confessional nature, a picture of Whittemore as an affectionate and concerned family man does emerge from his poetry.

Whittemore taught in the English Department at Carleton College in Minnesota for nearly twenty years beginning in 1947 and was for a part of that time chairman of the department. In 1964 he was consultant in poetry at the Library of Congress. In 1968 he moved to the University of Maryland, eventually becoming professor emeritus.

Whittemore is rightly well-known and admired as a magazine editor. From 1939 to 1953, he was the editor of *Furioso*, one of the liveliest literary publications of the period. What distinguished this magazine from all of its competitors was its fondness for comic parody and satire. This tradition was carried on with nearly equal distinction when Whittemore edited *The Carleton Miscellany* from 1960 to 1964. His work as the literary editor of *The New Republic* from 1969 to 1974 added some zest to the pages of that venerable publication.

Analysis

Reed Whittemore has published fewer poems than many of his contemporaries have done, and most of them have been written in an ironic vein. His targets are the pretentious—both romantic and bureaucratic, both individual and institutional—against which he sets his own balanced, moderate point of view. The poems imply that the realism at their center is all the modern world has to offer in the way of belief.

At times, Whittemore runs the risk of being merely a writer of light verse, a maker of clever rhymed jokes, but in his best work he combines the sensible note of comedy with a seriousness of theme. This combination, along with his subtle command of form and sound in verse, make him a poet of consequence.

Whittemore's first book, *Heroes and Heroines*, consists primarily of poems about literature and literary figures. It is an amusing book that explores
through a series of comic poems the idea of heroism in portraits of Don
Quixote, Lord Jim, Hester Prynne, Lady Ashley, Gulliver, and many other
characters from books. The poems display Whittemore's fondness for traditional verse forms—particularly the sonnet—his wit, and his interest in the
theme of heroism; yet it is a book of very limited range that only hints at his
potential as a poet.

In Whittemore's second book, *An American Takes a Walk*, that potential is
clearly displayed as he develops the comic tone that becomes the trademark
of his work. That tone can be seen in his often reprinted poem "Lines (Composed upon Reading an Announcement by Civil Defense Authorities Recom-
mending that I Build a Bombshelter in My Backyard)." The poem begins
with a description of the dugout that the speaker and his friends had built
as children and that he identifies with some vague notion of heroic fantasy,
"some brave kind of decay." Now he is being asked to dig another hole "under the new and terrible rules of romance." "But I'll not, no, not do it, not
go back," the poem proclaims; he knows that this time, if he conforms to
the government's wishes, he will not be able to return to "the grown-up's
house" as he had done as a child. This time the seeming child's play is play
in earnest, a deadly absurdity. As Howard Nemerov has pointed out, Whittemore's poetry is filled with images of entrapment and burial, and this poem
can be read as more than a satirical thrust at Civil Defense. It contains the
poet's rejection of safety and security as a kind of living death and seems to
long for some world where daring and risk have meaning.

The problem, however, Whittemore's work implies, is that a heroism that
risks all often leads to nothing. One of his funniest poems, "A Day with the
Foreign Legion," makes a number of tough statements about the failure of
heroic action, or its meaninglessness. The poem is based on a *Beau Geste*
version of the Foreign Legion as it appears in motion pictures, where, when
everything seems darkest, the characters make speeches that "serve as the
turning point":

> After which the Arabs seem doped and perfectly helpless,
> Water springs up from the ground, the horses come back,
> Plenty of food is discovered in some old cave,
> And reinforcements arrive led by the girl
> From Canada.

That is what usually happens, but in this instance it is too hot; there is no
magical ending and the audience is bitterly disappointed. The poem asks who
is to blame—the film, the projector, "the man in the booth, who hastened
away, as soon as the feature was over"? The poem answers, in a series of
purposely confusing repetitions, that none of them is to blame, or all of

them are, or possibly the culture is to blame. "It was the time, the time and the place, and how could one blame them?" The poem seems to be saying that in this time (modern) and this place (America) the world of romance and happy endings is finished.

The title poem, "An American Takes a Walk," mocks the idea of a tragic or sacred vision existing in America or American literature. When the American of the poem comes across a wood reminiscent of Dante's world of hell, it is a pleasant wood, hell in a "motherly habit."

> How in that Arden could human
> Frailty be but glossed?
> How in that Eden could Adam
> Be really, wholly lost?

The emphasis on innocence and on success in America, according to Whittemore, leads the American writer to adopt the demands of his culture. In "The Line of an American Poet," the poet writes for the market, following the supply-and-demand economy. He produces works, "Uniform, safe and pure," becoming another American success story.

Whittemore once described poetry "as a thing of the mind," saying that he "tends to judge it . . . by the qualities of the mind it displays" (*Poets on Poetry*, Howard Nemerov, editor). This emphasis on the mind, on intelligence, is an unusual one for a contemporary American poet. In recent years, the instinctual and the irrational have usually been seen as the sources of poetry. Whittemore's attitude is what leads him to reject the theatrical and fantastic, to be a realist and ironist. At the same time, however, it can be argued that this dominating intelligence in his work limits Whittemore, giving his poetry a kind of self-consciousness, a too-ready irony. He has written many poems about writing poems ("A Week of Doodle," "After Some Day of Decision," and "Preface to an Unwritten Text," for example, in *An American Takes a Walk*), about the difficulties of writing poems, about the fact that he has not written any poems. These pieces are often funny, but still they seem to point to some problem with his very notion of being a poet, a kind of debilitating self-awareness. At times he seems burdened with the idea of being a poet, as if it were a pompous occupation, apologizing for not offering a world view of proper scope for one who would call himself a poet.

In his next few volumes, Whittemore continues the style developed in *An American Takes a Walk*. His poems give an amusing picture of suburbia and the academic life, worlds where trivial things matter. Even the weather—as in "The Self and the Weather"—can depress one's mood. The poem begins by declaring that it is tiresome to talk about the weather and goes on to talk about it—very amusingly—at considerable length. The poet finds he cannot write on a rainy day, staring out the window "at wet leaves, wet grass, wet laundry and so on," but he feels that a better man, "any man of resolve, any man with a mission," would rise above the weather, rise to where it always was sunny, and write. Such a person, however, would write treatises, not poems, "for treatises seldom/ Traffic in weather as poems do." These treatises would be written in underground rooms where the outside world will be represented by "a picture by some gay cubist of what could not possibly/ Be wet leaves, wet grass, wet laundry, and so on."

The only new element in Whittemore's work at this time is found in a number of long, satiric poems written in rhyming, loosely metrical couplets. The purposely forced comic rhymes seem to imitate both Lord Byron and Ogden Nash. The targets range from the Beat poets to rocket scientists, and, although almost all the poems have amusing passages, they go on at entirely too great a length for their satiric purposes.

Although there is no revolutionary change in Whittemore's poetry after *An American Takes a Walk*, his poems do wear a somewhat more experimental guise, opening up in language and form, beginning with the new poems in *Poems, New and Selected* in 1967. In the six poems labeled "shaggy" (that is, "Flint Shaggy," "Geneva Shaggy," and so on), Whittemore slips into a black-faced comedian's voice reminiscent of the comic language of John Berryman's *Dream Songs* (1964). In other poems such as "The Bad Daddy," and from later volumes "Death," "The Mother's Breast and the Father's House," and "Marriage," he moves toward an irrational side of his psyche that his earlier work explicitly rejected. The picture of marriage is of pigs eating each other and death is the lord that lives in the marrow: "Holy illiterate . . . spider of bone." A kind of fierce bitterness overwhelms these poems at times, in a manner not seen in his previous poetry. In the poem "Clamming," Whittemore writes one of his most successful antiromantic poems in his more familiar, amusing style. The poem begins with the poet telling of how he often repeats a story about the time he was trapped on a sandbar while clamming as a little boy and faced the Long Island Sound as his possible fate. There is not much to the story, but he keeps telling it because "it serves my small lust/ To be thought of as someone who's lived." He cannot get away from his ego: "The self, what a brute it is. It wants, wants./ It will not let go of its even most fictional grandeur." Now he has a son, small and sickly, and he would like to protect him from the sea and other dangers, but a greater danger might be too much self-regard, as represented by the oft-told tale of clamming, and that he does not want to pass on to his son. Finally, his advice to his son is to be careful but not too careful: "Lest you care too much and brag of the caring/ And bore your best friends and inhibit your children and sicken/ At last into opera on somebody's sandbar. Son, when you clam,/ Clam." The plea for realism and modesty in the ending of "Clamming" sums up very nicely the attitudes and strengths of Whittemore's poetry.

In 1982, in *The Feel of Rock*, and more extensively in 1990, in *The Past, the Future, the Present*, Whittemore again created selected volumes of his previous poetry, adding a few new poems on both occasions. The smallness of the additions of new poems seems to show that Whittemore has been concentrating on the writing of prose in the 1980's rather than the writing of poetry.

A number of the new poems continue Whittemore's satiric expressions of dissatisfaction with modern American culture: "It's a terrible thing to come to despise one's country," he states in one of his poems, but he obviously thinks that the ideals of America have been lost in the current political and social scene. In "The Destruction of Washington" he imagines some future archaeologist exploring the destroyed capital. Whatever they discover, he hopes that at least their ignorance will be less than ours.

Whittemore also has begun exploring his childhood and the lives of his parents in a few poems in these two volumes. "Mother's Past" is about the inability of the mother to take good photos, always moving, or putting her finger in front of the lens. The photos are often of young people going off on automobile excursions, while the photographer—the mother—remains behind. The speaker is dissatisfied with the record of a life represented by the photos: "Ask how many were missed that it takes to make a good/ Past for a life or a book./ The answer is always more pictures than poor mother took."

In "The Feel of Rock" the early life of the speaker's home is portrayed in the ironies of the opening stanza:

> My father went broke on a shaded street.
> My mother drank there.
> My brothers removed themselves; they were complete.
> I kept to my room and slicked down my hair.

As the poem continues, the speaker realizes that he resembles the father in his loneliness and unhappiness. Then he goes on to think about his father's burial (the mother already dead); the feel of rocks becomes the gravestones of his family. On a later return to the cemetery, he loses himself amid the maze of stones and wonders where his father has gone and whether life is only the world of rocks.

In "The Feel of Rock" and "Mother's Past," Whittemore is risking a personal tone rarely seen before in his work. Although the poems have at times a tentative quality, they add a new element to the work of this always interesting writer.

Michael Paul Novak

Other major works

NONFICTION: *The Boy from Iowa*, 1961 (poetry and essays); *From Zero to Absolute*, 1968; *William Carlos Williams: Poet from Jersey*, 1975; *The Poet as Journalist*, 1976; *Pure Lives: The Early Biographers*, 1988; *Whole Lives: Shapers of Modern Biography*, 1989.

MISCELLANEOUS: *The Fascination of the Abomination*, 1963 (poetry, stories, and essays).

Bibliography
Dickey, James. *Babel to Byzantium*. New York: Farrar, Straus & Giroux, 1968. Dickey classifies Whittemore as essentially a satirist, but he modifies his praise of his work because of Whittemore's tendency not to go deeply and personally into his subjects.

Lieberman, Laurence. "New Poetry in Review." *Yale Review* 58 (Winter, 1968): 267-268. Lieberman praises Whittemore's poetry as perfectly pitched and displaying a flawless ear. He believes, however, that his targets of satire have become too familiar and feels that the poet seems satisfied in becoming a kind of "highbrow Ogden Nash."

Nemerov, Howard. *Poetry and Fiction: Essays*. New Brunswick, N.J.: Rutgers University Press, 1963. This is the most complete and sympathetic overview of Whittemore's poetry. Nemerov emphasizes Whittemore's concentration on heroism in action and its absence in modern society. He points out the frequency of the images of being locked up, walled in, or buried in the poetry and speculates that these images represent the isolation of the human condition.

Rosenthal, M. L. "Plastic Possibilities." *Poetry* 119 (November, 1971): 102-103. Rosenthal points out that even though Whittemore's poems often begin in joking self-irony, they can quickly turn to serious purposes in their conclusions. Whittemore's rejection of all romantic posturings determines the quality and tone of his poetry.

Whittemore, Reed. "Poetry as Discovery." In *Poets on Poetry*, edited by Howard Nemerov. New York: Basic Books, 1966. This is both an illuminating and a modest essay on Whittemore's discussion of his own work. He calls poetry "a thing of the mind," and he says that he judges it by the quality of the mind displayed. He also analyzes the relationship of poetry to self-discovery and the often melancholy conclusion of that discovery.

JOHN GREENLEAF WHITTIER

Born: Haverhill, Massachusetts: December 17, 1807
Died: Hampton Falls, New Hampshire; September 7, 1892

Principal poetry

Legends of New-England, 1831; *Moll Pitcher*, 1832; *Mogg Megone*, 1836; *Poems Written During the Progress of the Abolition Question in the United States*, 1837; *Poems*, 1838; *Lays of My Home and Other Poems*, 1843; *Voices of Freedom*, 1846; *Poems*, 1849; *Songs of Labor and Other Poems*, 1850; *The Chapel of the Hermits and Other Poems*, 1853; *The Panorama and Other Poems*, 1856; *The Sycamores*, 1857; *The Poetical Works of John Greenleaf Whittier*, 1857, 1869, 1880, 1894; *Home Ballads and Poems*, 1860; *In War Time*, 1863; *Snow-Bound: A Winter Idyl*, 1866; *The Tent on the Beach and Other Poems*, 1867; *Maud Muller*, 1869; *Among the Hills and Other Poems*, 1869; *Ballads of New England*, 1869; *Miriam and Other Poems*, 1871; *The Pennsylvania Pilgrim and Other Poems*, 1872; *Hazel-Blossoms*, 1875; *Mabel Martin*, 1876; *Favorite Poems*, 1877; *The Vision of Echard and Other Poems*, 1878; *The King's Missive and Other Poems*, 1881; *The Bay of Seven Islands and Other Poems*, 1883; *Saint Gregory's Guest and Recent Poems*, 1886; *At Sundown*, 1890.

Other literary forms

Besides his extensive poetry, John Greenleaf Whittier wrote numerous antislavery tracts, compiled editions of New England legends, edited various newspapers, and was active in Abolitionist politics. Whittier's *Legends of New-England*, his earliest collection, was followed by the antislavery arguments in *Justice and Expediency* (1833), and *The Supernaturalism of New England* (1847). Whittier's finest prose work is perhaps *Leaves from Margaret Smith's Journal* (1849), a Quaker novel in journal form. *Old Portraits and Modern Sketches* (1850) and *Literary Recreations and Miscellanies* (1854) followed, and the *Prose Works of John Greenleaf Whittier* were collected in two volumes in 1866.

Whittier also edited *Child Life* (1872) and *Child Life in Prose* (1874), as well as *Songs of Three Centuries* (1876). He wrote a masterful introduction to his edition of *The Journal of John Woolman* (1871), another notable American Quaker writer.

A full collection of Whittier's prose can be found in *The Writings of John Greenleaf Whittier* (1888-1889).

Achievements

Whittier was a remarkably prolific writer and reformer. As poet, editor, Abolitionist, and religious humanist, Whittier managed to produce more than forty volumes of poetry and prose during his lifetime, not counting his uncollected journalistic work. Through his antislavery poems he spoke for the conscience of New England, and he later celebrated the virtues of village life for an age that looked back upon them with nostalgia. Although honored and venerated as a poet during his later years, he was curiously guarded about his literary reputation, remarking to his first biographer, "I am a *man*, not a mere verse-maker." His belief that morality was the basis of all literature may have made him finally more of a moralist than a poet; his Quaker conscience would not permit him to produce "art for art's sake."

Early in life he patterned his verse after Robert Burns, writing dialect imitations of the Scottish poet to the extent of being called "the American Burns." He further corrupted his muse by imitating the worst of the popular, sentimental, and genteel verse of his age and did not achieve a distinctive poetic voice until midcareer. Like many a self-educated poet, Whittier lacked a clear sense of critical taste and judgment, especially in regard to his own work. He wrote too much too quickly and could not distinguish between his best poems and his inferior work. Even his later work is often tainted by melodrama, moralizing, and sentimentality. Yet when the worst has been said, the abiding strength of his work transcends its weaknesses.

His most obvious poetic strength is accessibility. Whittier wrote popular poetry that did not make great intellectual demands upon his readers. Unlike the modernists, who wrote for a select, highly educated audience, Whittier tried to reach the ordinary reader. Instead of composing dense, ironic, highly allusive verse requiring careful explication, Whittier's narratives and ballads were written in a common idiom that could be readily understood. His poetical materials were regional legend and folklore, topical events, and the personal resources of his Quaker faith. Their moral perspective is clear and forthright, at times didactic or moralistic, and it lacks the ambiguity or tentativeness favored by the New Critics. George Arms argues persuasively that Whittier and the other schoolroom poets simply cannot be appreciated according to current standards of taste, and so have been too often simply dismissed instead of being understood. Their strengths are seen as liabilities and they are faulted for lacking qualities foreign to their age.

The purview of Whittier's work was "common, natural things"—the realm of ordinary life. He rarely dealt with the extremes of human experience, except in some of his Abolitionist poems. He shared the optimism and piety of his age and held to a romantic view of nature and a belief in the moral progress of man. His sense of moral order and probity may seem merely quaint or old-fashioned to the modern reader, but his poems reflect moral convictions sincerely held. He devoted thirty years to the struggle against slavery and committed the better part of his talents and energy to that issue. If he lost his sense of social justice later in life and failed to comprehend the problems of an industrial society, that might well be excused by his age. Few men are capable of devoting themselves to more than one cause in a lifetime.

The alleged deficiencies in Whittier's poetics should also be judged in terms of his commitment to a popular rather than an academic style. Whittier favored a light, relaxed approach to his verse. Perhaps he overused mechanical rhymes, ballad meter, apostrophe, and hyperbole, but in his "Proem" he is frank to confess his limitations. His muse was not given to exalted flights, but spoke plainly for freedom and democracy. Whittier's readership steadily grew during his later years so that his reputation once seemed secure, but like those of the other Fireside Poets, it has suffered a sharp decline since his death. He is now read, if at all, as the author of "Snow-Bound: A Winter Idyl" and other nostalgic portraits of New England village life rather than as one of the leading poets of his age. Though his reputation may now be eclipsed by Walt Whitman, Emily Dickinson, and Herman Melville, no American poet of the nineteenth century better deserves the title of "poet of the common man" than Whittier.

Biography

John Greenleaf Whittier was born in Haverhill, Massachusetts, on December 17, 1807, in an old family homestead built by a Quaker ancestor. He was the second of four children in the family of John and Abigail Whittier, of old Quaker stock. Besides John Greenleaf, the Whittier children included an older sister Mary, a younger brother Matthew Franklin, and a younger sister Elizabeth Hussey. Several other relatives lived with the family, including a paternal grandmother, a bachelor uncle, and a maiden aunt. The poet's father, John Whittier, was an honest, industrious farmer who tilled his hard, rocky land in the Merrimack Valley with only marginal success. Whittier's mother, Elizabeth, was a model of quiet strength and deep refinement. She was noted in the community for her domestic industry and "exquisite Quaker neatness." The entire family attended Friends' services at Amesbury, nine miles away, even in poor weather.

Whittier's childhood was one of hard farm work (that eventually weakened his health) and the occasional freedom of the outdoors—a life of frugality, harmony, and affection later idealized in "Snow-Bound" and "The Barefoot Boy." There were few books in the Whittier household besides the Bible and *The Pilgrim's Progress* (1678), and the family depended for entertainment on the tales of his uncle Moses and the stories brought by itinerant Yankee peddlers and gypsies. Whittier's education was meager, consisting of sporadic attendance at the district school and several terms at Haverhill Academy. One of the local teachers, Joshua Coffin, introduced him to the poetry of Robert Burns, and made such a lasting impression on young Whittier that he was later commemorated in "To My Old School Master." As a boy, Whittier showed a natural gift for rhymes and verse, and wrote simple ballads in imitation of Robert Burns and Sir Walter Scott. His sister Mary sent one of these to the local newspaper, the Newburyport *Free Press*. The editor there,

William Lloyd Garrison, was so impressed that he paid a personal visit to the Whittiers to urge further education for their son. Whittier's father was said to have replied to Garrison, "Sir, poetry will not get him bread."

His father finally relented and Whittier was allowed to enter Haverhill Academy at the age of nineteen. To pay his expenses he learned the craft of shoemaking, a common winter vocation among New England country folk. Meanwhile, his poems continued to appear in the Haverhill *Gazette* and other publications. At Garrison's behest, Whittier entered the world of Boston journalism and at twenty-two became editor of the *American Manufacturer*, a Whig trade weekly. In the summer of 1829 he was called home by the illness and death of his father, which required him to manage the farm and provide for his family. Still unhappy with the drudgery of farm life, Whittier gladly accepted an invitation from Hartford, Connecticut, in July, 1830, to edit the *Weekly Review*. Unfortunately his health failed and Whittier was forced to resign from this attractive position within eighteen months and return to Haverhill in 1832. He was now twenty-five years old, ambitious, but without purpose or direction. A letter from Garrison in the spring of 1833 restored Whittier's spirits when he was invited to apply his talents to the Abolitionist Movement. From 1833 to the end of the Civil War, the abolition of slavery became the abiding goal of Whittier's life.

Immersion in Abolitionist politics made him a master of satire and invective, but at the expense of his literary gifts. Out of his new commitment came *Justice and Expediency*, and that same year he was elected to the National Anti-Slavery Convention in Philadelphia. Thus began a thirty-year career of antislavery advocacy and agitation. Several times he was exposed to the threat of mob violence and barely escaped personal injury. He later said that he was prouder of his Abolitionist work than of all his authorship, but this comment must be taken in the perspective of his career.

As a young man, Whittier had struggled to reconcile his worldly literary ambitions with his Quaker reticence and piety. As a poor country boy he had aspired to Boston gentility but lacked the education or means to move in Brahmin circles. One third of his poetry was written before he was twenty-five, though much of it was sentimental and imitative. When he shrewdly realized that poetry would not bring him the fame he sought, he turned to politics and reformism instead. The Abolitionist Movement gave him a focus for his talents and energies. He became involved in Essex County politics and by 1835 was elected to the Massachusetts Legislature. The following year he sold the Haverhill farm and moved to a small house in Amesbury, where he briefly edited the Amesbury *Village Transcript*. The next twenty years saw him editing various antislavery newspapers and writing numerous Abolitionist poems and articles. Much of this was obviously hackwork, but occasionally he would write a notable poem in the heat of indignation, such as "Massachusetts to Virginia," "Barbara Frietchie," or "Laus Deo." His reform efforts interfered with his lyric gifts as a poet, however, and his best work came later in life, in his fifties and sixties, especially after the Civil War. The War Between the States presented a particular dilemma to Whittier in pitting his antislavery sentiments against his Quaker commitment to nonviolence. He saw the need for emancipation, but did not approve of secession or the drift toward armed conflict. Yet he remained a loyal Unionist and wrote poems and broadsides in favor of the Union cause. Titles such as "Our Countrymen in Chains" and "The Sabbath Scene" are little more than propaganda, but Whittier was writing to appeal to the emotions and feelings of ordinary people, and these antislavery verses enjoyed great popular success. Next to Harriet Beecher Stowe, he was perhaps the most effective propagandist for the Abolitionist cause.

In his personal life, Whittier remained a resolute bachelor, despite several romantic attractions to Quaker admirers. He lived with his mother, two sisters, and a brother in Amesbury, and cherished the company of his family. Their successive deaths in the 1850's and 1860's, however, particularly the loss of his beloved sister Elizabeth in 1864, left him increasingly isolated. The idyllic poem "Snow-Bound" was written partially in memory of his tight-knit family, and with its publication in 1866 Whittier enjoyed his first large commercial success, and thereafter was able to live comfortably on his literary earnings. Henceforth his volumes of poetry came out regularly and sold well, but he was plagued with persistently poor health and never felt fully comfortable with his new fame or with the many visitors to his Amesbury cottage. Occasionally he would venture into Boston to join Ralph Waldo Emerson, Henry Wadsworth Longfellow, and Oliver Holmes at the Saturday Club, but more often he preferred to enjoy the simple company of his niece and her family at their country estate in Danvers.

After the war, Whittier had gradually become institutionalized as one of the Fireside Poets, and with this increased popularity came other honors. He served as a Harvard overseer from 1858 onward and as a trustee of Brown University from 1869 to 1892. Harvard also awarded him an honorary LL.D., in 1886, although Whittier was prevented by illness from attending the ceremony in person. On his seventieth birthday, his friends held a formal dinner in his honor, on which occasion Mark Twain embarrassed the guests when his humor misfired, his intended tribute being taken by some as parody.

In his later years, Whittier increasingly assumed the role of New England patriarch, invoking in his poems a sentimental and nostalgic view of village life. He felt out of touch with the changes in the postwar America of the Gilded Age, and increasingly withdrew to the quiet meditation of his Quaker faith. On September 3, 1892, he suffered a paralytic stroke, which led to his death six days later, on September 7, at the age of 84. Oliver Wendell Holmes spoke at his funeral, after which Whittier was buried in the Friends' section of the Union Cemetery in Haverhill, next to his parents and sister.

Analysis

In the collected edition of his work, John Greenleaf Whittier decided to arrange his poems by topic, in ten categories, rather than present them in chronological order. He also suppressed many of the early verses that had proved embarrassing to him so that the supposedly complete 1894 edition of *The Poetical Works of John Greenleaf Whittier* is not really definitive, though it reflects the poet's final intentions. This arrangement obscures Whittier's development as a poet, but it does tell something about his major concerns and about the poetic forms in which he felt most comfortable. These include antislavery poems, songs of labor and reform, ballads, narratives and legends, nature poems, personal poems, historical poems, occasional verses, hymns and religious lyrics, and genre poems and country idylls.

From Whittier's collected verse, perhaps a dozen or so titles are distinctive. These include "Ichabod," "Massachusetts to Virginia," "Barbara Frietchie," "Telling the Bees," "Laus Deo," "The Trailing Arbutus," "Skipper Ireson's Ride," "First-Day Thoughts," and of course "Snow-Bound." A few other selections should be mentioned—"In School-Days," "The Barefoot Boy," and "Dear Lord and Father of Mankind"—simply because they are part of America's popular culture.

Many of Whittier's Abolitionist poems are little more than crude propaganda, but with "Ichabod" he produced a masterpiece of political satire and invective. Cast in terms of a prophetic rebuke, the poem is directed at Daniel Webster, whose "Seventh of March" speech in favor of the Fugitive Slave Law aroused the wrath and enmity of many Northern Abolitionists, who accused him of selling out to slave interests. Whittier portrays Webster, in terms of bitter denunciation, as a leader who has betrayed his countrymen and extinguished the life of his soul. His audience would certainly have caught the disparaging reference to I Samuel 4:21, "And she named the child Ichabod, saying the glory is departed from Israel!" Webster, a contemporary "Ichabod" in his fall from glory, becomes the object of scorn and pity for his betrayal of the antislavery cause.

This same contentious tone is also evident in another antislavery poem, "Massachusetts to Virginia," which contrasts the free strength of the North with the moral decadence brought about by slavery in the South. The poem recalls that both Commonwealth States had stood united in the War for Independence, and appeals to that sense of common fellowship in freedom. Though some passages are marred by stock declamatory phrases and excessive use of formal diction and hyperbole, the poem ably makes its point and ends with a ringing slogan, "No fetters in the Bay State,—No slaves upon our Land!"

To a staunch Abolitionist, the ratification of the Thirteenth Amendment on December 18, 1865, was reason enough for an occasional poem, but Whittier's "Laus Deo" (literally "Praise God") expresses his personal jubilation at seeing a lifetime's work brought to completion. The poem describes the ringing of bells and firing of guns in Amesbury that accompanied the announcement that slavery had officially been abolished throughout the Union. The ten stanzas of trochaic tetrameter create a hymn of celebration and gratitude in which the Lord sanctions the righteousness of the Union cause.

On a more personal note, Whittier wrote many memorable verses in tribute to his Quaker faith, the finest of these perhaps being "First-Day Thoughts," in which he evoked the quiet grace and deep spirituality of the Friends' service. He captures the essence of Christian worship in the soul's contemplation of its Creator through "the still small voice" of silent meditation. This same note of profound spiritual depth and reverence for the inner life appears in his famous hymn, "Dear Lord and Father of Mankind," which was adapted from the last six stanzas of "The Brewing of Soma." This inner faith grew with age and led Rufus M. Jones to comment later that Whittier "grasped more steadily, felt more profoundly, and interpreted more adequately the essential aspects of the Quaker life and faith" than any other of his age.

Whittier's most lasting accomplishment, however, rests with his country idylls and genre poems, those set pieces and descriptive verses in which he evokes a memory of his childhood or presents an idealized view of the pleasures of rural life. In "The Trailing Arbutus," for example, a glimpse of this early spring flower on an otherwise cold and bitter day becomes the occasion for a moment of natural rapture. A better poem, "Telling the Bees," uses the New England custom of draping bee hives after a family death as a way of foreshadowing the narrator's sorrow at the loss of his beloved Mary. This particular poem, occasioned by the death of the poet's mother, contains some of his finest descriptive passages. Another genre poem, "In School-Days," treats of bashful love and childhood regrets nostalgically remembered, while "The Barefoot Boy" presents a stilted and somewhat generalized picture of rural childhood: only in the middle stanzas does the poem rise above platitudes to a realistic glimpse of the poet's actual boyhood. With "Skipper Ireson's Ride," Whittier turned a New England legend into the material for a memorable folk ballad, although at the expense of historical veracity. The poem's mock-heroic tone does not mask the cruelty of the incident, in which Old Floyd Ireson was "tarred and feathered and carried in a cart" by the women of Marblehead for allegedly failing to rescue the survivors of another sinking fishing vessel. However factually inaccurate, Whittier's version of the legend captures the essential qualities of mob behavior in what one critic has called the most effective nineteenth century American ballad.

"Snow-Bound," subtitled "A Winter Idyl," is probably Whittier's most lasting achievement. The founding of *The Atlantic Monthly* in 1857 had given him a steady market for his verse, and when the editor, James Russell Lowell, wrote to him in 1865 requesting a "Yankee pastoral," Whittier responded with "Snow-Bound," which was published in the February, 1866, issue. The epigrams from Agrippa von Nettesheim's *Occult Philosophy* (1533) and Ralph Waldo Emerson's "The Snow Storm" establish the parameters of the poem in what John B. Pickard has called the protective circle of the family and hearth against the ominous power of the winter storm. Through an extended narrative in four-beat rhymed couplets, Whittier recalls the self-sufficiency of his family and recounts their close-knit circle of domestic affection as seen through a week of enforced winter isolation. This theme is enhanced through a series of contrasts between light and dark, warmth and cold, indoors and outdoors, fire and snow. After taking the reader through the round of barnyard chores, the poet shifts his perspective indoors to describe the sitting room of the Whittier homestead. Part II of the poem begins with Whittier's recollections of the tales and stories the family shared during their long evenings before the fire, with father, mother, uncle, aunt, schoolteacher, and another female guest each taking turns with the storytelling. The evening's entertainment finally ends as the fire burns low in the hearth and each family member retires from the pleasant circle of light and warmth. Part III of the poem gradually shifts from the past back to the present, as the poet's memories of "these Flemish pictures of old days" gradually fade; just as the fireplace logs had earlier faded to glowing embers covered with gray ash, so the poet will now gradually relinquish these recollections that have warmed "the hands of memory." His concluding lines express the hope that these memories will touch other readers and uplift their hearts, like the fresh odors of newly cut meadows, or pond lilies' fragrance on a summer breeze. The shift in season enforces the contrast between past and present, distancing Whittier from his family, most of whom had since died.

While he was not a major poet, Whittier learned early from Robert Burns the value of the commonplace, and his best poetry reflects an affectionate understanding of New England country life. If his muse flew no higher than popular and occasional verse, at least he wrote well of what he knew best—the customs and folkways of Yankee farming; the spiritual resources of his Quaker faith, which taught him to place spiritual concerns over material needs; and the history and legends of Essex County. His most accomplished poems look ahead to Edwin Arlington Robinson and Robert Frost, who would further probe the diminished world of the New England farm and village. Whittier stands directly in this tradition. His reputation has held better than those of the other Fireside Poets, and he will continue to be read for his grasp of several essential truths: the value of family affections, the importance of firm moral character, and the simple attractions of country life.

Andrew J. Angyal

Other major works

LONG FICTION: *Narrative of James Williams: An American Slave*, 1838;

Leaves from Margaret Smith's Journal, 1849.

NONFICTION: *Justice and Expediency: Or, Slavery Considered with a View to Its Rightful and Effectual Remedy, Abolition*, 1833; *The Supernaturalism of New England*, 1847; *Old Portraits and Modern Sketches*, 1850; *Literary Recreations and Miscellanies*, 1854; *Whittier on Writers and Writing: The Uncollected Critical Writings of John Greenleaf Whittier*, 1950 (Edwin H. Cady and Harry Hayden Clark, editors); *The Letters of John Greenleaf Whittier*, 1975 (John B. Pickard, editor).

ANTHOLOGIES: *Child Life*, 1872; *Child Life in Prose*, 1874; *Songs of Three Centuries*, 1876.

MISCELLANEOUS: *Prose Works of John Greenleaf Whittier*, 1866; *The Journal of John Woolman*, 1871 (editor); *The Writings of John Greenleaf Whittier*, 1888-1889.

Bibliography

Kribbs, Jayne K., comp. *Critical Essays on John Greenleaf Whittier.* Boston: G. K. Hall, 1980. Part of the Critical Essays on American Literature series. Kribbs's extended introduction locates four periods of the poet's writing career and suggests in conclusion that the central question about Whittier is not how great, but how minor a figure he is in American literature. All the essays are written by respected scholars. Contains a bibliography and an index.

Leary, Lewis Gaston. *John Greenleaf Whittier.* Twayne's United States Authors series 6. New York: Twayne, 1961. Although this introductory study looks at Whittier's life and art, the poetry discussion is more useful than the biographical section, which contains some errors and no new information. Leary discusses the poet's limitations, especially as a critic, and gives his subject perspective with references to Nathaniel Hawthorne, Herman Melville, and Henry David Thoreau. Supplemented by a bibliography.

Miller, Lewis H. "The Supernaturalism of *Snow Bound.*" *New England Quarterly* 53 (1980): 291-307. A good reading on how Whittier broke through his usually plain style to create an impressive rhythm, tone, and syntax in his striking creation of a bleak landscape and snow-bound universe.

Pickard, John B. *John Greenleaf Whittier: An Introduction and Interpretation.* New York: Barnes & Noble Books, 1961. The book begins with a biographical summary; the last seven chapters are a critical guide to his work. Pickard discusses Whittier's control of local-color detail, the moralism of his nature poems, and the authenticity of his religious poems. Some of the poems discussed are "Last Walk in Autumn," "The Barefoot Boy," "Snow-Bound," and "The Double-Headed Snake of Newbury."

Wagenknecht, Edward. *John Greenleaf Whittier: A Portrait in Paradox.* New York: Oxford University Press, 1967. Wagenknecht leaves the usual methods of biography behind by arranging his facts and anecdotes topically rather than chronologically. The result is a vibrant and energetic portrait of Whittier that displays the richness of his inner and outer life. The thesis of this book is that many facets of Whittier's life seem paradoxical to one another. Includes a bibliography.

Warren, Robert Penn. *John Greenleaf Whittier's Poetry: An Appraisal and a Selection.* Minneapolis: University of Minnesota Press, 1971. In a sixty-page essay, Warren discusses "Snow-Bound," "Telling the Bees," "Ichabod," "To My Old Schoolmaster," and other poems addressing themes of childhood and nostalgia, as well as a controversial Freudian view of the poet's development. Includes thirty-six poems by Whittier.

Woodwell, R. H. *John Greenleaf Whittier: A Biography.* Haverhill, Mass.: Trustees of the John Greenleaf Whittier Homestead, 1985. This is the fullest biography, based on years of research. It is encyclopedic, but has a very good index. Woodwell's 636 pages are not highly readable, but he does include a useful review of Whittier's criticism.

RICHARD WILBUR

Born: New York, New York; March 1, 1921

Principal poetry

The Beautiful Changes and Other Poems, 1947; *Ceremony and Other Poems*, 1950; *Things of This World*, 1956; *Poems 1943-1956*, 1957; *Advice to a Prophet and Other Poems*, 1961; *Loudmouse*, 1963 (juvenile); *The Poems of Richard Wilbur*, 1963; *Walking to Sleep: New Poems and Translations*, 1969; *Digging for China*, 1970; *Opposites*, 1973 (juvenile); *The Mind-Reader: New Poems*, 1976; *Seven Poems*, 1981; *New and Collected Poems*, 1988.

Other literary forms

In addition to his success as a poet, Richard Wilbur has won acclaim as a translator. Interspersed among his own poems are translations of Charles Baudelaire, Jorge Guillén, François Villon, and many others. His interest in drama is most notably shown in his translations of four Molière plays: *Le Misanthrope* (1955, *The Misanthrope*); *Tartuffe* (1963); *École des femmes* (1971, *The School for Wives*); and *Les Femmes savantes* (1978, *The Learned Ladies*). In 1957, Random House published *Candide: A Comic Operetta* with lyrics by Wilbur, book by Lillian Hellman, and score by Leonard Bernstein. Wilbur admits that he attempted to write a play in 1952, but he found its characters unconvincing and "all very wooden." He turned to translating Molière, thinking he "might learn something about poetic theater by translating *the master.*" Wilbur has edited several books, including *A Bestiary*, with Alexander Calder (1955); *Poe: Complete Poems* (1959); and *Shakespeare: Poems*, with coeditor Alfred Harbage (1966). In 1976, Wilbur published *Responses, Prose Pieces: 1953-1976*, a collection of essays which he describes as containing "some prose by-products of a poet's life." Most of his manuscripts are in the Robert Frost Library at Amherst College. His early work is housed in the Lockwood Memorial Library at the State University of New York at Buffalo.

Achievements

Eschewing any obvious poetic version or formal, personal set of guidelines, Wilbur has come to be regarded as a master craftsman of modern poetry. Although he sees himself as an inheritor of the vast wealth of language and form used by poets before him, Wilbur has consistently striven to create and maintain his own artistic signature and control over his own work. Having begun his career immediately after World War II and having been exposed to what has been called "the Beat generation," Wilbur creates his poetry from an intriguing blend of imaginative insights and strict adherence to the niceties of conventional poetics. His is not the poetry of confession or hatred readily exemplified by Sylvia Plath, nor is it hallucinatory or mystical as is much of Allen Ginsberg's work.

Wilbur began to write poetry because the war prompted him to confront the fear and the physical and spiritual detachment brought about by a world in upheaval. He says that he "wrote poems to calm [his] nerves." It is this sense of imposed order on a disorderly world that has caused some readers to think of Wilbur's poetry as a distant investigation into human life addressed to a small, educated audience and delivered by a seemingly aloof but omniscient observer. Nearly all Wilbur's poems are metrical, and many of them employ rhyme. Perhaps if a feeling of detachment exists, it comes not from Wilbur the poet but from the very standards of poetic expression. Every persona established by a poet is, in Wilbur's words, "a contrived self." This voice is the intelligent recorder of experience and emotion. It is Wilbur's voice in the sense that, like the poet, the persona discovers relationships between ideas and events which are grounded in concrete reality but which lead to abstracted views of nature, love, endurance, and place. He uses concrete images—a fountain, a tree, a hole in the floor—to explore imagination. His flights into imagery are not sojourns into fantasy; they are deliberate attempts to be a witness to the disordered and altogether varied life around him.

Wilbur achieves brilliantly what he sees poetry doing best: compacting experience into language that excites the intellect and vivifies the imagination. His voice and the cautious pace at which he works are not to be taken as self-conscious gestures. They are, to use his word, matters demanding "carefulness." He finds "gaudiness annoying, richness not." Wilbur's poetry is rich; it is wealthy in imagery and plot and rhythmic movement. He seems to believe that language cannot be guarded unless it is used to carry as much meaning as it can possibly bear. This freedom with language is not prodigal but controlled. Betraying poetry's ancestry would be anarchy for Wilbur. At the heart of his canon is the verbal liberty he finds in formalism. Consequently, in each line he hopes that at least one word will disturb the reader, providing a freedom found only within the architectonics of poetry's conventions. His poems enjoy humor and quiet meditation, and they lend themselves easily to being read aloud. Because of the freedom the rules of poetry give to them, Wilbur's poems are energetic, and his persona, peripatetic.

Honored with degrees from numerous colleges and universities, Wilbur has also been the recipient of Guggenheim Fellowships (1952-1953, 1963) and the Prix de Rome (1954). *Things of This World* was awarded the Pulitzer Prize, the National Book Award, and the Edna St. Vincent Millay Memorial Award. In 1964, he was a corecipient of the Bollingen Prize for his translation of *Tartuffe*. In 1987 he was named Poet Laureate of the United States, an honor that was soon followed by the Aiken Taylor Award for Modern American Poetry.

Biography

Born to Lawrence and Helen Purdy Wilbur, Richard Purdy Wilbur was reared in a family which was moderately interested in art and language. His father was an artist, and his mother was a daughter of an editor with the *Baltimore Sun*. His maternal great-grandfather was also an editor and a publisher who established newspapers supporting the Democratic platform. In 1923, the family moved to a farm in North Caldwell, New Jersey, and Wilbur and his brother enjoyed their childhoods investigating nature, an activity which remains a strong focal point in his poems. His father's painting and his mother's link with newspapers led him at times to think of becoming a cartoonist, an artist, or a journalist. His love of cartooning continues, for he illustrated *Opposites* with bold line drawings. His interests were many, however, and he was encouraged by his family to explore any talents he wished. After graduating from Montclair High School in 1938, he entered Amherst College, where he edited the newspaper and contributed to *Touchstone*, the campus humor magazine. He spent summers hoboing around the country.

After graduation in 1942, Wilbur married Charlotte Hayes Ward (with whom he has had four children), joined the Enlisted Reserve Corps, and saw active duty in Europe with the 36th Infantry Division. At Cassino, Anzio, and the Siegfried line, he began writing poetry seriously, embarking on what he calls creation of "an experience" through a poem. He sent his work home where it remained until he returned from the war to pursue a master's degree in English at Harvard. The French poet André du Bouchet read the poems, pronounced Wilbur a poet, and sent the works to be published. They were released as *The Beautiful Changes and Other Poems* in 1947; the same year Wilbur received his degree from Harvard and was elected to the Society of Fellows.

His status as a poet established, Wilbur began his teaching career. From 1950 to 1954, he was an assistant professor of English at Harvard. Then, from 1954 to 1957, he served as an associate professor at Wellesley College; during that time his award-winning *Things of This World* was published. In 1957, he went to Wesleyan University as a professor of English. He stayed there until 1977, when he accepted the position of writer-in-residence at Smith College. He divides his time between Key West, Florida, and the Berkshire Mountains near Cummington, Massachusetts, where he occupies himself doing things which he says are "non-verbal so that I can return to language with excitement and move toward language from kinds of strong awareness for which I haven't instantly found facile words. It is good for a writer to move into words out of the silence, as much as he can."

Analysis

If readers were to limit their interest in Richard Wilbur's poetry to a discussion of imagery, they would be misunderstanding and distorting some of the basic premises upon which he builds his poetry. Just as he sees each of his poems as an independent unit free of any entanglement with other poems in a collection or with a superimposed, unifying theme, so he views the creation of a poem as an individual response to something noticed or deeply felt. Because all worthwhile poetry is a personal vision of the world, Wilbur heightens the tension and irony found in his poems by establishing a voice enchanted by what is happening in the poem but controlled so that the persona is nearly always a reasonable voice recording details and events in an entirely believable way. His sense of decorum, then, plays a major role in creating the relationship between reader and poet.

Readers often react to Wilbur's decorum in one of two ways: either they laud the fictive persona as a trustworthy human being, lacking deceit, or they hear him speaking from a plateau which is at best inaccessible to the reader because it is too distant from the mundane. Wilbur's decorum actually creates a median between these two extremes. Like Robert Frost, Wilbur believes that poetry must present shared experiences in extraordinary ways. His persona is not directed toward readers solely as readers of poetry. Rather, the voice is aimed sharply at defining the experiences that both readers and poet hold in common. Wilbur never talks *at* the reader, but rather, he addresses himself to the human condition. Often his voice is much more vulnerable and humorous than readers admit. Many of his poems are reminiscent of soliloquies. A reader may come to the poems the way a person may discover a man talking out loud to himself about personal experiences, all the while using the most imaginative, sonorous language to describe them. At his best, Wilbur provides moments when readers can recognize the deep humanity which runs through his work.

Although he looks for no overriding idea or central metaphor when he organizes a collection, Wilbur does return to themes which are at the heart of human life: nature, love, a sense of goodness and contentment, the search for direction, the need to feel a part of a larger unknown, a wider life. All of these topics are spiritual concerns. Unlike Edgar Allan Poe, whom he sees as a writer who ignores reality to construct a world colored by the fantastic, Wilbur grounds his spiritual wanderings in the world that readers know. In this respect, he is capturing what is abstract in the mesh of concrete imagery, a feat also successfully accomplished by Frost and Emily Dickinson.

Perhaps nowhere else do Wilbur's major themes so intelligently and ironically coalesce as in "Lamarck Elaborated," a poem dealing not only with nature and love but also with the inner and outer worlds that human beings inhabit. Mankind's place in these two worlds and his ability to balance them provide a common experience for both poet and reader. The inner world of man, represented by the senses and the intellect, perceives the outer world framed by nature which, in turn, has the power to shape man's ability to interpret what he senses to be the physical world. Chevalier de Lamarck, a French naturalist whose life straddles the seventeenth and eighteenth centuries, believed that the environment causes structural changes that can be passed on genetically. Although man may assign names to the animals, plants, and objects that surround him, he is unable to control the changes which may occur in nature and which may, in turn, change him. Man has adapted to nature. Paradoxically, mankind's attempts at analyzing the natural state of things leads him to "whirling worlds we could not know," and what he thinks is love is simply an overwhelming desire causing dizziness. The poem's voice records man's obsession with his place in a scheme he wishes to dominate but cannot. Literally and figuratively, the balance between the inner and outer worlds "rolls in seas of thought."

The balance implied in "Lamarck Elaborated" is also investigated in "Another Voice." Here Wilbur probes the soul's ability to do good when man's nature is often to do bad. How can the soul feel sympathy when evil has been committed? How can it transform violence into "dear concerns"? Can the "giddy ghost" do battle with malevolence? Wilbur seems to suggest that the soul's response should be one of endurance as it acknowledges evil without becoming evil. The soul may not be able to rid itself of its "Anxiety and hate," two powerful forces, but neither will it relinquish its quiet sympathy which serves as a witness for compassion.

Although "Another Voice" may conjure up a spirit of resignation as the poet ponders the weaknesses of the human soul, Wilbur's poetry contains many examples of contentment, complete happiness, and mature acknowledgment of human limitations. Wilbur reminds his readers that human beings cannot be or do all that they might wish to become or accomplish. "Running," "Patriot's Day," and "Dodwells Road" form a thematic triptych in which Wilbur muses about the stages of life and the reactions human beings have to these stages. The first poem is an account of the persona's memories of his boyhood and the abandonment that running provided. In the second, the persona is an observer of the Boston Marathon and of "Our champion Kelley who would win again,/ Rocked in his will, at rest within his run." The third poem presents the persona as both participant and observer. Having taken up the sport of jogging, as if to reaffirm his physical well-being, the speaker runs out of the forest and is brought to a halt by "A good ache in my rib-cage." He feels comfortable in the natural setting surrounding him, a "part of that great going." The shouts of two boys (possibly the persona's sons) and the barking of a dog break the quiet, and the speaker finds delight in their running and leaping. In a gesture as inevitable as it is moving, the speaker gives the "clean gift" of his own childhood, his own vigor, to the boys.

The voice that Wilbur assumes in his poems is often that of a person discovering or attempting to discover something unknown or removed. Usually the epiphany that the persona undergoes is centered around ordinary conditions or experiences. Sometimes the enlightenment produces extraordinary insights into human nature, the fragility of life, or the inexorable passage of time. A poem which manages to evoke poignancy, humor, and fear is "A Hole in the Floor," in which the speaker stands directly above an opening a carpenter has made "In the parlor floor." The use of the word "parlor" brings to mind turn-of-the-century home-life, a certain quaintness and security. Now that this *sanctum sanctorum* has been defiled, the speaker stares into the hole to view an unexpected scene. He is poised on the brink of a discovery and compares himself with Heinrich Schliemann, the excavator of Troy and Mycenae. He sees in the hole the vestiges of the house's origins: sawdust, wood shavings "From the time when the floor was laid."

Wilbur heightens the mythological tone of the poem by comparing the shavings to the pared skins of the golden apples guarded by the Hesperides in the garden on the Isles of the Blest. Although in the dim light the curly lengths of shaved wood may seem "silvery-gold," they remain concrete reminders of the carpenter's trade and of the creation of the structure in which the speaker now stands. If he senses that something primordial has been uncovered, he cannot quite convey his feelings. The speaker, of course, has given in to his own curiosity and wishes to be the explorer of unknown territories, the uncoverer of what had been private and hidden, but, at the same time, close by. Reveling in his investigation of the joists and pipes, he finally wonders what it is he thought he would see. He brings his consciousness back to the steady, mundane world of the parlor and upbraids himself for his curiosity and romanticism. He asks himself if he expected to find a treasure or even the hidden gardens of the Hesperides. Perhaps, he ponders, he has come face-to-face with "The house's very soul."

Unlike Frost's figure who is content to kneel by a well, see his own reflection, and then catch a glimmer of something at the bottom, Wilbur's speaker understands that what he discovers or believes he has discovered is something beyond the orderly, formal restrictions imposed upon him by the parlor. Somehow, the hidden realm on which the house stands adds an importance to what can in fact be known. Paradoxically, what the persona knows is his inability to fathom the unknowable, that "buried strangeness/ which nourishes the known." The parlor suddenly becomes "dangerous" because its serenity rests on uncertainty, darkness, and private beginnings. The "buried strangeness" not only resides at the foundation of the house, but it is also found in any human construction, a building, a passion, a theory, or a poem.

"A Hole in the Floor" is further representative of Wilbur's poetry because it balances two opposites, and these contraries work on several levels: curiosity and expectation, the known and the unknown, and reality and imagination. It is a complex and beautifully crafted poem. Other poems which also investigate the balance between opposites include "Another Voice," "Advice to a Prophet," "Gemini," "Someone Talking to Himself," and "The Writer." Wilbur's obvious pleasure in riddles is another example of this taut balance between the unknown and the known, the question and the answer, the pause and the reply. In addition, *Opposites*, charming and witty as it is, has this same tense equilibrium built into it.

The contrast between opposing ideas is probably most evident in what could be called Wilbur's "two-voice" poems, those in which he presents "two voices going against each other. One is a kind of lofty and angelic voice, the other is a slob voice, and these are two parts of myself quarreling in public." The poem "Two Voices in a Meadow," which begins *Advice to a Prophet and Other Poems*, juxtaposes a milkweed's flexibility with a stone's tenacity. The milkweed yields to the wind's power to carry its cherubic seeds to the soil, and the stone attributes the solid foundation of heaven to its immovable nature. In "The Aspen and the Stream," the tree and the brook carry on a dialogue in which the aspen's metaphysics are countered by the stream's no-nonsense, literal approach to its place in the universal scheme of life.

Sometimes Wilbur's interest in opposites takes the form of a study of reconciliation through religion. Such poems as "Water Walker" and "A Christmas Hymn" suggest his concern with religious doctrine and its influence on private action and public thought. At other times, the balance is jarred because the persona is duped into believing something false or is misled because of naïveté. A more gullible person than the one in "A Hole in the Floor," the character in "Digging for China" burrows into the earth thinking that he can reach China. The speaker digs and digs to no avail, of course, and becomes obsessed and then delirious, "blinking and staggering while the earth went round." Admitting his folly, he confesses that "Until I got my balance back again/ All that I saw was China, China, China." He returns to whatever balance he may have known before his futile attempt to reach the Orient, but he enjoys no enlightenment of the spirit.

The tense balance between knowledge and ignorance may appear in Wilbur's poems when the persona is confronted with an abstraction so amorphous and foreign that it cannot adequately be defined, as in "A Hole in the Floor." At other times, Wilbur allows his characters to confront ideas, events, or feelings which are much more readily and vividly recognized. In such cases, the emotions, although private, have a larger, perhaps a more cosmic significance added to them; these are shared emotions, easily identifiable because nearly all human beings have experienced them. Even if man stands on the edge or the margins of experience, he is from time to time thrust squarely into life's demands and responsibilities. Wilbur elucidates this idea in poems such as "Marginalia," in which "Things concentrate at the edges," and "Our riches are centrifugal."

Two poems which combine both the experience of living life fully and the experience of participating at its edges are "Boy at the Window" and "The Pardon." Both have titles which would befit paintings, and, indeed, Wilbur presents concrete stories colored and framed by his language and the structure of the poems themselves. Each has as its main character a boy who is both witness and participant. "Boy at the Window" is reminiscent of a classic Italian sonnet in its form and meter, although Wilbur divides the two sections into equal parts of eight lines each. Looking out from a window toward a snowman he has built, the boy is confronted by the "god-forsaken stare" of the figure "with bitumen eyes." The structure of the poem reinforces the balanced stares given by the boy and the snowman. Safe and warm, the boy intuitively knows that the snowman is an "outcast" from the world that the boy, himself, enjoys. The boy, however, does not mourn for the snowman; rather, the snowman "melts enough to drop from one soft eye/ A trickle of the purest rain, a tear." Surrounded as he is by "light" and "love," the boy understands, perhaps for the first time, fear and dread. The poem provides a quiet moment when the boy in his silence recognizes something about sin and futility and innocence and contentment. With its blending of childhood trust and energy with a maturer reflection on mankind's fall from grace, it evokes much the same mood as Dylan Thomas' "Fern Hill."

"The Pardon" has as its plot a boy's confrontation with the death of his dog. At first he refuses to accept the event and tries to mask the experience just as "the heavy honeysuckle-smell" masks the odor of the decaying body. Admitting fear and the inability to "forgive the sad or strange/ In beast or man," the child cannot bring himself to bury the dog he loved "while he kept alive." After the boy's father buries the dog, the child sleeps and dreams of the dog's coming toward him. The boy wants to "call his name" to ask "forgiveness of his tongueless head." His attempts are checked, however, and he feels betrayed by his horror and his guilt. The poem is told from the perspective of a grown man who is remembering his childhood. Knowing the gesture may be ludicrous or ineffective, he "begs death's pardon now." Whether redemption occurs or the guilt is lifted is not told, but the very act of confronting this long-ago event is in itself a mature gesture of reconciliation and remorse, covered, perhaps, with shame and embarrassment. The rhyme scheme of the poem also suggests the persona's growing control over the incident, a control made possible by the passing of years and the accumulation of experience. The boy lacked a perspective; the man he has become provides it. Like his father before him, the speaker hopes to have the strength and the will to bury the dog, if not literally, then at least symbolically. As the persona moves toward this strength, the rhyme scheme, chaotic at the poem's beginning, settles into an obvious, harmonious pattern which parallels the speaker's growing dominance over his sorrow.

Wilbur is known and admired for his short poems whose imagery and subjects are compacted by his mastery of language and poetic convention. As if to reaffirm his commitment to the richness of these standards, his later collections have included long, dramatic monologues which remind readers of the oral tradition in poetry. "Walking to Sleep" and "The Mind-Reader" are poems which invite Wilbur's audience to explore the frontier, the wilderness of conscious thought and subconscious ruminating. The poems are both accessible and cryptic. Nowhere else has Wilbur created such sustained narrations, such talkative, complex tellers of his tales. In fact, he has noted that "Walking to Sleep" requires eight minutes to read aloud. The narrators are both conjurers and straightforward friends. Readers wish to believe them, but, at the same time, their manipulative language and their careful choice of details and information suggest an artifice. Both poems deal with the equilibrium between what is private, sleep and thought, and what is public, consciousness and action. Readers are led through the poems by the narrators who help the audience balance its way as if on a tightrope. In addition, the poems seem to be inviting readers to lose themselves in their own minds, an activity calling for leisure, courage, and an eagerness to embrace the unknown and the uncontrollable.

On its surface, "Walking to Sleep" is a sensuous account of sleep, sweeping from scene to scene, mirroring the act of dreaming. It begins *in medias res*, and readers are asked to have the poise of a queen or a general as they give themselves over to sleep and, more important, to the devices of the poem itself. Wilbur explores in ways that are whimsical, horrifying, and provocative the images that appear to a sleeper and to a poet as well. The poem may well be an exploration into the origins of poetry, and the narrator-poet may be speaking to himself as much as he is to an audience. His only direct warning to himself and his readers is the speaker's suggestion that the imagination never be allowed to become too comfortable; it must remain "numb" with a "grudging circumspection." Readers can feel the rhythms of sleep and love, creativity, and balance in the poem just as vividly as they sense the rhythms of meter, imagery, humor, and resignation. The poem is a masterful work controlled by the limitless power of man's imagination.

"The Mind-Reader" deals with a man who thinks other people's thoughts. The narrator describes himself as a person condemned to finding what is lost, remembering what is forgotten, or foreseeing what is unknown. He is able to manipulate his listeners and his followers because of their superstitious awe of his ability, which they are afraid to disprove. He confesses that he "sometimes cheats a little," admitting that he has no clear, easy answers to give to questions about love, careers, or doubts. He sees his duties as being those of a listener rather than those of a man capable to prescience, and he wonders if "selfish hopes/ And small anxieties" have replaced the "reputed rarities of the soul." The irony in the poem is underscored when the speaker turns to his readers and asks them a question of huge, religious proportions. Like his audience, he now longs for guidance, "some . . . affection" capable of discovering "In the worst rancor a deflected sweetness." Ironically, he dulls his mind with drink and satiates himself with "concupiscence." To the great question of whether a gentle, proper, and completely honest, cosmic mind-reader exists, he has no answer.

In the past, Wilbur's craft has been narrowly defined as the poetry of a mind set apart from the everyday world that human beings inhabit. Although his interest in balance is evident, his keen insight into contraries and the inner and outer lives of his characters are equally important to an understanding of what he is attempting in his poems. His work focuses on the enlightenment of the human spirit, but it never denies the darker impulses or fears which are brought to bear when doubt, resignation, or apathy appear as challenges to the harmony that civilized man strives to achieve. His poems are not so much reaffirmations of the beauty of life as they are records of an attempt at order, an order certainly suggested by the conventions of poetry. These conventions govern a poetic talent whose use of subject, meter, rhyme, and imagery provokes the senses and provides an ordinary understanding of life in an extraordinary and uncompromising way.

Walter B. Freed, Jr.

Other major works

PLAYS: *The Misanthrope*, 1955 (translation); *Candide: A Comic Operetta*, 1956 (lyrics; book by Lillian Hellman, music by Leonard Bernstein); *Tartuffe*, 1963 (translation); *The School for Wives*, 1971 (translation); *The Learned Ladies*, 1978 (translation); *Andromache*, 1982 (translation); *Four Comedies*, 1982 (translation); *Phaedra*, 1986 (translation).

NONFICTION: *Responses, Prose Pieces: 1953-1976*, 1976; *On My Own Work*, 1983; *Conversations with Richard Wilbur*, 1990 (William Butts, editor).

MISCELLANEOUS: *A Bestiary*, 1955 (edited); *Modern American and Modern British Poetry*, 1955 (Louis Untermeyer and Karl Shapiro, editors). *Poe; Complete Poems*, 1959 (edited); *Shakespeare: Poems*, 1966 (edited); *The Narrative Poems and Poems of Doubtful Authenticity*, 1974 (edited).

Bibliography

Cummins, Paul F. *Richard Wilbur: A Critical Essay*. Grand Rapids, Mich.: Wm. B. Eerdmans, 1971. Defends Wilbur's poetry against the charge of passionless elegance; argues that the poet uses rhyme and meter skillfully to enhance tone and meaning. A largely thematic study. Includes a primary and a secondary bibliography (both of which, naturally, are dated), but no index.

Field, John P. *Richard Wilbur: A Bibliographical Checklist*. Serif series: Bibliographies and Checklists 16. Kent, Ohio: Kent State University Press, 1971. For the student wishing to make further forays into Wilbur's poetry and thinking, this volume provides a valuable detailed listing of the poetry collections and their contents, articles, stories, edited works, book reviews, interviews, and manuscripts. A list of secondary sources is also supplied.

Hill, Donald L. *Richard Wilbur*. New York: Twayne, 1967. The biographical chronology extends only through 1964. Devotes a chapter each to *The Beau-*

tiful Changes, Ceremony, Things of This World, and *Advice to a Prophet*, with both thematic and technical discussions. A final chapter looks at Wilbur's prose writings and evaluates his place among twentieth century poets. Notes, a bibliography, and an index are included.

Salinger, Wendy, ed. *Richard Wilbur's Creation.* Ann Arbor: University of Michigan Press, 1983. A rich collection featuring, in part 1, many previously published reviews of Wilbur's chief works through 1976; contributors include such luminaries as Louise Bogan, Randall Jarrell, Donald Hall, and John Ciardi. The second half presents more comprehensive critical essays on various aspects of the poet's themes and craft. Valuable for its scope and for the quality of its writing.

Wilbur, Richard. *Conversations with Richard Wilbur.* Edited by William Butts. Literary Conversations series. Jackson: University Press of Mississippi, 1990. The nineteen interviews collected here span about thirty years (beginning in 1962) and thus shed light on both changing times and the development of an important poet. Wilbur here responds to the critics who have labeled him as overly good-natured, lacking in passion, and too controlled. The poet also discusses how he approaches the writing of a poem, his opinions of creative-writing programs, and many other topics. Indexed.

_____. *On My Own Work.* Aquila Essays 20. Portree, Isle of Skye, Scotland: Aquila, 1983. This small book, apparently printed on an old-fashioned mimeograph, is hard to find. Yet it is worth the search for a student who wants to explore Wilbur's own concept of his poetry. Despite his demurrals—"the ideas of any poet, when reduced to prose statement, sound banal and mine are no exception"—he is unfailingly articulate and interesting.

OSCAR WILDE

Born: Dublin, Ireland; October 15, 1854
Died: Paris, France; November 30, 1900

Principal poetry

Ravenna, 1878; *Poems*, 1881; *The Sphinx*, 1894; *Poems in Prose*, 1894; *The Ballad of Reading Gaol*, 1898.

Other literary forms

Oscar Wilde wrote a number of plays produced successfully in his lifetime: *Lady Windermere's Fan* (1892), *A Woman of No Importance* (1893), *An Ideal Husband* (1895), and *The Importance of Being Earnest* (1895). Banned in London, his play *Salomé* was produced in 1893 in Paris with Sarah Bernhardt. Two plays, *Vera: Or, The Nihilists* (1880) and *The Duchess of Padua* (1883), were produced in New York after publication in England. Finally, two plays, *A Florentine Tragedy* (1906) and *La Sainte Courtisane*, were published together in the collected edition of Wilde's works in 1908. Wilde published one novel, *The Picture of Dorian Gray* (1891), serially in *Lippincott's Magazine*. Commercially and artistically successful with a number of his plays and his one novel, Wilde reached his peak in the early 1890's when he wrote little poetry. Wilde also wrote short stories and a number of fairy tales. His last prose work is a long letter, *De Profundis*, an apologia for his life. Parts of it were published as early as 1905, but the full work was suppressed until 1950.

Achievements

G. F. Maine states that the tragedy of Wilde is that he is remembered more as a criminal and a homosexual than as an artist. Readers still feel overwhelmed by Wilde's life just as his personality overwhelmed his contemporaries. His greatest achievement is in drama, and his only novel—*The Picture of Dorian Gray*—is still widely read. In comparison, his poetry is essentially derivative.

Wilde modeled himself on the poets of a tradition that was soon to end in English literature, and most of his poetry appears in the earlier part of his career. Within this Romantic tradition, Wilde had a wider range than might be expected; he could move from the limited impressions of the shorter poems to the philosophic ruminations of the longer poems. Yet behind each poem, the presence of an earlier giant lurks: John Keats, William Wordsworth, Algernon Charles Swinburne. Wilde's most original poem, *The Ballad of Reading Gaol*, is not derivative, and its starkness shows a side of Wilde not generally found in his other poems. Wilde's poetry is a coda, then, to the end of a tradition.

Biography

Oscar Fingal O'Flahertie Wills Wilde was born in Dublin, Ireland, on October 15, 1854. Flamboyance, so characteristic of the adult Wilde, was an obvious quality of both of his parents. His father was noted for physical dirtiness and love affairs, one of which led to a lawsuit and public scandal. Something of a social revolutionary, his mother published poetry and maintained a salon for intellectual discussion in her later years. Wilde grew up in this environment, showing both insolence and genius. He was an excellent student at all his schools. He attended Portora Royal School, Trinity College in Dublin, and then won a scholarship to Magdalen College, Oxford. At this time, John Ruskin was lecturing, and Wilde was influenced by Ruskin's ideas and style. More important, he heard and met Walter Pater, who had recently published his *Studies in the History of the Renaissance* (1873). It is Pater's influence that is most obvious in Wilde's development as a poet. While at Oxford, Wilde visited Italy and Greece, and this trip strengthened the love of classical culture so obvious in his poetry.

In the 1880's, as he developed as a writer, he also became a public personality. He toured the United States for about a year, and in both the United States and England he preached an aesthetic doctrine which had its origins in the Pre-Raphaelites and Pater. He married in 1883 and had two sons. Wilde serially published his only novel, *The Picture of Dorian Gray*, which immediately created a sensation with the public. Thereafter, he wrote a number of plays, most notably *Lady Windermere's Fan* and *The Importance of Being Earnest*.

Wilde's last decade involved the scandal over his homosexuality. His chief male lover was Lord Alfred Douglas, whose father, the Marquess of Queensberry, tried to end Wilde's liaison with his son and ruin Wilde socially. Consequently, Wilde sued the Marquess of Queensberry for libel but lost the case and also had his homosexuality revealed. Tried twice for homosexuality, he was found guilty and finally sentenced to two years at hard labor. From his prison experiences, Wilde wrote his most famous poem, *The Ballad of Reading Gaol*. Released from prison, he wandered over the Continent for three years, broken physically and ruined financially. He died in Paris at the age of forty-six.

Analysis

Oscar Wilde's poetry derives from the rich tradition of nineteenth century poetry, for, as Richard Aldington shows, Wilde imitated what he loved so intensely in the great poets of his century. Drawing from John Keats, Dante Gabriel Rossetti, William Morris, and Algernon Charles Swinburne, Wilde demonstrated an aestheticism like theirs in his lush imagery and in his pursuit of the fleeting impression of the moment. His poetry tries to capture the beautiful, as the Victorian critic John Ruskin had urged a generation earlier, but generally lacks the moral tone that Ruskin advocated. Wilde's poetry best fulfills the aesthetic of Walter Pater, who, in his *Studies in the History of the Renaissance*, advocated impressionism and art for art's sake. Indeed, Wilde paraphrased Pater's famous line of burning with a "hard, gemlike flame" in several of his poems.

Wilde published many poems individually before 1881, but his *Poems* of 1881 included almost all of these poems and many new ones. With this collection, he published more than half of the poetry that he was to produce. The collection of 1881 is a good representation of his aestheticism and his tendency to derivativeness. Wilde avoided the overtly autobiographical and confessional mode in these poems, yet they mirror his attitudes and travels as impressions of his life. The forms he tried most often in the collection were the Italian sonnet and, for longer poems, a six-line stanza in pentameter with an ababcc rhyme scheme. The smaller poetic output which followed the 1881 collection consists of a number of shorter poems, two longer poems, and *Poems in Prose*. The short poems break no new ground, *The Sphinx* heralds a decadence and a celebration of pain unequaled in the nineteenth century except by Swinburne a generation earlier. *The Ballad of Reading Gaol*, however, builds on Wilde's earlier efforts. Again, he avoids the confessional mode that one would expect, considering the horrors of incarceration out of which the poem grew. The persona of the poem is no longer an urbane mind observing nature and society, but a common prisoner at hard labor generalizing about the cruelties of humans and their treatment of those they love. In this poem, despite its shrillness and melodrama, Wilde struck a balance between his own suffering and art, a balance which the impressionism of his poetic talents made easier. He dealt, as an observer, with the modern and the sordid as he had dealt earlier with art and nature. *Poems in Prose* is Wilde's effort at the short parable, offering neither the impressionism nor the formal qualities of his other poems, but ironic parables which refute the pieties of his era. Here Wilde is at his wittiest.

Ravenna was Wilde's first long poem to be published, and it won the Newdigate prize for poetry while he was still at Oxford. Written in couplets, the poem deals with many of the themes which he developed for the 1881 collection; thus, *Ravenna* is the starting point in a study of Wilde's poetry. Like the later long poems, *Ravenna* develops through contrasts: northern and southern European cultures, innocence and experience, past and present, classical and Christian. As a city, Ravenna evokes all of these contrasts to the youthful Wilde.

The opening imagery is of spring, with a tendency to lushness typical of Keats. The boyish awe that Wilde felt in Ravenna is tempered, however, by recollection, for in the poem he is recalling his visit a year later. It is through recollection that he understands the greatness of the city, for in his northern world he has no such symbol of the rich complexity of time. What he learns from the English landscape is the passage of seasons which will mark his aging. He is sure, though, that with his love for Ravenna he will have a youthful inspiration despite his aging and loss of poetic powers.

Most of the poem is a poetic recounting of Ravenna's history. Wilde discusses the classical past of the city with reference to Caesar, and when he refers to George Gordon, Lord Byron's stay in the city, by association with Byron's last days in Greece, he imagines the region peopled with mythological figures; but the evening convent bell returns him to a somber Christian world. Recounting the Renaissance history of the city, Wilde is most moved by Dante's shrine. He closes the poem with references to Dante and Byron.

Wilde published twenty-eight sonnets in the 1881 collection, *Poems*, all of them Italian in form. Like his mentor Keats, Wilde used the sonnet to develop themes which he expanded in his longer poems. "Hélas," an early sonnet not published in the 1881 collection, is his artistic manifesto that sets the tone for all the poems that followed. "Hélas" finds Wilde rhetorically questioning whether he has bartered wisdom for the passion or impression of the moment. In the sonnets that follow, he clearly seems to have chosen such moments of vivid impression.

In several sonnets, Wilde alludes to the poets who molded his style and themes, including two sonnets about visiting the graves of Keats and Percy Bysshe Shelley in the Protestant cemetery in Rome. He identifies himself with Keats as he never identifies with Shelley, and rightly so, for Keats's style and themes echo throughout the 1881 collection. Wilde also refers directly to Keats in another sonnet, "Amor Intellectualis," and to other poets important to him: Robert Browning, Christopher Marlowe, and particularly Dante and John Milton. The sonnet "A Vision" is a tribute to Aeschylus, Sophocles, and Euripides. On a larger scale than the sonnets, the longer poem "The Garden of Eros" presents Wilde's pantheon of poets with his feelings about them.

Some of the sonnets have political themes; in a number of these, Wilde advocates freedom, occasionally sounding like a Victorian Shelley. He is concerned with the political chaos of nineteenth century Italy, a land important to him for its classical past; "Italia" is a sonnet about the political venality in Italy, but it stresses that God might punish the corrupt. In his own country, Wilde idealizes the era of the Puritans and Oliver Cromwell; the sonnet "To Milton" laments the loss of democracy in England and advocates a return to the ideals of the Puritan revolution. In "Quantum Mutata," he admires Cromwell for his threat to Rome, but the title shows how events have changed, for Victorian England stands only for imperialism. This attack on British imperialism informs the long poem "Ave Imperatrix," which is far more emotional in tone than the political sonnets.

A number of Wilde's sonnets express his preference for the classical or primitive world and his antipathy for the modern Christian world. These poems have a persona visiting Italy, as Wilde did in 1877, and commenting on the Christian elements of the culture; "Sonnet on Approaching Italy" shows the speaker longing to visit Italy, yet, in contemplating far-off Rome, he laments the tyranny of a second Peter. Three other sonnets set in Italy, "Ave Maria, Gratia Plena," "Sonnet Written in Holy Week in Genoa," and "Urbs Sacra Aeterna," have Wilde contrasting the grandeur and color of the classical world with the emptiness and greyness of the Christian world. It is in these poems that Wilde is most like Swinburne. In other sonnets, he deals with religious values, often comparing the Christian ideal with the corruption of the modern Church he sees in Italy, or Christ's message with the conduct of his sinful followers. In "Easter Day," Wilde depicts the glory of the Pope as he is borne above the shoulders of the bearers, comparing that scene with the picture of Christ's loneliness centuries before. In "E Tenebris," the speaker appeals for help to a Christ who is to appear in weary human form. In "Sonnet, On Hearing the Dies Irae Sung in the Sistine Chapel," Wilde criticizes the harsh picture of a fiery day of judgment and replaces it with a picture of a warm autumn harvest, in which man awaits reaping by and fulfillment in God.

Wilde's best religious sonnet, "Madonna Mia," avoids the polemicism of some of his other religious sonnets, showing instead an affinity with the Pre-Raphaelite painting and poetry of a generation earlier. This sonnet is Pater-esque in its hard impression, and it fulfills the credo suggested by the sonnet "Hélas." The picture Wilde paints in words is detailed: braided hair, blue eyes, pale cheeks, red lips, and white throat with purple veins; Wilde's persona is a worshiper of Mary, as Dante was of Beatrice.

"The Burden of Itys" is one of several long philosophic poems about nature and God to be found in the 1881 collection. Each of these poems has the same stanza form, a six-line stanza with an ababcc rhyme scheme; the first five lines are iambic pentameter, and the sixth is iambic heptameter. The stanza form gives a lightness which does not perfectly fit the depth of the ideas the poems present; it seems a form better suited to witticism than to philosophy.

Set in England close to Oxford, "The Burden of Itys" is similar in imagery and setting to Matthew Arnold's poems "The Scholar Gypsy" and "Thrysis." Wilde piles image on image of the flora of the region to establish the beauty of the setting, suggesting that the beauty of the countryside (and thus of nature in general) is holier than the grandeur of Rome. Fish replace bishops and the wind becomes the organ for the persona's religious reverie. By stanza thirteen, Wilde shifts from his comparison between Rome and nature to a contrast between the English landscape and the Greek. Because England is more beautiful than Greece, he suggests that the Greek pantheon could fittingly be reborn in Victorian England. A bird singing to Wilde, much like the nightingale singing to Keats, is the link between the persona imagining a revival of classical gods and actually experiencing one in which he will wear the leopard skin of a follower of Bacchus. This spell breaks, though, with another contrast, for a pale Christ and the speaker's religion destroy the classical reverie.

Brought back then to the Victorian world, as Keats was brought back to his world at the end of "Ode to a Nightingale," Wilde philosophizes and fixes the meaning of his experience in a way Keats never would have done. He stresses that nature does not represent the lovely agony of Christ but warm fellowship both in and between the worlds of man and animal. Even Oxford and nature are linked to each other, Wilde implies, as the curfew bell from his college church calls him back.

"Panthea" also works through dissimilarity, this time between southern and northern Europe, passion and reason, and classical and Christian thought. Wilde's rejection of the Church in "The Burden of Itys" is gentle, but in "Panthea" it is blatant. The gods have simply grown sick of priests and prayer. Instead, man should live for the passion and pleasure of an hour, those moments being the only gift the gods have to give. The poem emphasizes that the Greek gods themselves dwell in nature, participating fully in all the pleasures there. Their natural landscape, though, is not the bleak landscape of northern Europe, but the warm rich landscape of southern Europe.

Wilde proceeds to the philosophical theme of the poem, that one great power or being composes nature, and Nature, thus, subsumes all lives and elements and recycles them into various forms. For man to be reborn as flower or thrush is to live again without the pain of mortal existence; yet, paradoxically, without human pain, nature could not create beauty. Pain is the basis of beauty, for nature exists as a setting for human passion. Nature, in Wilde's words, has one "Kosmic Soul" linking all lives and elements. Wilde echoes lines of Keats and Pater, and, uncharacteristically, William Wordsworth; Wilde's affirmation proceeds with lines and images from Wordsworth's "Ode: Intimations of Immortality from Recollections of Early Childhood."

"Humanitad" is the longest of the philosophical poems in the 1881 collection, and it has much less in common with the other two philosophical poems than they have with each other. While spring is imminent, the speaker responds only to the winter elements still persisting. He emphasizes (paraphrasing Pater) that he has no fire to burn with a clear flame. The difference here is with the renewal of spring and spiritual exhaustion, and the speaker must look outside himself for some source of renewal. At one point, the poem turns topical by referring to ideals of simplicity and freedom: Switzerland, Wordsworth, and Giuseppe Mazzini. Wilde invokes the name of Milton as epitomizing the fight for freedom in the past; and, at the same time, he laments that there are no modern Miltons. Having no modern exemplar, Wilde also dismisses death and love as possible solutions for his moribund life. Turning to science, Wilde also rejects it. Wilde then has no recourse, and he faces a meaningless universe until he touches on mere causality after having rejected science.

Causality leads to God and creed, for causality is a chain connecting all elements. Nature, as in "Panthea," cannot help the speaker, for he has grown weary of mere sensation. Accordingly, he turns to the force behind nature (in this instance, God as Christ), although he rejects orthodoxy. He sees modern man's creed as being in process, for man is in the stage of crucifixion as he tries to discover the human in Christ and not the divine. The persona then sees his emptiness as the suffering leading to renewal. It is the full discovery of Christ's humanity which will make modern human beings masters of nature rather than tormented, alienated outcasts.

Just as Wilde drew from classical mythology for many of his poems and then contrasted the gray Christian world with the bright pagan world, he used Egyptian mythology in *The Sphinx* to picture a decadent sadistic sensuality as distinguished from a tortured Christian suffering. The situation in the poem is that a cat has crept into the speaker's room; to the speaker, the cat represents the Sphinx. Now, giving his imagination play, the speaker reveals his own sadistic eroticism, a subject that Wilde had not developed in other poems. The style also represents a departure for him; the stanzas consist of two lines of iambic octameter with no rhyme, resulting in a langorous slow rhythm in keeping with the speaker's ruminations about sensuality and sadism.

The cat as Sphinx represents the lush, decadent, yet appealing sensuality found in Egyptian mythology. In half of the poem, Wilde rhetorically questions the Sphinx about mythological figures of ancient Egypt, asking who her lovers were and at the same time cataloging the most famous myths of Egypt. Wilde settles on Ammon as the Sphinx's lover, but then he discusses how Ammon's statue has fallen to pieces, thus suggesting that the lover might be dead. Yet the Sphinx has the power to revive her lover; Ammon is not really dead. Having earlier referred to the holy family's exile in Egypt, Wilde now mentions that Christ is the only god who died, having let his side be pierced by a sword. Christ then is weaker than Ammon, and, in this way, Wilde suggests that pagan mythology is more vital than Christian mythology. The speaker's reflections on love become orthodox at the end; he feels he should contemplate the crucifix and not the Sphinx. He returns to a world of penitence where Christ watches and cries for every soul, but the speaker sees the tears as futile. The poem then raises the question of whether human beings can be redeemed from their fallen condition.

Wilde's most famous poem, *The Ballad of Reading Gaol*, is a departure from any of the poems he had published previously. Sometimes overdone emotionally, the poem uses the prison as a metaphor for life and its cruelties. Wilde is the observer rather than the subject; in this way, he distances himself from his own experiences. The poem raises the thematic question of why man is cruel to other men, so cruel that he always destroys what he loves. It is through cruelty that men kill or destroy the ones they love, just as the prisoner whom Wilde observes, and who is soon to hang, murdered his lover. The mystery of man's cruelty was the mystery of the Sphinx in Wilde's previous poem, but here the issue is the agony of the mystery rather than the decadent glory of cruelty, as in *The Sphinx*.

Wilde exploits the Gothic elements of the situation, dwelling on the macabre details of the grave of quicklime which dissolves the murderer's body. He uses the dread and gloom of the prisoners' lives to heighten the tone, but he often becomes shrill and melodramatic by emphasizing details such as the bag that covers the head of the condemned, tears falling like molten lead from the other prisoners as they observe the condemned, terror personified as a ghost, and the greasy rope used for the hanging. Ironically, the surviving prisoners are bedeviled by terror and horror, while the condemned dies calmly and serenely. Wilde uses a simple six-line stanza for a forcefully direct effect. The short lines alternate three and four feet of iambic pentameter with masculine rhyming of the second, fourth, and sixth lines. The stanza form is not one which suggests a reflective tone but rather a direct, emotional one.

The concluding motif of the poem is religious. The prison is a place of shame, where brother mistreats brother. Christ could feel only shame at what he sees his children do to each other there; but he rescues sinful man when he is broken by suffering and death. Even though the body of the hanged had no prayers said over it before interment in the quicklime, Christ rescued his soul. The surviving prisoners, their hearts broken and contrite, also gain salvation from the effects of their suffering.

Wilde's *Poems in Prose* was the last collection published of all his poems except *The Ballad of Reading Gaol*, and the reader hears a different voice from that of the other poems, satirical and paradoxical like William Blake's in *The Marriage of Heaven and Hell* (1790). In Wilde's hands, the prose poem is a debonair and provocative parable on religious subjects. More often than not in his six prose poems, Wilde is trying to shock the bourgeoisie out of complacency and religious orthodoxy.

"The Artist" sets the tone of the prose poems; in this piece, the artist forsakes the oppressive sorrow of Christianity for the pursuit of hedonism. It is this kind of ironic reversal which the other prose poems also develop. In "The Doer of Good," Christ returns to find sinners and lepers he has saved or cured delighting in the sin, no longer wrong, from which he saved them. The one person whom Christ saved from death wishes that Christ had left him dead. "The House of Judgment" ironically shows the sinner complaining that his earthly life was hellish, and, confronted now with Heaven, he has no conception of it after his life of suffering. The most moving of the six is "The Teacher of Wisdom," in which Wilde shows that the finest act of man is to teach the wisdom of God. A hermit, having attained the knowledge of God, refuses to part with it by giving it to the young sinner who is imploring him.

Frustrated, the sinner returns to sin, but, in so doing, extracts the knowledge from the hermit, who hopes to turn the sinner away from more sin. Fearing that he has parted with his knowledge, the hermit is consoled by God, who now, for his sacrifice, grants him a true love of God. In this parable, Wilde has transcended the satiric wit of the other parables to teach through irony.

Dennis Goldsberry

Other major works

LONG FICTION: *The Picture of Dorian Gray*, 1891.

SHORT FICTION: "The Canterville Ghost," 1887; *The Happy Prince and Other Tales*, 1888; *Lord Arthur Savile's Crime*, 1891; *A House of Pomegranates*, 1891.

PLAYS: *Vera: Or, The Nihilists*, 1880; *The Duchess of Padua*, 1883; *Lady Windermere's Fan*, 1892; *A Woman of No Importance*, 1893; *Salomé*, 1893 (in French), 1894 (in English); *The Importance of Being Earnest: A Trivial Comedy for Serious People*, 1895; *An Ideal Husband*, 1895; *A Florentine Tragedy*, 1906; *La Sainte Courtisane*, 1908.

NONFICTION: *Intentions*, 1891; *The Soul of Man Under Socialism*, 1895; *De Profundis*, 1905; *Letters*, 1962 (Rupert Hart-Davies, editor).

MISCELLANEOUS: *Works*, 1908; *Complete Works of Oscar Wilde*, 1948 (Vyvyan Holland, editor); *Plays, Prose Writings, and Poems*, 1960.

Bibliography

Ellmann, Richard. *Oscar Wilde.* New York: Alfred A. Knopf, 1988. This six-hundred-page study of Wilde's life and work will probably remain the definitive one for years to come. Ellmann argues that Wilde was conducting an examination of society and a reconsideration of its ethics. Not only has his best writing not lost its relevance, Ellmann believes, but his findings were always right. Supplemented by notes, a select bibliography, two appendices, and a detailed forty-nine-page index.

Eriksen, Donald H. *Oscar Wilde.* Boston: Twayne, 1977. This small volume is a useful corrective to studies of Wilde that see him and his work as anomalies of literature and history. After a brief chapter on Wilde's life and times, Eriksen makes critical and analytical assessments of his poetry, fiction, essays, and drama. A chronology, notes and references, an annotated bibliography, and an index supplement the text.

Gagnier, Regenia A. *Idylls of the Marketplace: Oscar Wilde and the Victorian Public.* Palo Alto, Calif.: Stanford University Press, 1986. This erudite study attempts to reach an understanding of Wilde by focusing less on his life and work and more on the relation of his work to his audiences. Leaning heavily on contemporary critical theory, it connects Wilde, Friedrich Engels, and Fyodor Dostoevski in ways that some may find more confusing than illuminating, but Gagnier's readings of the works are generally insightful and persuasive. Supplemented with a bibliography and an index.

Kohl, Norbert. *Oscar Wilde: The Works of a Conformist Rebel.* Translated by David Henry Wilson. Cambridge, England: Cambridge University Press, 1989. This scholarly study, representative of the most recent approaches to Wilde, interprets Wilde's works mainly through textual analysis, although it includes discussions of the society in which Wilde lived and to which he responded. Kohl argues that Wilde was not the imitator he is often accused of being but a creative adaptor of the literary traditions he inherited. Supplemented by detailed notes, a lengthy bibliography (the 1980 German edition contains 1,800 annotated entries), and an index.

Miller, Robert Keith. *Oscar Wilde.* New York: Frederick Ungar, 1982. This 152-page study is a useful introduction to Wilde and his work. The opening chapter reviews his biography, and subsequent chapters condense earlier critical analyses of *The Picture of Dorian Gray*, the plays, and the fairy tales. The sixth chapter discusses *The Ballad of Reading Gaol*, which Miller admires, and the last chapter contains an objective evaluation of Wilde as an aesthete and an artist. Includes a lengthy chronology, notes, a brief bibliography, and an index.

Raby, Peter. *Oscar Wilde.* Cambridge, England: Cambridge University Press, 1988. One of a series of excellent introductory critical studies to English and Irish authors. Includes biographical information because, Raby argues, it is most useful to see Wilde as indivisible from his works. The 1881 collection of poems, he says, makes it clear that Wilde's artistic purpose was a life's work. Supplemented with a chronology, notes, a bibliography, and an index.

Shewan, Rodney. *Oscar Wilde: Art and Egotism.* New York: Barnes & Noble Books, 1977. In this illuminating study, Shewan sees Wilde's attitude toward art reflected in John Keats and Percy Bysshe Shelley: Wilde devoted his career to exploring the self and applied his life to self-expression and self-dramatization. Supplementary material consists of a chronology, a bibliography, and an index.

C. K. WILLIAMS

Born: Newark, New Jersey; November 4, 1936

Principal poetry
A Day for Anne Frank, 1968; *Lies*, 1969; *I Am the Bitter Name*, 1972; *The Sensuous President*, 1972; *With Ignorance*, 1977; *Tar*, 1983; *Flesh and Blood*, 1987; *Poems 1963-1983*, 1988.

Other literary forms
In collaboration with classical scholars, C. K. Williams has written verse translations of two Greek tragedies: one, in 1978, of Sophocles' *Trachinai* (435-429 B.C.; *The Women of Trachis*), and the other, in 1985, of Euripides' *Bakchai* (405 B.C.; *The Bacchae*). The translations, as their notes indicate, are for the modern stage as well as for modern readers. Williams hopes for a flowering of the "kernel" of Sophocles' tragedy within the translator's historical moment, "a clearing away of some of the accumulations of reverence that confuse the work and the genius who made them." The translations are thus not staid or literal but do aim for thematic accuracy and life. Williams also translated poems from Issa under the title *The Lark. the Thrush. the Starling* (1983).

Achievements
Williams achieved early success in the era of cynicism and protest surrounding the Vietnam War. His early work sketches in a tough, cryptic style the nightmare visions of a God-forsaken world. *I Am the Bitter Name* is a howl of protest against the various corruptions of the world, lacking even the tonal variety and scant hope of his earlier work. Though powerful, Williams' protest poetry was seen by critics as an artistic dead end.

During the five-year interim between the publication of *I Am the Bitter Name* and *With Ignorance*, Williams remade his style, writing in long lines which fold back from the margin of the page and tell stories with proselike lucidity. The sense of human suffering and isolation common in the earlier poems remains, but the long-line poems narrate dramatic tales set in American cities: scenes of family life, recollections of childhood, and views from the windows of urban apartments. Exact description and conventional punctuation replace the blurred grammar and dreamlike flow of the earlier verse. The later Williams poses in his poems as a sympathetic survivor who, seeing clearly the complexities and disillusionment of contemporary life, shares astonishing personal associations with the reader.

Biography
Born November 4, 1936, in Newark, New Jersey, the son of Paul B. and

Dossie (née Kasdin) Williams, Charles Kenneth Williams was educated at Bucknell University and at the University of Pennsylvania, where he was graduated with a B.A. in 1959. In 1965, he married Sarah Jones, and they had one daughter, Jessica Anne, who figures in Williams' personal poems. At the Pennsylvania Hospital in Philadelphia, he founded a program of poetry therapy and was a group therapist for disturbed adolescents.

A Day for Anne Frank led to the publication of two volumes of poetry in 1969 and 1972 which established Williams as a protest poet of the Nixon era. He was a visiting professor at Franklin and Marshall College in 1977 and at the University of California at Irvine in 1978 before becoming professor of English at George Mason University. In addition, he has taught creative writing at various workshops and colleges, including Boston University and Columbia University.

A Guggenheim Fellowship in 1974 resulted in *With Ignorance*, the first book in his new style. In 1975, Williams married Catherine Mauger, a jeweler. They have one son. Williams was awarded the Bernard F. Conner Prize for the long poem by *The Paris Review* in 1983.

Analysis

Stylistic originality distinguished C. K. Williams' earliest work, and he has continued to evolve as a poet. Consistent in all periods of his work has been a "metaphysical" roughness and avoidance of merely literary polish. Meanwhile, he has treated frightening realities which are not conventionally subjects of poetry. His experimental style began with dreamlike lyrics with short run-on lines, sporadic punctuation, and startling leaps of image and diction. Strident in tone, sometimes shocking, the early poems found quick acceptance in the Nixon years.

Lies includes the long poem *A Day for Anne Frank*, which was published in a limited edition a year before it. In *Lies*, Williams anatomizes the horrors of modern history and existential despair. The absence of divine order grounds a series of nightmare visions with titles such as "Don't," "The Long Naked Walk of the Dead," "Loss," "Trash," "Downward," "Our Grey," and "It Is This Way with Men," which allegorizes men as spikes driven into the ground, pounded each time they attempt to rise. Williams' universe is the indifferent or hostile one of classic American naturalism, but it takes much of its apocalyptic substance from the Holocaust and from the Vietnam War. In spite of the negativity of his lyric outcries against suffering and waste, Williams' early poems burn, not only with terror but also with a passion that things should be better. Optimism, authority, and poetic form are smashed like atoms. Williams' complaint is that of the child-man against the parent-universe in which he finds himself an unloved stepson.

There is monotony, even callowness, in this stance, in improbable metaphors and scatological language flaunted for shock value—expressing a gnostic rejection of his prison-body in the inhospitable universe. Nevertheless, *Lies* was critically acclaimed for its fusion of moral seriousness and verbal ingenuity. It concludes with the long poem about Anne Frank, the quintessential victim of history; to borrow a comparison from one of Williams' poems, she was like a little box turtle run over by a bus. "It's horrible," he says in that lyric. *A Day for Anne Frank* displays the horrible motto "God hates you!"

I Am the Bitter Name takes the technique of *Lies* one step further toward the abolition of technique—one step too far, most critics have argued. More homogeneous than *Lies*, this collection appears to try for and achieve self-portraits of apocalyptic incoherence. The poet displays, piled like monstrous fish, the products of his vigorous dredging of his nightmare unconscious. Critic Jascha Kessler, in one of the more positive reviews of Williams' work, catalogs his strengths and failings: "the simplicity, clarity of diction, haste and jumbling of his thought by the unremitting stroboscopic, kaleidoscopic pulsing of a voice from thought to speech to image to unvoiced thought." Impressed that the source of Williams' expression is valid, calling the book "real poems," Kessler is nevertheless disoriented by it. Other critics were less positive, charging that Williams' passionate flailings missed their targets or even dismissing the poems as sentimental and blurred.

As the tonal consistency of *I Am the Bitter Name* suggests, and as his later work confirms, Williams is a deliberate experimental stylist. Purged of commas, capitals, and periods, the poems sprout unpredictable question marks, exclamation points, and quotations. The sense spills over the ends of the short, jagged lines, so that it becomes almost a rule in these poems that a line end does *not* signal a break in sense. The effect is one of breathlessness, of a mind that, insofar as it is conscious at all, barely understands what it is saying. The reader seems to be hearing the raw emotive material of poetry at the moment of creation. Williams' vocabulary, too, suggests breathless, regressive speech, almost childishly simple but scatological—especially in the political poems. The voice again suggests a righteous man-child, outraged to surreal protest by the extent to which the real God and the real governments betray his standards.

Sometimes the words in *I Am the Bitter Name* are explicitly political, as in "A Poem for the Governments." This poem offers itself as an onion to make governments cry for the family of the imprisoned Miguel Hernandes, whose family has nothing but onions to eat. Reminding "mr old men" how they have eaten Miguel and "everything good in the world," the poem becomes "one onion/ your history" and concludes self-referentially, "eat this." Such explicit ordering of metaphor, common in *Lies*, is not the rule in *I Am the Bitter Name*, where even poems on political subjects dissolve into cryptic collisions of word and image. "The Admiral Fan," for example, begins with a "lady from the city" removing her girdle and baring her "white backside" in a barnyard and dissolves into a vision of her dismemberment, apparently not only by farm animals but also by a Washington lobbyist in a long car. She is emptied of "dolls." Her breasts become "dawn amity peace exaltation" in a vegetable field identified—as the grammar blurs—with nothingness, and flashing stoplights. Like the poems of André Breton, these let go even of grammatical structure in submission to the uprush of image and emotion.

Between 1972 and 1977, Williams was divorced, was remarried, and received grants and teaching appointments; during this time, he dramatically reinvented his poetic style. Except for its closing title poem, *With Ignorance* withdraws from the nightmare abyss and grounds its associations on human stories expressed in conventionally punctuated long lines with all the clarity of good prose. The change was presumably as much psychological as stylistic. The mature Williams, turned forty, tells his daughter that he has already had the bad dreams: "what comes now is calm and abstract." Later, in "Friends," he stands outside the terrors of his earlier poems to observe that "visions I had then were all death: they were hideous and absurd and had nothing to do with my life." The style of these self-possessed reflections is easy informal prose, the style of a personal letter refined in its very plainness, which sets the stage in the more effective poems for sudden outbreaks of metaphysical anguish or human pathos equal to the best of his earlier verse.

In "The Sanctity," Williams remembers going home with a married coworker from a construction site and seeing homicidal hostility between his friend's mother and wife, and the coworker's rage—a dark side of his character wholly masked by the ironic idyll of the workplace. The construction site is the only place, apparently, where the workmen feel joy, where they feel in power. Printed sources prompt some of the incantatory stories: an SS officer spitting into a rabbi's mouth to help him defile the Torah, until they are kissing like lovers; a girl paralyzed by a stray police bullet. Williams draws, however, usually from his experience: a veteran met in a bar, a friend in a mental hospital, an old bum seen after a marital quarrel, a girl he "stabbed" with a piece of "broken-off car antenna" when he was eight. Here, in grotesque anecdotes, Williams again examines the irrational in human life, the inevitable discord and suffering, but with a sympathy for recognizable human faces and characters missing from most of his earlier work. Political concerns are implicit in the presence of veterans and police bullets, but there is no preaching. The one short poem not narrative is "Hog Heaven," which begins, "It stinks," and develops in biblical repetitions and variations an enveloping nausea for the flesh, a theme and method common in the protest poems but expanded here in limber, Whitmanesque lines.

Tar demonstrates greater mastery of the anecdotal long-line style, telling longer and more complex stories with more restraint and power and returning at times to openly political themes. The title poem recalls the day of the near-disaster at the Three Mile Island nuclear plant, which was also a day of roofing work on the narrator's apartment building. Without ceasing to be themselves, the workmen become both trolls from the underworld and representatives of vulnerable humanity, their black tar-pots associated with the nuclear threat to the north. Williams' old vision of the apocalypse is here, but the symbols are stronger because they move in a narrative with a persuasive surface of its own. Williams is reclaiming techniques many contemporary poets have abandoned to fiction. As he masters the long-line narrative style, the lines become less plain—not necessarily more ornate, but more susceptible to ornamentation without losing their naturalness and tone of the grotesque.

Some of the poems in *Tar* begin with nature imagery and are leavened by it, though the suffering face of the city still always shows. "From My Window," for example, begins with the first fragrances of spring, budding sycamore, crocus spikes, a pretty girl jogging—but this is only an overture to the movement outside the narrator's window of two alcoholic veterans, one of whom is in a wheelchair, and their tragicomic accident in the street, which reveals the unlovely, childlike nakedness of the crippled one. Like many of Williams' narratives, this one takes a sudden turn near the end, recalling the able-bodied veteran pacing wildly in a vacant lot in falling snow, struggling to leave his imprint while the buildings stare coldly down.

Tar is almost as much a book of short fictions as of poems; characters include a man falling in love with a black woman who walks her hideously ill dog outside his window, a boy awakening to night terrors in the city, a decaying luxury hotel taken over by drug users, mental patients, and old women. A pornographic tintype centers a fantasy on immigrant life; a welterweight fighter awakens memories of a German widow, a refugee following her husband's plot against Adolf Hitler, who encouraged her daughter's affair with the narrator—as if his Jewishness could expiate her guilt. Two of the most interesting poems, "Neglect" and "The Regulars," narrate no unusual events but are minimal narrative sketches of a bus layover in a faded coal town and old men in a neighborhood undergoing gentrification—short stories in their use of description and dialogue, but in the cadences of Williams' taut, long lines.

Some of the poems in *Tar* use quatrains, four long lines clustered and end-stopped. In *Flesh and Blood*, Williams invents and writes a sequence of lines in a form comparable to the sonnet in length and rhetorical structure, eight lines of about twenty syllables each, usually shifting direction after the fifth line. Moving away from the extended stories of earlier works, Williams does not lose focus on the pathos and character of the urban world, but, necessarily, his tales shrink into the frame—either to vignettes or to terse summaries like a gossiping conversation. Williams portrays victims of stroke and Alzheimer's disease, a poetry-loving bum, an unhappy wife, a sobbing child, a girlfriend who hates her body, and, in one subsequence, readers in a variety of places and poses.

There is always clarity in these portrait poems, usually wisdom and complexity, but little of the frenzy that burned in the earlier work. *Flesh and Blood* includes poems that develop allegorical subjects in abstract language, despite earlier critical disapproval of this method—particularly in "One of the Muses," the only poem in *Tar* which critics judged a failure. It is Williams' way, however, to take chances. His characteristic strength is his restlessness and formal creativity—his refusal to remain confined within a style after he has mastered it.

William H. Green

Other major works

TRANSLATIONS: *Women of Trachis*, 1978 (of Sophocles' play *Trachinai*; with Gregory Dickerson); *The Lark. the Thrush. the Starling*, 1983 (of poems by Issa); *The Bacchae*, 1985 (of Euripides' play *Bakchai*; with H. Golder).

Bibliography

Bawer, Bruce. Review of *Tar*, by C. K. Williams. *Poetry* 144 (September, 1984): 353-355. Praises *Tar* for its portraiture, citing "Waking Jed" and "The Color of Time" as the best of the collection. Compares Williams to Walt Whitman, but says the former has more warmth and intensity of feeling. Argues that *Tar* is a reminder not only of "what poetry is all about, but what life is all about." An appreciative review.

Coles, Robert. Review of *With Ignorance*, by C. K. Williams. *The American Poetry Review* 8 (July/August, 1979): 12-13. Likens Williams to Søren Kierkegaard because he stays in the world and watches while "groping for inner truth." Coles says Williams has achieved in these poems a "humble intelligence" and considers the task in these poems as a journey fraught with challenges.

Greiner, Donald J., ed. *American Poets Since World War II*. Vol. 5 in *Dictionary of Literary Biography*. Detroit: Gale Research, 1980. Contains brief critical commentary on Williams' long poem, *A Day for Anne Frank, Lies, I Am the Bitter Name*, and *With Ignorance*. Greiner describes Williams' earlier poetry as one of "futility and despair arising from a hostile universe." Says he depicts well the power of terror, but is less successful when working with images that seem "to have been created rather than experienced." Discusses *With Ignorance* and notes that when the poetry is less bitter it becomes better.

Marowski, Daniel G., and Jean C. Stine, eds. *Contemporary Literary Criticism*. Vol. 33. Detroit: Gale Research, 1986. The entry on Williams gives a brief overview of his work, followed by excerpts from important reviews.

Notes that *With Ignorance* marks an important change of direction in his work: longer, flowing lines and emphasis of character and dramatic development. Also discusses *Tar*, noting that it is considered his most accomplished volume.

Vinson, James, and D. L. Kirkpatrick, eds. *Contemporary Poets*. 4th ed. New York: St. Martin's Press, 1985. The entry on Williams lists his publications and a selection of critical studies. Comments on the "swift" and "brittle" tone of his early poems in contrast to his later poems, where Williams seems to be looking at things from a fresh perspective. Notes that Carolyn Kizer has called Williams "the most exciting poet alive."

WILLIAM CARLOS WILLIAMS

Born: Rutherford, New Jersey; September 17, 1883
Died: Rutherford, New Jersey; March 4, 1963

Principal poetry

Poems, 1909; *The Tempers*, 1913; *Al Que Quiere!*, 1917; *Kora in Hell: Improvisations*, 1920; *Sour Grapes*, 1921; *Spring and All*, 1923; *Last Nights of Paris*, 1929 (translation with Elena Williams); *Collected Poems, 1921-1931*, 1934; *An Early Martyr and Other Poems*, 1935; *Adam & Eve & The City*, 1936; *The Complete Collected Poems of William Carlos Williams, 1906-1938*, 1938; *The Broken Span*, 1941; *The Wedge*, 1944; *Paterson*, 1946-1958; *The Clouds*, 1948; *Selected Poems*, 1949; *Collected Later Poems*, 1950, 1963; *Collected Earlier Poems*, 1951; *The Desert Music and Other Poems*, 1954; *A Dog and the Fever*, 1954 (translation with Elena Williams); *Journey to Love*, 1955; *Pictures from Brueghel*, 1962; *Selected Poems*, 1985; *The Collected Poems of William Carlos Williams: Volume I, 1909-1939*, 1986; *The Collected Poems of William Carlos Williams: Volume II, 1939-1962*, 1988.

Other literary forms

William Carlos Williams is best known for his poetry, but he did not limit himself to that form. His short-story collections include *The Knife of the Times and Other Stories* (1932), *Life Along the Passaic River* (1938), *Make Light of It: Collected Stories* (1950), and *The Farmers' Daughters: The Collected Stories of William Carlos Williams* (1961). Among his novels are *The Great American Novel* (1923), *A Voyage to Pagany* (1928), and the Stecher trilogy, composed of *White Mule* (1937), *In the Money* (1940), and *The Build-Up* (1952), and his best-known collection of plays is *Many Loves and Other Plays* (1961). He also wrote criticism and an autobiography. His essay collections include *In the American Grain* (1925) and *Selected Essays of William Carlos Williams* (1954). In addition, he and his mother translated Philippe Soupault's *Last Nights of Paris* (1929) and Don Francisco de Quevedo's *A Dog and the Fever* (1954).

Achievements

Williams' recognition was late in coming, although he received the Dial Award for Services to American Literature in 1926 for the "Paterson" poem and the Guarantor's Prize from *Poetry* in 1931; Louis Zukofsky's Objectivist number of *Poetry* in 1931 featured Williams. The critics, other poets and writers, as well as the public, however, largely ignored his poetry until 1946, when *Paterson*, Book I appeared. From that time on, his recognition increased steadily. He was made a Fellow of the Library of Congress, 1948-1949, and appointed Consultant in Poetry to the Library of Congress in 1952, even though he never served because of political opposition to his alleged left-wing principles. In 1948 he received the Russell Loines Award for *Paterson*, Book II, and in 1950 the National Book Award for *Selected Poems* and *Paterson*, Book III; in 1953 he shared with Archibald MacLeish the Bollingen Prize for excellence in contemporary verse. Finally, in May, 1963, he was awarded posthumously the Pulitzer Prize and Gold Medal for Poetry for *Pictures from Brueghel.*

Biography

William Carlos Williams was born in Rutherford, New Jersey, on September 17, 1883. His father (William George Williams) was an Englishman who never gave up his British citizenship, and his mother (Raquel Hélène Rose Hoheb, known as "Elena") was a Puerto Rican of Basque, Dutch, Spanish, and Jewish descent. His father was an Episcopalian who turned Unitarian and his mother was Roman Catholic. He was educated at schools in New York City and briefly in Europe and was graduated with a medical degree from the University of Pennsylvania in 1909. After an internship in New York City and graduate study in pediatrics in Leipzig, he returned to his native Rutherford, where he practiced medicine until he retired. In 1909 he proposed to Florence (Floss) Herman and in 1912 they were married. Their first son, William Eric Williams, was born in 1914 and their second, Paul Herman Williams, in 1916.

Williams, a melting pot in himself, had deep roots as a second-generation citizen of the United States. From early in his life he felt that America was his only home and that he must possess her in order to know himself. Possessing the America of the past and the present would enable him to renew himself continually and find his own humanity. Unlike many writers of his generation who went to Europe, such as his friend Ezra Pound, Williams committed himself to living in America because he believed he had to live in a place to be able to grasp it imaginatively.

Williams met Ezra Pound when they were both at the University of Pennsylvania; their friendship was fierce and uneven throughout their lives. While at the University, he also met Hilda Doolittle (H. D.) and the painter Charles Demuth. In his early poetry, he imitated Pound and the Imagists, accepting the Imagist credo as presented in *Poetry*. His natural inclination was to treat things directly with brevity of language and without conventional metrics. He was also influenced by his painter friends, particularly by the cubists and the expressionists. Modern painters filled their canvases with mechanisms, and Williams called a poem a "machine made of words." During 1915 and 1916, he attended literary gatherings with the *Others* group and met Alfred Kreymborg, Marianne Moore, and Wallace Stevens.

He began writing poetry in a poetic wasteland that did not want new or experimental poetry. The poets who had been popularly admired were the three-name poets so greatly influenced by the English tradition. Walt Whitman was not regarded highly and Emily Dickinson was unknown.

Although he devoted much of his time to being a full-time physician in Rutherford, Williams was a prolific writer—a poet, short-story writer, novelist, playwright, essayist, and translator. He was neglected both by the general public and by the literary establishment for most of his career, and often in his frustration he erupted against his critics and other practicing poets. With the publication of *Paterson*, Book I, in 1946, however, he began to receive the recognition he felt he deserved.

During most of the last fifteen years of his life, he continued to write even though he was not in good health. In 1948, when he was sixty-five years old, he suffered a heart attack, and in 1951 he had his first stroke, which was followed by another serious one a year later. The next year he was hospitalized because of severe depression. Finally, in 1961, two years before his death, he gave up writing after he suffered a series of strokes. On March 4, 1963, at the age of seventy-nine, he died in Rutherford, where he had been born and had lived all his life.

Analysis

Like Walt Whitman, William Carlos Williams attempted to create an American voice for American poetry. Both Whitman and Williams wanted to record the unique American experience in a distinctively American idiom, a language freed from the constraints of traditional English prosody. Whitman, as Williams says in his autobiography, broke from the traditional iambic pentameter, but he had only begun the necessary revolution. It was then up to Williams to use "the new dialect" to continue Whitman's work by constructing a prosody based on actual American speech.

Williams' search for a new language using the American idiom was intertwined with his search for a new poetic measure. Although he wanted to recover the relationship between poetry and the measured dance from which he believed it derived, his concept of measure is elusive. He believed that Whitman's free verse lacked structure. Williams sought a new foot that would be fairly stable, yet at the same time was variable, a foot that was not fixed but allowed for variation according to what the language called for. While the traditional poetic foot is based on the number of syllables in a line, Williams based his poetic foot on "a measure of the ear." The proper measure would allow him to present the American idiom as controlled by the rhythm of American speech.

When Williams wrote his early poems, he had not yet developed his own poetical theory; he first wrote conventionally and then according to the Imagist credo. He created some very good pictures of "things" and his poems achieved a reality of their own, but they did not go beyond the particulars to express universal truths—something that involves more than merely re-creating data.

In "The Red Wheelbarrow," for example, all the reader is left with is the picture of the red wheelbarrow and the white chickens beside it standing in the rain. In "Poem" the cat climbs over the jamcloset into the empty flower pot; Williams conveys nothing more than this picture. Other examples of Williams' poems of this period include "The Locust Tree in Flower" (the locust tree in flower is sweet and white, and brings May again), "Between Walls" (behind the hospital in the cinders of the courtyard shine the pieces of a broken green bottle), and "This Is Just to Say" (the poet tells his wife he has eaten the plums she was saving in the icebox).

In "To a Poor Old Woman," Williams does not convey any meaning beyond the picture he evokes of an old woman munching on a plum that she has taken from a bag she is holding in her hand. He does, however, experiment with the way he places the words of the line "They taste good to her" on the page. He repeats the line three times. First, he puts all the words on one line without a period at the end of the line; then he writes "They taste good/ to her. They taste/ good to her." He is searching for the correct form to use—the elusive measure needed.

In the epic poem *Paterson*, Williams sought to cover the landscape of contemporary American society and to discover himself as an American poet. His twenty-year journey in *Paterson* is similar to that of Hart Crane in *The Bridge* (1930), Ezra Pound in the *Cantos* (1925-1972), and T. S. Eliot in *The Waste Land* (1922) and *Four Quartets* (1943). Just as Whitman revised the poems of *Leaves of Grass* (1855) continuously and frequently moved them from section to section within the volume, so Williams identified *Paterson* with his own continuing life as a poet.

Paterson consists of five books and a projected sixth; each book is made up of three sections. In "The Delineaments of the Giants" (*Paterson*, Book I, 1946), Mr. Paterson, as he wanders through the city Paterson, describes details of the town and the area around it: the valley, the Passaic Falls, and Garret Mountain. Williams creates a history for the city as he describes past and present inhabitants and events concerning both them and the city. In "Sunday in the Park" (*Paterson*, Book II, 1948), the persona walks through Garret Mountain Park on a Sunday afternoon; there he views the workers of Paterson in their Sunday leisure activities. "The Library" (*Paterson*, Book III, 1949) takes place in the library, where the persona searches to discover how best to express the aspects of the city of Paterson that he has described in the first two books. "The Run to the Sea" (*Paterson*, Book IV, 1951) takes place in two locales—New York City and an entrance to the sea. The first section consists mostly of dialogues between Corydon and Phyllis, and Phyllis and Paterson. The section involves Madame Marie Curie's discovery of uranium and a digressive discussion of economics in America. The final section of the fourth book presents accounts of events, mostly violent, concerning the inhabitants of Paterson; it ends with the persona and a dog headed inland after they have emerged from the sea. *Paterson*, Book V, which does not have a title, takes place in The Cloisters, a museum on the Hudson River in New York City. This book is shorter than the others and some critics refer to it as a coda to *Paterson*, Books I-IV. Having grown old, the persona contemplates the meaning of a series of unicorn tapestries in the museum.

Paterson can be difficult reading. The persona of the poem does not remain constant; moreover, "Paterson" refers to both the city and the man. There are a number of other personae in *Paterson* who are sometimes ambiguously fused. Paterson the city becomes Paterson the man, who is also a woman, who becomes the poet writing *Paterson*, who is also William Carlos Williams, a poet and a man.

In addition, Williams shifts from verse to prose without transitional devices, and there are many such shifts within verse passages, from persona to persona, and from subject matter to subject matter. The prose passages, sometimes taken directly from an exterior source, range from newspaper clippings and quotations from various books to letters by Williams' fictional personae.

Paterson is Williams' attempt to delineate his culture and to define himself poetically. The two quests are interrelated. Williams can present details of the America that he sees and describe aspects of her culture. He wants, however, to convey the truths in what he describes and the universals concerning his vision. To be able to do so, he must work out his poetic theory and discover himself as a poet.

In *Paterson*, Williams relied importantly on local particulars. First, he chose a city that actually existed. In *The Autobiography of William Carlos Williams* he writes of taking the city Paterson and working it up as a case, just as he worked up cases as a doctor. According to Joel Conarroe in *William Carlos Williams' "Paterson"* (1970), Paterson was a city that was similar to Williams' native Rutherford, but one that better possessed the characteristics that Williams needed for his poem. Paterson had existed since the beginnings of America and therefore had a history. It was a very American city with a diverse population, about a third of which was foreign-born. Located on the Passaic River with the Passaic Falls, Paterson was bounded on one side by Garret Mountain. Partially because of these natural resources, it was one of the first industrial cities in America. Furthermore, its industry grew steadily and it was often the scene of well-known strikes. Fortunately for the action of the poem, Paterson also suffered a major fire, flood, and tornado.

Williams peoples his poem with persons who actually existed and uses events that actually occurred. Often, in the prose passages, he gives the specifics about the inhabitants and events. In *Paterson*, Book I, Williams develops a history for the city of Paterson. He tells the reader the number of inhabitants of each nationality living in Paterson in 1870. He describes some of the inhabitants. David Hower, for example, is a poor shoemaker who in Feb-

Critical Survey of Poetry

ruary, 1857, while eating mussels, finds substances that turn out to be pearls. A gentleman in the Revolutionary Army describes a monster in human form, Pieter Van Winkle. His description is followed by the account of a 126-pound monster fish taken by John Winters and other boys. Mrs. Sarah Cumming, the wife of Reverend Hopper Cumming for two months, mysteriously disappears into the falls just after her husband turns from the cataract to go home. When the bridge that Timothy B. Crane built is being put across the falls, Sam Patch jumps to retrieve a rolling pin and thus begins his career as a famous jumper, a career that ends when he attempts to jump the falls of the Genesee River in 1829. The reader learns exactly what Cornelius Doremus owned when he died at eight-nine years of age and what each item was worth. At one time the men of Paterson ravage the river and kill almost all of its fish. Finally, the reader is told about Mr. Leonard Sandford, who discovers a human body near the falls.

In *Paterson*, Books II-V, Williams continues to present details about the geography, inhabitants, and events of Paterson; as the poem progresses, however, he relies less on prose from historical accounts in books and newspapers and more on letters, dialogues, and verse. The particulars also become more personally related to the fictional poet of the poem or to Bill (Dr. Williams). There are passages about the Indians who first lived in the area. Williams includes a tabular account of the specimens found when men were digging an artesian well at the Passaic Rolling Mill, Paterson, and an advertisement concerning borrowing money on the credit of the United States. Phyllis, an uneducated black woman, writes several letters to her father. Throughout the poem a woman poet (C. or Cress), another poet (A. G.), and Edward or E. D. (Edward Dahlberg) write letters to a person without a name, to Dr. Paterson, to Dr. Williams, and to Bill.

In addition to all of these particulars, Williams deals with aspects of American society. A major weakness of contemporary American culture is the inability of man to communicate with others and even with himself. In *Paterson*, Book I, Williams immediately introduces the problems with language faced by the inhabitants of Paterson. Industrialization is one of the sources of their difficulties; industrialization and materialism separate them from themselves and from each other. The people walk incommunicado; they do not know the words with which to communicate. It is as if they face an equation that cannot be solved, for language fails them. Although there is a torrent in their minds, they cannot unlock that torrent since they do not know themselves.

Sam Patch is an example of a man who dies incommunicado. Before he attempts to dive into the falls of the Genesee River, he makes a short speech. The words, however, are drained of meaning and they fail him. He disappears into the stream and is not seen until the following spring, when he is found frozen in ice, still locked in by his inability to communicate.

In the second part of *Paterson*, Book II, Williams describes Madame Curie's discovery of uranium, a discovery that he relates to the need in America for the discovery of a new credit system. This system would be like "the radiant gist" that Madame Curie discovered and would cure America's economic cancer, a condition contributing to man's inability to communicate. The lust for money and the industrialization of society cut man off from his roots and from other men.

Humanity's problems with language are reflected in the relationships between man and woman. The love of man and woman consummated in marriage should be a means of communication, but in contemporary society "divorce" is the common word: "The language/ is divorced from their minds." In *Paterson*, Book I, Williams tells of Mrs. Sarah Cumming, who after two months of marriage has everything to look forward to, but who mysteriously disappears into the falls after her husband turns his back on her. Marriage, then, is no answer to the problem of communication. The words locked in the "falls" of the human mind must be released. Immediately after the prose section about Mrs. Cumming comes the passage "A false language. A true. A false language pouring—a/ language (misunderstood) pouring (misinterpreted) without/ dignity, without minister, crashing upon a stone ear. At least/ it settled it for her."

In *Paterson*, Book II, as Paterson walks through Garret Mountain Park, the breakdown of language is reflected in the religious and sexual life of the Paterson workers as they spend their leisure time on a Sunday afternoon. A sermon by the itinerant evangelist Klaus Ehrens is a meaningless harangue; he does not communicate with those in the park. The relationship between man and woman is reduced to a sexual act of lust without meaning; it is not even an act that will produce children. Language and communication between male and female is exhausted. Ironically, B. is told in a letter by someone who has been caring for a dog that the dog *is* going to have puppies; animals, unlike humans, remain fertile.

The first section of *Paterson*, Book IV, is primarily a narrative consisting of dialogues between Corydon and Phyllis, and Phyllis and Paterson. In both relationships the participants fail to communicate successfully. Corydon is an old lesbian who is half-heartedly attempting to seduce Phyllis, a virgin. Paterson is also an unsuccessful lover of the young black nurse. Phyllis writes letters to her Pappy in uneducated English. In the last letter she tells him of a trip with Corydon to Anticosti—a name that sounds Italian but is French. The two women have a guide who speaks French with Corydon. Phyllis cannot understand what they are saying; she does not care, however, because she can speak her own language. The dialogues reveal relationships in which there is a potential for love and communication, but in which there is a failure to communicate.

Williams describes the predicament of Paterson, but he wants to convey the universals of American society and go beyond the "facts" to the "ideas." Being able to express the general through "things" is part of Williams' quest to define himself as a poet. *Paterson* is a search for the redeeming language needed to enable contemporary man to communicate; the quest itself, however, is valuable even if the redeeming language is not discovered.

In the "Preface" to *Paterson*, Williams states that the poem is the quest to find the needed language ("beauty") that is locked in his mind. Soon after, in *Paterson*, Book I, Williams indicates that he is attempting to determine "what common language to unravel." Mr. Paterson, the persona, will go away to rest and write. Thus, Williams begins his quest for the redeeming language.

Paterson, Book I, ends with a quotation from *Studies of Greek Poets* (1873) by John Addington Symonds in which Symonds discusses Hipponax's attempt to use a meter appropriate for prose and common speech. Symonds also notes that the Greeks used the "deformed verse" of Hipponax for subjects dealing with humanity's perversions. Thus, the Greek poets devised a prosody suitable to their society, just as Williams seeks a measure to express American society.

Throughout *Paterson*, several letters by the woman poet C., or Cress, interrelate the theme of man's failure to communicate, especially through heterosexual love, and the poet's function to solve this problem of language. The longest of her letters, covering six-and-one-half pages, appears at the end of *Paterson*, Book II. In it she complains about woman's wretched position in society. She is particularly upset about her relationship, or lack of relationship, with Dr. P. She has tried to communicate intimately and has shared thoughts with him that she has not shared with anyone else. He has rejected her. She accuses him of having used her; he has encouraged her first letters only because he could turn them into literature and use them in his poem. As long as her letters were only literature—a literature divorced from life—their relationship was satisfactory, but when she attempted to use her letters to communicate on a personal level, he turned his back on her. When her writings became an expression of herself, their friendship failed. She thus expresses an idea that E. D. had stated earlier in the poem—that the literary work and its author cannot be separated. An artist derives a unity of being and a freedom to be himself when he achieves a successful relationship between the externals, such as the paint, clay, or language that he uses, and his shaping of these externals.

In *Paterson*, Book II, the persona goes to the library to try to learn how, as a poet, to express the details of the city described in the first two books. The library contains many acts of communication, but all of them are from the past and will not serve the poet in his quest for the redeeming language that will free man and himself. The poet in the poem, and Williams himself by implication, have failed to communicate, both as poets and as men.

Briefly at the beginning of *Paterson*, Book III, Williams suggests the need for an "invention" without which the old will return with deadly repetitiveness. Only invention will bring the new line that in turn brings the new word, a word that is required now that words have crumbled like chalk. Invention requires the poet to reject old forms and exhausted words in order to find the new-measured language. Throughout this book there is destruction and violence. The natural disasters that occurred in Paterson (the flood, the fire, and the tornado) and made it necessary for the inhabitants to rebuild sections of the city suggest the poet's search in which he finds it necessary to destroy in order to create. The poet does not find what he is searching for, because both the invention and words are lacking. Nevertheless, he continues his search for "the beautiful thing."

Near the end of *Paterson*, Book III, the poet experiments with form and language. On one page Williams places the lines almost at random. It is as if someone has taped various typed lines carelessly on the page without making sure that the lines are parallel or that they make sense when read. There are numbers and words in both English and French. The reader is invited to consider the meanings evoked by "funeral *designed*," "plants," and "wedding bouquets." On the following page there are four passages in which the words are abbreviations meant to be a phonological representation of the words of an illiterate person. Immediately after these passages appears the tabular account of the specimens found when a water well is being dug. Water brings life and rebirth. The poet wants to unlock the language of the falls that had filled his head earlier and to create the new-measured language. He concludes that "*American poetry is a very easy subject to discuss for the/ simple reason that it does not exist.*"

In *Paterson*, Book IV, Williams returns to Madame Curie's "radiant gist"; the poet hopes to make a similar discovery in his poetry so that he can heal those who suffer from an inadequate language. The poet reminds himself that his "virgin" purpose is the language and that he must forget the past. At the end of the book he emerges from the sea, which has been presented in terms of violence, and heads inland eating a plum and followed by a dog that has also been swimming in the sea. Williams concludes that "This is the blast/ the eternal close/ the spiral/ the final somersault/ the end." Williams suggests process in this end; the end is a spiral similar to a Möbius strip in which the end is always a return to the beginning.

Again Williams interrelates the poet's art and the process of love. Both are a means of communication between man and woman and a way for a person to discover himself; both, he explains in *Paterson*, Book V, involve a paradox. The virgin's maidenhead must be violently destroyed in the sexual act for her to realize her potential to create another human being. The poet must destroy past forms to discover the form appropriate for his time; Williams must reject the language and form of past poetry to create the new-measured language that will express contemporary American society and provide for communication among men.

Paterson, Book V, contains a question and answer section in which Williams discusses his theory of poetry. Poetry is made of words that have been organized rhythmically; a poem is a complete entity that has a separate existence. If the poem is any good, it expresses the life of the poet and tells the reader what the poet is. Anything can be the subject of poetry. The poet in America must use the American idiom, but the manner in which the words are presented is of the greatest importance. Sometimes a modern poet ignores the sense of words. In prose, words mean what they say, but in poetry words present two different things: what they actually mean and what their shape means. Williams cites Pieter Brueghel as an artist who saw from two sides. Brueghel painted authentically what he saw, yet at the same time served the imagination. The measured dance, life as it is presented in art by the imagination, is all that man can know. The answer to the poet's quest is that "We know nothing and can know nothing/ but/ the dance, to dance to a measure/ contrapuntally,/ Satyrically, the tragic foot." The poet presents life in a form appropriate to the time in which he lives; he presents the particulars of life that are a contrast or interplay of elements directed by his sexual desires and need for love, his humanity.

It is in the poems that Williams wrote during the last ten years of his life that he achieves greatness—the poems collected in *The Desert Music and Other Poems*, *Journey to Love*, and *Pictures from Brueghel*. In these, he uses the new-measured language he had sought in *Paterson*, Books I-V; but, more importantly, he goes beyond "things" to "ideas." The poems are more than pretty subjects; in them he discovers "the beautiful thing."

Some of the best poems of this period are "The Descent," from *Paterson*, Book II; "Paterson: Episode 17," in *Paterson*, Book III; "To Daphne and Virginia"; "The Sparrow (To My Father)"; "A Negro Woman"; "Self-Portrait"; "The Hunters in the Snow"; "The Wedding Dance in the Open Air"; "The Parable of the Blind"; "Children's Games"; "Song," beginning "Beauty is a shell"; "The Woodthrush"; and "Asphodel, That Greeny Flower."

When Williams was asked in 1961 to choose his favorite poem for an anthology called *Poet's Choice*, he selected "The Descent" from *Paterson*, Book II. He said that he had been using "the variable foot" for many years, but "The Descent" was the first in that form that completely satisfied him. "Asphodel, That Greeny Flower," from *Journey to Love*, is another poem in which Williams truly succeeds, and a discussion of that poem provides a good summary to a discussion of Williams' poetry.

In "Asphodel, That Greeny Flower" Williams uses his new-measured language, containing "fresh" words (the American idiom) written in a measure appropriate to his times and controlled by the rhythm of American speech ("the variable foot" in the triadic stanza). He is also concerned with creating a poem that has its own existence and is a "thing" in itself. Williams draws from the particulars of American life and his own life to evoke images of America and American culture; now that he has discovered the new-measured language, however, he can express universal truths about America and her culture. The poem at the same times expresses Williams' life as a poet and points to what he is and believes.

Williams uses his new-measured language to capture the flow of American speech as well as to reinforce and emphasize the content and meaning of the poem. For example, in one passage the measure of the lines suggests the urgency of the present, then slows into memory and reminiscence and finally into silence. At another point, Williams' measure gives the sense of the rolling sea. James Breslin in *William Carlos Williams: An American Artist* (1970) discusses in detail Williams' use of the American idiom presented in "the variable foot" and triadic stanza.

Williams uses natural details such as the asphodel, the honeysuckle, the bee, the lily, the hummingbird, apple blossoms, strawberries, the lily-of-the-valley, and daisies. He uses particulars from his own life: a trip he took with his wife, a time he was separated from her, and their wedding day. He makes references to his own poetry; a young artist likes Williams' poem about the broken green bottle lying in the cinders in the hospital courtyard and says he has heard about, but not read, Williams' poem on gay wallpaper.

The new-measured language enables Williams to draw from the facts and details of the local to reach the realm of the imagination and convey truths about humanity. He begins the poem by addressing the asphodel, but immediately, his "song" becomes one addressed to his wife of many years, not to the flower. Throughout the poem there is constant shifting between the image of the asphodel and Floss, as well as a fusing of the two particulars. The flower at times becomes a symbol. As Breslin explains, the poem is a continuing process as the "things" expand to the "ideas" beyond them, and the truths expressed contract back into the particular images.

The poem is a realistic love song that conveys the nature of the man who is the poet creating the poem. He asks his wife to forgive him because too often medicine, poetry, and other women have been his prime concerns, not her and their life together. The asphodel becomes a symbol of his renewed love for her in his old age. He can ask for her forgiveness because he has come to realize that love has the power to undo what has been done. Love must often serve a function similar to that of the poet, for the poet also must undo what has been done by destroying past forms in order to create new ones.

In "Asphodel, That Greeny Flower" Williams regrets that he has reached a time when he can no longer put down the words that come to him out of the air and create poems. Through the details of his poetry, he has attempted to express the general truths of the imagination. With his old age, however, he has gained knowledge that makes him optimistic. "Are facts not flowers/ and flowers facts/ or poems flowers/ or all words of the imagination,/ interchangeable?" "Flowers" or "facts," "poems" and "words of the imagination" are interchangeable, for everything is a work of the imagination. What is important is that love is a force of the imagination that rules things, words, and poems; love is life's form for poetry. Through love and poetry, all men will be able to communicate. Both love and works of the imagination, be they artistic endeavors or otherwise, are creative powers that are men's means of escaping death. This is the universal truth, the "idea" that Williams has come to, through the particulars of his poetry and his life.

Sherry G. Southard

Other major works

LONG FICTION: *The Great American Novel*, 1923; *A Voyage to Pagany*, 1928; *White Mule*, 1937; *In the Money*, 1940; *The Build-Up*, 1952.

SHORT FICTION: *The Knife of the Times and Other Stories*, 1932; *Life Along the Passaic River*, 1938; *Make Light of It: Collected Stories*, 1950; *The Farmers' Daughters: The Collected Stories of William Carlos Williams*, 1961; *The Doctor Stories*, 1984.

PLAYS: *Many Loves and Other Plays*, 1961.

NONFICTION: *In the American Grain*, 1925; *A Novelette and Other Prose*, 1932; *The Autobiography of William Carlos Williams*, 1951; *Selected Essays of William Carlos Williams*, 1954; *The Selected Letters of William Carlos Williams*, 1957; *The Embodiment of Knowledge*, 1974; *A Recognizable Image*, 1978; *William Carlos Williams, John Sanford: A Correspondence*, 1984; *William Carlos Williams and James Laughlin: Selected Letters*, 1989.

Bibliography

Coles, Robert. *William Carlos Williams: The Knack of Survival in America.* New Brunswick, N.J.: Rutgers University Press, 1975. This examination of Williams' work aims at an understanding of Williams as a poet and writer who was fascinated with the meaning and values of America. Coles offers a study of both poems and stories. Includes a bibliography and an index.

Fisher-Wirth, Ann W. *William Carlos Williams and Autobiography: The Woods of His Own Nature.* University Park: Pennsylvania State University Press, 1989. In this work, the author considers certain works by Williams as autobiography. Although this book is not a comprehensive survey of Williams' writing, it does add new insight into Williams' conception of the self and its relationship to the world. Offers passing treatments of *Kora in Hell* and *Paterson.* Supplemented by thorough notes and an index.

Townley, Rod. *The Early Poetry of William Carlos Williams.* Ithaca, N.Y.: Cornell University Press, 1975. In this work, both the life and art of Williams are examined. The author gives critical attention to both Williams' emotional and spiritual crises and examines the imaginative world of his early poems. Contains bibliographical references and an index.

Whitaker, Thomas R. *William Carlos Williams.* Boston: Twayne, 1989. This work provides a useful key to Williams' writing. The primary focus of Whitaker's study is the works themselves and not Williams' biographical or literary history. One of Twayne's United States Authors series. Includes a chronology, a selected bibliography, and an index.

Williams, William Carlos. *Interviews with William Carlos Williams.* Edited by Linda Wagner-Martin. New York: New Directions, 1976. Contains an introduction by Linda Wagner-Martin. Williams speaks candidly about himself and his work. Includes bibliographical references and an index.

YVOR WINTERS

Born: Chicago, Illinois; October 17, 1900
Died: Palo Alto, California; January 25, 1968

Principal poetry

The Immobile Wind, 1921; *The Magpie's Shadow*, 1922; *The Bare Hills*, 1927; *The Proof*, 1930; *The Journey, and Other Poems*, 1931; *Before Disaster*, 1934; *Poems*, 1940; *The Giant Weapon*, 1943; *To the Holy Spirit*, 1947; *Collected Poems*, 1952, revised 1960; *The Early Poems of Yvor Winters, 1920-1928*, 1966; *The Poetry of Yvor Winters*, 1978.

Other literary forms

Though Yvor Winters believed his poetry to be his principal work, he was, during his lifetime, better known as a critic. His criticism was virtually coextensive with his poetry, the first published essays appearing in 1922 and the last volume in 1967. Controversial because of its wide-ranging and detailed revaluations of both major and minor writers in American, British, and French literature, the criticism indirectly but indisputably illuminates his own work as poet: by suggesting explanations for the changes it underwent, for the main styles he attempted, and even for details in individual poems.

His single short story, "The Brink of Darkness" (1932; revised 1947), is autobiographical. Its setting (the Southwestern United States) and subject matter (hypersensitivity in isolation, the advent of death, psychological obsession to the brink of madness, the recovery of identity) are those of many poems, especially early ones, in the Winters canon.

Achievements

Among his contemporaries, Winters was something of an anomaly. Instead of moving from traditional to experimental forms, he seemed to many readers to reverse that process. Before 1928, his published work was largely what is loosely called free verse, influenced by such diverse sources as the Imagists and French Symbolists, possibly Emily Dickinson, and certainly translations of Japanese and American Indian poetry. After 1930, Winters' published work used traditional metric and rhyme patterns exclusively. He appeared to stand against all the main poetic currents of his time.

At no time, however, early or late, did his poetry ignore modern influences. Among the poets he continued most to admire and emulate were Charles Baudelaire, Paul Valéry, Thomas Hardy, Robert Bridges, and Wallace Stevens. His effort consistently was to make use of the most fruitful traditions among all at his disposal, not merely those in fashion. Thus, many of his later poems are written in the great plain style of the Renaissance. In his most distinctive work, Winters tried to combine the sensitivity of perception which the recent associative and experimental methods had made possible with the rational structures characteristic of the older methods. The result was something unique in modern poetry. Even before his death, his influence was beginning to be felt in such poets as Edgar Bowers, J. V. Cunningham, Catherine Davis, Thom Gunn, Janet Lewis, N. Scott Momaday, Alan Stephens, and others.

In his criticism also, Winters went his own way, challenging accepted opinions and making enemies in the process. Not only did he define what he believed were mistaken and possibly dangerous directions in the thinking and methods of many American poets, novelists, and prose writers, but also, in his final volume, *Forms of Discovery: Critical and Historical Essays on the Forms of the Short Poem in English* (1967), he offered new and for many readers unpopular perspectives on the history of the short poem, both in Great Britain and in the United States. His criticism, however, is not primarily destructive in bent. For one thing, he revised the reputations of many distinguished poets who had already begun to sink into oblivion, such as George Gascoigne, Fulke Greville, and Charles Churchill from the older periods; Bridges, T. Sturge Moore, and Frederick Goddard Tuckerman from more recent times. For another, he found forgotten poems and qualities of major writers that deserved attention—such poets as Ben Jonson, George Herbert, Henry Vaughan, Hardy, Stevens, and Edwin Arlington Robinson. Finally, he formulated coherent theories about poems, and in fact all literary forms, as works of art, theories to which his own work as a poet and his evaluations of the work of others consistently subscribe. To ignore or dismiss this copious and wide-ranging body of work is to overlook one of the clearest, most precisely analytical, and most disturbingly persuasive voices in American criticism.

Of all the honors he received during his lifetime, Winters said he was proudest of an issue of the Stanford undergraduates' magazine, *Sequoia*, which paid tribute to him in 1961. In 1960, he received the Bollingen Award from Yale University for his poetry, and in 1961, the Harriet Monroe Poetry Award from the University of Chicago. Having served on the faculty of Stanford University since 1928, Winters was made full professor in 1949, and in 1962 he became the first holder of the Albert L. Guerard professorship in English. In 1961-1962, a Guggenheim grant enabled Winters to complete the work on his last volume of criticism. By the end of his life, he was beginning to receive the acclaim that is due him. In 1981, *The Southern Review* honored him with an entire issue devoted to studies of his life and work.

Biography

Born in the first year of the twentieth century, Arthur Yvor Winters spent his earliest years in Chicago and in Eagle Rock (an area of Los Angeles), California. The landscape of Southern California near Pasadena provides the setting for two major poems in heroic couplets, "The Slow Pacific Swell" and "On a View of Pasadena from the Hills." Later, he returned to Chicago, was graduated from high school, and for one year attended the University of Chicago, where, in 1917, he became a member of the Poetry Club, which, in his own words, "was a very intelligent group, worth more than most courses in literature." By then he had begun to study his contemporaries—Ezra Pound, William Carlos Williams, Stevens, William Butler Yeats—and the diverse poetic styles appearing in the little magazines.

In 1918, having contracted tuberculosis, he was forced to move to Santa Fe, New Mexico, confined to a sanatorium for three years. The debilitating fatigue and pain, the resultant hypersensitivity to sound and sight and touch, and the sense of death hovering were experiences indelibly etched in his poetry then and later. In 1921, Winters began teaching grade school—English, French, zoology, boxing, basketball—in a coal-mining camp called Madrid, and he taught high school the following year in Cerrillos. These five years in the Southwestern United States were a slow period of recovery in isolation, a time when his own study of poetry continued and his correspondence with many contemporary poets was active. It was also the time of his earliest publications. The landscape of New Mexico suffuses the poetry of his first four volumes.

In the summer of 1923, Winters began the academic study that would eventually bring him to Stanford for his doctorate, earning a B.A. and an M.A. in romance languages, with a minor in Latin from the University of Colorado. The skills he acquired enabled him to translate many poems from French and Spanish (including thirteenth century Galician) and, between 1925 and 1927, to teach French and Spanish at the University of Idaho at Moscow. During this period, he married Janet Lewis, later a distinguished novelist and poet, whom he had met in 1921 on a return visit to Chicago; their wedding was in 1926 in Santa Fe, where she, too, had gone to cure tuberculosis. Together now, they moved to Stanford in 1927, when Winters was twenty-six years old; then, under the tutelage of his admired mentor in Renaissance studies, William Dinsmore Briggs, he began the systematic study of poetry in English that occupied him for the rest of his life.

Winters' life in California as a teacher, husband, father, and involved citizen is reflected everywhere in his later poetry. He became a legend at Stanford. Depending on which students were reporting, he was dogmatic, shy, reasonable, surly, kind, hilarious, humorless, a petty tyrant, or an intellectual giant. His disciples and detractors felt intensely about him; few were indifferent. The marriage of Winters and Janet Lewis was a lasting and loving one, and it nurtured their independent careers as writers. His daughter Joanna was born in 1931 and his son Daniel in 1938. Hardly one to withdraw into an ivory tower, Winters liked to get his hands dirty. The raising and breeding of Airedale terriers was a lifelong activity. He kept goats and a garden. He became deeply involved with the trial of David Lamson, a friend unjustly accused of murdering his wife. During World War II, he served as a Citizens' Defense Corps zone warden for Los Altos. These experiences are the kinds of occasions he wrote about in his later work.

Before his retirement from Stanford in 1966, Winters had already endured the first of two operations for cancer, the disease that killed him in 1968. His final effort as a writer, amid acute pain, was to see his last book, *Forms of Discovery*, through to publication after the death of his publisher and old friend, Alan Swallow.

Analysis

The change in poetic forms from experimental to traditional—from Imagistic free verse to formalist poetry using the traditional plain style or post-Symbolist imagery—which Yvor Winters' poetry exhibits after 1930 is so dramatic that it is easy to overlook the continuity of certain stylistic features and thematic preoccupations throughout his career. From the very beginning of his poetic life, he abhorred an indulgent rhetoric in excess of subject matter; always he attempted an exact adjustment of feeling to intellectual content. He paid strict attention to the value of each word as an amalgam of denotative, connotative, rhythmic, and aural properties; to the integrity of the poetic line and the perfect placing of each word within it; and to the clarity and economy of a style that avoids cliché. A poem was for him a means of contemplating human experience in such a way that the meaning of that experience and the feelings appropriate to the meaning are precisely rendered.

Thematic continuity exists also. His first volume of poems, *The Immobile Wind*, whatever immaturities of style it may exhibit, contains themes that he worked and reworked in all of his poems thereafter. As a collection, it speaks of man alone in an empty universe whose end is death, whose choices are existence or creation. Man lives and observes. If this is all, life remains an unrealized potential, the experience of which may be beautiful or terror-ridden but will lack the possibility of meaning which the artist may be able to create. To do this, the artist must choose his reality, must will it; to create his own world, he must give over the things of this one, for this world is merely phenomenal, the raw material of vision, a means at best, not an end: "And all these things would take/ My life from me." The end for all is death, and, in addition for the artist, the possibility of awareness. Religion offers no solace. The subject of the book is the poet, his growth and mission and death. The images in *The Immobile Wind* are sharp and self-contained and their meanings elusive; as one reads through these poems, however, the subjects and images repeat themselves, interweaving, and patterns of meaning begin to emerge.

In its continual allusiveness to itself and to its own images and in its occasional obscurities, *The Immobile Wind* is an irritating book, but it is not impenetrable. More accessible is *The Magpie's Shadow*, which consists of a series of six-syllable poems (a few stretch to seven) grouped according to the season of the year. Each is intended to convey a sharp sense impression; each as an evocation of a season is evocative also of the passage of time and hence of change and death. "The Aspen's Song," from the summer section, is characteristic: "The summer holds me here." That is the poem. The aspen tree is celebrating its moment of being alive, a moment that creates an illusion of permanence and immobility, an illusion because the summer is transient and the motion of change is there in the tree at every moment. The motion/stasis paradox of this image—present also in the oxymoronic title *The Immobile Wind*—recurs through Winters' poetry. No doubt inspired by translations of American Indian and Japanese originals, it also may be seen as an early manifestation of what he later came to call the post-Symbolist method: the sharp sensory image of metaphysical import.

The Bare Hills is Winters' last and most successful book devoted entirely to experimental forms. It is divided into three sections. The first, called "Upper River Country: Rio Grande," consists of twelve poems, each describing a month of the year; together, they are emblematic of the poet's progress through life, the poet growing more sensitive to the beauty and brutality around him and more aware of the meaninglessness of life and the inevitability of death. The second, called "The Bare Hills," consists of seven groups of three, four, or five poems each; it tells of the poet surrounded by death and cruelty but trying to learn, feeling inadequate to his task of creation, lacking an audience: he has but "this cold eye for the fact; that keeps me/ quiet, walking toward a/ stinging end: I am alone. . . . " The third section, called "The Passing Night," consists of two prose poems describing a bleak landscape of endless cold, a minimal level of existence, almost void of hope; the poet waits and remembers and observes, and that is all.

In many of these poems, Winters is continuing to experiment with the evocative image. For example, here is the third of four stanzas from one of the finest poems in this collection, "The Upper Meadows":

> Apricots
> The clustered
> Fur of bees
> Above the gray rocks of the uplands.

Out of context, the images seem vivid, perhaps, but randomly juxtaposed; in context, which has been describing the dying leaves at the advent of autumn, the transience of these living beings—apricots and bees—is felt, reinforced by the final stanza, ending with this line: "But motion, aging." The landscape evoked in the poem is beautiful, vibrantly alive, and dying. In an early review of *The Bare Hills*, Agnes Lee Freer called it "a book inspiring in its absolute originality."

The Proof exhibits the transition from experimental to traditional forms. The first half of the volume consists of poems in the Imagistic/free verse manner of his early work; the second half contains several sonnets and a few poems in various traditional stanzaic patterns. Winters himself has said, "It was becoming increasingly obvious to me that the poets whom I most admired were Baudelaire and Valéry, and Hardy, Bridges, and Stevens in a few poems each, and that I could never hope to approach the quality of their work by the method which I was using." He had come to believe that, in poems of firm metrical pattern, more precise and hence more expressive rhythmical and aural effects were possible, the result being the communication of greater complexity of feeling. To this belief he adhered for the rest of his life.

"The Fable," originally a blank-verse sonnet but reduced to ten lines in the *Collected Poems*, is illustrative. After describing the sea, which "Gathers and washes and is gone," he writes:

> But the crossed rock braces the hills and makes
> A steady quiet of the steady music,
> Massive with peace
>   And listen, now:
> The foam receding down the sand silvers
> Between the grains, thin, pure as virgin words,
> Lending a sheen to Nothing, whispering.

The sea is the wilderness surrounding us, emblematic of the empty universe and, in its ceaseless motion and ominous quiet, the process of dying. In the first line of this passage, the reversed feet in the first and third positions are metrical irregularities that, by contrast, emphasize the slow evenness of the next two lines, an evenness that recalls the quiet heaving of the sea itself. The sibilant sounds in the fourth line quoted are also descriptively accurate and metaphysically charged: the sound of the sea washing through the sand is the voice of the emptiness itself, of "Nothing, whispering."

His next volume, *The Journey and Other Poems*, consists of eight poems in heroic couplets. The first, "The Critiad," his longest poem, is an attempt to create satirical portraits in the manner of Alexander Pope; Winters chose to preserve neither it nor the last poem, "December Eclogue," in his collected works. The other six poems, most of them longer than his usual efforts, are among his most original, for they put the heroic couplet to new uses. "The Journey" through Snake River Country, for example, describes in forty-four lines a train trip at night through Wyoming and arrival at a destination in the morning. On a descriptive level, the poem is detailed and exact. On a symbolic level, it depicts a journey through hell, at the end of which the poet emerges intact from his spiritual trial. The following lines describe the poet's sudden awareness of the brutal and meaningless wilderness, the landscape of despair:

> Once when the train paused in an empty place,
> I met the unmoved landscape face to face;
> Smoothing abysses that no stream could slake,
> Deep in its black gulch crept the heavy Snake,
> The sound diffused, and so intently firm,
> It seemed the silence, having change nor term.

The poet has been describing the violence and squalor of life in the towns the train has passed through, and now he contemplates the empty landscape that harbors those towns. Descriptively, the language is very exact: The abysses are "Smoothing"—that is, being smoothed and stretching for endless distances—because of the river's ceaseless motion; the river's sound is diffused but also there, inevitably, forever, having neither change nor termination. One finds again the motion/stasis paradox which here is also a sound/silence paradox. In this quiet scene, decay is alive and busy; the river is the Snake, evil, eternal, obliterating all "Deep in its black gulch." Iambic pentameter couplets have not been used in this way before.

The next volume, *Before Disaster*, is a miscellaneous collection of poems in traditional forms: quatrains of three, four, or five feet; some sonnets; a few poems in rhymed couplets of varying line lengths. The subject matter is equally various: personal, as in "To My Infant Daughter" and "For My Father's Grave"; mythological, as in "Midas," "Orpheus," and "Chiron"; occasional, as in "Elegy on a Young Airedale Bitch Lost Some Years Since in the Salt-Marsh," "The Anniversary," "On the Death of Senator Thomas J. Walsh," "Dedication for a Book of Criticism," and so on. Here is the final stanza from a poem in the plain style called "To a Young Writer":

> Write little; do it well.
> Your knowledge will be such,
> At last, as to dispel
> What moves you overmuch.

Nothing could be plainer or seem simpler, but what is conveyed is a weighty sense of classical restraint and control, the power of realized truth.

All the collections that follow are republications of old work, supplemented with either some new work or old work never before published in a book. The 1960 revision of his *Collected Poems*, however, represents something more than merely a new grouping. Even though it is a selection, hence incomplete, it arranges in chronological order the poetry he wished to keep, beginning with four poems from *The Immobile Wind* and ending with his last poems, "At the San Francisco Airport" and "Two Old-Fashioned Songs." Thus, it is a record of Winters' poetic life. The poems it contains are meditations on a wide variety of subjects: on the greatness of historical heroes, such as Socrates, Herman Melville, John Sutter, and John Day; on the greatness of legendary heroes, such as Theseus, Sir Gawaine, and Hercules; on the evil that people do, as in the poems that deal with World War II; on the vast beauty of the world, in such things as an orchard, a dirigible, California wine, the ancient manzanita, a Renaissance portrait, "summer grasses brown with heat," the "soft voice of the nesting dove," and so on; and on the ever-encroaching wilderness and our proximity to death: "Ceaseless, the dead leaves gather, mound on mound." The book is a reflection of a great mind, one at every moment intellectually alive as well as hypersensitive to physical reality. To read it is to partake of the richness, the depths of Winters' inner life. Because the poems exhibit the three very different methods Winters perfected— free verse, traditional plain style, and post-Symbolist imagery—to read the book is to understand something of poetry as an art. If Winters' belief in the power of literature to alter one's being is true, it is to change for the better as well.

Joseph Maltby

Other major works

SHORT FICTION: "The Brink of Darkness," 1932, revised 1947.

NONFICTION: *Primitivism and Decadence: A Study of American Experimental Poetry*, 1937; *Maule's Curse: Seven Studies in the History of American Obscurantism*, 1938; *The Anatomy of Nonsense*, 1943; *Edwin Arlington Robinson*, 1946; *In Defense of Reason*, 1947; *The Function of Criticism: Problems and Exercises*, 1957; *Forms of Discovery: Critical and Historical Essays on the Forms of the Short Poem in English*, 1967; *The Uncollected Essays and Reviews of Yvor Winters*, 1973.

Bibliography

Gelpi, Albert. "Yvor Winters and Robinson Jeffers." In *A Coherent Splendor*. Cambridge, England: Cambridge University Press, 1987. Gelpi notes that Winters' early poems belie his critical precepts. They display the strong influence of Ezra Pound and William Carlos Williams, despite Winters' furious anti-Romantic denigration of both poets in his criticism. Winters strongly identified with the California landscape, as can be seen in *The Magpie's Shadow*. Gelpi compares his attitude to the West with that of Robinson Jeffers.

Gunn, Thom. "On a Drying Hill." In *The Occasions of Poetry*. San Francisco: North Point Press, 1985. Gunn, himself a noted poet, was a student of Winters at Stanford University. He describes Winters' strong personality and his efforts to convert his students to his critical principles. Foremost among these was the rejection of Romantic poetry. Winters sometimes surprised his pupils by praising the vivid images of the Romantic Hart Crane. His poetry and criticism emphasize the portrayal of individual details.

Kaye, Howard. "The Post-symbolist Poetry of Yvor Winters," *The Southern Review* 7, no. 1 (Winter, 1971): 176-197. Winters' poetry strongly evokes landscape. His ability to portray the external world in a precise manner was remarkable. In Kaye's view, Winters counts as one of the great twentieth century poets. His stress upon rationality and control reflects a fear of being overwhelmed by death and strong emotion. Winters' struggle with his emotions is a leitmotif of his poetry. He attempted to extirpate his own Romantic tendencies.

Rexroth, Kenneth. *American Poetry in the Twentieth Century.* New York: Herder, 1971. Rexroth contends that Winters was the true exile of his generation of writers. Most of his friends went to Paris, but health problems forced Winters to live in a dry climate. His move to Northern California kept him isolated, and his criticism became cranky and cliquish. He was an important poet who created an original variant of neoclassicism.

Wellek, Rene. "Yvor Winters." In *A History of Modern Criticism: American Criticism, 1900-1950.* Vol. 6. New Haven, Conn.: Yale University Press, 1986. Wellek gives a characteristically careful summary of the principles that underlie Winters' poetry and criticism. A poem should express a moral judgment. The judgment, based on absolute moral values, is ideally incapable of being paraphrased. Winters deprecated the expression of emotion not under the strict dominance of reason. His own poems often show the sort of emotion he in theory rejected. Although he held narrow views, he brought to attention the question of the truth of poetry.